MONTGOMERY COLLEGE LIBRARY
GERMANTOWN CAMPUS

MYTH, LEGEND, AND CUSTOM
IN THE OLD TESTAMENT

*the text of this book is printed
on 100% recycled paper*

THEODOR H. GASTER

Myth, Legend, and Custom in the Old Testament

A comparative study
with chapters from Sir James G. Frazer's
Folklore in the Old Testament

VOLUME II

HARPER TORCHBOOKS
HARPER & ROW, PUBLISHERS
NEW YORK, EVANSTON, SAN FRANCISCO, LONDON

Folklore in the Old Testament (3 vols.) by Sir James G. Frazer was published by Macmillan & Company, London, 1918.

MYTH, LEGEND, AND CUSTOM IN THE OLD TESTAMENT. Copyright © 1969 by Theodor H. Gaster. All rights reserved. Printed in the United States of America. No part of this book may be used or reproduced in any manner without written permission except in the case of brief quotations embodied in critical articles and reviews. For information address Harper & Row, Publishers, Inc., 10 East 53rd Street, New York, N.Y. 10022. Published simultaneously in Canada by Fitzhenry & Whiteside Limited, Toronto.

First HARPER TORCHBOOK edition published 1975

STANDARD BOOK NUMBER: 06-138640-5 (vol. I)
06-138641-3 (vol. II)

75 76 77 78 79 10 9 8 7 6 5 4 3 2 1

Contents*

Preface	xxi
Introduction	xxv
Notes to Introduction	liii–lv

VOLUME I
THE PENTATEUCH
GENESIS

In the Beginning

1. Creation as shaping	3
2. Primordial water	3
3. Primordial wind	4
4. The firmament	5
5. The separation of heaven and earth	6
6. "God saw that it was good"	6
7. The primal upsurge	6

Adam and Eve

▲ 8. Man formed from earth or clay	8
9. Man animated by divine breath	19
10. Man made in the image of God	21
11. Woman:	21
formed from Man's rib	
the woman in Paradise	

The Garden of Eden

12. The Earthly Paradise	24
13. The location of Paradise	25
east	

* ▲ indicates passages incorporated from Sir James G. Frazer's *Folklore in the Old Testament*.

	west	
	in the sky	
14.	The Waters of the Garden	26
	the "Confluence of the Two Streams"	
	the Paradisal River and the Four Streams	
	the Paradisal Fountain	
15.	The land of gold and gems	28
16.	The food of Paradise	29
17.	The Trees of Paradise	32
	the Tree of Life	
	the Tree of the Knowledge of Good and Evil	
18.	The Serpent	35
	as guardian	
	the "subtil beast"	
	▲ the cast skin	
	▲ the falsified message	
19.	The Cherubim	48
20.	The Revolving Sword	48
21.	The role of man	49

Cain and Abel

22.	Behind the Biblical Story:	51
	smith and herdsman	
	the rivalry of professions	
23.	"Sin crouches at the door"	55
24.	The mark of Cain	55
▲ 24a.	*Excursus*	56
25.	Abel's blood	65
26.	The errant ghost	69
▲ 27.	The contagion of bloodshed:	69
	the banishment of homicides	
	bloodshed renders the soil barren	
28.	The curse of wandering	72
29.	The Land of Nod	73
30.	Other interpretations	74

The Song of Lamech

31.	An ancient war cry	76
	battle taunts	

Adah and Zillah
"If Cain be avenged sevenfold"

The Sons of God and the Daughters of Man

32. "Sons of God" — 79
    properties conveyed through sexual intercourse
    the mortal span

The Deluge

▲ 33–45. Deluge stories around the world — 82
46. The mountain of deliverance — 128
47. The dispatch of the birds — 129
48. The rainbow — 130

The Tower of Babel

▲ 49. Scaling heaven — 132
▲ 50. The confusion of tongues — 135
51. Babel — 138

The Patriarchs

ABRAHAM

52. Abraham and Melchizedek — 139
▲ 53. "Cutting" a covenant — 140
54. Seeing the fourth generation — 156

SODOM AND GOMORRAH

55. Entertaining angels unawares — 156
    the submerged city
    itinerant strangers as gods in disguise
56. Blinding for impiety — 158
57. Taboo on looking back — 159
58. The pillar of salt — 160

59. The proposed sacrifice of Isaac — 161

JACOB

60. Twin culture-heroes — 163
    hostile twins

61. The hairy man	164
62. The sinister redhead	164
▲ 63. Jacob steals the blessing	165
sacrificial skins in ritual	
the New Birth	
▲ 64. Jacob at Bethel	182
dreams of the gods	
the heavenly ladder	
the sacred stone	
▲ 65. Jacob at the Well	193
66. Jacob's marriage	199
67. Reuben and the mandrakes	200
68. The theft of the *teraphim*	200
69. Stealing the heart	201
▲ 70. The covenant at the cairn	201
71. Jacob at Maḥanaim: The Furious Host	204
▲ 72. Jacob at the ford of Jabbok	205
the mysterious adversary	
the shrinking sinew	
73. Guardian angels	212
74. Jacob's last words	214

JOSEPH

75. The bloodstained coat	215
76. Potiphar's wife	217
▲ 77. Joseph's cup	218
77a. One hundred years and ten	222

EXODUS

Moses

▲ 78. Moses in the bulrushes	224
79. Moses at Horeb	230
the Burning Bush	
the removal of shoes	
80. The three proofs of Moses' commission	232
81. The rod of Moses	233
82. The incident at the inn	234
83. The death of Moses	234

The Exodus

84. The "finger of God"	236
85. The escorting angel	236
▲ 86. The Passage through the Sea of Reeds	237
87. The Song at the Sea	240
87a. Sweetening bitter waters	241
88. Manna—the "Bread of Angels"	242
▲ 89. The ox that gores	243
▲ 90. Not to seethe a kid in its mother's milk	250
▲ 91. The golden bells	263

LEVITICUS 279

NUMBERS

▲ 92. The poison ordeal	280
93. Leprosy as punishment	300
94. The soul as shadow	301
95. The Blossoming Rod	301
96. The Covenant of Salt	301
97. The Song at the well	302
98. Balaam	303

professional cursing
Augur consulted before battle
Balaam as a typical soothsayer
Balaam's oracles

99. Balaam's ass

DEUTERONOMY

100. Aborigines as giants	311
▲ 101. Boring a servant's ear	312
102. Cultic transvestism	316
103. Moses' farewell song	318

'Elyôn
children fed on honey and curd
the howling waste
the pupil of the eye
Resheph and Qeṭeb

Notes for sections 1–103   323–407

VOLUME II

FORMER PROPHETS

JOSHUA

104.	Joshua at Jericho	411
	"the walls came tumblin' down"	
	the circumambulation of the walls	
	the *seven* circuits	
	the trumpets	
105.	Foundation-sacrifice	413
106.	"Sun, stand thou still"	414

JUDGES

107.	The mutilation of captives	416
108.	Captives fed on scraps	417
109.	The Song of Deborah	418
	long-haired warriors	
	riding high and sitting low	
	"Awake, awake, Deborah, utter a song"	
	the cursing of Meroz	
110.	Gideon	419
	Gideon's fleece	
	Gideon's men	
111.	The purple of kings	422
▲ 112.	Jotham's parable	423
113.	The navel of the earth	428
114.	Sowing a city with salt	428
115.	Jephthah's vow	430
116.	Shibboleth	433
117.	Samson	433
	Samson as a solar hero	
	Samson and the foxes	
	Samson's riddle	
	▲ Samson and Delilah	
118.	The woman divided into twelve parts	443
119.	The rape of the women of Shiloh	444

RUTH

120.	Levirate marriage	447
121.	Covering with a garment in token of protection	448

Samuel

122.	Gestures of adoption	448
123.	Removing the shoe	449
124.	Falling to the ground	451
124a.	Leaping over the threshold	451
125.	Of mice and men	451
126.	Death for looking into the Ark of the Lord	453
127.	Qualifications for kingship	454
128.	Eyes brightened by eating honey	454
129.	Agag	455
	walks "delicately"	
	is hewn asunder	
130.	Battle taunts	457
131.	Beheading fallen foes	457
▲ 132.	The bundle of the living	457
▲ 133.	The Witch of Endor	462
134.	Mutilation of fallen foes	475
135.	Signs of mourning	475
136.	Bloodshed renders soil infertile	475
137.	The "holder of the spindle"	475
138.	Taboo on touching the Ark of the Lord	476
139.	Shaving and shearing	476
140.	The Uriah letter	478
141.	Regnal names	479
142.	The coal on the hearth	479
143.	Absalom and his father's concubines	480
144.	King's misconduct affects soil	481
145.	A Hebrew Niobe	482
▲ 146.	The sin of a census	483

Kings

147.	Abishag	489
148.	The ritual of enthronement	489
149.	Asylum at the altar	490
▲ 150.	The judgment of Solomon	491
151.	The dedication of the Temple	494
152.	Settlement of disputes beside the altar	495

CONTENTS

▲ 153. Solomon and the Queen of Sheba — 495
154. Hand withers for impiety — 497

Elijah

155. The "man of God" — 498
▲ 156. Elijah and the ravens — 498
157. "Measuring" the sick — 503
158. The confrontation on Carmel — 504
    Baal
    the fire upon the altar
    the limping dance and the gashing with knives
    Elijah's taunts
    rain-stones
    the filling of the trench with water
    Elijah on the summit of Carmel
    the raincloud
159. The ascension of Elijah — 511
160. The mantle of Elijah — 512
161. Harlots bathe in Ahab's blood — 513
162. Baal Zebub, "Lord of the Flies" — 514

Elisha

163. Waters purified by salt in new vessels — 516
164. Elisha called "baldpate" — 517
165. The inexhaustible cruse — 518
165a. Elisha revives a dead boy — 519
166. Bathing cures leprosy — 519
    waving in magic
167. Iron floats — 520
168. The use of corpses in magic — 521
▲ 169. Yahweh's lions — 522
170. The horses and chariots of the sun — 524

Notes for sections 104–170 — 526–562

LATTER PROPHETS

Isaiah

171. Whispering in charms — 565
▲ 172. Soul-boxes — 566

173.	Waistcloths and shoestrings	567
174.	Seraphim	567
175.	Invaders characterized as "tails of smoking firebrands"	567
176.	"A virgin shall conceive": Immanuel	568
177.	Gibbering ghosts and mediums	570
178.	Cursing by king and god	570
179.	The dawn of salvation	571
180.	"Lucifer, son of the morning"	571
181.	The fate of Sargon	572
182.	Flying serpents	573
183.	Shaving the beard in mourning	573
184.	The gardens of Adonis	573
185.	The rebel constellations	574
186.	Leviathan	575
187.	The "Name of the LORD" as his agent	577
188.	The haunts of demons	577
189.	Hairy devils	578
190.	Lilith	578
191.	The loom of life	580
192.	Heaven as a muslin curtain	580
193.	Battle vaunts	580
193a.	The combat against the Dragon	580
194.	The Suffering Servant	580
195.	The faery city	582
196.	Gad and Meni	584

JEREMIAH

197.	Man from stones	586
198.	Land made barren through unchastity	586
199.	Passing children through fire	586
200.	Creation of heaven and earth	588
201.	"The wind and the rain" fissures for the rain promptuaries for the wind	589
202.	Rites of mourning ▲ cuttings for the dead funeral meats	590
203.	The ritual lament	604

Contents

204.	Invoking the earth	604
205.	Rachel weeping for her children	605
205a.	David *redivivus*	606

Ezekiel

206.	Cherubim	607
207.	Ezekiel's vision of heathen worship	607
208.	Trapping the soul	615
209.	Yahweh's scourges	617
210.	The righteous Daniel	618
211.	Salting newborn children	618
212.	Rites of divination	619
	crossroads	
	belomancy	
	hepatoscopy	
213.	The fallen paragon	621
214.	Pharaoh and the Nile	624
215.	The parable of the cedar	626
216.	The dimming of the sun	627
217.	Kôshar, the god of minstrelsy	628
218.	The thread of life	628
219.	The navel of the earth	628

The Minor Prophets

220.	Introductory	630

Hosea

221.	Hosea and the pagan festivals	632
222.	Gomer, daughter of Diblaim	636
223.	Gomer's children	637
224.	Stripping a divorcee	637
225.	Marriage formulas	639
226.	*Ephôd* and *teraphîm*	639
227.	David *redivivus*	640
228.	El the Bull	640
229.	The bread of mourners	640
230.	Oil in the making of covenants	640

Joel

231.	Joel and the pagan festivals	642
232.	The dimming of the sun	647
233.	The foe from the north	647

Amos

234.	Amos and the pagan festivals	648
235.	Judgment by fire	649

Jonah

236. The story of Jonah 652
    sailing with an "unholy" person
    man cast overboard to allay storm
    swallowed and disgorged intact
    Jonah's prayer
    animals dressed in mourning

Micah

237.	Prophecy by puns	657
238.	Casting sins into the sea	659

Nahum

239.	The burden of Nineveh	661
240.	"The mills of God grind slowly"	666

Habakkuk

241. "Hush before the Lord" 668
242. The prayer of Habakkuk 668
    God as rising sun
    Yahweh's two escorts
    Resheph
    waves as horses
    lightning as arrow
    sun and moon halted
    "threshing" foes
    mortification before harvest

Zephaniah

    243. Zephaniah and the pagan festivals   679
    244. Ravens in ruins   685

Zechariah

    245. Zechariah and the pagan festivals   686
    246. *Teraphîm*   687

Malachi

    247. Malachi's picture of the Last Days   688
           the Messenger
           the fiery ordeal
           doom on sorcerers
           God's record
    248. The sun of righteousness   689
    249. The Second Coming of Elijah   690

Notes for sections 171–249   692–737

THE HOLY WRITINGS

Psalms

    250. The divine adoption of kings   741
    251. Seeing the face of God   743
    252. The breakers of Death   743
    253. The bonds of Death   745
    254. Riding a cherub   745
    255. The heavenly sieve   746
    256. Lightning as an arrow   746
    257. Walking round the altar   746
    258. A Canaanite psalm?   747
    259. Paradisal bliss   752
    260. Magical waters   752
    261. An ancient Hebrew wedding song   753
    262. Mountains in midsea   757
    263. The far reaches of the North   758
    264. Death as a shepherd   758

265.	Bottled tears	759
266.	Yahweh's processional	759
267.	The Book of Fate	764
268.	The combat against the Dragon	764
269.	Demon shafts	764
270.	Food of angels	765
▲ 271.	The bird sanctuary	765
272.	The heavenly and earthly Zion	766
273.	The throne founded on righteousness	769
274.	The winged soul	769
275.	A coven of demons	769
276.	From Canaanite hymn to Israelite psalm	771
277.	Renewing youth like the eagle	772
278.	Heaven as a garment	772
279.	The wings of the wind	773
280.	The clouds as chariots	773
281.	The kindly stork	773
282.	The bread of angels	773
283.	The right hand	773

284.	The ritual of enthronement
	    installation
	    right hand
	    footstool
	    allegiance
	    king as priest
	    king as champion
	    the chalice
		773

285.	Jordan turned back	781
286.	Snares of Death	781
287.	Tears fertilize	781
288.	The winds of fortune	783

JOB

289.	Introductory	784
290.	The Devil's wager	785
291.	The Sons of God	785
292.	Satan	785
293.	Signs of mourning	786
294.	Mother Earth	786

295.	Rousing Leviathan	787
296.	Father's knees	788
297.	The weary dead	789
298.	The sons of Resheph	789
299.	Guard over Sea and Dragon	790
300.	Orion	790
301.	The whip of God	790
302.	The disappearing shadow	791
303.	The hawsers of the heart	791
304.	The King of Terrors	792
305.	God's net	793
306.	Razed foundations and faery gold	793
307.	The shades beneath the waters	794
308.	Binding waters in clouds	795
309.	The pillars of heaven	795
310.	The Dragon in the net	796
311.	The thread of life	796
312.	The legend of the phoenix	796
313.	The negative confession	797
314.	Blowing kisses to sun and moon	798
315.	Man pinched out of clay	799
316.	Cattle presage storms	799
317.	Gold from the north	799
318.	Stars divine	799
319.	Rain from bottles	800

Proverbs

320.	Introductory	801
321.	The house that sinks down to Death	801
322.	Ants store food in summer	802
323.	Pointing the finger	802
324.	Wisdom as God's master craftsman	803
325.	The seven pillars of Wisdom	803
326.	The Fountain of Life	804
327.	The lamp of the soul	804
328.	Coals of fire on the head	805
329.	Mythological riddles	806
330.	'Aluqah the vampire	807

The Song of Songs

331. Introductory	808
332. The banner of Love	811
333. Apples and love	811
334. Solomon's groomsmen	812
335. The "Terror by Night"	813
336. The separable soul	813
337. The dance of Maḥanaim	813
338. The Reshephs of love	814

Lamentations

339. Dirges over cities; the weeping "daughter of Jerusalem"	815
340. The limping meter	818
341. Sitting apart	819
▲ 342. The silent widow	819
343. Cannibalism in a time of famine	825
344. Drinking gall	826
345. Gravel and dust in the mouth	826
346. The king as the life-breath of his people	826
347. The king's shadow	827

Esther

348. Introductory	829
349. The Iranian background:	834
the court at Susa	
the royal banquet	
the one hundred and eighty days	
"men who know the law"	
the seven who saw the king's face	
the crazy edict	
the royal crown	
Haman's boast	
"whom the king delights to honor"	
covering the head	

Ecclesiastes

350. The telltale bird	838

Notes for sections 250–350   839–876

Addenda	*Volume I*	409
	Volume II	877
List of Abbreviations	*Volume I*	417
	Volume II	885
Index of Motifs	*Volume I*	423
	Volume II	891
Index	*Volume I*	427
	Volume II	895

Preface

This book is an attempt to gather into one place all that can be derived from Comparative Folklore and mythology for the interpretation of the Old Testament. It grew out of the publishers' invitation to me to prepare an updated edition of Sir James G. Frazer's *Folklore in the Old Testament* on the lines of what I had previously tried to do for his *Golden Bough*. Very soon after I set to work, however, it became increasingly apparent that, to produce a work of any real use, I should have to go beyond that specification. For Frazer's book is, in fact, simply a collection of disjointed disquisitions on various points of folklore, which either take the Old Testament as their point of departure or try to wind up with it. In no sense does it offer complete coverage of the field, and more is left out than is put in. Moreover, although these essays may be invaluable in themselves, their connection with the Bible is often tenuous and sometimes even depends on false philology.

What I have done, then, is to go through the Old Testament from cover to cover and pick out, verse by verse, anything on which Comparative Folklore or mythology may throw light. In this effort, I have kept my sights not only on elucidating the overt sense of the text but also on recovering by the aid of such material the undercurrents of thought and the subliminal elements of the writers' minds; for it is obvious that in order fully to appreciate any work of art, attention must be paid not only to what the author expresses but also to what has—albeit subconsciously—impressed itself upon him. In other words, the background of a picture is just as important as the foreground.

The enormous amount of material that had to be digested has made it necessary for me to be terse, rather than discursive. I have not gone in for literary frills, since this is designed primarily as a work of reference. At the same time, I have made a special point of including ample references to the more elusive monographs and articles which have appeared on any particular theme in learned periodicals published since 1900. In this respect, the reader's attention is directed to the heading "Literature" at the top of certain sections of the notes. Because titles are cited recognizably in the notes, it has not seemed necessary to overburden the book with a separate bibliography.

What is here assembled covers not only stories and myths but also customs and popular concepts. These last are often enshrined in the words and expressions used in the original Hebrew, and in such cases I have had perforce to get a little philological. I have, however, always consulted the convenience of the man who wants to eat the meal without bothering too much about the recipe or the cooking, and I have therefore tried always to separate the kitchen from the dining room—which means that I have relegated purely technical matter to the notes, which the lay reader can skip.

The work is based on a card file, now running to more than 17,000 items, which I have been assembling for the past thirty-five years. I do not claim that everything here presented is of equal significance or even relevance. Like my great predecessor, I have found it hard at times to avoid flying off at a tangent; popular usages and concepts are so closely interwoven that one has often to bring in purely secondary and tangential material in order to unravel what comes as a tangled complex. Nor do I claim for a moment that all of the interpretations of Scriptural passages here offered are equally valid or that all of them are definitive. Many are simply suggestions. I hope, however, that—as is so often the case with Frazer's work—even when theories and deductions are rejected, the actual collection of material may still prove useful to students in other contexts.

I should like also to forestall, right here at the start, the oft-expressed objection that bringing cargo from the seven seas may be a pleasant pastime for treasure-seekers, but is not a sound procedure for a scientific expedition. A lot of people these days look down their noses at the Frazerian method of comprehensive comparison on the grounds that it jumbles together material drawn from different climes and centuries. In the present case, it is claimed, it is methodologically frail to institute parallels between Biblical beliefs and practices and those of peoples who lived (or live) much later and in quite other environments. To this it may be rejoined that, unless specifically stated, such comparisons are never intended to imply direct cultural contacts or borrowings, but merely to illustrate patterns of thought and feeling, to show the variety with which certain basic notions have been expressed in different times and places, and to suggest, on the strength of cumulative analogues, the true (or original) significance of things which may now be seen only in a distorting mirror. In precisely the same way, *semantic* parallels between diverse languages are no less valid and instructive because those languages themselves are unrelated. Indeed, in both cases the diversity enhances, rather than diminishes, the significance of the comparison. Moreover, in *interpreting* any one or other particular custom I have generally used the control of *context*, choosing that explanation which best accords with the acknowledged tenor and meaning of other usages with which it is ceremonially associated. True, some of the explanations may even then be incorrect, but this seems a calculated risk worth taking, for while, on the one hand, some things in the

Old Testament may thus become distorted, on the other hand, some may otherwise be missed.

Finally, where does Frazer come in? My original commission was to edit him, and I am afraid that, instead, I have smothered him. For one thing, I have, with a few exceptions, reserved for a future volume all matter dealing with legal institutions (e.g., ultimogeniture). For another, I have cut out the whole of his lengthy disquisition on the worship of trees and stones, as now merely repeating what may readily be found in any number of standard works on Comparative Religion. Let me say, then, that apart from this I have here retained what I could, and have marked it dutifully and piously with the notations ▲ and ▼ at the beginnings and ends of the relevant sections of the text. In the notes the sign ▲ is placed at the beginning only. Moreover, in such cases I have enclosed my own additions, both in the text and in the notes, between square brackets. The reader may be assured, therefore, that Frazer is indeed here, and I would add only that even in the parts which he did not write he is likewise here in a very real sense. However much his methods and conclusions may be decried today as imperfect and outmoded, the fact remains that nobody who works in this general field and who can now command a wider view and a better perspective can fail to recognize that he does so largely by standing on the master's shoulders.

*   *   *

I have had no help from colleagues in preparing this book, and have indeed been constrained, over these long years, to plow a lonely furrow. The field is not yet sufficiently cultivated, and the ground is still very hard. Perhaps the reader will make allowances for this fact.

On the other hand, I would here record with deep gratitude the generous and ready assistance which I have received over the years from the Simon R. Guggenheim and Lucius N. Littauer Foundations and from Columbia University's Council for Research in the Social Sciences. My warmest thanks are due also to Miss Eleanor Jordan, of Harper & Row, who spent laborious days and endless care in knocking a difficult manuscript into shape. She has made me appreciate more keenly what Elijah must have felt in the wilderness when those succoring ravens at last hovered into sight.

T.H.G.

Introduction

The folklore of the Old Testament consists of stories, songs, customs, institutions, and idioms. It is the residue of what Israel inherited from her pagan ancestors or adopted and adapted from her neighbors.

I. MYTH AND STORY

Major elements of this heritage are *myth* and *story,* but these are usually modified or recast to suit the outlook and taste of a later age. The ancient landmarks are not dishonored, but new building changes their aspect and the surrounding scene.

Myth in Genesis

In the earlier chapters of the Book of Genesis the traditional stories are retold, as often as not, in order to exemplify the current situation of man or some general and continuing principle. Thus, the time-hallowed myth of the wind which swept the primordial waters becomes a paradigm of how the creative spirit brings order out of chaos, while that of the expulsion of the first man and woman from Paradise for eating the fruit of knowledge is retold to illustrate man's constant sacrifice of innocence to intellect.

Myth in the Prophets

The prophets, too, employ the ancient myths in a special way. The primary function of an Old Testament prophet was to trace and expound the continuing plan and purpose of God in passing events. This involved recognizing characteristic traits of his operations, and to do so the prophets drew upon *mythological* as well as historical precedents. Thus, the defeat of Israel's enemies and oppressors could be regarded as a repetition, on the stage of events, of his mythological discomfiture of the primeval Dragon; while the eventual restoration of the monarchy could be portrayed by applying to David the ancient myth of the king or hero who, like Arthur or Barbarossa, had not really died but would someday return to his people in their hour of need.

Ancient Near Eastern parallels

A hundred years ago, most of such mythological allusions would have passed unnoticed. Today, however, thanks to the rediscovery through archaeological exploration of so much of Mesopotamian, Canaanite, Hittite, and Egyptian literature, it is possible at long last to recognize that, for all its distinctive qualities, the Old Testament is in fact saturated with the popular lore of the Ancient Near East. The notion, for instance, that water preceded all things (§2) likewise occurs in Babylonian and Egyptian mythology, both of which likewise attest the creation of man from clay (§§8, 315). Similarly the story of the Faery Garden (Eden) finds a parallel among the Sumerians; and that of the forbidden dalliance of the Sons of God with the daughters of men (§32) revolves around a theme which recurs in a Hittite legend. Again, the narrative of the Deluge (§33) is found in substantially the same form— including such details as the construction of the ark and the dispatch of the birds—in the far older Babylonian Epic of Gilgamesh. That this legend was indeed current in divers parts of the Ancient Near East is evidenced by the fact that fragments of Hittite and Hurrian (Horite) versions have actually been recovered and that a portion of the Babylonian recension has actually turned up in the ruins of the Palestinian city of Megiddo. Take, likewise, the tale of the rivalry between Jacob and Esau (§60). The contest between the more or less civilized man and his savage and shaggy antagonist appears earlier in the same Babylonian myth; while the familiar tale of Joseph and Potiphar's wife finds a parallel in an Egyptian folktale of the thirteenth century B.C. (§76). So too, the exposure of the infant Moses in the bulrushes reproduces, with appropriate change of scene, an earlier legend associated with Sargon, king of Agade (§78).

Mythological figures

It is likewise from Ancient Near Eastern sources that we at last learn the true character of several mythological figures mentioned allusively in the Old Testament. It is now apparent, for instance, that the familiar *cherub* was not —as formerly supposed—a nightgowned angel, but simply the equivalent of the Mesopotamian *karibu,* a form of griffin, so that the cherub who guards the entrance to Eden is but a variant of fairy tale's Dragon Who Guards the Treasure; and that on which the Lord rides (Ps. 18:10) of the Garuda bird of the Indic Vishnu and of otherworldly mounts in other cultures (§19). Similarly, behind the statement, in the story of Cain and Abel (Gen. 4:7), that "Sin croucheth at the door" we can now recognize an allusion to the demonic "Croucher" of Mesopotamian popular belief (§23), and behind the various references to Resheph, formerly rendered as a common noun meaning "flame," the Canaanite plague-god of that name (§§103, 242, 269, 298, 338). Leviathan, the monster vanquished primordially by Yahweh and destined to be vanquished again at the end of the present era (Isa. 27:1), is now seen to be but a Hebraization of Leviathan vanquished by Baal in an earlier Canaanite myth from Ras Shamra-Ugarit (§§186, 295); while the broad theme of the Conquest of the Dragon—probably reflecting the seasonal subjugation of floods—has its counterparts in Sumerian, Babylonian, and Hittite myths, as well as many parallels in European folktale and custom.

Other characters of ancient myth similarly make their appearance in the Old Testament. The members of the heavenly court, for example, are still designated as *benê elōhîm,* or *benê El,* "sons of God," as in the Ugaritic texts (§§**32, 291, 318**); the Babylonian *lilith,* or demonic hag, is classed among the demons who inhabit desolate places (§**190**); Kôshar, the Canaanite god of minstrelsy, is mentioned as the archetype of the musician (§**217**); the Lord of Hell bears the ancient Sumerian name of "King of Terrors" (§**304**); and the virtuous Daniel of the Ugaritic *Poem of Aqhat* is cited by the prophet Ezekiel as the legendary paragon of righteousness (§**210**).

Mythological allusions

Near Eastern sources also enable us to detect mythological allusions which are not fully spelled out and which would otherwise elude us. In Isaiah's "Daystar (KJV: Lucifer), son of the morning," for example, and in Ezekiel's "fallen paragon" we may now recognize figures who have in fact several congenors in ancient mythology (§§**180, 213**); while the "pleasant plantings" which Isaiah excoriates as a heathen abomination can now be identified as the equivalent of the familiar "gardens of Adonis"—seedboxes ritually watered and made to germinate as a symbol of the resurrection of the dead or discomfited spirit of vegetation (§**184**). The bound "Fool" (Heb.: *Kesîl*) of Job 38:31 now reveals himself as a form of Orion (§**300**); while an allusion to the widespread legend of the phoenix is recognized by some scholars in another passage of the same book (§**312**).

A peculiarly fascinating instance of the way in which Ancient Near Eastern sources may throw light on the origins of a Biblical story is afforded by the tale of how the first woman was created from the rib of the first man and named Eve, "mother of all the living." This, it would now seem, was motivated simply by the fact that in Sumerian cuneiform script the two signs NIN.TI could be read alternatively as "Lady of the Rib" or as "Lady of Life." The Hebrew compiler, who had such a cuneiform original before him, was therefore prompted to incorporate two alternative interpretations of that name (§**11,a**).

Mythological vocabulary

Sometimes ancient myths (and usages) survive only in a chance word or phrase, as when *we* speak of Cupid or the Muses, or employ such terms as *martial, jovial, protean, tawdry,* and *melancholy.* The vocabulary of the Old Testament is full of such relics. Take, for instance, the familiar description of the Promised Land as one *flowing with milk and honey.* This expression comes straight out of ancient legends about the Earthly Paradise, for that is one of the characteristic features of that blessed realm.[1] Conversely, the several references to "the gates of Death" (Ps. 9:13; Job 38:17), or of Sheol (Isa. 38:10), echo traditional portrayals of the netherworld as a subterranean or otherworldly city. So too, when Isaiah denounces Babylon as "one who has been playing Rahab" (Isa. 14:4), he is alluding to the well-known myth of the arrogant and blustering Dragon who was so called; and of the same order is the designation of Egypt by that name (Isa. 30:7; Ps. 87:4). Again, in the Song of Songs (8:6), the pangs of love are styled "fiery *reshephs* (RSV: flashes of fire)," whereby they are compared to the assaults of the ancient Canaanite plague-god, just as we might speak of *Cupid's darts.*

Occasionally, to be sure, the allusions are not quite so patent, and the recognition of them cannot go beyond a suspicion or guess. Who is to say, for example, whether the Book of Job's description of disease as "the firstborn of Death" (18:13) is simply an *ad hoc* poetic image or an echo of ancient mythology? Similarly, when the dance of the Shulammite is likened, in the Song of Songs (7:1), to "the dance of Maḥanaim," the words may possibly allude to some variant of the tale recounted in Genesis 32:1–2 (§**71**), wherein the Phantom Host there associated with that place were portrayed, as in parallel stories elsewhere, as a troupe of celestial dancers (e.g., in Greek mythology, the rout of Artemis). Such a mythological allusion is possible, but it is by no means certain, and scarcely transcends the bounds of conjecture.

Mythological clichés

Popular stories have their characteristic phrases, tenaciously preserved through centuries of retelling. "Fee, fi, fo, fum," for example, is an integral element of *Jack and the Beanstalk,* and "Grandma, what big eyes you have!" of *Little Red Riding Hood.* A mere reference to such phrases is sufficient to evoke the entire tale. So, in the poetry of the Old Testament, there is evidence of a standard mythological vocabulary, drawn from traditional pagan prototypes.

The primeval Dragon is "smitten" (Isa. 51:9 [LXX]; Ps. 68:21; Job 26:12) or "roared at" (Isa. 50:2; Ps. 104:7), as in the Canaanite texts from Ras Shamra-Ugarit; the contumacious Rahab is "stilled" or "given his quietus" (Isa. 14:4; 30:7; Job 38:11);[2] the abode of God is in "the far recesses of the north" (Isa. 14:13; Ps. 48:2), as likewise in the Ugaritic myths; the members of the heavenly court are "sons of God" (Gen. 6:2, 4; Pss. 29:1; 89:6; Job 1:6; 2:1; 38:7), as in Canaanite and Akkadian; Yahweh "chariots upon the clouds" (Isa. 19:1; Ps. 104:3), as does Baal; and Leviathan is described as "the fleeing serpent"[3] and "the twisted serpent" (Isa. 27:1; Job 26:13)—precisely the same epithets as are used in an Ugaritic text to define that fell monster.

Parallels among primitive peoples

But "not from eastern windows only." Many of the stories related in the Old Testament are by no means peculiar to the Ancient Near East, but are simply particular forms of tales current elsewhere in the world.

The story of the Earthly Paradise, for instance, is found alike in the Ancient

Near East, Classical, and primitive cultures, and contains the same details of the special food forbidden to mortals and of the central river (or fountain) which is the primary source of earth's waters and which is diffused by four streams flowing to the four quarters (§§12–16). Similarly, if we dismiss as secondary the detail of her formation from the rib of Adam (see above), Eve would have been in the Garden from the beginning, and she thus becomes simply a Hebrew version of the seductive Fairy Mistress, a fairly ubiquitous figure in folktales of the Earthly Paradise or the Enchanted Realm (§§11,b, 321). Again, legends of a primeval deluge which destroyed the first race of men and from which only one or a few specially pious persons were spared, though often severely localized, are a feature of almost all primitive mythologies, and usually include the incident of deliverance in an ark or special vessel and the grounding of it on a high mountain (§§33–45). So too the Tower of Babel finds analogues in several primitive stories revolving around the theme of men's impious attempt to scale heaven, and the confusion visited upon them (§49).

Nor are these the only examples. Likewise familiar to all students of Comparative Folklore are the tale of the man who, like Abraham, entertains angels unawares (§55); of the city which, like Sodom and Gomorrah, is submerged or destroyed through the impiety or inhospitality of its inhabitants (§55,a); of the man or woman transformed, like Lot's wife, into a pillar of salt (sometimes, into stone) as a punishment for disobedience (§58); of the twin culture-heroes who, like Jacob and Esau, quarrel while still in the womb (§60); of the Phantom Host which appears on a dark or stormy night, even as the host of angels or otherworldly beings appeared to Jacob at Maḥanaim (§71); of the coat dipped, like Joseph's, in the blood of a wild beast, to feign that its owner had met his death by ravin (§75); of the rejected siren who brings false charges, like Potiphar's wife, against the object of her passion (§76); of the hero exposed, like Moses, at birth (§78); of the miraculous parting of waters (§86); of the rash vow whereby, like Jephthah, a man is obliged to sacrifice his own offspring (§115); of the "Uriah Letter" (§140); the Judgment of Solomon (§150), and the Ascension of Elijah (§159); of the king who, like David, will posthumously return to his people (§§205,a 227); and of the man, like Jonah, swallowed by a fish but subsequently disgorged intact (§236).

It is worth pointing out, however, that in citing such parallels from *primitive* cultures special caution is necessary, for many of them may in fact be nothing but "playbacks" of the Biblical stories picked up from Christian missionaries and then elaborated or garbled. Thus, when a tale from Tahiti tells of a first woman named Ivi created from the rib of the first man,[4] it is not difficult to recognize the Scriptural Eve masquerading in native garb. Similarly, when we are told in a story from the island of St. Cristoval that the first woman was fashioned out of *red* clay,[5] it is easy to detect the influence of a popular piece of Biblical exegesis, which connects the name Adam and the *adamah,* or "earth," whence he was taken, with the Hebrew word *adôm,* "red." This is the kind of thing that a missionary might very well have absorbed in his seminary days and then passed on in his retelling of the Scriptural narrative, only to have it served up by the natives to a later generation of eager anthropologists!

Localization of myths

Storytellers often lend added interest to their tales by giving them a local setting familiar to their listeners; and this device appears also in the Old Testament. Thus, the mythical Earthly Paradise is located (not without a strain on geography) somewhere in Mesopotamia (§13), and two of the four mythical rivers which issue from it are identified with the Tigris and Euphrates (§14). Similarly, the mythical tower reared to heaven (§49) is equated with the great stepped temple (*ziggurat*) of Babylon; and the concomitant motif of the confusion of tongues—well-attested elsewhere—serves fancifully to explain the name of that city, i.e., Babel-Babble (§51). Again, the widespread tale of the submerged city is located at Gomorrah, on the shores of the Dead Sea, simply because the name Gomorrah suggests a Semitic word meaning "flood, submerge" (§55,b); and the story of the traveler who has to wrestle with the spirit of a stream before he can cross it is located, on the same principle, at the Ford of Jabbok, simply because that name suggests the Hebrew word *'abaq,* "wrestle" (§72). The celestial army—a variant of the European Phantom Host—is encountered by Jacob at Maḥanaim, because Maḥanaim can be interpreted to mean "twin camps" (§71)! In the same way too, the "red man" (Heb.: *'adôm*), who is the antagonist of the hero in many folktales relating to the rivalry of culture twins, is identified with Edom, the eponymous hero of the Edomites (§62).

Telltale names

Another device for enhancing popular interest is to give the characters of a story arbitrary or invented names significant of their roles. One recalls at once Aristophanes' Lysistrata, "Madame de Mobilisation," who seeks to "bring the boys back home" from the Peloponnesian War, as well as Shakespeare's Doll Tearsheet or Constable Goodman Dull, and Sheridan's redoubtable Mrs. Malaprop. In precisely the same way, in the Old Testament stories, Samson's leman is called Delilah, or "Coquette," and the contumacious Dragon whom Yahweh subdues is Rahab, "Sir Bluster," or Leviathan, "Wriggly." By the same token too, Cain wanders to the quite fictitious land of Nod, a name which itself means "wandering."

Reinterpretation

In course of time, the original purport of a story often comes to be forgotten, and the traditional details are then reinterpreted in accordance with the understanding of later generations. There are several examples of this in the Old Testament.

The story of Cain and Abel, for instance, revolved originally around the rivalry of the smith and the herdsman, for that is what the names themselves really denote. For the Scriptural writer, however, it is simply a didactic, moral tale about the first murder, and its several traditional elements, such as the wandering and marking of the smith—originally designed to indicate the characteristic trait of his occupation and his sacrosanct status—have taken on an entirely different complexion (§§**22, 24**). The ceremony of walking around a city or area as a symbol of establishing title to it—a ceremony attested in several parts of the world—has lost its significance for the Biblical historian and become but a triumphal march around the beleaguered Jericho (§**104**). The ancient notion that the human body consists of *twelve* essential parts is likewise lost to the author of the gruesome tale in the Book of Judges (ch. 19) concerning the ravished wife who was dissected into twelve pieces; to him this is motivated only by the desire of her husband to send a portion of her, as a grim warning, to each of the twelve tribes of Israel (§**118**)! In somewhat similar fashion, the original meaning of the acts performed by Elijah in his celebrated confrontation with the prophets of Baal on Mt. Carmel no longer comes through in the Scriptural narrative. The twelve stones which he erected on the spot, and which really represented a familiar feature of rain-making rites, are interpreted as twelve slabs used to reconstitute the wrecked altar of Yahweh—one for each of the tribes of Israel! Similarly, the loud cries uttered in that same ceremony are taken to be invocations to Baal, whereas Comparative Folklore suggests that they were originally imitations of thunder in a magical procedure (§**158**).

Myth as propaganda

Sometimes, too, a deliberately polemical note is introduced in these reinterpretations of pagan usages. Thus, the ceremony of passing children through fire in order to "sain" them against evil powers—a ceremony which is likewise well-attested elsewhere—is represented as a form of human sacrifice (§**199**).

Nowhere, perhaps, is this form of transmutation more in evidence than in the story of Esther, which appears to have originated as a tale told in the harems about the shrewdness of a woman in frustrating a jealous intrigue at the Persian court. In the Biblical version, however, it has become the foiling of a plot against the Jews, and the story has been so reshaped as to explain at the same time the characteristic features of a local festival (*Purim*).

Political use of myth

The adaptation of the ancient tales may also be determined by *political* considerations. Thus, the traditional story of the Rival Twins is taken, as we have seen, to symbolize the relations between Israel and her eastern rival, Edom

(§60); while the "hero" of the time-hallowed legend of the divine paragon who was ousted from Paradise for his overweening pride is paradigmatically identified by the prophet Ezekiel with the proud king of Tyre, destined for a fall (§213). So, too, in Psalms 47:3 and 98:1–3, the mythical monsters whom, in the old myth, the storm-god defeated in order to acquire or assert his kingship, are converted into hostile nations whom Yahweh subdues in order to evince his sovereignty and achieve salvation for his people; and when Joel speaks (2:20) of God's eventually removing "the northerner" from the territory of his people, he is transmuting the mythological figure of the demon from the north into a specific political foe of Israel (§233).

An especially instructive example of this process is afforded by the brief (and probably truncated) story of the cursing of Canaan in Genesis 9:20–27. Canaan is excoriated because his father Ham looked upon Noah's nakedness. The original version of this tale evidently revolved around the belief—paralleled elsewhere—that one must not look upon a kinsman's genitals lest one cast the evil eye on his procreative powers. (This belief seems, indeed, to underlie the express commandments in Leviticus 18:6–7). Now, in terms of the story itself, there is, to be sure, nothing odd (as critics have supposed) in the fact that Ham's son, rather than himself, is cursed. The point is simply that because Noah had been made to suffer indignity from his son, so Ham, who perpetrated the offense, will suffer indignity from *his,* for Canaan will be condemned to be the slave of his brothers. But this old story is given a political complexion: it signifies the subjugation of the Canaanites by the Israelites and the Philistines, and Cain is made a son of Ham because, when the story was written, the land was largely a vassal of Egypt, who was regarded as a son of Ham (cf. Gen. 10:6).

Aetiological myths

Another way of accommodating general stories to a local scene is to use them *aetiologically*—that is, as explanations of familiar names or of current customs and institutions. Thus, when Jacob wrestles with the mysterious antagonist, the scene is laid near a place called Penuel, the name of which is taken to mean Face-of-God, on the grounds that the hero there beheld the face of a divine being (god), yet survived. Similarly, when the adversary maims him in the ischiac nerve—a detail which recurs in parallel stories elsewhere—this serves to account for the fact that the Israelites refrain from eating the ischiac nerve of animals (§72).

A particularly interesting example of this process occurs in the story of Jephthah's daughter, told in the Book of Judges. When she learns that she has been doomed to be sacrificed, as the result of her father's rash vow, she begs to be allowed to go with her companions and roam upon the hills for two months. In commemoration of this, adds the Biblical storyteller, "Israelite maidens go to bewail the daughter of Jephthah for four days every year." Here a popular folktale has been used to explain the widespread custom of bewailing the crops or the vanished spirit of fertility at seasonal ceremonies (§115).

Suppression

There are also cases in which details of the older stories have been deliberately *suppressed* in order to accommodate the whole to a new outlook. In many cultures, for instance, the separation of heaven from earth is the subject of a distinct myth. Thus, in the Mesopotamian Epic of Creation (*Enuma Elish*), it is said to be accomplished by Marduk's splitting the vanquished Tiamat lengthwise, "like an oyster," and then using the upper part of her body to constitute the firmament, and the lower the bedrock of the earth; while the Hittite *Story of Ullikummi* refers to a cleaver by which the sundering was effected. There are likewise Egyptian myths on the subject, and in several primitive cultures the separation is represented as the forced severance of Father Sky and Mother Earth when they were locked in conjugal embrace. The compiler of Genesis, however, eschews these mythological fancies, because they are out of keeping with his own monotheistic outlook: heaven is parted from earth solely by the fiat of God (§5). Again, in the story of Cain and Abel, the *débat* between the smith (Cain) and the herdsman (Abel), which was part and parcel of the original tale and which is, in fact, a characteristic element of this entire genre, has been excised as irrelevant to the new complexion given it by the Biblical writer. Indeed, in this case, the excision is made quite blatantly by the simple expedient of leaving a gap in the text (§22)!

In the same way too, in the story of the dalliance of the sons of God with the daughters of men (Gen. 6:1-4), the fate of the former (elaborated, to be sure, in later pseudepigraphic and rabbinic literature) is omitted from the Biblical version, because it was alien to the compiler's purpose in retelling the tale: he wanted simply to account for the limitation of human life to a maximum of one hundred and twenty years (§32)!

A further instance of this process appears in the narrative of the Deluge. In general, this hews close to the earlier versions in the Babylonian Epic of Gilgamesh and in the *Story of Atraḥasis*.[6] Yet, one important detail is missing: the eventual translation of the hero to the Blessed Isle, where he enjoys immortality. To the Israelite writer, no one could be immortal, and the inclusion of such a patently mythological detail would impair the moral import which he was seeking to give to the ancient tale.

II. THE ROLE OF MYTH IN THE OLD TESTAMENT

Thus far we have been discussing the bearing of specific ancient and primitive myths upon specific passages of the Old Testament. But this raises the larger question: What is the role of myth *per se* in the Old Testament in general—that is, in the articulation of Israel's peculiar genius and message or, in theological terms, in the process of divine revelation? It is to this that we must now address ourselves.

In the first place, then, it should be recognized that myth is not (as often supposed) simply something ancient and archaic, subsequently superseded by logical and philosophical forms of discourse. Myth, or *mythopoeia,* is an independent and autonomous faculty of the mind which may operate at any time and in any age, alongside of intellection and speculation. Its characteristic is that it envisages and expresses things in terms of their impact, not of their essence; it is impressionistic, not analytic, and it finds its expression in poetry and art rather than in science. Its concern is with experience, not with categorization; it articulates a present, existential situation in general, continuous terms, translating the punctual into the durative, the real into the ideal.

From this it follows that the individual's relation to myth is necessarily one of *involvement*. Myth depicts his own situation by means of a particularizing story, but in the final analysis he is a participant, not merely an auditor or spectator.

Coming now to the myths and stories of the Old Testament, the essential thing about them is that they are paradigms of the continuing human situation; we are involved in them. Adam and Eve, characters in an ancient tale, are at the same time Man and Woman in general; we are all expelled from our Edens and sacrifice our happiness to the ambitions of our intellects. All of us metaphorically flee our Egypts, receive our relevation, and trek through our deserts to a promised land which only our children or our children's children may eventually enjoy. In every generation God fights the Dragon, and David fells Goliath. We all wrestle with angels through a dark night.

Not infrequently the real lesson of such a myth strikes home only when the light of Comparative Folklore is shed upon it; and this holds good not only for ancient stories but also for ancient institutions and usages. The whole process of ritual ablutions, for example, gains added meaning and pertinence when it is realized that to the Scriptural writers bathing in "living waters" meant immersion in the primal, uncontaminated essence of existence, and not simply the removal of impurity. So too, the primitive practice of carrying one's god around in a chest (ark) is more than a piece of crude hocus-pocus; it is an expression, in unsophisticated terms, of the necessity of the divine presence in the wilderness of our lives. Or again, the tinkling bells on the robes of the high priest, which protected him from death when he entered the holy of holies, are more than a primitive apotropaic device to scare demons: they are a reminder of the ambivalent nature of the divine and otherworldly, which alarms as well as attracts.

All of this is not mere allegorization, nor it is not something read in later on the basis of more sophisticated philosophies. These implications are inherent in the myths and usages from the beginning. Behind the concept of demons lies the feeling which inspires it, the existential situation which this archaic idiom articulates. A bride, for instance, who veils her face as a disguise from evil spirits is simply a girl scared of the hazards of marriage; and when a family welcomes the ghosts of its ancestors at a seasonal festival, what is really implied is the lively sense that the past is involved in the present and that we are haunted by our memories and traditions.

Things which *we* can express today by rational and speculative categories were articulated by our remote forebears in impressionistic images, and it is these images that inform myths. *We* might say, for example, that an apprehension of Natural Law involves the ability of men to transcend their diurnal experiences, and of the transcendent to be concentrated and objectified in the immediate. But these are abstract—almost metaphysical—terms which had not been developed at the time the bulk of the Old Testament was written. For a Biblical writer, the same truth will be expressed by saying that for the Law of God to be received by men, man must go up the mountain, and God come down. *We* can say, if we adopt a teleological view of history, that the obscurities which envelop human existence will eventually yield to the progress of science and insight. Malachi, borrowing an image from ancient iconography, says that in the Last Days the sun of righteousness will arise with healing in its wings. *We* can say that tyranny, obfuscation, and evil will eventually be eliminated by a clearer understanding of the real principle of the universe and the ground of existence. Isaiah says that in the end the Lord, with his strong and grim sword, will smite Leviathan, the crooked serpent, the primeval marplot, who may be temporarily chained, but who has yet to be slain.

Even God does not escape this more primitive mode of articulation; it is, indeed, the price of his revelation. *We* can speak of the Absolute, the Principle of Nature, the Cosmic Ground, the dynamics of history, and the ultimate referent of experience, and when we speak of these things in terms of a *being,* we are indulging in deliberate *personification*—that is, we are applying to what we can envisage as concepts the characteristics and attributes of a distinct category, that of personality. But to the writers of the Old Testament, no such transference (or *metaphor*) was involved; there were no *two* entities arbitrarily identified with each other. The Absolute, the Principle of Nature, the dynamics of history, and so forth were *persons*—beings, not ideas—and man apprehended them not by intellectual subscription to a concept but through social relationship with a Being. The God who led the Israelites out of Egypt by his strong hand and outstretched arm *was* indeed the dynamic of history, but he was that as a person, not a personification. The wind is the breath of God; the thunder is his voice. These are not just literary images or conceits; wind and thunder are here parts of a person, not impersonal forces.

Comparative Folklore helps us to recover this primitive stance, to envisage the world by other than dialectic definitions. It retrieves a lost dimension of experience. It has become customary of late to call this approach by the name of *mythopoeia*. I should prefer to call it poetry. It is, as Cassirer pointed out, the stuff of the affective, as distinct from the intellectual, side of the mind, and equally determines meaning and significance. It must be recognized, however, that these two sides of the mind are not watertight compartments; they tend continually to overflow into each other. The immediacy and urgency of myth and ritual inevitably recede as men's developing powers of detached analysis provide an alternative to sympathetic involvement; and when that happens, the survival of traditional forms comes to depend more on their esthetic appeal than on their functional efficacy. Ritual turns into art, and myth is increasingly replaced by philosophy or science. Conversely, however, art and philosophy continue to draw on myth and ritual. The Old Testament stands in the stream of this development. Mythic modes of expression become literary *metaphors,* and survive only vestigially, as when *we* speak of Cupid or the Muses.

This raises a delicate problem, for in the case of ancient texts it is often exceedingly difficult, if not impossible, to determine whether a metaphor is live or dead—that is, whether the underlying myth is still a matter of popular belief or whether that original belief has evaporated into a mere verbal conceit. We know, for instance, that disease and bodily affliction were anciently regarded as the assaults of demons; yet, when Saul declares (II Sam. 1:9), "Cramp (or, Agony) has seized me," is Cramp (or Agony) to be spelled, so to speak, with a capital letter, or is the expression merely an idiomatic relic, as when *we* speak of a heart *seizure?* Similarly, when Resheph is said (Hab. 3:5) to attend upon Yahweh, or when the pangs of love are described as "fiery *reshephs*" (Song of Songs 8:6), do the writers really have in mind the figure of the Canaanite plague-god of that name, or is this simply a case of metonymy? This is a problem which I will not even attempt to resolve, but it must at least be mentioned.

Myth, as an extension of existential experience, is thus the natural language of Religion. It is, in fact, what transmutes historical data into religious truth. The Exodus from Egypt is a historical datum; it becomes a matter of religion only when myth has portrayed it in paradigmatic terms. The Crucifixion is likewise a historical datum, but what, for a Christian, distinguishes the agony of Jesus from that of the two thieves is the factor of *salvation*—that is, the introduction into the story of that mythic element which expresses the hearer's own situation and concern. To be sure, such symbolic significance, issuing as it does out of the hearer's own experience, is necessarily variable, even though the actual story line may remain constant. Thus, the particular Egypt from which men escape today may not be that one from which the Israelites departed, and in our own day and age the Dragon may be Automation or what not. Accordingly, it is not to be supposed that when ancient mythological stories are used in the Old Testament they were necessarily interpreted by the Scriptural writers within their primal frame of reference. To name but one significant point of difference, mythological characters (like demons and dragons) which originally represented independent powers in a world not yet regarded as a systematic cosmos have somehow to be subsumed to the overarching authority of Yahweh and to be depicted as elements within the economy of his dispensation. But it is just this plasticity which gives the old myths their continuing validity and relevance, and which makes the mythic mode of expression the supreme vehicle for the living Word of God. In many and divers ways has God spoken to our fathers . . . and still speaks.

III. CUSTOM AND BELIEF

Light on popular beliefs

It is not only by supplying *literary* parallels that Comparative Folklore throws light on the Biblical narratives and, indeed, on the Old Testament in general. No less significant is the contribution which it makes by clarifying particular beliefs, customs and superstitions implicit in it. The notion, for instance, that the earlier inhabitants of the Holy Land were *giants* links up at once with a belief entertained by many peoples in order to account for megaliths (§**100**). The statement, in the Book of Samuel, that Agag, the king of the Amalekites, when brought before the prophet, came "with limping gait (EV: delicately)," hypocritically chanting a dirge, stands in an arresting light when it is observed that a limping dance was (and still is) a characteristic feature of mourning ceremonies in the Near East (§**129**). The epithet, "baldpate," hurled by the urchins at the prophet Elisha, acquires added force when it is related to the widespread belief that a hairless man is impotent (§**164**). The fact that both Jacob and Moses incorporate predictions of the future into their farewell speeches is elucidated by the well-attested ancient notion that a dying man has the gift of prophecy (§**74**). So too, when Abel's blood cries out from the ground, the idea becomes fully intelligible only when the narrative is aligned with the worldwide belief that the blood is the seat of the *élan vitale* and thus a substitute for the outraged ghost (§**25**).

The entire story of Jacob's encounter with the "unco" being at the Ford of Jabbok is revealed by Comparative Folklore to be a pastiche of familiar popular notions. The mysterious antagonist is simply the personified current of the stream; he must vanish ere daybreak, in accordance with a belief which prevails everywhere concerning witches, elves, fairies, nixes, and nocturnal spirits. His name must remain undivulged, because the name is an essential part of the identity, so that knowledge of it can furnish control over a person; *nomina omina sunt* (§**72**).

The world and man

There are likewise many parallels in the Old Testament to beliefs entertained elsewhere concerning the features of the world and the nature and destiny of man.

The firmament is portrayed as a metal strip (Heb.: *raqî'a*; §**4**). Heaven and earth alike rest on pillars (§309). Misconduct, especially on the part of the king, can impair the fertility of the soil (§§144, 198). Fire can purge a man from evil spirits (§199). The sun is portrayed by the prophet Malachi as winged—a concept which also finds expression in Ancient Near Eastern art (§248). The wind flits across the primeval deep like a bird (Heb.: *merȧhepheth:* §3).

The blood is the seat of life (§§9, 25). The heart or soul can leave a man temporarily in moments of stress; it can be *ex-cited* out of him (§336), and deception is called "stealing the heart" (§69). Conversely, the soul can be prevented from escaping by being bound to the body by fillets (§208).

Leprosy or similar disfigurement of the skin is a punishment for impiety (§93); so is blindness (§56). A man's strength or essential self can lie in his hair (§§117, 164), and the hair is therefore shorn when he suffers legal disgrace (§139) or, in rites of mourning, when he participates in that diminution of the corporate life which is entailed by the death of a kinsman (§135). Life itself can be portrayed as a thread, snapped at death (§§218, 311); and Death binds men in his toils (§§253, 286). At the moment of demise, a man's soul may be said to take wing like a bird (§274); and the ghosts of women who die in childbirth haunt the uplands seeking their babes (§205).

Common ideas about *animals* also find parallels in the Old Testament. The serpent, for instance, is shrewd and wily (§18). Certain beasts, like Balaam's ass, can "flair" ghosts or other invisible beings (§99). The stork is renowned for its kindliness to its young, and is therefore called *ḥasîdah,* "the kindly."

Traces of *popular medicine* may also be recognized by the comparative method. Thus, when Reuben supplies his temporarily barren mother with mandrakes as an aid to further conception, his action can be explained by the persistent popular tradition that the mandrake is an aphrodisiac (§67); while when the lovesick maiden in the Song of Songs begs to be "stayed" with apples (or quinces), she is drawing on an equally widespread belief that the fruits in question are an antidote to the effects of powerful emotion or to irregular movements of the heart (§333).

To folk medicine likewise belongs the action of David's counselors in placing the beauteous virgin Abishag in his bed to warm him in his old age. This action, we are told expressly, had no sexual implications. It is elucidated immediately by the popular belief that the aura of the young can rejuvenate the ageing—a belief which, as late as the eighteenth century, prompted certain superannuated English gentlemen (including members of the cloth) to rent accommodation in girls' boarding schools (§147)!

To the realm of popular usages belong also several references to *magical* procedures, such as waving (§166) and whispering (§171), the employment of *new* implements (§166), the use of bells (§91) and of salt (§211) to forefend evil spirits, and the practice of divination at crossroads (§212,a).

Sometimes, to be sure, it is difficult to distinguish between folk medicine and magic, as when the bones of a holy man are said to resuscitate an adjacent corpse (§**168**), or when a prophet "stretches himself out" upon a dead or moribund boy to revive him (§**157**).

There are also sundry references to standard types of *taboo*. In addition to the ban on divulging names, to which we have already referred, there is the curse implicit on taking a census. Here we have the familiar proscription of *counting:* to know the number of anything can be as perilous as knowing its name, for it can equally enable one to control its identity (§**146**). No less widespread is the taboo involved in the story of how Lot's wife was forbidden to look back on leaving Sodom (§**57**).

Lastly, among standard *ritual procedures* mentioned in the Old Testament and illumined by Comparative Folklore it will suffice to cite the references to animal and even human scapegoats (§**194**), to the necessity of silence in the presence of a god (§**241**), to the custom of accompanying offerings with salt, and to that of circuiting the altar in worship—this last originally a method of warding off evil spirits (§**257**).

IV. FOLKLORE AND LITERARY GENRES

It is not only on the *content* of Old Testament literature but also on its *form* that Comparative Folklore throws interesting new light.

It has been observed increasingly in recent years that there is often a close connection between forms of literature and traditional patterns of ritual or public ceremony. An outstanding example is the development of drama out of the program of seasonal festivals,[7] and scholars have suggested that a ritual background may likewise be detected in divers hymns of the Indic Rig Veda,[8] in the Scandinavian Elder Edda,[9] in some of the odes of the classic Chinese *Book of Songs,*[10] and in the English Mummers' Play.[11] In the same way, several of the literary *genres* of the Old Testament seem to have been conditioned by the exigencies of ritual or cultic ceremonies for which they were originally designed.

Dirges

Dirges, for example, are usually composed in a halting, or scazonic, meter.[12] Whereas a normal Hebrew verse—there are, of course, variations—usually consists in two half lines of parallel sense, each containing *three* accentual beats (e.g., *A snáre have ye béen to Mizpáh, / a nét outspréad on Tabór:* Hos. 5:1), in dirges the last beat of the second half is cut off, to produce a distinctly *limping* effect (e.g., *Outdoórs they líe on the gróund, / my yóung men and óld; / My yóuths and máidens áll / fáll by the swórd:* Lam. 2:21). Now, it so happens that a characteristic feature of Near Eastern funerals is a lamentation chanted while the mourners circle around the bier *with a curious limping step.* It is not difficult to see, therefore, that the peculiar meter must have been designed originally to "mark the pace" in this ceremony, even though it subsequently came to survive simply as a literary convention.

Funeral dirges were (and still are) customarily intoned by female relatives of the deceased or by professional wailing women. This in turn led to the literary convention of putting laments over fallen cities into the mouth of an imaginary female inhabitant. Threnodies of this type have indeed come down to us from ancient Mesopotamia (where they hark back to Sumerian times), and it is to this ritual origin that we may now trace the characteristic style of the Biblical Book of Lamentations, much of which is similarly put into the mouth of a mourning "daughter of Zion."

Psalms of asylum

Likewise rooted in popular custom is the literary form of certain psalms (e.g., Pss. 7, 17, 26), in which a suppliant beseeches the favorable judgment of God against men who are laying charges against him. These psalms are characterized by a more or less standard structure and by the presence, in a more or less stereotyped sequence, of certain clichés. They usually begin with the statement that the suppliant is seeking *refuge* in Yahweh. They then appeal to him specifically as a *judge* (or a "prober of hearts"), and—in juridical language—identify the suppliant with the "righteous" or innocent party, and his accusers or opponents with the "wicked," or guilty. The latter are said to be *pursuing* (i.e., persecuting) him, and to be setting traps and ambushes for him. The Psalmist protests his innocence, sometimes exonerating himself of specific offenses, and on one occasion (Ps. 7:3) contenting himself with the blanket formula, "I have not done *this*," i.e., so-and-so, evidently to be filled in as required. Again in legal terms, Yahweh is sometimes besought to find the Psalmist's antagonists *guilty* and to make them *pay indemnity* (Heb.: *ha'ashîmēm*).

Such compositions were evidently conditioned in the first place by the Ancient Near Eastern practice of providing asylum at shrines and altars for men pursued by vendettas. They became the temporary guests of the resident deity and could therefore claim the protection of their host, in accordance with the established convention of bedouin society. The practice of adjudicating disputes beside the altar is mentioned specifically in the Old Testament itself in connection with Solomon's dedication of the Temple (I Kings 8:31–32), and one recalls that both Adonijah and Joab fled to the altar to escape the royal wrath. The formal procedure evidently involved the recitation under oath of a "negative confession," protesting innocence of specific charges (§313). If the suppliant lied, the god himself would exact retribution, but if he was indeed guiltless, he might in this way escape an unjust and peremptory fate.

Some of these Biblical "psalms of asylum" seem, indeed, to have been adapted from compositions in use at pagan sanctuaries, for it is significant that when they mention the name of Yahweh, that name often overloads the meter, suggesting that it is a later insertion.[13]

Kingship psalms

In the same way, too, psalms which begin with the words, *The Lord has become king* (EV: The Lord reigneth) are now generally recognized to have been patterned after a traditional style of hymn composed for the annual enthronement of the deity at the New Year festival. To the Hebrews the ceremony was, in all likelihood, no longer a living thing, but the style survived as a literary convention.

A good example of this type is Psalm 93, which boldly transfers to Yahweh the mythic exploits attributed to Baal in the Canaanite myths from Ras Shamra: he subdues sea and river, ensconces himself as king in "the height," and occupies a glorious palace (§**276**).

Hallelujah

The familiar *Hallelujah* at the beginning or end of a psalm is likewise the relic of an ancient popular usage. The Hebrew word *hallel,* which came to mean "praise," is really an onomatopoeic word (like *yell, howl,* etc.) expressive of inarticulate shouting or screaming. Now, among primitive peoples, the earliest form of prayer—as, in fact, of song in general—consists precisely in such ecstatic ejaculations. It is, for instance, by the frantic chanting of meaningless syllables that certain Australian aborigines seek to produce rainfall;[14] while the Yamana of Tierra del Fuego have been observed to perform their ritual dances to such inarticulate cries as

ha ma la, ha ma la, ha ma la, ha ma la,
O la la la la,   la la la la   la

and their neighbors, the Selk'nam perform in the same way.[15] So too among the Veddas of Ceylon a common prayer is the equally meaningless

tan tandinanan tandinana
tanan tandina tandinana[16]

and similar chants are intoned in the Peyote cult of the North American Arapaho.[17] In pre-Islamic usage, such shouting, accompanied by a skipping march (*ṭawāf*) around the altar, was indeed known as *tahlīl*. It survives in the modern *dhikr,* or wild shriek, and its counterpart may be heard at any "hot gospel" rally.

Out of this inarticulate ejaculation there develops in time the *invocation* of the holy name, e.g., *ya Allah, iō Bacche,* etc.—a development illustrated, on a more profane level, by the substitution of *"Jesus!", Madonna mia,* or *sacre nom de Dieu* for the original *oh, ah, ouch,* in modern swearing.[18]

This in turn produces the *elaborated invocation,* in which the name is tricked out with laudatory epithets, e.g., *Allah akbar* (Allah is mighty), *Holy, holy, holy, is the Lord of Hosts,* etc. This is the ancient Arabic *takbīr* ("aggrandizement") or *tasbīḥ* ("laudation") and the Greek *epiklēsis*. A good Biblical example is Exodus 34:6–7 (which really represents what Moses cried out to God, rather than vice versa, as commonly supposed): *Yahweh, Yahweh, a god compassionate and gracious, long-suffering and of abundant kindness and fidelity* (or, *truth*), etc.

Finally comes the stage where the epithets are validated by lengthier descriptions of the god's deeds, exploits and qualities; this yields the full-fledged *hymn*.

Taunt-songs

Again, it was a common custom in antiquity to open hostilities with an exchange of taunts and boasts between the opposing armies or their commanders. It is thus that Marduk and Tiamat preface their combat in the Babylonian Epic of Creation (*Enuma Elish*), and in the Old Testament, David and Goliath follow suit, each boasting the prowess of his god, much in the manner of the "My-dad-can-lick-your-dad" of brawling schoolchildren today. The practice is by no means confined to the Orient. The Welsh thought that such invective (*glam dichen*) could actually inflict physical damage on an opponent, and a crossfire of "taunt (*nith*)-songs" is a recognized method of settling disputes among the inhabitants of Greenland. Among the Arabs this produced a special genre of martial poetry, known as *hijâ*-verse, and literary specimens of this may be found in the Old Testament in the bellicose little Song of Lamech (Gen. 4:23–24) and in the utterances of Balaam, the seer commissioned by the king of Moab to "curse" the invading Israelites (§§**31, 98**).

Ballad

Lastly, there is the *ballad*. A ballad—as the very name implies—is primarily a song accompanying a dance, and its literary structure is determined by that fact. Leading characteristics of the ballad are therefore: (a) a *refrain,* designed to permit the various sections of the dancers each to utter the crucial exclamation, and (b) constant *repetition of keywords,* often tricked out with elaborations or "incremental supplements,"[19] matching the constant return of the dancers to their original positions and the constant elaboration of steps and movements. Often, too, an important word is repeated with emphasis at the end of a verse or stanza, like a final crashing chord of the accompanying music. Other characteristic features are an initial appeal to the audience to "listen," and a rapid, almost jerky transition (or "leap") from incident to incident, chiming with the rapid transitions in the dance. In short, a ballad is choreography in words—at least in its pristine form.

All of these features appear in the Biblical Song of Deborah (§**109**), which may therefore be regarded as a specimen of this genre:

1. The song is put into the mouth of the woman Deborah herself, and she is expressly bidden (v. 12) to bestir herself and sing.

2. There is an opening invocation (v. 3) to "hearken" and "give ear," as in the English ballads of *Richard of Almaigne* ("Sitteth all stille, ant herkneth to me"), *King Edward the First* ("A-stounde herkneth to my song"), *The Heir of Linne* ("Lithe and listen, gentlemen, / To sing a song I will beginne"), *Jemmy Dawson* ("Come, listen to my mournful tale, / Ye tender hearts and lovers dear"), *The Birth of Saint George* ("Listen, lords, in bower and hall, / I sing," etc.) and *George Barnwell* ("All youths of fair England . . . / to my song give ear"). Moreover, that this form is indeed ancient is shown by its presence in the Canaanite *Hymeneal of Nikkal and Yariḫ* from Ras Shamra-Ugarit ("Hearken, ye songstresses"), the Hittite *Myth of the Kingdom of Heaven* ("Let the mighty gods now hearken"), and the Biblical *Song of Lamech* ("Adah and Zillah, hear my voice, / Womenfolk of Lamech, give ear to what I say").

3. A refrain, "Bless ye the Lord," appears at the end of verses 2 and 9, and it has been suggested[20] that it was meant to be repeated also, as a kind of antiphon, elsewhere in the song.

4. Certain keywords are constantly repeated, with characteristic "incremental elaboration," e.g.:

> v. 4: The skies *also dripped*,
> the clouds also *dripped water*.[21]
> v. 7: *They ceased from law and order*,[22]
> in Israel *they ceased*,
> until I, Deborah, *arose*,
> *arose*, a mother in Israel.
> v. 13: *Then marched* a mere remnant against stalwarts,
> *the army of the Lord marched* for me . . . .
> v. 19: Came *kings, they fought*;
> then *fought the kings of Canaan*.
> v. 21: *The brook of Kishon* swept them away,
> *the brook* . . . .[23]
> *the brook Kishon*.
> v. 23: They came not *to the help of the Lord*,
> *to the help of the Lord* amid the warriors.
> v. 24: *Blessed above women* be Jael,
> *among women* in the tent *be she blessed*!
> v. 27: *Between her feet he crouched, he fell* . . .
> *between her feet he crouched, he fell*;
> where he crouched, there fell he subdued.

5. The important word *Israel* is repeated emphatically—a kind of ringing cry (almost like "Texas! Texas!" at a ball game) at the end of clauses or stanzas, in verses 2, 3, 5, 7, 8, 9, and 11, and the word *warriors* in verses 13 and 23.[24]

6. Incidents are linked rapidly and almost mechanically by the constant repetition of the word, *then* (verses 8, 11, 13, 19, 22).

7. Likewise characteristic of the ballad are the introductory clauses giving the setting in time:

> v. 2: When men loosed all restraint(?) in Israel.
> v. 4: When thou didst go forth, O Lord, from Seir;
> when thou didst march from the territory of Edom.
> v. 6: In the days of Shamgar, the son of 'Anat,
> in the days of Jael . . . .

This recalls the typical opening of many an English and Scottish ballad, e.g., *The Tournament of Tottenham* ("It befel in Tottenham, on a dire day"); *Fair Rosamond* ("Whenas King Henry ruled this land, / The second of that name"); and *The Brave Lord of Willoughby* ("The fifteenth of July, / with glistening spear and shield, / A famous fight in Flanders / was foughten in the field").

8. Then there is the rhetorical question, designed to enhance suspense and to give the dancers an opportunity for a resounding burst of song by way of reply. Admittedly, this is not evident in our present Hebrew text, but without altering a single letter and by simply redividing the consonants of the first word (viz., *mî qôl* for *mi-qôl*), it may be readily elicited from a clause in verse 11 which has thus far baffled commentators:

> *What is this noise of people huzzah-ing*[25]
> *between the water-troughs?*
> *Why, they are recounting there*
> *the triumphant acts of the Lord!*

This again recalls a similar device in the English and Scottish ballads, e.g., " 'Who have we here?' Lord Bodwell said," in *The Murder of the King of Scots*, or the more poetic, "Ye highlands, ye highlands, / Oh, where have ye been? / They hae slain the Earl of Murray / and hae laid him in the green."

9. Lastly, the virtually onomatopoeic words of verse 22:

> *'az hal^{e}mū 'iqbê sūsîm*[26]
> *dah^{a}rôt dah^{a}rôt 'abbirāw*

which may be rendered approximately,

> *Then hammered the hoofs of his horses;*
> *stamp, stamp, stamp went his stallions,*

may likewise have been accompanied by a vigorous stamping of feet on the part of the dancers.

The whole song, then, may be put into the category of the song-with-dance (i.e., *ballad*), wherewith, as we are told expressly in the Old Testament itself, women welcomed their menfolk when they returned victorious from battle. It thus provides an excellent example of the manner in which popular custom conditioned literary form.

Something of the same sort may be recognized also in the song which Moses and the children of Israel are said to have sung after they had crossed the Sea of Reeds dryshod (Exod. 15). Here too we have the same introductory phrase, *I will sing of the Lord,* and the same repetition of crucial words, with "incremental supplements":

> v. 2: This is *my God,* and I will extol him,
> *my father's god,* and I will exalt him;
> v. 4: Pharaoh's chariots and army
> he hurled in the *sea;*
> his picked captains sank
> in the *Sea of Reeds;*
> v. 16: *Until thy people passed over,* O Lord,
> *until this people whom thou hadst gotten passed over.*

There is likewise the same emphasis upon a cardinal word at the end of a clause or stanza:

> v. 1: horse and mount he threw into the *sea;*
> v. 4: Pharaoh's chariots and army
> he hurled in the *sea;*
> v. 8: The deeps congealed in the heart of the *sea;*
> v. 10: Thou didst blow with thy breath (wind);
> then covered them the *sea;*
> v. 19 (perhaps an excerpt from another song):
> When Pharaoh with his horses and chariots
> entered the *sea;*
> when with his horsemen
> (he entered) the *sea,*
> the Lord turned back on them
> the waters of the *sea,*
> but the Israelites walked on dry land
> in the midst of the *sea.*

There is also the same type of rhetorical question:

> v. 11: Who is like thee 'mid the gods, O Lord,
> who 'mid the holy ones (LXX) so majestic as thee . . . ?

And it is said expressly (v. 20) that at the same time Miriam and the womenfolk "went forth with timbrels and dance" and also sang.

A new look at the Minor Prophets

These, however, are not the only instances of the relation of literary forms to popular usages. Comparative Folklore also makes an important contribution to the understanding of the Minor Prophets by illuminating the cultic background against which they spoke.

If we line up the successive images and metaphors used by a minor prophet, these may often be found to coincide with the various elements of ritual ceremonies connected with pagan seasonal festivals. This suggests that the prophets were often delivering their messages in terms of satire upon such apostatic performances. Thus, when a prophet speaks of Yahweh's *pouring out his wrath like water* (Hos. 5:10), he may be taking a sly dig at the pagan ceremony of pouring water as a rain-charm (§221). Similarly, when he says that *Yahweh will search out Jerusalem with lamps* (Zeph. 1:12), he may be deriding the "heathen" custom of staging torchlight processions through the city in seasonal rites (§243). And when he warns his recalcitrant countrymen that Yahweh is about to *hold a banquet, and has already invited his guests* (Zeph. 1:7), he may be alluding pointedly to the fact that a standard feature of the cultic myths associated with pagan seasonal celebrations was the banquet tended by or to the god in order to re-cement his ties with his worshipers (§243). Other examples of such use of satire are given in the body of this work.

If this basic supposition is correct, an important conclusion follows for the literary analysis of the prophetic books. Instead of fragmentizing them and regarding them as compilations from different hands simply because they seem sometimes to pass too rapidly and inconsequentially from one theme to another, we may now rather try to fit the apparently disconnected pieces into a single over-all pattern of seasonal ceremonies, and thereby vindicate the unity of the whole. Thus, when the Book of Joel passes from a picture of devastation and mourning to a description of Yahweh's final war against the heathen and of the assize at which he will judge them, there is no need to assume that the themes are unrelated and that the several prophecies therefore proceed from different authors. For the fact is that the usual pattern of seasonal festivals is that an initial period of mortification and abstinence—symbolizing the eclipse of life at the close of the agricultural year—is followed by a mimetic battle between Old and New, Life and Death, Rain and Drought, Summer and Winter, or the like, which is mythologized as the defeat by the god of his contumacious opponents (e.g., the victory of Marduk over Tiamat and her allies in the Babylonian New Year myth, of the Hittite Weather-god over the Dragon in the cult-legend of the Feast of Purulli, and of Baal over Yam and Mot in the Canaanite poems from Ras Shamra). Then, in turn, comes the divine assembly at which the order of the world and the fates of men are determined for the incoming year. Joel, therefore, may have been preaching against the background of this consecutive program, and the seeming incoherence and inconsequence disappear (§231).

That there was, indeed, an undercurrent of such allusive satire in these prophetic utterances is seemingly indicated by the striking conclusion of the Book of Hosea (14:9)—a book in which the same pattern can be discerned:

> Whoever is wise will understand these things,
> whoever is discerning will know them.

These words may be read as a Hebrew equivalent of the familiar *Verbum sapienti sat* (A word to the wise).

V. THE SPOKEN WORD

Popular literature is *heard*, rather than *read*, and the influence of recitation is present everywhere in the Old Testament.

"Hear ye"

1. The reciter draws his audience by an introductory invitation to the crowd to listen, somewhat like the *oyez* of the town crier. So the prophets often begin with the cry, *Hear ye* or *Give ear*.

Cante-fable

2. To keep his audience awake and interested, a storyteller often punctuates his narrative, at appropriate places, with popular songs, in which all may join. This device is common to many cultures, and is characteristic especially of early Arabic romances (*sāj*). It is known technically as *cante-fable*. A good example in the Old Testament is the song put into the mouth of the Israelites after crossing the Sea of Reeds dryshod (Exod. 15). So too, when the prophet Jonah is ensconced in the belly of the "great fish," and the story comes to a logical and dramatic standstill until he is disgorged, he is represented as spending the intervening time chanting a prayer which consists largely of liturgical clichés paralleled in the Book of Psalms and elsewhere. This was evidently chanted by the audience; they were spending the "intermission," so to speak, intoning snatches from a Hebrew *Hymns Ancient and Modern!* Again, after telling the story of Cain and Abel, the narrator starts reciting the family tree of the former's descendants. This, to be sure, is tedious stuff for an audience which has gathered to hear a good story. But the storyteller knows how to relieve their boredom. When he comes to Lamech, Cain's descendant in the fifth generation, he suddenly interpolates a little war song chanted by a tribe named the Lamechites, and deftly foists it upon the ancient worthy (§**31**). So also, in the equally tedious account of the stages by which the Israelites crossed the wilderness in their exodus from Egypt, when the narrator gets to their halt at a place named Beër, and when he realizes that his audience is nodding or dozing, he rouses their flagging interest by introducing a popular song chanted annually when a new *beër*, or water pit, was dug.

Repetition of messages

3. When the story requires that a message be conveyed, it is often repeated *in extenso* (cf. Gen. 24:22–49). This device likewise characterizes the older

Sumerian, Akkadian, and Ugaritic epics, and it is found also in the Iliad and Odyssey, in the Kalevala (though there perhaps only through Lönnrot's editing), and elsewhere. It originated, we may suggest, in the exigencies of *recitation:* the crowd of listeners was constantly swelling, and newcomers had to be kept abreast of the story. This was a way of doing so.[27]

Oracles in verse

4. It is likewise, perhaps, to the factor of oral communication that we should attribute the convention of delivering oracles—and hence prophecies—in verse.[28] To be sure, in moments of enthusiasm speech is apt anyway to fall into cadences, as anyone who reads Cicero or listens to an inspired orator or an enraptured preacher can easily test. But in the case of oracles something else seems also to be involved. A man would often *send,* rather than *go,* to consult an oracle, and it was, of course, essential that the messenger should report the divine words *verbatim,* without distortion or error due to lapse of memory. In this situation, verse would have served as a mnemonic technique, and at the same time have guaranteed accuracy, for any involuntary garbling or deliberate falsification would have been readily betrayed (unless the messenger were exceptionally clever or skillful) by resultant defects of scansion. (This, of course, does not apply to oracles derived from omens, divination, or astrology, for these were interpretations of signs—commentaries, as it were, on actual phenomena—rather than communications of spontaneous outbursts. Nor does it apply to oracles which may have been written down on tablets. We are speaking only of those which had to be reported by word of mouth.)

Deictic expressions

5. Yet another evidence of the influence of recitation upon literary form and style is afforded by the use of the adverbs *there* and *thither* in contexts where they would be intelligible only if accompanied by a gesture on the part of the speaker. Job, for example, declares in a famous passage (1:21) that not only did he come naked from the womb but that he will also return *thither* in the same condition. Nobody, however, returns to his mother's womb, naked or otherwise; yet, the expression is clarified immediately once it is realized that the story was told *orally* and that at this point the narrator (like Job himself) must have *pointed to the earth* (§**294**). Similarly, when the prophet Habakkuk, portraying the advent of the Lord in terms of sunrise, remarks (3:4) that, although the first glow has indeed streaked the mountains, *"there* lies the hiding-place of his might," the phrase becomes intelligible and vivid only when one sees it as accompanied by a wave of the speaker's hand toward the region below the horizon, whence the full glory of the sun is yet to emerge.

Of the same order, too, is the expression, "May the Lord do thus and more to me," used so often in the swearing of oaths. This again is meaningless except in the context of *recitation*, when the narrator would have accompanied the words by drawing his finger across his throat, or the like.[29]

Distortion and modernization

6. Literature which is passed down by word of mouth naturally undergoes verbal changes in successive generations. Anyone who has studied the textual variants of traditional ballads, songs or stories will not need to be told that constant modernization of vocabulary is part and parcel of the process of transmission. We must expect the same sort of thing in the Old Testament; and indeed we find it. In Psalm 68:4, Yahweh is acclaimed as "he who rides across the deserts," the Hebrew for which is *rōkeb ba-ʿarābôth*. This, however, is simply a misunderstanding and consequent modification of a very similar expression, *rōkeb ʿarāPHôth*, "he that rides upon the clouds," which is a standard epithet of Baal in the Canaanite poems from Ras Shamra-Ugarit. It is not a mere textual corruption (as many modern scholars suppose),[30] but a popular distortion, of the same order as that which turned the *girasole* into the *Jerusalem* artichoke or the London tavern called the *El Infanta de Castille* into the *Elephant and Castle*.

Nor are such changes wrought only by the mouths of the "common folk"; learned editors and professional antiquarians also play their hands in the process. One recalls, for instance, what Bishop Percy did to the reliques of ancient English poetry, and how the meticulous Ritson pilloried him for such sacrilege; how Walter Scott occasionally prettified the Scottish ballads; and how Wilhelm Grimm modified and stylized the peasant language of the famous *Household Tales*. There is similar evidence of the "learned sock" in the Old Testament. To be sure, in some cases the archaic language of the traditional myths and stories is retained intact by dint of usage, just as the British still speak of "lords puisne" and we of the Capitol. Thus, the epithets which characterize Leviathan in Isaiah 27:1 and Job 26:13 are archaic and recur nowhere else in the Hebrew Scriptures; while in Ezekiel's parable of the Fallen Paragon (28:14) the word which describes the cherub with wings *outspanned* (viz., *mimšaḥ*) is likewise an archaic, not a current, term.[31]

On the other hand, however, there are clear evidences elsewhere of "Percyfication" on the part of ancient editors—changes due not to *oral* misunderstanding but to failure to interpret written words which happen to have grown obsolete. An instructive illustration of what took place in such later redaction of traditional material is afforded by comparing two versions of the same saying in the Book of Proverbs—a cumulative anthology of time-honored aphorisms. In 12:23 we are told that *a prudent man conceals (his) knowledge,* but in 13:16 that *a prudent man acts with knowledge.* Now, the point here is that what came later to be understood as the normal Hebrew word for *acts* (viz., *yaʿaśeh*) was really an archaic word (viz., **yaʿaśeh;* cf. Arabic *ʿ-sh-y*) meaning *conceals.* The one version, therefore, even though it misinterpreted it (or was it itself misunderstood even later), at least preserved the original term of the traditional proverb; the other, though it did *not* misinterpret it, "Percyfied" it, substituting the current term (Heb.: *k-s-h*).[32]

Similar modernization can be recognized elsewhere. David's lament for Saul and Jonathan, for example, contains in the present text the obscure lines:

> *Ye mountains of Gilboa,*
>   *be there no dew nor rain upon you,*
>   *ye fields of offerings* (Heb.: *śᵉdê tᵉrūmôth*)!

We now know, however, from a passage in one of the Ras Shamra poems, that this bizarre reading is simply a later editor's attempt to "correct" a very similar archaic expression (viz., *šeraʽ tᵉhômôth*) which really meant "neither upsurge of the deeps," and referred to the ancient belief that the earth is watered by the cosmic ocean in the form of rain from above and of the upwelling of springs from below.[33]

Take, again, Samson's famous riddle in Judges 14:14: *What is the eater out of which has come something to eat, the strong out of which has come something sweet?* The answer, as we know, was *a lion infested by bees carrying honey,* but it has been observed that in the original version the point evidently depended—as so often in riddles—on a play of words, an archaic Hebrew word for *honey* being identical in form with that for *lion,* while *the eater* was a common popular expression for a ravening beast (§**117**).

Another example of the same process may be detected in Psalm 82:7, where it is said of those who claimed to be gods and celestial beings that

> Nevertheless ye shall die like men,
>   and fall *like one of the princes.*

As most scholars have recognized, the word *princes* is here somewhat odd, for what the context demands is surely a reference to the myth of the "fallen angels." In later Hebrew, however, "princes" came indeed to be a common designation for angels, and it is therefore plain that it has here been substituted for some more archaic term. What that term was is anybody's guess. It may be suggested, perhaps, that it was *Nephilim,* a term for the primeval giants (associated with the fallen angels) in Genesis 6:4 and Numbers 13:33, for whatever that term may really have meant, it could have come to be derived fancifully from the Hebrew word *n-ph-l,* "fall," and this would provide a singularly effective play on words![34]

These examples, taken together with parallel phenomena in popular literature everywhere, should warn us, incidentally, against the prevalent tendency of Bible scholars to assume that a given work or passage must necessarily have been *composed* at a late date merely because it contains words or grammatical constructions of demonstrably late vintage. In the case of works which may have come down orally, all that such evidence really indicates is the late date of the extant *redaction*.³⁵

VI. FOLKLORE AND TEXTUAL CRITICISM

Another contribution which Comparative Folklore makes to the understanding of the Old Testament is that it sometimes enables us to vindicate the authenticity of the traditional text against arbitrary modern emendations.

Thus, in Deuteronomy 32:10 (**§103**), the unusual expression, "howling wilderness," has taxed the ingenuity of commentators, and the Hebrew words have therefore been variously "corrected." But Comparative Folklore reveals that among the bedouin the desert is popularly known as "the place of ululation" because the shrill winds which sweep across it are regarded as the howling or shrieking of demons.

Again, in Ezekiel 28:14 (**§213**), the paragon who is cast out of Paradise is said to have walked there originally *amid fiery stones* (Heb.: *'abnê esh*). Not so, say several modern scholars, deftly altering the Hebrew text: he walked *amid beings divine* (Heb.: *bᵉnê el*)! But Comparative Folklore shows that Paradise is often pictured as a place of precious stones, and a Mesopotamian lexical text actually specifies "fiery stone" as the name of a particular gem. The dulled radiance of the celestial jewels is thus restored.

In Psalm 68:22 (**§266,a**), Yahweh declares that he is able to retrieve men from Bashan and from the depths of the sea. The reference to Bashan, a region east of the Jordan, has puzzled Biblical scholars, and by clever manipulation of the Hebrew text (i.e., *mi-<ki>bshan <esh>* for the traditional *mi-Bashan*) the verse has therefore been made to assert that Yahweh rescues men *from the fiery furnace*. Comparative Folklore shows, however, that in the mythology of the Canaanites, Bashan and Sea (Yam) were the names of dragons which the god Baal was said to have subdued. Moreover, the archaic words for "capture" and "muzzle"—words actually used in the Canaanite myth—can indeed be recognized behind those traditionally rendered, "retrieve, bring back." Hence it becomes apparent that the Biblical poet was simply adapting a time-honored myth: what the verse really says is that Yahweh is able to make a captive of the Dragon and to muzzle Sir Sea in the depths.

In Ezekiel 24:17, eating the *bread of men* (Heb.: *leḥem 'anāshîm*) is described as a rite of mourning. This too has baffled modern exegetes, as it already baffled the translators of the ancient Aramaic and Latin Versions, and the phrase has therefore been emended, by the omission of but a single letter (viz., *leḥem 'ônîm*) to *bread of mourners*—an expression which actually occurs in Hosea 9:4. The fact is, however, that one of the purposes of funeral meals is to re-cement the ruptured ties of the community, and this is the basic meaning of the word rendered "men." Indeed, even at the present day, its exact equivalent (*awnâse, waniseh*) is a not uncommon term among Arabs for funeral meats![36]

In Amos 8:14 the recalcitrant Israelites are charged with swearing loyalty to false gods and with taking oaths by the formula, *As the way* (Heb.: *DeReK*) *of Beersheba lives!* This clearly makes no sense, and modern scholars have therefore emended the traditional text to read, *As thy (god) Dod* (Heb.: *DôDᵉKā*) *lives, O Beersheba,* on the assumption that Dod (literally, Beloved) was the name of a heathen deity. But our increased knowledge of ancient Canaanite religion now discloses that the Hebrew consonants traditionally vocalized as *DeReK*, "way," are really to be read *DôRᵉKā*, "thy pantheon," the word *dôr* being a standard name for the circle or family of the pagan gods![37]

In Hosea 6:11 (§**221**) the prophet threatens reprobate Israel in the words, *Yahweh has set a harvest for you!* Modern critics, unable to penetrate the meaning of these words, have blithely finagled them to read, *Yahweh has laid up abominations for thee!* But, apart from the fact that abominations are elsewhere always something perpetrated *against* Yahweh rather than *by* him, this facile emendation overlooks the point, which Comparative Folklore demonstrates, that the prophet is preaching against the background of pagan seasonal celebrations. His ringing cry to the harvesters that Yahweh has another kind of harvest in store for them is therefore singularly effective, particularly since it comes as the climax of his speech. Thus, in more senses than one, Comparative Folklore removes an abomination.

A final example is furnished by Hosea 8:6 (§**228**). In the traditional text this reads:

> *That calf of thine, O Samaria, is a stinking thing*
> . . . .
> *For out of Israel is he;*
> *a workman made him, and he is no god.*

The penultimate line is notoriously difficult, and once again various emendations have been proposed. But once again Comparative Folklore clarifies what is otherwise obscure; for the fact is that, by mere redivision of the Hebrew consonants, the words rendered, *For out of Israel is he* can be read, *For who is (this) El the Bull,* and from texts discovered at Ras Shamra-Ugarit we now know that this was a common designation of the supreme god of the Canaanites.[38]

NOTES

INTRODUCTION

1. See: H. Usener, in Rhein. Mus. 57 (1902), 177–92; I. Guidi, in RB 12 (1903), 241 ff.; T. H. Gaster, Thespis[2], 222; Stith Thompson, MI, F 701.1.
2. The Hebrew word is *sh-b-th*. In Isa. 30:7 it lies concealed beneath the impossible reading, *Rahab hem shabeth*, which must be corrected to *Rahab ha-mashbath*. In Isa. 14:4 the concocted verb *marhēbah*, "she that plays the role of Rahab," was misunderstood by the early Jewish editors and therefore distorted to *madhēbah*, which, however, is barely translatable. The correct reading can be restored from the Greek (Septuagint) and Syriac versions, and from the Dead Sea Isaiah scroll.—In Job 38:11 the mythological allusion has again been lost by the displacement of a single letter: for *ū-phô' yāshîth bi-ge'ôn gallêkā* read *ū-phô' yishbôth ge'ôn gallêkā*.
3. This is simply the conventional rendering of Heb. *bārī^aḥ*, but it is by no means certain; for other explanations, see: W. F. Albright, in BASOR 83 (1941) 39, n.3 ("ancient, primeval"); T. H. Gaster, in JRAS 1944.47, n.49 ("sinister"); C. Rabin, in JTS 47 (1946), 38–41.
4. Cf. J. G. Frazer, FOT, ed. min., 5.
5. C. E. Fox, The Threshold of the Pacific (1924), 238.
6. For translations, cf. ANET 43–44 (Sumerian); 93 ff. (Akkadian); 104 ff.
7. See: Gilbert Murray, in Jane Harrison's Themis (1912), 314 ff.; Jane Harrison, Ancient Art and Ritual (1913); F. M. Cornford, The Origin of Attic Comedy[2], ed. T. H. Gaster (1961).
8. E.g., Rig Veda ix.112; cf. L. von Schroeder, Mysterium und Mythus (1903).
9. Bertha S. Phillpotts, The Elder Edda and Scandinavian Drama (1920).
10. B. Schindler, in Orient and Occident: Moses Gaster Anniversary Volume (1936), 498–52.
11. See: R. J. E. Tiddy, The Mummers' Play (1923).—A similar theory has been applied to the Italian *maggio* and *bruscello:* P. Toschi, Dal dramma liturgico alla rappresentazione sacra (1940); V. de Bartholomaeis, Le origini della poesia drammatica italiana (1924); S. Fontana, Il maggio (1929); G. Cocchiara, Le vastasate (1926). Cf. also: R. Stumpfl, Kultspiele der Germanen als Ursprung des mittelalterlichen Dramas (1956).
12. On this meter (called conventionally *qînah*), cf. K. Budde, in ZAW 2 (1882), 1–52; 3 (1883), 11.
13. E.g., Pss. 7:1, 4, 7, 9; 17:1, 14; 26:1, 6, 12.
14. A. C. Bouquet, Sacred Books of the World (Penguin 1954), 27–28.
15. M. Gusinde, Die Feuerland Indianer (1931–37), ii.115, 1139–40.
16. C. G. and B. Z. Seligmann, The Veddas (1911), 366.
17. B. Nettl, Music in Primitive Culture (1956), 23.—On this subject in general, cf. C. M. Bowra, Primitive Song (Mentor Books, 1964), 64 f.
18. A clear reference to such cries may be recognized in the Old Testament itself in Psalm 68:4, which should be rendered: *"Cast up a highway for him who rides across the deserts, (to the cry,) 'Yah is his name!'"*; cf. Exod. 15:3.
19. Cf. F. Gummere, The Popular Ballad (reprint, 1959), 117 ff.; S. Mirsky, "The Origin of Anadiplosis in Hebrew Literature," in Tarbiz 28 (1959), 171–80 (Hebrew).

20. I. W. Slotki, in JTS 33 (1932), 341–54.

21. The repetition of the verb is deliberate, and no emendation is required.

22. An approximate rendering of Hebrew $p^e rāzôn$ (cf. Arabic f-r-z; Akkadian $parṣu$), the exact meaning of which is still unknown.

23. Hebrew, $qiddūmîm$ (G. A. Smith: "spates"), the exact meaning of which is unknown. At all events, it is an "incremental addition," and hence should not be emended into a verbal form, e.g., $qidd^e mam$, "confronted them," as in LXX.

24. In Psalm 68, the word $Elôhîm$ ("God") is similarly repeated throughout at the beginning or end of clauses and stanzas; vv.2, 3, 4, 5, 6, 7, 8, 9, 10, 16, 17, 18, 19, 22, 25, 27, 29, 32, 33, 35, 36 (*bis*). If this is indeed a structural device, the recognition of it would invalidate Albright's view (in Mowinckel Festschrift, 1955.1–12) that the psalm is really but a string of disconnected *incipits* of ancient hymns.

25. With George Adam Smith, I take $m^e haṣ^e ṣîm$ to be onomatopoeic. For the sentiment, cf. Euripides, *Medea*, 67–69. As anyone knows, who has traveled in the East or in the Greek islands, the local fountain or washing place is always a center of chatter and gossip.

26. Reading, with most modern scholars, $sūsîm, dah^a rôth$ for the $sūs mi$-$dah^a rôth$ of the received text; $sūs$-ma (with archaic -ma) would also be possible.

27. Another device derived from recitation is the use of *gradated numbers* (e.g., "twice, . . . nay, thrice") for dramatic effect; cf. ANET 46, 1. 48 (Sumerian); J. Friedrich, in OLz 1937.518, n. 1 (Hittite); C. H. Gordon, Ugaritic Handbook (1947), 34 (Ugaritic); Od. 3. 115 f., 5.306; Sophocles, Ajax 433 (Greek); K. Krohn, Die folkloristische Arbeitsmethode (1926), 80 (Finnish). Cf. also Humpty Dumpty's "I told them *once*, I told them *twice*;/They would not listen to advice," and the Duchess' "I beat him *once*, I beat him *twice*;/I beat him till he sneezes," in *Alice through the Looking-Glass*.

28. Note that in Herodotus, oracles are usually reproduced in Greek hexameters.

29. I Sam. 3:17; 14:44; 20:13; II Sam. 3:9; I Kings 2:23; II Kings 6:31, etc. A similar expression occurs in Arabic, e.g., Tabari, Annales, ed. M. J. de Goeje (1897–1901), i.852,2; ii.453,12.

30. So, for instance, RSV. But this strains the normal sense of the verb $sôlū$, "cast up a highway," which has then to be twisted to mean "Lift up a song." This ruins the point: the god who normally careers through the sandy tracts of the desert is to have a level highway prepared for his triumphant progress. For the sentiment, cf. Isa. 40:3.

31. Cf. Akkadian $mašāḫu$; Vulgate actually renders *extentus*.

32. Cf. I. Eitan, in JQR, N.S. 14 (1923), 46 f.

33. H. L. Ginsberg, in JBL 57 (1938), 209–13.

34. The same process may perhaps be recognized in Micah 1:11. The prophet is excoriating various cities of Judah by playing on their names. Concerning Beth ha-Eṣel he observes that *Lamentation has taken from you its* standing-place (Heb.: '$emdāthô$). Here, I suggest, the point lies in the fact that the name suggests an archaic word *$eṣel$ (akin to Arabic $aṣl$) meaning "firm root." This word may originally have stood in the text and have been replaced later by a more familiar term.

35. These *oral* modifications of archaic words and phrases must be sharply distinguished from cases in which ancient spellings in a *written* text baffled later scribes and were therefore "emended." Two arresting examples of the latter process are: (*a*) Ps. 68:19, *Thou hast asscended on high, hast led captives in thy train, hast received tributes* among men, where *among men* (Heb.: $bā$-$ādām$) is a "correction" of an archaic bdm, "from their hands"; (*b*) Ps. 16:3, *I will not pour their libations* out of blood, *nor take their names upon my lips*, where *out of blood* (Heb.: mi-dam) is again a "correc-

tion" of the same archaic *bdm*, "with (my) hands." Yet another illuminating example occurs in Balaam's oracle, Num. 24:23; see below, §**98**.

36. G. Schumacher, in MDPV 1904.75 f.; J. Morgenstern, Rites of Birth, Marriage and Death among the Semites (1966), 149.

37. F. Neuberg, in JNES 9 (1950), 215–17; cf. T. H. Gaster, in Orientalia 11 (1942), 60.

38. This interpretation is due to Tur Sinai.

FORMER PROPHETS

Joshua

104 Joshua at Jericho Josh. 6:1-21

(a) "The walls came tumblin' down"

Despite extensive excavation of the site, archaeology can as yet say nothing definite about an Israelite invasion of Jericho. In the opinion of many scholars, the Biblical narrative really reflects the reminiscence of an earlier capture of the city by pre-Israelite Hebrews (Ḫabirû).[1] In any case, the account clearly incorporates several purely folkloristic traits.

(b) The circumambulation of the walls

Thus, Joshua's celebrated march around the walls of the beleaguered city is based, in all probability, on the widespread custom of laying claim to territory by so tracing out its bounds.[2] Such circuitory marches often formed part of the ceremonies at the installation of kings.—In Egypt, for example, the new pharaoh circumambulated the fortified wall in a festal procession on the day of his enthronement. The ceremony, called "the circuit of the wall" (*phrr ḥ inb*), was said to be as old as the time of Menes, the first monarch of United Egypt.[3]—Similarly, the Hittite king had to tour his realm at the annual winter festival of Nuntariyashas;[4] while in the Canaanite Poem of Baal, discovered at Ras Shamra-Ugarit, that god makes the rounds of "seventy-seven towns, eighty-eight cities" in order to assert his new kingship over gods and men.[5]—In India, the rajputs marched ceremoniously around a temple or stupa at the time of their installation;[6] and in Malaya, a new sultan was required to perambulate his territory seven times on the same occasion.[7]—In 1875, the new king of Thailand ritually circuited his palace and city at the time of his enthronement,[8] and the practice likewise figures in many African installation ceremonies.[9] A familiar survival of it is the ceremony of "beating the bounds" in British popular usage.[10] The local vicar marches around the confines of the parish in solemn procession; every so often a choirboy, or some other functionary, is lifted by his legs and his head "bumped" on the boundary line. The custom was observed as late as the twenties of the present century at such places as East Barnet, Datchet in Buckinghamshire, Bexhill, and St. Clement's parish in Hastings, Sussex.[11] It is recorded also from various rural areas of Germany.[12]

History records several instances in which territory was acquired by circumambulation.—Thus after Horatius Cocles had delivered Rome by his celebrated defense of the bridge against the Etruscans, the grateful city awarded him all the territory which he could encompass in a circuit traced out by his chariot.[13]—Similarly, in 496, Clovis awarded to the abbot John of Reomans all the land he could circuit while riding on an ass;[14] and some two centuries later, Dagobert, king of the Franks, gave to St. Florent as much of the land of Kircheim, in Alsace, as he could traverse riding on an ass while the king bathed and dressed.[15] It was in the same way, too, that King Waldemar of Denmark rewarded St. André in 1205; the holy man was granted all the territory he could encircle riding on a nine-day-old colt, while the king was bathing.[16] Of like tenor also is a legend current at Maccarese (ancient Castel St. Giorgio), near Rome, which tells of a knight who combatted a local dragon on condition that he might claim for himself as much land as he could cover at a gallop on a single day.[17]

(c) The seven circuits

Joshua's men, we are told, circuited the walls of Jericho for seven successive days. On each of the first six days, they made the rounds once, but on the seventh day, seven times. They were accompanied by seven priests blowing trumpets ahead of the ark of the Lord.

This emphasis on the sacred number seven shows clearly that the Biblical writer *is modeling his account upon a ritual ceremony,* and such ritual circumambulation is indeed attested in many parts of the world.—In ancient Rome, for instance, it was the custom in times of peril to circuit the city in a ceremony called *amburbium;*[18] and annually on the Feast of Lupercalia (Feb. 15) men were ritually scourged around its bounds.[19]—Ritual perambulations of this kind survived into Christian usage;[20] and it is recorded of both Dagobert (628-38) and Hugh Capet (967-96) that they used to march ceremoniously around cities, not only to assert possession of them but also to ensure public peace and well-being.[21]—The ancient kings of Sweden likewise made a practice of marching around cities in a reverse direction to the sun's as a means of securing their safety.[22]

The purpose of this procedure was to form a closed circle which might obstruct the entry of demons and noxious influences. As we shall see later (below, §257), altars were commonly circuited in this way during acts of worship; so was a bridal couple, and so too was the bier of the dead.—It has been suggested also that the rite was sometimes designed to keep the gods or beneficent spirits of a place accessible and to prevent their slipping away.[23] It is obvious, however, that when the Biblical writer patterned his account after the ancient ritual, he could not have had this meaning in mind, for the gods of Jericho would have been hostile to the invading Israelites and the latter would therefore have had no reason to keep them where they were; and as for their own god, far from being within the beleagured city, he was in fact accompanying his people in their circuits in the form of his sacred ark!

(d) The trumpets[24]

On the seventh day, seven priests preceding the ark of the Lord blew seven times upon their trumpets. Thereupon the people uttered a loud shout and the wall collapsed.

Stories of magic horns the blasts of which raze walls are by no means uncommon in folktales the world over,[25] and it is therefore not at all impossible that the Biblical narrative is indebted to the influence of such popular lore. It should be observed, however, that noise is everywhere regarded as a method of expelling demons and hostile powers. Thus, New Year, regarded universally as a "critical" period, is very commonly inaugurated by the beating of drums, the rattling of kettles, the cracking of whips, the firing of guns, the ringing of bells, etc., in order to forefend noxious spirits which might otherwise infest it.[26] The Navaho, for example, employ a "groaning stick" on that occasion;[27] the Zuni of Mexico resort to the use of bull-roarers;[28] so do also the Kafirs of Africa.[29] In Estonia, hammers are beaten, and kettles rattled.[30] So too, it is common practice to sound drums, etc. at eclipses in order to frighten away the demon who is believed to be attacking the sun or moon;[31] while ancient Greek legend tells how King Salmoneus of Elis once tied kettles to his chariot in a bizarre attempt to intimidate Zeus![32] Not impossibly, then, the sounding of the trumpets before Jericho reflects a time-honored rite of frightening or expelling hostile demons in this fashion.

It is noteworthy that both the ancient Greek (Septuagint) Version of the Bible and the historian Josephus (*Ant.* VI.1.5) play down the miraculous character of the incident. The latter says that the trumpets were blown only *in order to encourage the troops.* Living in Roman times, he probably had in mind the *tuba concionis,* or "trumpet of assembly" which customarily rallied Roman soldiers to battle,[33] and in the shout uttered by Joshua's men he evidently saw the equivalent of the united war cry which the Romans used to emit before battle in order to strike terror into the heart of the foe.[34]

105 Foundation-sacrifice   6:26

After the destruction of Jericho, Joshua imposed an oath on the people never to rebuild it. The formula of the oath declared that anyone who might venture to do so would have to lay the foundations at the cost of his eldest son, and set up the gates at that of his youngest. This dire prediction, we are told, was fulfilled later during the reign of Ahab, when Hiel of Bethel had indeed to sacrifice in this way his eldest son, Abiram, and his youngest, Segub.[1]

The reference is to the worldwide institution of the *foundation-sacrifice:* at the construction of a new building a human being or animal is slain and buried under the threshold as an offering to spirits, demons, or deceased ancestors who might otherwise bring misfortune or ruin upon it.[2]

Popular tradition associated the sacrifice of a maiden in this way with the foundation of such famous Syrian cities as Antioch and Laodicea;[3] while the Arabic version of *The Travels of St. John, son of Zebedee* relates that a young girl was buried alive under the foundations of a bathhouse threatened by a satanic spirit.[4] Indeed, until recent times the belief persisted in various parts of the Orient that a Turkish bath had to be rendered immune from accidents and untoward influences by the inaugural sacrifice or inhumation of a Negro or Sudanese.[5]

Among the Arabs of Syria and Palestine,[6] and likewise among the peasantry in modern Greece,[7] it is common practice to slay a cock, ram, or lamb at the building of a house and to let the blood flow freely over the foundation stone; while the custom of human or animal sacrifice on such occasions is abundantly attested in European folklore.[8] In Papua, two old people, deemed expendable, are sacrificed whenever a "men's house"—that is, a communal meeting place for males—is completed.[9]

Nor is the custom confined to the actual building of a house: among Arab peasants, jinns or evil spirits are similarly placated when new land is broken up.[10]

Sometimes, as in ancient Mesopotamian and Palestinian buildings, images and figurines are substituted for real human beings.[11] On the other hand, however, the discovery of infant skeletons in the foundations of houses excavated at such sites as Gezer, Megiddo, and Ta'anek[12] is not necessarily to be interpreted as evidence of foundation-sacrifice, for it was in any case a not uncommon practice in the East to bury children in the corners of rooms.[13]

106 "Sun, stand thou still" 10:12–14

Joshua delivered the inhabitants of Gibeon from a threatened attack by the Amorites. In a popular song quoted by the Scriptural writer, that victory is said to have been attended by a singular miracle:

> Said the LORD in the sight of Israel:
> "Sun, on Gibeon be still,
>   and Moon in the Vale of Aijalon!"
> So sun stood still, and moon stayed
>   until the nation took vengeance on its foes.[1]

Agamemnon prayed to Zeus for a similar miracle at Troy,[2] and such magical manipulation of the luminaries is a not uncommon motif in folktales.[3] Hera, says Homer, ordered the sun to set betimes so as to facilitate an attack of the Achaeans upon the Trojans.[4] Conversely, when Zeus was enjoying Alcmene, he commanded the sun to bank its fires and stay at home, so that the night might be prolonged, and at the same time Hermes bade the moon travel thrice more slowly than usual;[5] and this boon was granted by Athene when Odysseus was reunited with Penelope.[6]

The motif recurs both in German[7] and Australasian popular tales,[8] and even finds place in hagiography. Once, we are told, when St. Ludwin wished to perform ordination on the same day both at Rheims and Laon, the day was miraculously lengthened to enable him to accomplish this pious intent.[9]

Some scholars, to be sure, have attempted to dilute the miraculous element in our Biblical story.[10] It has been suggested, for instance, that what really happened was that, at Joshua's request, the hailstorm which had been harassing the Amorites, and which the Scriptural writer expressly mentions, lasted from noon on the day of battle until the following noon, blocking out the light of both sun and moon![11] An alternative explanation which has been proposed is that the Hebrew word conventionally rendered "be still" does not mean that the sun actually halted its course, but only that it desisted from aiding the Gibeonites, since Joshua wanted to confute their trust in heavenly bodies and demonstrate that the victory came from Yahweh![12]

The poem which the writer quotes is said to have formed part of the now lost *Book of Jashar*. This work is mentioned again in II Samuel 1:18 as the source of David's famous Lament over Saul and Jonathan; while in the Greek (Septuagint) Version the song chanted by Solomon at the dedication of the Temple is quoted as an excerpt from the Book of *Shîr*, i.e., Song, and many scholars regard this as a corruption of Jashar. Ostensibly, the name would mean *The Book of the Upright,* but to explain this as a generic designation of the heroes there commemorated seems, to say the least, a trifle strained. Since ancient compositions were usually known by their opening words (e.g., the Babylonian poems *Enuma Elish* and *Ludlul bêl nimêqi*), and since we have elsewhere in the Bible (Exod. 15:1; Judg. 5:1) excerpts of songs actually introduced by the word *yashar* "he sang" (or *va-tashar,* "she sang"), it is not impossible that the book really derived its name from this standard prefatory phase.

Judges

107 The mutilation of captives Judg. 1:5–7

During their invasion of Canaan, the men of Judah capture a prince of Bezek (modern Ḥirbet Bezḳa, near Gezer) and amputate his thumbs and big toes.

The mutilation of the captured prince was not simply an act of savagery; it was designed to prevent his ever again taking up arms or marching to war.

The Greeks and Romans sometimes adopted the same practice.[1] Thus, when the Athenians captured the island of Aegina, in 458 B.C., they cut off the right hand of every enemy soldier, "lest he should again carry a spear or throw a lance";[2] and when the city of Uxellodunum (Puy d'Isolu?) surrendered to Julius Caesar in 52 B.C., he ordered the hands of any who had borne arms to be amputated.[3]

By an extension of the same idea, it has been a not uncommon practice among diverse peoples to mutilate the corpses of the slain in order to immobilize their vengeful spirits. The aborigines of Tasmania, for example, used to sever the right thumb of fallen foes lest their ghosts be able thereafter to wield a spear;[4] and similar mutilation was commonly practiced by Greek murderers upon their victims.[5] Clytaemnestra, we are told, so mangled Agamemnon;[6] and Lycurgus, king of the Edonians, cut off the extremities of his son Dryas whom he had struck dead with an ax in a fit of madness.[7] According to one account, murderers used even to attach the severed parts to their own clothing;[8] and an earlier instance of this is afforded by a Canaanite myth from Ras Shamra-Ugarit in which the goddess 'Anat hangs the shorn limbs of her slaughtered foes from her girdle.[9]

Sometimes, however, it was the criminal himself who was so treated. In an Ambrosian illustrated manuscript of the Iliad, Dolon, the Trojan spy slain by Diomedes (10.34), is shown with hands and feet bound;[10] and at Travancore they used to cut off the heels of a murderer when he was hanged to prevent his ghostly feet from "running to do evil."[11]

Sometimes, too, it is the perfectly innocent dead who are thus "disabled." The Romans, for instance, made a practice of cutting off a finger of the deceased before cremation;[12] and in early graves discovered at Gezer, in Palestine, the fingers of infants are buried separately.[13]

Often, for the same reason, the dead were *beheaded*. Thus, the kings of Assyria frequently refer in their annals to impaling the heads of their enemies,[14] and Herodotus informs us that this was also standard practice among the Scythians.[15] Greek legend furnishes instances of this custom in the cases of Eurystheus,[16] Antaeus,[17] Cyecnus,[18] and Oenomaeus;[19] while Evenus, the father of Marpessa, is said to have cut off the hands of his daughter's unsuccessful suitors and to have nailed them to the walls of his house.[20] Coming down to more recent times, Giraldus Cambrensis tells us that once, in the time of Fitzstephen, Irish foot soldiers placed some two hundred enemy heads at the feet of Dermitius, prince of Leicester.[21] In certain parts of Armenia[22] and Africa,[23] if a person falls sick after a funeral, the body of the deceased is disinterred and beheaded; and a case is on record in which a Chinese felon, condemned to death, begged not to be decapitated, so that he would not be immobilized in the next world.[24]

Other parts of the body were likewise mutilated. Constantine, for instance, is said to have cut off the noses of fallen foes,[25] and similar mutilations are attested among the Celts[26] and Berbers,[27] in Dahomey,[28] in Persia,[29] and in New Caledonia,[30] while in the ancient Mesopotamian Epic of Gilgamesh the hero chops off the testicles (or haunches?) of the divine *Ālu*-bull after he has slain it.[31] William of Newbury relates that a Galway chieftain once captured a cousin of Henry II (1154–89), plucked out his eyes and his tongue, and severed his genitals[32]—an act of barbarism which may nevertheless have had its origins in superstition. It is recorded also that during the Greek War of Independence a fallen soldier from the island of Santorini (Thera) was mutilated by the enemy out of fear that he was a vampire.[33]

Lastly, it may be mentioned that among the Cheyenne Indians of North America the tribal sign, which consists in drawing the right index finger several times across the left forefinger, is commonly interpreted to indicate "cut finger" or "cut wrists" and "is said to be derived from their custom of cutting off the fingers and hands of slain enemies."[34]

108 Captives fed on scraps

The prince of Bezek reconciles himself to this fate by observing that God has requited him in kind for the fact that "seventy kings with their thumbs and big toes cut off used to gather scraps under my table."

There is an interesting parallel to this in a Canaanite mythological poem from Ras Shamra-Ugarit. The supreme god El invites the other gods to a banquet. Those who acknowledge him and are therefore regarded as his friends are offered viands, whereas those who do not, and are therefore regarded as "gate-crashers," are ordered to be "beaten with a stick (till they sink) under the table."[1]

In the Middle Ages, adulteresses were sometimes punished by being fed on scraps with the household dogs;[2] and the same ignominy was occasionally imposed as a penance.[3]

109 The Song of Deborah

(a) Long-haired warriors

The initial words of the Song of Deborah, rendered in RSV *That the leaders took the lead in Israel,* could also mean *When men let grow their hair in Israel* (AJV).[1] If this latter rendering be correct, we may see in them an allusion to the custom, attested alike in Greek,[2] Arabic,[3] Icelandic,[4] Swiss,[5] and Spanish[6] sources, whereby warriors kept their hair unshorn because it was regarded as an "index" or seat of their lives and strength.[7] In the Iliad the Achaeans are regularly described as "long-haired," and this has been thought to refer to the same usage;[8] while it is known that in Greek practice generally men who were bent on blood-vengeance kept their beards untrimmed until their mission had been accomplished.[9]

(b) Riding high and sitting low

The words, *Ye that ride on roan asses, yet that sit upon rugs* (lit. *cloaks*), constitute what is called a merism, that is, a figure of speech in which a whole is expressed in terms of two contrasting parts, e.g., *officers and men,* for *army,* or *dollars and cents* for *cash.* The expression thus embraces the entire population by specifying its two extremes.

He who rides on the ass is the grandee. In Amorite texts from the ancient city of Mari, "rider on the ass" (*rakib emerim*) is the title of a municipal officer.[10] On the other hand, he who sits, or squats, on his coat[11] is a lowly beggar by the wayside. The contrast is well illustrated by the Palestinian Arab proverb, "A prince remains a prince, even on a mat (*el 'amir ulauw innuh 'al ḥaṣīr*),"[12] while the words, "He is on the mat (*hū 'al ḥaṣireh*)" are, like the English, "He is on the floor," a common colloquial expression for utter abasement.[13]

Curiously enough, a Sumerian poet expresses this contrast between lord and commoner in precisely the opposite terms. In the Epic of Gilgamesh and Agga, the nobles are those "who are raised with the sons of the king," while the lowly poor are those "who press the donkey's thigh."[14]

Roan (RSV: tawny) asses are especially prized by the Arabs, and Arab stallions from the Nejd are usually of roan or chestnut color.[15] The Hebrew word so rendered, however, could also mean *white,*[16] and it is therefore worth observing that in other cultures riding on white steeds is indeed attested as a mark of distinction. In ancient Greece, for example, this was a sign of royalty or nobility,[17] and the Dioscuri, or Heavenly Twins, who were indeed known as "kings" or "lords" (*anakte*),[18] were said to ride on white horses.[19]

So too were their Indic counterparts, the Aśvins. In the Biblical Book of Revelation,[20] the King of Kings and his warriors ride on white horses; and the expression, "the man on a white horse," has become proverbial for an imperialistic ruler. In his final tenth avatar, say the Hindus, Vishnu (Kalki) will appear riding on a white horse.

(c) "Awake, awake,[21] Deborah, utter a song." 12

The reference is not to the present song but to that customarily chanted by the womenfolk when the warriors return with the loot. It is in this way that Saul and David were greeted after the slaying of Goliath,[22] and in Psalm 68:12 we are assured that once Yahweh takes command on the field of battle, one can rest assured that in due course a veritable army of women will come forth to cheer the victors.[23] The custom still prevails among bedouin Arabs.[24]

(d) The cursing of Meroz 23

The "messenger (EV: angel) of Yahweh" who bade the Israelites curse Meroz for not coming to their help need not have been an angel, as is commonly supposed. He may have been simply the augur or "counsellor" who, as we have seen (above, §**98**) accompanied armies and advised their leaders as the spokesman of the god.

The site of Meroz has not yet been identified. Not impossibly, the introduction of this curse into the Song was motivated by a popular tradition which derived its name from a Semitic word meaning "calamity, doom," i.e., *Cry doom on Doomsville*.[25]

110 Gideon

(a) Gideon's fleece[1] 6:36–40

Gideon, leader of the Israelites, spreads a fleece on the ground at night. If it remains dry, while everything around it is covered with dew, this will be interpreted as a sign that Israel will overcome a coalition of Moabites, Amalekites, and others that has been mobilized against it. In the morning, however, the fleece is sopping wet. After imploring God's clemency, Gideon tries again the following night. This time the fleece remains dry.

The idea that rain can fall miraculously in one place and leave the surrounding area dry, or vice versa, is a commonplace in legends of saints.[2] Rabbi Ḥoni ben Dosa, says the Talmud, could stand in a drawn circle and by the effect of his prayer cause rain to fall all around him while none fell on him.[3] So too, when the body of Bishop Cerbonius of Populonium, on the isle of Elba, was being brought back to his see, heavy rain accompanied the voyage, but not a drop fell on the ship itself.[4] Again, when Fulgentius, Bishop of Otricoli, found himself surrounded by Goths who were praying to the sun, he drew a circle, stood within it, and remained dry while a downpour miraculously drenched them.[5] In like manner, Albinus of Angers was once able to stand immune in a rainstorm;[6] and St. Patrick, while observing the divine office in the open air, found that he and his disciples remained dry while it poured in torrents all around them.[7] Bishop Aridius of Limoges could ride through rain without becoming wet;[8] and tales of the same general import were told, in the twelfth, fourteenth, and fifteenth centuries, concerning Gudwal, Petrocus, and Antoninus.[9]

The same motif appears also in connection with holy places. Rain never fell, says the Talmud, on the altar of the Temple in Jerusalem;[10] and similar legends were current in Classical antiquity concerning the statue of Diana at Rhosus,[11] the temple of Venus at Paphos, and that of Minerva at Nea.[12] The privilege was granted also to the home of John the Evangelist at Ephesus,[13] and to the uncovered grave of the Lady Mary in the Valley of Jehosaphat;[14] while William of Malmesbury relates the same thing of the churches built by Aldhelm of Sherbourne in Dorsetshire, England.

Nor, indeed, is the notion excluded from secular tales, for it forms a leading motif in a modern story from the Balkans.[15]

(b) Gideon's men[16]   7:1–8

▲ *Gideon rallies the Israelites against attack by the Midianites, Amalekites, and neighboring bedouins. But Yahweh fears that if the whole army of Israel triumphs over the whole army of their foes, the people may be puffed up with pride and, forgetting Him to whom alone they could owe the success of their arms, claim that "Our own hand hath saved us." To prevent this deplorable illusion, he commands Gideon to dismiss to their homes all the fearful and craven-hearted and to retain only the valiant and brave. Twenty-two thousand recreants readily avail themselves of this leave of absence, leaving only ten thousand stalwarts to face the enemy. Even that number, however, appears too large to Yahweh. So the whole force is ordered to march down to the river, and the word is given to drink water. Immediately a marked distinction is observed in the manner in which the command is carried out. The great majority of the men kneel down and, applying their mouths to the water, imbibe it by suction. Three hundred, however, scoop it up in their hands and, lifting it to their mouths, lap it up with their tongues like dogs. These three hundred are chosen for the campaign.*

The test is one of alertness: the men who drink standing up instead of lying down show themselves more watchful and ready to meet any sudden emergency, such as an attack from the rear. The point may be well illustrated by noting corresponding differences in the modes of drinking adopted by various primitive peoples, for these suggest that the custom of throwing water into the mouth with the hand, instead of kneeling or lying down and applying the lips to the stream, is characteristic of men like hunters or porters whose occupation renders it either unsafe or difficult to employ the other posture.

Speaking, for instance, of the Ogieg or Wandorobs of East Africa, Captain C. H. Stigand observes that "they drink from a stream on all fours, putting their mouths down to the water. Practically every other tribe drink, when no vessel is available, with the hand. They either take up water with one hand or both, or throw up water with the right hand and catch it in the mouth. The latter is the way most caravan porters drink."[17] Among the Bambalas of the Congo valley "water is the commonest drink, and in the village cups are used for drinking purposes; but on a march the water is thrown into the mouth with the hand; they lie down on their stomachs and, bending the fingers, scoop up the water without spilling a drop, though the hand never touches the mouth in the process."[18] When the Namaquas, a Hottentot tribe of South-West Africa, are out hunting, they always drink by throwing water into their mouths with their fingers, and they trace the custom to the Hottentot Adam or first man, who one day, hunting a lion, saw the animal lying in wait for him under a large mimosa tree beside a pool of water. The first man's dogs, on coming to the spot, lay down, lapped up the water, then shook themselves and frisked about. But the first man, more cautious, knelt down, holding his spear in his left hand, and drank the water by throwing it into his mouth with two fingers, while all the time he kept a sharp eye on the lion. When man and dogs had thus refreshed themselves, they attacked the lion and soon made an end of him. Since that time the Namaquas have always drunk water in the same way when they are out hunting.[19]

Again, a native of Cambodia, travelling through the forest, "ought not to drink by putting his mouth to the water, if he wishes not to be despised by tigers and other fierce animals. Let him drink by throwing water into his mouth with his hand, for then the denizens of the woods will respect him."[20] So, too, "a thirsty Samoan, in coming to a stream of water, stoops down, rests the palm of his left hand on his knee, and, with the right hand, throws the water up so quickly as to form a continued jet from the stream to his mouth, and there he laps until he is satisfied."[21] Similarly, the New Caledonians stoop till their head is a few inches above the water, and then throw the liquid into their mouth with one hand till their thirst is quenched.[22]

Commenting on the story of Gideon's men, a missionary to Melanesia observes that "this lapping of the water like a dog by Gideon's army was unintelligible to me until I came to the New Hebrides. Standing one day by a stream I heard a noise behind me like a dog lapping water. I turned and saw a woman bowing down and throwing the water rapidly into her mouth with her hand. This satisfactorily explained the action of Gideon's men. It showed care and watchfulness; for they could walk along the stream lapping the water as they went; and an enemy was less likely to take them unawares than if they bent on their knees to drink. Most of the natives, however, bend down and touch the water with their lips as the rejected men of Gideon's army did."[23]

[Similarly too, among the Arunta of Australia medicine men are instructed never to lie down or kneel when they wish to drink water, but always to use a small receptacle.[23a]] ▼

111 The purple of kings 8:26

Purple,[1] or deep red, was the favored color of royalty or nobility in ancient times.

The Babylonian king wore a deep red garment, called *lamḫuššu*, which means just that.[2] Plutarch tells us that Artaxerxes of Persia was similarly clad.[3] The Cilician god Sandon is said to have worn a deep red robe, called *sandyx*,[4] and in the Homeric Hymn to Dionysus, he is depicted as being similarly attired.[5] In the Book of Daniel, to be clothed in purple is a sign of distinction;[6] and in the Book of Lamentations the nobility are described as "reared on purple."[7] Greek tyrants likewise wore purple,[8] and the *trabea* affected by the ancient kings of Rome was a toga striped with purple.[9] Romulus is said to have worn a deep red cloak.[10] The Jewish mystical classic, the *Zohar*, relates that in the fourth hall of Paradise those who mourn for Zion or who have been martyred for their faith stand clad in purple garments.[11]

All of this is simply a particularization of the more general use of red—the color of blood—as a means of fortifying oneself with extra life and thus counteracting hurtful elements or demons.[12] Babylonian magicians wore red garments, and this color was also affected in rites of expiation and in those concerning the dead.[13] Red pigment was applied to the eye to cure it from the assault of eye disease;[14] and the god Marduk himself smeared red ochre on his lips before he engaged the monster Tiamat in battle.[15] At the ancient Mexican festival of Titill, which was primarily a commemoration of the dead, the image of the god was clothed in red.[16] Red threads were wound by Jews around the throats of children to forefend sickness,[17] just as among the Tupis of Brazil the godfather of a child paints it red soon after its birth,[18] and in Japan a red cross is sometimes hung in a house to ward off demons.[19] Among the Greeks and Romans, red skeins had to be used for the symbolic "binding" of victims in homeopathic magic.[20] In England and elsewhere, red bands are tied around the thighs of a woman in labor, for apotropaic purposes;[21] and among the Tarascos of Mexico, babies are so bound for the same reason.[22] In Irish folklore, a man assailed by the "wee ones" sits up with a red handkerchief bound around his head. "Always red, if the fairies are about," says the rector's widow who records this superstition.[23] In the Canaanite *Poem of Aqhat*, discovered at Ras Shamra-Ugarit, one of the central characters is instructed to wash and rouge himself before performing a ritual ceremony.[24] Among the native tribes of Western Victoria (Australia), objects stolen in order to work magic on their owners have to be rubbed with red clay;[25] and among the Galelas and Tobelorese of Halmahera, the faces and bodies of boys are smeared with reddened water to ensure their wellbeing.[26] The Tlingits of Alaska paint children's noses red to the same end.[27]

Red animals are commonly used in cathartic rites.[28] The ancient Hindus offered red goats to the Aśvins;[29] and in Egypt oxen which were sacrificed had to be red.[30] In Israel, the ashes of a red heifer removed the effects of violating taboo—a custom preserved by the Samaritans until as late as 1348 and still current among the Falashas of Ethiopia.[31]

The altar in the Mosaic sanctuary was spread with a red cloth.[32] Red stones (e.g., coral, red agate, red jasper, carnelian) are used by Mediterranean peoples as a protection against the evil eye.[33]

Among the Greeks, red was the favorite funereal and chthonic color.[34] Hector's bones, for instance, were wrapped in red cloths.[35] Red is likewise the funereal color—to cite but two modern instances—in Ashanti[36] and among the Gypsies.[37] Similarly, among the Tartars of the Crimea and Southern China, as also among the Arabs of Egypt and in modern Greece and Albania,[38] the bridal veil is often red, as was the Roman *flammeum*.[39] "Scarlet stuff" was used in Israelite ritual to decontaminate persons who had recovered from leprosy or vitiligo;[40] and on Roman holidays, the faces of the divine images were painted red with *minium*.[41]

See also above, §62, concerning *red-haired persons*.

▲ 112   Jotham's parable[1]   9:7–15

In the mouth of Jotham the fable of the trees would seem to be a democratic, or perhaps rather theocratic, satire on kingship, for according to him all the noble and useful trees declined the office, so that in despair the trees were driven to offer the crown to the meanest and most useless of their number, who accepted it only on a condition which practically involved the destruction of the aristocracy of the woods, the cedars of Lebanon. The distrust of monarchy which the parable implies was natural enough in the honest son of an honest patriot, who had refused to rule over his people, and had declared that the rule of God was better than the rule of man; and the same distrust of kings and the same preference for a theocracy are expressed still more plainly by the Hebrew historian who records, with evident reluctance and regret, the institution of the monarchy under Saul. But apart from any political application the story of the rivalry between the trees for the primacy would seem to have been popular in antiquity. [Thus, a cuneiform text from the city of Ashur, the ancient capital of Assyria, tells the story of a quarrel between the tamarisk and the palm-tree, each claiming superiority over the other. The tamarisk boasts that it supplies the wood for axes which break open the dry clods, and also for plows and threshing wains. The palm retorts, however, that *its* wood furnishes the keels of ships, the roofs of houses, and many a domestic tool.[1a]] In Greek dress, the theme appears in one of the fables of Aesop. The fir-tree, we read, one day said boastfully to the bramble, "You are good for nothing, but I am useful in roofs and houses." To which the bramble replied, "O wretched creature, if you only remembered the axes and the saws that will chop and cut you, glad enough would you be to be a bramble instead of a fir."[2] Again, a pomegranate and an apple-tree disputed with each other as to which was the more fruitful, and when the dispute was at its height, a bramble called out from a neighbouring hedge, "O my friends, do let us stop fighting."[3] In these fables, it should be noted, as in Jotham's parable, the bramble is involved in a discussion with trees of higher pretensions.

The same theme was treated much more elaborately by the Alexandrian poet Callimachus in a poem, of which a copy, written on papyrus, was discovered in Egypt during the winter of 1905–1906. The verses unfortunately are mutilated and incomplete, but so far as they go they describe a contest for supremacy between a laurel and an olive-tree, in which, up to the point where the manuscript breaks off, the olive-tree appears to get much the better of the argument. So far as the lines can be read or probably restored, the fable runs as follows:[4]

"The ancient Lydians say that once on a time the laurel contended with the olive on Mount Tmolus. For the laurel was a tall tree and fair, and fluttering her branches thus she spoke: 'What house is there at whose doorposts I am not set up? What soothsayer or what sacrificer bears me not? The Pythian prophetess, too, she sits on laurel, eats of laurel,[5] lies on laurel. O foolish olive, did not Branchus heal Ionia's sons with but a stroke of laurel and a few muttered words, what time Phoebus was wroth with them? I go to feasts and to the Pythian choral dance, I am given as a prize in games, and the Dorians cut me at Tempe on the mountain tops and bear me thence to Delphi, whene'er Apollo's rites are solemnized. O foolish olive, no sorrow do I know, nor mine the path that the corpse-bearer treads. For I am pure, and men tread me not under foot, for I am holy. But with thee they crown themselves whene'er they are about to burn a corpse or lay it out for burial, and thee they duly spread under the dead man's ribs.'

"So spake she boasting; but the mother of the oil answered her calmly: 'O laurel, barren of all the things I bear, thou hast sung like a swan at the end. . . . I attend to the grave the men whom Ares slays, and [am spread under the heads] of heroes who [died gloriously]. And when children bear to the tomb their white-haired grandam or Tithonus old, I go with them and on the path am laid, (helping them) more than thou (doest help) the men who bring thee from Tempe's dale. But as for that thou spakest of, am not I a better prize than thou? for are not the games at Olympia greater than the games at Delphi?[6] But silence is best. Not a word more concerning thee shall I so much as mutter, neither good nor bad. Yet lo! the birds that perch among my leaves are twittering thus: "Who found the laurel? It was the earth who brought it forth as she brings forth the ilex, the oak, the galingale, or other woodland things. But who found the olive? Pallas it was, when she contended for the shore with him who dwells amid the sea-weed, and the ancient one gave judgment, he the man with snaky limbs below.[7] That is one fall for the laurel! But of the immortals, who honours the olive, and who the laurel? Apollo honours the laurel, and Pallas honours the olive, which she found. In that they are alike, for I distinguish not between the gods. But what is the laurel's fruit? How shall I use it? It is good neither to eat nor to drink nor to anoint one's self with. But pleasing is the olive's fruit in many ways, both as a food and as an unguent. . . . That is, I think, the laurel's second fall. And then what is the tree whose leaves the suppliants hold out? The olive's leaves. That is the laurel's third fall." But plague on these birds, will they never stop? They must still be chattering! Impudent crow, is thy beak not sore with croaking? "Whose trunk is it that the Delians preserve? It is the olive's, which gave a seat to Leto." ' . . . So spake the olive. But the laurel's rage swelled at the words, and the smart struck deeper than before. [And now an ancient spreading thorn-bush][8] spoke up, for she was not far from the trees. 'O my poor friends,' quoth she, 'do let us cease, lest we carry the quarrel too far. Come, let's give over bickering.' But the laurel glared daggers at the thorn, and thus she spake: 'O cursed wretch, don't preach patience to me, as if thou wert one of us. Thy very neighbourhood chokes me. By Phoebus, by Persephone, talk not of reconciliation! Slay me rather!' "

At this point the poem breaks off in the manuscript, and we cannot say how the quarrel between the trees ended, but from the poet's evident partiality for the olive, we may conjecture that the subsequent verses described the triumph of that pacific, fruitful, and useful tree over the bellicose, barren, and boastful laurel. What tree or shrub it was that attempted to intervene as peacemaker in the strife, and got small thanks for its pains from one at least of the disputants, we cannot say for certain, since the Greek text at this point is mutilated; but the analogy of Aesop's fable, in which a bramble attempts to end a dispute between a pomegranate and an apple-tree, suggests that the humble bush may have played the same benevolent but thankless part in the poem of Callimachus, and the suggestion is borne out by the sharp way in which the proud laurel turns on the would-be mediator, whose claim to meddle in a quarrel between trees she contemptuously rejects ("as if thou wert one of us").

[A similar fable concerning the rivalry of the pomegranate-tree and the bramble occurs in the Aramaic version of the celebrated Romance of Aḥikar, inscribed on a palimpsest papyrus of the late fifth century B.C. discovered, in 1906–7, at Elephantine in Upper Egypt. The bramble, we read, once taunted the pomegranate-tree by asking why anyone who tried to touch its fruit had always to encounter a mass of thorns. "True," rejoined the pomegranate tartly, "but you yourself offer nothing else."[8a]]

The rivalry between the trees appears to be a favourite theme of Armenian fables. For example, in one of them it is said that the plants held a council to decide which of them deserved to reign over the rest. Some proposed the date-palm, because he is tall and his fruits are sweet. But the vine resisted the proposal, saying, "It is I who diffuse joy; it is I who deserve to reign." The fig-tree said, "It is I, for I am sweet to the taste." The thorn said, "The honour should be mine, because I prick." Each of them thought himself better than the rest, and imagined that he could dispense with them. As for the date-palm, on reflection he perceived that the trees would not let him reign, because they were loth to share their honours with others. He said, "It belongs to me rather than to anybody else to be king." The other trees admitted his claim to a certain extent. They said, "Thou art tall and thy fruits are sweet, but thou lackest two things. Thou does not bear fruit at the same time that we do, and thou art not suitable for building. Besides, thou art so tall that it is impossible for many people to enjoy thy fruit." He answered, "I shall become king and make you princes, and after accomplishing my time I shall still reign over your sons." He set the kingdom in order, naming the rest to various offices. The vine he made chief cupbearer, the fig-tree consul, the thorn head executioner, the pomegranate head physician; other plants were to serve for medicines, the cedars for building, the forests for fuel, the bushes for prison; each was assigned its special task.[9]

A Malay story tells of a dispute between the plants as to their respective claims to precedence. Once upon a time, we are informed, the maize-plant boasted, saying, "If rice should cease to exist, I alone should suffice to sustain mankind." But the liane and the jungle yam each made a like boast, and as the parties could not agree, the case was brought before King Solomon. Said Solomon, "All three of you are perfectly right, albeit it were perhaps better that the maize-plant should sustain mankind because of his comradeship with the bean." Thereat the wrath of the liane and the yam waxed hot against the maize-plant, and they went off together to hunt for a fruit-spike of the jungle fig-tree whereon to impale him, but found none. And meanwhile the maize-plant, hearing news of their quest, set to work to find arrow-poison. And when he found it he poisoned the jungle yam therewith, wherefore to this day the jungle yam has narcotic properties. Then the jungle yam, being wroth thereat, speared the maize-plant in his turn, wherefore to this day the cobs of the maize are perforated. And the maize-plant, reaching out in turn, seized the pointed shoot of a *wilang* (?) stem and wounded the liane therewith. At this juncture the parties to the quarrel went before the prophet Elijah who said, "This matter is too great for me, take ye it before Solomon." And Solomon said, "Let them fight it out between them, that the rage of their hearts may be appeased." Wherefore there was battle between them for twice seven days. And when the twice seven days were needed, the battle being still undecided, the combatants were parted, and a space was set between them by Solomon. And the jungle yam he made to sit down, and the liane to lie down. But the maize-plant and the bean he made to stand together.[10]

Jotham's parable seems to have enjoyed a special popularity during the

Middle Ages, for we find it detached from its Biblical setting and inserted in various collections of fables which were derived, directly or indirectly, from Phaedrus. In some of these collections the story is taken with but slight verbal changes from the Vulgate,[11] but in a Latin version of the fables which pass under the name of the mediaeval French poetess Marie de France, the writer has handled the theme more freely. The trees, so runs the fable, once assembled and consulted about choosing a king. A tall and spreading tree proposed the vine for the kingly office, but the vine refused on the ground that he was weak and could do nothing without a support. So the trees offered to choose the whitethorn, saying that he deserved to reign because he was strong and handsome. But the whitethorn declined the offer, declaring that he was not worthy to reign because he bore no fruit. Several other trees were proposed, but they all excused themselves for various reasons. At last, when no tree could be found that would consent to be king, the broom got up and said, "The sceptre is mine by rights, because I desire to reign and I ought to be king, for my family is most opulent and noble." But the other trees answered the broom, "In the whole family of trees we know none meaner or poorer than thee." The broom replied, "If I am not made king, never will I honour him whom ye shall elect, neither will I love those who appoint another than me." The trees said to him, "What, then, will you be able to do to us if you do not love our king or us?" The broom answered, "Though I seem to you mean and needy, yet could I do that which I had thought to do if I were king." And they all asked him what that was. He said to them, "I had thought to prevent any tree from growing that stands under me or over me." "It is likely enough," replied the others, "that thou couldst do that to us if thou wert king and powerful; but what thinkest thou canst thou do when we are stronger than thou?" But the broom did not answer the question, he only said, "I cannot harm you without injuring myself. Yet I will carry out my intention. I can cause," said he, "that any herb or tree that is under me shall cease to grow, and that any that is above me shall wither. But to do that it is necessary that I myself should burn. Therefore I wish to be consumed with fire, with all my kindred that are about me, in order that those trees which deem themselves great and noble may perish with me in the flames."[12]

This fable is plainly nothing but a feeble expansion of the parable of Jotham.

[When the bramble says to the trees (v. 15), "If in good faith you are anointing me king over you, then come and take refuge in my shade (shadow)," the author of the fable is introducing a clever play on a popular expression associated with kingship. For in the royal letters of Assyria, persons under the special protection of the king, or officials traveling on missions of state are frequently said to be "in his shadow."[12a] Similarly, too, in an Egyptian inscription of Pharaoh Pi-ankhi (about 720 B.C.), courtiers entreat him to "set us in thy shadow."[12b] Not impossibly these expressions refer, if only metaphorically, to being sheltered under the royal parasol.[12c]] ▼

113 The navel of the earth   9:37

When Abimelech and his men come down from Mt. Gerizim to attack the city of Shechem, they are described by the enemy commander as "coming down from the navel of the earth (RSV: *center of the land*)."

Many ancient and primitive peoples identify their main city or principal shrine with the "navel" or center of the earth—the point where the world axis (often portrayed as a mountain), which reaches from the mid-point of heaven to the mid-point of the netherworld, penetrates its surface.[1] The idea is widely attested among the Sumerians and Semites of Mesopotamia.[2] Cities like Nippur, Larsa, and Sippar, for instance, were so regarded, while the great temple of Marduk in Babylon was held to be "the link between heaven and earth."[3] In Jewish tradition this is said likewise of Jerusalem;[4] and as late as the second and third century of the Common Era, the *omphalos* or navel of the earth was portrayed on coins from the whilom Phoenician city of Tyre.[5] Moreover, to this day, the Samaritans so characterize Gerizim, their sacred mountain, to which specific reference is made in our Biblical passage.[6]

In Greece this idea was entertained about Delos, Delphi, Pythoi, Paphos (in Cyprus), and other shrines;[7] and among the Arabs about the Ka'aba at Mecca.[8] The Hindus speak in the same vein of the mythical Mt. Meru in the Himalayas,[9] and the Buddhists of the spot where the Master received enlightenment under the banyan-tree.[10] That the Celts too shared the notion "is evidenced by such words as *medinemetum, mediolanum* which exist even today in French place names. . . . In the village of Armany (district of La Roche) can be found a 'Middle-of-the-Earth-Stone.' "[11] The notion obtains also among the Pygmies of Malacca,[12] and "seems, indeed, to be part of the symbolism of pre-historic monuments."[13]

114 Sowing a city with salt

After the defeat of the men of Shechem, Abimelech razed their city and strewed salt upon it.

The action is not unparalleled in the Ancient Near East. In a treaty concluded, around 750 B.C., between Barga'yah, king of a yet unidentified realm named K-t-k, and Matta'el, king of Arpad, in Syria, the curse is invoked on the latter that, if he break faith, his city "shall be sown with natron and salt."[1] Similarly, King Ashurbanipal of Assyria (688–33 B.C.) boasts that he "sowed with salt" the vanquished cities of Elam.[2] Moreover, in later times, Attila employed the same device after his conquest of Padua, and Frederick Barbarossa after the capitulation of Milan.[3]

In ancient and primitive thought salt has various connotations, and the practice has therefore been explained in several different ways.

(i) The older commentators saw in it *a symbol of devastation,* salt being indeed mentioned in this sense elsewhere in the Old Testament itself, viz., Jeremiah 17:6 ("saltland"||"wilderness"); Zephaniah 2:9 ("nettles and saltpits and a waste for ever"); Psalm 107:34 ("salty waste" × fruitful land"); and Job 39:6 (||"steppe").

(ii) Others, however, have suggested that it was *a symbol of sterility invoked as retribution for a breach of covenant*,[4] such as the men of Shechem are said explicitly (9:22) to have committed against Abimelech. This explanation is supported by the terms of the aforementioned ancient treaty, and salt is so used symbolically in the military oath of the Hittites: "[The officiant] places salt in their hands . . . and speaks as follows: '. . . Whoever breaks these oaths, shows disrespect to the king of the Hatti (Hittite) land, and turns his eyes in hostile fashion upon the Hatti land, . . . let him be scattered like salt! Just as salt has no seed, even so let that man's name, seed, house, cattle and sheep perish!' "[5]

(iii) A third view is that strewing a city with salt was *a means of putting it under a ban*.[6] The ban (Heb.: ḥerem) was a form of taboo, and since tabooed objects were regarded as numinous or "charged," they were treated in the same way as those deemed sacred.[7] Salt, we know, was often used to consecrate and purify the latter.[8]

(iv) The practice has been interpreted also as *a means of purifying the soil from the contamination of bloodshed*[9] This, of course, would likewise be based on the general use of salt as a purifying agent.

(v) Lastly, it has been suggested that the real purpose of the action was *to avert the vengeful spirits of the slain*—in this case more specifically, of Abimelech's seventy murdered brothers.[10] Salt, on account of its incorruptibility, is widely employed as a means of forefending demons or noxious spirits (see below, §**211**) and, as we have seen (above, §**26**), fear of the vengeful ghosts of the slain played an important role in ancient and primitive belief.

The first of these explanations is, on the whole, the most plausible. What argues especially in its favor is the fact that salt is often mentioned alongside of other substances which certainly symbolize devastation. Thus, in the aforementioned ancient Syrian treaty, as again in the inscription of Ashurbanipal and in a record of the early Hittite king, Anittas of Kussara, the vanquished city is sown also with *cress* or weeds,[11] and in the Hittite myth of the Snaring of the Dragon (Illuyankas), the same is done to a house consigned to destruction;[12] while in Deuteronomy 29:23 salt is conjoined with *brimstone*.[13] Furthermore, against the view that the practice was a form of curse for violation of a covenant it is to be observed that when Ashurbanipal strewed salt over the cities of Elam no such breach of faith was in fact involved; the Assyrian monarch was simply invading them on an imperialistic rampage. Significant too is the fact that in an Assyrian list of omens, salt "sprouting" from the soil is mentioned as a bad sign.[14]

It may be added, as a matter of curious interest, that the practice was based on the effect of salt on weeds and topsoil only; if it is sunk to the roots of vegetation, it in fact stimulates growth![15]

115 Jephthah's vow   11:30–40

(a) *Jephthah, the Gileadite, champion of Israel, makes a vow that if Yahweh will grant him victory over the Ammonites who are waging war against his people, he will sacrifice to him the first person who meets him when he returns home. He is met by his daughter, who is his only child.*

Parallels to this story are to be found in the popular lore of several peoples.[1] The best known is probably the Greek legend of Idomeneus, king of Crete. Caught in a storm on his return from the Trojan War, he vowed to Poseidon, god of the sea, that he would sacrifice to him whomever he would first meet when he landed safely on his native shores. This turned out to be his own son.[2]

A similar tale was told by the Greeks about Maeander, the son of Cercaphos and Anaxibia. At war with the people of Pessinus, in Phrygia, he vowed to the Great Mother that if she granted him victory he would sacrifice to her the first person who came out to greet him when he returned home. The first to do so was his own son, Archelaos, together with his mother and sister.[3]

In modern European versions of the tale, it tends to be combined with the familiar theme of the prince bewitched into the form of an animal. From Hesse, Germany, for example, comes the story of a man who went on a journey and promised his youngest daughter to bring back to her a singing and soaring lark. When, however, he at last espied one, a lion stepped forth, ready to devour him. Thereupon the merchant promised the beast that if it would spare him and permit him to take the bird, he would give it the first thing that met him when he returned home. This turned out to be the daughter herself. However, the story has a happy ending, for the lion proves to be a handsome prince who has been bewitched but is eventually freed from the spell.[4]

A variant of this tale from Lorraine makes the promised gift a talking rose. This is found in the courtyard of a castle, but is guarded by a white wolf. A similar bargain is struck, with a similar result, but here too the wolf turns out to be an enchanted prince. In this case, however, the story does not end happily, for an equally familiar motif is tacked on to it: the wolf swears the girl to secrecy about his true identity, but she betrays it, and he instantly falls dead.[5]

Yet another variant, this time from Hanover, makes the prize a *Löwenblatt,* and the protector of it a black poodle. Once again, the same pact is concluded, with the same result, but here the additional element is introduced that the girl's father, a king, at first tries to palm the animal off with a goosegirl and then with a false princess. The fraud is detected each time, but when the real daughter is at last delivered up, it turns out that the poodle is really an enchanted prince.[6] (In versions of the same story from Schleswig-Holstein the enchanted prince takes the form of a bear or white wolf.[7])

As told in the Tyrol, it is a traveling merchant who promises his youngest daughter to bring her a leaf that dances, sings, and plays. The leaf, however, is guarded by a serpent who exacts the same bargains, again with the same result, but who is eventually revealed to be a bewitched youth.[8]

In a Lithuanian version it is a king who sets out for Vilna to find a woman who will clean and tend his palace. His youngest daughter, however, offers to do this herself, if he will bring her back a mat woven of living flowers. On the way home, he finds in a forest a wolf wearing a hood of just such blossoms. Same bargain; same result; and, once again, the wolf is really an enchanted prince.[9]

The story is known also in Sweden, but there it is a king who loses his way in a wood and is guided out of it by a man in a gray cloak, who demands as the price of his services the first person whom the king encounters on returning to his palace. It turns out, of course, to be his youngest and favorite daughter. He at first tries to palm off her two older sisters. The man sends them back, but when the youngest girl is indeed delivered to him, he once again proves to be an enchanted prince or nobleman.[10]

Somewhat similar in detail, but revolving around the same theme, is another Swedish story which tells how a mermaid once released a king's ship in exchange for a promise to give him the first thing which the king met on his return. It was his own son.[11]

In a Danish version, it is a dwarf who rescues a king from a swamp upon similar conditions. The eventual victim of the rash vow is the king's own son and heir, who has been born to him while he was on his travels.[12]

Nor is the story confined to Europe. An Arabic poem, dating before the time of Mohammed, relates how Al-Mundhir, king of Ḥira, once vowed that on a certain day each year he would sacrifice the first person he saw. On one occasion this turned out to be his favorite, 'Abid.[13]

> **(b)** *Jephthah's daughter, on hearing of the fate in store for her, begs her father to spare her for two months so that she may "go and wander*[14] *about on the mountains and bewail my virginity, along with my companions." This he grants. "It then became a custom in Israel,"* adds the writer, *"that Israelite maidens went year by year to lament the daughter of Jephthah the Gileadite four days in the year."*

Modern scholars see in this a story based on the ancient and primitive custom of annually bewailing the dead or ousted spirit of fertility during the dry or winter season.[15] That spirit would here have been personified, like Persephone in Greek myth, as a female.

"Such lamentation for Osiris in Egypt, Attis in Asia Minor, and Adonis in

Syria are well known.[16] Similarly, in the Babylonian Epic of Gilgamesh (vi.46–47) and again in the poem of the Descent of Ishtar to the Netherworld (rev. 56–57)[17] mention is made specifically of the annual weeping of Tammuz. Moreover, an early Babylonian text published by Reisner[18] and another of Arsacid date[19] define the month of Tammuz (July) as a period of wailing (*tekiltu*), ritual mourning (*rikis sipitti*) and weeping (*bikîtum*);[20] while an old Assyrian almanac prescribes weeping for its second day.[21] This seasonal ululation, which obtained likewise in the Greek cult of Demeter and Kore,[22] survived, indeed, into the Christian era, for a medieval Arabic antiquary records the performance of it at Harran.[23] It is true that recent studies have thrown considerable doubt upon the time-honored identification of Tammuz with the spirit of fertility,[24] but for our present purpose this is not really important, for the analogy to the rite performed by Jephthah's daughter could still stand, even if Tammuz was in fact bewailed for other reasons.

The wailing for these seasonal spirits is, *au fond,* a mythological rationalization of an even more primitive custom of howling and shrieking at harvest ceremonies. "The Egyptians, says Diodorus, used to shed tears and cry upon Iris at the first cutting of the corn,[25] and their summer festival was marked, according to Herodotus, by the chanting of a doleful lay called Maneros[26]—a distortion of the Egyptian words, *maa n per.k,* "come to thy house,"[27] which constitute the initial phrase in seasonal dirges for Osiris which have actually come down to us.[28] The custom is attested also at a much later date by Firmicus Maternus, who reproaches the pagan Egyptians for "lamenting over the crops and wailing over the growing seed."[29]

In Mesopotamia, the harvest was accompanied by a ritual cry known as *alalu,* or "ululation";[30] and Plutarch informs us that the traditional cry at the Attic vintage festival of Oschophoria was *eleleu.*[31] Similarly, according to a writer quoted by Athenaeus, the ritual dirges uttered in the mysteries of Demeter and Kore went under the name of *iouloi* (or *houloi*), i.e., "howls."[32] . . . Lamentations were likewise a characteristic feature of the Eleusinian mysteries."[33]

The two-months which Jephthah's daughter spends in such rites correspond to the double-month of the early (10th cent. B.C.) Palestinian agricultural calendar discovered at Gezer,[34] and to the system of reckoning employed by the pre-Islamic Arabs.[35]

As for the four days of annual wailing in Israel, that is best illustrated by the Attis mysteries, where the god was ceremoniously interred on March 22, to be resurrected three days later.[36] As has often been observed, this survives in the third-day resurrection in Christianity, and there would appear to be a distinct allusion to it in Hosea 6:2.

Lastly, it should be noted that the ritual ululations are frequently satirized by the Hebrew prophets themselves (e.g., Hos. 7:14; Joel 1:5; Amos 5:16–17; Zeph. 1:10), showing the prevalence of this practice in popular Palestinian usage (see below, §221).

116 Shibboleth

> *The Ephraimites at first refuse aid to Jephthah and his men against the Ammonites. When they subsequently offer their services, Jephthah treats them as opportunistic "johnnies-come-lately," and when they retort that the Gileadites are simply secessionists from Ephraim, he sets his men against them and cuts off their retreat by occupying the fords of the Jordan. Any fugitive Ephraimite who tries to pass himself off as a Gileadite is made to repeat the word shibboleth (ear of corn). But, invariably, he pronounces it sibboleth, thereby betraying himself. In this way no less than forty-two thousand Ephraimites meet their death.*

The device employed in this famous story has been repeated on several historical occasions.[1] Thus, when the English defeated the Danes on St. Bryce's day (November 13), 1002, fugitive enemies were detected by being made to utter the words "Chichester Church," which they pronounced, "Shishshester Shersh."[2] Similarly, during Wat Tyler's uprising in 1381, "many Flemings lost their heads" because "they could not say, 'Bread and cheese,' but said instead, 'Case and Brode.'"[3] Again, when the Frisians defeated the forces of William IV, Count of Holland, near Stavoren, in 1345, they recognized escaping Hollanders by making them recite verses, which they mispronounced.[4]

117 Samson

▲ Among the grave judges of Israel the burly hero Samson cuts a strange figure. That he judged Israel for twenty years we are indeed informed by the sacred writer, but of the judgments which he delivered in his judicial character not one has been recorded, and if the tenor of his pronouncements can be inferred from the nature of his acts, we may be allowed to doubt whether he particularly adorned the bench of justice. His talent would seem to have lain rather in the direction of brawling and fighting, burning down people's cornricks, and beating up the quarters of loose women; in short, he appears to have shone in the character of a libertine and a rakehell rather than in a strictly judicial capacity. Instead of a dull list of his legal decisions we are treated to an amusing, if not very edifying, narrative of his adventures in love and in war, or rather in filibustering; for if we accept, as we are bound to do, the scriptural account of this roystering swashbuckler, he never levied a regular war or headed a national insurrection against the Philistines, the oppressors of his people; he merely sallied forth from time to time as a solitary paladin or knight-errant, and mowed them down with the jawbone of an ass or any other equally serviceable weapon that came to his hand. And even on these predatory expeditions (for he had no scruple about relieving his victims of their clothes and probably of their purses) the idea of delivering his nation from servitude was to all appearance the last thing that would have occurred to him.

In the extravagance of its colouring the picture of Samson owes more to the brush of the story-teller than to the pen of the historian. The marvellous and diverting incidents of his career probably floated about loosely as popular tales on the current of oral tradition long before they crystallized around the memory of a real man, a doughty highlander and borderer, a sort of Hebrew Rob Roy, whose choleric temper, dauntless courage, and prodigious bodily strength marked him out as the champion of Israel in many a wild foray across the border into the rich lowlands of Philistia. For there is no sufficient reason to doubt that a firm basis of fact underlies the flimsy and transparent superstructure of fancy in the Samson saga. The particularity with which the scenes of his life, from birth to death, are laid in definite towns and places, speaks strongly in favour of a genuine local tradition, and as strongly against the theory of a solar myth, into which some writers would dissolve the story of the brawny hero. ▼

(a) Samson as a solar hero[1]

The basis of the solar-myth theory is as follows: (i) The name Samson derives from the Hebrew word *shemesh,* meaning "sun," and much of the action takes place near Beth-Shemesh (mod. Tell Rumeileh), presumably an ancient shrine of the sun-god, where solar myths would very probably have been current.[2] (ii) The story of how Samson burned up the standing grain and olive crop of the Philistines by sending into their fields foxes with firebrands tied to their tails (15:4-6) might well represent the action of the scorching sun. (iii) The shearing of Samson's locks at the instigation of Delilah (16:16-19) might, in the same way, reflect the curtailment of the sun's rays by the shades of the night.[3]

In the light of Comparative Folklore, however, this interpretation can no longer be sustained. The incident of the foxes has, as we shall see, several parallels in other cultures, in all of which it possesses no symbolic significance, but can be readily explained as based either on a well-established ritual practice or an equally well-documented military stratagem. There are likewise plenty of analogues to the story of how a hero was enfeebled by the shearing of his locks, and in none of them does he bear a name which has anything whatsoever to do with the sun.[4] What is more, we now know both from Mesopotamian and from Canaanite sources that Samson (or its equivalent) was in fact a not uncommon name among ordinary mortals.[5]

(b) Samson and the foxes   15:4-5

Samson's first exploit was the firing of the Philistines' grainfields by sending into them foxes with lighted torches tied to their tails.

Modern scholars have advanced two alternative explanations of this incident, each based on popular practice. According to the one, it reflects, albeit in a distorting mirror, *a traditional ritual usage designed to remove mildew from crops.* The Roman poet Ovid tells us that at the annual Festival of Ceres (on April 19) it was customary to send into the fields foxes with firebrands tied to their tails.[6] Although he explains it on quasi-historical grounds, this custom (which is attested also by the fabulist Babrius)[7] was really a form of lustration by fire, mildew and other noxious elements being thereby consumed. Similarly, among the Arabs, foxes with torches attached to their tails were sometimes dispatched into the cornfields as a charm to promote rainfall and fertility;[8] while in European folklore the fox itself often personifies mildew because it is of the same color.[9] Moreover, in Paris and in parts of Savoy, foxes are (or once were) occasionally burned or singed in the midsummer bonfires,[10] though, admittedly, this may have been simply a ceremonious way of getting rid of the invaders.

The other explanation of Samson's exploit sees in it a *military stratagem*—part of the guerrilla tactics employed at the time by the Israelites against the Philistines.[11] For this an excellent parallel is offered by Livy's account of how Hannibal scared the Roman troops at Lake Trasimene, in 217 B.C., by launching into their fields oxen with firebrands tied to their horns.[12] In the same way, too, when in 1262 the Mongols were encamped against the Arabs in a field outside Aleppo, the latter frightened them off by dispatching into their midst foxes and hounds with torches attached to their tails;[13] and the redoubtable Timur (Tamurlane) is said to have routed an Indian army, in 1397, by striking panic in its elephants at the sight of a host of camels carrying flaming torches.[14] There is an interesting variation of this theme in the Icelandic *Heimskringla* of Snorri Sturluson. Harald of Norway, we read, was laying siege to a large and populous town in Sicily, but came to realize that its walls were too stout to be broken down and that its townsmen had plenty of provisions with which to hold out. So "he thought up a scheme: he told his birdcatchers to catch the small birds that nested within the town and flew out to the woods each day in search of food. Harald had small shavings of fir tied to the backs of the birds, and then he smeared the shavings with wax and sulphur and set fire to them. As soon as the birds were released they all flew straight home to their young in their nests in the town; the nests were under the eaves of the roofs, which were thatched with reeds or straws. The thatched roofs caught fire from the birds, and although each bird could only carry a tiny flame, it quickly became a great fire; a host of birds set roofs alight all over the town. One house after another caught fire, and soon the whole town was ablaze. At that all the people came out of the town, begging for mercy."[15]

(c) Samson's riddle 14

The Biblical writer accounts for Samson's exploit as an act of revenge for a thwarted love affair. Samson, runs the story, had picked a wife from among the Philistines at Timnah (modern Tibneh, west of Beth Shemesh). At the wedding feast, as a typical Oriental form of entertainment, he had posed a riddle to the assembled company of thirty guests, but the bride had wheedled the solution out of him and had revealed it. In high dudgeon, Samson had betaken himself to Ashkelon and there slain thirty Philistines. Outraged at this savagery, his father-in-law had thereupon canceled the marriage, giving the girl to the best man and denying Samson any access to her. At this, Samson took three hundred foxes, turned them tail to tail, attached lighted torches to each pair of tails, and sent them into the Philistine's fields at the time of the wheat harvest.

The riddle which Samson's guests were invited to solve was to identify the object described in the following jingle:

> *It comes from "the eater"*
> *'tis something you eat,*
> *—from something fierce,*
> *but itself is sweet.*

The answer was, honey (14:18).

It has recently been shown that the point of the riddle lies—as usually—in a play on words.[16] The Hebrew word for *honey*, viz., *arî*, is identical in outward form with one meaning *lion*. The latter is the "something fierce." It is also "the eater," for this was a popular designation both among the Canaanites and (later) among the Arabs for a carnivorous beast.[17]

▲ (d) Samson and Delilah 16

The art and skill of the storyteller reveal themselves most clearly, however, in the account of the catastrophe which befell his hero through the wiles of his treacherous mistress, Delilah, who wormed from him the secret that his great strength lay in his hair, and then betrayed him to his enemies by having it shorn.

The story revolves around the widespread belief that the strength, or very life of men (especially of heroes), resides in their locks.[18] Thus, the natives of Amboyna, an island in the East Indies, used to think that their vigor would desert them if their locks were shorn. A criminal under torture in a Dutch court once persisted in denying his guilt until his hair was cut off, when he immediately confessed. One man, who was tried for murder, endured without flinching the utmost ingenuity of his torturers till he saw the surgeon standing by with a pair of shears. On asking what they were for, and being told that it was to shave his hair, he begged that they would not do it, and made a clean breast. In subsequent cases, when torture failed to wring a confession from a prisoner, the Dutch authorities made a practice of cutting off his hair.[19] The natives of Ceram, another East Indian Island, still believe that if young people have their hair cut they will be weakened and enervated.[20]

In Europe it used to be thought that the maleficent powers of witches and wizards resided in their hair, and that nothing could make any impression on these miscreants so long as they kept their hair on. Hence in France it was customary to shave the whole bodies of persons charged with sorcery before handing them over to the tormentor. Millaeus witnessed the torture of some persons at Toulouse, from whom no confession could be wrung until they were stripped and completely shaven, when they readily acknowledged the truth of the charge. A woman also, who apparently led a pious life, was put to the torture on suspicion of witchcraft, and bore her agonies with incredible constancy, until complete depilation drove her to admit her guilt. The noted inquisitor Sprenger contented himself with shaving the head of the suspected witch or warlock; but his more thoroughgoing colleague Cumanus shaved the whole bodies of forty-one women before committing them all to the flames. He had high authority for this rigorous scrutiny, since Satan himself, in a sermon preached from the pulpit of North Berwick church, comforted his many servants by assuring them that no harm could befall them "sa lang as their hair wes on, and sould newir latt ane teir fall fra thair ene."[21] Similarly in Bastar, a province of India, "if a man is adjudged guilty of witchcraft, he is beaten by the crowd, his hair is shaved, the hair being supposed to constitute his power of mischief, his front teeth are knocked out, in order, it is said, to prevent him from muttering incantations. . . . Women suspected of sorcery have to undergo the same ordeal; if found guilty, the same punishment is awarded, and after being shaved, their hair is attached to a tree in some public place."[22] So among the Bhils, a rude race of Central India, when a woman was convicted of witchcraft and had been subjected to various forms of persuasion, such as hanging head downwards from a tree and having pepper rubbed into her eyes, a lock of hair was cut from her head and buried in the ground, "that the last link between her and her former powers of mischief might be broken."[23] In like manner among the Aztecs of Mexico, when wizards and witches "had done their evil deeds, and the time came to put an end to their detestable life, some one laid hold of them and cropped the hair on the crown of their heads, which took from them all their power of sorcery and enchantment, and then it was that by death they put an end to their odious existence."[24]

[On the other hand, an ancient Mesopotamian magical text tells us that witches themselves contrived to pluck out hairs from their intended victims in order to work their evil upon them;[24a] and everyone knows of the use in spells of "a hair of the dog that bit you."

Nor are these the only illustrations of this widespread belief. In many cultures, as we have seen, warriors have to go unshorn lest they lose their power.[24b] A child's hair may not be cut during its first year, since this would prejudice its chances of survival.[24c] Among the Pennsylvania Dutch a woman may not cut her husband's hair lest he become enfeebled and impotent.[24d]

Elsewhere baldness is regarded as a sign of debility.[24e] Moreover, because the hair (like the fingernails) is symbolic of the total self, it is often surrendered in *rites de passage,* when a person "changes identity" by transition from one stage of life to another. In ancient Greece, for example, girls dedicated their tresses to Artemis when they reached puberty;[24f] and elsewhere brides are shorn at marriage,[24g] as are nuns when they become "brides of Christ." It is this belief too that underlies the Teutonic custom of shearing the locks of an adulteress[24h]—a custom known also to the Babylonians, Arabs, and Jews[24i] as also that of cutting the hair of prisoners[24j] or criminals.[24k] So also, the hair is sometimes surrendered in token of adoption, as among the Pawnee Indians of North America.[24l] It is related of Boson, king of Provence, that he had his hair cut off and dedicated to Pope John VIII when the latter adopted him; this signified surrender of personality.[24m]]

It is no wonder that a belief so widespread should find its way into fairy tales which, for all the seeming licence of fancy, reflect as in a mirror the real faith once held by the people among whom the stories circulated. The natives of Nias, an island off the west coast of Sumatra, relate that once upon a time a certain chief named Laubo Maros was driven by an earthquake from Macassar, in Celebes, and migrated with his followers to Nias. Among those who followed his fortunes to the new land were his uncle and his uncle's wife. But the rascally nephew fell in love with his uncle's wife and contrived by a stratagem to get possession of the lady. The injured husband fled to Malacca and besought the Sultan of Johore to assist him in avenging his wrongs. The Sultan consented and declared war on Laubo Maros. Meanwhile, however, that unscrupulous chief had fortified his settlement with an impenetrable hedge of prickly bamboo, which defied all the attempts of the Sultan and his troops to take it by storm. Defeated in open battle, the wily Sultan now had recourse to stratagem. He returned to Johore and there laded a ship with Spanish mats. Then he sailed back to Nias, and anchoring off his enemy's fort he loaded his guns with the Spanish mats instead of with shot and shell, and so opened fire on the place. The mats flew like hail through the air and soon were lying thick on the prickly hedge of the fort and on the shore in its neighbourhood. The trap was now set and the Sultan waited to see what would follow. He had not long to wait. An old woman, prowling along the beach, picked up one of the mats and saw the rest spread out temptingly around her. Overjoyed at the discovery she passed the good news among her neighbours, who hastened to the spot, and in a trice the prickly hedge was not only stripped bare of the mats but torn down and levelled with the ground. So the Sultan of Johore and his men had only to march into the fort and take possession. The defenders fled, but the wicked chief himself fell into the hands of the victors. He was condemned to death, but great difficulty was experienced in executing the sentence. They threw him into the sea, but the water would not drown him; they laid him on a blazing pyre, but the fire would not burn him;

they hacked at every part of his body with swords, but steel would not pierce him. Then they perceived that he was an enchanter, and they consulted his wife to learn how they might kill him. Like Delilah, she revealed the fatal secret. On the chief's head grew a hair as hard as a copper wire, and with this wire his life was bound up. So the hair was plucked out, and with it his spirit fled.[25] In this and some of the following tales it is not merely the strength but the life of the hero which is supposed to have its seat in his hair, so that the loss of the hair involves his death.

Tales like that of Samson and Delilah were current in the legendary lore of ancient Greece. It is said that Nisus, king of Megara, had a purple or golden hair on the middle of his head, and that he was doomed to die whenever that hair should be plucked out. When Megara was besieged by the Cretans, the king's daughter Scylla fell in love with Minos, their king, and pulled out the fatal hair from her father's head. So he died.[26] According to one account it was not the life but the strength of Nisus that was in his golden hair; when it was pulled out, he grew weak and was slain by Minos.[27] In this form the story of Nisus resembles still more closely the story of Samson. Again, Poseidon is said to have made Pterelaus immortal by giving him a golden hair on his head. But when Taphos, the home of Pterelaus was besieged by Amphitryo, the daughter of Pterelaus fell in love with Amphitryo and killed her father by plucking out the golden hair with which his life was bound up.[28] In a modern Greek folk-tale a man's strength lies in three golden hairs on his head. When his mother pulls them out, he grows weak and timid and is slain by his enemies.[29] Another Greek story, in which we may perhaps detect a reminiscence of Nisus and Scylla, relates how a certain king, who was the strongest man of his time, had three long hairs on his breast. But when he went to war with another king, and his own treacherous wife had cut off the three hairs, he became the weakest of men.[30]

[Celtic lore tells similarly how Blodenwedd disabled Llew Llaw by cutting off his hair and exposing him, at the vulnerable moment, to attack by her lover, Gromas; and in Irish legend, Blathnat is said likewise to have deprived Cu Roi of his strength and then invited her lover Cuchularin to slay him.[30a] The same motif appears also in Norse mythology: Loki shears the golden tresses of Sif, the wife of Thor.[30b] Stories of the same tenor are to be found also in The Arabian Nights[30c] and in Turkish popular tales.[30d]]

Sometimes the hero's strength is said to lie not in his hair but rather in some external object such as an egg or a bird.

A Russian story relates how a certain warlock called Kashtshei or Koshchei the Deathless carried off a princess and kept her prisoner in his golden castle. However, a prince made up to her one day as she was walking alone and disconsolate in the castle garden, and cheered by the prospect of escaping with him she went to the warlock and coaxed him with false and flattering words, saying, "My dearest friend, tell me, I pray you, will you never die?" "Certainly not," says he. "Well," says she, "and where is your death? Is it in your dwelling?" "To be sure it is," says he, "it is in the broom under the threshold." Thereupon the princess seized the broom and threw it on the fire, but although the broom burned, the deathless Koshchei remained alive; indeed not so much as a hair of him was singed. Balked in her first attempt, the artful hussy pouted and said, "You do not love me true, for you have not told me where your death is; yet I am not angry, but love you with all my heart." With these fawning words she besought the warlock to tell her truly where his death was. So he laughed and said, "Why do you wish to know? Well then, out of love I will tell you where it lies. In a certain field there stand three green oaks, and under the roots of the largest oak is a worm, and if ever this worm is found and crushed, I shall die." When the princess heard these words, she went straight to her lover and told him all; and he searched till he found the oaks and dug up the worm and crushed it. Then he hurried to the warlock's castle, but only to learn that the warlock was still alive. Then the princess fell to wheedling and coaxing Koshchei once more, and this time, overcome by her wiles, he opened his heart to her and told her the truth. "My death," said he, "is far from here and hard to find, on the wide ocean. In that sea is an island, and on the island grows a green oak, and beneath the oak is an iron chest, and in the chest is a small basket, and in the basket is a hare, and in the hare is a duck, and in the duck is an egg; and he who finds the egg and breaks it, kills me at the same time." The prince naturally procured the fateful egg and with it in his hands he confronted the deathless warlock. The monster would have killed him, but the prince began to squeeze the egg. At that the warlock shrieked with pain, and turning to the false princess, who stood smirking and smiling, "Was it not out of love for you," said he, "that I told you where my death was? And is this the return you make to me?" With that he grabbed at his sword, which hung from a peg on the wall; but before he could reach it, the prince had crushed the egg, and sure enough the deathless warlock found his death at the same moment."[31]

A Serbian story relates how a certain warlock called True Steel carried off a prince's wife and kept her shut up in his cave. But the prince contrived to get speech of her, and told her that she must persuade True Steel to reveal to her where his strength lay. So when True Steel came home, the prince's wife said to him, "Tell me, now, where is your great strength?" He answered, "My wife, my strength is in my sword." Then she began to pray and turned to his sword. When True Steel saw that, he laughed and said, "O foolish woman! my strength is not in my sword, but in my bow and arrows." Then she turned towards the bow and arrows and prayed. But True Steel said, "I see, my wife, you have a clever teacher who has taught you to find out where my strength lies. I could almost say that your husband is living, and it is he who teaches you." But she assured him that nobody had taught her. When she found he had deceived her again, she waited for some days and then asked him again about the secret of his strength. He answered, "Since you think so much of my strength, I will tell you truly where it is. Far away from here there is a very high mountain; in the mountain there is a fox; in the fox there is a heart; in the heart there is a bird, and in this bird is my strength. It is no easy task, however, to catch the fox, for she can transform herself into a multitude of creatures." Next day, when True Steel went forth from the cave, the prince came and learned from his wife the true secret of the warlock's strength. So away he hied to the mountain, and there, though the fox, or rather the vixen, turned herself into various shapes, he contrived, with the help of some friendly eagles, falcons, and dragons, to catch and kill her. Then he took out the fox's heart, and out of the heart he took the bird and burned it in a great fire. At that very moment True Steel fell down dead.[32]

In another Serbian story we read how a dragon resided in a water-mill and ate up two king's sons, one after the other. The third son went out to seek his brothers, and coming to the water-mill he found nobody in it but an old woman. She revealed to him the dreadful character of the being that kept the mill, and how he had devoured the prince's two elder brothers, and she implored him to go away home before a like fate should overtake him. But he was both brave and cunning, and he said to her, "Listen well to what I am going to say to you. Ask the dragon whither he goes and where his great strength is; then kiss all that place where he tells you his strength is, as if you loved it dearly, till you find it out, and afterwards tell me when I come." So when the dragon came home the old woman began to question him, "Where in God's name have you been? Whither do you go so far? You will never tell me whither you go." The dragon replied, "Well, my dear old woman, I do go far." Then the old woman coaxed him, saying, "And why do you go so far? Tell me where your strength is. If I knew where your strength is, I don't know what I should do for love; I would kiss all that place." Thereupon the dragon smiled and said to her, "Yonder is my strength in that fireplace." Then the old woman began to kiss and fondle the fireplace; and the dragon on seeing it burst into a laugh. "Silly old woman," he said, "my strength is not there. It is in the tree-fungus in front of the house." Then the old woman began to fondle and kiss the tree; but the dragon laughed again and said to her, "Away, old woman! my strength is not there." "Then where is it?" asked the old woman. "My strength," said he, "is a long way off, and you cannot go thither. Far in another kingdom under the king's city is a lake; in the lake is a dragon; in the dragon is a boar; in the boar is a pigeon, and in the pigeon is my strength." The secret was out; so next morning, when the dragon went away from the mill to attend to his usual business of gobbling people up, the prince came to the old woman and she let him into the mystery of the dragon's strength. Needless to say that the prince contrived to make his way to the lake in the far country, where after a terrible tussle he slew the water-dragon and extracted the pigeon, in which was the strength of the other unscrupulous dragon who kept the mill. Having questioned the pigeon, and ascertained from it how to restore his two murdered brothers to life, the prince wrung the bird's neck, and no doubt the wicked dragon perished miserably the very same moment, though the storyteller has omitted to mention the fact.[33]

Similar incidents occur in Celtic stories. Thus a tale, told by a blind fiddler in the island of Islay, relates how a giant carried off a king's wife and his two horses, and kept them in his den. But the horses attacked the giant and mauled him so that he could hardly crawl. He said to the queen, "If I myself had my soul to keep, those horses would have killed me long ago." "And where, my dear," said she, "is thy soul? By the books I will take care of it." "It is in the Bonnach stone," said he. So on the morrow when the giant went out, the queen set the Bonnach stone in order exceedingly. In the dusk of the evening the giant came back, and he said to the queen, "What made thee set the Bonnach stone in order like that?" "Because thy soul is in it," quoth she. "I perceive," said he, "that if thou didst know where my soul is, thou wouldst give it much respect." "That I would," said she. "It is not there," said he, "my soul is; it is in the threshold." On the morrow she set the threshold in order finely, and when the giant returned he asked her, "What brought thee to set the threshold in order like that?" "Because thy soul is in it," said she. "I perceive," said he, "that if thou knewest where my soul is, thou wouldst take care of it." "That I would," said she. "It is not there that my soul is," said he. "There is a great flagstone under the threshold. There is a wether under the flag; there is a duck in the wether's belly, and an egg in the belly of the duck, and it is in the egg that my soul is." On the morrow when the giant was gone, they raised the flagstone and out came the wether. They opened the wether and out came the duck. They split the duck, and out came the egg. And the queen took the egg and crushed it in her hands, and at that very moment the giant, who was coming home in the dusk, fell down dead.[34]

Once more, in an Argyleshire story we read how a big giant, King of Sorcha, stole away the wife of the herdsman of Cruachan, and hid her in the cave in which he dwelt. But by the help of some obliging animals the herdsman contrived to discover the cave and his own lost wife in it. Fortunately the giant was not at home; so after giving her husband food to eat, she hid him under some clothes at the upper end of the cave. And when the giant came home he sniffed about and said, "The smell of a stranger is in the cave." But she said no, it was only a little bird she had roasted. "And I wish you would tell me," said she, "where you keep your life, that I might take good care of it." "It is in a grey stone over there," said he. So next day when he went away, she took the grey stone and dressed it well, and placed it in the upper end of the cave. When the giant came home in the evening he said to her, "What is it that you have dressed there?" "Your own life," said she, "and we must be careful of it." "I perceive that you are very fond of me, but it is not there," said he.

"Where is it?" said she. "It is in a grey sheep on yonder hillside," said he. On the morrow, when he went away, she got the grey sheep, dressed it well, and placed it in the upper end of the cave. When he came home in the evening, he said, "What is it that you have dressed there?" "Your own life, my love," said she. "It is not there as yet," said he. "Well!" said she, "you are putting me to great trouble taking care of it, and you have not told me the truth these two times." He then said, "I think that I may tell it to you now. My life is below the feet of the big horse in the stable. There is a place down there in which there is a small lake. Over the lake are seven grey hides, and over the hides are seven sods from the heath, and under all these are seven oak planks. There is a trout in the lake, and a duck in the belly of the trout, an egg in the belly of the duck, and a thorn of blackthorn inside of the egg, and till that thorn is chewed small I cannot be killed. Whenever the seven grey hides, the seven sods from the heath, and the seven oak planks are touched, I shall feel it wherever I shall be. I have an axe above the door, and unless all these are cut through with one blow of it, the lake will not be reached; and when it will be reached I shall feel it." Next day, when the giant had gone out hunting on the hill, the herdsman of Cruachan contrived, with the help of the same friendly animals, which had assisted him before, to get possession of the fateful thorn, and to chew it before the giant could reach him; and no sooner had he done so than the giant dropped stark and stiff, a corpse.[35] ▼

118 The woman divided into twelve parts   19

A levite, sojourning beside the highlands of Ephraim, has a concubine who hails from Bethlehem, in Judah. She deceives him by consorting with other men, and finally takes off for her hometown. He goes to fetch her back, and is hospitably received by her father. On the return journey, the party is accommodated overnight at Gibeah, a city in the territory of Benjamin, by an aged fellow-Ephraimite who has encountered the levite in the street after everyone else has refused him lodging. Hooligans, however, surround the house and demand that the old man's guest be surrendered to them for unnatural purposes. The old man offers his own virgin daughter and his guest's concubine instead. They choose the latter and abuse her all night. At dawn the levite finds her lying in a faint on the threshold. He takes her back to his hometown, but there slices her into twelve parts which he distributes "throughout all the territory of Israel." Thus the concubine pays in the end for her infidelity to him.

This gruesome story is, of course, simply a variant of the folktale related in the Book of Genesis (ch. 19) concerning Lot and the angels. Upon it, however, there has been engrafted the moralizing theme of "the postman always rings twice."

In the original version of the tale, the *twelve* parts into which the hapless woman is severed probably had nothing whatever to do with the twelve tribes of Israel, this being simply an Israelization of an older märchen-motif. They may have been the twelve parts in which the human body was anciently believed to consist. This notion is well attested, for instance, among the Hittites,[1] and in one Hittite ritual for curing sickness, the patient is magically healed by treatment of the twelve limbs of a sacrificial beast.[2]

Twelvefold offerings were likewise common. Thus, in a funeral ritual it is expressly prescribed that twelve loaves be placed beside the cremated corpse,[3] and at a subsequent stage of the proceedings the fleeces of twelve unblemished sheep are dedicated to the gods.[4] Similarly, in a ritual designed to expel pestilence, provision is made for the presentation of twelve vessels and twelve loaves of bread;[5] while in another, for the removal of evil spirits from a palace, twelve loaves of *ḫuri*-bread and twelve of some other kind are presented.[6]

Nor was this twelvefold offering confined to the Hittites. In the Homeric Hymn to Hermes, a sacrifice is likewise divided into twelve parts, but these are rationalized as having been presented to the twelve Olympian deities.[7]

By a similar development the twelve stones erected by the prophet Elijah on Mt. Carmel, in what was really an ancient rain-making ritual, are associated in the Scriptural account (I Kings 18:31) with the "twelve tribes of the sons of Jacob" and are said to have been built into an altar of Yahweh (see below §158).

119 The rape of the women of Shiloh 21:16–24

In vengeance for the outrage perpetrated by the men of Gibeah, the Israelites vowed never to give their daughters in marriage to any member of the tribe of Benjamin. Subsequently, however, after a reconciliation had been effected, it occurred to them that maintenance of this ban would result eventually in the extinction of a tribe of Israel. They therefore devised a way of circumventing the vow. The Benjaminites were informed that an annual festival was about to be celebrated at Shiloh, at which maidens would come out to dance. They were advised to lie in ambush in the vineyards and then pounce on the girls, taking whomever they desired. This they did.

On the face of it, the story here related is perfectly natural and intelligible. A country carnival is an obvious place for sex-starved males to go stalking mates. Indeed, throughout the centuries young men have been known to eye girls in church, and E. W. Lane, in his *Manners and Customs of the Modern Egyptians,* paints a vivid picture of the similar enterprise of Arabs in the mosque at Cairo.[1]

A close parallel to the incident here related is afforded, however, by the familiar Roman legend of the rape of the Sabine women at the agricultural festival of Consualia (in August).[2] "In the early days of Rome," runs the story, "the population consisted chiefly of broken men who had taken refuge in the asylum opened for them by Romulus. As the neighboring peoples refused to give their daughters in marriage to these ruffians, Romulus was obliged to resort to stratagem to procure wives for his subjects. So he issued a proclamation that he was about to celebrate the solemn games in honor of the equestrian Neptune. Many people flocked from the neighborhood of Rome to witness the spectacle; in particular the Sabines came in great force with their wives and children. When the games were about to begin, and the spectators were on the tiptoe of expectation, the young Roman men rushed upon them, singled out the likeliest young women, and carried them off. After some ado they succeeded in pacifying the damsels and so won brides for themselves."[3]

In the same way the Messenians are said, in Greek legend, to have carried off maidens from neighboring Laconia during the celebration of a festival of Artemis at Limnae.[4]

It has been suggested also that the famous Greek myth which tells how Persephone was abducted by Hades (Pluto) while gathering flowers may reflect a similar practice.[5] For, while it is true that the rape of maidens in such circumstances is something of a stock situation in Greek poetry,[6] "there is some evidence of a widespread custom of the ceremonial [i.e., ritual] gathering of flowers in spring, analogous to the modern Greek May Day Festival of Flower-gathering.[7] Herosantheia (or Heroantheia) was a Peloponnesian festival of this kind."[8]

It is possible, however, that our Biblical story is, *au fond,* an etiological legend told originally to account for an ancient practice of mass-mating at seasonal festivals.[9] Designed to regenerate and refecundate the human community at those regular intervals when its corporate life seemed to have completed a cycle, this practice is widely attested both in antiquity and among modern primitive peoples.[10] It obtained—to cite but a few examples—at the Roman festival of Anna Perenna on the Ides of March;[11] while among the Pipiles of Central America copulation takes place in the fields at the moment the first seeds are sown.[12] Similarly, in parts of the Ukraine, married couples copulate in the fields on St. George's Day (April 23) in order to promote the fertility of the crops and to achieve the renewal of the topocosm—that is, the corporate life of the area.[13] In certain districts of Portugal they likewise roll together in the meadows, in a ceremony called *rebolada,* before the reaping of flax, in May.[14] In Java, husbands and wives adopt the same practice as a means of stimulating the growth of rice;[15] while in Amboyna men indulge in mimetic sexual intercourse with trees whenever the harvest is threatened.[16] So too among the Hereros of South West Africa[17] and among various

Bantu tribes[18] mass-mating and sexual promiscuity are obligatory at specific seasons of the year; while the Garos of Assam encourage men and women to sleep together after certain major seasonal festivals.[19]

In a more ceremonial form of the custom, the king has at the same time to indulge in a ritual marriage with a chosen bride.[20]

An attenuated survival of this usage may be recognized in popular traditions that certain crucial days of the year are particularly auspicious for the choosing of husbands and wives.[21] The Talmud tells us, for example, that it was customary in Jerusalem to choose brides on the Day of Atonement—that is (originally), during the period of austerity and purification preceding the autumnal harvesting of fruits—and on the 15th day of the month of Ab (August), the occasion of an ancient festival.[22] Similarly, in some parts of England, St. Roch's day (August 16) and St. Luke's day (October 18) were deemed especially propitious for the choosing of mates.[23] In the same way too it is the custom in Spanish Galicia for girls to repair at harvest time to a duly selected barn, where their ardent swains make love to them;[24] and among the Thompson River Indians of British Columbia husbands and wives are chosen at a seasonal festival held in the "spring house."[25]

A further attenuation is the European popular custom of compulsory kissing or "lifting" on certain days of the year.[26] "Kissing fairs" and "hocking days" (cf. German *hoch,* "high") are well attested. Thus, in the Arad commune of Nagyhalmagy, in Hungary, a *markt* is (or was) held annually on March 15, at which women may be kissed without risk of rebuff.[27] Similarly, in certain parts of England, girls may be "lifted" with impunity on May 15; and at Hungerford, in Berkshire, the second Thursday after Easter is "hocking day," when the "tuttimen" go about the streets lifting or "hocking" the women and exacting a kiss from each.[28] Analogous, of course, is the religiously observed Yuletide custom of kissing under the mistletoe—a custom which derives, as every folklorist knows, from the cruder primitive usage of compulsory promiscuity at seasonal festivals.[29]

Ruth

120 Levirate marriage

The Book of Ruth turns largely around the ancient institution of levirate marriage. A discussion of this belongs within the sphere of law rather than folklore. Since, however, certain elements of traditional custom are involved, the subject cannot be altogether excluded from this work. For the reader's convenience I therefore append a representative bibliography:

M. Burrows, in JBL 59 (1940), 23–33; id., in BASOR 77 (1940), 2–14; id., The Basis of Israelite Marriage (AASOR, No. 15); D. Jacobson, The Social Background of the OT (1942), 290 ff.; I. Mendelsohn, in The Biblical Archaeologist 11 (1948), 24 ff.; J. Mittelmann, Das althebräische Levirat (1939); H. Schaeffer, Social Legislation of the Primitive Semites (1915), 57–64; I. Mattuck, in Kaufmann Kohler Festschrift (1913), 210–22; S. A. Cook, The Laws of Moses and the Code of Hammurabi (1903), 144, n. 3; S. R. Driver, ICC on Deut. 25:6 f.; W. W. Davies, in The Christian Advocate 63 (1888), 820 f.; W. Redslob, Die Levirat-Ehe bei den Hebräern (1836); Rauschenbusch, De lege leviratus (1765).

For analogies in the Middle Assyrian Law Code (§43), cf. B. Cruvelier in RB 34 (1925), 524–46; G. R. Driver and J. C. Miles, The Assyrian Laws (1935), 240–50.

For a parallel in the Hittite Law-Code (§193), cf. A. Goetze, ANET 196; O. Gurney, The Hittites (1952), 101 f.

Among some bedouin tribes the brother of a man deceased must marry his widow: J. Burckhardt, Bedouins and Wahabys (1830), i.112; B. Jacob, Altarabische Parallelen zum AT (1897), 14; J. Wellhausen, Die Ehe bei den Arabern (1893), 435 f. Sometimes his nephew must do so, even if he himself has murdered the husband: C. A. Doughty, Travels in Arabia Deserta (1888), i.506; ii.20.

Cf. also the *niyoḡa*—marriage of a betrothed widow in the Laws of Manu, ix.59–64, and the so-called *čakar*—marriage among the Iranians and Parsis.

Among the Bushmen of South Africa a widow who does not remarry must be supported by her deceased husband's brother: C. G. Seligmann, Races of Africa (1930), 29.

On the institution in general, see: E. Westermarck, A History of Human Marriage (1921), iii.208 ff.; R. Briffault, The Mothers (1927), i.761; J. G. Frazer, Pausanias (1898), iii.198–200.

121 Covering with a garment in token of protection — Ruth 3:9

Ruth asks Boaz to cast his garment over her in token of his protection.

Covering with a garment is in several cultures a recognized method of taking a person under one's protection; indeed, the very word "protect" carries this meaning. In Ezekiel 16:8 Yahweh declares that he "adopted" the infant Israel by spreading his garment over him, and in pre-Islamic times this was the manner in which an Arab son took over his father's relicts.[1] It was by this gesture too that Mohammed "married" the Jewess Safiya after the battle near Khaibar;[2] and even in modern times it was customary in the Sinai peninsula for bridegrooms to cast their mantles over their brides.[3] So too, in the marriage ceremony of the Russian Orthodox Church, the bridegroom casts the lap of his gown over the bride;[4] and it is related of Maria Cantacuena that she spread out her cloak and wrapped it around the children she adopted.[5]

In a figurative sense, reference is made to this custom in one of the pseudepigraphic *Odes of Solomon,* dating (probably) from the first century of the Common Era: *I have been prepared against the coming perdition,* says the passage, *in that I have been placed under God's garment of nondestruction, and in that he has enfolded me in life immortal and embraced (kissed) me.*[6]

An interesting variation of this usage was the European practice whereby children who had been born to a couple out of wedlock could be legitimized by being covered with the nuptial veil or the pallium of the altar when their parents married. Such children were known as *pueri mantellati* or—in German—*Mantelkinder.*[7] The custom was observed in Scotland as late as the nineteenth century.[8] A fascinating survival of it may perhaps be detected in the Jewish custom of spreading a prayer shawl (*ṭallîth*) over the heads of minors when they are called to the rostrum for the reading of the Lesson at the annual Festival of Rejoicing in the Law (*Simḥath Torah*). The synagogal service on that occasion is cast in the form of a symbolic wedding between Israel and the Law (Torah), and it is in extension of that symbolism that children, who are not normally eligible to be called to the reading of the Lesson from it until they attain the age of religious majority, are fancifully "legitimized" *ad hoc!*[9]

122 Gestures of adoption — 4:16

Naomi takes the child born to Ruth and Boaz and lays him on her bosom. Thereby she becomes his foster-mother.

Placing a child upon the bosom was a gesture of adoption. It symbolizes suckling, and it could be performed by men as well as by women. The Count of Edessa, for instance, so adopted Baldwin.[1] The custom is well attested in

European usage,² but that it is indeed ancient and obtained also in the Orient is indicated not only by our present passage but also, it would seem, by Psalm 2:7, where, by the emendation of a single letter in the original Hebrew, the obscure and ungrammatical phrase usually rendered (as in RSV), *I will tell of the decree of the Lord: He said to me, You are my son, today I have begotten you,* may be made to yield the sense, *"I gather thee unto my bosom"—so saith the Lord unto me—"Thou art my son, this day have I acknowledged thee mine offspring."*³

A variant of the custom of placing a child on the bosom to symbolize adoption is mentioned in an ancient Mesopotamian document: if the real parents of a child wished to reclaim it from a foster-mother, they placed before it a vessel (*kabduqû*) filled with human milk. This likewise symbolized suckling.⁴

123 Removing the shoe   4:7–12

The symbolic meaning of removing the shoe as a gesture of divorce or repudiation¹ has been variously explained.

(i) Some scholars would illustrate it from the fact that in Arab ceremonies of divorce the man sometimes removes his shoe, saying, "she was my slipper; I cast (her) off."² Furthermore, a wife is sometimes called figuratively a "shoe" (*na'l*), and the expression "to tread" is used of sexual intercourse.³

(ii) In documents from the Mesopotamian city of Nuzi, dating from the fifteenth century B.C., a pair of shoes sometimes represents a "legal" payment of formal or fictional character.⁴ That the same custom obtained later among the Israelites has been inferred from references in the Book of Amos (2:6; 8:6) to the transgression of selling the needy for a pair of shoes; while, according to the Greek (Septuagint) text of I Samuel 12:3, the aged Samuel declared to Israel: *Whose calf* (Heb.: *ox*) *have I ever taken? Or whose ass have I ever taken? Or whom of you have I ever overmastered and oppressed? Or from whose hand have I ever taken a bribe or* a pair of shoes (i.e., a purely fictitious payment, to deprive him of his property)?⁵ In the present writer's opinion, however, the connection is doubtful, because in our passage the significance surely lies in the pulling off of the shoe, not in the shoe itself.

(iii) A third explanation derives from the fact that in those same documents from Nuzu "lifting the foot" is a technical term for releasing property.⁶ This, however, really belongs to quite a different order of ideas. "Lifting the foot" is simply the opposite of "putting one's foot down" or setting someone or something "under one's heel" as a gesture of subjugation. The expression is used in this sense alike in the Old Testament itself (Ps. 8:7) and in Ugaritic⁷ and Phoenician sources.⁸ The Egyptians planted their feet on vanquished foes,⁹ and in the Babylonian Epic of Creation the god Marduk does likewise to the vanquished Tiamat;¹⁰ while the Romans spoke similarly of "laying all things underfoot."[11] The lifting of the foot would therefore very naturally imply release from such domination, but this is surely quite different from *the pulling off of a shoe*.

(iv) A curious interpretation advanced by some Jewish authorities (e.g., Jehiel of Paris) is that the drawing off of the shoe was simply the customary gesture of mourning.[12] When the potential levir refused to "raise up seed" for his deceased brother, the latter was indeed dead, and the widow signified this by drawing off the levir's shoe.

Not impossibly, the true explanation lies in the fact that the shoe was a symbol of authority; the ceremonial removal of it therefore indicated that such authority had been surrendered. True, we cannot yet authenticate such symbolism from any Ancient Near Eastern source, but in support of this interpretation it may be noted that, according to some later rabbinic authorities, a glove may be substituted for the shoe,[13] for this can be brought into relation with the custom, which persisted in English usage until recent times, of bestowing a pair of gloves "by way of delivery or investiture, in sales or conveyances of lands and goods."[14]

Samuel

124 Falling to the ground   I Sam. 3:19

Yahweh favors Samuel and "does not let any one of his words fall to the ground."

What falls to the ground loses its inherent power and is no longer "whole."[1] Folklore expresses this idea in custom as well as in language. Pythagoras, for instance, forbade his followers to pick up anything that had fallen from the table,[2] and this became a law at Croton.[3] The same practice obtained also among the Romans[4] and the ancient Prussians.[5] In Greece it was held that whatever falls on the ground belongs to the "heroes,"[6] or ancestral spirits; while a modern German superstition assigns it to the Devil.[7]

When herbs are plucked, says Pliny, care must be taken that they are not subsequently dropped,[8] and the same caution is elsewhere prescribed concerning the gathering of stones.[9] Material used in magic or medicine was likewise believed to lose its efficacy if it fell.[10] Thus, a Greek spell for forcing locked doors instructs the operator to "take the navel of a firstborn ram, without letting it fall on the ground."[11]

124a Leaping over the threshold   5:5
See below, §243.

125 Of mice and men   5:6—6:5

The Philistines capture the ark of Yahweh. He retaliates by sending an epidemic of hemorrhoids.

Individuals who commit sacrilege or transgression are punished by blindness (**§56**), leprosy (**§93**), or paralysis (**§154**). Hence, when a whole people does so, this entails an epidemic.

Folklore knows several parallels to the incident here related. Callimachus tells us that when, in 652 B.C., Lygdamus led a host of Cimmerians against the temple of Artemis at Ephesus, the goddess turned her shafts upon them, and "no man of them was destined to return to Scythia";[1] and the lexicographer Hesychius adds that, on the score of this episode, "Scythian desolation" became a proverbial expression.[2] The shafts of Artemis, like those of her brother Apollo, and like those said in European folklore to be shot by elves, were the strokes of plague or disease.[3] Similarly, according to Herodotus, when some of the Scythians pillaged the shrine of Aphrodite (i.e., Astarte) at Ascalon, the outraged goddess visited upon them what he calls "the female sickness"—that is, an atrophy of the organs of generation.[4] Of the same tenor too, is a story related, in the fourth century C.E. by Ammianus Marcellinus, the last of the major Roman historians. He says that after the Romans had sacrilegiously deported the image of Apollo of Seleucia to the Palatine in Rome, certain soldiers peered into a crevice in the original Syrian temple in the hope of finding hidden treasure; whereupon a sudden and widespread contagion ensued.[5] Lastly, Dictys Cretensis, in his fabled narrative of the Trojan War, relates that after Agamemnon had impiously slain the sacred hind of Artemis, a plague broke out and grew in intensity from day to day, until everything fell prey to it.[6]

> *The Philistines decide to send the ark to the Israelites, but their priests and diviners advise that the restoration be accompanied by a tresspass-offering, or indemnity. The latter includes five golden images of mice, one for the lord of each of the five Philistine cities of Palestine.*

The association of plague—especially bubonic plague—with mice was certainly observed in antiquity, even though the causal connection may still have been unknown; and it survives in European folklore.[7] Strabo tells us, for example, that the Iberians of Spain were regularly "tormented by vast swarms of mice, from which pestilential diseases have frequently ensued";[8] and it is a common superstition among the peasants in Germany that a procession of mice forebodes an epidemic;[9] while in Bohemia the mouse is (or was) popularly regarded as a symbol of plague and war.[10]

Some scholars have sought to discover an instance of this belief in the Old Testament itself. In the Second Book of Kings it is related that when Sennacherib laid siege to Jerusalem in 701 B.C., he was prevented from actually penetrating the city because "an angel of Yahweh went forth and smote in the camp of the Assyrians an hundred fourscore and five thousand men."[11] Now, according to Herodotus, when the same invader marched upon Egypt, he was stopped at the last moment by the fact that field mice gnawed the quivers and shield handles of his men overnight. Combining these two accounts, it has been suggested that Herodotus has garbled the details of an incident which really took place on the outskirts of Jerusalem and which consisted in the sudden onset of a plague brought by mice.[12] To be sure, this ingenious suggestion is not without its difficulties, first because the story of how rodents achieved an army's defeat by gnawing at its bowstrings is indeed paralleled elsewhere,[13] and second because, as Andrew Lang acutely pointed out,[14] the Father of History speaks specifically of *field* mice, and these do not in fact carry infection!

Be this as it may, mice are indeed associated in popular lore with gods who send or avert plague.[15] The prime example of this is Apollo. Apollo, as we know, was, among other things, a god of plague.[16] It is he who, in the

Iliad, shoots the shafts of pestilence at the Greeks before Troy;[17] who, in the Odyssey, kills Rhexenor through illness,[18] and whom Melanthios bids slay Telemachus,[19] and Penelope bids slay Antinous.[20] His arrows are called "arrows" of pestilence,"[21] and he is said once to have inflicted a plague on the Libyans.[22] In a Graeco-Phoenician bilingual inscription from Cition, in Cyprus, he is explicitly identified with the Phoenician plague-god, "Resheph of the arrow,"[23] and a place named Arsuf (i.e., Reshephville), near Jaffa, was known in Seleucid times as Apollonias.[24] Conversely, he was also the healer or averter of plague, bearing such titles as "Healer" (Akesios)[25] and "Physician" (Iatros).[26] Now, in several parts of the Greek world Apollo was known as Smintheus,[27] and this derives from an old Cretan word, *sminthos*, meaning "mouse."[28] At Hamaxitos the god was definitely associated with mice,[29] and at Chryse the sculptor Skopas embellished his statue with a mouse at its feet.[30] Here, then, we have the plague-god explicitly associated with mice, and what makes this the more interesting and the more pertinent to our Biblical narrative is that the Philistines are said to have come from Crete.[31] In sending the golden mice to Yahweh to avert plague they would therefore have been transferring to Israel's god a standard practice traditionally associated with his counterpart in their own religion. Such, at least, is the construction which many scholars have put upon this incident. A word of caution, however, is not inappropriate, for we must not lose sight of the possibility that Apollo Smintheus was not a plague-god at all, but simply one who kept mice away from the fields.[32]

It has been suggested also that Apollo's sister Artemis, who was likewise a sender and averter of pestilence, provides yet another example of a plague-deity associated with mice, for at Therapne, on the border of Arcadia, she was known by the curious epithet Mysia,[33] which may be explained, perhaps, from the word *mus*, "mouse."[34] Moreover, at Lysoi in Arcadia she was worshiped beside a spring in which mice were fabled to come to life and have their being.[35] A survival of this or an analogous mouse-goddess has been recognized in the figure of St. Gertrude who is said specifically to protect from mice and from diseases[36] and who is often portrayed accompanied by a mouse.[37]

126 Death for looking into the Ark of the Lord   6:19

When the Philistines were returning the captured Ark of the Lord to the Israelites, certain men of Beth Shemesh looked inside it. In retribution for this impiety the Lord slew them.

On the significance of this offense, see below, §138. The traditional text gives the number of those slain as "seventy men, five thousand men." The absence of the copula shows that the two numbers are variants. Folklore clarifies the variation, for the fact is that both seventy and five thousand are conventional round numbers in Hebrew.[1] The latter was evidently considered too implausible and was therefore duly "corrected." Both readings were then preserved side by side.[2]

127 Qualifications for kingship   9:21; 10:23; 16:7

Saul, chosen to be king of Israel, is "goodlier" and taller than any one of the people.

The king, in ancient and primitive thought, is the epitome of his people's corporate life and fortune. Therefore he must be without blemish and (at least in theory) physically superior to everyone else.

Examples of this belief are legion. Concerning the pretender Absalom it is said expressly, in the Old Testament itself, that he was the most beautiful man in Israel and "without blemish from top to toe";[1] while in the Babylonian *Epic of Creation*, Marduk, who becomes king of the gods, is described as the tallest among them and as endowed with a "surpassing stature."[2] According to Herodotus, Xerxes I was likewise the tallest and most handsome of the Persians;[3] and Athenaeus tells us that among the ancient Ethiopians the most handsome man was appointed king.[4]

In the Canaanite (Ugaritic) *Poem of Baal*, the god Ashtar though recommended by the queen goddess Asherat as "terrific" (*'ariṣu*), is disqualified from succeeding him after he has disappeared into the netherworld, because he is too small: "his head does not reach to the top of the throne, nor his feet to the footstool."[5] Similarly, the Konde of Lake Nyassa keep the king under surveillance before installing him, "lest, being a weakling, he should be a menace to the land";[6] while among the Varozwe, a Shona tribe of Africa, "absence of bodily blemishes was considered absolutely necessary in the occupant of the throne."[7]

A natural corollary is that the king is deposed or killed as soon as he shows signs of old age, debility, or physical defect. When Uzziah-Azariah of Judah became a leper, says the Book of Kings, the reins of government passed to his son Jotham.[8] In similar vein, in the Canaanite (Ugaritic) *Epic of K-r-t*, that monarch's upstart son, Yaṣṣib, claims the throne from him on the grounds that he has become sick and feeble, merely talks "blather" and is unable to dispense justice, redress oppression, or succor the widow and orphan.[9] In Western Africa, it is likewise the general rule that kings are dethroned or slain by reason of bodily defect. This is standard practice; for example, among the Fazoql, the Shilluk of the White Nile, the Bunyoro, the Kibanga of the Upper Congo, the Hausa of Northern Nigeria, and the Zulus.[10]

128 Eyes brightened by eating honey   14:24–30

When the Israelites engaged the Philistines at Beth-aven, Saul adjured his men to abstain from food until victory was won. Some of them found a honeycomb, but carefully refrained from tasting in obedience

> to the king's command. Saul's son, Jonathan, however, cavalierly broke the taboo, but instead of dire consequences found that as soon as the honey touched his lips, his eyes brightened.

Involved in this story is a widespread tradition of folk medicine. The physicians of ancient Egypt prescribed honey for diseases of the eyes,[1] and the Greeks followed suit. Aristotle says that honey relieves dullness of vision,[2] and Dioscorides that it removes "whatever darkens the pupils."[3] Galen too recommended it for affections of the eyes,[4] and Pliny speaks in the same sense, adding that it is useful against cataract, and was employed for such purposes in India.[5] Celsus[6] and Marcellus of Bordeaux[7] likewise endorse it as a nostrum in diseases of the eyes; while even in modern times it has been held efficacious against trachoma.[8]

This is merely a particular application of the idea that honey is regenerative and expels or averts evil spirits.[9] Hindus and Moslems smear it on the lips and gums of newborn babes,[10] and in Greek myth this is said to have been done both to the infant Zeus[11] and to the infant Dionysus.[12] In the pseudepigraphic story of Joseph and Asenath, the archangel Michael provides the Egyptian princess with a honeycomb by the use of which she achieves both purification and immortality;[13] while in the Finnish Kalevala, the slain hero Lemminkainen is revived by magic honey.[14] Initiants into the mysteries of Mithra were given honey as a means of regeneration.[15] Jews still eat honey at New Year, and in Babylon, honey was offered at the dedication of new images of the gods at the Akîtu (New Year) festival.[16] An ancient Egyptian charm prescribes honey as a means of keeping away the child-stealing witch.[17]

For the same reason rivers of honey are characteristic of the Golden age, and are said to flow in Paradise (see above, §14).

129 Agag

(a) Agag walks "delicately"   15:32

> *Agag, king of the Amalekites, defeated by Saul, is led into the presence of the prophet Samuel. He comes walking "delicately" and exclaiming, "Bitter indeed is death."*[1]

The Hebrew word rendered "delicately" really means "with limping gait."[2] The reference is to a custom observed at Semitic funerals, whereby the mourners shuffle around the bier with a peculiar limping or hopping step.[3] An excellent description of the rite is given by Roger in his *La terre saincte*, published in 1664,[4] while Lane, in his famous *Manners and Customs of the Modern Egyptians*, informs us that

it is customary among the peasants of Upper Egypt for the female relations and friends of a person deceased to meet together by his house on the first three days after the funeral, and there to perform a lamentation and a strange kind of dance.

They daub their faces and bosoms and parts of their dress with mud; and tie a rope girdle . . . round the waist. Each flourishes in her hand a palm-stick or a nebroot (a long staff), or a drawn sword [so to forefend demons], and dances with a slow movement, and in an irregular manner; generally pacing about and raising and depressing the body.[5]

The custom was reported also by Wetzstein, the German consul at Damascus, as current among the peasants of Syria in the nineteenth century, and it was there known by the same term (*ma'id*) as in our Biblical text.[6] In Arabic and Syriac, the word "to skip, hop" (*r-q-d, r-q-ṣ*) also denotes the performance at a funeral of a special kind of limping dance,[7] and in an ancient Mesopotamian syllabary, the corresponding Akkadian word (*ruquddu*) is listed as the technical term for a professional mourner.[8] The term seems also to occur, as early as the fourteenth century B.C., in the Canaanite (Ugaritic) *Poem of Aqhat* in connection with the mourning for him by his father, Daniel.[9]

Not impossibly, it was because they had to accompany this limping dance that Hebrew dirges were usually composed in a peculiar limping (scazontic) meter, achieved by truncating the final beat of what would otherwise be a verse consisting of two balanced halves, each with three corresponding accents, e.g.,

> Outdóors they líe on the gróund
> yóung men and óld;
> My yóuths and máidens áll
> are sláin by the swórd;[10]

The point of our Scriptural narrative is, then, that Agag, like an archhypocrite, approaches the prophet in the manner of a mourner, intoning a typical dirge!

(b) Agag is hewn asunder   15:33

Samuel orders Agag to be hewn in pieces, as a condign punishment for his savagery.

Agag is not merely slain; he is slain "before Yahweh at Gilgal," and he is slain in a special way. This indicates that he became the victim of a ritual ceremony, and that ceremony is admirably illustrated from Arab sources. After a successful foray, the Arabs, we are told, used, before dividing the spoil, to select from it one choice beast which they sacrificed and upon the flesh of which they then feasted.[11] The technical name for the victim was *naqi,* which means properly "that which is split, rent, hewn." The Saracens, says Nilus, did not always use an animal for this purpose; by preference they would select a handsome boy.[12] It has therefore been suggested that the hewing asunder of Agag "before Yahweh" represents an earlier Israelite example of the same practice.[13] The *raison d'être* was probably the recementing by commensality (see above, §52) of kinship ties after the losses incurred in warfare or on forays.

130 Battle taunts   17:43–48
See above, §31.

131 Beheading fallen foes   17:46, 51
David cuts off the head of the defeated Goliath.

The decapitation of slain enemies is a widely attested custom. To confine ourselves to the ancient Semites: the Assyrian monarch Ashurbanipal boasts that he so treated his foes;[1] while a relief on a gate at Zenčirli, in North Syria (8th cent. B.C.), depicts a victorious warrior riding with the head of his victim in his hand.[2] Among the pre-Islamic Arabs it was likewise the custom to take the head of a vanquished enemy as trophy,[3] and in Persia, during Sassanian times, such heads were hung up in the fire-temple.[4]

This was not, however, simply an act of savagery. It was of a piece with the custom of cutting off the hands, lest the ghosts of the slain should move them again to take up arms.[5] The head was popularly regarded as one of the seats of the personal "genius," or individuality.[6] The Romans, for example, regarded the forehead as sacred to the genius natalis, and touched it in praying to him.[7] In Yoruba it is held that the principal of each man's three indwelling spirits, called Odori, dwells in the head.[8] In Cambodia[9] and in the Marquesas Islands,[10] the head is taboo, and in Thailand it is forbidden to touch the head of a fallen or sleeping man with the foot; those who thus come into contact with it must build chapels to the earth-demon to avert ill-omen; so too must the persons touched.[11]

An interesting survival of these ideas occurs in a recent Catholic work on baptism, where it is contended that "the water must touch the *head* . . . for the human soul functions principally in the head."[12]

Thus, the purpose of beheading a fallen foe is to accompany the destruction of his body with the annihilation of his "genius."

▲ 132 The bundle of the living   25:29

The traveller who, quitting the cultivated lands of central Judea, rides eastwards towards the Dead Sea, traverses at first a series of rolling hills and waterless valleys covered by broom and grass. But as he pursues his way onward the scenery changes; the grass and thistles disappear, and he gradually passes into a bare and arid region, where the wide expanse of brown or yellow sand, of crumbling limestone, and of scattered shingle is only relieved by thorny shrubs and succulent creepers. Not a tree is to be seen; not a human habitation, not a sign of life meets the eye for mile after mile. Ridge follows ridge in monotonous and seemingly endless succession, all equally white, steep, and narrow, their sides furrowed by the dry beds of innumerable torrents, and their crests looming sharp and ragged against the sky above him as the traveller ascends from the broad flats of soft white marl, interspersed with flints, which divide each isolated ridge from the one beyond it. The nearer slopes of these desolate hills look as if they were torn and rent by waterspouts; the more distant heights present the aspect of gigantic dustheaps. In some places the ground gives out a hollow sound under the horse's tread; in others the stones and sand slip from beneath the animal's hoofs; and in the frequent gullies the rocks glow with a furnace heat under the pitiless sun which beats down on them out of the cloudless firmament. Here and there, as we proceed eastward, the desolation of the landscape is momentarily lightened by a glimpse of the Dead Sea, its waters of a deep blue appearing in a hollow of the hills and contrasting refreshingly with the dull drab colouring of the desert foreground. When the last ridge is surmounted and he stands on the brink of the great cliffs, a wonderful panorama bursts upon the spectator. Some two thousand feet below him lies the Dead Sea, visible in its whole length from end to end, its banks a long succession of castellated crags, bastion beyond bastion, divided by deep gorges, with white capes running out into the calm blue water, while beyond the lake rise the mountains of Moab to melt in the far distance into the azure of the sky. If he has struck the lake above the springs of Engedi, he finds himself on the summit of an amphitheatre of nearly vertical cliffs, down which a rugged winding track, or rather staircase, cut in the face of the precipice, leads to a little horse-shoe shaped plain sloping to the water's edge. It is necessary to dismount and lead the horses carefully down this giddy descent, the last of the party picking their steps very warily, for a single slip might dislodge a stone, which, hurtling down the crag, and striking on the travellers below, would precipitate them to the bottom. At the foot of the cliffs the copious warm fountain of Engedi bursts in a foaming cascade from the rock amid a verdurous oasis of luxuriant semitropical vegetation, which strikes the wayfarer all the more by contrast with the dreary waterless wilderness through which he has been toiling for many hours. Hebrews called Jeshimmon, or desolation, the wilderness of Judea. From the bitter but brilliant water of the Dead Sea it stretches right up into the heart of the country, to the roots of the Mount of Olives, to within two hours of the gates of Hebron, Bethlehem, and Jerusalem.

To these dismal wilds the hunted David fled for refuge from the pursuit of his implacable enemy Saul. While he was in hiding there with the band of broken men he had gathered round him, he was visited by Abigail, the wise and beautiful wife of the rich sheep-farmer Nabal, whom the gallant outlaw had laid under a deep obligation by not stealing his sheep. Insensible of the services thus rendered to him by the caterans, the surly boor refused with contumely a request, couched in the most polite terms, which the captain of the band had sent in for the loan of provisions. The insult touched the captain's nice sense of honour to the quick, and he was marching over the hills at the head of four hundred pretty fellows, every man of them with his broadsword buckled at his side, and was making straight for the farm, when the farmer's wife met him on the moor. She had soft words to soothe the ruffled pride of the angry chieftain, and, better perhaps than words, a train of asses laden with meat and drink for the sharp-set brigands. David was melted. The beauty of the woman, her gentle words, the sight of the asses with their panniers, all had their effect. He received the wife, pleading for her husband, with the utmost courtesy, promised his protection, not without dark hints of the sight that the sun would have seen at the farm next morning if she had not met him, and so dismissed her with a blessing. The word was given. The outlaws faced to the right-about, and, followed no doubt by the asses with their panniers, marched off the way they had come. As she watched those stalwart, sunburnt figures stepping out briskly till the column disappeared over the nearest ridge, Abigail may have smiled and sighed. Then, turning homeward, she hastened with a lighter heart to the house where her boorish husband and his hinds, little wotting of what had passed on the hills, were drinking deep and late after the sheepshearing. That night over the wine she wisely said nothing. But next morning, when he was sober, she told him, and his heart died within him. The shock to his nervous system, or perhaps something stronger, was too much for him. Within ten days he was a dead man, and after a decent interval the widow was over the hills and far away with the captain of the brigands.

Among the compliments which the charming Abigail paid to the susceptible David at their first meeting, there is one, which deserves our attention. She said, "And though man be risen up to pursue thee, and to seek thy soul, yet the soul of my lord shall be bound in the bundle of life with the Lord thy God; and the souls of thine enemies, them shall he sling out, as from the hollow of a sling." No doubt the language is metaphorical, but to an English writer the metaphor is strange and obscure. It implies that the souls of living people could be tied up for safety in a bundle, and that, on the contrary, when the souls were those of enemies, the bundle might be undone and the souls scattered to the winds. Such an idea could hardly have occurred to a Hebrew even as a figure of speech, unless he were familiar with an actual belief that souls could thus be treated. To us, who conceive of a soul as immanent in its body so long as life lasts, the idea conveyed by the verse in question is naturally preposterous. But it would not be so to many peoples whose theory of life differs radically from ours. There is in fact a widespread belief among savages that the soul can be, and often is, extracted from the body during the lifetime of its owner without immediately causing his death. Commonly this is done by ghosts, demons, or evil-disposed persons, who have a grudge against a man and steal his soul; for if they succeed in their fell intent and de-tain long enough, the man will fall ill and die.¹ For that reason people who identify their souls with their shades or reflections are often in mortal terror of a camera, fearing lest the photographer who has taken their likeness has abstracted their souls or shades along with it.

Sometimes, however, souls are extracted from bodies with a kindly intention. The primitive seems to think that nobody can die properly so long as his soul remains intact, whether in or out of the body; hence he infers that if he can contrive to draw out his soul and stow it away in some place where nothing can injure it, he will be for all practical purposes immortal so long as it remains unharmed and undisturbed. Hence in time of danger the wary savage will sometimes carefully extract his own soul or the soul of a friend and leave it, so to say, at deposit account in some safe place till the danger is past and he can reclaim his spiritual property. For example, many people regard the removal to a new house as a crisis fraught with peril to their souls; hence in Minahassa, a district of Celebes, a priest then collects the souls of the whole family in a bag, and keeps them there till the danger is over.² Again, in Southern Celebes, when a woman's time is near, the messenger who goes to fetch the doctor or midwife takes with him a chopping-knife or something else made of iron. The thing, whatever it is, represents the woman's soul, which at this dangerous time is believed to be safer outside of her body than in it. Hence the doctor must take great care of it, for were it lost the woman's soul would with it be lost also. So he keeps it in his house till the confinement is over, when he gives back the precious object in return for a fee.³ In the Kei Islands a hollowed-out coco-nut, split in two and carefully pieced together, may sometimes be seen hanging up. This is a receptacle in which the soul of a newly-born infant is kept lest it should fall a prey to demons. For in those parts the soul does not permanently lodge in its tabernacle of clay, until the clay has taken a firm consistency. The Eskimos of Alaska adopt a similar precaution for the soul of a sick child: the medicine-man conjures it into an amulet and then stows the amulet in his medicine-bag, where, if anywhere, the soul should be out of harm's way.⁴ In some parts of South-Eastern New Guinea, when a woman walks abroad carrying her baby in a bag, she "must tie a long streamer of vine of some kind to her skirt, or better still to the baby's bag, so that it trails behind her on the ground. For should the child's spirit chance to wander from the body it must have some means of crawling back from the ground, and what so convenient as a vine trailing on the path?"⁵

But perhaps the closest analogy to the "bundle of life" is furnished by the bundles of *churinga,* that is, flattened and elongated stones and sticks, which the Arunta and other tribes of Central Australia keep with the greatest care and secrecy in caves and crevices of the rocks. Each of these mysterious stones or sticks is intimately associated with the spirit of a member of the clan, living or dead; for as soon as the spirit of a child enters into a woman to be born, one of these holy sticks or stones is dropped on the spot where the mother felt her womb quickened. Directed by her, the father searches for the stick or stone of his child, and having found it, or carved it out of the nearest hard-wood tree, he delivers it to the headman of the district, who deposits it with the rest in the sacred store-house among the rocks. These precious sticks and stones, closely bound up with the spirits of all the members of the clan, are often carefully tied up in bundles. They constitute the most sacred possession of the tribe, and the places where they are deposited are skilfully screened from observation, the entrance to the caves being blocked up with stones arranged so naturally as to disarm suspicion. Not only the spot itself but its surroundings are sacred. The plants and trees that grow there are never touched: the wild animals that find their way thither are never molested. And if a man fleeing from his enemies or from the avenger of blood succeeds in reaching the sanctuary, he is safe so long as he remains within its bounds. The loss of their *churinga,* as they call the sacred sticks and stones thus associated with the spirits of all the living and all the dead members of the community, is the most serious evil that can befall a tribe. Robbed of them by inconsiderate white men, the natives have been known to stay in camp for a fortnight, weeping and wailing over their loss and plastering their body with white pipeclay, the emblem of mourning for the dead.[6]

It would be rash to assert that the ancient Semites ever conserved their souls for safety in such sticks and stones, but it is not rash to affirm that some such practices would explain in a simple and natural way the words of Abigail to the hunted outlaw.

[There are, however, other possible explanations:

(a) The Hebrew word rendered *bundle* can also mean *wallet,*[6a] and in that case we may aptly compare the words of an Old Babylonian letter: "May thy god (lord) and thy goddess keep thee as (in) the wallet which they hold in their hands."[6b] A similar expression occurs also in the literature of the Mandeans of Iraq and Iran.[6c]

(b) L. Oppenheim has pointed out that at Nuzi, a city in Upper Mesopotamia which flourished in the fifteenth century B.C., it was apparently the custom to "keep tabs" on sheep and goats sold, sacrificed, moved for shearing and the like by means of pebbles. One pebble represented each animal, and could be transferred to a particular receptacle reserved for each category. An ovoid clay pouch so used has actually been discovered.[6d] O. Eissfeldt has suggested that the Biblical idiom refers to such a usage, the wish of Abigail being that the king's "soul," or life, may be included among the pebbles deposited in the pouch reserved for those who are to be kept alive.[6e] Marvin Pope records a similar method of checking guests and "no-shows" at social functions in Jerusalem,[6f] and it may be added that this device was also once used in the United States to register ballots at elections,[6g] and that it underlies the expression "to blackball," i.e., to exclude, or doom to rejection.] ▼

▲ 133   The Witch of Endor   28

> *Saul, frightened by the massing of the Philistines at Shunem, consults the oracle of the Lord, but this is denied him. He then goes in disguise to a witch who is clandestinely practicing her forbidden craft at Endor. He asks her to conjure the spirit of Samuel from the netherworld. The witch reports that she sees an* elohim, *or otherworld being, coming up. He looks like an old man wrapped in a mantle. Saul recognizes him as Samuel.*

The practice of necromancy was shared by the Hebrews with other peoples of the Ancient Near East.[1] A clear reference to it appears to be contained in the twelfth canto of the Gilgamesh epic. There the hero Gilgamesh is represented mourning for his dead friend Eabani. In his sorrow he appeals to the gods to bring up for him the soul of his departed comrade from the nether world. But one after another the deities confess themselves powerless to grant his request. At last he prays to Nergal, the god of the dead, saying, "Break open the chamber of the grave *and open the ground,* that the spirit of Enkidu, like a wind, may rise out of the ground." The deity graciously listened to his prayer. "He broke open the chamber of the grave and opened the ground; and caused the spirit of Enkidu to rise out of the ground like a wind." With the ghost thus summoned from the vasty deep Gilgamesh converses, and learns from him the mournful state of the dead in the nether world, where is the devouring worm and all things are cloaked in dust. However, the gloominess of the picture is a little relieved by the information which the apparition vouchsafes as to the solace which the rites of burial afford to the souls of warriors fallen in battle, compared with the deplorable condition of those whose corpses have been suffered to welter unburied on the field.[2]

The ancient Greeks were familiar with the practice of evoking the souls of the dead in order either to obtain information from them or to appease their wrath. It would seem that the practice of calling up the shades from the nether regions was not carried on by necromancers at any place indiscriminately, but was restricted to certain definite spots which were supposed to communicate directly with the underworld by passages or apertures, through which the spirits could come up and go down as they were summoned or dismissed. Such spots were called oracles of the dead,[3] and at them alone, so far as appears, could legitimate business with the shades of the departed be transacted. There was one at Aornon in Thesprotis, where the legendary musician Orpheus is said to have called up, but in vain, the soul of his loved and lost Eurydice.[4] The whole vicinity of this oracular seat would seem to have been associated with, if not haunted by, the spirits of the dead; for the names of the infernal rivers were given to the neighbouring waters. Beside it ran the Acheron[5] and not far off flowed the Cocytus,[6] "named of lamentation loud heard on the rueful stream." The landscape combines the elements of grandeur, solitude, and desolation in a degree that is fitted to oppress the mind with a sense of awe and gloom, and thereby to predispose it for communion with supernatural beings. No wonder that in these rugged mountains, these dreary fens, these melancholy streams, the ancients fancied they beheld the haunts of the spirits of the dead.

Another oracle of the dead was established at Heraclea in Bithynia. The Spartan King Pausanias, who defeated the Persians in the battle of Plataea, resorted to this oracle, and there attempted to summon up and propitiate the ghost of a Byzantine maiden named Cleonice, whom he had accidentally killed. Her spirit appeared to him and announced in ambiguous language that all his troubles would cease when he should return to Sparta. The prophecy was fulfilled by the king's speedy death.[7]

We have no information as to the mode in which the ghosts were supposed to appear and reply to questions at these places; hence we cannot say whether the phantoms revealed themselves to the inquirer himself or only to the wizard who conjured them up; nor again do we know whether the person who was favoured with these manifestations beheld them awake or in dreams. However, at some Greek oracles of the dead the communication with the souls of the departed is known to have taken place in sleep. Such, for example, was the custom at the oracle of the soothsayer Mopsus in Cilicia. Plutarch tells us that on one occasion the governor of Cilicia, a sceptic in religion and a friend of Epicurean philosophers, who derided the supernatural, resolved to test the oracle. For that purpose he wrote a question on a tablet, and without revealing what he had written to anybody he sealed up the tablet and entrusted it to a freedman with orders to submit the question to the ghostly seer. Accordingly the man slept that night, according to custom, in the shrine of Mopsus, and next morning he reported to the governor that he had dreamed a dream. He thought he saw a handsome man standing by him, who opened his mouth, and, having uttered the single word "Black," immediately vanished. The friends of the governor, who had assembled to hear and to quiz the messenger from the other world, were at a loss what to make of this laconic message, but no sooner did the governor himself receive it than he fell on his knees in an attitude of devotion. The reason for this very unusual posture was revealed when the seal of the tablet was broken and its contents read aloud. For the question which the governor had written therein was this, "Shall I sacrifice a white bull or a black?" The appropriateness of the answer staggered even the incredulous Epicurean philosophers, and as for the governor himself, he sacrificed the black bull and continued to revere the dead soothsayer Mopsus to the end of his days.[8]

The pious Plutarch, who reports with obvious satisfaction this triumphant refutation of shallow infidelity, has related another incident of the same sort which was said to have occurred in Italy. A certain very rich man named Elysius, a native of the Greek city of Terina in Bruttium, lost his son and heir, Euthynus, by a sudden and mysterious death. Fearing that there might have been foul play in this loss of the heir to all his riches, the anxious father had recourse to an oracle of the dead. There he offered a sacrifice, and then, in accordance with the custom of the sanctuary, he fell asleep and dreamed a dream. It seemed to him that he saw his own father, and begged and prayed him to help in tracking down the author of his son's death. "For that very purpose am I come," answered the ghost, "and I beg you will accept my message from this young man," pointing, as he said so, to a youth who followed at his heels, and who resembled to the life the son whose loss Elysius mourned. Startled by the likeness, Elysius asked the young man, "And who are you?" to which the phantom answered, "I am your son's genius. Take that." So saying, he handed to Elysius a tablet inscribed with some verses, which declared that his son had died a natural death, because death was better for him than life.[9]

In antiquity the Nasamones, a tribe of northern Libya, used to seek for oracular dreams by sleeping on the tombs of their ancestors;[10] probably they imagined that the souls of the departed rose from their graves to advise and comfort their descendants. A similar custom is still practised by some of the Tuaregs of the Sahara. When the men are away on distant expeditions, their wives, dressed in their finest clothes, will go and lie on ancient tombs, where they call up the soul of one who will give them news of their husbands. At their call a spirit named Idebni appears in the form of a man. If the woman contrives to please this spirit, he tells her all that has happened on the expedition; but if she fails to win his favour, he strangles her.[11]

The most elaborate description of the evocation of a ghost in Greek literature is to be found in Aeschylus's tragedy, *The Persians*. The scene of the play is laid at the tomb of King Darius, where Queen Atossa, the wife of Xerxes, is anxiously waiting for news of her husband and the mighty host which he had led against Greece. A messenger arrives with tidings of the total defeat of the Persians at Salamis. In her grief and consternation the queen resolves to summon up the ghost of Darius from the grave, and to seek counsel of him in the great emergency. For that purpose she offers libations of milk, honey, water, wine, and olive oil at the tomb, while at the same time the chorus chants hymns calling on the gods of the nether world to send up the soul of the dead king to the light of day. The ghost accordingly emerges from the earth, and learning of the disaster that has befallen the Persian arms, he gives advice and warning to his afflicted people.[12] In this account it is clearly implied that the ghost appears in broad daylight, and not merely in a dream, to those who have evoked it; but whether the poet is describing a Greek or a Persian form of necromancy, or is simply drawing on his own imagination, we cannot say for certain. Probably the description is based on rites commonly performed by Greek necromancers, either at the regular oracles of the dead, or at the graves of the particular persons whose ghosts they desired to consult. The Pythagorean philosopher Apollonius of Tyana is reported by his biographer Philostratus to have conjured up the soul of Achilles from his grave in Thessaly. The hero appeared from the barrow in the likeness of a tall and handsome young man, and entered into conversation with the sage in the most affable manner, complaining that the Thessalians had long since ceased to bring offerings to his tomb, and begging him to remonstrate with them on their negligence.[13] In Pliny's youth a certain grammarian named Apion professed to have evoked the shade of Homer and questioned the poet as to his parents and his native land, but he refused to reveal the answers which he received from the ghost; hence later ages have not benefited by this bold attempt to solve the Homeric problem at the fountain head.[14]

The poet Lucan has given us, in his usual tawdry bombastic style, a tedious report of an interview which, according to the bard, Sextus Pompeius, son of Pompey the Great, had with a Thessalian witch before the battle of Pharsalia. Anxious to learn the issue of the war, the unworthy son of a great father, as Lucan calls him, has recourse, not to the legitimate oracles of the gods, but to the vile arts of witchcraft and necromancy. At his request a foul hag, whose dwelling is among the tombs, restores an unburied corpse to life, and the soul thus temporarily replaced in its earthly tabernacle tells of the commotion which it has witnessed among the shades at the prospect of the catastrophe so soon to befall the Roman world. Having delivered his message, the dead man requests as a particular favour to be allowed to die a second time for good and all. The witch grants his request, and considerately erects a pyre for his convenience, to which the corpse walks unassisted and is there comfortably burnt to ashes.[15] Thessalian witches were certainly notorious in antiquity, and it is likely enough that necromancy was one of the black arts which they professed; but no reliance can be placed on Lucan's highly coloured description of the rites which they observed in evoking the ghosts. More probable is the account which Horace gives of the proceedings of two witches, whom he represents as pouring the blood of a black lamb into a trench for the purpose of calling up ghosts to answer questions.[16] Tibullus speaks of a witch who conjured up the shades from their tombs by her chants;[17] and in the reign of Tiberius a highborn but feeble-minded youth, named Libo, who dabbled in the black arts, requested a certain Junius to evoke the spirits of the dead for him by incantations.[18]

More than one of the wicked Roman emperors are said to have had recourse to necromancy in the hope of allaying those terrors with which the memory of their crimes, like avenging spirits, visited their uneasy consciences. We are told that the monster Nero never knew peace of mind again after he had murdered his mother Agrippina: he often confessed that he was haunted by her spectre and by the Furies with whips and burning torches, and it was in vain that by magic rites he conjured up her ghost and attempted to appease her anger.[19] Similarly, the crazed and bloody tyrant Caracalla imagined that the phantoms of his father Severus and of his murdered brother Geta pursued him with drawn swords, and to obtain some alleviation of these horrors he called in the help of wizards. Among the ghosts which they evoked for him were those of the emperor's father and the Emperor Commodus. But of all the shades thus summoned to his aid none deigned to hold converse with the imperial assassin except the kindred spirit of Commodus, and even from him no words of consolation or hope could be elicited, nothing but dark hints of a fearful judgment to come, which only served to fill the guilty soul of Caracalla with a fresh access of terror.[20]

The art of necromancy has been practised by barbarous as well as civilized peoples. In some African tribes the practice has prevailed of consulting the ghosts of dead kings or chiefs as oracles through the medium of a priest or priestess, who professed to be inspired by the soul of a deceased ruler and to speak in his name. For example, among the Baganda of Central Africa a temple was built for the ghost of each dead king, and in it his lower jawbone was reverently preserved; for curiously enough the part of his body to which the ghost of a dead Baganda man clings most persistently is his jawbone. The temple, a large conical hut of the usual pattern, was divided into two chambers, an outer and an inner, and in the inner chamber or holy of holies the precious jawbone was kept for safety in a cell dug in the floor. The prophet or medium, whose business it was from time to time to be inspired by the ghost of the dead monarch, dedicated himself to his holy office by drinking a draught of beer and a draught of milk out of the royal skull. When the ghost held a reception, the jawbone, wrapt in a decorated packet, was brought forth from the inner shrine and set on a throne in the outer chamber, where the people assembled to hear the oracle. On such occasions the prophet stepped up to the throne, and addressing the spirit informed him of the business in hand. Then he smoked one or two pipes of homegrown tobacco, and the fumes bringing on the prophetic fit he began to rave and speak in the very voice and with the characteristic turns of speech of the departed monarch; for the king's soul was now supposed to be in him. However, his rapid utterances were hard to understand, and a priest was in attendance to interpret them to the inquirer. The living king thus consulted his dead predecessors periodically on affairs of state, visiting first one and then another of the temples in which their sacred relics were preserved with religious care.[21]

Again, among the Banyoro, another tribe of Central Africa, in the Uganda Protectorate, the ghosts of dead kings were consulted as oracles by their living successors. Over the king's grave a mound of earth was raised, with a flat top which was covered with a grass carpet and overlaid with cow-skins and leopard-skins. This served as the throne where the king's ghost was supposed to take its seat at any ceremony. Before this throne offerings were presented to the ghost, and there also requests were made, when the reigning king wished to consult his father on matters of state or when sickness appeared in the royal household. At the grave a large hut was built, and in it were lodged guards, whose duty it was to watch over the tomb and to present the offerings to the worshipful ghost.[22]

Among the Basoga of the Central District, in the Uganda Protectorate, the souls of dead chiefs are in like manner consulted as oracles through the medium of women, who act as their interpreters or prophets. When a chief has been dead and buried for some months, his ghost appears to one of his kinsmen and tells him, 'I' wish to move." On being informed of the ghost's desire, the new chief orders the grave of his predecessor to be opened and the skull removed. When the skull has been dried and enclosed in skins, the chief sends for a woman, who must be a member of the clan to which the nurse of the late chief belonged. To her he commits the duty of guarding the skull, interpreting the wishes of the ghost, and attending to its wants. She also receives a she-goat, a cow, and a hen, which are to provide food for the ghost. Having received her commission and the provender, the woman is escorted to a place called Nakazungu, on the Mpologoma river, where a large house is built for her. There the skull is deposited in a shrine or temple, which is deemed the house of the ghost, and there the woman becomes possessed by the ghost and reveals his wishes. Thither, too, the new chief sends offerings to the spirit of his father. However, the skull and the ghost remain in this place of honour only during the life of his successor. When the next chief dies, the old skull and the old ghost are compelled to vacate the premises and shift their quarters to a wooded island in the river, where the skulls and ghosts of all former chiefs are permanently lodged. No house there shelters them from the inclemency of the weather. Each skull is simply deposited in the open, with a spear stuck in the ground beside it. The prophetess who attended to its wants in the temple accompanies the skull to its long home in the island, and there she may continue to interpret the wishes and views of the ghost to any who care to consult it. But few people think it worth while to make a pilgrimage to the old ghosts in this oracular Golgotha or Place of Skulls in the forest; most persons prefer to ask the advice of the new ghost in the temple. Thus fashion runs after novelty in the world of the dead as in the world of the living.[23]

Among the Bantu tribes who inhabit the great tableland of Northern Rhodesia the spirits of dead chiefs sometimes take possession of the bodies of live men or women and prophesy through their mouths. When the spirit thus comes upon a man, he begins to roar like a lion, and the women gather together and beat the drums, shouting that the chief has come to visit the village. The possessed person will predict future wars, and warn the people of approaching visitations by lions. While the inspiration lasts, the medium may eat nothing cooked by fire, but only unfermented dough. However, this gift of prophecy usually descends on women rather than on men. Such prophetesses give out that they are possessed by the soul of some dead chief, and when they feel the divine afflatus they whiten their faces to attract attention, and they smear themselves with flour, which has a religious and sanctifying potency. One of their number beats a drum, and the others dance, singing at the same time a weird song, with curious intervals. Finally, when they have worked themselves up to the requisite pitch of religious exaltation, the possessed woman drops to the ground, and bursts out into a low and almost inarticulate chant, which amid the awestruck silence of the bystanders is interpreted by the medicine-men as the voice of the spirit.[24]

Again, among the Barotsé, a Bantu tribe of the Upper Zambesi, the souls of dead kings are consulted and give their responses through the mouth of a priest. Each royal tomb is indeed an oracle of the dead. It stands in a beautiful grove, and is enclosed by a palisade covered with fine mats, like the palisade which surrounds the residence of a living king. Such an enclosure is sacred; the people are forbidden to enter it, lest they should disturb the ghost of him who sleeps below. A priest acts as intermediary between the royal ghost and the people who come to pray to him at the shrine. He alone has the right to enter the sacred enclosure; the profane multitude must stand at a respectful distance. Even the king himself, when he comes to consult one of his ancestors, is forbidden to set foot on the holy ground. He kneels down at the entrance, claps his hands, and gives the royal salute, which is solemnly returned by the priest from within the enclosure. Then the suppliant, whether king or commoner, makes his petition to the worshipful spirit and deposits his offering; for no man may pray at the shrine with empty hands. Inside the enclosure, near the entrance, is a hole, which is supposed to serve as a channel of communication with the spirit of the deified king. In it the offerings are deposited. Often they consist of milk, which is poured into the hole; more solid offerings, such as flesh, clothes, and glass beads, become the property of the priest after they have lain for a decent time beside the sacred aperture. The spirits of dead kings are thus consulted on matters of public concern as well as by private persons on their own affairs. All over the country these temple-tombs may be seen, each in its shady grove; hence no man need have far to go to seek for ghostly counsel at an oracle of the dead.[25]

Among the Ewe-speaking Negroes of South Togoland, when the funeral celebration is over, it is customary to summon up the soul of the deceased. His relations take cooked food to the priest and tell him that they wish to bring water for the spirit of their departed brother. The priest accordingly receives food, palm-wine, and cowry-shells at their hands, and with them retires into his room and shuts the door behind him. Then he evokes the ghost, who on his arrival begins to weep and to converse with the priest, sometimes making some general observations on the difference between life in the upper and in the under world, sometimes entering into particulars as to the manner of his own death; often he mentions the name of the wicked sorcerer who has killed him by his enchantments. When the dead man's friends outside hear the lamentations and complaints of his ghost proceeding from the room, they are moved to tears and cry out, "We pity you!" Finally, the ghost bids them be comforted and takes his departure.[26] Among the Kissi, a tribe of Negroes on the border of Liberia, the souls of dead chiefs are consulted as oracles by means of the statuettes which are erected on their graves. For the purpose of the consultation the statuettes are placed on a board, which is carried by two men on their heads; if the bearers remain motionless, the answer of the spirit is assumed to be "No"; if they sway to and fro, the answer is "Yes."[27] In the island of Ambrym, one of the New Hebrides, wooden statues representing ancestors are similarly employed as a means of communicating with the souls of the dead. When a man is in trouble, he blows a whistle at nightfall near the statue of an ancestor, and if he hears a noise, he believes that the soul of the dead kinsman has entered into the image; thereupon he recounts his woes to the effigy and prays the spirit to help him.[28]

The Maoris of New Zealand feared and worshipped the spirits of their dead kinsfolk, especially dead chiefs and warriors, who were believed to be constantly watching over the living tribesmen, protecting them in war and marking any breach of the sacred law of taboo. These spirits dwelt normally below the earth, but they could return to the upper air at pleasure and enter into the bodies of men or even into the substance of inanimate objects. Some tribes kept in their houses small carved images of wood, each of which was dedicated to the spirit of an ancestor, who was supposed to enter into the image on particular occasions in order to hold converse with the living. Such an ancestral spirit (*atua*) might communicate with the living either in dreams or more directly by talking with them in their waking hours. Their voice, however, was not like that of mortals, but a mysterious kind of sound, half whistle, half whisper.[29]

An Irishman, who lived long among the Maoris and knew them intimately, witnessed many such exhibitions of necromancy, and has described one of them in detail. The priests, he tells us, undertook to call up the spirit of any dead person for a proper fee. On this particular occasion the ghost evoked was that of a very popular young chief (*rangatira*), whom the Irishman had known intimately, and who had been killed in battle. At the request of his nearest friends, a priest engaged to call up the dead man's spirit to speak to them and answer certain questions which they wished to put. The interview took place at night in a large house common to the whole population, where fires cast a flickering light through the gloom. The priest retired to the darkest corner. All was expectation, and the silence was broken only by the sobbing of the sister and other female relations of the dead man. About thirty persons were seated on the rush-strewn floor. At last, when the fire had died down, leaving only a heap of glowing charcoal, a voice issued from the darkness solemnly saluting the assembly. It was answered by a cry of affection and despair from the dead chief's sister, a fine handsome young woman, who rushed, with both arms distended, into the darkness from which the voice proceeded. She was instantly seized round the waist and restrained by main force by her brother, till, moaning and fainting, she lay still on the ground. At the same instant another female voice was heard from a young girl, who was held by the wrists by two young men, her brothers, "Is it you? is it you? truly is it you? *ane! ane!* they hold me, they restrain me; wonder not that I have not followed you; they restrain me, they watch me, but I go to you. The sun shall not rise, the sun shall not rise, *ane! ane!*" Here she fell insensible on the floor, and with the sister was carried out. Afterwards the ghost conversed with his brother in strange melancholy tones, like the sound of the wind blowing into a hollow vessel, and he answered a woman's inquiry about her dead sister. Having satisfied her affectionate anxiety, the ghost next requested that his tame pig and his double-barrelled gun might be given to the priest. The Irishman now struck in and questioned the ghost as to a book which the dead chief had left behind him. The ghost indicated correctly the place where the volume had been deposited, but on being pressed to mention some of its contents he took an abrupt leave of the assembly, his farewell sounding first from the room, next from deep beneath the ground, then from high in air, and finally dying away in the darkness of night. The company broke up after midnight, and the Irishman retired to rest. But he was soon wakened by the report of a musket, followed by the shouts of men and the screams of women. Hastening in the direction from which the sounds proceeded, he saw in the midst of a crowd, by the light of a burning house, the lifeless and bleeding body of the young girl who had said that she would follow the spirit to the spirit land. She had kept her word, having secretly procured a loaded musket and blown herself to pieces. The voice of the priest said, close to the Irishman, "She has followed her *rangatira*."[30]

In Nukahiva, one of the Marquesas Islands, the priests and priestesses claimed to possess the power of evoking the spirits of the dead, who took up their abode for the time being in the bodies of the mediums and so conversed with their surviving relatives. The occasion for summoning up a ghost was usually the sickness of a member of the family, on whose behalf his friends desired to have the benefit of ghostly advice.[31]

At the initiation ceremonies, which they observe every year, the Marindineeze, a tribe on the southern coast of Dutch New Guinea, summon up the souls of their forefathers from the underworld by knocking hard on the ground with the lower ends of coco-nut leaves for an hour together. The evocation takes place by night.[32] Similarly at their festivals the Bare'e-speaking Toradjas of Central Celebes evoke the souls of dead chiefs and heroes, the guardian spirits of the village, by beating on the floor of the temple with a long stick.[33]

The Sea Dyaks of Borneo believe that the souls of their dead friends live and revisit them on earth. They are invoked in times of peril and distress; and on the hilltops or in the solitude of the jungle a man will often go by himself and spend the night, hoping that the spirit of a dead relative may visit him and reveal to him in a dream some charm by which he may extricate himself from his difficulties and grow rich and great.[34]

Among the Kayans of Borneo, when a dispute has arisen concerning the division of a dead man's property, recourse is sometimes had to a professional wizard or witch, who summons up the ghost of the deceased and questions him as to his intentions in the disposal of his estate. The evocation, however, cannot take place until after the harvest which follows upon the death. When the time comes for it, a small model of a house is made for the temporary accommodation of the ghost and is placed in the gallery of the common house, beside the door of the dead man's chamber. For the refreshment of the spirit, moreover, food, drink, and cigarettes are laid out in the little house. The wizard takes up his post beside the tiny dwelling and chants his invocation, calling upon the soul of the deceased to enter the soul-house, and mentioning the names of the members of his family. From time to time he looks in, and at last announces that all the food and drink have been consumed. The people believe that the ghost has now entered the soul-house; and the wizard pretends to listen to the whispering of the soul within the house, starting and clucking from time to time. Finally, he declares the will of the ghost in regard to the distribution of the property, speaking in the first person and mimicking the mode of speech and other peculiarities of the dead man. The directions so obtained are usually followed, and thus the dispute is settled.[35]

The Bataks of Central Sumatra believe that the souls of the dead, being incorporeal, can only communicate with the living through the person of a living man, and for the purpose of such communication they choose an appropriate medium, who, in serving as a vehicle for the ghostly message, imitates the voice, the manner, the walk, and even the dress of the deceased so closely, that his surviving relations are often moved to tears by the resemblance. By the mouth of the medium the spirit reveals his name, mentions his relations, and describes the pursuits he followed on earth. He discloses family secrets which he had kept during life, and the disclosure confirms his kinsfolk in the belief that it is really the ghost of their departed brother who is conversing with them. When a member of the family is sick, the ghost is consulted as to whether the patient will live or die. When an epidemic is raging, the ghost is evoked and sacrifices are offered to him, that he may guard the people against the infection. When a man is childless, he inquires of a ghost through a medium, how he can obtain offspring. When something has been lost or stolen, a ghost is conjured up to tell whether the missing property will be recovered. When any one has missed his way in the forest or elsewhere and has not returned home, it is still to a ghost, through the intervention of a medium, that the anxious friends apply in order to learn where the strayed wayfarer is to be sought. If a medium is questioned as to how the ghost takes possession of him, he says that he sees the ghost approaching and feels as if his body were being dragged away, his feet grow light and leap about, human beings seem small and reddish in colour, the houses appear to be turning round. But the possession is not continuous; from time to time during the fit the ghost leaves the medium and plays about. When the fit is over, the medium is often sick and sometimes dies.[36]

Necromancy has been practised by man amid Arctic snow and ice as well as in tropical forests and jungles. Among the Eskimo of Labrador we read of a shaman who used to oblige his friends by calling up the spirits of the dead, whenever the living desired to inquire concerning the welfare of the departed, or the whereabouts of absent relatives at sea. He would first blindfold the questioner, and then rap thrice on the ground with a stick. On the third rap the spirit appeared and answered the shaman's questions. Having supplied the information that was wanted, the ghost would be dismissed to his own place by three more raps on the ground. This sort of necromancy was called "conjuring with a stick" (*kilu'xin*). A similar method of evoking the souls of the dead is employed by the Eskimo of Alaska. They believe that the spirits ascend from the under world and pass through the body of the shaman, who converses audibly with them and, having learned all he desires, sends them back to their subterranean abode by a stamp of his foot. The answers of the ghosts to his questions are supposed by sceptics to be produced by ventriloquism.[37]

In China, the practice of necromancy was always common, and in recent times the practitioners were chiefly old women. Such necromancers, for example, abound in Canton and Amoy. During his residence at Canton, Archdeacon Gray witnessed many exhibitions of their skill, and he describes one of them as follows: "One day, in the month of January 1867, I was the guest of an old lady, a widow, who resided in the western suburb of the city. She desired to confer with her departed husband, who had been dead for several years. The witch who was called in, was of prepossessing appearance and well-dressed; and she commenced immediately to discharge the duties of her vocation. Her first act was to erect a temporary altar at the head of the hall in which we were assembled. Upon this she placed two burning tapers, and offerings of fruits and cakes. She then sat on the right side of the altar, and, burying her face in her hands, remained silent for several minutes. Having awakened from her supposed trance or dream, she began to utter in a singing tone some words of incantation, at the same time sprinkling handfuls of rice at intervals upon the floor. She then said that the spirit of the departed was once more in the midst of his family. They were greatly moved, and some of them burst into a flood of tears. Through the witch as a medium, the spirit of the old man then informed the family where he was, and of the state of happiness he was permitted to enjoy in the land of shades. He spoke on several family topics, and dwelt upon the condition of one of his sons who, since his death, had gone to the northern provinces of China—references which evidently astonished the members of the family who were present, and confirmed their belief in the supernatural powers of the female impostor before them. There can be no doubt that she had made suitable inquiries beforehand. After exhorting his widow to dry her tears, and on no account to summon him again from the world of shades, in which he was tolerably happy, the spirit of the old man retired."[38]

According to the account of a native Chinese author, it is customary in the province of Shantung to consult the ancestral spirits (*shen*), in the female apartments, when a member of the family is sick. The medium employed for the purpose is an old witch who dances, playing a tambourine and making grimaces, and is therefore called the dancing spirit. "But this practice," he proceeds, "flourishes specially in the capital of the empire, where even young married women in respectable families perform it from time to time. In the hall of the house they place on the table stands which are filled with meat, and goblets full of spirits, and they light large candles, so that it is clearer there than in the daytime; then the woman, tucking up her petticoat, draws up one leg and hops like a *shang-yang*,[a] while two grasp her arms, and support her on either side. She babbles in a monotonous tedious way, now in a sing song, now as if uttering conjurations, now with a flow of words, then with only a few, without any modulation or tune. Meanwhile drums are wildly banged in the apartment, so that their thunder stuns one, and in their noise the words which come from her opening and closing lips are far from distinct. In the end she droops her head, looks askance, and wants help to stand erect; but for her supporters she would tumble. But suddenly she stretches out her neck and jumps one or two feet into the air, and all the women in the apartment shiver and regard her with terror; thereupon she exclaims, 'The ancestor comes and eats!' Now they blow out the lights, so that it is pitch dark everywhere. Silent the bystanders stand in the dark, and speak not a word to each other; indeed, owing to the confused noise, nothing they might say would be understood. After a while they hear the woman mention with a shrill voice the (deceased) father or mother-in-law, or the husband or sister-in-law, by the name by which he or she was familiarly known, this being a sign to the whole company to re-light the candles. With outstretched necks they now ask the medium whether good or evil is to be expected, and in the mean time they inspect the goblets, baskets and cups, to find them altogether emptied; and they try to read on her face whether the spirit is contented or not; and, full of respect, they address a series of questions to her, which she answers as readily as an echo."[39]

The practice of calling up the spirits of the dead for consultation is said to be very common in Amoy, where the necromancers are professional

[a] A fabulous one-legged bird.

women. Among the male sex the reputation of these ladies for strict veracity seems not to stand very high, for to tell a man, in common parlance, that he is "bringing up the dead" is almost equivalent to saying that he is telling a lie. Hence these female necromancers often prefer to confine their ministrations to their own sex, lest they should expose their high mysteries to the derision of masculine sceptics. In that case the session is held with closed doors in the private apartments of the women; otherwise it takes place in the main hall, at the domestic altar, and all inmates of the house are free to attend. Many families, indeed, make a rule to question, by means of these witches, every deceased relation at least once not long after his or her death, in order to ascertain whether the souls are comfortable in the other world, and whether anything can be done by family affection to ameliorate their condition. An auspicious day having been chosen for the ceremony, the apartment is swept and watered, because spirits entertain an aversion to dirt and dust. To allure the ghost, food and dainties, together with burning incense, are placed on the domestic altar, or, should the conference take place in a secluded room, on an ordinary table. In the latter case, when the medium has come, it is necessary for one of the women to go to the altar, where the tablets are deposited in which the souls of the dead members of the family are believed to reside. Having lighted two candles and three incense-sticks at the altar, she invites the ghost to leave its tablet and follow her. Then, with the incense between her fingers, she slowly walks back into the room, and plants the sticks in a bowl or cup with some uncooked rice. The medium now goes to work, chanting conjurations, while she strums a lyre or beats a drum. In time her movements grow convulsive, she rocks to and fro, and sweat bursts from her body. These things are regarded as evidence that the ghost has arrived. Two women support the medium and place her in a chair, where she falls into a state of distraction or slumber, with her arms resting on the table. A black veil is next thrown over her head, and in her mesmeric state she can now answer questions, shivering, as she does so, rocking in her seat, and drumming the table nervously with her hands or with a stick. Through her mouth the ghost informs his relations of his state in the other world and what they can do to improve it or even to redeem him entirely from his sufferings. He mentions whether the sacrifices which are offered to him reach their destination intact or suffer loss and damage in process of transmission through the spiritual post; he states his preferences and he enumerates his wants. He also favours his kinsfolk with his advice on domestic affairs, though his language is often ambiguous and his remarks have sometimes little or no bearing on the questions submitted to him. Now and then the medium holds whispered monologues, or rather conversations with the ghost. At last she suddenly shivers, awakes, and raising herself up declares that the ghost has gone. Having pocketed the rice and the incense-sticks in the bowl, she receives her fee and takes her departure. "The various phases in the condition of the medium during the conference are, of course, taken by the onlookers for the several moments of her connection with the other world. Yet we remain entitled to consider them to be symptoms of psychical aberration and nervous affection. Her spasms and convulsions pass for possession, either by the ghost which is consulted, or by the spirit with which she usually has intercourse, and which thus imparts to her the faculty of second sight by which she sees that ghost. And her mesmeric fits confessedly are the moments when her soul leaves her, in order to visit the other world, there to see the ghost and speak with it. Her whispering lips indicate conversation with her spirit, or with the ghost which is consulted. It may be asked, why, since this ghost dwells in its tablet on the altar, her soul should travel to the other world to see it. We can give no answer."[40]

[The witch of Endor is described in the Hebrew text as "a woman who owns (or controls) an *'ob*" (KJV: "that hath a familiar spirit"; RSV: "a woman who is a medium"). This technical term (which recurs elsewhere in the Old Testament[40a]) has long proved a puzzle to interpreters. The older view was that it was the common Hebrew word for "bottle" and referred to a common belief —familiar especially from the story of Aladdin—that genii or familiar spirits can be kept in bottles.[40b] To this day, for example, the Galelas and Tobelorese think they reside in earthen pots.[40c] In a Canaanite (Ugaritic) poem from Ras Shamra, however, the "portmanteau" word *ilib* occurs with the sense of "ancestral spirit,"[40d] and W. F. Albright has ingeniously suggested that this is made up of *il* "god, otherworld being," and the Canaanite cognate of our puzzling *'ob*.[40e] The former would then relate to the fact that the beings whom the witch saw ascending from the netherworld are indeed described in the Hebrew text by the comparable term *elohim*, likewise meaning "gods, otherworld beings"; while the latter might then be explained from the Arabic term *'abā*, "return" in the sense of our *revenant*, or the Danish *gienfard, gienganger*.[40f]] ▼

134 Mutilation of fallen foes II Sam. 31:14
See above, §107.

135 Signs of mourning 1:2, 11
See below, §§202, 293.

136 Bloodshed renders soil infertile 1:21
See above, §27.

137 The "holder of the spindle" 3:29
Abner, a supporter of Saul, consorts with one of his master's concubines. Upbraided for this, he decides to transfer his allegiance to David. The latter receives him cordially, but David's general, Joab, nurses a grudge against the new ally because he has been responsible

476 SAMUEL

for the slaying of his (Joab's) brother, Asahel. Unbeknown to his royal master, he summons Abner to the capital and there settles the score by stabbing him. When David hears of this, he pronounces upon Joab the curse that his household may never be without "a leper or one that holds the spindle[1] or one that falls by the sword or one that lacks bread."

The sense of David's curse is that Joab's progeny may suffer disease, effeminacy, ill-fortune in war, and starvation. The expression, "one that holds the spindle," implies one who is fit only to do woman's work, and it represents a common form of commination in the Ancient Near East. Thus, in the treaty of Mat'ilu of Arpad, the curse is invoked that if either party violate the provisions of the agreement, "he shall become like a whore, and his people like women";[2] while in an inscription of Esarhaddon, now in Berlin, Ishtar, "queen of combat and battle," is besought to turn the manhood of the perfidious into womanhood.[3] Similarly, in a Hittite ritual text, the punishment prescribed for disloyal citizens is that they be dressed in female clothing, handed a spindle, and blinded.[4]

138 Taboo on touching the Ark of the Lord 6:6–7

As David was bringing the sacred ark of Yahweh to Jerusalem, his new capital, the oxen which were drawing it stumbled. A certain Uzza caught hold of it, to steady it. This, however, was deemed sacrilege, and "God struck him down on the spot . . . and he died."

That which is "holy" and otherworldly—what the Scots call "unco"—may not be touched or approached by a mundane and mortal creature, except he be in a state of absolute purity, lest it thereby become contaminated and lose its "mana."[1]

The incident here recorded has two illuminating parallels in Classical lore. When Troy was burning, we are told, Ilus took the Palladium—a counterpart of the Biblical ark—from the shrine of Athene (or whatever the native goddess may have been called) in order to rescue it from the flames. He was instantly blinded[2]—the standard punishment for sacrilege.[3] The same fate also befell Metellus when he tried to snatch that sacred object from a fire in the temple of Vesta.[4] (Both, it may be added, eventually had their sight restored.)

139 Shaving and shearing 10:1–6

When the king of the Ammonites died, David sent a message of condolence and goodwill to his son and successor, Hanun. The latter's counselors, however, were suspicious of David's envoys and, on their advice, Hanun had them arrested and "shaved off half of the beard of each, and cut off their garments in the middle, at their hips, and sent them away." David naturally resented this, and when the Ammonites perceived that they had "become odious" to him,[1] they decided to forestall his reprisals by hiring Syrian mercenaries to mount an attack upon Israel.

Comparative Folklore suggests a new interpretation of this bizarre incident. In Arab custom there are two different reasons for forcibly shaving a man's beard. The one is as a gesture of reconciliation: the "blood-avenger" of a slain man settles accounts with a repentant murderer by shearing his locks instead of cutting his throat.[2] Thus the sheikh of Bweme in Adjlun told S. I. Curtiss that one of the recognized ways in which a blood-avenger claims satisfaction and makes peace with his kinsman's slayer, in lieu of accepting payment or security or demanding surrender of property, is to cut off some of the latter's hair. Similarly, a bedouin wanderer informed the same scholar that when a murderer brings to the avenger the customary sacrifice of peace and reconciliation, "the avenger shaves off some of his (the murderer's) beard." They then "kiss each other on the head and beard. If the avenger refuses to claim damage from the murderer, he shaves off the lock of hair on his forehead and lets him go."[3]

Similarly, among the Druzes, "if a murderer believes that he and his family are too weak to defend themselves against the family of the murdered man, he goes to the nearest relative of the latter with a cord or a cloth about his neck. He excuses himself by pleading that since he is a man of honor, he could not avoid committing the murder, since the other had applied a dishonorable epithet to him. He then gives the blood-avenger, amid compliments, full freedom to take his life. Then the relative of the murdered man is obliged to forgive him. Nevertheless, this does not proceed quite so inconsequentially. The wronged man has a barber brought to shave off the beard of the murderer.[4]

"Among the Tiāhā a parallel practise is found. When a prisoner is taken in war, and they do not wish to put him to death, he is led to the encampment, where a corner of his head below the temples is shaved, and he is let go free."[5]

It is also customary, however, to shear a prisoner's locks in token of his subjection and surrender of personality (see above, §117).[6]

In the light of these usages the incident here recorded takes on quite a different complexion. Hanun, it may be suggested, really intended no insult. He was simply accepting a final reconciliation between the Israelites and the Ammonites by a gesture customary in such circumstances among his own people. David, however, interpreted it in the other sense, namely, as an indication that Hanun was treating Israel as a subjected people surrendering to him. Such an explanation gives point to the Ammonites' subsequent amazement at David's reaction; they were surprised that what they had meant to signify reconciliation had been so misunderstood that they had now "become odious" to those with whom they had sought to be friends.

140 The Uriah letter [11]

David consorts with Bathsheba, the beautiful wife of Uriah, a paladin at his court. To further the intrigue, he sends Uriah with a letter to Joab, the commander of the army. The letter orders Joab to place Uriah in an exposed position in battle against the Ammonites. This is done, and Uriah is killed.

This is but a Hebrew version of a widespread folktale.[1] The most familiar parallel is the Greek story of Bellerophon.[2] Sthenoboea,[3] the wife of Proetus, becomes infatuated with him and tries to seduce him. When he rejects her advances she plays the role of Potiphar's wife and falsely accuses him to her husband. Thereupon Proetus sends him with a letter to his (Proetus) father-in-law Iobates, requesting the latter to have him killed. Accordingly, Iobates dispatches him to fight the fearsome Chimaera. Bellerophon, however, mounts his winged horse Pegasus and shoots the monster from the air. He is then sent on other adventures designed to be fatal, but in each case emerges unscathed. Iobates then relents, marries Bellerophon to his daughter, and eventually bequeathes to him his kingdom.

An Indian version appears in one of the tales of Somadeva's Ocean of Story, where King Adityavaraman similarly disposes of his vizier Sivavaraman, whom he suspects of an intrigue with one of his concubines.[4]

Often the story takes the twist that the fatal letter is intercepted; the intended victim alters the name or someone else changes the contents to his advantage.[5] Thus, in Saxo's *Historia Danica,* Hamlet's wicked uncle Fengon sends him, with two companions, to England, bearing a letter to the English king requesting that monarch to put him to death. Hamlet, however, changes his own name to that of his companions, and they perish in his stead. This incident was taken over by Shakespeare who identified the two victims as Guildenstern and Rosencrantz.[6] Similarly, in Grimm's story of *The Devil with Three Golden Hairs,* a king tries to prevent a youth from marrying his daughter, as fated. Encountering him while on his travels, the king sends him to the palace with a letter to the queen, ordering her to have him killed. On the way, however, the youth rests in a robbers' hut. The robbers change the letter so that it orders the youth's marriage to the princess.[7] Again, in an Arabic version, the poet Mutalammis is given a letter ordering his death. He destroys it, but his companion Tarafah, who bears a similar missive, does not do so, and perishes. The motif recurs also in the Scandinavian Edda,[8] and stories of the same tenor are likewise reported from modern Greece[9] and Hungary.[10]

141 Regnal names   12:24-25

>   *Bathsheba bears to David a son whom he calls Solomon. The child is subsequently renamed Jedidiah, "beloved of Yahweh," the change being made formally by the prophet Nathan.*

In ancient times, as we have seen (above, §72), a person's name was not simply a verbal appellation, but a manifestation of his essential self. Kings, popes, and members of holy orders therefore assume new names when they enter upon their careers and thus assume, as it were, new characters. The custom goes back to ancient Egypt, and appears to have been fairly widespread in the Near East.[1]

The name Jedidiah, "beloved of Yahweh," is not chosen arbitrarily. It is the Hebrew equivalent of a title commonly affected in the Ancient Near East. Mesopotamian kings, for example, were often styled *naram ili,* "beloved of the god," or *migir ili,* "favored by the god";[2] while in the Canaanite myths discovered at Ras Shamra, "Prince (*zbl*) Sea" bears the common epithet *mdd Il,* "beloved (friend) of El (God),"[3] and Môt, god of sterility and of the netherworld, is termed similarly *ydd Il.*[4]

142 The coal on the hearth   14:7

>   *Joab, anxious to reconcile David to his upstart son, Absalom, sends to him a clever woman of Tekoa whom he instructs to win the king over by means of a parable. Clad in mourning, she tells David that she is the mother of two sons, one of whom killed the other during a quarrel. The clan is now demanding the manslayer's death, but this will mean that "they will extinguish the one coal that is left (on the hearth)."*

>   Put out the light, and then put out the light
>   Shakespeare, *Othello,* V.ii.7.

The hearthfire is universally regarded as the symbol of family life. When it dies out, the family is extinct.

The idea is expressed several times in the Old Testament; compare, for instance, Job 18:5-6: "The light of the wicked is put out, and the spark of his fire doth not shine; the light in his tent is darkened, and his lamp above him is put out"; *ibid.* 21:17: "Dimmed is the light of the wicked"; Proverbs 13:9; 24:20: The lamp of the wicked is put out"; *ib.* 20:20: "Whoso curseth his father or his mother, his lamp shall be put out"; II Samuel 21:17: "Then David's men sware unto him, saying 'Thou shalt go no more out with us to battle, lest thou quench the lamps of Israel." Mesopotamian texts likewise mention the extinction of the hearthfire or the oven as a sign of family misfortune,[1] and it has been suggested that the Sumerian word for "heir" (IBILA) really means "one who keeps the oil (lamp) burning (I(A)+BIL)."[2] In Arabic idiom, the extinction of a light is likewise a synonym for disaster.[3]

The image is well known also to Classical writers.[4] Ovid, for instance, speaks of "extinguished hearths" as a symbol of exile,[5] and both Tibullus[6] and Martial[7] of the "ever-burning fire on the hearth" as betokening bliss and contentment.

A modern Greek belief on the island of Zacynthos (Zante) is that a light burns for every human life in the realm of Charos, god of death; when one of them goes out, a man dies.[8] Similarly, an English popular superstition holds that guttering candles betoken death,[9] and analogous notions appear in German folklore.[10]

Among the Tonga, Sothe, and Venda-Bantu tribes of Southeast Africa,[11] as also among the Zulus,[12] it is the practice to extinguish the main communal fire at the death of a chieftain; while among the Cwana, fires are put out at moments of public calamity, as when an epidemic occurs.[13] Along the same lines, a burning brazier was carried before Spartan[14] and Hellenistic kings.[15]

Conversely, the maintenance of the household fire implies the preservation of the home. Yahweh promises to "give a lamp to David and his sons for ever,"[16] and in the Canaanite Poem of Aqhat one of the reasons why a man wants a son is that he shall have someone "to make his smoke ascend from the ground."[17]

143 Absalom and his father's concubines   16:20-23

Absalom, in order to rally popular support for his ambitions, is anxious to demonstrate an open breach with David. On the advice of Ahitophel, he does so by publicly indulging in sexual relations with David's concubines.

There is more to this incident than an act of affront. Ahitophel's advice is based on the ancient custom whereby a son and heir inherited all of his father's wives and concubines except his own mother. This was, so to speak, part of the act of succession.

The custom is attested both in Semitic and in Classical sources. Molaika, wife of the Calif Ali, was thus "inherited"; so was Amina, the wife of Abu Mo'ayyit, and so too was the Fahmite widow of the Calif Omar.[1] Robertson Smith suggests[2] that desire to establish succession was what motivated Reuben to consort with Jacob's concubine, Bilhah,[3] and that when Ish-bosheth accused Saul's uncle and supporter, Abner, of consorting with the former's concubine, what he really meant was that Abner was not disinterested but conniving to secure the succession for himself.[4]

In the Odyssey, Telegonus, the son of Odysseus, "inherits" Penelope,[5] and Telemachus inherits Circe.[6] So too Herakles charged his son Hyllus to marry Iole when he came of age.[7] Several cases of this practice may be cited also from Syro-Roman times.[8]

144 King's misconduct affects soil   21:1–9

Because Saul had slain the Gibeonites, with whom Israel had concluded a treaty, the Lord sent a three-year famine during the reign of Saul's successor, David.

The king is the epitome of his people's life and destiny. Misconduct, like debility, on his part therefore impairs the fertility of the soil and the general welfare.[1]

In a Hittite text it is stated that a twenty-year blight has resulted from sins committed by the royal household,[2] and similar ideas appear in ancient Mesopotamian literature.[3] In the Canaanite (Ugaritic) *Epic of K-r-t,* drought follows that monarch's neglect of a vow he has made to the goddess Asherath;[4] while in an Aramaic treaty of the eighth century B.C., between the king of K-t-k and the king of Arpad, a seven-year scourge is invoked as sanction in case of breach by either party.[5]

In parts of Africa, drought is attributed to the king's unchastity,[6] and this is likewise a common theme of Irish legend[7] and of European folktales in general.[8] Ammianus Marcellinus, the last of the major Roman historians, has an interesting passage anent this concept. "Among the Burgundians," he tells us, "the king is removed from power and deposed by ancient rite, if during his reign the fortunes of war suffer reverse or the earth refuses to yield substantial crops." "The Egyptians," he adds, "used in the same way to attribute such disasters to their rulers."[9]

All of this, of course, is merely a particular application of the wider principle that misconduct in general—and especially, sexual misconduct—is reflected in the condition of the soil.[10] Thus the Kayans of Borneo hold that adultery is punished by the spirits, who withold crops;[11] while the Negroes of Loango suppose that the intercourse of a man with an immature girl is punished by God with drought.[12] Job, protesting that he is no adulterer, declares that if he were, "fire would root out all my produce"; and in the Book of Leviticus we are told that misconduct pollutes the land and causes it to "vomit forth its inhabitants."[13] Indeed, in several passages of the Old Testament the same Hebrew word describes the infertility of the soil as normally denotes the defilement of a woman through unchastity.[14]

Conversely, a land prospers under a good king. For this reason, ancient Semitic monarchs, like Azitawad of Adana[15] and Zakir of Hamath,[16] both of the eighth century B.C., make a point, in their triumphal inscriptions, of boasting that during their reigns crops were abundant. So too, in Homer's Odyssey, Odysseus (still unrevealed to her) tells Penelope that her fame has risen to the broad heavens, "like that of a blameless king who is god-fearing and holds to justice . . . so that, through him, the black earth bears barley and wheat, and the trees burgeon with fruit, and the sheep breed in the plains, and the sea teems with fish."[17] The greatest bliss that could be invoked on a new king was, in fact, that he might serve as a symbol of his people's peace and prosperity. "May he be in the land," says the Psalmist, "like an expanse of corn which waves in the breeze on the hilltops; may he be like the fruit which in Lebanon grows, and may men blossom forth out of the city like grass of the earth."[18]

145 A Hebrew Niobe   21:10

In retribution for the massacre perpetrated by Saul, the Gibeonites request of David that seven of Saul's sons be handed over to them and be hung up before the Lord on a hill at Gibeon. David consents, but Rizpah, one of Saul's concubines, whose sons have been included among the seven, keeps continuous vigil over the bodies "from the early days of harvest until the rains, fell." David, told of her devotion, orders the bones collected, along with those of Saul and Jonathan, and gives them honorable burial. Thereupon, the Lord is propitiated, and the famine ends.

(a) Rizpah is usually regarded as a kind of Hebrew Niobe,[1] but perhaps, in its original form, the story revolved around the widespread notion that the *essential vitality of a person lies in the bodily fluids,*[2] *so that a corpse must be "watered" before it can be assured of eventual resurrection.* It is for this reason that, for example, Arabs often make a practice of burying the dead near water,[3] and in an ancient Arabic poem the spirit of a deceased man prays that his burial mound as well as himself may "drink from the thunderclouds and raindrops."[4] The Babylonians made a practice of pouring water over the dead,[5] and a very common belief in Europe is that rain at a funeral is lucky;[6] as the English proverb puts it, "Blessed is the dead the rain rains on."[7] Not impossibly, there is an allusion to this idea in the words of Job 21:32–33:

> When he is borne to the grave,
> Watch is kept o'er his tomb;
> the clods of the valley are sweet unto him.

Associated with this notion is the belief that dew revives the dead. Mentioned already by Isaiah (*Thy dead shall live; those whom I have made corpses shall arise, for thy dew is a shimmering dew*),[8] the "dew of resurrection" features prominently in later Jewish folklore.[9]

(b) As we have seen in the story of Cain and Abel (above §14), the unavenged spirits of the slain can affect the fertility of the soil by causing drought or blight. Rizpah therefore keeps her vigil until the auspicious moment—the time when the rains would normally descend. At that time her action is reported to David, and he becomes anxious that the spirits be appeased.

What is here related is admirably illustrated by an incident recorded by

Plutarch. A plague broke out in Rome, and the Pythian oracle was consulted. It advised that the wrath of Saturn and the spirits (manes) of those unjustly slain should be appeased. Thereupon Lutatius Catulus created a temple to Saturn containing an altar with four faces.[10]

▲ 146 The sin of a census   24

The Lord is angry with the Israelites, so he inspires David to commit a crime which will bring dire consequences upon them. The crime is the taking of a census.

[To be able to identify a thing precisely is, in ancient and primitive thought, to have potential control over it. It is for this reason, as we have seen (above, §72), that knowledge of a person's name is all-important in working magic against him and, conversely, it is for this reason that otherworld beings refrain from disclosing it. To know the exact number of things can produce the same result. Accordingly, all over the world we find a popular resistance to taking a census, counting cattle, crops or fruits, and even to revealing one's age.]

This curious superstition is especially well attested among the Negroid races of Africa. For example, among the Bakongo of the Lower Congo "it is considered extremely unlucky for a woman to count her children one, two, three, and so on, for the evil spirits will hear and take some of them away by death. The people themselves do not like to be counted; for they fear that counting will draw to them the attention of the evil spirits, and as a result of the counting some of them will soon die. In 1908 the Congo State officials, desiring to number the people for the purpose of levying a tax, sent an officer with soldiers to count them. The natives would have resisted the officer, but he had too many soldiers with him; and it is not improbable that fights have taken place between whites and blacks in other parts of Africa, not that they resisted the taxation, but because they objected to be counted for fear the spirits would hear and kill them."[1] Similarly among the Boloki or Bangala of the Upper Congo, "the native has a very strong superstition and prejudice against counting his children, for he believes that if he does so, or if he states the proper number, the evil spirits will hear it and some of his children will die; hence when you ask him such a simple question as, 'How many children have you?' you stir up his superstitious fears, and he will answer: 'I don't know.' If you press him, he will tell you sixty, or one hundred children, or any other number that jumps to his tongue; and even then he is thinking of those who, from the native view of kinship, are regarded as his children, and desiring to deceive, not you, but those ubiquitous and prowling evil spirits, he states a large number that leaves a wide margin."[2]

Again, the Masai of East Africa count neither men nor beasts, believing that if they did so the men or beasts would die. Hence they reckon a great multitude of people or a large herd of cattle only in round numbers; of smaller groups of men or beasts they can reckon the totals with tolerable accuracy without numbering the individuals of the groups. Only dead men or dead beasts may be counted one by one, because naturally there is no risk of their dying again in consequence of their numeration.[3] [The Loango have a similar reluctance to numbering their cattle;[3a] while] the Wa-Sania of British East Africa "most strongly object to being counted, as they believe that one of those who were counted would die shortly afterwards."[4] To the Akamba, another tribe of the same region, the welfare of the cattle is a matter of great concern; hence the people observe certain superstitious rules, the breach of which is believed to entail misfortune on the herds. One of these rules is that the cattle may never be counted; so when the herd returns to the village, the owner will merely cast his eye over it to discover if a beast is missing. And in this tribe the unluckiness of counting is not limited to cattle, it extends to all living creatures, and particularly to girls.[5] On the other hand, another authority on the Akamba tells us that "there does not appear to be any superstition against counting stock; if a man has a large herd he does not know the number, but he or his wives when milking would quickly notice if a beast with certain markings was not present. A man however knows the number of his children but is averse to telling any one outside his family. There is a tradition that a man named Munda wa Ngola, who lived in the Ibeti Hills, had many sons and daughters, and boasted of the size of his family, saying that he and his sons could resist any attack from the Masai; one night however the Masai surprised him and killed him and his people, and the countryside considered that this was a judgement on him."[6] Again, among the Akikuyu, another tribe of British East Africa, "it is difficult to arrive at figures, even approximately correct, with regard to the size of the families. The natural method of conversing with the mothers as to the number of their children is soon found to be, to say the least, a tactless proceeding. It is considered most unlucky to give such figures. The inquiry is politely waived, with a resquest to 'come and see.' . . . The objection to giving family statistics was discovered not to be in force amongst other members than the parents; at any rate it did not seem to affect those Kikuyu boys who were continually in touch with us. These answered readily any questions as to the number of their father's wives, their grandfather's wives, and their respective children, and seemed to have a good acquaintance with their relations."[7] The Gallas of East Africa think that to count cattle is an evil omen, and that it impedes the increase of the herd.[8] To count the members of a community or company is reckoned by the Hottentots to be of very evil augury, for they believe that some member of the company will die. A missionary who once, in ignorance of this superstition, counted his workpeople, is said to have paid for his rashness with his life.[9]

The superstitious objection to numbering people seems to be general in North Africa; in Algeria the opposition offered by the natives to all French regulations which require an enumeration of the inhabitants is said to be based in great measure on this aversion to be counted. Nor is this repugnance limited to the counting of persons; it is exhibited also in the counting of measures of grain, an operation which has a sacred character. For example, at Oran the person who counts the measures of grain should be in a state of ceremonial purity, and instead of counting one, two, three, and so on, he says "In the name of God" for "one"; "two blessings" for "two"; "hospitality of the Prophet" for "three"; "we shall gain, please God" for "four"; "in the eye of the Devil" for "five"; "in the eye of his son" for "six"; "it is God who gives us our fill" for "seven"; and so on, up to "twelve," for which the expression is "the perfection for God."[10] So in Palestine, at counting the measures of grain, many Mohammedans say for the first one, "God is one," and for the next, "He has no second," then simply "Three," "Four," and so on. But "there are several unlucky numbers, the first being five, and therefore, instead of saying the number, they often say 'Your hand,' five being the number of the fingers; seven is another unlucky number, strange to say, and is passed over in silence, or the word 'A blessing' is used instead; at nine Moslems often say, 'Pray in the name of Mohammed'; eleven also is not unfrequently omitted, the measurer saying, 'There are ten,' and then passing on to twelve."[11] Perhaps such substitutes for the ordinary numbers are intended to deceive evil spirits, who may be lying in wait to steal or harm the corn, and who are presumably too dull-witted to comprehend these eccentric modes of numeration.

In the Shortlands group of islands, in the Western Pacific, the building of a chief's house is attended by a variety of ceremonies and observances. The roof is heavily thatched at each gable with thatch made of the leaves of the ivory-nut palm. In collecting these leaves the builders are not allowed to count the number, as the counting would be deemed unlucky; yet if the number of leaves collected should fall short of the number required, the house, though nearing completion, would be at once abandoned.[12] Thus the loss entailed by a miscalculation may be heavy, and from its possible extent we can judge how serious must, in the opinion of the natives, be the objection to counting the leaves, since rather than count them they are prepared to sacrifice the fruit of their labour. Among the Cherokee Indians of North America it is a rule that "melons and squashes must not be counted or examined too closely, while still growing upon the vine, or they will cease to thrive."[13] Once on a time the officer in charge of Fort Simpson, in British Columbia, took a census of the Indians in the neighbourhood, and very soon afterwards great numbers of them were swept away by measles. The Indians attributed the calamity to their having been numbered.[14] The Omaha Indians "preserve no account of their ages; they think that some evil will attend the numbering of their years."[15]

Similar superstitions are widespread in Europe. [The Roman poet Catullus tells Lesbia that they should "confound" the number of their kisses lest evil-minded persons cast the evil eye on them or bewitch them with spells;[15a] and

Muretus, the sixteenth-century scholar, notes that in his day Italian peasants avoided counting the fruit on a tree.[15b] The Lapps used to be, and perhaps are still unwilling, to count themselves and to declare the number, because they feared that such a reckoning would both forebode and cause a great mortality among their people;[16] [and Swedish fishermen still deem it unpropitious to count their catch[16a]]. In the Highlands of Scotland, "it is reckoned unlucky to number the people or cattle belonging to any family, but more particularly upon Friday. The cowherd knows every creature committed to his charge by the colour, size, and other particular marks, but is perhaps all along ignorant of the sum total of his flock. And fishermen do not care to confess the number of salmon or other fish which they have taken at a draught or in a day, imagining that this discovery would spoil their luck."[17] Though this account is derived from a writer of the eighteenth century, similar superstitions are known to have prevailed in Scotland far into the nineteenth century, and it is probable that they are not extinct at the present time. In Shetland, we are told, "counting the number of sheep, of cattle, of horses, of fish, or of any of a man's chattels, whether animate or inanimate, has always been considered as productive of bad luck. There is also said to have been an idea prevalent at one time, that an outbreak of small-pox always followed the census being taken."[18] Among the fisher folk on the north-east coast of Scotland on no account might the boats be counted when they were at sea, nor might any gathering of men, women, or children be numbered. Nothing aroused the indignation of a company of fisherwomen trudging along the road to sell their fish more than to point at them with the finger, and begin to number them aloud:

> Ane, twa, three,
> Faht a fishers I see
> Gyain our the brigg o' Dee,
> Deel pick their muckle greethy ee.[19]

So the fish-wives of Auchmithie, a village on the coast of Forfarshire, used to be irritated by mischievous children, who counted them with extended forefingers, repeating the verse:

> Ane, twa, three!
> Ane, twa, three!
> Sic a lot o' fisher-wifies
> I do see!

And the unluckiness extended to counting the fish caught or the boats in the herring-fleet.[20]

In Lincolnshire, England, "no farmer should count his lambs too closely during the lambing season. [As a French proverb puts it, *Brebis comptées, le loup les mange* (Number your sheep, and the wolf will eat them).[20a] I have seen a shepherd in obvious embarrassment because his employer knew so little of his own business that, though usually the most easy of masters, he would insist on learning every morning the exact number of lambs his flock had produced. For a cognate reason, it may be, some people when asked how old they are reply, 'As old as my tongue, and a little bit older than my teeth.' Gaidoz remarks in *Melusine* (ix. 35) that old people ought not to tell their age, and when importuned to reveal it they should answer that they are as old as their little finger. Inhabitants of Godarville, Hainault, reply, 'I am the age of a calf, every year twelve months' ";[21] [and Sardinian peasants have been known to resort to similar evasions[21a]]. In England, the superstitious objection to counting lambs is not confined to Lincolnshire. A friend, whose home is in a village of South Warwickshire, wrote to me some years ago, "Superstitions die hard. Yesterday I asked a woman how many lambs her husband had. She said she didn't know, then, perceiving the surprise in my face, added, 'You know, sir, it's unlucky to count them.' Then she went on, 'However we haven't lost any yet.' And her husband is postmaster and keeps the village shop, and, in his own esteem, stands high above a peasant."[22]

In Denmark they say that you should never count the eggs under a brooding hen, else the mother will tread on the eggs and kill the chickens. And when the chickens are hatched, you ought not to count them, or they will easily fall a prey to the glede or the hawk. So, too, blossoms and fruit should not be counted, or the blossoms will wither and the fruit will fall untimely from the bough.[23] In North Jutland people have a notion that if you count any mice which the cat has caught, or which you chance to discover, the mice will increase in number; and if you count lice, fleas, or any other vermin, they also will multiply in like manner.[24] It is said to be a Greek and Armenian superstition that if you count your warts they will increase in number.[25] On the other hand, it is a popular German belief that if you count your money often it will steadily decrease.[26] In the Upper Palatinate, a district of Bavaria, people think that loaves in the oven should not be counted, or they will not turn out well.[27] In Upper Franconia, another district of Bavaria, they say that, when dumplings are being cooked you should not count them, because if you do, the Little Wood Women, who like dumplings, could not fetch any away, and deprived of that form of nutriment they would perish, with the necessary consequence that the forest would dwindle and die. Therefore to prevent the country from being stripped bare of its woods, you are urged not to count dumplings in the pan.[28] [Elsewhere in Germany, it is considered unlucky to count fruit on a tree or fish which have been caught.[28a]]

On the whole we may assume, with a fair degree of probability, that the objection which the Israelites in King David's time felt to the taking of a census rested on no firmer foundation than sheer superstition, which may have been confirmed by an outbreak of plague immediately after the numbering of the people.[28b] [A striking parallel comes from Tiraspol, in Russia, where, in 1897, some twenty-eight persons buried themselves alive in order to escape a census, which they regarded as sinful.[28c] Similarly, it was reported from England, in the nineteenth century, that "some regard with feelings of strong antipathy our decennial census, and it is only the compulsion of the law which induces them to comply with this national means of ascertaining the state of the population."[28d]] To this day the same repugnance to count or be counted appears to linger among the Arabs of Syria, for we are told that an Arab is averse to counting the tents, or horsemen, or cattle of his tribe, lest some misfortune befall them.[29]

At a later time, Hebrew Law so far relaxed the ban upon a census as to permit the nation to be numbered, on condition that every man paid half a shekel to the Lord as a ransom for his life, lest a plague should break out among the people.[30]

[On the popular level, however, the superstition continued among the Jews into relatively modern times, for the mystical Kabbalists laid it down that "Satan has power over things that have been counted."[30]] ▼

Kings

147 Abishag I Kings 1:1-4

In David's old age, a beautiful maiden, Abishag of Shunem, is brought to him to lie in his bosom and keep him warm, though she does not serve as a concubine.

What is here involved is the principle known technically as *osphresiology*. This asserts that new vigor can be imparted to the aged and infirm by physical contact with, or proximity to, young persons.[1]

The physician Marcellus Empiricus of Bordeaux (4th cent.) recommends a poultice for chronic disorders of the stomach which had the same effect as though the patient were *adverso pectore cujuslibet tepefactus*.[2]

In eighteenth-century England "there was a belief that the breath of young women might be helpful in prolonging life. . . . One physician actually took lodgings in a girls' boarding-school for this purpose. 'I am myself,' wrote Philip Thicknesse in 1779, 'turned of sixty, and in general, though I have lived in various climates, and suffered severely both in body and mind, yet having always partaken of the breath of *young women, wherever they lay in my way*, I feel none of the infirmities which so often strike the eyes and ears in this great city of sickness [Bath] by men many years younger than myself.'"[3]

148 The ritual of enthronement 1:9, 33, 38

Adonijah, a pretender to the throne of David, stages a ceremony of installation and anointment at a certain stone beside the Fuller's Spring (En Rogel), near Jerusalem.[1] David retaliates by having his son Solomon formally anointed beside another spring, named Gihon.

(a) Water, as we have seen (above, §2), was the source of all primal virtues and wisdom. Accordingly, ancient kings often claimed descent from water-goddesses or asserted that they had been drawn out of the waters shortly after birth. In Southeast Asia, for example, the king is said to be the child of a mortal man and a *nagi*, or water-nymph.[2] In Indonesia, the kings of San-fo-ts'i were called for this reason "sperm of a naga" (*long tsin*);[3] while the Emperors of China, Palaung and Pagan were believed to have sprung from the union of Prince Thuriya, son of the sun, and the nagi of Thusandi, and the king of Palembang claimed that his parents were King Souran and the daughter of a submarine monarch.[4]

Alternatively, the special qualities of kingship were imparted by baptism at the time of installation. Thus, in the Hindu ceremony of *abhiṣeka*, or royal consecration, water taken from the sacred River Sarasvatī is sprinkled over the king's head and addressed: "O water, that art naturally a giver of kingship, give kingship to X."[5] The ceremony is called Sprinkling-with-Kingly-Dignity.[6] Similarly, in Egypt, the Pharaoh was baptized at his enthronement by the gods of the four quarters of the earth.[7]

Among the Sumerians of Mesopotamia, Ea, god of the primeval deep, was said to impart "intelligence" (IGI.GAL) to new kings.[8] This claim became, in fact, something of a standard cliché; it occurs in the inscriptions of Eanadu,[9] Entemena,[10] and Ur-Bau[11] of Lagash, as well as in those of Lugalzagissi of Uruk[12] and even in the Code of Hammurapi of Babylon.[13]

The power of special waters features also in European folktales.[14] In a Basque story, a hero who has subdued a dragon is unable to kill it until the princess whom he has rescued throws a bottle of water in his face; this gives him extra strength.[15] Similarly, in a Russian tale, a hero named Gol insists that a princess fortify him with "the water of heroes."[16]

(b) If water imparts strength and wisdom, stone imparts durability—especially since this is often regarded as emanating from a god who dwells within it.

Anglo-Saxon kings were customarily anointed standing on a stone at Kingston-on-Thames,[17] and to this day the throne of the king of England is mounted on the celebrated Stone of Scone when he is crowned in Westminster Abbey. Swedish monarchs likewise stood on a stone when they were installed at Uppsala, and the same practice is recorded also as current at the installation of kings at Antanarivo and Ambohimanga in Madagascar.[18] In Scotland, the chief of the Celtic O'Donnels was inaugurated on a special stone (called Flagstone), set on a mound; while the chief of the clan M'Donald was crowned "king of the isles" while standing on a sacred stone. A cylindrical obelisk said to have been used in connection with the enthronement of chieftains still stands in the Rath-na-Riegh. Similarly, German emperors and Lombard kings took their coronation oaths beside a stone pillar which now stands before the Church of St. Ambrosio at Milan.[19]

(Coronation beside a pillar, rather than directly on a stone, seems to be implied in two passages of the Old Testament itself. In Judges 9:6, Abimelech is installed as king "beside the oak of the pillar at Shechem";[20] while in II Kings 11:14, the priest Jehoiada crowns Joash while the latter "stands beside the pillar, according to custom."[21])

149 Asylum at the altar   1:50; 2:28

When Adonijah hears what has happened, he flees in terror of Solomon and rushes to lay hold on the "horns" (knobs) of the altar. Later, Joab, who has supported him, does likewise.

Altars and sanctuaries were regarded throughout the Ancient Near East as places of asylum.[1] This is simply an extension of the common bedouin convention whereby a man who repairs to another's tent, touches the ropes, or eats three handfuls of food (be it only salt) can claim protection for a minimum of three days.[2] When men resort for refuge to an altar or sanctuary they are therefore styled "guests" of the god or goddess.

A Canaanite text of the fourteenth century B.C. from Ras Shamra-Ugarit mentions "guests of the sacred enclosure" (*gr ḥmt*),[3] and a mythological poem from the same site invokes upon an assassin who is still at large the curse that he may find himself perpetually seeking asylum as "a guest of the sanctuary" (*gr bt il*).[4] Right of asylum continued in Phoenician temples until relatively late times; we have evidence of it at the sanctuary of Melqarth at Tyre[5] and at the temple in Daphne, near Antioch,[6] even in the Hellenistic age, and "guests" (*grm*) are listed, in the fourth century B.C., among the personnel of a temple at Kition, in Cyprus.[7] Moreover, Tacitus tells us that the Emperor Tiberius instituted an inquiry into abuses of the system at Paphos and Amathus, on the same island.[8] In Arabic usage, a suppliant beside the Ka'aba at Mecca is known as a "guest of Allah" (*jār Allah*),[9] and Yakūt tells us that right of asylum prevailed in pre-Islamic times at the holy places of Jalṣ and Fals.[10]

A man pursued by a vendetta, or in danger of such pursuit, could seek refuge at an altar or sanctuary, where, under oath, he could protest his innocence in the form of a "negative confession" ("I have not lied, stolen, murdered," etc.). The god himself would then punish him if the oath were false.[11] It is, indeed, in this sense that we are to understand the Psalmist's statement that he who "walks blamelessly, does what is right, speaks truth in his heart, and . . . harms not his fellow" is fit to be a guest (RSV: sojourn) in the Lord's tent.[12]

The right of asylum at sanctuaries was, in fact, so standard an institution in Israel that the law of Exodus 21:14 finds it necessary expressly to withdraw it in cases of deliberate homicide.

Nor was this right by any means confined to the Semites. Classical writers tell us that after Ajax had violated Cassandra, the goddess Athene prevented the Greeks from sailing home from Troy. Thereupon they sought to kill the miscreant, but he fled to an altar and thus found safety.[13] Similarly, the Heraclids, fleeing from Eurystheus, found asylum beside the altar of Mercy at Athens.[14]

In Christian tradition, churches afford asylum. A decision of the American courts, however, has recently (1968) denied this right to draftees seeking thus to avoid military service.

▲ 150 The judgment of Solomon   3:16–28

Two harlots come before Solomon to seek his judgment. Each, at about the same time, has borne a son in the same house. The one declares: We were alone in the place. During the night this woman ac-

cidentally smothered her child. While I was asleep, she took mine, laid it in her bosom, and put her dead child in mine. When daylight came, I saw what she had done. The other replies that the live child is indeed hers, and the dead child that of ther accuser. Solomon orders the child to be cut in half. The one woman immediately cries out, "No; no! Give her the child whole!" The other, however, says, "No, divide it." In this way the true mother is revealed.

Like much else that is told of King Solomon, this anecdote has the air rather of a popular tale than of an historical narrative. True or false, it has passed into folk-lore, having been incorporated into that vast legendary literature of the Jains, which as yet has been only partially explored by European scholars. Four of these Indian versions of the story have been discovered in recent times;[1] they all bear a family resemblance to each other and to their Hebrew; original. It will be enough to cite one of them, which runs as follows:

A certain merchant had two wives; one of them had a son and the other had not. But the childless wife also took good care of the other's child, and the child was not able to distinguish, "This is my mother, that is not." Once on a time the merchant, with his wives and his son, went to another country, and just after his arrival there he died. Then the two wives fell to quarrelling. One of them said, "Mine is this child," and the other said just the same. One said, "It is I who am the mistress of the house"; and the other said, "It is I." At last they carried the dispute before a royal court of justice. The presiding minister of justice gave an order to his men, "First divide the whole property, then saw the child in two with a saw, and give one part to the one woman and the other part to the other." But when the mother heard the minister's sentence, it was as if a thunderbolt, enveloped in a thousand flames, had fallen on her head, and with her heart all trembling as if it had been pierced by a crooked dart, she contrived with difficulty to speak. "Ah, sire! Great minister!" she said, "it is not mine, this child! The money is of no use to me! Let the child be the son of that woman, and let her be the mistress of the house. As for me, it is no matter if I drag out an indigent life in strange houses; though it be from a distance, yet shall I see that child living, and so shall I attain the object of my life. Whereas, without my son, even now the whole living world is dead to me." But the other woman uttered never a word. Then the minister, beholding the distress of the former woman, said, "To her belongs the child, but not to that one." And he made the mother the mistress of the house, but the other woman he rebuked.[2]

[This celebrated story has far more parallels in world folklore than Frazer has cited.[2a]

An Indian (Prakrit) tale, for instance, tells of two women who set out for a feast, each with an infant child. While they are sleeping in a forest, a wolf kills one of the children. Its mother substitutes it for that of her companion before the latter wakes. At the court of Gopicandra a wise parrot advises that the child be cut in half. The true mother reveals herself by demurring.[2b]

A Buddhist Jataka tale, preserved in a Singalese version of the fifth or sixth century C.E., relates that a female cannibal demon (*yakinni*) once stole the child of a woman who was bathing. The demon and the mother appealed to Buddha for judgment. He drew a line on the ground and ordered them to draw the child across it in a tug of war. The true mother refused.[2c]

Again, in a Tibetan tale, a man has both a wife and a concubine. The former is barren, but the latter bears a son. When the man dies, the wife claims the son as hers in order to inherit the estate. The sage Vičakha orders a tug of war. The true mother refuses.[2d]

A Chinese story of the same type by Ying Shao (178–97 C.E.) is quoted in Mo Tsing's *Yilin,* dating from the time of the Tang Dynasty (7th–9th centuries C.E.). This is based in turn on an earlier work by Chung-Yung of the Liang Dynasty (546–56 C.E.). A charming translation of it will be found in Lin Yutang's *The Wisdom of China.*[2e] From China also comes the celebrated Story of the Chalk Circle (*Huei-lan-ki*), based on a corpus of plays (*Yuen-jin-pe-chang*) compiled under the Yuen rulers (1259–1368). In this version, Pao-Čing, chief of the city, orders the child to be pulled out of a circle drawn in chalk on the ground. The true mother objects.[2f]

Nor is it only in the classic literature of the country that the story is known. A modern Chinese folktale tells of two women who contend for possession of a child. The wife of the mandarin suggests that a live fish be put into its clothing and that it then be thrown into the water. When the true mother sees the fish struggling to get free and thereby harming the infant, she plunges in to rescue him, thus proving the truth of her claim.[2g] In another version, the child is ordered, as in the Biblical tale, to be cut in two.[2h]

There is also an Iranian version of the tale;[2i] while in a Bosnian variant, which otherwise follows the Scriptural narrative, the wise decision is attributed to the celebrated sage and wit, Nasreddin Hodja.[2j]

Different in detail, but identical in basic theme, is a tale from Cairo recorded by a Paduan traveler in the eighteenth century. Two men claim the paternity of a child. The judge orders it starved for three days and then fed a bowl of milk. The child gulps and slops. The "false" father chides it for its bad manners; the true father pitifully excuses it.[2k]

The story is also portrayed—of all places—on a wall painting at Pompeii. Since the characters are there depicted as pygmies, and since there are in the same room frescoes of hippopotami and crocodiles, it has been suggested that the tale may have been of Egyptian origin;[2l] but, as the famous folklorist Gaidoz pointed out, this need indicate only that the artist was an Egyptian or worked under Egyptian influence, not that the story itself came from Egypt.[2m]

Other representations of the tale are to be found in the grave chamber of the Villa Pamphili[2n] and in a house near the Farnesina in Rome.[2o]

Theodor Benfey claimed that the story was of Tibetan provenience,[2p] but this view is not accepted by more recent scholars. Hermann Gunkel suggested, on the other hand, that it came ultimately from India and dealt, in its original form, with the claims of two women to the same man's estate, for in India a childless widow has no rights to inheritance.[2q] ▼

151 The dedication of the Temple · 8

Solomon builds a temple to the LORD in Jerusalem, and dedicates it in the seventh month of the year, at the onset of the rainy season. The Scriptural writer gives the text of a hymn which the king is said to have recited.

The date of the dedication of the Temple is not fortuitous; it follows an ancient precedent of installing the god of rainfall and fertility in a new fane after he has vanquished the marplot of Chaos and the contumacious dragon who tries either to impound the waters or else to send them in floods at the onset of the wet season. This triumph and enthronement, which inaugurated the world order in the past, was thought to be repeated each year and therefore formed the central theme of myths recited at the New Year Festival. Examples are the Canaanite *Poem of Baal,* the Mesopotamian Epic of Creation (*Enuma Elish*) and the Hittite myth of the Slaying of the Dragon (Illuyankas).[1]

The date chosen is also important in the solar year, for it is the time of the autumnal equinox.[2] In the Canaanite myth, a major role is assigned for this reason to the sun-goddess (*Š-p-š*).[3]

Against this background, the song intoned by Solomon at the dedication ceremony takes on a new significance. In the traditional Hebrew text it runs as follows:

> *YAHWEH said that he would dwell in thick cloud.*
> *A lofty house have I indeed built for thee,*
> *a place for thee to dwell in for ever.*

This, however, obscures the point, for the crucial opening line has dropped out! It can be restored, however, from the ancient Greek (Septuagint) Version, and it contains, significantly, an allusion to the sun at its zenith.[4] Now, a Hebrew word for zenith was *zebul*,[5] and the "lofty house" which Solomon declares that he has indeed built for Yahweh is, in the original, "a *zebul*-house." The whole point now becomes clear as the sunlight itself: the little poem is a sublime satire on the pagan rites, the implication being that the new temple of Yahweh is to enshrine him perpetually in a blaze of glory, whereas the sun can always be obscured by cloudmists! The point can be baldly reproduced as follows:

> *Yahweh set the sun on high*
> *In the topmost of the sky,*
> *But then in turn he bade it dwell*
> *Where the cloudmists round it swell.*
> *Yet, for Thee Thyself right here*
> *I a lofty house uprear,*
> *Where, as at Thy zenith-tide,*
> *Thou for evermore may'st bide!*[6]

152 Settlement of disputes beside the altar   8:31–32
See §§149, 271.

▲ 153 Solomon and the Queen of Sheba   10

According to Israelite tradition King Solomon was a sage whose reputation for wisdom spread to the ends of the earth, and from all quarters kings sent envoys to Jerusalem to profit by the sagacity and learning of the Hebrew monarch.[1] Amongst the rest the Queen of Sheba, not content to receive at second hand the treasures of knowledge which he dispensed to his hearers, came in person from her home in southern Arabia to question Solomon with her own lips and to listen to his wise answers. We are told that she put riddles to him, and that he read them all; not one of them did he fail to answer.[2]

In Central Celebes similar stories are told of contests of wit between the rival Rajahs of Loowoo and Mori. It is said, for example, that the Rajah of Mori, hearing reports of the other's greatness, resolved to test his power and glory. For this purpose he sent him an iron staff bent into a loop, with a request that he would straighten it out. The Rajah of Loowoo put the staff in a furnace, and when it was red-hot, he straightened it out, as he had been requested to do. Having performed the task set him, he now in his turn tested his rival by sending the Rajah of Mori a tube of sago, baked in a bamboo and bent into a loop while it was still warm. This tube he begged the Rajah of Mori to straighten out The Rajah of Mori accordingly set to work on the tube of sago, but do what he would, he could not straighten it out. If he tried to do it when the sago was dry, the tube threatened to break in his hands; if he tried to do it when the sago was damp, by being dipped in water, the tube dissolved; and if he warmed it up to dry it again, the sago melted into a solid mass. So in this trial of skill the Rajah of Loowoo got the better of the Rajah of Mori.

However, in another story the Rajah of Mori contrives to defeat his rival. The Rajah of Loowoo had sent him a piece of cotton with a request that he would draw out all the threads. This the Rajah of Mori contrived to do, and having executed the task, he sent the Rajah of Loowoo in return a piece of bark-cloth with a request that the Rajah would be so good as to draw out all the threads from *that*. In vain the Rajah of Loowoo struggled to disentangle all the fibres of the bark; at last he had to give it up and acknowledge that the Rajah of Mori was at least his peer.

Yet another story, however, reverses the parts played by the two potentates and assigns the superiority to the Rajah of Loowoo. It is said that the Rajah of Loowoo came to visit the Rajah of Mori, and that the two sat up late at night talking by the light of a resin-torch, after all the other folk in the palace had gone to sleep. As the torch guttered and threatened to go out, the Rajah of Mori took a stick and directed the flow of resin so that the flame burst out again as bright as ever. Now this is a task which is usually performed by a slave, and the good-natured Rajah only did it with his own hands because all his slaves were abed. However, his astute rival at once took advantage of his politeness to place him in a position of inferiority. "Because you have snuffed the torch," said he to the Rajah of Mori, "you are less than I, and you must pay me homage." The crestfallen but candid Rajah of Mori acknowledged the justness of the observation, and confessed the superiority of the Rajah of Loowoo.[1]

If we had the Queen of Sheba's version of her interview with King Solomon, we might perhaps discover that in the war of wit she was at least able to hold her own against the Hebrew monarch.

In the dreary wilderness of the Koran, which by comparison with the glorious literature of the Old Testament remains an eternal monument of the inferiority of the Arab to the Hebrew genius, we read how Solomon tested the discernment of the Queen of Sheba by overlaying his court of audience with glass, and how the Queen of Sheba, falling into the trap, mistook the glass for water and drew up her skirts to wade through it.[2] Later Arab tradition has not unnaturally dwelt by predilection on the visit of a native Arab princess to the wise king at Jerusalem, and has adorned or disfigured the simple theme by many fanciful details. Among the rest it enlarges on the trivial incident of the glassy pavement. Envious or malignant demons had whispered, so it is alleged, in Solomon's ear that the Queen had hairy legs or the feet of an ass, and in order to prove or disprove the truth of the accusation the sage king resorted to the expedient of the crystal floor. When the Queen raised her skirts to wade through the imaginary water, Solomon saw that the story of her deformity was a vile calumny, and, his too susceptible heart receiving a strong impression of her charms, he added her to the numerous ladies of his harem.[3] At Jerusalem the legend is told to this day, and the very spot where the incident happened is pointed out. It is a few yards within the gate called Bâb el Asbât, or the Gate of the Tribes, the only gateway now left open in the eastern wall of the city. Here down to the summer of 1906 there stood an old bath house, which dated from the days of the Saracens, but which, according to tradition, had been built by King Solomon for the use of the Queen of Sheba.[4]

The deception of the crystal pavement occurs also as an incident in the great Indian epic, the *Mahabharata*. We there read how on one occasion the dull-witted king Duryodhana mistook a sheet of crystal for a sheet of water, and tucked up his skirts to wade through it; how another time he on the contrary mistook a lake of crystal water for dry land, and fell splash into it with all his clothes on, to the amusement of the spectators and even of his own servants; how he tried to pass through a crystal door, which he supposed to be open, but knocked his brow against its hard surface till his head ached and his brains reeled; and how after this painful experience, he came to an open door, but turned away from it, because he feared to encounter the obstruction of crystal again.[5]

Despite the resemblance between the two stories in the Koran and the *Mahabharata,* neither the prophet nor the poet can well have copied directly the one from the other, the prophet because he did not read Sanskrit, and the poet because he died before the prophet was born. If they did not both draw independently from the well-spring of fancy an incident, for the creation of which an imagination less than Miltonic might conceivably have sufficed, they may have borrowed it from a popular tale which circulated alike in the bazaars of India and the tents of Arabia. ▼

154 Hand withers for impiety   13:4

An ecstatic ("man of God") appears at Bethel and denounces the pagan practices of Jeroboam. The king stretches out his hand to lay hold of him, but it withers.

This is a common motif in later Christian legend. In the apocryphal Infancy gospel, Salome doubts the virgin birth of Jesus, whereupon her hand withers. She is cured only when an angel descends from heaven and when she touches the child's swaddling bands.[1] Similarly, when Aurelius (270 C.E.) ordered St. Vitus, then only twelve years old, to be scourged for worshiping Christ, both the lictor's and his own hand withered, though the latter was subsequently healed by the saint.[2] So too it is related of the Empress Eudoxia (c. 400 C.E.) that she once tried to force her way into the cathedral at Constantinople after Chrysostom had expressly barred her from it and ordered it shut and bolted in her face. The soldier who, at her command, raised his ax to burst open the doors found his arm paralyzed. Only when the empress withdrew did Chrysostom heal him.[3]

Elijah

155　The "man of God"

Elijah is described as a *man of God*.[1] So are Moses,[2] Samuel,[3] and Elisha,[4] as well as the anonymous messengers of Yahweh who come to Eli at Shiloh,[5] to Jeroboam at Bethel,[6] and to the parents of Samson.[7] The term does not refer, as in modern speech, to piety or devotion, but characterizes men subject to suprasensuous experiences;[8] it is virtually the equivalent of *shaman,* and it is significant that in the cases of Elijah and Elisha it is applied to them in connection with quasi-magical performances on their part.

In precisely the same way, the Hittites used the expression "man of the gods" to denote one who was crazed or who possessed the mantic powers of a soothsayer,[9] and a verb formed from the word "god" signified this type of "possession."[10] The Arabs likewise called a mantic "he of Allah";[11] while the Greeks spoke of him as "one with a god inside him"[12] or as "one seized by a god."[13] So too among the Japanese, the victim of a hypnotic trance is known as "one to whom a god has attached himself";[14] and in the language of the Quiché of Peru, "the word *huaca* is the most general term for the divine, but *huaca runa,* "divine man," means "one who is crazy."[15]

(It should be observed that the Hebrew expression does not really mean "man of God"—with a capital G—but simply one possessed by the supernormal. In the same way, the Suffering Servant of Isaiah who is said, in the usual rendering, to be "smitten of God" [53:4] is simply one who has been plagued by demonic influences—what the Arabs would call "jinn-struck" [*majnun*].)

▲ 156　Elijah and the Ravens　　　　　　　　　　17:2–6

According to the Hebrew historian, the first mission entrusted by God to the prophet Elijah was to go to Ahab, king of Israel, and announce to him that neither dew nor rain should fall on the land for several years. But having discharged his divine commission, the ambassador of the deity was not left to perish in the long drought. For the word of the Lord came to him, saying, "Get thee hence, and turn thee eastward, and hide thyself by the brook Cherith, that is before Jordan. And it shall be, that thou shalt drink of the brook; and I have commanded the ravens to feed thee there." So Elijah went and dwelt by the brook Cherith, that is before Jordan. And the ravens brought him bread and flesh in the morning, and bread and flesh in the evening; and he drank of the brook. But it came to pass after a while that the brook dried up, because there was no rain in the land.

The brook Cherith has been identified with the Wady Kelt, which descends eastward from the highlands of Judea and opens out on the plain of the Jordan not far from Jericho. The glen is one of the wildest and most romantic in Palestine. It is a tremendous gorge cleft through the mountains, shut in by sheer precipices, and so narrow that the bottom scarcely measures twenty yards across. There the stream forces its way through brakes of cane, rushes, and oleanders, the strip of verdure contrasting with the nakedness of the rocky walls on all sides. In its depth and narrowness the ravine reminds the traveller of the famous defile which leads through the red cliffs to Petra. A magnificent view into the glen is obtained from some points on the road which leads down from Jerusalem into the valley of the Jordan. After traversing for hours the almost total desolation which marks that long descent through the bare, torrent-furrowed limestone hills, the wayfarer is refreshed by the sight of the green thread far below, and by the murmurous sound of water which comes up, even on autumn days after the parching drought of summer, from the depths of the profound ravine. Peering over the giddy brink he may see ravens, eagles, and huge griffon-vultures wheeling beneath him.[1]

To this wild solitude, where water seldom fails throughout the year, the prophet Elijah may well have retired to live out the years of drought which he foresaw and foretold, and there he may have tarried with no neighbours but the wild beasts and the wild birds.

[The story of the helpful (or grateful) birds who bring food to a man (especially a hero) in distress is a favorite of popular literature in many lands.[1a] Achaemenes, the ancestor of the Persian kings, is said to have been nurtured by an eagle;[1b] and of Semiramis, the wife of Ninus, mythical founder of Nineveh, it is related that she was fed in childhood by doves until found by the shepherd Simmas.[1c] Ptolemy I and his mother Arsinoe are two others who are reputed to have been succored by an eagle after they had been exposed to die;[1d] and according to Ovid, Romulus and Remus were fed by a woodpecker when the wolf failed them.[1e] In Indic myth, the beauteous Sakuntala, abandoned in a forest after birth, is tended by birds.[1f]

The theme appears frequently in legends of Christian saints.[1g] St. Catherine, imprisoned by Maxentius, is fed for twelve days by a dove.[1h] St. Vitus, fleeing the persecution of the Christians in Sicily (303), is fed on the way to Naples by an eagle.[1i] St. Peter, the hermit of the Lower Thebaid (341), is fed daily for sixty years by a crow.[1j] St. Auxentius is fed daily at Sinope by a pigeon.[1k] St. Cuthbert (7th cent.) is fed by rooks on the isle of Farne.[1l]]

There was, however, a special propriety in the employment of ravens to minister to the prophet in the wilderness; for the raven has often been regarded as a bird of omen and even as itself endowed with prophetic power. [Indeed, the expression, "to have the foresight of a raven," was proverbial in the British Isles.[1m] Examples of this belief are legion. A Babylonian magician, for example, advises King Esarhaddon (680–69 B.C.) that it presages ill if a raven flies into a house carrying something in its bill;[1n] while an ancient Mesopotamian manual of divination says that if a raven croaks when an army is setting out, this betokens coming defeat.[1o]] The Greeks, for their part, deemed the bird sacred to Apollo, the god of prophecy, and Greek augurs drew omens from its croaking;[2] [while one of Aesop's fables relates that the goddess Athene came to hate it because she grew jealous of its prophetic powers.[2a]] Persons who sought the gift of divination, says Porphyry, used to eat the hearts of ravens, believing that they thus acquired the bird's prophetic soul.[3] The Romans credited the raven with the ability to foretell rain and storm. [Vergil, for instance, records the belief that a raven, stalking up and down on the sands and croaking, was calling for rain.[3a] Similarly, Horace called it a "water-augur,"[3b] and Aelian, writing in the second century C.E., says that it foretells tempests.[3c]]

In European folklore the raven is preeminently an omen of death and misfortune. [There are several allusions to this in English literature.[3d] Lady Macbeth exclaims in a famous passage,

> The raven himself is hoarse
> That croaks the fatal entrance of Duncan
> Under my battlements;[3e]

and in Butler's *Hudibras* the question is put:

> Is it not om'nous in all countries
> When crows and ravens croak on trees?[3f]

The bird was particularly ill-omened if it croaked directly over a housetop. Says John Gay in his pastoral, *The Dirge:*

> And with hoarse croakings warn'd us of our fate;[3g]
> The boding raven on her cottage sat,

and in Shakespeare's *Othello* occur the lines:

> it comes in my memory
> As doth the raven, o'er the infected house,
> Boding to all.[3h]

Nor is this notion confined to Europe. It is attested equally in Australia[31] and in America,[3j] while] the Lillooet Indians of British Columbia imagine that he who has a raven for his guardian spirit possesses the gift of prophecy.[4]

The sagacity and solemn deportment of this sable bird may have had much to do with throwing a glamour of mystery and sanctity about it. According to an eminent authority the raven is "probably the most highly developed of all birds. Quick-sighted, sagacious, and bold, it must have followed the prehistoric fisher and hunter, and generally without molestation from them, to prey on the refuse of their spoils, just as it now waits, with the same intent, on the movements of their successors; while it must have likewise attended the earliest herdsmen, who could not have regarded it with equal indifference, since its now notorious character for attacking and putting to death a weakly animal was doubtless in those days manifested. Yet the raven is no mere dependent upon man, being always able to get a living for itself; and, moreover, a sentiment of veneration or superstition has from very remote ages and among many races of men attached to it—a sentiment so strong as often to overcome the feeling of distrust not to say of hatred which its deeds inspired, and, though rapidly decreasing, even to survive in some places until the present time."[5]

Pliny tells a story which strikingly illustrates the veneration in which the raven was popularly held at Rome, when Rome was at the height of her glory. Under the reign of Tiberius it happened that a pair of ravens had built their nest on the roof of the temple of Castor and Pollux. One of the young birds in time flew down, stalked into a shoemaker's shop, and took up its quarters there, the shoemaker not venturing to molest a creature which he looked upon with religious awe, partly perhaps for its own sake and partly for the sake of the holy place where it had been hatched. Every morning the sagacious bird flew out of the shop, perched on the rostra in the forum, and there in a distinct voice saluted the emperor and his two sons, Drusus and Germanicus, by name, after which he greeted in an affable manner the people passing to their business. Having discharged these offices of civility he returned to the shop. This he continued to do regularly for many years, till at last another shoemaker in the neighbourhood killed the bird, either out of spite, as was suspected, at the custom which the raven brought to his rival, or, as the shoemaker himself alleged, in a fit of passion because the bird had befouled the shoes in his shop. Whatever his motive, it was a bad day's work for him; for the people, thunderstruck at the death of their old favourite, rose in their wrath, drove the corbicidal shoemaker from his shop, and never rested till they had the miscreant's blood. As for the dead raven, it received a public funeral, which was attended by thousands. The bier was supported on the shoulders of two Ethiopians as black as the corpse they carried; a flute-player marched in front discoursing solemn music, while wreaths of flowers of all sorts, carried in the procession, testified to the general respect and sorrow for the deceased. In this impressive manner the funeral cortege made its way to the pyre, which had been erected two miles out on the Appian Way. The historian concludes by remarking that the bird received a grander funeral than many a prince before him, and that the death of the fowl was more signally avenged than the murder of Scipio Africanus.[6]

Among the qualities which have procured for the raven a certain degree of popular veneration may be its power of imitating the human voice. That power is attested not only by Pliny's anecdote but by modern writers. Thus Oliver Goldsmith affirms that "a raven may be reclaimed to almost every purpose to which birds can be converted. He may be trained up for fowling like an hawk; he may be taught to fetch and carry like a spaniel; he may be taught to speak like a parrot; but the most extraordinary of all is, that he can be taught to sing like a man. I have heard a raven sing the Black Joke with great distinctness, truth, and humour."[7] And Yarrell, in his *History of British Birds,* writes, "Among British birds, the power of imitating the sounds of the human voice is possessed in the greatest perfection by the raven, the magpie, the jay, and the starling. In proof of this power in the raven, many anecdotes might be repeated; the two following, derived from unquestionable authorities, are perhaps less known than many others: 'Ravens have been taught to articulate short sentences as distinctly as any parrot. One, belonging to Mr. Henslow, of St. Alban's, speaks so distinctly that, when we first heard it, we were actually deceived in thinking it was a human voice: and there is another at Chatham which has made equal proficiency; for, living within the vicinity of a guard-house, it has more than once turned out the guard, who thought they were called by the sentinel on duty.' "[8]

It is possible, too, that the raven's habit of preying on the human dead may have helped to invest it with an atmosphere of mystery and awe; for as savages commonly suppose that they themselves can acquire the desirable properties of the dead by eating some part of their corpses, so they may have imagined that birds of prey, which batten on the slain, absorb thereby the wisdom and other qualities which the dead men possessed in their lifetime. This suggestion is supported by the analogy of the superstitious veneration in which the hyena is held by many tribes of East Africa; it appears to arise in large measure from the custom, which these tribes observe, of exposing their dead to be devoured by hyenas. For example, the Nandi, who follow that practice, hold hyenas in great respect, and believe that the animals talk like human beings and converse with the spirits of the dead. When several children in one family have died, the parents will place a newly-born babe for a few minutes in a path along which hyenas are known to walk, hoping that the brutes will intercede for the child with the spirits of the dead and induce them to spare its life. If such a child lives, it receives the name of Hyena.[9] Similarly the Bagesu and the Wanyamwesi, two other tribes of East Africa who throw out their dead to be devoured by hyenas, regard these animals as sacred and often take the cry of a hyena in the evening to be the voice of the last person who died in the neighbourhood. The Wanyamwesi say that they could not kill a hyena, because they do not know whether the creature might not be a relation of theirs, an aunt, a grandmother, or what not.[10] These beliefs appear to imply that the souls of the dead are reborn in the hyenas which devour their bodies. Thus the practice of exposing the dead, combined with the belief in the transmigration of human souls into animal bodies, may suffice to establish an imaginary kinship between men and beasts and birds of prey, such as hyenas, eagles, vultures, and ravens. How far its predatory habits have contributed to surround the raven in particular with that degree of respect which it enjoys among the vulgar, is a question which might be worth considering.

[Otto Gruppe has suggested,[10a] however, that the specification of ravens as the succorers of Elijah has in fact quite a different explanation. The raven, he says, is simply a substitute for the *eagle* who, at least in Greek legend, was believed to be the purveyor of celestial ambrosia. It was on such food that, in the original form of the story, the prophet was nourished. If it be asked why specifically the raven was substituted, the answer may lie in the fact that this bird appears to obtrude itself on the attention of the traveler all over the desolate region, from Jerusalem to the Dead Sea, in which the Biblical story plays.

Yet a third possibility is that the raven was specified because of a belief that it was especially adept at bringing succor in thirsty climes, seeing that, according to Classical writers, it reared its own young in the hottest and driest period of the year.[10b]

At all events, whichever explanation be adopted, the prevalence of the story in so many different parts of the world sufficiently disposes of the prosaic suggestion advanced by some Biblical scholars that the Hebrew word '*orebim,* "ravens," should really be read '*Arabim,* "Arabs"![10c]] ▼

157 "Measuring" the sick   17:7–24

Elijah revives the dead son of the woman of Zarephath by placing him on his own bed and then stretching himself out upon him thrice.

The same story is told, with significant variations, about Elisha (II Kings 4:32–37). There the prophet not only stretches himself upon the child, but also "places his mouth upon its mouth, his eyes upon its eyes, and his hands upon its hands" until "the flesh of the child becomes warm."

The Hebrew word rendered "stretched himself out" means literally "measured himself." Two ideas appear to be combined. The first is that a sick or dead person can be cured or revived by having the "essence" of a numinous or holy being superimposed upon him. This is, *au fond,* an extreme expression of the notion which underlies the touching of or by a holy man, or of the king's curing scrofula by touch.¹ Analogous too is the old German usage whereby pregnant women used to measure a wick around a saint's image and then tie it round their own bodies.²

The other idea is that the measuring of a sick person effects a cure. This also may be illustrated from old German lore. In the medieval Bîhtebuch, the confessant is asked whether he has ever allowed himself to be measured by witches; while in the Liegnitz district old women called "measurers" (Messerinnen) used to measure people from head to foot to see whether they had consumption.³ The basic notion underlies our own popular expression, "to take a man's measure, size him up."

Note also the threefold repetition of the action—a characteristic feature of magical procedures,⁴ as also of folktales.⁵

(It should be observed that in the Elisha version of the story the point of the prophet's action has been forgotten, and the writer substitutes for the term "stretched himself out" the more neutral "bent over." The ancient Greek (Septuagint) translators were likewise unaware of the true import, for they substituted for the crucial word the simpler, "he *breathed into* (ἐνεφύσησεν) the child.")

158 The confrontation on Carmel 18

For several months the soil had suffered a severe drought. Elijah, the prophet of the LORD (Yahweh), seized the opportunity to discredit the growing faith in Baal, the Canaanite god of rain. He therefore staged a dramatic "competition" on Mt. Carmel between the latter's priests and himself. Each party was to erect altars, offer sacrifices, and call on its god with appropriate rites. The god who answered by consuming the sacrifice by fire from heaven would be the winner.

The pagan priests went through their accustomed ritual, gashing themselves with knives until their blood flowed and performing a limping dance about the altar, while they cried loudly, "Baal, answer us!" Nothing happened. It was then Elijah's turn. The prophet erected an altar made out of twelve stones. Then he dug a trench around it and filled it with water poured from twelve vessels. This done, he taunted his antagonists by bidding them call "in a loud voice" because their god might perchance be asleep or away or otherwise preoccupied. Finally, he offered the sacrifice. Fire descended miraculously from heaven, and the multitude shouted, "Yahweh—He is the god!"

Few stories in the Old Testament can be more amply illustrated by Comparative Folklore and Religion than that of the contest between Elijah and the prophets of Baal on Mt. Carmel. What is involved in this incident is, essentially, a competition in rain-making during a period of drought. Each side employs standard, established rain-making techniques, but by the time the traditional story came to be written down, the true significance of these techniques had long been forgotten. It is only by their recurrence elsewhere that we are now able to recover it and thus to reconstruct the incident as it may really have occurred.

(a) Baal

The first thing to observe, then, is that Baal, the rival of Yahweh, to whom the pagan prophets address themselves, is not just a vague and general god of the heathen. To the Canaanites he was specifically the *god of rainfall*. In the *Poem of Baal,* discovered at Ras Shamra-Ugarit (14th cent. B.C.), it is said expressly that when the furrows of the fields are parched, it is because Baal has been neglecting his duty or is absent from the earth;[1] while in the same poem, when the supreme god El grants permission to Baal to have a palace of his own, he expresses the hope that thenceforth Baal will send his rains at appropriate seasons, and not merely by caprice.[2] Again, in the Ugaritic *Poem of Aqhat,* when King Daniel learns of the murder of his son, he prays that Baal may withhold his rains from the polluted soil.[3] The Arabic writer Bukhari defines "land of Baal" as "soil watered by fountains or clouds";[4] while in the Jewish Mishnah "field of Baal" is cited as a popular designation of land watered by rain rather than by artificial irrigation.[5]

> That there was indeed an ancient sanctuary on Carmel is suggested by the fact that even in later Roman times it was still regarded as a traditional holy place.[6] Tacitus tells us that Carmel was the name of a god as well as of a mountain,[7] and his statement is confirmed by the discovery there, in recent years, of a stone foot dedicated to Zeus Heliopoleites Carmelos—clearly a Hellenized form of the more ancient local deity.[8] Similarly, Suetonius says that in the days of Vespasian, the mountain was the seat of an oracle;[9] and the neo-Platonic philosopher Jamblichus, writing in the reign of Constantine, characterizes it as "sacred above all mountains and out-of-bounds to the vulgar."[10]

(b) The fire upon the altar

The proof of whether Yahweh or Baal is the true god lies in which of them answers his suppliants by sudden, unlit fire upon the altar.

Gods are, to a large extent, personifications of what *we* would call natural forces. Lambent fire of unknown origin was therefore regarded as a manifestation of their presence. It was in this form, for instance, that the deity revealed himself both to Gudea, governor (*ensi*) of the Sumerian city of Lagash,[11] and to Moses.[12] The mysterious appearance of so-called "automatic fire" on an altar was therefore considered in antiquity a token of divine favor.[13] Pausanias tells us that when Seleucus, together with Alexander, offered sacrifice to Zeus at Pella, the wood on the altar blazed automatically,[14] and he reports also that at Hierocaesarea, in Lydia, he himself saw upon an altar ashes which burst into flame when priests prayed over them.[15] Valerius Maximus mentions a similar "miracle" at Egnatia,[16] and in one of Vergil's Eclogues, a sudden blaze upon an altar is deemed an auspicious omen.[17] Conversely, the extinction of altar-fire was taken to indicate the withdrawal of the god or goddess.[18]

The production of such fire by hocus-pocus was, we are told, part of the stock-in-trade of ancient magicians. Pausanias says that it was a common feature of Iranian magic,[19] and other Classical writers declare that it was a common trick on the part of profane conjurers.[20] Maximus, for example, is said to have made a statue of Hecate laugh and to have caused the torches in her hands to light up automatically.[21] On a more exalted level, Caesarius von Heisterbach attributes similar feats to several Christian saints.[22] It has therefore been suggested by some scholars that Elijah practiced a similar feint, surreptitiously substituting naphtha (kindled by the sun or by a concealed mirror) for the water which he is said to have poured over the altar![23] Sober readers, however, will scarcely be fired by this suggestion; one might as well try to identify botanically the species of beanstalk which Jack climbed! Moreover, it has been shrewdly pointed out that, since Elijah performed *in the late afternoon*, the sun would in any case scarcely have been strong enough to work such a trick.[24]

(c) The limping dance and the gashing with knives

> *After dressing the altar, the priests of Baal commence their performance by limping beside* (KJV, wrongly: *leaping upon*) *it. Then they gash themselves with knives, "as was their wont," until the blood flows.*

The prophets of Baal were performing a type of ritual dance which is attested also from other sources. Heliodorus (3rd cent. B.C.), in his romance *Aethiopica,* describes how Tyrian seafarers performed a dance of "hops and skips" in honor of the local god, "Heracles," i.e., Melqarth. "They now jumped with light leaps," he says, "and now limped along on the ground."[25] His account is doubly pertinent to our theme, because the cult of Baal, against which Elijah was contending, appears to have been promoted in Israel especially by Jezebel, the Tyrian princess whom King Ahab had married. Again, from Deir al Qaʻla, near Beirut, comes an inscription of the third century B.C. which mentions specifically a "Baal of the Skipping Dance" (*Baʻal marqôd*);[26] while Herodian, the historian of the Roman Empire, paints a graphic picture of the Emperor Heliogabalus (218–22 C.E.) executing a dance around the altar of his god at Emesa (Homs), in Syria.[27]

The custom is also known elsewhere. In modern Palestine, for instance, Arabs sometimes dance and leap with bent knees as a means of magically producing rain;[28] while on a curious bas-relief found at Aricia (La Riccia), near Rome, men and women are depicted "tripping the light fantastic" in the

Romanized cult of Isis.[29] Analogous procedures are reported also from India[30] and Iceland.[31]

The limping dance was, as we have seen (above, §**129**), associated especially with *funeral ceremonies,* and it is thus that it is to be interpreted also in the present instance. We now know, from the mythological poems discovered at Ras Shamra-Ugarit, that when drought beset the land, it was popularly believed that Baal had sunk into the netherworld, and the cry went up, *"Baal is dead!"*[32]

It is likewise as a *funeral rite* for Baal that we should understand the concomitant action of his prophets, when they "gashed themselves with knives and lancets, as was their wont, until the blood gushed out upon them." Such laceration was and still is a common rite of mourning in many parts of the world, its primary purpose being to revivify the deceased.

The practice was common in cults revolving around the figure of a dying and reviving god of fertility.[33] Herodotus tells us, for example, that as a part of the worship of Osiris in the Egyptian city of Busiris, "at the conclusion of the sacrifice, the whole crowd, men and women alike, proceed to beat themselves in honor of the god . . . while the Carian element of the population go even further, gashing their faces with knives."[34] Similarly, when Lucian of Samosata (2nd cent. C.E.) describes the rites performed at the temple of "the Syrian Goddess" at Hierapolis (Membij), he makes a point of telling us that "on certain days a crowd flocks into the temple, and the sacred eunuchs (*galli*) in great number perform "the ceremony of men" (i.e., castrate themselves) and gash their arms."[35]

As is well known, orgiastic cults of this type, imported largely from Asia Minor, attained something of a vogue in Rome from the dawn of the Imperial Age onward, and Roman authors frequently allude to this characteristic practice of laceration.[36] Particularly lurid is the description given by the poet Tibullus, who says of the exotic priestess of such a cult:

> Frenzied, with battle-ax she rends her arms,
> And o'er the image of the goddess sheds
> Her streaming blood, unheeding. There she stands,
> The blade plung'd in her side, her bosom torn.[37]

Similarly, his contemporary, Propertius, poses the agonizing question:

> Why should any man with sacred spear
> Gash his own arms and tear his flesh to shreds,
> The while those mad, wild Phrygian cries ring out?[38]

while Statius (c. 61–96 C.E.) compares the melee of battle, with its clashing spears and freely flowing blood, to an orgy in the cult of the Asianic Mother-goddess, when her devotees pour pell-mell out of her temple, gashing their arms in frenzy.[39]

In such ceremonies, however, it is also possible that the shedding of blood served quite a different purpose. As we have seen (above, §**144**), drought and blight were popularly regarded as the consequence of misconduct. Hence, as Pettazzoni has suggested, the underlying idea may have been to eliminate "sin" from the inner man along with the discharge of his blood, i.e., his contaminated vital essence. Blood-letting for this purpose actually obtains in the Malaccas, among the Bechuanas of South Africa, the Yuchi Indians of California, the Aztecs and Totonacs of Mexico, in Nicaragua, Guatemala, Peru, and China, and it is attested also in ancient Greece.[40]

Again, it should not be overlooked that in some parts of the world, bloodletting is an act of imitative magic, to produce rain.[41] In Java, for instance, people thrash themselves in times of drought until the blood flows,[42] and in Eggibiu, a region of Ethiopia, they stage sanguinary conflicts to the same end.[43]

(d) Elijah's taunts

> *The prophets of Baal receive no response from him. Thereupon Elijah taunts them, bidding them, "Cry aloud, for he is a god. Maybe he is engaged or busy,[44] or on a journey; maybe he is asleep, and will wake."*

There is a subtle point in these taunts, and Comparative Folklore brings it out. *Elijah is deliberately satirizing certain standard pagan procedures.* Thus, when he urges his opponents to "cry loudly," he is mocking the practice of magically promoting thunderstorms (and hence rainfall) by imitating its loud noise. In many parts of the world, for instance, bull-roarers are used for this purpose;[45] the Zuñi of Mexico also crack whips,[46] and at Tartu, in Estonia, men rattle kettles and bang with hammers.[47] Similarly, when Elijah bids the prophets of Baal to arouse the god because he may be asleep, he is taking a sly dig at the custom in pagan temples of awakening the god each morning or in times of distress.[48] "Awake, O Judge!" says an Egyptian pyramid text of the third millennium B.C., "Rouse thyself. O Thoth! Awake, ye sleepers! Awake, ye that dwell in Kenset!"[49] and Porphyry tells us that the ceremony of waking the god was part of the Egyptian daily ritual even in Roman times.[50] At Delphi, the Greek Dionysus was similarly roused by the Thyades,[51] as was Bacchus at Rome.[52] Nor indeed was the usage unknown to the Hebrews themselves; Yahweh was roused daily in the Second Temple by an order of priests called "awakeners" ($m^{e‘}ôr^{e}rîm$), who chanted the words, "Awake, Lord! Why sleepest thou?" (Ps. 44:23),[53] and thrice in the Psalms, Yahweh is bidden "Awake!"[54] At Tyre there was an annual ceremony of awakening the god "Herakles" (i.e., Melqarth) in the month of Peritios;[55] and it has been suggested that an official called "he who makes the god stand up" (*m-q-m i-l-m*), who is mentioned in connection with various Phoenician temples, was really the priest who roused him every morning.⁵⁶

The general tenor of Elijah's taunts, it may be added, finds a striking parallel in a passage of the *Deipnosophistae* (Banquet of the Learned) by the Greek grammarian, Athenaeus (c. 230 C.E.). "When," we read, "Demetrius Poliorketes returned to Athens from Leucas and Corcyra, the Athenians welcomed him with an extraordinary ovation . . . dancing and singing praises to the effect that he was the only true god, whereas the others were asleep or away from home or had no ears."⁵⁷

(e) Rain-stones

> It is now Elijah's turn. He first takes twelve stones and with them builds an altar to Yahweh. Then, after dressing that altar, and digging a trench around it, he orders twelve barrel-fulls of water to be poured over it. The water also fills the trench.

The Biblical writer explains the prophet's action as the renovation of an altar of Yahweh which had been overthrown, and interprets the twelve stones as symbolic of the twelve tribes of Israel. Comparative Folklore suggests, however, that this is simply an *interpretatio israelitica* of a more ancient practice.

"Stones," says Frazer in *The Golden Bough*,⁵⁸ "are often supposed to possess the property of bringing on rain, provided they be dipped in water or sprinkled with it. . . . In a Samoan village a certain stone was carefully housed as the representative of the rain-making god, and in time of drought his priests carried the stone in procession and dipped it in a stream. . . ."⁵⁹ At Sagami in Japan there is a stone which draws down rain whenever water is poured on it.⁶⁰ In Behar people think to put an end to drought by keeping a holy stone named Narayan-chakra in a vessel of water. . . ."⁶¹ At Barenton, Breton peasants used, when they needed rain, to draw water from a special fountain and pour it over a slab.⁶² "On Snowdon, . . . a row of stepping-stones runs out into the Black Lake (Dulyn), and if anyone steps on the stones and throws water so as to wet the farthest stone, which is called the Red Altar, 'it is but a chance that you do not get rain before night, even when it is hot weather.' "⁶³ At Uskub, in Turkey, in a time of drought, both Christians and Moslems set up a fallen altar of Jupiter Optimus Maximus and poured wine over it.⁶⁴ Analogous procedures are reported also from Africa, India, and Mexico.⁶⁵ Often, too, the ceremony has been transmogrified into the Christian rite of dipping the statue of a saint in water.

It has been suggested that the celebrated *lapis manalis* at Rome was originally such a "rain-stone" and came later to be integrated with the cult of Jupiter in order to give sanction to traditional prayers and sacrifices associated with it.⁶⁶ According to Pliny, the theory underlying the use of "rain-stones" was that they housed the rain-spirit, and that the latter could be "manipulated" by inciting or influencing other spirits who were resident there.

The selection of *twelve* stones need originally have had no reference to the twelve tribes of Israel, for twelve is often used as a round number in ancient rituals.

The ritualistic twelve appears again in the twelve barrels of water poured over the stones, and here the major religious character of the procedure comes out even more clearly in the fact that the aspersion is made in *three* installments, such threefold iteration ("holy, holy, holy") being commonplace in such cases.

(f) The filling of the trench with water

This may likewise be interpreted as a procedure designed to procure water for the parched soil, for it possesses an arresting parallel in an ancient custom performed both in Syria and in Greece to the same end. When the ground was dry, it was believed that the waters of the subterranean ocean, which normally welled up in the form of springs, had disappeared down a crevice; by pouring more water into a ditch, they could be made to rise and overflow.[67] The custom is mentioned by Lucian as having been performed twice yearly in the temple of the Syrian Goddess at Hierapolis (Membij). The water, he says, was brought from the sea and poured out within the sacred precincts. It passed down into a chasm, identified in local myth with that which had received the waters of the Deluge.[68] A similar procedure has been witnessed in recent times at Tyre,[69] and it has been suggested that this was also the real purport of a strange rite performed by the Greeks on the last day of the Mysteries at Eleusis. "They fill two vessels (*plēmochoai*)," says the grammarian Athenaeus, "and, turning with one towards the east, and with the other towards the west, recite over them a ritual formula." The rite, he adds, was mentioned in the now lost Cretans of Euripides, where it was said expressly that the contents of the vessels were poured into a "chasm of the earth."[70]

(g) Elijah on the summit of Carmel

> *After the fire had duly fallen upon the altar of Yahweh, and the assembled multitudes have therefore acknowledged him as the true god, Elijah repairs, accompanied only by his servant, to the top of the mountain. There he "bows himself to the ground and puts his face between his knees." Six times he bids his servant look out to sea, but each time the lad brings back word, "There is nothing." The seventh time, however, he reports: "Behold, a little cloud is rising from the sea, like a man's hand." Presently the heavens lower, and rain falls.*

To put one's head between one's knees would normally suggest a gesture of despondency, and the expression indeed occurs in this sense both in Egyptian[71] and in Ugaritic.[72] Elijah, however, has just scored an impressive triumph, and it is therefore difficult to see why he should be in despair. Accordingly, it may be suggested—albeit with reserve—that what he really did was to adopt a posture of divinatory trance, for this may be illustrated by the fact that to this day just such a posture is characteristic of fetish-women in Guinea during the act of divination.[73]

(h) The raincloud

The comparison of the raincloud to a man's hand finds an interesting parallel in Finnish and Estonian folklore, where a thundercloud is envisaged as "a little man with a copper hand who, rising from the water, becomes a giant."[74]

159 The ascension of Elijah

> *Elijah and his disciple Elisha are walking beside the Jordan. Suddenly they are parted from each other by a fiery chariot driven by fiery horses. Elijah is caught up in a stormwind and raised to heaven. He vanishes from Elisha's sight.*

This is simply a Hebrew version of the well-known folktale of the *Wild Hunt* (E 501), the gist of which is that a deity or famous historical character rides across the sky on stormy nights, or appears in moments of crisis, accompanied by a ghostly troop of followers. In Teutonic folklore, the host is usually known as the *wütendes Heer,* or Wild Host, but this is simply a popular corruption of *Wotan's Heer,* i.e., the army of Wotan, or Odin. An earlier form of it has been seen by some scholars in the bacchic routs of Artemis and Dionysus in Greek belief, for these are sometimes said to be celestial.[1]—Tales of the Wild Hunt are ubiquitous, and it would be tedious to cite them in detail. It is, however, especially pertinent that the Hunt often appears as an army of old soldiers who "never die, but simply fade away."[2] Dio Halicarnassus, for example, speaks of it specifically as a "celestial *army,*"[3] and it is so designated also in Spanish tradition. Indeed, it is in this form that it is said to have been seen near Worms in 1098,[4] at the siege of Byzantium by Philip II of France in 1204,[5] and at the battle of Mons in World War I (Aug. 23, 1914).—Arthur of Britain is reported so to have appeared at various times in the forests of Brittany, in Savoy, in parts of Scotland, and—as late as the nineteenth century—at Cadbury Castle, in Somerset.[6]—In Germany, similar tales are told about Rupprecht and other national heroes.[7]

All the characteristic details of the Wild Hunt occur in our Biblical narrative. Thus (a) it is often said to appear beside a body of water[8] as here it appears beside the River Jordan—a notion evidently derived from the rising of mists from rivers, lakes, and marshes. (b) It is usually accompanied by a chariot or wagon.[9] (c) It exhales fire, is wreathed in fire, and leaves a trail of sparks.¹⁰ (d) It appears on stormy nights, is heralded by a storm, and disappears in a storm, or in a sudden blast of wind.¹¹

When Elijah disappears, Elisha exclaims: *My father, my father! the chariots of Israel and the horsemen thereof!* In these words the Biblical writer merely works in a standard cliché, for exactly the same expression is employed also by King Joash when Elisha himself falls sick (II Kings 13:14). In both of their present contexts, the words clearly mean no more than that the hero in question is tantamount in power and prowess to an entire protective army;¹² but it may be suggested that originally they possessed quite a different meaning and were intended to identify the ghostly chariot and horses as those of Jacob—the ancestral hero of the Israelites.¹³ The expression, *My father, my father,* would then be simply an exclamation of surprise or alarm, exactly like the Arabic *ya abu, ya abu,* commonly employed in this way.¹⁴

Combined with that of the Wild Hunt is the equally familiar motif of the *translation of a hero to heaven.*¹⁵—The god Mithra, for instance, was said to have been borne aloft in the chariot of the sun after his earthly mission had been fulfilled.¹⁶—Hercules, too, was believed to have ascended in a cloud from his funeral pyre;¹⁷ and Roman emperors were held to ride with the Sun-god after death. A papyrus from Egypt has Phoebus announce the death of Trajan by saying, "I have just ridden with Trajan in a chariot drawn by white horses";¹⁸ and even on the tombs of very humble persons a chariot is often figured to suggest their lot in the afterlife.¹⁹

160 The mantle of Elijah 19:19

In primitive thought, "clothes makyth man" in a very real sense, since a person's garments are considered not merely as vestments but as part of his essential self. Conferment of them upon another therefore signifies transference of personality. It is, indeed, for this reason that a king is clothed in traditional robes; he inherits a traditional "self."¹

In Morocco, chieftains exchange cloaks or turbans as earnests in concluding covenants; they thereby pledge themselves.² Similarly, one can work magic against a person if one secures even the smallest portion of his clothing, as does Simaetha in Theocritus' famous idyll.³

The belief has curious offshoots. The clothes of the Mikado, for example, are so sacred—that is, so intimately bound up with his divine "self"—that it is fatal for anyone to wear them;⁴ while a man who dons the robes of a Maori chieftain, will face certain death,⁵ just as in Fiji, a similar act of presumption entails a special disease.⁶

Conversely, removal of clothes implies loss of identity or extreme self-abasement. It was for this reason that worshipers often appeared before their gods *in puris naturalibus,* though here the additional factor of possibly contaminating the divine also operates.⁷ It is for this reason too that mourners and penitents doffed their garments, and that divorcees were stripped when dismissed from their husbands.[8] A particularly interesting example of this symbolism occurs in a Jewish anecdote concerning one Rabbi David ben Daniel of Mosul who pronounced a ban (*ḥerem*) on detractors of the philosopher Maimonides. They could clear themselves only if they asked forgiveness at the sage's tomb and deposited their turbans upon it, i.e., symbolically divested themselves of their offending "selves."[9]

The haircloth worn by Elijah[10] was, of course, a characteristic sign of humility. Manu prescribed similarly that the devout should wear garments of cow hair.[11] Buddhist monks are sometimes encouraged to wear rags, and rags[12] were likewise worn in penance in medieval Christendom.[13] Strabo tells us that at Palmetum, in the Suez area, men and women who guarded the sacred grove of palms wore skins.[14]

161 Harlots bathe in Ahab's blood 22:38

The harlots were not merely having fun; they were giving themselves a tonic and probably also, in their estimation, a beauty treatment. "The blood is the life,"[1] and throughout the ages it has been believed that bathing in it can reinvigorate the body and cure afflictions of the skin.[2] Pliny tells us, for instance, that the ancient Egyptians used to bathe in blood as a cure for leprosy or elephantiasis;[3] while from modern India comes the story of a woman who had lost her child and was told by a fakir to bathe daily in a boy's blood in order to ensure that her next would be healthy.[4] In Bechuanaland, the blood of a goat is sprinkled over a sick man to cure him;[5] while among the Caribs a newborn boy is "anointed" with drops of his father's blood so that the latter's vitality and courage may be transmitted to him.[6] Constantine, we are told, desisted from this practice only as the result of a vision; while, on the other hand, in one version of the notorious "blood-libel,"[7] Richard I of England is alleged to have been advised by a Jew to bathe in the blood of a newly slain child in order to gain strength and relieve bodily infirmities.[8] Bathing in the blood of a bull (*taurobolium*) or of a ram (*criobolium*) was also one of the principal rites of regeneration in the so-called Mystery Religions of the Hellenistic age.[9]

The notion is introduced frequently into popular legend and fiction.[10] Thus, in one of the "vampire tales" included in Somadeva's *Ocean of Story* (*Kathasaritsagara*), the Indian princess Mrigenkavati, wife of Sahasranika, asks for a bloodbath to cure her malady;[11] and in the medieval English romance of *Amys and Amylion,* one of those knightly brothers has his two children slain so that their blood may relieve the other of leprosy.[12] In the Arthurian cycle of legends, Galahad is told by the maiden daughter of King Pellinore that in a certain castle lies a lady sick to death who can recover only if she is anointed with the blood of a pure princess;[13] and very much the same thing is related in Longfellow's *Golden Legend* concerning Prince Henry who lies sick of a strange disease in the castle of Vautberg, on the Rhine.[14] A Jewish legend associates the medieval bloodbath with the pharaoh who oppressed the Israelites in Egypt;[15] and the basic motif occurs also in Syrian,[16] Tibetan,[17] German,[18] Italian,[19] and Czech[20] folktales.

Sometimes the regenerative blood is absorbed by *drinking* rather than bathing.[21] The ancient Scythians, for example, mutilated the bodies of fallen foes and drank their blood in order to imbibe their strength;[22] and a medieval chronicler says the same of the Hungarians,[23] while in the *Nibelungenlied* the brave Burgundians so use the blood of the Huns whom they have slain in battle.[24] Similarly, it is recorded that when the Count of Montmorency was put to death at Toulouse in 1632, the troops drank his blood in order to fill their veins with his intrepid valor;[25] and the Iroquois are said to have done likewise when the Jesuit missionary Jean de Brébeuf was martyred by them in 1648.[26] Moreover, even at the present day, the wounded Somali sucks his blood in order to regain his strength,[27] and it is customary among huntsmen in Upper Austria to quaff the blood of a newborn beast so as to acquire what they call "a sturdy breast."[28]

When, in 1483, Louis XI of France lay near to death, he attempted to revive himself by daily draughts of the blood of young children.[29] On the same principle the blood of slain dragons or monsters is credited in legend with medicinal and regenerative properties. Sifrit, it will be remembered, became invulnerable by drinking the blood of Fafnir,[30] and in the German romance of Kudrun, Hagen drinks the blood of a monster whom he has killed; while in a Danish legend an ailing king can be cured only by drinking dragon's blood.[31] In allusion to such legends a well-known Rhenish wine is still called *Drachenblut*.

162 Baal Zebub, "Lord of the Flies" II Kings 1:2, 3, 6, 16

Ahaziah, king of Israel, falls from an upper window of his palace at Samaria. He sends to the heathen god Baal Zebub of Ekron to inquire whether he will live.

The Hebrew word *zebūb* means "fly," but why should Ahaziah send to a Lord of Flies to inquire whether he would recover from sickness?

Scholars have cited in explanation the apparent analogies of the Greek god Zeus *apomyios* (Averter of Flies)[1] and of the demon Myagros (Driver of Flies), worshiped at Aliphora in Arcadia,[2] both of whom were, it is asserted, regarded as averters of pestilence. The apparent analogy, however, is really no analogy at all, for the deities in question were not in fact averters of pestilence in general; they were simply propitiated before sacrifice in order to keep flies away from the altar.[3] Besides, Ahaziah fell from a window; so why, in any case, should he resort to a god who averted plague?

An alternative explanation is, therefore, that Baal Zebub, "Lord of the Flies," was a god who gave oracles through the buzzing of flies. Such an oracle indeed existed—to cite but one arresting example—at the holy well of Kirkmichael in Bannfshire, Scotland.⁴ There seems, however, to be no evidence of such a practice on Semitic soil.

Yet, even if the fly was not an averter of plague or a giver of oracles by means of buzzing, he may well have been a symbol of death and disease, for this idea is widespread both in the ancient world and in modern folklore.⁵ Thus, in the Iranian Avesta, the demon of death (*Naças*) is said to take the form of a fly.⁶ In Greece, Eurynomos, the demon of decay and putrefaction, is similarly portrayed;⁷ and so too is death in several parts of Africa.⁸ In medieval Europe, plague and sickness were commonly represented as flies.⁹ In the French areas of Switzerland, witches are said to send blue flies against men in order to bring death or sickness upon them;¹⁰ while a legend current at St. Gall tells of a beldam who brought death by stinging in the form of a fly.¹¹ In German folklore the Devil its often depicted as a fly;¹² and among the Lapps, Finns, and Norwegians flies are popularly regarded as demons in disguise.¹³

If, however, Ahaziah resorted to Baal Zebub as a god of death, he probably did so only on the basis of a popular etymology of that deity's name. For the god of Ekron was, in all probability, a *Philistine,* not a *Semitic,* deity, so that the word which the Hebrews interpreted as *zebūb,* "fly," would really have been a like-sounding *Philistine* term, of quite different meaning.¹⁴

Elisha

163 Waters purified by salt　　　　　　　　　　　　　　**II Kings 2:19 ff.**

The men of Jericho complain to Elisha that, despite the pleasing location of the city, there is no water and the ground is barren. The prophet fills a new cruse with salt and casts it into a spring. Instantly the waters are "healed."

Contamination is attributed in ancient and primitive thought to the machinations of demons. Salt, being an incorruptible substance, is universally regarded as potent against them.[1] It was for this reason, for instance, that newborn children were commonly "salted" among the Hebrews[2] and Greeks,[3] as they are still by Balkan peasants[4] and by the Todas of Southern India.[5] The Arabs protect children from the evil eye by placing salt in their hands on the eve of the seventh day after birth; the following morning, the midwife or some other woman strews it about, crying, "Salt in the eye of all who look with malice!"[6] The Germans used to put salt under a child's tongue as soon as it was born,[7] and in the Catholic rite of baptism this is still done as a means of exorcizing the Devil. Laotian and Thai women "wash" with salt after childbirth as a protection against demons;[8] and in the northern counties of England a sachet of salt is tucked into a baby's clothing on its first outing.[9] As late as 1946, a couple was arraigned at Trowbridge, Wiltshire, for burning salt over a child in order to stop it from crying. The father attributed the cries to witchcraft, and pleaded in defense that "he felt he had to counteract the evil influences that were around."[10] The basis of such practices lies—in the words of an old writer—in the belief that witches and warlocks, "like their master, the Devil, abhor salt as the emblem of immortality." Indeed, because of its potency against them witches allowed no salt in their kitchens, and no salt was used in their "Devil's feasts."[11]

By similar reasoning, the Romans made use of salt in purificatory rites, e.g., to avert the fulfillment of a bad dream.[12]

The properties attaching to salt extended, of course, to saline waters. Thus the well of Zeus Asbamaios, which was of that character, was held to afford special protection against evil influences,[13] while Clement of Alexandria records a superstition that water drawn from three wells and mixed with salt provided immunity against the "princes of darkness."[14]

Elisha places the salt in a *new* bowl. The efficacy of a magical procedure can be impaired if the material used has been contaminated. Accordingly, it is commonly specified in charms and recipes that only *new* vessels and implements may be employed.[15] Thus, in the great Greek magical papyri there is frequent reference to *new* pots and bowls,[16] and Pliny likewise endorses this requirement.[17] Similarly, the medieval Jewish book of magic entitled *The Sword of Moses* lays it down that a *new* potsherd is to be used for inscribing charms designed to "make a man follow thee,"[18] to fructify a barren tree,[19] to cure a sick dog,[20] and to send plague;[21] while in modern Egyptian folklore it is held that a murdered person's ghost can be pinned down by driving a *new* nail into the ground at the scene of the crime.[22]

The same provision applied in more formal ritual. Thus—to cite but a few examples—at the games celebrated in honor of Poseidon at Onchestos, the race had to be run by a *new-broken* colt;[23] and a *new* cart was required to transport the ark of Yahweh to Jerusalem.[24] So too the Roman poet Tibullus, in entreating the acceptance of an offering, stresses that it has been presented in pure, i.e., hitherto unused, vessels.[25]

164 Elisha called "baldpate" 2:23

Urchins in the city of Bethel mock Elisha as he passes by, crying after him "Baldpate."

The urchins who cried "Baldpate" after Elisha were simply behaving like all ill-bred children everywhere, and the modern reader cannot but be a trifle shocked at the prophet's humorless and savage reaction. Behind the insult, however, lies an interesting piece of folklore. As we have seen (above, §117), hair is popularly regarded as the seat of vitality. Accordingly, a bald man was, in antiquity, an object not only of fun but also of opprobrium, because he was believed to have lost his vital essence and consequently to be impotent. Aristotle says, for example, that baldness is due to loss of semen,[1] and that boys maimed in the sexual organs do not grow beards.[2] Hairy men, he says also[3]—and in this Pliny agrees with him[4]—have the strongest sexual bent, and the sexual appetite even of mares can be extinguished by cutting off their manes.[5] The belief survives in our own concept of the "hairy-chested he-man" and in the superstition current among British schoolboys that, if they masturbate, they will lose their strength and their hair will fall out.

In Balkan folkore a bald man is regarded as outside the human race and cannot marry;[6] while a popular German expression for the Devil is "Baldpate" (*Kahlkopf, Snoyen*).[7]

The bald man was a constant butt of jokes in Classical antiquity.[8] Indeed, Juvenal is said to have been banished to Egypt for ridiculing the baldness of

Nero—which, in fact, other writers did too.[9] Jesters at banquets were commonly bald, to raise a laugh from the guests, and this custom continued into medieval times.[10]

165 The inexhaustible cruse 4:1–7

At Zarephath, Elisha is given hospitality by a poor widow. She has only a handful of meal in a barrel and a little oil in a cruse, but, at the prophet's request, she makes a cake for him before serving herself and her son. The prophet promises her that neither the barrel nor her cruse will ever be empty throughout the time of drought. So it turns out.

This is simply a Hebrew version of the familiar folktale, known technically as *Tischlein deck' dich,* the theme of which is that scant food is miraculously increased as a reward for hospitality to itinerant gods or saints.[1]

The theme is best known to Western readers from the tale, *Vom süssen Brei* in the Grimm collection,[2] but it has plenty of parallels elsewhere. An Indian variant tells, for instance, how in similar circumstances a single grain of rice was made to yield inexhaustible sustenance;[3] while in a modern Turkish version it is a coffee mill that becomes endowed with this magical property.[4] From the Pelew Islands comes the tale of a magic bird, called Peaged arsai, which alights beside a poor boy and sets before him a single morsel of meat and some *toro.* "What good is that?" cries the lad. "I am hungry!" "Then eat, only eat," replies the bird, and lo and behold, every time the boy takes a bite, what he eats is immediately replaced. When he is so full that he cannot manage a single further bite, and is therefore constrained to break the Pelew custom of eating either everything served at a meal or taking the leftovers with one, and when in this dilemma, he looks anxiously at the bird, the latter cries, "Enough! Finished!" and the miraculous increase stops.[5]

Finnish and Hungarian versions relate how a poor girl is enabled to feed a guest to satiety from three grains of corn which continuously multiply, and how a samovar miraculously develops twelve spouts, each yielding a different drink.[6]

In Classical literature we have, of course, the famous story of Philemon and Baucis who entertain Jupiter and Mercury out of their scant store, only to discover to their amazement that every time the wine bowl is emptied, it fills up again of its own accord.[7] The story served as the subject of well-known paintings by Bramantino (1455–1536) and the Zuccari, and was especially popular with Flemish, Dutch, and German artists of the seventeenth century. It was likewise adopted frequently (under the influence of the New Testament story of the Loaves and Fishes) in Christian hagiologies.[8]

The Western versions of the tale have been traced to a lost comedy (*Thēria*) by the Greek playwright Kratês (c. 470 B.C.),[9] but the theme itself may perhaps be recognized, at a far earlier date, in a Canaanite mythological text from Ras Shamra-Ugarit, our extant copy of which goes back to the fourteenth century B.C. This text relates how two sons of the supreme god El, distinguished from birth by a voracious appetite, are left by him to forage for themselves on the edges of the steppeland. There they encounter a man (possibly an official) storing grain. They beg him for bread and wine, but he replies—the text is incomplete—that he has only a meager quantity of either. Nevertheles, they break into his store and eat lavishly. The text then continues with lines which have been imperfectly preserved but which seem to say that what had at first been small quantities of grain and drink now become larger quantities and that the jar of wine becomes full. Now, this text was composed for a celebration in honor of those two gods, and it is difficult to see why they should have been thus honored unless they had compensated their greedy consumption of the victuals with some promise for future increase. The celebration, so the text says clearly, took place at the time when the sun was ripening the grapes and the vines were blooming. It would seem possible, therefore, that this explanatory myth turned on the theme of *Tischlein deck' dich:* the generous host was rewarded by a promise of increase and prosperity—a promise that the steppeland, seemingly barren, would yet yield produce year by year—as in fact it does. The annual fulfillment of the promise would thus have been the occasion of the festival for which the text was designed![10]

165a Elisha revives a dead boy 4:34

This is a duplicate of the incident related concerning Elijah (see above, §157).

166 Bathing cures leprosy 5:10

Naaman, commander-in-chief of the king of Syria, is a leper. At the suggestion of a handmaid, appeal is made to Elisha. The prophet bids him to bathe seven times in the Jordan.

(a) What is involved in this procedure is not ablution, or the washing off of impurity, but what we may call *illution*—the washing *in* of the properties of primordial waters (see above, §2), here identified as the River Jordan. This, indeed, is the real meaning of *baptism* in general; and it is worthy of note that among the Mandeans of Iraq and Iran the baptismal river is still called Jordan.

The Biblical incident served as a precedent in later Jewish magic, for the medieval collection of charms entitled *The Sword of Moses* says that a leper can be cured if he dips seven times in a river.[1]

The vital essence can, however, be renewed also by an infusion of *blood,* for "the blood is the life" (see above, §26).[2] Such immersion in blood, says Pliny, was common in Egypt;[3] while the Emperor Constantine is said to have desisted from this practice only when so warned by a vision.[4] In Somadeva's *Ocean of Story*, the Indian princess Mṛigavāti asks to bathe in blood to cure herself of an ailment;[5] and in the medieval romance of Amys and Amylion two children are slain to provide blood through which one of the heroes may be cured of leprosy.[6] Tales of the same purport are to be found in Basile's *Pentamerone*,[7] and in Sicilian,[8] German,[9] Syrian,[10] and Tibetan lore.[11] A rabbinic legend (*midrash*) has it that the Pharaoh of the Exodus suffered from leprosy and therefore bathed daily in the blood of the Hebrew children whom he ordered slain;[12] while, *en revanche*, a variant of the infamous "blood libel" asserted that Richard I of England had been advised by a Jew to achieve the same end by bathing in the blood of a slain newborn child.[13] Similarly, in 1870 a Moslem butcher in Northern India, who had lost a son, was told by a Hindu fakir that if he washed his wife daily in blood, his next child would be healthy.[14] In Bechuanaland, the blood of a goat is poured over a sick person.[15]

(b) Waving in magic

> *Naaman is at first indignant since he expects an instant cure by a mere waving of the prophet's hands over his body and deems the prosaic instructions given him something of an insult to his dignity. Urged by his servants, however, he eventually complies and is healed.*

Waving motions are a common feature of magical procedures; their purpose is to *diffuse* the otherworldly quality by which the magic is worked.[16]

In the Hittite myth of Telepinu, the divine sorceress Kamrusepas makes waving motions to remove from him all the anger and umbrage which have caused him to withdraw his ministrations from the earth;[17] and the same technique is mentioned in other Hittite texts.[18] Moslem midwives sometimes wave vessels full of water over the heads and feet of newborn babes in order to forefend demons;[19] and at Moslem weddings the bride's mother sometimes sprinkles red-dyed water in a waving motion over the bridegroom.[20] At Hoshangabād, in Northern India, it is customary to wave a handful of corn over a sick person, thereby conveying to him the essence of healthy development;[21] and in parts of Afghanistan three shots of pepper are waved in the face of a person believed to be possessed by a demon.[22]

Waving motions were likewise made over offerings in Israelitic ritual—evidently as a survival of an earlier device for keeping off evil influences.[23] This was the practice at the ordination of the high priest,[24] at the presentation of *shelamim* (EV: "peace-offerings"),[25] guilt-offerings,[26] and first fruits,[27] in the ceremony of trial by ordeal,[28] and at the consecration of nazirites.[29]

167 Iron floats 6:5–7

> *The guild of professional prophets ("the sons of the prophets") complain to Elisha that their quarters are too constricted. He bids them repair to the banks of the Jordan and there construct a more com-*

> *modious abode. One of the guild asks him to accompany them and bring along his servants to help in the work. While they are felling timber, one of the laborers drops his ax into the water—a disaster heightened by the fact that he had it only on loan from someone else! The prophet thereupon cuts down a stick and throws it toward the spot where the ax fell. Instantly the ax floats on the surface.*

The miracle of floating iron occurs in Christian hagiology.[1] A novice clearing the bank of a lake near the monastery of St. Clement at Monte Cassino accidentally dropped the head of his ax into the water. St. Benedict (480–543) laid his hands on the haft; instantly the iron head rose and fitted itself to the handle.[2] It was thus too that St. Leufredus retrieved an ax dropped into the water by one of the monks at La Croix (738 C.E.).[3] Similarly, while St. Wolfram was sailing from Candebec to Frisia, St. Vando, during the celebration of the Mass on board, accidentally dropped the paten and it fell into the water. Wolfram took a stick and dipped it into the waters. The paten then floated on the surface.[4]

168 The use of corpses in magic 13:21

The life essence or any special qualities which once inhabited the dead can, according to widespread popular belief, be transferred to the living and afford them extra strength when their own is failing. By an extension of this idea, a dead person may himself be reanimated, if brought into contact with the bodily remains of a saint, since the latter are endowed with numinous properties.[1]

An Arabic superstition holds that if one lies between the graves of holy men, one can be relieved of fever;[2] and in parts of Germany it is believed that one can acquire health by disturbing the dead.[3] In Armenia, a piece of a dead man's hand is given to a sick person;[4] and similarly in Ireland a dead man's hand can cure ailments.[5] This latter belief obtained also among the Jews, and is mentioned in the Talmud.[6] Analogously the Romans thought that one could induce health by stroking a patient with a dead man's hand,[7] and that a tooth drawn from a cadaver could cure toothache.[8] In Thomas Hardy's story, *The Withered Arm* (included in his *Wessex Tales*), touching the neck of a man who had been hanged is said to effect a cure;[9] and certain primitive tribes of South Africa maintain that magic can be worked from a decoction of the left hand and foot of a person slain for ritual purposes.[10] A trial for murder committed to this end was reported in 1957.[11] In much the same vein Pliny declares that the hair of a man who has been crucified protects from quartan fever;[12] while Jewish sources record a popular notion that a barren woman can induce conception by applying to her person the water or soap in which a corpse has been washed.[13]

The bodies of the dead can also be used magically to inflict harm. The Belep of New Caledonia, for example, believe that they can disable an enemy from flight through magic worked with the leg bone of a dead foe;[14] and the ancient Greeks seem to have thought that to set a young male child on a tomb would be to rob him of his manhood by infecting him with the impotence of the dead.[15] A South Slavonian housebreaker often begins operations by throwing a dead man's bone into the house. "May you have as much chance of waking," he says cynically of the sleeping inmates, "as has this bone!"[16]

▲ 169 Yahweh's Lions 17:24–28

[*In 722* B.C. *the king of Assyria invaded the territory of Israel, deported its inhabitants, and replaced them by people drawn from his own dominions. The latter, of course, did not worship Yahweh, and when the God of Israel saw how they ignored him, he "sent lions among them, which killed some of them." On hearing of this, the Assyrian monarch ordered one of the deported priests of Yahweh to be repatriated in order to teach the newly settled population "the law of the god of the land."*]

The incident illustrates a not uncommon belief that every land has its own local deity, who can be propitiated only by the natives of the country, since they alone are acquainted with the particular form of religious ritual which he expects.[1] For example, the Toradjas of Central Celebes hold that "every district has its own earth-spirit, or rather earth-spirits, which can only be invoked by members of the tribe which inhabits the district." Hence, when a man has obtained leave to lay out a rice-field in the territory of another tribe, and the time comes for him to make an offering to the earth-spirit Toompoo ntana, "Owner of the Ground," "the stranger always invites for that purpose the help of one of the garden-priests of the tribe in whose land he has come to dwell, because they say that such a stranger does not know how he ought to invoke the spirit of that land; he is not yet accustomed to that earth-spirit."[2]

Again, among the aboriginal tribes of the Upper Niger valley, the Earth is a very important deity, whose worship is cared for by a priest called the Chief of the Earth. Each village, as a rule, has its Chief of the Earth, who is the religious, but not the political, head of the community, being charged with the duty of offering sacrifices to Earth and the other local deities, and of acting generally as the indispensable intermediary between the gods and the people. For example, it is his business to sacrifice for good crops at sowing, to offer thank-offerings after harvest, to perform the rites necessary for procuring rain in seasons of drought, and to make atonement whenever Earth has been offended by the spilling of human blood on the ground, whether in murder or in simple assault and battery.[3] Moreover, as representative of the Earth-deity, and therefore himself master of the earth, it is the prerogative of the priest to grant permission to dig graves and to prescribe their dimensions.[4]

This important priesthood continues to be filled by members of the old aboriginal race under the rule of an alien people, the Mossi, who have invaded and conquered a large part of the country. "The existence of these Chiefs of the Earth among the Mossi is explained very probably by the superposition of the conquering on the conquered race. When the Mossi invaded and conquered the country, in proportion as they spread their dominion they put men of their own race at the head of all the villages and cantons to ensure the submission of the vanquished population. But they never thought—and this is a notion to be found in the whole of West Africa—that they were qualified to offer sacrifices to the Earth-god of the place and the local divinities. It was only the vanquished, the ancient owners of the soil, with which they continued in good relations, who were qualified for that. Hence the old political head of the aborigines was bound to become naturally a religious chief under the rule of the Mossi. Thus we have seen that the king (*Moro-Naba*) never himself offers the sacrifices to Earth at Wagadugu, nor does he allow such sacrifices to be offered by his minister of religion, the Gandé-Naba. He lays the duty on the king of Wagadugu (*Wagadugu-Naba*), the grandson of the aborigines, who as such is viewed favourably by the local divinities. Similarly, when he sacrifices to the little rising-grounds in the neighbourhood of Wagadugu, he commits the charge of the offerings and sacrifices to the local chief. But what the king (*Moro-Naba*) actually does now at Wagadugu, the Mossi kings (*naba*) doubtless did formerly, more or less everywhere after the conquest, as soon as the submission of the aborigines was assured. Hence the institution of the Chiefs of the Earth (*Tensoba*)."[5]

The historian has not described the rites and ceremonies by which the Israelitish priest at Bethel succeeded in staying the ravages of the man-eating lions; we can, therefore, only compare the intention, but not the form, of the rites and ceremonies which a priest of one of the aboriginal tribes in India at the present day performs for the purpose of staying the ravages of man-eating tigers and laying the ghosts of such persons as have fallen victims to the ravening maw of these dangerous brutes. The Baigas (or Bygas) are one of the wildest of the primitive Dravidian tribes that roam the dense *sal* forests which clothe the hills of Mandla in the Central Provinces of India. They lead a very secluded life in the wilderness, and down to the middle of the nineteenth century, when they first came under the exact observation of English officers, they were even more solitary and retired than they are now.[6]

In the country where they dwell they are regarded as the most ancient inhabitants and accordingly they usually act as priests of the indigenous gods.[7] Certainly there is reason to believe that in this part of the hills they are predecessors of the Gonds, towards whom they occupy a position of acknowledged superiority, refusing to eat with them and lending them their priests or enchanters for the performance of those rites which the Gonds, as newcomers, could not properly celebrate. Among these rites the most dangerous is that of laying the ghost of a man who has been killed by a tiger. When such an event has taken place, the Baiga priest or enchanter proceeds to the scene of the catastrophe, provided with articles, such as fowls and rice, which are to be offered to the ghost of the deceased. Arrived at the spot, he makes a small cone out of the blood-stained earth to represent either the dead man or one of his living relatives. His companions having retired a few paces, the priest drops on his hands and knees, and in that posture performs a series of antics which are supposed to represent the tiger in the act of destroying the man, while at the same time he seizes the lump of blood-stained earth in his teeth. One of the party then runs up and taps him on the back with a small stick. This perhaps means that the tiger is killed or otherwise rendered harmless, for the priest at once lets the mud cone fall into the hands of one of the party. It is then placed in an ant-hill and a pig is sacrificed over it. Next day a small chicken is taken to the place, and after a mark, supposed to be the dead man's name, has been made on the fowl's head with red ochre, it is thrown back into the forest, while the priest cries out "Take this and go home." The ceremony is thought to lay the dead man's ghost, and at the same time to keep the tiger from doing any more harm. For the Baigas believe that if the ghost were not charmed to rest, it would ride on the tiger's head and incite to fresh deeds of blood, guarding at the same time from the attacks of human foes by his preternatural watchfulness.[8]

If we cannot suppose that the Israelitish priest at Bethel performed a similar pantomime for the repression of man-eating lions among the woods of Samaria, we shall perhaps be justified in assuming that the rites which he did celebrate were neither less nor more effectual than those which the jungle-priests of Mandla still observe for a like purpose over the blood-stained earth in their native forests. At all events, with these parallels before us we can better appreciate the gross religious impropriety of which the foreign settlers in Palestine were deemed to be guilty, when they began by completely ignoring the old god of the land; it is no wonder that he is represented as being nettled at such treatment and as taking strong measures to impress his claims on the attention of the newcomers. ▼

170 The horses and chariots of the sun   23:11

He also removes the model horses and burns the model chariots set up by previous kings at the entrance to the Temple in honor of the sun.

The idea that the sun drives a chariot was commonplace in the Ancient Near East. Shamash, the sun-god of the Mesopotamians, is described in their literature as "the Charioteer" (*rakib narkabti*),[1] and in a Phoenician inscription of the eighth century B.C., from Zenčirli, in Syria, he is associated with another called Rkb-el, which would seem to denote a divine charioteer.[2] Pottery models of horses and chariots, found at pre-Israelite levels in several Palestinian cities, have been related by some scholars to such a solar cult, but this is doubtful.[3]

The concept is likewise well attested outside the Semitic world.[4] In the Indic Rig Veda, Surya, the sun-god, rides a chariot,[5] and a similar notion attached to the sun among the Iranians.[6] The chariot of the sun is not mentioned, however, in the Iliad and Odyssey, but first occurs among the Greeks in the Homeric Hymns[7] and in Hesiod.[8] Thereafter it becomes a commonplace.[9]

A cognate concept is that of the *horses* of the sun.[10] The Iranian Avesta speaks of "the sun's swift steeds,"[11] and horses were dedicated and sacrificed to the solar deity.[12] The Rhodians offered a chariot and four horses annually to the sun;[13] and the Spartans sacrificed horses to the sun on Mount Taygetus.[14] A similar practice was observed, says Herodotus, by the Massagetae of Turkestan;[15] while the Romans annually threw a chariot and horses into the sea in honor of the sun.[16] The Icelandic saga of Hrafnkell revolves around a horse consecrated to Frey, a solar deity;[17] and in medieval Sweden, the day of St. Etienne, the Christian successor of Frey, was dedicated to horses.[18]

NOTES

JOSHUA

104 Joshua at Jericho
(a) "The walls came tumblin' down"
 1. See: G. E. Wright, Biblical Archaeology (1960), 47 f.

(b) The circumambulation of the walls
 2. P. Saintyves, Essais de folklore biblique (1902), 177–204; W. Pax, in WS 8 (1937), 1–88.
 3. K. Sethe, Untersuchungen, iii (1905), 133–35; J. Vandier, La religion égyptienne (1949), 181 f.; S. A. B. Mercer, The Religion of Ancient Egypt (1949), 351.
 4. A. Goetze, Kleinasien[1] (1933), 154.
 5. T. H. Gaster, Thespis[2], 193 f.
 6. The ceremony was called *pradaksina;* see: M. Eliade, Patterns in Comparative Religion (1958), 373 f.; C. H. Tawney, Ocean of Story (1880), i.190–93.
 7. R. O. Winstedt, in JRAS 1945.139 f.
 8. W. Simpson, The Buddhist Praying Wheel (1896), 275.
 9. Tor Irstam, King of Ganda (1944), 176 ff.
 10. Brand-Ellis, Popular Antiquities of Great Britain (1882–83), i.197 f.; T. F. Thiselton Dyer, British Popular Customs (1876), 204 ff., 208–11; 213 f.; E. M. Hull, The Folklore of the British Isles (1928), 77–80; E. M. Leather, The Folklore of Herefordshire (1912), 149–51.
 11. A. R. Wright, English Folklore (1928), 44–45.
 12. P. Sartori, Sitte und Brauch (1910–14), iii.168, 216, 268.
 13. Livy, ii.10; Valerius Maximus, iii.2, 1.
 14. Bouquet, Recueil des historiens de la Gaule (1840 ff.), iv.
 15. M. Diemer, Légende dorée de l'alsace (1905), 115–18.
 16. J. Michelet, Origin du droit français (1837), 63–64.
 17. Il Messagero (Rome), Sept. 8, 1967, p. 3.

(c) The seven circuits
 18. Lucan, Phars. i.592 ff.; Apuleius, Met. iii, init.; Servius, on Virgil, Ecl. iii.77.
 19. Plutarch, Romulus xxi.4; Ward Fowler, Roman Festivals at the Period of the Republic (1899), 319; J. G. Frazer, The Fasti of Ovid (1929), vol. ii, p. 335 f.; E. Samter, in ARW 16 (1913), 137 ff.
 20. Saintyves, loc. cit.
 21. Gesta Ambrosiensium, apud Scriptores Rer. Franc., x.228.
 22. Michelet, op. cit., 128.
 23. M. Haberlandt, in Corr. Bl. d. Ges. f. Anthropol., Ethnol., und Urgeschichte, 21.9.

(d) The trumpets
 24. P. Haupt, in WZKM 23 (1909), 355–65.
 25. Stith Thompson, MI, D 1562.3; Bolte-Polivka, i.464 ff.; Aarne-Thompson, Types, #569.
 26. T. H. Gaster, New Year (1955), 45–49; Frazer-Gaster, NGB §41.

27. W. Matthews, in RBEW 5 (1887), 435 f.
28. E. O. James, in ERE x.562b.
29. D. Kidd, The Essential Kafir (1904), 333.
30. W. Mannhardt, Antike Wald- und Feldkulte (1877), 342n.
31. Cf. A. H. Krappe, La genèse des mythes (1938), 135, R. Lasch, in ARW 3 (1900), 97 ff.
32. Apollodorus, Bib. i.9, 7.
33. Livy, vii.36; viii.7, 32.
34. Caesar, Bell. Civ. iii.92; Livy, vii.36; Sallust, Catiline 60.

105 Foundation-sacrifice

1. I Kings 16:34.
2. See: P. Sartori, in Zs. f. Ethnologie 30 (1898), 1–54; S. Baring-Gould, in Murray's Magazine, 1 (1887), 363–77; H. Trumbull, The Threshold Covenant (1896), 45 ff.; H. Naumann, Primitive Gemeinschaft-kultur (1921), 70 ff.—For the Semitic field, see: S. A. Cook, in W. Robertson Smith, The Religion of the Semites³ (1927), 632 f.; F. W. S. O'Neill, in ET 21 (1909), 43 f.
3. Joh. Malalas, 37; 200; 203.
4. Ed. Mrs. A. S. Lewis, p. 43.
5. T. Canaan, in JPOS 6 (1927), 63; cf. Mishnah, Ohol. 18.7; Niddah 7.4.
6. S. I. Curtiss, Ursemitische Religion im Volksleben des heutigen Orients, tr. H. Stocks (1913), xvi f., 73, 209, 219, 229.
7. J. G. Frazer, GB iii.89.
8. See, for example: S. Gaidoz, in Mélusine 4 (1888), No. 2; P. Sébillot, Le folklore de France (1904–7), 165 ff.; A. H. Krappe, Balor with the Evil Eye (1927), 165 ff.; Revue Celtique 41 (1924), 187.
9. K. Landtmann, in Acta Acad. Aboensis, 1920, i.5.
10. C. A. Doughty, Arabia Deserta (1888), i.136; ii.100, 198.
11. Cf. R. A. S. Macalister, Gezer (1902–9), ii.426 ff.; ATAOB², ii, fig. 231 (Gezer); A. Lods, Israel (1930), 114.—J. Gray, Archaeology and the Old Testament World (Torchbook ed., 1965), 45, identifies images buried in Palestinian houses with the *teraphim*, or household gods (see above, §68), but I see no authority for this.
12. H. Vincent, Canaan d'après l'exploration récente (1907), 282 ff.; A. Lods, Israel (1930), 113 ff.; S. A. Cook, The Religion of Ancient Palestine in the Light of Archaeology (1925), 84 ff.
13. Vincent, loc. cit.; T. Canaan, in JPOS 4 (1925), 8n.; 6 (1927), 118, n.3; A. B. Cook, Zeus ii (1925), 1059.

106 "Sun, stand thou still"

1. There are further allusions to this miracle in Hab. 3:11; Ecclus. 46:4–7.
2. Iliad 2.413 ff.
3. Stith Thompson, MI, D 2146.1; cf. Plautus, Amphitryo 113 f.; A. Dillmann, Comm. on Jos. 10:12.
4. Iliad 18.439 f.
5. Hesiod, Shield 1–56; Pindar, Isthm. vii.5; Lucian, Dial. deorum 10; Apollodorus, Bib. ii.4, 7–8; Hyginus, fab. 28; Seneca, Phaedra 315.
6. Odyssey 23.241 ff.
7. P. Zaunert, Deutsche Märchen seit Grimm (1912–23), 143.
8. C. Schirren, Die Wandersagen der Neuseeländer (1856), 37 ff.
9. Acta Boll., Sept. viii.171; H. Delahaye, The Legends of the Saints (1961), 51.
10. See in general: Badger, in PEFQS, July 1900; S. Birch, ib., April 1900; Matthes, in ThT 1908.461–94; Kelly, in ET 1909.566; B. Alfrink, in StC 24 (1949), 238–69;

J. de Fraine, in Verbum Domini 28 (1950), 227–36; Van der Busche, in Collationes Gandavenses, ii/1 (1951), 48–53.—Standard Bible commentaries are full of tiresome homiletical nonsense about this incident.

11. R. C. Fuller, in Scripture iv/10 (1951).

12. E. C. Brewer, Dictionary of Miracles, 295 f.—It may be pertinent, alternatively, to compare the Hebrew word with the Arabic *d-w-m,* used specifically of *the sun's turning in its course.*

JUDGES

107 The mutilation of captives

1. Xenophon, Hist. gr. ii.1, 31; Plutarch, Lysander 9; Cicero, De officiis iii.11; Valerius Maximus ix.2, ext. 8.

2. Aelian, VH ii.29.

3. Caesar, Bell. Gall. viii.44.

4. A. Oldfield, in Trans. Ethnol. Soc. of London 3 (1865), 287.

5. Cf. Hesychius, Photius, s.v. *maschalismata;* Schol. on Ap. Rhod., Argon. iv.477; E. Riess, in Rhein. Mus. 49 (1894), 182 f.; F. Dümmler, in Philologus 56 (1897), 13 ff.; E. Rohde, Psyche[1], 322–26; O. Gruppe, Gr. Mythol. (1906), 903, n.1; Metzger, in Mélanges Chas. Andler (Strasbourg 1924), 251–68; J. G. Frazer, Apollodorus, vol. i, p. 328, n.1.

6. Aeschylus, Choephoroe 349 (v. T. G. Tucker, Comm. in loc.); Sophocles, Electra 439 (v. Schol. in loc.).

7. Apollodorus, Bib. iii.5, 1.

8. Rohde, loc. cit.; R. C. Jebb, Electra of Sophocles (1892–1900), 211 ff.

9. V AB, B 5–13; tr. H. L. Ginsberg, ANET 136. Cf. Strabo, 5.302; Diod. Sic., 5.29. Cf. also G. L. Gomme, Ethnology in Folklore (1892), 148.

10. A. Baumeister, Denkmäler des klass. Altertums (1855–88), i.460 f., fig. 506.

11. S. Mateer, The Land of Charity (1871), 203 ff.

12. Festus, 135 Lindsay, s.v. *os resectum.*

13. PEFQS 1903.32 ff.

14. E.g., Shalmaneser, in ANET 277; Esarhaddon, ib., 290.

15. Herodotus, iv.103.—Certain tribes in Borneo do the same thing: J. G. Frazer, GB vii.294 ff.

16. Strabo, viii.6, 19, p. 337; Apollodorus, Bib. ii.8, 1.

17. Apollodorus, Bib. ii.5, 11.

18. Ib., ii.7, 7.

19. Ib., Epitome ii.5.

20. Scholiast on Iliad 9.557; Eustathius, in loc., p. 776.

21. Giraldus Cambrensis, Conquest of Ireland, i.4; cf. G. L. Gomme, Ethnology in Folklore (1892), 149.

22. M. Abeghian, Das Armenische Volksglaube (1899), 11.

23. J. B. Labat, Relation historique de l'Ethiopie occidentale (1732), i.208.

24. J. Jones, in Trans. Ethnol. Soc. of London, 3 (1865), 138; E. B. Tylor, Primitive Culture, ii.35.

25. E. Gibbon, The Decline and Fall of the Roman Empire, ed. J. B. Bury, v.186.

26. Silus Italicus, 4.213; Diod. Siculus, 14.115; Livy, 10.26; Strabo, 198. Cf. M. W. Dunbar, History of Antiquity (1877–87), i.176.

27. Ibn Batuta 17, ed. S. Lee.

28. A. Dalzel, History of Dahomey (1793), 76.

29. J. Morier, A Second Journey through Persia (1818), 186.
30. ERE, s.v. Mutilation.
31. Epic of Gilgamesh vi.161. (E. Speiser, in ANET 85, renders "right thigh.").
32. William of Newbury, G. Nub. 281.
33. J. C. Lawson, Modern Greek Folklore and Ancient Greek Religion (reprint, 1964), 435 ff.
34. J. Mooney, The Ghost-Dance Religion (reprint, 1965), 264.

108 Captives fed on scraps

1. Ugaritica V (1967), i.6–8: $dyd^cnn\ y^cdb\ lhm\ lh,\ wdl\ yd^cnn\ ylmn\ tht\ tlhn$.
2. G. Kittredge, "Arthur and Gorlagon," in Harvard Studies and Notes in Philology and Literature, 8 (1903), 252n.; Stith Thompson, MI, Q 478.2–3.—This practice lends itself readily to incorporation as a motif in the widespread story of the adulteress who mistreats a dog which eventually betrays her to her husband: see E. J. Gibb, The History of the Forty Vizirs (1886), 331 f., and versions of the legend of Robert of Sicily cited by Kittredge, loc. cit.
3. Stith Thompson, MI, Q 523.3.

109 The Song of Deborah

(a) Long-haired warriors

1. The Hebrew expression is, bi-$ph^eroc^a\ ph^erac^ôth\ b^e$-$Yisraël$. The verb p-r-^{c} means primarily, "to break loose, be unrestrained," and is then used metaphorically of behaving lawlessly (Prov. 29:18), or of keeping the hair untrimmed (Lev. 10:16; 13:45). Hence, the only legitimate translations are, *When men cast off restraint* (i.e., *inhibitions*), or *When locks flowed freely in Israel*. For my own part, I confess that the former seems to me more likely, since it provides a stricter parallel to the following, *When men offered themselves freely* (i.e., *volunteered*).—RSV's rendering is based on the fact that in Deut. 32:42, where the crucial word recurs in the expression, *the head of $p^erac^ôth$ of the enemy*, it has been traditionally taken to mean "leaders." This, however, is tenuous, for that verse can equally well be rendered, *I will make my arrows drunk with blood . . . with the blood of the slain and the captives—(blood) from the long-haired heads of the enemy*, as RSV itself indeed translates it.
2. W. H. Roscher, ed., Lex. Myth, s.v. Achilles.
3. J. Wellhausen, Reste d. arab. Heidentums² (1897), 123.
4. Edda vii.116; cf. S. Bugge, Heldensage (1889), 222 f. (*Haralds haarfagres Løfte*).
5. O. Jegerlehner, Oberwallis (1906), 308, #39.
6. S. Boggs, in FCC 90.53, #400* B.
7. See in general: Frazer-Gaster, NGB, §§167, 502; Bolte-Polivka, ii.413 ff.; Eitrem, Opferritus und Voropfer der Griechen und Römer (1915), 400; E. Bi., s.v. Nazirite. See also below, §117, d.
8. Gilbert Murray, The Rise of the Greek Epic (1907), 123.—It has been objected that the Myceneans are known to have worn their hair long in any case; see fully: D. L. Page, The Homeric Iliad (1963), 243, 282, nn.67–68.
9. Nicetas, Lacon, Chronogr. v.260; G. L. von Maurer, Das griechische Volk (1835), 10.

(b) Riding high and sitting low

10. G. Dossin, ARM i.45; 5–6; 72.6, etc.; cf. A. Salonen, in AOr. 17/ii.320; S. Feigin, in Studies in Memory of Moses Schorr (1944), 227–40.
11. RSV's *rich carpets* misses the point. The Hebrew word *middîn*, admittedly difficult, is best taken as an "Aramaic" plural of *mad, madū*, "cloak." LXX and Vulgate's *in judgment* arises from fanciful combination of the word with *dîn*, "judgment," but

this involves impossible syntax.—An alternative suggestion is that *m-d-n* should be interpreted after the Ugaritic *m-d-l,* "caparison," and that (by adding *'ayr,* "male donkey," at the end) the clause should be rendered, "Ye who sit on caparisoned [male donkeys]"; cf. D. Hillers, *apud* W. F. Albright, Yahweh and the Gods of Canaan (1968), 49, n. 102. But this destroys the pointed contrast between *riding* (rkb), *walking* (hlk) and *sitting* (yšb). Furthermore, I know of no other place where *y-š-b* ("sit") is used of *being mounted.*

12. T. Canaan, in JPOS 19 (1939), 225, No. 38.
13. Ib.
14. Tr. S. N. Kramer, ANET 44.
15. G. Jacob, Studien in arabischen Dichtern, ii (1894), 115; G. A. Doughty, Arabia Deserta (1888), ii.231.
16. The word is $s^eḥôrôth$; see GB[16], s.v. $ṣāḥôr$. Vulg. renders "gleaming" (*nitentes*).
17. Pindar, Pyth. i.66; Sophocles, Electra 706.
18. Pausanias, ii.32, 7; Sophocles, frag. 871.2, Nauck; CIA iii.1015.
19. Pindar, Pyth. i.127.
20. Rev. 19:11, 14.

(c) "Awake, awake, Deborah, utter a song"

21. This conventional rendering is not quite accurate. Deborah was wide awake. What the Hebrew word really means here is "vent your passion."
22. I Sam. 18:7 ff.
23. RSV: *The Lord gives the command; great is the host of those who bore the tidings.* But this misses the force of the Hebrew original. The first clause is *conditional,* and in the second, the word rendered *those that bore the tidings* is feminine. Moreover, the description of them as *a great host* is the whole point of the verse: the victorious army of men will be greeted by what amounts to another vast army of their joyous womenfolk!
24. Doughty, op. cit., i.452; G. Jacob, Das Leben der vorislamischen Beduinen (1895), 125.

(d) The cursing of Meroz

25. Cf. Heb. *rôzî-li,* "woe is me!" (Isa. 24:16), and Arabic cognate. The name of the city may really have been Hurrian, with the characteristic ending *-zzi;* on the latter, see: E. Speiser, Mesopotamian Origins (1930), 141; A. L. Oppenheim, in WZKM 44 (1937), 206; T. H. Gaster, in JRAS 1935.38, n.117.

110 Gideon

(a) Gideon's fleece

1. E. Nestle, in ARW 12 (1909), 154–58; W. Schultz, in OLz 1910.241–45.
2. H. Günthert, Die Christliche Legende des Abendlandes (1910), 78 f., whence our examples are taken.
3. TB Yoma 53[b].
4. Günthert, loc. cit.
5. Ib.
6. Venantius Fortunatus, Vita S. Albini, c.7; Monumenta Germaniae historica, auct. antiqu. iv[2], 29.
7. Jocelin, Vita 17.
8. Gregory of Tours, Hist. x.29.
9. See: A. Franz, Die kirchliche Benediktionen im Mittelalter, ii (1909), 16 f., as cited by Günthert.
10. TB Yoma 21[a].

11. Günthert, loc. cit.
12. Ib.
13. Bernardi Itinerarium, in Tobler, Descriptiones terrae sanctae (1874), 94.
14. Günthert, op. cit., 173.
15. J. v. Hahn, Griech. u. albanes. Märchen (1864), i.227.

(b) Gideon's men

16. See: S. Tolkowsky, in JPOS 5 (1925), 69–74; D. Daube, in JJS 7 (1956), 155–61; Y. Yadin, The Art of Warfare in Biblical Lands (1963), ii.257.
17. C. H. Stigand, The Land of Zini (1913), 274 ff.
18. E. Torday, Camp and Tramp in African Wilds (1913), 85.
19. T. Hahn, in Globus, 12/ix.277; id., Tsuni- || Goam, The Supreme Being of the Khoi-Khoi (1881), 71.
20. E. Aymonier, in Cochinchine Française, Excursions et Reconnaissances, No. 16 (Saigon 1883), 165.
21. G. Turner, Nineteen Years in Polynesia (1861), 332.
22. Labillardière, Relation du voyage à la recherche de la Pérouse (1800), ii.196.
23. W. Gunn, The Gospel in Futuna (1914), 276.
23a. Paul Radin, Primitive Religion (reprint, 1957), 114.

111 The purple of kings

1. On purple dye in antiquity, cf. E. Bask, Dissertatio de purpura (Uppsala 1686); G. Wilckius, De purpura varia speciatim regia (Wittenberg 1706); A. Steger, Diss. de purpura sacra dignitatis insigni (Leipzig 1744); B. Roswall, Diss. de purpura (Lund 1750); A. Dedekind, Ein Beitrag zur Purpurkunde. Appendix to Neue Ausgabe seltenen Schriften über Purpur (1898); H. Blümner, Purpureus (1892); J. B. Mayor, Thirteen Satires of Juvenal (1872), ad i.27; Faymonville, Die Purpurfarberei d. versch. Kulturvölker d. Klass Altertums (Diss., Heidelberg 1900). Cf. also: Rachel Carson, The Sea Around Us (Mentor Books ed.), 148.
2. W. Muss-Arnolt, Assyrian Dictionary, s.v.
3. Plutarch, Artaxerxes 5.
4. Joh. Lydus, De magistratibus iii.64.
5. Homeric Hymn to Dionysus, 5–6.
6. Dan. 5:7, 16, 29.
7. Lam. 4:5.
8. Horace, Odes i.35, 2; see fully: J. B. Mayor, on Juvenal i.27.
9. Pliny, HN viii.195; ix.136; Livy, i.41, 6; Cicero, Brutus 56; Servius, on Vergil, Aen. vii.612; J. G. Frazer, The Fasti of Ovid (1929), ii.33 (on i.37).
10. Plutarch, Romulus 14.
11. Zohar, i.38^b–39^b.
12. F. von Duhn, "Rot und Tot," in ARW 7 (1906), 1–24; Eva Wunderlich, Die Bedeutung der roten Farbe im Kultus der Griechen und Römer, RVV 20/i (1927); I. Scheftelowitz, in ZAW 39 (1921), 117 f.; E. Samter, Geburt, Hochzeit und Tod (1911), 190 f.; P. Henisch, Die Trauergebräuche bei den Israeliten (1931), 59 ff.; G. B. Luquet, L'art et la religion des hommes fossiles (1926), 185; L. Deubner, De incubatione (1909), 25; H. Kees, "Farbensymbolik in aegyptischen religiösen Texten," in Nachr. Akad. Wiss. Göttingen, Phil.-hist. Kl. 11 (1943).
13. W. Schrank, Babyl. Sühnriten (1908), 28 ff.; K. Frank, Babyl. Beschwörungsreliefs (1908), 44; H. Zimmern, Ritualtafeln (1901), #26.i.14–15; G. Furlani, La relig. bab. e assira (1929), ii.167, 351.
14. E. Ebeling, Tod und Leben (1923), No. 30, A. 25.
15. Enuma Elish iv.61.

16. ERE viii.616.
17. TB Shabbath vii.11; see on this: I. Scheftelowitz, Schlingen- und Netzmotif (1912), 32 ff.
18. Globus, 89.60.
19. G. H. Simon, in JAF 65 (1952), 291.
20. Theocritus, Id., ii.2; Petronius, Satyricon 131; Pap. London 46.402, Wünsche. (The reference in Pap. Paris, Suppl. Gr. 574.2704 to wrapping an amulet in a *red* skin is here inapposite. It is to be explained by the fact that codices were commonly bound in red leather: see Catullus, xxxvii.6–7; T. Birt, Antikes Buchwesen [1882], 64 f.).
21. Folklore 9 (1898), 79; T. H. Gaster, The Holy and the Profane (1955), 13; A. E. Crawley, The Mystic Rose² (1927), i.333.
22. C. Lumholtz, Unknown Mexico (1902), ii.423.
23. Mrs. Wm. Hunt, in Folk-Lore 44 (1938), 194.
24. I Aqhat 204.
25. Crawley, op. cit., i.158.
26. Ib., ii.19.
27. R. Briffault, The Mothers (one-vol. ed., 1963), 248.
28. K. Latte, in ARW 26 (1928), 41 ff.
29. Satapatha Brahmana V.5.4, 1; cf. A. B. Keith, in JRAS 1938.603.
30. J. G. Frazer, GB, ed. min., 380.
31. Num. 19:2; cf. R. Patai, in JQR, N.S. 20 (1939), 59–70.
32. Num. 4.13.
33. E. A. W. Budge, Amulets and Superstitions (1930), 314.
34. Plutarch, Lyc. 27; Artemidorus, i.77; Aeschylus, Eumenides 1028. See fully: E. Rohde, Psyche⁷, ch. v, n.61.
35. Iliad xxiv.796.
36. G. Parrinder, La religion en Afrique centrale (1950), 134.
37. T. W. Thompson, in Journal of the Gipsy Lore Society, 3.1.
38. D. Seligmann, D. böse Blick (1910), 252–57.
39. Festus, s.v. *flammeum* = p. 89, ed. Mommsen.
40. Lev. 14:2 ff.
41. Pliny, HN xxxiii.11; Plutarch, Quaest. Rom. 98; Arnobius, Adversus nationes vi.10; Vergil, Ecl. vi.20; x.27; Tibullus, i.1, 17 (v. Kirby Smith in loc.). Cf. also: E. Nestle, in Philologus 50.501 ff.

▲ **112 Jotham's parable**

[1. Cf. M. Adinolfi, in Rivista Biblica Italiana 7 (1959), 322-42; H. Gunkel, Das Märchen im AT (1917), 16 ff.; W. Wienert, Die Typen der griechisch-röm. Fabel, FCC 56 (1925), 73–74; E. Ebeling, Die babylonische Fabel . . . , MVOG 2/iii (1927); id., in JCS 4 (1950), 215–22; R. J. Williams, "The Fable in the Ancient Near East," in A Stubborn Faith: W. A. Irwin Volume (1956), 3–26.]

[1a. KARI ##145, 324; cf. B. Meissner, Babylonien und Assyrien, ii (1925), 428 f.]
2. Fabulae Aesopicae #125, Hahn; Babrius, fab. 64.
3. Fab. Aesop. #385, Hahn.
4. A. S. Hunt, Oxyrinchus Papyri, vii (1910), 39 ff. [R. Pfeiffer, ed., Callimachi Fragmenta (1925), 51 ff.; H. Diels, "Orientalische Fabeln in griechischen Gewand," in Internat. Wochenschrift f. Wiss., 4 (1910), 995 ff.]
5. The Greek says, *"sings* of laurel," but the text is probably to be emended, as suggested by Diels. The prophetess chewed laurel as a mode of inspiration: Lucian, Bis accusatus 1; Tzetzes, Scholia on Lycophron 6; [Plutarch, E apud Delphos 2; id., De Pythiae oraculis 6; cf. A. Abt, Apologie des Apuleius (1908), 77 ff.].
6. An olive wreath was the prize at Olympia; a laurel wreath at Delphi.

7. An allusion to the contest of Athene and Poseidon for possession of Attica: [Herodotus, viii.55; Ovid, Met. vi.70 ff.; cf. J. G. Frazer, Apollodorus (1921), vol. ii, p. 78a].
8. The text is here fragmentary. The words in brackets are supplied by Diels.
[8a. Aḥiqar xi.168 f.; tr. H. L. Ginsberg, ANET², 429.]
9. F. Macler, in JA, N.S. 19 (1902), 467 ff.
10. W. Skeat, Fables and Folktales from an Eastern Front (1901), 13–15.
11. L. Hervieux, Les fabulistes latines: Phèdre et ses anciens imitateurs (1884), ii.589 ff., 761.
12. Ib., 581 ff.
[12a. See fully: A. L. Oppenheim, in BASOR 107 (1947), 7–11.]
[12b. Pi-ankhi 53.]
[12c. This suggestion is made by Oppenheim, loc. cit.]

113 The navel of the earth

1. M. Eliade, Patterns in Comparative Religion (1958), 231 f., 374 ff.; id., The Eternal Return (1955), 12 ff.; W. M. Roscher, Omphalos (1913); id., Neue Omphalosstudien (1915); id., in Sitzb. Kön. Ges. d. Wiss. 80 (1918), 2 ff.; R. Meninger, in Wörter und Sachen 5 (1913), 43–91; 6 (1914) [critique of Roscher]; W. Gaerte, in Anthropos 5 (1916), 956–79; A. S. Pease, in UCILL 8 (1923), 535 (on Cicero, De Divinatione lxvi.15).
2. A. J. Wensinck, The Ideas of the Western Semites concerning the Navel of the Earth (1916); A. Jeremias, Handbuch d. altorientalischen Geisteskultur² (1936), 33 f.; T. H. Gaster, Thespis², 183.
3. E. Burrows, in The Labyrinth, ed. S. H. Hooke (1935), 45–70.
4. Ezek. 38:12; Enoch 26:1; Jubilees 8:2; Tertullian, Contra Marcionem ii.196; A. Jellinek, Beth ha-Midrash (1853–78), v.63; Ethiopic Synaxaria, in Dillman's Chrestomathia 16 [Calvary]. Cf. M. Grünbaum, in ZDMG 31 (1887), 199; J. Jeremias, in Ἄγγελος II (1926), ii.92 ff.
5. S. A. Cook, The Religion of Ancient Palestine in the Light of Archaeology (1925), 164.
6. M. Gaster, in ZAW 17 (1911), 448.
7. Pausanias, x.13, 7; Pindar, Pyth., iv.4; vi.3; Plutarch, Moralia 409E; Lucian, De saltatione 39, 147; Strabo, x.65. See: Robert-Preller, Griech. Mythologie⁴ (1894), 226; Jane Harrison, Themis² (1927), 396; A. B. Cook, Zeus ii (1925), 166–68; O. Gruppe, Gr. Mythol. (1906), 723, n.2.
8. Ibn Haukal, Oriental Geography, ed. Ouseley (1800), 2.
9. W. Kirfel, Die Kosmographie der Inder (1920), 18.
10. Kalingabodhi Jataka, #479; H. T. Francis and E. J. Thomas, Jataka Tales (Jaico paperback, 1957), 317.
11. P. Saintyves, Corpus de folklore préhistorique en France, ii (1936), 327.
12. P. Schebesta, Les Pygmées (1940), 156.
13. Gaerte, op. cit.; Eliade, Patterns, loc. cit.

114 Sowing a city with salt

1. Sujin (Sefiré) Inscription, 17; tr. F. Rosenthal, ANET², 504.
2. Annals vi.79 = Luckenbill, ARAB ii. §811.
3. Encyclopaedia Biblica, s.v. Salt.
4. F. C. Fensham, in The Biblical Archaeologist 25 (1962), 48–50.
5. KBo VI.34, ii.15 ff.; tr. A. Goetze, ANET 353.
6. W. R. Smith, The Religion of the Semites² (1894), 454, n.1.
7. Cf. EBib., s.v. Ban; F. Schwally, Semitische Kriegsaltertümer, i (1901), 37.

8. Cf. Lev. 2:13 (see: Dillmann, in loc.); Ezek. 43:24. So too among the Greeks and Romans: Theocritus, Id. xxiv.97; Tibullus iii.4, 10; J. G. Frazer, The Fasti of Ovid (1925), ii.142 f., 283; Arnobius, Adv. nationes ii.67. See also: Grimm-Stallybrass, TM 1047.
9. S. Gevirtz, in VT 13 (1963), 56–62.
10. A. M. Honeyman, in VT 3 (1953), 192–95; A. Jirku, Materialen zum Volksreligion Israels (1914), 13 ff.
11. Trans. A. Goetze, ANET 126; cf. T. H. Gaster, Thespis², 261.
12. B. Hrozný, in AOr 1 (1929), 273 ff.; tr. J. Friedrich, AO 24/ii.6.—The operative word is Akkadian *siḫlu*; Aramaic *šeḥalîn*; Hittite *zaḫliya(s)*; see on this: J. Friedrich and B. Landsberger, in ZA, N.F.7 (1931), 313 f.
13. Cf. Gen. 19:24; Ezek.: 38:22; Ps. 11:8. Note, however, that in Theocritus, Id. xxiv.97 brimstone is mentioned along with salt as a purifying agent.—Tiglath-Pileser (Pr. vi.14) says that he strewed "*ṣipu*-stones" over a conquered city, but what this means is uncertain.
14. M. Jastrow, Religion Babyloniens und Assyriens (1905–12), ii.716.
15. E. P. Deatrick, in The Biblical Archaeologist 25 (1962), 41–47.

115 Jephthah's vow

(a)

1. See: Stith Thompson, MI, S 241; W. Baumgartner, in ARW 18.240 ff.; E. Oca, in RBCalz. 26 (1965), 167–71; Th. Barbes, in ThT. 1909.137–43; Feilberg, Bidrag til en Ordbeg over Jyske Almusmal (1886–1914), i.404; ii.647a; Andrejev, in FCC 69.58, 62, 225n.; M. Cox, Cinderella (1893), 511.
2. Servius, on Vergil, Aen. iii.121 f.; xi.264; First and Second Vatican Mythographers, in Scriptores rerum mythicarum Latini, ed. G. H. Bode (1834), i.195, 210.—The story is here combined, as in the Swedish version (see n.11), with the familiar motif that an embroiled sea must be appeased by a human sacrifice; on this, see below, §236 (Jonah).
3. Plutarch, De fluviis ix.1.
4. Grimm's Tales, #88.
5. E. Cosquin, Contes populaires de Lorraine (n.d.), ii.215–17.
6. C. and Th. Colshorn, Märchen und Sagen (1854), #20. Cf. also: P. Zaunert, Deutsche Märchen seit Grimm (1919), 303 ff.
7. K. Müllenhoff, Sagen Märchen und Lieder der Herzogthümer Schleswig-Hollstein und Lauenberg (1843), 285–88.
8. Ch. Schneller, Märchen und Sagen aus Wälschtirol (1867), #25.
9. A. Leskien and K. Brugmann, Litauische Volkslieder und Märchen (1882), #23.
10. Bolte-Polivika, i (1913), 16 ff.
11. B. Thorpe, Yule-Tide Stories (1853), 44 f.
12. Svend-Grundtvig (tr. Mulley), Fairy Tales from Afar (1900), 166.
13. C. J. Lyall, Ancient Arabian Poetry (reprint, 1930), p. xxviii.

(b)

14. The traditional Hebrew text reads, "and go down" (*wᵉ-yaradtî*); the correction (*wᵉ-radtî*) is due to Robertson Smith. It may be added that the emended reading corresponds to the term employed in mythological accounts of the search for the vanished deity, viz., Bion, Epitaphion Adōnidos 18: *alalētai*; Homeric Hymn to Demeter, 43: *strōphat'*. Note also the use of the same word in this connection in a Babylonian commentary on the rites of the Akitu festival, VAT 9555. 29 *ši-i ta-ta-rad* (cuneiform text: *ta-da-ra*; correxit Langdon).
15. T. H. Gaster, Thespis², 30 ff.
16. J. G. Frazer, GB vii (Spirits of the Corn and Wild), ch. vii; A. Moret, in An-

nuaire de l'hist., de phil., et d'hist. orientales 3 (1935), 311 ff.; H. Hepding, Attis (1903), 128, 186. For the weeping in the Babylonian Akitu rites, cf. VAT 9555.29.
17. CT XV, Pl. 48.
18. G. Reisner, Sumerisch-babyl. Hymnen aus Tontafeln Griechischer Zeit (1896), 145, iii. 12–15.
19. ZA 6 (1891), 243. 34.
20. S. Langdon, Babylonian Menologies and the Semitic Calendars (1935), 120 f.
21. R. Labat, in RA 38 (1941), 28.
22. Cf. Proclus, on Plato, Rep. i.215 Kroll; Marius, Vita Procli, c.33 Boissonade.
23. D. Chwolson, Die Sabier (1856), ii.27.
24. O. R. Gurney, in JSS 7 (1962), 147–60; E. M. Yamauchi, in JBL 84 (1965), 283–90.
25. Diodorus Siculus, i.14.
26. Herodotus, ii.79; cf. Julius Pollux, iv.54; Pausanias, ix.29, 7; Athenaeus, 620A.
27. H. Brugsch, Die Adonisklage und das Linoslied (1852), 24; A. Wiedemann, Herodots zweites Buch (1890), 24–26.
28. J. de Hoorack, Les lamentations d'Isis et de Nephthys (1866); E. A. W. Budge, Osiris and the Egyptian Resurrection (1911), ii.59–66; A. Moret, Mystères égyptiennes (1913), 24–26.
29. De errore prof. relig., ii.7 (addressed to the Egyptians); cf. also: Diod. Sic. i.14, 2; A. Moret, La mise à mort du dieu en Égypte (1927), 19 ff.
30. A. L. Oppenheim, in BASOR 103 (1946), 11–14.—For a similar custom in modern Palestine, see: G. Dalman, Arbeit und Sitte in Palästina, i (1928), 566.
31. Plutarch, Theseus 22 (reading *spendontes,* with Cornford, for the *speudontes* of the MSS.).
32. Semus, quoted by Athenaeus, iv.618 f.; cf. E. Spanheim, In Callimachi hymnos Observationes (1697), 649.
33. E. Rohde, Psyche[2] (1897), 289.
34. D. Diringer, Le iscrizioni anticho-ebraiche palestinesi (1934), 1–20; tr. W. F. Albright, ANET 320.
35. A. Jeremias, The Old Testament in the Light of the Ancient East, tr. Beaumont (1911), ii.168.
36. H. Hepding, Attis (1903), 151 ff.

116 Shibboleth

1. See: Notes and Queries 10/x (1908), 408; 10/xi (1909), 36, 233.
2. E. C. Brewer, Dictionary of Miracles, 228.
3. C. L. Kingsford, ed., Chronicles of London (1827), 15.
4. A. M. Kramer, in Notes and Queries, 10/xi (1909), 36.

117 Samson

(a) Samson as a solar hero

1. Cf. I. Goldziher, Hebrew Mythology, tr. R. Martineau (1877), 392–446; E. Stucken, Astralmythen (1907), i.70–75; H. Steinthal, in Zs. für Völkerpsychologie und Sprachwissenschaft 2 (1862); H. Stahn, Die Simsonsage (1908); A. Smythe Palmer, The Samson-saga and Its Place in Comparative Religion (1913); P. Carus, The Story of Samson (1907); S. Reinach, Samson. Bibl. de vulgaris. du Musée Guimet (1912); H. Gunkel, in Internat. Monatsschrift für Wiss., Kunst und Technik, 1913.875–94. Even W. F. Albright once leaned to this view (JBL 37 [1919], 130), but he subsequently modified it (JPOS 1 [1922], 51, n.2).—A. Lods, in Actes du congrès internat. d'histoire des religions, 1923.504–16, and again in Israel (1930), 406, while conceding that Samson was originally a solar hero, thinks that the story was of pre-Israelitic

Horite provenience. Manoah, the father of Samson (a name which does not recur in the O.T.) is, he claims, simply the eponymous hero of the Horite clan of Manaḥat (possibly modern el-Menaḥ, near 'Ain Šams) mentioned in Gen. 36:23, and Samson himself a doublet of Sheshai, the pre-Israelitic giant of Hebron (Num. 13:22; Jos. 15:14). The connection of Manoah with Manaḥat was previously adumbrated by Robertson Smith in EBib., s.v. Samson.

2. Zorah (modern Sara'a), the hometown of Samson's father, Eshtaol (modern Eshwa), Timnah (mod. Tibneh), where Samson took a Philistine bride, and the Valley of Sorek (mod. Wadi Sarar), where Delilah lived, all lie within a five-mile range of Beth Shemesh (mod. Tell Rumeileh).

3. Cf. Greek *komē;* Latin *coma,* both "tress" and "ray."

4. Stith Thompson, MI, K 976.

5. Babylonian Shamshanu, BEUP ix.7, 20; Ugaritic Špšyn, RS 80.i.20; 321.ii.25; Špš (a man's name), RS 80.i.11; 321.iv.6. Cf. also Babylonian Shimshai (S. Daiches, in OLz 11.277) and Biblical Shimshai (Ezra 4:8).

(b) Samson and the foxes

6. Ovid, Fasti iv.680 ff.

7. Babrius, fab.i.11.

8. I. Goldziher, Muhammedanische Studien (1889–90), i.35; J. Wellhausen, Reste d. arabischen Heidentums[2] (1897), 167.

9. O. Preller, Röm. Mythologie[3] (1875), ii.43 f.; F. Baethgen, Beiträge zur sem. Religionsgeschichte (1888), 170 f.

10. J. W. Wolf, Beiträge zur deutschen Mythologie (1852–57), ii.388; Subsidia i (1873), 269.

11. R. Hartmann, in ZAW 31 (1911), 69–72.

12. Livy, xxii.16 f. This, however, may have been simply part of a "scorched earth" policy, such as the forces of Julian later (A.D. 323) employed against the Persians: Ammianus Marcellinus, xviii.7.

13. Maqrizi, tr. Quatremière (1837–45), I.i.179; Sihab ad-Din ibn Faḍallah al'-'Omari, Al-ta'rif bil-muṣtlaḥ aš-Šarif (Cairo 1894), 201 f.

14. John Schiltberger, ed. Neumann, 78, as quoted by Hartmann, loc. cit.

15. M. Magnusson and H. Palsson, King Harald's Saga (1966), 52 f.

(c) Samson's riddle

16. H. Bauer, in ZDMG.1912.473 f.; see also: J. R. Porter, in JTS 13 (1962), 106–9.

17. Cf. the mythological beasts called "eaters" (*aklm*) in the Ugaritic *Hunting of Baal* (75 Gordon, i.26, 36), and the Arabic *'akīl,* "eater," as an epithet of the lion: Freytag, Lex. Arab., s.v.

▲ **(d) Samson and Delilah**

[18. Frazer-Gaster, NGB §§26, 500–02; Schredelseker, De superstitionibus Graecorum quae ad crines pertinent (Diss. Heidelberg 1913); L. Sommer, Das Haar im Religion und Aberglauben der Griechen (Diss. Munich 1912); O. Waser, in ARW 16 (1913), 381 ff.; H. Günthert, in Sitzb. Heidelb. Akad. Wiss., 1915.11 f.; O. Gruppe, Griech. Mythologie (1906), 187, n.2; 882, nn.2 ff.; S. Reinach, Samson (1912), 23 f.; G. A. Wilken, Verspreide Geschriften (1912), iii.551 ff.; W. R. Smith, The Religion of the Semites[3] (1927), 342, n.2; HWbDA, iii.1258; Stith Thompson, MI, D 1831; J. Morgenstern, Rites of Birth, Marriage, Death and Kindred Occasions among the Semites (1966), 84 ff.; W. Abt, Apologie des Apuleius (1908), 179 ff.—Sommer, op. cit., thinks that this belief underlies the Homeric references to swearing by the beard (Iliad 2.501 ff.; 8.371; 10.454).—In Jewish legend, the strength of Judah is said to have resided in his hair: L. Ginzberg, Legends of the Jews, v.277, 354.]

19. F. Valentyn, Oud en Nieuw Oost-Indien (1724–26), ii.143 ff.—Several of the folklore parallels here cited were first adduced by G. A. Wilken in his essay, "De Simsonsage," reprinted in his De Verspreide Geschriften (1912), iii.551–79.
20. J. G. F. Riedel, De sluik- en kreishaarige rassen tusschen Selebes en Papua (1886), 137.
21. J. G. Dalzyell, The Darker Superstitions of Scotland (1834), 637–39.
22. W. Crooke, Popular Religion and Folk-Lore of Northern India (1896), ii.281.
23. Ib.
24. B. de Sahagun, Histoire des choses de la Nouvelle Espagne, tr. D. Jourdanet and R. Simeon (1880), 374.

[24a. KAR II.80.32 (= Ebeling, Quellen, i [1918], 29, 32): *šarta imlušu*.]

[24b. See above, §**109**.]

[24c. Zs. für Mythologie 2.336; 4.299; Notes and Queries 1/vi (1852), 312; II.xii (1861), 500; VI/vi (1882), 249, 416.]

[24d. E. M. Fogel, Beliefs and Superstitions of the Pennsylvania Germans (1915), #1831.]

[24e. See below, §**164**.]

[24f. Sozomen, v. 10, 7; E. Samter, Familienfeste der Griecher und Römer (1901), 64 ff.; A. B. Cook, Zeus i (1923), 68.]

[24g. E.g., in the steppes of Russia: R. Chambers, The Book of Days (1880), i.721; in Prussia: F. Nork, Die Sitte und Gebräuche d. Deutscher, etc. Das Kloster, xii (1849), 163; at Trapani, Sicily: H. N. Hutchinson, Marriage Customs (1879), 275; in Japan: Notes and Queries III/ii (1862), 67; among the Kaffirs of Natal: J. Shooter, The Kaffirs of Natal (1857), 75; among Jews: T. H. Gaster, The Holy and the Profane, 106 f.]

[24h. J. Grimm, Deutsche Rechtsaltertümer³ (1881), ii.287; H. Vordemfelds, Die germ. Religion in der deutschen Volksrechten, RVV 18/i (1923), i.113 ff.; K. Müllenhoff, Deutsche Altertumskunde, iv (1920), 309 f.—During the Hitler regime in Germany, the Nazis cut off the hair of "Aryan" women who engaged in liaisons with Jews. —The custom was known also to the Slavs: F. S. Krauss, Sitte und Brauch der Südslaven (1885), 192 f.]

[24i. A. Poebel, Legal and Business Documents from the Time of the First Dynasty of Babylon (1909), No. 48.14–16; I. Goldziher, Muhamm. Studien (189–90), i.85; J. L. Burckhardt, Travels in Nubia (1819), 146: A. Büchler, in WZKM 18.91–138.]

[24j. See below, §**139**.]

[24k. Morgenstern, op. cit., 238 f.; cf. Isa. 7:20.]

[24l. J. O. Dorsey, in MAFLS 8.113, No. 31.]

[24m. E. C. Brewer, Dictionary of Phrase and Fable, s.v. Adoption by hair.]

25. J T. Nieuwenhuisen and H. C. B. Rosenberg, in Verhandl. van het Batav. Genootschap van Kunsten en Wetenschappen, 30 (1863), 110 ff.; cf. H. Sundermann, Die Insel Nias (1905), 71.
26. Apollodorus, Bib. iii.15, 8; Aeschylus, Choephoroe 612 ff.; Pausanias, i.19, 4; Ciris 116 ff.; Ovid, Met. viii.8 ff.
27. Tzetzes, Scholia on Lycophron, 650.
28. Apollodorus, Bib. ii.4, 5 and 7.
29. J. G. von Hahn, Griechische und Albanesische Märchen (1864), i.217; a similar story, ib., ii.282.
30. B. Schmidt, Griechische Märchen (1877), 91 f. The same writer found in the island of Zacynthus [Zante] a belief that the whole strength of the ancient Greeks resided in three hairs on their chests, and that it vanished whenever those hairs were cut, but returned if they were allowed to grow again: see: B. Schmidt, Das Volksleben der Neugriechen (1871), 206. [A variant in a Greek folksong relates that once, during

the Turkish domination, an agha managed to overcome a Greek hero in combat but could not kill him until an obliging stork fortuitously plucked out some of his hair: Lucy Garnett, Greek Folk Poesy (1896), ii.175.]

[30a. Robert Graves, The Greek Myths (1955), i.310.]

[30b. H. van d. Leyen, Deutsches Sagenbuch (1920), i.26 f. Like the story of Samson and Delilah, this too is often interpreted as a solar myth.]

[30c. W. Henning, The Thousand and One Nights, xii.67.]

[30d. R. Menzel, Bilur Köschk (1923), 16.]

31. A. Dietrich, Russian Popular Tales (1857), 21–24.

32. C. Mijatovich, Serbian Folk-Lore, ed. W. Denton (1874), 167–72; F. S. Krauss, Sagen und Märchen der Südslaven (1883–84), i.164–69.

33. A. H. Wratislaw, Sixty Folk-tales from Exclusively Slavonic Sources (1889), 224–31.

34. J. F. Campbell, Popular Tales of the West Highlands[2] (1890), i.7–11.

35. D. MacInnes, Folk and Hero Tales (1890), 103–21.

118 The woman divided into twelve parts

1. KUB IX.4, i.3 ff., 22 ff.; iii.33 ff.; IX.34, ii.23 ff., 38 ff.; cf. T. H. Gaster, Thespis[2], 307 f.

2. KUB IX.4 and 34 (duplicates); cf. A. Goetze, The Hittite Ritual of Tunnawi (1933), 42 ff.—For analogous magical practices based on the assumed number of the bodily parts, see: F. Boll, Sphaera (1903), 471 ff.; S. Eitrem, Papyri Osloenes, i (1925), 41 ff.

3. KUB XXX.15, i.11.—Curiously enough, a Christian epitaph of the early 5th cent., discovered at Tanagra, in Boeotia, calls for the regular offering to the dead of *"twelve round loaves and goodly wines"*; cf. H. Musarillo, in Theological Studies 11 (1950), 567–69; id., The Fathers of the Primitive Church (1966), 264.—In SMSR 23 (1952), 19, I have suggested that the sacrifice of the *twelve* Trojans at the funeral of Patroclus (Iliad 23.175 f.) was simply a cruel variation on such twelvefold funeral offerings. It is noteworthy that Homer shows the same distaste for this gruesome story (ib., 176) as does our Biblical writer for the ancient Hebrew tale (cf. Judg. 19:30)!

4. Ib., i. 23–24.

5. KUB IX.32; tr. J. Friedrich, AO 24/iv.12.

6. KUB IV.12; tr. Friedrich, ib., 14.

7. Homeric Hymn to Hermes, 128. Twelvefold sacrifices among the Greeks are mentioned also by Eustathius on Iliad 6.93; cf. also: Sophocles, Trachiniae 760 f.

119 The rape of the women of Shiloh

1. E. W. Lane, Manners and Customs of the Modern Egyptians (Minerva Library ed., 1890), 396.

2. Livy, i.9; Plutarch, Romulus 14; Ovid, Fasti ii.139 ff.

3. This account is taken from J. G. Frazer, The Fasti of Ovid (1929), ii.311.

4. Pausanias, iv.4, 2; iv.16, 9; iv.31, 3; Strabo, viii.4, 9.

5. L. R. Farnell, Cults of the Greek States (1896–1909), ii.124; cf. also: Roscher's Lexicon d. Griech. Mythologie, ii.1313.

6. E.g., Euripides, Ion 857; Helen 242–48; Hypsipyle, fr. 734; Plutarch, Ait. phys. 217F.

7. Allen-Sikes-Halliday, The Homeric Hymns[2] (1936), 128 f.

8. Hesychius, Photius, Lexx., s.v. μασχαλισμος.

9. Cf. T. H. Gaster, Thespis[2] (1961), 41.

10. Frazer-Gaster, NGB §§118–21, and Additional Notes thereto.

11. Ovid, Fasti iii.523 f. (v. Frazer, in loc.); W. Ward Fowler, The Roman Festivals of the Period of the Republic (1899), 50–54.

12. H. H. Bancroft, Native Races of the Pacific States (1856–76), ii.719 f., iii.507.
13. W. W. Mannhardt, Mythologische Forschungen (1884), 341.
14. R. Gallop, Portugal (1936), 11. For analogous customs in England, see: Brand-Ellis, Popular Antiquities of Great Britain (1882–83), i.181. So too in Germany: Mannhardt, op. cit., 340; T. Siebs, in Zs. für Volkskunde 3 (1893), 277.
15. G. A. Wilken, in De Indische Gido, June 1884, p. 958.
16. J. G. Frazer, GB ii.100.
17. P. Brincker, in Mitt. f. orient. Sprachen zu Berlin, 3 (1900), 2.
18. H. Fehlinger, Sexual Life of Primitive Peoples (1921), 23.
19. A. Playfair, The Garos (1909), 68.
20. T. H. Gaster, Thespis², 78 f., 413 ff.; see below, §176.
21. E. Westermarck, A Short History of Human Marriage (1926), 28.
22. Mishnah, Ta'anith iv.8.
23. W. C. Hazlitt, Dictionary of Faith and Folklore (1905), 193.
24. Howes, in Folk-Lore 40 (1929), 56 f.
25. L. Spence, in ERE iii.67ª.
26. Gaster, op. cit., 41 f.
27. Lorenz, in ARW 17 (1915), 342.
28. A. R. Wright, English Folklore (1928), 43.
29. For a different explanation, see: L. Spence, Myth and Ritual in Dance, Games and Rhyme (1947), 42 f.

RUTH

121 Covering with a garment in token of protection

1. G. W. Freytag, Einleitung in d. Stud. d. arab. Sprache (1861), 223; G. A. Wilken, Das Matriarchat bei den alten Araben (1864), 69; G. Jacob, Das Leben der vorislamischen Beduinen (1895), 58 f.; id., Altarabische Parallelen zum AT (1897), 27 f.— A paper on this usage (ḥil'at) was read by F. W. Buckler before the Twentieth International Congress of Orientalists at Brussels in 1928, but I have been unable to trace publication of it.
2. Ibn Hisham, ed. Wüstenfeld, 763.
3. J. L. Burckhardt, Bedouins and Wahabys (1830), 213.
4. H. N. Hutchinson, Marriage Customs of Many Lands (1897), 199.
5. Zs.f. Vk. 20 (1910), 146.
6. Odes of Solomon 28:5. J. Rendell Harris renders the crucial phrase, "I have been set on his immortal pinions," but I think the Syriac word k-n-ph-â here has the meaning "skirt" rather than "pinion." Cf. also Gesenius, Thesaurus, s.v. k-n-f.
7. Ducange, iii.114c, s.v. pallio cooperire. Hommel, Jurisprudentia numismatibus illustrata (1763), 214–18; J. Grimm, Deutsche Rechtsaltertümer³ (1881), i.220; F. Nork, Die Sitten und Gebräuche der Deutschen. Das Kloster xii (1849), 161.—There is an interesting reference to this custom in a letter (Ep. 13) of Robert Grosseteste, the great bishop of Lincoln, to William de Raleigh, bishop of Winchester.* Raleigh replies that he has verified this usage in English law on the authority of Richard de Luce, a jurist of the time of Henry III. John Selden, in his Table Talk, also alludes to it.
8. Notes and Queries, I/vii (1853), 17, 243 f.; A. L. Gilchrist, in Folk-Lore 49 (1938), 192 f.
9. T. H. Gaster, Customs and Folkways of Jewish Life (1965), 132 f.

---

* Du Cange says strangely, *Walter* Raleigh, who lived some three centuries later and whose connection with cloaks was, as we know, something else again!

122 Gestures of adoption

1. F. Liebrecht, Zur Volkskunde (1879), 439.
2. L. Kohler, in ZAW 29 (1909), 312–14; Zs. f. Vk. 20 (1910), 140 ff.; J. Grimm, Deutsche Rechtsaltertümer³ (1881), i.219, 638.
3. I.e., for *'aSaPPeRaH 'eL HôQ*, read *'ôSîPHeKaH 'eL HeQî*. The emendation is due to H. Torczyner (Tur Sinai); see also: H. Ringgren, in ZAW 64 (1952), 123. Note that the Hebrew word *'-s-ph*, which is thus restored to the text, is indeed the technical term for adoption: cf. Ps. 27:10 and post-Biblical usage.
4. B. Landsberger, *Ana ittišu* (1937), 51–57.

123 Removing the shoe

1. Cf. Deut. 25:9; see: L. Dürr, in OLz 41 (1938), 410–12.
2. R. Burton, Land of Midian (1857), ii.197; I. Goldziher, Abh. arab. Philologie (1896–99), i.47; W. R. Smith, Kinship and Marriage in Early Arabia (1885), 269.
3. J. L. Burckhardt, Bedouins and Wahabys (1830), i.113.
4. HSS V.17, 76; tr. E. Speiser, AASOR 10 (1930), 63–64, 66. See also: E. A. Speiser, in BASOR 77 (1940), 15 ff.
5. I.e., for the traditional text, which reads *We'aᶜLîM ᶜêNi Bô*, "(From whose hand have I ever taken a bribe) to blind my eyes therewith?" the Greek Version presupposes, by a change of but a single letter, *WeNa'Laim 'āNū Bî*, "Or a pair of shoes? Testify against me!"
6. E. R. Lacheman, in JBL 56 (1937), 53–56.
7. II Aghat vi.44–45.
8. Aztwd Inscription from Karatepe; tr. F. Rosenthal, ANET², 499 f.
9. J. G. Wilkinson, The Ancient Egyptians (1878), ii.337.
10. Enuma Elish iv.104, 118; tr. E. A. Speiser, ANET 67.
11. Vergil, Aen. vii.99 f.; Livy, xxxiv.22. Cf. also *pedem opponere;* Ovid, Pont. iv.6–7.
12. Cf. J. D. Eisenstein, JE, s.v. Halizah.
13. L. Lewy, in MGWJ 62 (1918), 178–85.—For other Jewish interpretations of the custom, see: M. Guttmann, in Wissensch. Zeitschr. für jüd. Theologie 4 (1839), 61–87; A. Büchler, in ZAW 21 (1901), 81–92; J. Nact, in JQR 6 (1915), 1–22.
14. F. Thiselton Dyer, Domestic Folklore (n.d.), 92.—For a similar usage in Germany, see HwBDA, i.1405.

SAMUEL

124 Falling to the ground

1. H. Spencer, Principles of Sociology (1897), i.318; E. Rohde, Psyche⁷ (1921), 245, n.1.
2. Diogenes Laertius, viii.34.
3. Jamblichus, Vita Pythag. 126.
4. Pliny, HN xxviii.27.
5. C. Hatknoch, Alt und neues Preussen (1684), 188.
6. Aristophanes, frag. 291, Dindorf (= Athenaeus, 427E).
7. A. Wuttke, Der deutsche Aberglaube der Gegenwart³ (1900), §458.
8. Pliny, HN xxviii.6.
9. Orphica, Lithica 383.
10. S. Eitrem, Papyri Osloenses i (1925), 114 f.
11. Eitrem, op. cit., Text 1.313.

125 Of mice and men

1. Callimachus, Hymns iii.251–58.
2. Lex., s.v. *Skythôn erêmia*. The expression is echoed in Aeschylus, Prometheus Vinctus 1–2.
3. O. Gruppe, Griech. Mythologie (1906), 1269 ff.
4. Herodotus, i.105 f.
5. Ammianus Marcellinus xxiii.6, 24; cf. B. Gildersleeve, in AJP 29 (1908), 97 f.; P. Svoronos, in Journ. internat. d'archéologie num. 13 (1911), 115 f.
6. De bello Troiano i.19.
7. For examples, see: J. V. Grohmann, Apollo Smintheus und die Bedeutung der Mäuse in der Mythologie der Indogermanen (1862), 28 f.; HWbDA vi.43.
8. Strabo, iii.4, 18.
9. A. Wuttke, Der deutsche Volksaberglaube der Gegenwart[2] (1925), 201.
10. Grohmann, loc. cit.
11. II Kings 19:35.
12. Herodotus, ii.141; see: A. Godley, in CR 15 (1901), 194 ff.; J. H. Moulton, ib., 281 f.; J. Oestrup, in Noeldeke Festschrift (1906), ii.86 ff.; D. M. Robinson, in AJP 29 (1908), 97, n.1.
13. Cf. Strabo, xiii. §604.—For a Chinese parallel, cf. F. Liebrecht, Zur Volkskunde (1879), 13.
14. CR 15 (1901), 319 f.
15. J. U. Powell, "Rodent Gods in Ancient and Modern Times," in Folk-Lore 40 (1929), 173 ff.
16. F. G. Welcker, Kleinere Schriften (1844–67), iii.33–45.
17. Iliad 1.39 ff.
18. Odyssey 7.64.
19. Odyssey 17.251.
20. Ib., 494.
21. Iliad 1.10; Lycophron, 1205; Apollodorus, Bib. ii.103; Macrobius, Sat. i.17, 9; Gruppe, op. cit., 1238 f.
22. Macrobius, Sat. i.17, 24.
23. CIS I.110 (341 BC); G. A. Cooke, A Text-Book of North Semitic Inscriptions (1903), 55 f.
24. F. Clermont-Ganneau, Récueil d'archéologie orientale (1888–1907), i.176 ff.
25. At Elis: Pausanias, vi.24, 6; cf. Euripides, Andromache 880.
26. Aristophanes, Birds 584; Gruppe, op. cit., 1238, n.4.
27. Grohmann, op. cit.; Gruppe, op. cit., 1229, n.2; A. Lang, Custom and Myth[2] (1885), 103–20 [superficial]; J. G. Frazer, GB viii.282 f.; A. H. Krappe, in ARW 33 (1936), 40–46; id., in Class. Phil. 36 (1941), 133–41.
28. Scholiast, on Lycophron 1303; Schol., on Iliad 1.39 (ed min., Heyne [1834] i.12).
29. Aelian, Hist. animal. xii.5.
30. Strabo, xiii.1, 45. Menandros, *Peri epideiktiôn*, in Rhetores Graeci, ed. Spengel (1856), iii.445 f., identifies Apollo with Horus. It is therefore not without interest that porcelain images of mice dedicated to Horus have been found in Egypt: Lang, op. cit., 113.
31. In Amos 9:7 they are said to have come from Caphtor, usually identified with Crete. On this identification, see: T. H. Gaster, Thespis[2], 163. Cf. also Deut. 2:3.
32. Polemo, quoted by Scholiast on Iliad 1.39; cf. Gruppe, op. cit., 1229.—The Chams of Indo-China have a rude idol called Good Rat whom they propitiate when rats infest fields excessively: E. Aumonier, in BPHR 24 (1891), 236; J. G. Frazer, GB viii.283.

33. Pausanias, iii.20, 9.
34. So S. Wide, Lakonishe Kulte (1893), 118; A. H. Krappe, in Class. Phil. 39 (1944), 178–93.
35. Pseudo-Aristotle, Mirab. auscult. 125 (137); cf. Wide, op. cit., 119.
36. F. Panzer, Bayerische Sagen und Gebräuche (1848–56), ii.157.
37. C. L. Rochholz, Deutsche Glaube (1897), i.158.—In a painting at Strasbourg Cathedral, for instance, she is portrayed surrounded by mice; while on a metal collar preserved in the Collegiate Church at Nivelles, Belgium, she has a mouse on the hem of her garment: Powell, op. cit., 177; Krappe, in Class. Phil. 36 (1944), 138. It should be observed, however, that "in medieval tradition the souls of the departed were believed to spend the first night in the Great Beyond with St. Gertrude" (Krappe, loc. cit.; Grohmann, op. cit., 34, 38), and souls were commonly assumed to take the form of mice: H. Pfannenschmid, Germ. Erntefeste (1878), 163, 433; J. Wellhausen, Reste d. arab. Heidentums[2] (1897), 152; Matthew of Paris, quoted by M. Cox, Introduction to Folklore[2] (1897), 43. This, therefore, may be what is intended. But even so, this may be simply a Christian interpretation of the mouse's association with the older plague-goddess who had been transmogrified into St. Gertrude. We know, in fact, that in pre-Christian times the cult of a Teutonic goddess of death, variously named Nehalennia or Hludana, flourished in Belgium, and it has long been suspected that St. Gertrude is but her Christian successor: Krappe, loc. cit.; H. Güntert, Kalypso (1919), 62.

126 Death for looking into the Ark of the Lord

1. For 5000 as a round number, cf. Judg. 8:10; 20:45; I Sam. 17:5.
2. RSV omits the "five thousand."

127 Qualifications for Kingship

1. II Sam. 14:25; see: R. Patai, in HUCA 20 (1947), 155 ff.
2. Enuma Elish i.99.
3. Herodotus, vii.187.
4. Athenaeus, xiii.20.
5. II AB, i.59–60; cf. T. H. Gaster, Thespis[2], 218 f.
6. D. R. Mackenzie, The Spirit-ridden Konde (1925), 72 f.
7. S. S. Doran, in South African Journal of Science 15 (1918), 397.
8. II Kings 15:5.
9. Krt C, vi.44 f.; tr. H. L. Ginsberg, ANET 148[a].
10. Frazer-Gaster, NGB §190.

128 Eyes brightened by eating honey

1. B. F. Beck, Honey and Health (1938), 86.
2. Aristotle, De animal. hist. ix.40, 21; Probl. ined. i.2.
3. Dioscorides, ii.
4. Galen, xi.34, xii.70; xiii.731, etc.—A recipe inscribed on a marble tablet (after A.D. 138) probably from the temple of Asclepius on an isle in the Tiber, prescribes honey for sick eyes: Dittenberger, Sylloge[2], 807.15 ff.; A. Deissmann, Light from the Ancient East[2] (1911), 132.
5. Pliny, HN xi.37, 38; xxix.128.
6. Celsus, vi. 34.
7. Beck, op. cit., 88.
8. Ib., 118.
9. E. N. Fallaize, in ERE vi.770; Stith Thompson, MI, D 1338.9.
10. Beck, op. cit., 223 f.; W. R. Smith, in Journal of Philology 14.125; J. Wellhausen,

Reste d. arab. Heidentums² (1897), 173; J. Morgenstern, Rites of Birth, Marriage, Death and Kindred Occasions among the Semites (1966), 34–35. Photographs of the ceremony appeared in Life magazine, July 12, 1954, p. 52.
 11. Vergil, Georgica iv.451.
 12. Ap. Rhodius, Argon. iv.1136.
 13. Cf. J. A. Fabricius, Codex pseudepigraphus Veteris Testamenti (1722), 780–81.
 14. Kalevala, runo xv.385 ff.; tr. Kirby (Everyman's Library ed.), i.159 f.
 15. Headlam-Knox, Herodas (1922), 271.
 16. KB vi/2, 48.21.
 17. Translated in ANET 328. The charm dates from the 13th cent. B.C.

129 Agag

(a) Agag walks "delicately"

 1. The traditional Hebrew text reads, *Surely the bitterness of death is past*, but the Hebrew word *sar*, rendered *is past*, is probably a mere variant of the following *mar*, which means *is bitter*, rather than *bitterness of*. The Greek (Septuagint) Version so reads the phrase.
 2. The word is $m^ednît$, which KJV and RV (after Symmachus and the Aramaic Targum) vocalize $ma^{ca}danît$ and derive from ^{c}-d-n, "be delicate." But it should really be read $m^{ec}ôdanît$, from m-^{c}-d, "totter, stagger," as both the Greek Septuagint and the Latin Vulgate recognized.
 3. See: A. J. Wensinck, Some Semitic Rites of Mourning and Religion (1917), 43; H. Jahnow, Das hebräische Leichenlied (1923), 75, n.6.
 4. E. Roger, La terre saincte (1664), 265.
 5. Minerva Library ed. (London 1890), 488.
 6. J. Wetzstein, in Zs. für Ethnologie 5 (1873), 296 ff.
 7. Jahnow, loc. cit.; Wensinck, loc. cit.; S. A. Cook, in Essays and Studies presented to Wm. Ridgeway, ed. E. C. Quiggin (1913), 397 ff.
 8. BM 83–1–18, 1846, rev. i.6–7 T. G. Pinches, in PSBA 18 (1896), 253. The Sumerian equivalent is LÚ. TU. IGI. GUGU(?), which Pinches interprets as "one who weeps with troubled eye."
 9. III Aqhat 189 (reading: *ltm mrqdm*); see: T. H. Gaster, Thespis², 370 f.
 10. Lam. 2:21.

(b) Agag is hewn asunder

 11. Abu ᶜObaida, Ham, 458; Reiske, An. Musl. i.26 ff., of the notes; Lisan al-ᶜarab x.240; cf. W. Robertson Smith, The Religion of the Semites³ (1927), 491 f.; J. Wellhausen, Reste d. arab. Heidentums² (1887), 112.
 12. Nilus, in Migne, PG lxxix.66.
 13. Smith, loc. cit.

131 Beheading fallen foes

 1. KB ii.197.
 2. Cf. A. Jeremias, The Old Testament in the Light of the Ancient East (1911), ii.183, fig. 165.
 3. G. Jacob, Das Leben der vorislamischen Beduinen (1895), 28, n.2 (where full references are given).
 4. Th. Noeldeke, Aufsätze zur pers. Geschichte (1887), 90; cf. also: Firdausi, i.129, 8; i.324, 141, ed. Vullers.
 5. See above, §107.
 6. R. B. Onians, The Origins of European Thought, etc. (1951), 95 ff.; J. A. MacCulloch, ERE, s.v. Head; Frazer-Gaster, NGB §174.

7. Servius, on Vergil, Ecl. vi.3; Aen. iii.607.—K. Bethe, in Rhein. Mus. 62 (1907), 465, so explains the Homeric expression, *amenêna karêna* (Odyssey 10.521, 536; 11.29, 49), but L. Radermacher, in ARW 11 (1908), 414, objects that this refers simply to the fact that the people were counted *per capita!*
8. A. B. Ellis, The Yoruba-speaking Peoples of the Slave Coast (1894), 125 ff.
9. R. Verneau and Pennatier, in L'Anthropologie 36 (1921), 317.
10. J. Langsdorff, Reise um die Welt (1812), i.115 f.
11. A. Bastian, Die Völker des östlichen Asiens (1866–71), ii.256.
12. Rev. Francis Connell, Baptism (1938), 13 f.

132 The bundle of the living

1. On the concept of the external (or separable) soul, see: Frazer-Gaster, NGB, §§148–49, and additional note, p. 123.
2. P. N. Wilken, in Mededeelingen van wege het Nederlandsche Zendeling-genootschap, 7 (1863), 146 ff.
3. B. F. Matthes, Bijdragen tot de Ethnologie van Zuid-Celebes (1873), 74.
4. J. A. Jacobsen, Reisen in die Inselwelt des Banda-Meeres (1896), 199.
5. H. Newton, In Far New Guinea (1914), 186.
6. B. Spencer and F. J. Gillen, The Native Tribes of Central Australia (1899), 128–36; cf. iid., The Northern Tribes of Central Australia (1904), 257–82.
[6a. E.g., Prov. 7:20.]
[6b. VS XVI.1 (= P. Kraus, Altbabylonische Briefe 1931, 49, 51), 11–12: *be-el-ki u be-li-it-ki ki-ma ki-[si] sá qa-ti-šu-nu li-iṣ-ṣu-ru-ki.*]
[6c. M. Lidzbarski, Ginza, r., p. vii; E. S. Drower, The Canonical Prayerbook of the Mandaeans (1949), 80, n.4 (in reference to *laufa*).]
[6d. L. Oppenheim, in JNES 18 (1959), 121–28.]
[6e. O. Eissfeldt, in BASW 105 (1960), 60 f.]
[6f. M. Pope, Job (Anchor Bible, 1965), 104.]
[6g. The present writer acquired at a country fair in Vermont an antique ballot box designed for such a purpose.]

▲ 133 The Witch of Endor

1. Cf. CT, XXIII; A. Jeremias, The Old Testament in the Light of the Ancient East (1911), ii.184 f.
2. Epic of Gilgamesh xii.78 ff.; tr. Speiser, ANET 98 f.
3. *Nekyomanteia,* less commonly *nekromanteia* or *psychomanteia.*
4. Pausanias, ix.30, 6.
5. Herodotus, v.92, 7.
6. Pausanias, i.17, 5.
7. Plutarch, Cimon 8; id., De serâ numinis vindictâ, 10. Cf. Pausanias, iii.17, 8 f.
8. Id., De defectu oraculorum 45.
9. Id., Consolatio ad Apollonium, 14.
10. Herodotus, iv.172.
11. H. Duveyrier, Exploration du Sahara: les Touareg du Nord (1864), 415.
12. Aeschylus, Persae 600–838.
13. Philostratus, Vita Apollonii iv.16.
14. Pliny, Nat. Hist. xxx.18.
15. Lucan, Pharsalia xi.413–830.
16. Horace, Sat. i.26–29.
17. Tibullus, i.2, 47 ff. [with Kirby Smith's commentary, in loc.].
18. Tacitus, Annals ii.271 ff.
19. Suetonius, Nero xxxiv.4.
20. Dio Cassius, lxxvii.15.

21. J. Roscoe, in JRAI 31 (1901), 129 ff.; 32 (1902), 44 ff.; id., The Baganda (1911), 283–85; id., "Worship of the Dead as Practised by some African Tribes," in Harvard African Studies, 1 (1917), 39 ff.
22. Id., The Northern Bantu (1915), 53.
23. Ib., 226 ff.
24. C. Goldsbury and H. Sheane, The Great Plateau of Northern Rhodesia (1911), 83.
25. E. Beguin, Les Ma-rotsé (1903), 120–23.
26. J. Spieth, Die Religion der Eweer in Süd-Togo (1911), 238.
27. H. Néel, in L'Anthropologie, 24 (1913), 461.
28. F. Speiser, Two Years with the Natives in the Western Pacific (1913), 206.
29. E. Shorthand, Traditions and Superstitions of the New Zealanders[2] (1856), 81–96.
30. Old New Zealand, by a Pakeha Maori (London 1884), 122–28.
31. M. Radiguet, Les derniers sauvages: la vie et les moeurs aux Îles Marquises[2] (1882), 226–32. (The author first went to the Marquesas Islands in 1842.)
32. J. Viegen, in Tijdschrift van het Koninklijk Nederlaandsch Aardrijkskundig Genootschap, Second ser. 29 (1912), 149; A. J. Gooszen, in BTLVNI, 69 (1914), 377.
33. N. Adriani and A. C. Kruijt, De Bare'e-sprekende Toradja's van Midden-Celebes (1912–14), i.330.
34. E. H. Gomes, Seventeen Years among the Sea-Dyaks of Borneo (1911), 142.
35. C. Hose and W. McDougall, The Pagan Tribes of Borneo (1912), ii.38 ff.
36. J. Warneck, Die Religion der Batak (1909), 89 ff.
37. E. W. Hawes, The Labrador Eskimo. Canada, Department of Mines, Geological Survey, Memoir 91 (1916), 132.
38. J. H. Gray, China (1878), ii.22 ff.
39. J. J. M. de Groot, The Religious System of China, vi (1910), 1330 ff.
40. Ib., 1332–35.
[40a. E.g., Lev. 19:31; Deut. 18:11; Isa. 8:19; 19:3; 29:4; I Chron. 10:13. Cf. Th. Noeldeke, in ZDMG 28.667.]
[40b. See fully: J. Negelein, "Die Luft- und Wasserblase im Volksglauben," in ARW 5 (1902), 145–49.]
[40c. Zs. für Ethnologie 17 (1875), 86.]
[40d. II Aqhat i.27, 45; cf. T. H. Gaster, Thespis[2], 334.]
[40e. Archaeology and the Religion of Israel (1942), 203, n.31.]
[40f. For these terms, see: Grimm-Stallybrass, TM, 915.]

137 The "holder of the spindle"

1. KJV (following the Greek Septuagint and many of the older commentators) misses the point by rendering, *one that leaneth on a staff*, i.e., is crippled or feeble. But the Hebrew word (*pelek*) definitely means "spindle," not "staff."
2. MVAG 1898.234 f. Cf. Nah. 3:13: "Thy people in the midst of thee are women."
3. Berlin Esarhaddon Stele (= KB VI/i.62 ff.), rev. 56 f.
4. KBo VI.34; cf. T. H. Gaster, Thespis[2], 367.

138 Taboo on touching the Ark of the Lord

1. See Frazer-Gaster, NGB §§170–80 (and Additional Notes).
2. Plutarch, Greek and Roman Parallel Hist., c.17.
3. On blinding as a standard punishment for sacrilege, see above, §56.
4. Plutarch, loc. cit.

139 Shaving and shearing

1. The Hebrew original says more directly, "had become a stench."
2. See: J. Morgenstern, Rites of Birth, Marriage, Death and Kindred Occasions among

the Semites (1966), 84 ff.; P. Jaussen, Coutumes des arabes au pays de Moab (1908), 94 ff.
3. S. I. Curtiss, Ursemitische Religion im Volksleben des heutigen Orients, tr. H. Stocks (1913), 246–51.—A similar usage has been reported from the Sinai Peninsula: W. E. Jennings-Bramley, in PEFQS 1907.34 f.
4. F. Niebuhr, Reisebeschreibung nach Arabien (1774–1857), ii.431, as quoted by Morgenstern, loc. cit.
5. Morgenstern, op. cit., 86.
6. ᶜAntar, tr. Hamilton, i.149; ii.30; iii.92 f.; I. Goldziher, Muhamm. Studien (1889–90), i.250; Kitab al-Aghani, ed. Bulac (A.H. 1285), xii.128, 1; G. A. Wilken, Ueber das Haaropfer, etc. (1886–97), iii; W. Robertson Smith, The Religion of the Semites³ (1927), 325n.

140 The Uriah letter

1. Stith Thompson, MI, K 978; H. Gunkel, Das Märchen im AT (1921), 132; Bolte-Polivka, i.286 ff.; A. Aarne, Finnische Märchenvarianten (FCC 33), 64 ff., 91.
2. Iliad 6.155 ff.; Apollodorus, Bib. ii.3; Hyginus, fab. 57; Tzetzes, Schol. on Lycophron 171 id., Chiliades vii.816 ff.; Euripides wrote a tragedy (now lost) on this subject.
3. Homer calls her Anteia.
4. Somadeva, Ocean of Story, i.52; cf. Penzer, ch. xiii.
5. Stith Thompson, MI, K 511.
6. Shakespeare, Hamlet, V.ii; cf. J. Schick, "Hamlet in China," in Jahrbuch der deutschen Shakespeare-Gesellschaft, 50 (1914), 31 ff.
7. Jacob and Wilhelm Grimm, Kinder- und Hausmärchen, #29. The story comes from Zwehrn, the Main district, and Hesse.
8. F. v. d. Leyen, Märchen in der Göttersagen der Edda (1898), 19.
9. B. P. Kretschmer, Neugriechische Märchen (1917), 205; J. G. von Hahn, Griechische und Albanesische Märchen (1864), 162.
10. E. Sklarek, Ungarische Märchen (1901), 26.

141 Regnal names

1. On such "regnal names," see: A. M. Honeyman, in JBL 67 (1948), 13 ff.; A. Alt, in Bertholet Festschrift (1950), 219; S. Hermann, in Wiss. Zs. des Karl Marx Universität Leipzig. Gesellsch. u. sprachwiss. Reihe, iii (1953–54), i.55; R. de Vaux, Les institutions de l'Ancien Testament, i (1958), 165 f.
2. Examples are cited in R. Labat, Le caractère religieux de la royauté assyro-babylonienne (1939), 113 f.
3. II AB, ii.34; v.12; vii.3–4; V AB, D 35–36.
4. II AB, vii.46–47; I*AB, ii.8, 13; vi.31.

142 The coal on the hearth

1. KB VI/2.132, ii.86–87; cf. P. Haupt, in JBL 33 (1914), 166; 35 (1916), 319; B. Landsberger, in OLz 19 (1916), 33–39; A. Ungnad, Babylonische Briefe (1914), #229; P. Koschaker and A. Ungnad, Hammurabis Gesetze (1923), §1741; S. Smith, Isaiah XL–LV (1944), 164.
2. F. Thureau Dangin, in RA 10.93–97.
3. A. Schultens, Liber Iobi (1737), 440 f.
4. Fustel de Coulanges, The Ancient City (Anchor Books ed.), 25, n.2; F. Kirby Smith, on Tibullus i.1, 5. Cf. also: Aeschylus, Choeph. 629; Theocritus, Id., ii.51; Propertius, iv.8, 43; Ovid, Heroides xix.151–54.
5. Ovid, Tristia i.3, 44.

6. Tibullus, i.1, 6.
7. Martial, x.47, 4; xi. 56, 4.
8. B. Schmidt, Das Volksleben der Neugriechen (1871), 24c; D. C. Hesseling, Charos (1897), 53.
9. E. Thomas, in Notes and Queries, 6/iv (1881), 74.
10. J. Grimm, DM[4], 812 f.
11. O. Petersson, Chiefs and Gods (1953), 214 f.; E. J. and J. D. Kriege, The Realm of a Rain Queen (1947), 168.
12. A. C. Bryant, The Zulu People (1949), 469.
13. Petersson, op. cit., 339.
14. J. G. Frazer, GB ii.363 f.
15. Quintus Curtius, iii.3, 9; Clem. Rom., hom. ix.6 (ii.245 Migne). Cf. A. B. Cook, Zeus ii (1925), 34, n.1, citing A. C. Eschenbach, Diss. Acad., 519 ff. (which I have not seen); W. Otto, "Zum Hofzeremoniell der Hellenismus," in Epitymbion Swoboda (Reichenberg 1927), 194 ff.
16. II Kings 8:19; Ps. 132:17.
17. II Aqhat i.28, but the interpretation is uncertain, and some scholars think that the reference is to the evocation of the father's ghost in the form of a wisp of smoke.

143 Absalom and his father's concubines

1. W. Robertson Smith, Kinship and Marriage in Early Arabia[2] (1903), 107 ff.
2. Ib.
3. Gen. 35:22; 49:4.
4. II Sam. 3:7.
5. Apollodorus, Epitome vii.37; Hyginus, fab. 127.
6. Eugammon of Cyrene, Telegony, abstracted by Proclus; see: EGF, ed. Kaibel, 57 f.
7. Sophocles, Trachiniae 1216 f.; Ovid, Met. ix.278 ff.; Apollodorus, Bib. ii.7, 7.
8. Bruns-Sachau, §§109 f.

144 King's misconduct affects soil

1. See above, §127.
2. Prayer of Mursilis, II; A. Goetze, in Kleinas. Forschungen 1 (1930), 175; O. Gurney, in Annals of Art and Archaeology 27 (1940), 27, 37.
3. C. Virolleaud, L'astrologie chaldéenne, IIème suppl., ix.42; Ier suppl. (Adad), lix.26; R. Labat, Le caractère réligieux de la royauté assyro-babylonienne (1939), 121 f.
4. Krt = ANET 148 (iii); cf. T. H. Gaster, The Oldest Stories in the World (1952), 199, 206 f.; id., in JQR 37 (1946), 285 ff.
5. Tr. F. Rosenthal, ANET[2], 504.
6. J. G. Frazer, The Fasti of Ovid (1929), vol. ii, p. 297.
7. J. MacCulloch, Celtic Mythology (1918), 72.
8. Cf. Stith Thompson, MI, Q 552.3.
9. Ammianus Marcellinus, xxviii.5, 14.
10. See: E. Spanheim, on Callimachus, Artemis 125 f.; Plato, Legg. 906; M. Delcourt, Stérilités mysterieuses et naissances maléfiques dans l'antiquité classique (1938), 17; R. Patai, in JQR, N.S. 30 (1939), 59–69; id., Man and Temple (1947), 151–52.
11. A. W. Nieuwenhuis, Quer durch Borneo (1904–07), i.367.
12. R. E. Dennett, At the Back of the Black Man's Mind (1906), 53, 67–71.
13. Job 31:11 f.
14. The word is $ḥ$-n-p; cf. Isa. 24:5; Jer. 3:1, 2, 9; Ps. 106:38.
15. Tr. F. Rosenthal, in ANET[2], 499 f.
16. Ib.
17. Odyssey 19.109 f.

18. Ps. 72:16. (There is no need to emend the traditional text, as do several modern scholars.)

145 A Hebrew Niobe

(a)

1. The expression is due to Hugo Winckler, Geschichte Israels, ii.241.
2. R. B. Onians, The Origins of European Thought about the Body, etc. (1951), 213 (*aiōn* as liquid), 285 f.; Hippocrates, A 11 Diels; M. A. Canney, Givers of Life (1923), 55; M. Eliade, Patterns in Comparative Religion (1958), 193–99.
3. C. A. Doughty, Arabia Deserta (1888), i.349; W. E. Jennings-Bramley, in PEFQS 1907.26 f.; I. Goldziher, in ARW 13 (1910), 20 ff.; J. Morgenstern, Rites of Birth, Marriage, Death . . . among the Semites (1966), 122 f.
4. Goldziher, op. cit., 45, cited in connection with our Biblical passage by A. Jirku, Die Dämonen und ihre Abwehr im AT (1912), 65 f.
5. CT XVI, PL. 10. v.10–14. It must be conceded, however, that this may have been connected with the belief that *the dead are thirsty;* see: T. H. Gaster, Thespis², 334.
6. J. V. Grohmann, Aberglauben und Gebräuche aus Böhmen und Mähren (1864), 189; G. Lammert, Volksmediziniches und medizinisches Aberglaube in Bayern (1869), 105; C. L. Rochholz, Deutsche Glaube und Brauch im Spiegel der heidnischen Vorzeit (1870), i.198; A. le Braz, La légende de la Mort chez les Brétons américains (1923), i.365; E. M. Fogel, Beliefs and Superstitions of the Pennsylvania Germans (1915), 91, #361; Geiger, in HWbDA i.996; A. H. Krappe, The Science of Folklore (1930), 222.
7. W. C. Hazlitt, Dictionary of Faiths and Folklore (1905), i.249; A. R. Wright, English Folklore (1928), 21; H. M. Hyatt, Folk-Lore from Adams County, Illinois (1935), ##10039–44.
8. Isa. 26:19.
9. Syr. Apoc. Baruch 29:7; 73:2; Slavonic Enoch 22:9; TJ Berakoth v.9ᵇ; Taᶜanith i.63ᵈ; TB Hagigah 12ᵇ; Pirqê de R. Eliezer 34 (end); cf. L. Ginzberg, The Legends of the Jews (1909 sqq.), v.11, n.22.

(b)

10. Plutarch, Par. Graec. et Rom. 9, quoting Critolaus.—Saturn is here obviously the god of sowing.

▲ 146 The sin of a census

1. J. H. Weekes, Among the Primitive Bakongo (1914), 292.
2. Id., Among the Congo Cannibals (1913), 136.
3. M. Merker, Die Masai (1904), 152.
[3a. Pechuel-Loesche, in Zs. f. Ethnologie 10 (1878), 234.]
4. W. E. H. Barrett, in JRAI 41 (1911), 36.
5. C. Dundas, in JRAI 43 (1913), 501 ff., 526.
6. C. W. Hobley, Ethnology of A-Kamba and Other E. African Tribes (1910), 165.
7. W. S. and K. Routledge, With a Prehistoric People (1910), 135 f.
8. P. Paulitschke, Ethnographie Nordest-Afrikas (1896), 31.
9. T. Hahn, in Globus, 12.227.
10. E. Doutté, Magie et Religion dans l'Afrique du Nord (1908), 179 ff. For special expressions used in counting measures of corn in Morocco, see: E. Westermarck, Ceremonies and Beliefs Connected with Agriculture, etc. (1913), 31 ff.
11. C. T. Wilson, Peasant Life in the Holy Land (1906), 212 ff.
12. G. Brown, Melanesians and Polynesians (1910), 204.
13. J. Mooney, "Myths of the Cherokee," in 19th Annual Report of the Bureau of American Ethnology (1900), i.424.

14. R. C. Mayne, Four Years in British Columbia and Vancouver Island (1862), 313.

15. E. James, Account of an Expedition from Pittsburgh to the Rocky Mountains (1823), i.235.

[15a. Catullus, 5.11–13; 7.11–12.]

[15b. Cited by Robinson Ellis, Comm. on Catullus, 5.11.]

16. C. Leemius, De Lapponibus Finmarchiae eorumque linguâ, vitâ, et religione pristinâ Commentatio (1767), 499.

[16a. Lilian Eichler, The Customs of Mankind (1924), 667.]

17. J. Ramsay, Scotland and Scotsmen in the Eighteenth Century, ed. A. Allardyce (1888), ii.449.

18. J. R. Tudor, The Orkneys and Shetland (1883), 173; C. Rogers, Social Life in Scotland (1884–86), iii.224 ff.

19. W. Gregor, Notes on the Folk-Lore of the North-East of Scotland (1881), 200.

20. County Folk-lore, vii. Fife, collected by J. E. Simkins (1914), 418.

[20a. Quoted by Robinson Ellis, Comm. on Catullus, 5.12.]

21. Mabel Peacock, in Folk-Lore, 12 (1901), 179.

[21a. F. Nork, Das Kloster, xii (1849), 761.]

22. Letter from William Wyse, 2/25/1908.

23. H. Feilberg, "Die Zahlen im dänischen Brauch und Volksglauben," in Zs. für Ver. f. Volkskunde, 4 (1894), 383.

24. Ib., 384.

25. W. Henderson, Notes on the Folk-Lore of the Northern Countries of England and the Borders (1879), 140.

26. A. Wuttke, Der deutsche Volksaberglaube[2] (1869), 384, §633.

27. Ib., 378, §620.

28. A. Witzschel, Sagen, Sitten, und Gebräuche aus Thüringen (1878), 285, §100.

[28a. Am Urquell, 6 (1895), 10.]

[28b. See now: E. A. Speiser, "Census and Ritual Expiation in Mari and Israel," in BASOR 149 (1958), 17–25.]

[28c. I. Stchoukine, Le suicide collectif dans le Raskol russe (Paris 1903), cited by H. J. Rose, in ERE xii. 22[b].]

[28d. T. F. Thiselton-Dyer, Domestic Folklore[2] (n.d.), 133.]

29. J. Burckhardt, Travels in Nubia (1819), 741.

30. Exod. 30:11–16. The passage is assigned by most modern scholars to a late section of the Priestly Code (P), of exilic or post-exilic date.

[30a. F. Nork, Das Kloster, xii (1849), 761.]

KINGS

147 Abishag

1. See: A. Hagen, Die sexuelle Osphresiologie (Berlin 1901), 191–219 ("Shunamitism").

2. Marcellus Empiricus, De medicamentis empiricis, ed. Helmreich (1889); cf. E. Riess, in The New York Latin Leaflet, May 2, 1904.

3. T. H. White, The Age of Scandal (Penguin ed., 1962), 32 ff.

148 The ritual of enthronement

1. The spring lay on the boundary line between Judah and Benjamin: Jos. 15:1, 7; 18:11, 16; II Sam. 17:17. Josephus (Ant. viii.14, 4) locates it in the King's Garden.— The stone is called "the stone of Zoheleth," and since the Hebrew word z-ḥ-l means

"to creep," this is commonly rendered "Serpent's Stone." For a fascinating, though highly speculative, explanation of the name, see: R. Eisler, in OLz 16.397 f. Cf. also: G. von Rad, in TLZ., 72 (1947), 211–16.

2. J. Przyluski, "La princesse à l'odeur de poisson et la nagi dans les traditions de l'Asie orientale," in Études asiatiques, 2 (1925), 276. Cf. also: M. Eliade, Patterns in Comparative Religion (1958), 208 f., who suggests that the descent of Greek heroes from water-goddesses (e.g., Achilles) may reflect the same idea.

3. Przyluski, loc. cit.
4. Eliade, op. cit., 209.
5. Rajendralala Mitra, Indo-Aryans (London-Calcutta 1881), ii.3, 37 ff., 46 ff.; cf. E. Crawley, Oath, Curse and Blessing (Thinker's Library, No. 40), 87.
6. Satapatha Brahmana, V.iii.3; cf. A. Weber, Ueber die Königsweihe den Rajasâya (1893), 4, 33 f., 42–45, 110–17.
7. A. H. Gardiner, in JEA 36 (1950), 3–12.
8. E. Dhorme, Les religions de Babylonie et d'Assyrie (1945), 34; G. Furlani, La religione babilonese e assira (1928), i.129.
9. ISA, 38–39.
10. Ib., 67–68.
11. Ib., 94–95.
12. Ib., 218–19.
13. Code, rev. xxiv, 26 ff. (Meek, in ANET, renders "insight").
14. J. McCulloch, The Childhood of Fiction (1905), 71.
15. W. Webster, Basque Legends (1879), 22.
16. J. T. Naake, Slavonic Fairy Tales (1874), 28.
17. Grant Allen, The Evolution of the Idea of God (Thinker's Library ed., 1931), 78 f.; cf. A. Kuhn, Indogermanische Studien, i.334.
18. Antanarivo Annual, 1892.485, 492 f.; A. van Gennep, Tabou et totémisme à Madagascar (1904), 82.
19. Grant Allen, loc. cit.
20. But the meaning of the Hebrew text is not entirely certain.
21. Here too the translation is not entirely certain. The Hebrew word, *'ammud*, rendered "pillar," in accordance with its usual sense, could here mean "dais" (cf. Akkadian *kussu nimêdi*).

149 Asylum at the altar

1. See: M. Lohr, Das Asylwesen im Alten Testament (1930); W. Robertson Smith, Religion of the Semites[3] (1927), 75–77, 149, 543; L. Wenger, "Asylrecht," in RAC i.836–44; J. G. Frazer, Totemism and Exogamy (1910), i.96 ff.; E. Westermarck, The Origin and Development of the Moral Ideas (1906), ii.628 ff.
2. Smith, op. cit., 76; id., Kinship and Marriage in Early Arabia[2] (1894), 48–52; Hariri, ed. de Sacy, 177.
3. RS 2.27–28.
4. III Aqhat, 151 ff.; cf. T. H. Gaster, Thespis[2], 364 f.
5. Diodorus, xvii.41.8.
6. Strabo, xvi.2.6; II Macc. 4:33. Cf. also: B. W. Head, Historia Nummorum (1887), Index, iv, s.v.
7. CIS i.86 A 15, B 10; G. A. Cooke, North Semitic Inscriptions (1903), 67 f.
8. Tacitus, Ann., iii. 60 f.
9. Smith, op. cit., 77.
10. Yacut, ed. Wüstenfeld, s.vv. Jalsad, Fals; cf. J. Wellhausen, Reste des arabischen Heidentums[2] (1897), 52–54. See further: Quatremère, "Les asyles chez les Arabes," in Mém. Acad. Inscr., 15 (1845), 307 ff.; I. Goldziher, Muhammedanische Studien, i

(1889), 236 ff.; G. Jacob, Altarabische Parallelen zum Alten Testament (1897), 12, points out that to the bedouin graves sc. of saints are the main asyla.
11. See below, §313.
12. Ps. 15:1 ff.
13. Apollodorus, Epitome 5.23; Aretinus, Ilii Persis, summarized by Proclus = EPG, ed. Kinkel, 49 ff.
14. Apollodorus, Bib., ii.8.1; Schol. on Aristophanes, Knights, 1151.

▲ 150 The judgment of Solomon

1. L. P. Tessitori, "Two Jaina Versions of the Story of Solomon's Judgment," in The Indian Antiquity, 43 (1913), 148–52. The writer gives all four versions; two of them had been published previously by his fellow-countryman, F. L. Pulle.
2. This version of the story is from the Antarakathâsamgraha of Râjasekhara, a work apparently of the 14th cent.
[2a. The most exhaustive treatment will be found in F. M. Goebel, Juedische Motive in maerchenhaften Erzaehlungsgut (Gleiwitz 1932). Cf. also: Gaidoz, in Mélusine iv, Nos. 14, 15, 19; V. Chauvin, Bibliographie des oeuvres arabes (1892–1922), vi.63, No. 231; R. Köhler, Kleinere Schriften, ed. J. Bolte (1898–1900), 531; T. Zachariae, in Zs. f. Volkskunde 16.136 f.; A. Hertel, Geist des Ostens (1913), 6 f.]
[2b. Vikramodaya, No. 14 in Hertel's Pančatantra (1914), 154; Id., Panchakyana-Wartikka (1923), 157 f. A Tamil version is preserved in the Kathmanjari.]
[2c. Jataka, No. 546; T. Steele, An Eastern Love Story, Kusa Jatakaya (1871), 247–57; T. Rhys Davids, Buddhist Birth Stories (1880), i, pp. xiv–xvi.]
[2d. Tibetan Dsanglun; cf. J. J. Schmidt, in Mélusine, iv.367; F. A. von Schiefner, in Mélanges asiatiques, 8.527; F. A. von Schiefner and W. Ralston, Tibetan Tales (1882), 120; F. Köhler, in Zs. f. Missionsk. 42 (1927), 65–68 dates this version to the 7th cent.]
[2e. Lin Yutang, The Wisdom of China (1955), Sect. "Chinese Tales."]
[2f. Klein, Geschichte des Dramas (1865–86), iii.460 ff.]
[2g. The Academy, April 16, 1887, p. 275.]
[2h. N. B. Dennys, The Folklore of China (1876), 139.]
[2i. J. Gladwyn, Persian Moonshee[2] (1840), i.132.]
[2j. F. S. Krauss, cited by Gaidoz, in Mélusine, iv.414.]
[2k. Lumbroso, in L'archivio per lo studio delle tradizione popolari, 2 (1883), 574.]
[2l. Lumbroso, in M. R. Ac. d. Lincei, iii/9 (June 3, 1883); R. Engelmann, in Hermes 39 (1904), 146–54.]
[2m. Gaidoz, in Mélusine, iv.414 f.]
[2n. Abh. Bayer, Akad., Phil. Kl. 8 (1856–58), i.3, 9.]
[2o. E. Samter, in Archäologischer Anzeiger, 1898. 50.]
[2p. Th. Benfey, Pančatantra (1859), ii.544.]
[2q. H. Gunkel, Märchen im Alten Testament (1921), 144 f.]

151 The dedication of the Temple

1. See fully T. H. Gaster, Thespis[2] (1961), where the subject is worked out in detail.
2. The coincidence did not escape the ancient rabbis: see TJ Sanhedrin 18[b].
3. Gaster, op. cit., 47 f.
4. H. St. John Thackeray, The Septuagint in Jewish Worship (1921), 76 ff.
5. Hab. 3:5.
6. Some technicalities need to be discussed in order to reinforce the argument. (*a*) The missing opening line may be restored, after the Greek Version, to read, Šemeš hêḳin ba-šamayim (or Šemeš bašamayim hêḳin), which would mean ostensibly, "He (i.e., Yahweh) fixed the sun in heaven," but it is worthy of note that in Akkadian, the

equivalent of the verb *hêḳîn* is used specifically in speaking of a heavenly body which reaches its zenith (see: G. Meier, in AfO 12 [1938], 240, n.24; R. C. Thompson, Reports, #206; M. Jastrow, Rel. Bab. u. Assyr. [1905–12], ii.614, n.6). To this in turn corresponds the word *mākôn*, the fixed place now built for Yahweh (cf. Exod. 15:17); (*b*) the emphatic, "I have indeed built" (Heb.: *banôh banîthî*) now receives its proper emphasis.

▲ **153 Solomon and the Queen of Sheba**

1. N. Adriani and A. C. Kruijt, De Bare' e-sprekende Toradja's van Midden-Celebes (1912–14), i.133.
2. Koran, Sura 27 (tr. E. H. Palmer).
3. W. Hertz, "Die Rätsel der Königin von Saba," reprinted in his Gesammelte Abhandlungen (1905), 419 ff. In Arab tradition, the queen's name is Balqis.
4. J. E. Hanauer, Folk-Lore of the Holy Land (1910), 97 ff.
5. The Mahabharata, tr. M. N. Dutt (1895), ch. xlvii. Cf. C. Lassen, Indische Alterthumskunde, i^2 (1867), 825; G. A. Grierson, "Dwryodhana and the Queen of Sheba," in JRAS 1913.684 ff.; W. Crooke, ib., 685 f.; C. H. Tawney, ib., 1048. Tawney cites another parallel in an Indian tale: "In the Jyotishkavadana, 108, artificial fishes which can be set in motion by machinery, appear under a crystal floor. The entering guest takes this for water, and is therefore about to remove his shoes"; see: F. A. von Schiefner, Tibetan Tales, tr. W. R. S. Ralston (1882), 361, n.2. In the Jerusalemitan version of the story, a stream of water, with fish swimming in it, flowed under the crystal pavement: Hanauer, loc. cit.

154 Hand withers from impiety

1. Protevangelium xiv.18 ff.; M. R. James, The Apocryphal New Testament (1924), 47; Cotton MS, Pageant xv, "The Miraculous Birth and the Midwives," in W. Hone, Ancient Mysteries (1823), 71. Cf. also: Gospel of Pseudo-Matthew 13 = James, op. cit., 74.
2. E. Kinesman, Lives of the Saints (1623), 381.
3. Socrates, Hist. Eccles. vi.16.

ELIJAH

155 The "man of God"

1. Heb.: *'îš ha-'elôhîm*.
2. Deut. 33:1; Jos. 14:6; Ezra 3:2; Ps. 90:1.
3. I Sam. 9:6–8, 10.
4. II Kings 4:7.
5. I Sam. 2:27.
6. I Kings 13:1.
7. Judg. 3:5, 8 (cf. also v.2). In a somewhat attenuated sense, Nehemiah (12:24, 36) so characterizes David.
8. Cf. H. Duhm, Der Verkehr Gottes mit den Menschen im AT (1926), §11. Duhm compares the "man of God" with a dervish; ib., 61.
9. *Siunan antuhsas*: BoTU 23A, ii.32; cf. A. Goetze, in Kleinasiatische Forschungen 1 (1929), 219, n.3; O. Gurney, in AAA 27 (1940), 27, n.20.
10. ^{LÚ}DINGIR^{LIM}-*niyant-* (= *siuniyant-*): Ehelolf, in ZA, N.F. 9 (1936), 180. *siyuniahh-:* BoTU 23B, iv.15.
11. *Dhu Allah:* I. Goldziher, Abh. z. ar. Phil. (1896–99), 18.—It is often asserted

that there is an Arabic verb *aliha*, derived from Allah, which has a similar meaning, but this is simply a variant of *waliha*; see: A. Fischer, in Islamica 1.390–97.

12. *Entheos:* e.g., Aeschylus, Eumenides 17; Agamennon 1209; Plato, Phaedrus 244*b*.
13. *Theoleptos:* Aristotle, Ethics E 1.1.4; *theolêpsia:* Plutarch, ii.763A.
14. *Kangakari:* W. Aston, in ERE xi.470[b].
15. D. G. Brinton, Religions of Primitive Peoples (1889), 59 (citing Middendorf's Keshua Wörterbuch, s.v.).

▲ 156 Elijah and the Ravens

1. E. Robinson, Biblical Researches in Palestine[2] (1856), i.557 f.
[1a. See: R. Basset, Mille et un contes (1925–27), iii.295; A. Wesselski, Märchen des Mittelalters (1925), 249, #57; H. Gunkel, Das Märchen in A.T. (1921), 34.]
[1b. Aelian, HA xii.21.]
[1c. Diodorus, ii.4; cf. G. Binder, Aussetzung (1964), 163 f.]
[1d. Suidas, Lex., s.v. *lagôs;* cf. F. Cumont, Études syriennes (1917), 82 ff.]
[1e. Ovid, Fasti iii.37, 54.]
[1f. Kalidasa; Shakuntala and Other Writings, tr. A. W. Ryder (1939).]
[1g. Cf. P. Toldo, in Studien zur vergleichende Literaturgeschichte, II (1902), 87 ff.]
[1h. Metaphrastes, Lives.]
[1i. Guérin, Vie des saints[12] (1892), viii.29 f.]
[1j. Jerome, Life of Paul, First Hermit of Egypt.]
[1k. Brewer, loc. cit.]
[1l. Les petits Bollandistes, iii.550.]
[1m. K. Macaulay, History of St. Kilda (1765), 174.]
[1n. Letter of Balasi: R. F. Harper, Assyrian and Babylonian Letters belonging to the K Collection in the British Museum (1892–1914), #353 = R. H. Pfeiffer, State Letters of Assyria (1935), 3334; cf. J. Hunger, Babylonische Tieromina nebst griechisch-römischen Parallelen (1909), 33.]
[1o. Rm. ii.138; Bezold, Catalogue 1650; M. Jastrow, Rel. Bab. u. Assyr. ii (1912), 808.]
2. Aelian, HA i.48.
[2a. Cf. A. S. Pease, Comm. on Cicero, De Divinatione, vol. ii, p. 76.]
3. Porphyry, De abstinentia ii.48.
[3a. Vergil, Georgica i.388 ff.]
[3b. Horace, Odes iii.17, 3.]
[3c. Aelian, HA viii.7; Geoponica i.37. Cf. O. Keller, "Rabe und Krähe im Altertum," in Jahresber. d. wiss. Vereins f. Volkskunde und Linguistik (Prague 1873), 8 ff.]
[3d. Cf. Brand-Ellis, Popular Antiquities of Great Britain, iii (1849), 210–12.]
[3e. Shakespeare, Macbeth, I.v; C. Swainson, The Folklore and Provincial Names of British Birds (1886), 9 f.; T. F. Thiselton Dyer, The Folk-Lore of Shakespeare (1883), 149 f.
[3f. Samuel Butler, Hudibras, II, iii.707.]
[3g. Quoted by Brand-Ellis, loc. cit.]
[3h. Shakespeare, Othello, IV.i.]
[3i. JRAI 20.90.]
[3j. H. R. Schoolcraft, Indian Tribes of the United States (1853–56), iv.491. Cf. also: W. A. Clouston, "Folklore of the Raven," in Saxby's Birds of Omen (1893), 20.]
4. J. Tait, The Lillooet Indians (1906), 283.
5. A. Newton, Dictionary of Birds (1893–96), 766.
6. Pliny, HN x.121–23.
7. Oliver Goldsmith, History of the Earth and of Animated Nature (1776), v.226.
8. W. Yarrell, History of British Birds (1843), ii.68 ff.

9. A. C. Hollis, The Nandi (1909), 7, 70 ff.
10. J. G. Frazer, Totemism and Exogamy (1910), iv.305.
[10a. O. Gruppe, Griechische Mythologie (1906), 820, n.1.]
[10b. Petronius, frag. 26 Buecheler; Fulgentius, i.13.]
[10c. E.g., J. Gray, in The Interpreter's Bible, in loc.]

157 "Measuring" the sick

1. Gaster-Frazer, NGB §76; E. Law Hussey, in The Archaeological Journal, No. 39.
2. Grimm-Stallybrass, TM 1163.
3. Ib., 1165.
4. Cf. S. Eitrem, Opferritus und Voropfer der Griechen und Römer (1915), 485; O. Gruppe, in Bursians Jahresberichte 186 (1921), 281; O. Weinreich, in ARW 20.474.
5. Cf. G. Huet, Les contes populaires (1923), 72.

158 The confrontation on Carmel

Literature: H. H. Rowley, "Elijah on Carmel," in BJRL 43 (1960), 190–219 (with exhaustive bibliography of recent studies); R. de Vaux, "Les prophètes de Baal sur le Mont Carmel," in Bulletin du Musée de Beyrouth 5 (1941), 8–20; E. Würthwein, in Zs. für Theologie und Kirche, 59 (1962), 131–44.

(a) Baal

1. I AB iv.26–27, 37–38.
2. II AB v.68–69 = T. H. Gaster, Thespis^2, 185.
3. I Aqhat 25–45 = Gaster, op. cit., 358.
4. Bokhari, 95 Bulac; cf. Gaster, op. cit., 130, n.13.
5. TB, Sheb. ii.19; Sukkah iii.9; Ter. x.11; cf. Epstein, in ZAW 33 (1913), 82–83.
6. Cf. K. Galling, in Alt Festschrift (1953), 105 ff.; O. Eissfeldt, "Der Gott Karmel," in Sitzb. d. deutsch. Akad. d. Wiss. zu Berlin, Kl. für Sprachen, Literatur u. Kunst, 1953/i; A. Alt, Kleine Schriften (1953), 135 ff.
7. Tacitus, Hist. ii.78; cf. K. Scott, in JRS 24 (1934), 138 ff.
8. Avi-Yonah, in IEJ 2 (1952); summarized in SOTS Book List, 1954, p. 60.
9. Suetonius, Vespasian 5.
10. Jamblichus, Vita Pythag. iii (15).

(b) The fire upon the altar

11. Gudea Cylinder 1 = F. Thureau Dangin, Die sumer. Königsinschriften (1907), 102 f.
12. Exod. 3:3 ff.
13. Cf. E. Dodds, The Greeks and the Irrational (1957), 294, 307, n.95.
14. Pausanias, i.16.
15. Id., v.27.
16. Valerius Maximus, viii.2, 111.
17. Vergil, Ecl. viii.106; cf. also: Servius, on Vergil, Aen. xii.20; Solinus, v. 23.
18. F. Bötticher, in Philologus 25 (1867), 34.
19. Pausanias, v.27, 5 f.
20. Athenaeus, 19E; Julius Africanus, Kestoi, ed. Vielleford; cf. also: Hippolytus, Ref. haeres. iv.33; Dodds, loc. cit.
21. Enapius, Vita soph. 475; Migne, PG xii.12.
22. Caesarius von Heisterbach, Dial. Mirac. vii.46.
23. F. Hitzig, Gesch. d. Volk Israels (1869), 176; R. H. Kennett, in Old Testament Essays (1928), 91 ff.; A. Lucas, in PEQ 1945.5 f. Reference is made to a similar manner of kindling altar-fire, mentioned in II Maccabees 1:29 ff.
24. Cf. Rowley, op. cit., 211 f.

(c) The limping dance and the gashing with knives

25. Heliodorus, Aethiopica iv.17, 1.
26. C. Clermont-Ganneau, in Réc. d'archéol. orientale, i (1888), 101 f.; R. Pietschmann, Gesch. d. Phönizier (1889), 220; F. Cumont, in P-W ii (1896), 2834 f.; S. Ronzevalle, in Rev. archéol. Sér. IV/ii (1903), 29 f.
27. Herodian, v.5, 9; cf. Heliodorus, Aethiopica iv.5, 9.
28. R. Patai, in HUCA 14 (1939), 255. This, however, may be a leaping, rather than a limping, dance, and that is something quite different, concerning which see: Frazer-Gaster, NGB §23 (with Additional Note).
29. R. Paribeni, Notizie degli scavi (1919), 106 f.; F. Cumont, Les religions orientales dans le paganisme romain[4] (1929), Pl. viii.2 (facing p. 90). See on this: de Vaux, op. cit., 111; H. Gressmann, AO 23/viii (1923), 27.
30. Encyc. Brit.[10], vii.795.
31. S. Eitrem, Opferritus und Voropfer d. Griechen und Römer (1915), 479.
32. I*AB, i.6 = Gaster, op. cit., 213.
33. Cf. T. H. Gaster, Thespis[2], 213.
34. Herodotus, ii.61.
35. Lucian, De dea Syria 50.
36. E.g., Seneca, Agamemnon 686 ff.; Minucius Felix, Octav. xxiv.4; Apuleius, Met. viii.28; Horace, Sat. ii.3, 223; Lucan, Pharsalia i.365; Lucian, Asin. 37; Jamblichus, De mysteriis iii.4; cf. H. Hepding, Attis (1903), 159 f.; H. Graillot, Le culte de Cybèle (1912), 305 f.; F. Cumont, op. cit., 50–51 and nn.; T. Noeldeke, in ARW 10 (1907), 149 ff.
37. Tibullus, i.6, 44 f.
38. Propertius, ii.22, 15.
39. Statius, Theb. x.170.
40. R. Petazzoni, Confession des péchés (1931), i.151n.; 149, n.4; id., in SMSR 1930.285; id., La Confessione dei Peccati, iii (1936), 24, 38.
41. Frazer-Gaster, NGB §41 (with Additional Note).
42. J. Kreemer, in Mendel. Zendel. 30 (1886), 113.
43. Fr. Coulbeaux, in Missions catholiques 30 (1898), 455.

(d) Elijah's taunts

44. The meaning of the assonantal phrase, $kî\ sîaḥ\ w^e$-$kî\ sîg\ lô$ is uncertain. LXX paraphrases, "And maybe he is busy." So too Vet. Lat. Vulgate has *aut in diversorio est*. RSV renders, "Either he is musing or he is gone aside" (i.e., to the privy); KJV, "Either he is talking, or he is pursuing." I take the phrase as simply an example of the figure of speech known to Arab grammarians as *itba*^{c}, whereby effect is heightened by juxtaposing like-sounding words, one of which may be invented *ad hoc;* e.g., in English, "helter-skelter, pell-mell," etc. In that case, an approximate rendering would be, "He is all a-hustle and a-bustle," "he is in a stir and a stew"; "he is huffing and puffing around"; "he is in a dizzy tizzy."
45. Frazer-Gaster, NGB §41; D. Kidd, The Essential Kaffir (1904), 333.
46. E. O. James, in ERE x.562[b].
47. W. Mannhardt, Antike Wald-und Feldkulte (1877), 342n.
48. De Vaux, loc. cit.
49. A. Erman, Die Literatur d. Aegypter (1923), 37.
50. De abstinentia iv.9. See: A. Moret, Le rituel du culte divin journalier en Égypte (1902), 121 ff.; W. Spiegelberg, in ARW 23 (1925), 348; Cumont, op. cit., 89, 241, n.84.
51. Plutarch, De Iside et Osiride 35.
52. Inscription published in Jahreshefte d. oester. Archeol. Instituts 7 (1904), 93.

53. The order was abolished by John Hyrcanus: Mishnah, Ma‛aser Sheni v.15; Soṭah ix.10.
54. Pss. 7:7; 59:5; 88:65.
55. Menander, quoted by Josephus, Antiqu. Jud. viii.5.3; cf. Athenaeus, ix. 47; Stark, in SSGW 8 (1856), 132.
56. The title occurs on: (*a*) Larnax Lapethou iii = A. M. Honeyman, in Le Muséon 51 (1938), 288 (4th cent. B.C.); (*b*) a Rhodian inscription: A. Maiuri, Annuario della regia scuola di Atene, 2 (1916), 267–69; (*c*) Carthaginian inscriptions: CIS i.227, 260–62, 351, 377; Rép. i. ##13, 360, 537, 553, 554, 1569; (*d*) Jol (Shershel) 2 = G. A. Cooke, A Text-book of North Semitic Inscriptions (1903), #57.4. Cf. de Vaux, op. cit., 17 f.
57. Athenaeus, vi.253, b-f.

(e) Rain-stones

58. Frazer-Gaster, NGB §52. On the subject in general, see: R. Eisler, in Philologus 68 (1909), 42, n.222; M. Eliade, Patterns of Comparative Religion (1958), 226 f.; G. A. Wainwright, The Sky-Religion in Egypt (1938), 76; G. F. Kunz, The Magic of Jewels and Charms (1915), 5 f., 34; W. J. Perry, The Children of the Sun[2] (1926), 392; J. Rendell Harris, in Folk-Lore 15 (1905), 427 ff., 434 ff.; Notes and Queries III/iv (1864), 338.
59. G. Turner, Samoa, a hundred years ago and long before (1884), 145.
60. W. G. Aston, Shinto (1905), 330.
61. W. Crooke, Popular Religion and Folklore of Northern India (1896), i.75 f.
62. J. Rhys, Celtic Heathendom (1888), 184.
63. Ib., 185 f.
64. F. A. Hasluck, in Annual of the British School at Athens 21 (1914–16), 78.
65. Margaret Murray, in ZÄS 51 (1913), 131; S. G. Mitra, in Folk-Lore 9 (1898), 277.
66. Frazer-Gaster, loc. cit.; L. Deubner, in Neue Jahrb. 27 (1911), 334, n.3.

(f) The filling of the trench with water

67. O. Gruppe, Griech. Mythologie (1906), 446.—That Elijah's act was a magical rite is argued also by: P. Volz, Das Neujahrfest Yahwehs (1912), 31; R. Dussaud, Les origines canaanéennes du sacrifice israélite (1921), 205 f.; R. Patai, in HUCA 14 (1939), 256 f.; S. Mowinckel, Religion und Kultus (1953), 99; N. H. Snaith, in Interpreter's Bible, iii.157. It is denied, however, by R. de Vaux, Élie, 63; S. Garofalo, La Sacra Biblia (1951), 141.
68. Lucian, De dea Syria 13; Melito, in Cureton's Spec. Syr. (1885), 45.
69. Volney, Voyages en Syrie et en Égypte (= Études pol. de la Syrie [1787], ii.197).
70. Athenaeus, 496A; cf. Euripides, frag. 592, Nauck; Proclus, Tim. v.293^b (v. Bötticher, in Philologus 24 [1886], 235).

(g) Elijah on the summit of Carmel

71. Sinuhe R (= Pap. Berlin 3022), 10; W. C. Hayes, in JNES 7 (1948) 9, n.44 (*tp ḥr m* } *st*).
72. RS 137.23, Gordon (*tǵly rišthm lẓr brkhm*); cf. J. B. Bauer, in Hermes 87 (1959), 383 f.; A. Jirku, in ZDMG 103 (1953), 372.
73. Römer, Guinea, 57; Schlegel, Ewe-sprache, p. xvi, as quoted by E. B. Tylor, Primitive Culture, ii.221.

(h) The raincloud

74. S. Baring-Gould, Curious Myths of the Middle Ages (New York 1884), 201 f.

159 The ascension of Elijah

1. Dilthey, in Rhein. Mus. 25 (1870), 321 ff. See further: F. Schönwerth, Aus der Oberpfalz (1857–59), ii.149 ff.; O. Gruppe, Griech, Mythologie (1906), 406, n.l; 762; 840, n.5; 854, nn.5 ff.; 1203; 1209, n.2; 1293.
2. J. Grimm, DM[4], 768 ff.; Sartori, in Zs. f. Vk. 4 (1894), 289 ff.; A. Kuhn, in Zs. f. deutsch. Altertum 6 (1848), 13 ff.; W. Mannhardt, Antike Wald- und Feldkulte[2] (1904–5), i.149 ff.; H. Meisen, Die Sagen vom wütenden Heer und vom Wilden Jäger (1925); A. Endter, Die Sage vom wilden Jäger (Diss. 1933); V. Schweda, Die Sagen vom Wilden Jäger, etc. (1915); H. Plischke, Die Sage vom Wilden Heer im deutschen Volke (1914); E. S. Hartland, The Science of Fairy Tales (1891), 234 ff.; Ch. Hilscher, Diss. de exercitu furioso (1688, 1702).—In France, the Host is known as *mesnie furieuse*.
3. Dio. Hal. x.2.
4. Grimm-Stallybrass, TM 1591.
5. FHG iv.151.27.
6. F. Liebrecht, Des Gervasius von Tilbury Otia Imperialia (1856), 173–211.
7. J. Grimm, DM[4], loc. cit.
8. Schweda, op. cit., 13; Stith Thompson, MI, E 501.12.4.
9. Plischke, op. cit., 36; Stith Thompson, MI, E 501.10.3.
10. Schweda, op. cit., 28–29; Stith Thompson, MI, E 501.7.6, 1–4.
11. Plischke, op. cit., 55; Stith Thompson, MI, E 501.11.4; Plischke, op. cit., 37; Stith Thompson, MI, E 501.16.5.—Storms likewise occur at the death of witches: G. Kittredge, Witchcraft in Old and New England (1929), 158 f., 477, n.64.
12. In much the same way, in the old song chanted when the Ark of the Lord was brought back after a campaign, it was described as the equivalent of the "myriads (and) thousands of Israel": Num. 10:36.
13. Israel would then mean simply, Jacob. For a similar learned misunderstanding of a popular expression, we may refer to the famous words, *Is Saul also among the prophets?* (I Sam. 10:11, 12; 19:24), for—as Robert Eisler ingeniously suggested—the Hebrew word *shaūl* (Saul) may there have meant originally, "one loaned to the temple."
14. The expression, *y ad ad*, "Oh, daddy, daddy" (paralleled by *y um um*, "Oh, mummy, mummy") occurs in the same sense in the Ugaritic text, The Gracious Gods, 32.
15. E. Rhode, Psyche [7] (1921), ii.375, n.1.
16. J. Vermaseren, Mithras (Urban Bücher, 1965), 84 f.
17. Sophocles, Trach. 1193 ff.; Euripides, Heraclidae 910 ff.; Ovid, Met. x.134–275; Apollodorus, Bib. ii.158 ff.—Late Greek sources, however, discard the element of the fiery chariot. In Lucian, Hermot. vii, Heracles simply *flies* to heaven, and in Lysias, iii.11, he simply *disappears*.
18. Kornemann, in Klio 8.278; F. Cumont, The Mysteries of Mithra (1903), 157.
19. F. Cumont, After Life in Roman Paganism (1923), 157.

160 The mantle of Elijah

1. A. E. Crawley, ERE, s.v. Dress; cf. also: A. Jirku, in ZAW 37 (1917–18), 109–25.
2. E. Westermarck, The Origin and Development of the Moral Ideas (106–8), ii.623.
3. Theocritus, Id., ii.53–54.
4. E. Kaempfer, "History of Japan," in J. Pinkerton's Voyages and Travels (1808–14), vii.717; cf. E. Crawley, Oath, Curse and Blessing (1934), 99.
5. R. Taylor, Te ika Maui[2] (1870), 164.
6. J. G. Frazer, GB[3] (1911–15), iii.131.

7. See above, §79.
8. See below, §218.
9. S. Dahn, in Me'oroth: Quarterly for Oriental Jews. Special Issue for the 750th Anniversary of Maimonides (Tel Aviv 1954), 25.
10. Cf. P. Joüon, in Biblica 16 (1935), 74–81.—Haircloth is mentioned also in Zech. 13:4 as the characteristic garb of prophets.
11. SBE xxv.449.
12. H. Kern, Manual of Indian Buddhism (1896), 75.
13. Westermarck, op. cit., ii.356; Crawley, ERE v.569.
14. Strabo, xvi.4, 8; cf. W. Robertson Smith, The Religion of the Semites[3] (1927), 437 f.

161   Harlots bathe in Ahab's blood

1. See above, §25.
2. Cf. H. C. Trumbull, The Blood Covenant (1887), 116 ff., 224; H. L. Strack, Der Blutaberglaube (1892), 14 ff., 44 f.; L. Kohler, in ZAW 34 (1914), 147; E. W. Lane, Manners and Customs of the Modern Egyptians[1] (1836), i.33; H. Gunkel, Das Märchen im AT (1921), 142.
3. Pliny, HN xxvi.5.
4. W. Crooke, The Popular Religion and Folklore of Northern India (1896), ii.172 f.
5. R. Moffatt, Missionary Labours and Scenes in Southern Africa (1842), 277.
6. H. Spencer, Principles of Sociology (1876–82), i.116.
7. Notes and Queries, Feb. 28, 1857.
8. Strack, op. cit., 36 ff.
9. *Taurobolium:* H. Hepding, Attis (1903), 196 ff.; S. Angus, The Mystery-Religions and Christianity (reprint, 1966), 94 ff. *Criobolium:* C. A. Lobeck, Aglaophamus (1829), 797; A. Dieterich, Eine Mithrasliturgie[2] (1922), 157 ff.; E. Rohde, Psyche[7] (1921), ii.421 ff.
10. J. Dunlop, Geschichte der Prosadichtung, ed. and tr. F. Liebrecht (1851), 135.
11. N. M. Penzer, The Ocean of Story (1923 sqq.), i.97.
12. Trumbull, op. cit., 117.
13. Ib., 120 f.
14. E. W. Cox and E. H. Jones, Popular Romances of the Middle Ages (1871), 292, as cited by Trumbull, op. cit., 121 f.
15. Midrash Rabbah, on Exod. 2:23.
16. E. Prym and A. Socin, Syrische Sagen und Märchen (1881), 73.
17. F. A. Schiefner, Tibetan Tales (1882), 160.
18. E.g., Grimm's story "Faithful John"; Bolte-Polivka, i.56 ff.; G. Huet, in Le Moyen Age, 21 (1919), 162–84.
19. G. Basile, Pentamerone, ix.3; L. Gonzenbach, Sicilianische Märchen (1870), 354 (with R. Köhler's notes).
20. J. Grohmann, Sagen aus Böhmen (1863), 268.
21. Frazer-Gaster, NGB §393.
22. Herodotus, iv.26.
23. O. Hovorka and A. Kronfeld, Vergleichendes Volksmedizin (1908–9), i.180.
24. Cox and Jones, op. cit., 310.
25. Chateaubriand, Mémoire d'autre tombe, iii.120.
26. P. Parkman, The Jesuits in Northern America in the Seventeenth Century[20] (1885), 389.
27. P. Paulitschke, Ethnographie Nordost Afrikas i (1886), 186.
28. Hovorka-Kronfeld, op. cit., ii.29.
29. Chronique de France, 1516, feuillet 202, as cited by Soane, in Notes and Queries, Feb. 28, 1857.

30. Norma L. Goodrich, The Medieval Myths (1961), 142.
31. A. Aarne and S. Thompson, Types of the Folk-Tale (1928), #305; Stith Thompson, MI, D 1500.1.9.3.

162 Baal Zebub, "Lord of the Flies"

1. Pausanias, v.14, 1.
2. Ib., viii.26, 7.
3. Cf. FHG iii.197; Aelian, NA ii.18; v.17; Antiphanes, in Fragmenta Comicorum Graecorum, ed. Meineke, iii.134; A. B. Cook, Zeus ii (1925), 781–83; L. R. Farnell, Cults of the Greek States (1896–1909), i.45.
4. R. A. S. Macalister, The Philistines (1914), 91–93.
5. O. Keller, Antike Tierwelt (1909–13), ii.448 ff.
6. Vendidad vii.2; viii.71.
7. Pausanias, x.28, 7.
8. K. Knortz, Die Insekten in Sage (Annaberg 1910), 88.
9. A. Wuttke, Der deutsche Volksaberglaube der Gegenwart[5] (1900), 207; ARW 2.132.
10. Schweiz. Archiv für Volkskunde 25.190.
11. J. Kuoni, Sagen des Kantons S. Gallen (St. Gallen 1903), 5.
12. Grimm-Stallybrass, TM iii.998 f.; HWbDA ii.1626 f.; G. Simrock, Deutsche Mythologie (1874), 95, 479.
13. G. Kittredge, Witchcraft in Old and New England (1929), 180 f.—The Lithuanians had a fly-god called *mussubinbiks*.
14. A monster called *žbb* is mentioned in a Ugaritic text: 'nt iii.43.—W. C. Graham and H. G. May, Culture and Conscience (1936), 154, accepting the connection with *zebub* "fly" as authentic, observe that "the Philistines readily and easily adopted that type of nature-worship, which had probably been brought to that region [i.e., Ekron] by the Hyksos." This view (anticipated by F. C. Movers in JA 1878.220–25) goes beyond the evidence.

ELISHA

163 Waters purified by salt

1. T. H. Gaster, The Holy and the Profane (1955), 13–14; O. Gruppe, Griech. Mythologie (1906), 889, n.3.
2. Ezek. 16:4.
3. Galen, De sanitate tenenda, i.7.
4. E. Samter, Geburt, Hochzeit und Tod (1911), 152, n.6.
5. W. H. Rivers, The Todas (1906), 265 ff.
6. E. W. Lane, Arabian Society in the Middle Ages (1883), 188.
7. A. Wuttke, Deutscher Volksaberglaube der Gegenwart[2] (1900), 91; E. Mogk, ERE ii.633[a]; J. Grimm, DM[2] (1844), ii.999.
8. C. Bock, Temples and Elephants (1884), 260.
9. Notes and Queries 6/iii (1881), 73 f.
10. Manchester Guardian Weekly. March 22, 1947.
11. Grimm-Stallybrass, TM 1049.
12. Tibullus, iii.4, 9–10.
13. Strabo, xii.2, 6.
14. Clem. Alex., Strom. vii.4, 37.
15. J. G. Frazer, GB[2], ii.230; S. Eitrem, Opferritus und Voropfer der Griechen und Römer (1915), 38 f.

16. K. Preisendanz, Die griech. Zauberpapyri (1928–31), iv.2952, 3191; S. Eitrem, Papyri Osloenses i (1925), 100; Pap. Holn., col. ix.42; xii.5; Kyranides, p. 58.18; 77.32; Index of Wessely's Zauberpapyrus in Wiener Denkschriften xxiv, xlii, s.v. *kainos*.
17. Pliny, HN xxii.76, 85; cf. also: Marcell. Empir., xxvi.107.
18. M. Gaster, The Sword of Moses (1896), #46.
19. Ib., #57.
20. Ib., #58.
21. Ib., #69.
22. A. H. Sayce, in Folk-Lore 2.389.
23. Homeric Hymn to Apollo, 231.
24. II Sam. 6:3.
25. Tibullus, i.1, 38.

164 Elisha called "baldpate"

1. Aristotle, Problemata 878^b, 21 ff.; 879^b, 23 ff.; cf. R. B. Onians, The Origins of European Thought about the Body, etc. (1951), 232–33.
2. Id., De gener. animalium 746^b.21 ff.
3. Id., Fr. vii.285.8; Probl. 880^a.35 ff.
4. Pliny, HN xi.39.
5. Aristotle, Hist. anim. vi.57^b, 9; Pliny, HN viii.42, 164.
6. Zs. f. Vk. 9 (1899), 68; Flügel, Volksmedizin und Aberglaube im Frankenwald (1863), 62 f.
7. Grimm-Stallybrass, TM 1606 (*snoyen, kahlkopf*).
8. Mayor, on Juvenal, v.171; cf. also: Aristophanes, Clouds 540 f.; Brunck, Analecta ii.311 (= Lucian, Epigr. gr. 18).
9. Mayor, loc. cit.
10. Dunlop-Liebrecht, Gesch. der Prosadichtungen (1851), 72a.

165 The inexhaustible cruse

1. Bolte-Polivka, i.361; ii.438. G. Jacob, Märchen und Traum (1923), 47, regards it as a dream-motif!
2. Grimm's Märchen, ed. 1819, #103.
3. A. L. H. von Polier, Mythol. des Indous (1809), ii.45.
4. J. Kunos, Ozman-török népköltesi-gijütemeny (Budapest 1887–89), #17.
5. P. Hambruch, Südseemärchen (1916), #37.
6. A. Löwis of Menar, Finnische und estnische Volksmärchen der Weltliteratur (1922), 36, #10; E. Sklarek, Ungarische Märchen, N.F. (1909), 54, 66; cf. H. Gunkel, Das Märchen im A.T. (1925), 58 f.
7. Ovid, Met. viii.679–80.
8. P. Toldo, Studien zur vergl. Literaturgeschichte, 6 (1906), 289–97; H. Günter, Die christliche Legende des Abendlandes (1910), 97.
9. Bolte-Polivka, i.361.
10. Cf. T. H. Gaster, Thespis^2, 434 f.

166 Bathing cures leprosy

(a)

1. M. Gaster, The Sword of Moses (1896), #46.
2. H. C. Trumbull, The Blood Covenant (1887), 116 ff.; H. Strack, Das Blut im Glauben und Aberglaube (1900); Dunlop-Liebrecht, Ges. d. Prosaliteratur (1851), 135.
3. Pliny, HN xxvi.5.
4. Notes and Queries, Feb. 28, 1857.
5. Tawney-Penzer, Ocean of Story (1924–28), i.97.

6. Ellis, Early English Romances, 597 f.
7. G. Basile, Pentamerone, ix.3.
8. L. Gonzenbach, Sicilianische Märchen (1870), 354 (with R. Köhler's notes).
9. J. Grohmann, Sagen aus Böhmen (1863), 268.
10. E. Prym and A. Socin, Syrische Sagen und Märchen (1881), 73.
11. A. Schiefner and W. R. S. Ralston, Tibetan Tales (1882), 60.
12. L. Ginzberg, Legends of the Jews (1909 ff.), v.413, n.10; cf. Midrash Rabbah on Exod. 2:23.
13. Strack, op. cit., 36 ff.
14. W. W. Crooke, Popular Religion and Folklore of Northern India (1896), ii.172 f.
15. R. Moffatt, Missionary Labours and Scenes in Southern Africa (1842), 277; Trumbull, op. cit., 324.

(b) **Waving in Magic**

16. I. Scheftelowitz, Das stellvertretende Huhnopfer (1914), 28 f.
17. T. H. Gaster, Thespis[2], 310. (The Hittite term is *waḥnu-*.)
18. KUB IX 13 + XXIV.5, obv. 26 ff. = M. Vieyra, in RHR 118 (1939), 121 f.; tr. A. Goetze, ANET 355.
19. S. Seligmann, D. böse Blick (1910), ii.236.
20. Ib., ii.256.
21. W. Crooke, Popular Religion and Folklore of Northern India[2] (1896), i.153.
22. Seligmann, op. cit., i.383.
23. Heb.: *tenūphah*. Cf. the expression *tšnpn* in a Canaanite ritual tariff from Ras Shamra-Ugarit: RS 23.6, Gordon.
24. Exod. 29:26; Lev. 8:29.
25. Lev. 7:30; 9:21; 10:15.
26. Lev. 14:12, 24.
27. Lev. 23:11, 20.
28. Num. 5:26.
29. Num. 6:20.

167 Iron floats

1. E. C. Brewer, Dictionary of Miracles, 133.
2. Gregory the Great, Dialogues, book ii.
3. Guérin, Vies des saints[12] (1892), vii.188.
4. L'abbé Corblet, Hagiography of the Diocese of Amiens, quoted in Brewer, loc. cit.

168 The use of corpses in magic

1. O. Weinreich, Antike Heilungswunder (1910), 64; I. Scheftelowitz, Altpales. Bauernglaube (1925), 122 f.; T. J. Pettigrew, On Superstitions Connected with the History and Practice of Medicine and Surgery (1844), 100; E. S. McCartney, in Papers of the Michigan Academy of Science, Arts and Letters 16 (1931), 189–90; Frazer-Gaster, NGB §§26–27, and Additional Notes.
2. P. Kahle, in Palest. Jahrbuch, vii.112.
3. Am Urquell, 4.70.
4. M. Abeghian, Der armenische Volksglaube (1899), 11.
5. W. Wood-Martin, Traces of the Elder Faiths in Ireland (1911), i.295.
6. TB Giṭṭin 69[b].
7. Pliny, HN 28.45.
8. Ib.
9. Cited by McCartney, loc. cit.
10. Frazer-Gaster, loc. cit.

11. New York Herald Tribune, June 6, 1957.
12. Pliny, HN xxviii.41.
13. TB Sanhedrin 47ᵇ.
14. Fr. Lambert, Moeurs et supersitions des Néo-Calédoniens (Nouméa 1900), 30 f.
15. Hesiod, Works and Days, 750 ff.
16. F. S. Krauss, Volksglaube und religiöser Brauch der Südslaven (1890), 146.

169 Yahweh's Lions

1. W. Robertson Smith, The Religion of the Semites² (1894), 92 ff.
2. N. Adriani and A. C. Kruijt, De Bare'e-sprekende Toradja's van Midden-Celebes (1912–14), ii.233, 345 f.
3. L. Tauxier, Le Noir du Sudan pays Mossi et Gourounsi (1912), passim.
4. Id., 267 f., 310, 320.
5. Id., 461, 567 f.
6. J. Forsyth, The Highlands of India (1871), 357 f., 359 ff.; R. V. Russell, Tribes and Castes of the Central Provinces of India (1916), ii.77, 80.
7. Russell, op. cit., ii.78.
8. Forsyth, op. cit., 362 f.; Russell, op. cit., ii.84.

170 Horses and chariots of the sun

1. M. Jastrow, Rel. Bab. u. Assyriens (1905–12), 461.
2. G. A. Cooke, A Text-Book of North Semitic Inscriptions (1903), 165.
3. W. C. Graham and H. G. May, Culture and Conscience (1936), 242 f.
4. See: Stith Thompson, MI, A 724; Frazer-Gaster, NGB §56 and Additional Notes; A. B. Cook, Zeus i (1923), 205 f.; J. A. MacCulloch, Celtic Mythology (1918), 198; K. Helm, Altgerm. Religionsgeschichte (1913), i.178, 256; A. H. Krappe, La genèse des mythes (1938), 85 f.; M. O. Howey, The Horse in Magic and Myth (1923), 114 f.
5. Rig Veda i.115, 3–4; viii.60, 3; ix.63, 8. Cf. N. M. Penzer, The Ocean of Story (1924–28), i.143, n.2; ii.150 f.
6. Xenophon, Cyrop. viii.3, 4, 12.
7. Hom. Hymns ii.63; iii.69; iv.69; v.88; xxviii.44; xxxi.15.—However, in Odyssey 23.244 Eos (Dawn) rides a chariot.
8. Hesiod, fr. 67, Rzach.
9. E.g., Pindar, Ol. vii.71; Sophocles, Ajax 845, 857; Euripides, Phoen. 1–3; cf. O. Robert, Theogonie und Götter⁴ (1894), 431; O. Gruppe, Griech. Mythologie (1906), 381, n.14.
10. Cf. R. Eisler, in ARW 9 (1908), 150 f.; L. V. Schröder, Mysterium und Mimus (1908), 429 ff.; Krappe, loc. cit.
11. Vendidad xxi.5 (20); cf. Herodotus, vii.55.
12. Qunitus Curtius, iii.3, 8, 11.
13. Festus, s.v. October equus.
14. Pausanias, iii.20, 4.
15. Herodotus, i.216.
16. J. G. Frazer, The Fasti of Ovid (1929), ii.165–66.
17. Krappe, loc. cit.
18. J. W. Boecler, in Scriptores rerum Livonicarum, ii.674; J. Negelein, Germ. Mythologie (1912), 84; Krappe, loc. cit.

LATTER PROPHETS

Isaiah

171 Whispering in charms   **Isa. 3:3**

The LORD threatens to remove from Judah and Jerusalem every soldier and warrior, every governor and prophet, every wizard and senator, every petty official and nabob, every counsellor, every man expert in magic and charms.

The Hebrew word rendered *charm* means properly *whisper*, and is so used regularly in Semitic magic.[1] Charms are whispered, murmured, or hissed,[2] not only among the Semites, but also everywhere else for two reasons. First, this keeps the secret formula from the ears of "outsiders." Second, in the case of black magic, this prevents the spell's working on persons for whom it was not intended.

The whispering of spells is mentioned in other passages of the Old Testament itself. In Psalm 41:8 the writer complains that "all that hate me whisper against me," and that this refers specifically to magical incantations is evident from the fact that immediately afterward comes an allusion to the well-attested practice of pouring a magical substance over a man in order to bewitch him (see below, §260). Similarly, in Psalm 58:5 reference is made to a deaf adder "which will not hearken to the voice of *charmers*," and the same Hebrew word is employed. In Mesopotamian magical texts the spell is said to be "chirped" like a sparrow's song;[3] and in Arabic, the recitation of runes is expressed by the imitative word *waswas*, suggesting a hiss.[4] Lucian, in his entertaining *Dialogues of the Demi-monde*, speaks of a witch who "murmurs her spell" over and over again;[5] while German warlocks are said habitually to have resorted to a low-pitched croon.[6]

Instructions to punctuate the words of a charm with hisses are a feature of several ancient magical texts that have come down to us. Such rubrics appear, for instance, in the famous Second Leyden Papyrus and in the equally well-known incantation which its editor Dieterich took mistakenly for a liturgy in the cult of Mithra.[7] An Aramaic magical document from Nippur includes the notation *sh, sh,* indicative of hissing;[8] and so too does a celebrated Ethiopic charm known as the *Net of Solomon*.[9] Tibullus, the Roman poet, speaks of conjuring ghosts by emitting a strident sound;[10] and Petronius says of certain witches that "they began to screech, so that you might have thought a hound was chasing a hare."

In the latter half of the nineteenth century there arose in the Tuamotu islands in the Pacific a cult of "Hissers" who hissed loudly to evoke the dead. Soft hissing sounds, interpreted by priests in a trance, were returned from the roof of the house of worship.[11]

▲ 172 Soul-boxes   3:20

After describing, in a strain of Puritan invective and scorn, the haughty daughters of Zion who tripped about with languishing eyes, mincing steps, and tinkling feet, Isaiah proceeds to give a long catalogue of the jewels and trinkets, robes and shawls, the veils and turbans, all the finery and frippery of these fashionable and luxurious dames. In his list of feminine gauds he mentions "houses of the soul." The expression thus literally translated is unique in the Old Testament. Modern translators and commentators, following Jerome, render it "perfume boxes," "scent-bottles," or the like. Not impossibly, however, these "houses of the soul" were *amulets in which the soul of the wearer was supposed to lodge*. Nor, indeed, are the two interpretations mutually exclusive; for in the eyes of a people who, like the Hebrews, identified the principle of life with the breath, the mere act of smelling a perfume might easily assume a spiritual aspect; the scented breath inhaled might seem an accession of life, an addition made to the essence of the soul. Hence it would be natural to regard the fragrant object itself, whether a scent-bottle, incense, or a flower, as a centre of radiant spiritual energy, and therefore as a fitting place into which to breathe out the soul whenever it was deemed desirable to do so for a time. Far-fetched as this idea may appear to us, it may seem natural enough to the folk and to their best interpreters the poets:

> I sent thee late a rosy wreath,
>   Not so much honouring thee
> As giving it a hope that there
>   It could not wither'd be;
> But thou thereon didst only breathe
>   And sent'st it back to me;
> Since when it grows, and smells, I swear,
>   Not of itself but thee![3]

But if beauty can thus be thought to give of her life, her soul, to the soul of the rose to keep it fadeless, it is not extravagant to suppose that she can breathe her soul into her scent-bottle. At all events these old-world fancies, if such indeed they are, would explain very naturally why a scent-bottle should be called a "house of the soul." Poets perceive by intuition what most of us have to learn by a laborious collection of facts. Indeed, without some touch of poetic fancy, it is hardly possible to enter into the heart of the people. A frigid rationalist will knock in vain at the magic rose-wreathed portal of fairyland. The porter will not open to Mr. Gradgrind. ▼

173 Waistcloths and shoestrings   5:27

> *Not a waistcloth is loose,*
> *Not a sandal-thong broken.*

This has more than a literal meaning. In ancient thought, "clothes makyth man" in a very real sense, being regarded not merely as vestments, but as an integral part of the person or "self." Accordingly, the loosening of the waistcloth or shoestrings means that their wearer has himself "become undone." The former idiom occurs in the Old Testament; in Job 12:21 it is said of Yahweh that "he pours contempt on princes and looses the waistband of the strong," while, according to Isaiah 45:1, Cyrus was called by Yahweh to "subdue nations and ungird the loins of kings." Similarly, in a Canaanite mythological text from Ras Shamra-Ugarit, the god Baal is warned by his adversary Mot that if he tussles with him, the girdle of his robe—which is heaven itself (see below, §278)—will become loosed.[1]

The loosening or snapping of shoestrings was also interpreted, however, as signifying the removal of impediments, and was therefore considered a *good* omen. A character in one of Menander's comedies calls on the gods to send him good fortune, seeing that his shoestring has indeed snapped,[2] and John of Salisbury relates that when Mark the evangelist accidently broke his sandal thong when leaving ship on a proselytizing mission to Alexandria, he gave thanks for this good omen.[3] Both Cicero[4] and Pliny[5] mention the practice of deriving omens from the loosing of latchets; and this superstition obtained in the Hebrides as late as the nineteenth century.[6]

174 Seraphim   6:2

> *Isaiah sees a vision of the LORD seated on a high and lofty throne, with six-winged seraphs hovering around him.*

The six-winged seraphim have been traditionally identified as flaming angels, but this rests solely on a fanciful association of the word with the Hebrew *ś-r-ph*, "burn." In Isaiah 14:29, the winged seraph is described as the offspring of an adder; and in Numbers 21:6, 8 and Deuteronomy 8:15 "seraph-serpents" are said to inhabit the wilderness, just as Herodotus speaks of fiery serpents which dwell there.[1] It is therefore more likely that we are to see in the seraph a mythological demon, and it may then be identified with the grim six-winged creature holding a serpent in either hand, who is portrayed on a relief of the eighth century B.C. from Tell Ḥalaf, in Syria.[2] An Egyptian word *srrf*, which may be related, appears to mean "griffin" or "dragon."[3]

175 Invaders characterized as "tails of smoking firebrands"   7:4

We often miss the full point and irony of a prophetic utterance by failing to recognize a piece of folklore on which it is based. So, in the present instance, the real meaning is lost unless it is realized that Isaiah is alluding to what must have been a popular military stratagem of striking terror in an enemy by dispatching foxes through the battlefield with blazing torches tied to their tails. This, for instance, was the tactic adopted by Samson against the Philistines (see above §117).

Thus interpreted, added point is lent to the fact that the prophet is ordered to deliver his message of encouragement against the invaders in the vicinity of "the conduit of the Upper *Pool*," i.e., destined to quench the brands, and "on the highway to the Fuller's *Field*."

(This interpretation also avoids the necessity of twisting the Hebrew word [*zanab*], which normally denotes "tail" into the meaning "stump," as is usually done [LXX: *faggots;* RSV: *smoldering stumps;* MOFFATT: *faggots*]).

176 A virgin shall conceive:[1] Immanuel 7:14–16

When Rezin, king of Syria, and Pekah, king of Israel, unite to attack Judah, the latter's king Ahaz receives assurances from Isaiah that the LORD will yet protect his people. A sign of things to come will be that a young woman will conceive and bear a son, and name him Immanuel, i.e., "God is with us." From earliest infancy, the child will feed on curds and honey.

This famous prophecy is susceptible of two alternative interpretations:

1. The reference is purely general, i.e., an era of such prosperity will ensue that any young woman now pregnant will be justified in naming her child Immanuel, "God is with us." This interpretation is supported by the fact that the words "Behold, the young woman (*ǵlmt* = Heb.: *'almah* of our text) shall bear a son" occur as part of a hymeneal in a Canaanite text from Ras Shamra-Ugarit,[2] suggesting that they were a traditional marriage formula, somewhat like the Italian *fighli maschi!*

2. The reference is to an ancient myth which told of the birth of a Wondrous Child as a presage of the coming of Age of Bliss.[3] This myth—familiar especially from Vergil's *Fourth Eclogue*—was a "projection" of a Seasonal Rite at which the Spirit of the New Year, and hence of returning fertility and increase, was represented as the newborn offspring of a "sacred marriage" between the king (impersonating the god) and a hierodule (impersonating the goddess). This "marriage" is well-attested in the Ancient Near East.[4] It was a recognized element of the New Year festivities at Babylon, and other Mesopotamian cities.[5] Toward the end of the third millennium B.C., the inscription on a statue of Gudea, governor of Lagash, refers to "bringing wedding-gifts on New Year's Day, the festival of the goddess Baú";[6] while a cylinder of the same ruler speaks of the marriage of that divine bride and the god Ningirsu.[7] Similarly, a long Sumerian hymn describes the spreading of the nuptial couch for the "sacred marriage" of Idin-Dagan, third king of the Isin dynasty (ca.

1918–1897 B.C.) and the goddess Innini.[8] Further, a late commentary on the New Year (*Akîtu*) festivities in Babylon relates how, on the eleventh day of the month of Nisan, the god Marduk "speeds to the marriage";[9] while the same and other documents also describe the nuptials, at Borsippa and Calah, of the god Nabu and the goddess Tashmetu in the following month of Adar.[10] Lastly, brick couches used in this ceremony have actually been found in the ancient temple at Mari,[11] while the ceremony itself is starkly reproduced on a seal from Tell Asmar.[12]

Egyptian texts give evidence of a similar "sacred marriage" between the god Horus and the goddess Hathor celebrated annually at Edfu on the first day of the month of Epiphi (May-June), and followed three days later by the conception of the younger Horus.[13] So too, a feature of the Theban festival of Opet, held annually in the autumn month of Paophi (December-January), was the "sacred marriage" of the god Amon and the goddess Mut;[14] while an inscription in the temple at Deir-el-Bahri, accompanying reliefs which depict the event, describes the mating of god and goddess, impersonated (on the "punctual" and ritual level) by the pharaoh and his consort.[15]

The rite also obtained in ancient Greece. Aristotle informs us, for instance, that the Boukolikon at Athens was primitively the scene of Dionysus' "sacred marriage" with the king's consort;[16] while Lucian describes a three-day festival, blasphemously travestied by the false prophet Alexander, at which the nuptials of Leto and the birth of Apollo, and those of Koronis and the birth of Asklepios, were celebrated.[17] Moreover, the anonymous author of the Philosophoumena relates that at one stage of the Eleusinian Mysteries the hierophant "shouted and exclaimed in a loud voice, 'Holy Brimo hath given birth to a holy child, Brimos' ";[18] while we are told by Strabo that the birth of Zeus was enacted ritually in Crete.[19] Both marriage and nativity survive, albeit in attenuated and garbled form in the modern mumming plays performed in Thessaly, Macedonia, Epirus, and in the Northern Islands of Greece on such crucial seasonal dates as New Year, May Day, and the like; for the leading characters of those plays are often a bride and a groom, and the upshot of the dramatic action is the birth of a prodigious child.[20]

The offspring of the "sacred marriage" was, as we have seen, regarded as divine; and a standard term for a temple-woman in Phoenician was *ǵlmt,* the exact equivalent of the Hebrew word rendered "young woman (KJV: *virgin*)" in the scriptural text.[21] Hence, the prophet speaks of such a woman's bearing a son, who should be named Immanuel, i.e. (on this interpretation), "*a god is with us.*"

The seasonal festival at which the "sacred marriage" was celebrated often coincided with the winter solstice, wherefore the child was identified as the re-emergent sun[22]—an idea eventually adopted (through Hellenistic channels) by Christianity, which came to observe that date as the birthday of him who was regarded as Lux Mundi.[23]

If this second interpretation be adopted, the prophecy may be linked to that in 9:1 ff. ("Unto us a child is given," etc.), and the solstitial background of the underlying rite will lend added point to the words: *The people that walked in darkness have seen a great light; they that dwelt in a land of gloom—over them has daylight shone!*[24]

177 Gibbering ghosts and mediums   8:19

Consult the mediums and the wizards who chirp and mutter.

On chirping and muttering in magic, see above, §**171**. It was especially appropriate in necromancy, because in the folklore of most peoples, the ghosts of the dead are believed to gibber or to speak in a thin, piping voice. This is known technically as the *sursurrus necromanticus*.[1]

Homer says, for example, that the spirit of the deceased ascended from the netherworld like smoke, emitting twittering sounds;[2] and Vergil has the shades of the departed "lift their feeble voices."[3] Horace,[4] Lucan,[5] Statius,[6] Ovid,[7] Petronius,[8] and Claudian[9] describe them in the same way. Nor is this notion confined to the ancient world. The Zulus of Africa call ancestral spirits "whisperers" (*imilozi*);[10] the aborigines of New Zealand say that they whistle,[11] the Solomon Islanders that they speak in a "low whisper,"[12] and the Polynesians that they squeak;[13] while the Algonquins declare that shadow-souls chirp like crickets.[14] Among the Arabs, it is deemed appropriate to whistle when talking to devils.[15]

178 Cursing by king and god   8:21

Apostates, says the prophet, will be visited with hardship and hunger. They will then become embittered and start pronouncing curses by their king and their gods.[1]

A curse, like an oath, can be effective only if it is pronounced in the name—that is, on the authority—of that which has power.[2] To cite but two representative examples from contemporary primitive cultures: among the Melanesians, curses are usually invoked in the name of a *li'oa*, or powerful spirit,[3] while on Banks Island, *vagona*, the direst execrations, consists in procuring the intervention of a supernatural force.[4]

In accordance with this principle, it was customary in the Ancient Near East to pronounce curses or swear oaths in the name either of the god, as the source of continuous and indesinent power, or of the king, as his punctual embodiment, or of both. The oath by the god (*niš ili*, or *niš zikir ili*) is frequently mentioned in Mesopotamian texts,[5] while in the time of the Amorite dynasty of Hammurapi (seventeenth century B.C.),[6] and later at Nuzi, oaths by the king became particularly common.[7] In Egypt, oaths were often sworn by the god Thoth and the pharaoh combined;[8] and it is to be noted that in Genesis 42:15 Joseph swears by the life of the latter.

179 The dawn of salvation   9:1

> *The people who walked in darkness*
> *have seen a great light;*
> *they who dwelt in a land of gloom,*
> *on them has daylight shone.*

These famous words are perhaps a quotation from an ancient poem, for a perfect parallel to them may be found in a Mesopotamian oracular text, which reads: *He that dwelt in darkness unlit now exults, he sees the light of the sun!*[1]

180 "Lucifer, son of the morning"   14:12–15

> *In 705 B.C., Sargon of Assyria, who had been threatening Judah, was defeated in battle in a distant land. Isaiah scornfully compares the fallen monarch to a certain Hêlal, son of Dawn (EV: "Lucifer, son of the Morning"), who aspired to enthrone himself on the mountain of the gods, but was thrust down into the netherworld.*

Sargon, it would seem, was not only defeated, but also abandoned on the battlefield and left to perish. The fallen monarch is fancifully identified with the central character of an ancient myth relating how an overweening upstart who threatened the supremacy of the Most High God was eventually thrust from heaven to the nethermost Pit.

Stories of such celestial upstarts indeed occur in the literature of the Ancient Near East. A Cappadocian cuneiform tablet, dating about 2000 B.C., tells of a female deity who was cast from heaven by the supreme god Anu because of some evil, jealous, or rebellious purpose on her part.[1] Sanchuniathon, the Phoenician mythographer, tells how "Kronos," after removing his father "Ouranos" from sovereignty in heaven and seizing power for himself, became apprehensive of his brother "Atlas" and cast him from heaven into a deep cavern in the earth. Unfortunately, however, we are not yet able to recognize the Phoenician (or Canaanite) gods who lie beneath the Greek names which Sanchuniathon's translator, Philo of Byblus, has fastened upon them.[2] Hittite myth tells likewise of a struggle between the gods for the hegemony in heaven. Originally, we are told, Alalu ruled. After nine years, Anu deposed him. Nine years later, Anu was in turn dethroned by Kumarbi.[3] In another Hittite tale, a monster called Hahhimas—evidently a form of Jack Frost—after paralyzing the earth and seizing a number of gods who have been dispatched to bring relief, eventually threatens to scale heaven and attack the supreme weather-god. The upshot of this threat is unknown to us, since only a portion of the text has been preserved, but from the fact that the tale is told in connection with the worship of the sun and of one of the gods whom Hahhimas is said to have seized, it is apparent that he was defeated—that is, thrust down from heaven—and order restored.[4]

The Greek myth of the *Theomachia,* or battle of the gods, in which Ouranos is dethroned by Kronos, and the latter in turn by Zeus, is, of course, well known from Hesiod's *Theogony,*[5] and has been frequently compared in recent years with the Hittite story of Kumarbi.[6]

Stories of the removal of rebellious angels or celestial beings from heaven may be detected even in the Old Testament itself. Ezekiel (28:11 f.) likens the king of Tyre to an upstart thrust from the paradisal "mountain of the gods," and his picture is evidently derived from a traditional Phoenician myth familiar to the object of his scorn (see below, §**213**). Again, in Psalm 82:6 f., wicked rulers who arrogate to themselves divine status and honors are warned that they are really men after all and are destined "to fall like one of the princes," where there is possibly an allusion to a story about "fallen angels."[7]

The tale was a favorite of pseudepigraphic literature,[8] where the upstarts are usually identified with the mysterious angelic "watchers" of the Book of Daniel, or with the impious "sons of God" who, in the story related in Genesis 6:1–3, consorted with the daughters of men and are seemingly associated with beings called *nephilîm*—a name popularly derived from the Hebrew *n-ph-l,* "fall" (see above, §**32**).

181   The fate of Sargon   14:18–20

> *While all the kings of the nations,*
> *yea, all of them, rest in glory.*
> *each in his separate tomb,*
> *thou art cast forth without a grave,*[1]
> *like a (fallen) twig bemired,*[2]
> *swathed in the (spattered) robes*
> *of murdered men,*
> *of those whom the sword has transpierced*
> *—a trampled corpse!*
> *With those that (duly) go down*
> *to the bedrock of the Pit*
> *thou art not joined in burial. . . .*

There is a subtle point of folklore in this excoriation of the Assyrian king: *he is condemned to wander like an errant and restless ghost,* for it was a common belief of the Mesopotamians—as it is of many other peoples—that those who had died by the sword enjoyed no repose in the netherworld.[3]

The point is caught up in the succeeding verses, where it is said that Babylon will be reduced to "a possession of the hedgehog, and pools of water," for these are the typical haunts of ghosts (see below, §**188**).

We do not know where exactly Sargon met his defeat, but an Assyrian text has his son Sennacherib order the soothsayers to inquire what sin his father had committed that he was not buried in his own "house."

182 Flying serpents   14:29

Flying serpents are said in Numbers 21:6–8 and in Deuteronomy 8:15 to haunt the wilderness, and in Isaiah 30:6 to dwell in the inhospitable tracts of the Negev. They belong to the large class of mythical animals familiar from travelers' and sailors' yarns, and are mentioned again by Herodotus.[1] Lucan too speaks of the "flying serpents of the Arabs" (*Arabum volucer serpens*),[2] and references to them (*ḥaiyê ṭaiyara*) are to be found also in native Arab sources.[3] Among the Indians of Canada, lightning is portrayed as a flying serpent.[4]

183 Shaving the beard in mourning   15:2
See §§135, 293.

184 The gardens of Adonis   17:10

> RSV: *Though you plant pleasant plants,*
> *and set out slips of an alien god,*
> *though you make them grow on the day that you*
>   *plant them,*
> *and make them blossom in the morning that you sow,*
> *yet the harvest will flee away*
> *in a day of grief and incurable pain.*

These lines allude to the widespread custom of planting little seedboxes at crucial times in the seasonal calendar, watering them for a few days, and then regarding their germination as symbolic of revitalized fertility or even of the resurrection of the dead god (or spirit) of vegetation. "It is the custom," says a scholiast on Theocritus, "to plant wheat and barley in seedboxes during the festival of Adonis, and to call what is thus planted 'gardens of Adonis' ";[1] and references to such "gardens" are indeed made by Euripides,[2] Plato,[3] Theophrastus,[4] and other Greek writers.[5] "Just before New Year," reports the Jewish scholar Rashi in the eleventh century, "Jews plant seedboxes, water them, and watch them grow. They are kept until the Day of Atonement [ten days later]";[6] and the custom still survives among their modern co-religionists in parts of Italy.[7] In both Sicily[8] and Sardinia,[9] women sow wheat in plates shortly before Easter. These are then kept in a dark place and watered daily. Plants soon shoot up, and are tied with red ribbons. The plates are deposited on tombs along with effigies of the dead Christ, which are made up in Catholic and Greek Orthodox churches on Good Friday. The rite symbolizes the Resurrection.

In ancient Egypt, a similar custom was observed annually, to represent the resurrection of Osiris;[10] while in parts of India analogous ceremonies celebrated the seasonal revival of vegetation. Thus, at Udeipur, barley is sown in a small trench, then watered and heated artificially until the grain sprouts, whereupon the young women distribute the sprigs to the men, who wear them in their turbans.[11] Similarly, too, among the Oraons and Mundas of Bengal, it is customary for the daughters of the village headman to sow blades of barley, mixed with turmeric, in moist, sandy soil. When presently they sprout, the girls carry them in baskets to the karma tree, in the central dancing place. They are set down beside it to stimulate its growth.[12]

The prophet's allusion to such "gardens of Adonis" is more apparent in the original Hebrew than in the usual English versions; for what is rendered *pleasant plants* is really *plants of Na'amans,* and Na'aman ("comely, pleasant") seems to have been an ancient Semitic byname of Adonis.[13] Indeed, this name is believed to underlie the name *anemone,* which the Arabs call "the wounds of Na'aman" and which is held to have been stained red by the god's blood.[14]

185 The rebel constellations 24:21–23

> *It shall come to pass on that day*
> *that the LORD will punish the host of heaven in heaven,*
> *and the kings of the earth on the earth.*
> *They will be gathered together as prisoners in a pit;*
> *they will be imprisoned in a prison*
>
> . . . .
>
> *The moon will be confounded*
> *and the sun ashamed,*
> *for He who is indeed the LORD of HOSTS*
> *will reign in Mount Zion and in Jerusalem,*
> *and his glory be fully displayed*
> *before the elders of his court!*

The prophet is alluding to an ancient myth which told how, in primeval times, the supreme god imprisoned certain rebellious powers in subterranean vaults, himself asserting his sovereignty and establishing the world order. Thus, in the Mesopotamian Epic of Creation, the victorious Marduk imprisons them in "cells,"[1] and elsewhere in Akkadian literature they are commonly styled "the bound (or, chained) gods."[2] Similarly, in the Biblical Book of Revelation, the angelic allies of Satan are "cast down to the earth."[3] The analogy, in Greek myth, of the contumacious Cyclopes and Titans, similarly dispatched to Tartaros by Ouranos, will spring readily to mind.[4]

In later ages, these ousted rebels came to be identified with *stars* or *planets.*[5] Enoch, for example, sees in hell "seven stars like great burning mountains." Inquiring about them, he is told that what he is beholding is "the prison for the stars and host of heaven," who primevally "transgressed God's command by not coming forth at the right time."[6] So too Jude speaks of "wandering stars (Greek: *asteres planētai*) for whom nether darkness has been reserved for ever";[7] while in an Aramaic magical incantation from Nippur reference is made to "the seven stars (i.e., planets) and the twelve signs of the Zodiac which have been sealed until the great Day of Judgment,"[8] and allusion to the same myth is found in the liturgy of the Mandaeans of Iraq and Iran.[9]

It will be observed that in our quotation of the Biblical text one line has been omitted owing to uncertainty about the translation. It can mean either "And they shall be deprived of a large number of their days,"[10] or "And after many days they shall be visited." If the former rendering be adopted, the reference will be simply to the "blank days" of incarceration. If, however, we prefer the latter, the prophet's words may be understood to hark back to the ancient myth, for the Mesopotamian epic indeed speaks of Marduk's eventually having mercy on the vanquished gods and removing their yoke,[11] while a text published by T. G. Pinches describes how the god went down to their prison and freed them.[12] Enoch too says that they will be bound only for ten thousand years,[13] and the Aramaic charm that they will ultimately witness "a great hour of release."[14]

(It is possible also that the prophet is indulging in studied irony, for the Hebrew words (viz., *p-q-d* and *'a-s-f*) here rendered "punished" and "gathered together" are also military terms meaning "muster" and "assemble troops."[15] The idea would then be that Yahweh, the Lord of Hosts, will indeed muster the celestial hosts and assemble the earthly kings—not, however, for a victorious campaign but simply to mass them for judgment and to round them up like captives led to prison!)

186 Leviathan   27:1

Eschatology is cosmogony in the future tense: the age to come will be inaugurated in the same way as was the present age—by the Lord's subjugation of the rebellious Dragon of chaos and disorder. This myth is itself the counterpart of a ritual, surviving sporadically in folk usage, whereby the dragon of the nether waters is subdued at the beginning of the year, lest he prevent them from rising and moistening the earth or lest he send them in devastating flood.[1]

Ancient Near Eastern literature knows several forms of this myth. In Sumeria, it was related that the god Ninurta (or, in another version, the goddess Inanna) had primevally vanquished a draconic marplot and channeled the subterranean waters between the banks of the Tigris and Euphrates.[2] In Babylon, a myth recited at New Year (Akitu) related how, at the gray beginning of time, Marduk had conquered the draconic Tiamat and thus established the order of the world.[3] The Hittites likewise recited at New Year (Puruli) the tale of how the Weather God (or, in another version, a mortal named Hupasiyas) had overcome the primordial Dragon (Illuyankas) and how, in consequence of his triumph, rainfall had been assured.[4]

In a long mythological poem discovered at Ras Shamra-Ugarit, Baal, the Canaanite god of rainfall and fertility, does battle against Yam, *alias* Nahar, the genius of sea and streams, and, by subduing him, acquires dominion over gods and men and is able to regulate the seasons of the rains.[5] It is this feat which the prophet here appropriates to Yahweh and projects into the future. His very words, and especially the unusual epithets ("fleeing" and "tortuous") which he applies to the Dragon, reproduce exactly the lines of the older text, in which Baal is said to smite "Leviathan, the fleeing serpent" and the "Dragon Tortuous."[6]

The myth evidently enjoyed considerable popularity in Israelite folklore, for there are several allusions to it in the poetic books of the Old Testament, the Dragon being variously named Leviathan (Wriggly), Rahab (Blusterer), or Tannin (Sea-monster).

Thus (a) Isaiah himself elsewhere (51:9–10) describes Yahweh as he who hewed the Blusterer (Rahab) in pieces, transfixed the Dragon (Tannin), and dried up the sea (Yam).

(b) Habakkuk, envisioning the imminent approach of Yahweh to deliver his people from their oppressors, asks rhetorically (3:8) whether he is again about to launch an attack, as of old, upon Sea (Yam) and River (Nahar).

(c) In Psalm 74:13–14, Yahweh is addressed as the ancient King who by his strength broke up the sea (Yam), shattered the heads of the Dragon (Tannin), and crushed those of Leviathan.

(d) Similarly, in Psalm 89:9–10, Yahweh is pictured as establishing dominion over the proud and towering sea (Yam) and crushing the Blusterer (Rahab) like a slain man.

(e) In Psalm 93, Yahweh is hailed as a god who has acquired kingship and stabilized the world by subduing the contumacious rivers and sea.

(f) Lastly, the afflicted Job likens himself in one passage (7:12) to the sea (Yam) and Dragon (Tannin) whom Yahweh of old put under guard; and in another (26:12–13) he describes his God as having of old quelled the sea (Yam) by his strength and smitten the Blusterer (Rahab) by his skill.

In a manner characteristic of ancient myths, this tale was later embodied in a spell against evil spirits, for in an Aramaic incantation from Nippur demons are exorcized by "the charm which operated against the sea (Yam) and against Leviathan the Dragon (Tannin)," and it is said of the latter that he was smitten by "a fate laid upon him by God."[7]

Parallels to the story abound outside the Semitic area. In Indian mythology, one of the principal feats of Indra was the defeat of the monster Vrtra and the release of the waters which the latter had "impounded."[8] In Greek myth, we have the familiar victory of Zeus over Typhon (though the marine aspects of the monster have been obscured),[9] and among the Teutons that of Thor over Midhgardsormr, the serpent who encircles the earth.[10]

The name Leviathan is a fanciful invention of popular lore. It means properly "Coiling" or "Wriggly," and the monster is also called, both here and in the Canaanite text from Ugarit, 'Aqaltan, "the Tortuous." Similarly, in a Ugaritic charm against snakebite, a mythological serpent is called '-q-š-r, which means, in the same way, "Twist-and-Twine,"[11] while in Egyptian incantations of analogous type, a cobra is designated "Head-rearer."[12]

187 The "Name of the LORD" as his agent 30:27–28

> Behold, the Name of the LORD comes from afar,
> burning with his anger and with thick rising smoke;
> his lips are full of fury.
> and his tongue is like a devouring fire;
> his breath is like an overflowing torrent
> that reaches up to the neck.

In Semitic thought, a person's *name* is, as we have seen (above, §72), his *manifested identity,* not merely a *verbal appellation.* When, for instance, God does something "for His name's sake," he is simply being true to his known and revealed character, and the more correct translation is, *true to his nature.* Since, however, a god may reveal himself through envoys or appointed agents, any such may also be described as his "name." In the mythological poems from Ras Shamra-Ugarit, the goddess Ashtareth is styled "the name of Baal,"[1] and she is so characterized also in an inscription of Eshmun'azar of Sidon, of the fifth century B.C.[2]

The personified "Name of the LORD" is here portrayed in terms of the typical ogre of folktales.[3] The prophet's words reproduce to a nicety the description of Ḥumbaba, the Rübezahl of the sacred wood, in the Mesopotamian Epic of Gilgamesh. *His roar is like the flood-storm, his mouth is fire, his breath is death* (or, *pestilence*).[4] The monstrous Typhon is similarly depicted in Greek myth.[5]

188 The haunts of demons 34:13–14

Deserts and solitary places, including ruins, on account of their eeriness, are universally regarded as inhabited by demons. Mesopotamian magical incantations, for example, speak of them constantly as haunting the wilderness, and it is thither that they are exorcized.[1] The same notion obtains also in Arabic folklore,[2] and is likewise mentioned in the Talmud and other Jewish sources.[3] In Syriac, Thomas of Marga's *History* says expressly that devils come from ruins in the form of black ravens;[4] and an Ethiopic prayer specifies the wasteland as their normal abode.⁵ In a Canaanite mythological text from Ras Shamra-Ugarit, Baal is assailed in the desert by certain demonic creatures, called "renders" and "devourers" especially fashioned by El to lure him to his doom;⁶ and it is in the desert that Jesus is tempted by Satan.⁷ In Iranian belief, Ahriman and his evil spirits inhabit the desert;⁸ and a similar European superstition is alluded to both by Milton in his *Comus*⁹ and by Burton in his *Anatomy of Melancholy*.¹⁰ Marco Polo records that he found the same idea current in the Far East,¹¹ and in more recent times it has been reported from Mongolia.¹² Somewhat analogous is the belief of the Finns that demons frequent the sequestered tracts of Lapland.¹³

In ancient Mesopotamia, the netherworld—the other natural habitat of demons—was sometimes described as a plain.¹⁴

189 Hairy devils   34:14

The satyr shall cry to his fellow

The Hebrew word rendered *satyr* means simply *hairy one* (Vulgate: *pilosus*), and thus reflects a common belief in hirsute demons who frequent desolate places. The belief is attested alike in Aramaic magical texts from Nippur¹ and in pre-Islamic Arabic sources;² while a familiar Moslem story relates that Bilkis, queen of Sheba, was revealed as of demonic descent by the fact that she had hair on her ankles.³ The Mandaeans of Iraq and Iran speak of a shaggy female demon named Kaftâr who appears at full moon;⁴ and Teutonic folklore knows of scrawny and scraggy demons called *scrats*.⁵ Both Ephialtes, the proverbial *incubus*, and Pan are sometimes portrayed in ancient Greek folklore as goat-shaped satyrs.⁶ (The Hebrew word which we have been discussing can also mean simply "goat.")

190 Lilith   34:14

In the future, the ruins of Edom will be haunted by demons; the night-hag will make herself at home there.

The word rendered "night-hag" is *lilith*. The rendering is based on a traditional, but quite erroneous, association of it with the Hebrew *lāyil*, "night." In reality, it derives from the Sumerian *lil*, "wind." In the form *lîlu* it was then adopted by the Semites of Mesopotamia as the name of a demon; and the corresponding feminine is *lilîtu*, whence *Lilith*.¹ Lilu, Lilitu, and "the handmaid of Lilu" (*Ardat Lîli*) constituted a triad of what were originally perhaps no more than wind-spirits.² Later, however—possibly through false etymology of their names—they came to be regarded as night wraiths or nocturnal demons, Lilith herself becoming the *succuba*, or faery sylph who consorted with men in sexual dreams.

As early, however, as the eighth century B.C., Lilith was in turn confused—at least in Syria—with what had originally been the quite distinct demonic figure of the child-stealing witch, known to the Mesopotamians as Lamashtu.³ This we know from a curious amuletic plaque of that date discovered at Arslan Tash (ancient Ḥadatu) in the Upper Euphrates Valley. This plaque was designed to protect an expectant mother from Lilith's asaults, and the beldam is there portrayed, in two different representations, as a vixen swallowing a diminutive human figure and as a winged monster. The accompanying inscription names her explicitly "Lilith," "Winged One" (*'aftâ*), and "Strangleress" (*Ḥaniqatu*).⁴

In this aspect Lilith has worldwide analogues.⁵ The Hittite knew of a demonic beldam called "the Strangleress" (*Wesuriyanza*) who was exorcized by taking her image down to a river and then giving her a sop of bread conveyed to her in the mouth of a fish.⁶ Among the Semites of Mesopotamia she was portrayed as a hideous hybrid monster with a lion's head, ass's teeth, and bird's claws, holding a snake in either hand and suckling a dog and a pig at her breasts.⁷ A Babylonian text now in the Yale collection describes her explicitly as "strangling children,"⁸ and she was exorcized by being sent downstream in a boat⁹—a magical practice still observed in Indonesia.¹⁰ The Egyptians saw her as a female who slipped into the house under cover of darkness and with face averted.¹¹ The Greeks were acquainted with her in several guises.¹² As Empousa, she had one foot made of brass and the other of cow dung. Alternatively, she was known as Dame Donkey-legs (*Onoskelis*),¹³ or as *Mormō*, "Bogey,"¹⁴ or as *Mormolukeion*, "Vixen-bogey."¹⁵ She was also named Gello—a name which is probably connected with the word *ghoul* (properly "blood-sucker") but which was popularly interpreted as that of a lady-love of Zeus whose children had been slain by the jealous Hera and who took her revenge on human mothers!¹⁶ Again, she was recognized in the form of an owllike vampire, or as a plain owl (*Bubo*),¹⁷ and, above all, a screeching nightjar, or strix. The later became one of her standard names in later European folklore; in the Balkans she is still called Strygoi; in Switzerland, Streggele; and in Italian, *strega* is, of course, the normal word for "witch."¹⁸

The parallels are, in fact, virtually endless; and the method of forefending her has now become virtually standard. Alike in the Balkans, in Ethiopia, and among more superstitious Jews it is customary for expectant mothers to carry an amulet the text of which describes how a saintly character (variously identified as St. Sisinnius or as the prophet Elijah) once encountered the beldam and her companions and exorcized her, in the name of God, by forcing her to disclose her various aliases. These were then recorded, and whenever a pregnant woman carries them on her person or has them written up in her chamber, the demons are rendered powerless.¹⁹

The varied migrations of this charm against Lilith may be seen in the fact that even in its modern Jewish form mention is made—incongruously and as a meaningless magical formula—of the names of S.S. Sisinnius and Sinoe, while the aliases of the beldam include *Aello*, "Stormwind," and *Okypodē*,

"Swift-footed," the two analogous harpies mentioned by the Greek poet, Hesiod![20] Even Shakespeare alludes to the charm, for in *King Lear* occurs the familiar doggerel:

> Saint Withold footed thrice the [w]old;
> He met the night-mare and her nine-fold;
> Bid her alight
> And her troth plight,
> And aroint thee, witch, aroint thee!

In light of her common identification with owls, nightjars, and the like, it will now be clear why the prophet associates her, in our passage, with jackals, ostriches, and kites. In Malaya she is likewise identified with a screech owl and known as *langsuyar*;[22] while a popular Jewish name for her is Bruxa or Bruesche, which is simply the Portuguese *broxa*, "nightjar."[23]

191 The loom of life 38:12

> Like a weaver I have rolled up my life,
> He cuts me off from the loom.

On the concept of *life as a thread*, see below, §218.—A striking parallel to the prophet's phrase is afforded by the modern Greek euphemism, "His spindle is wound full (*mazōthēke to koubar' tou*) for "he died."[1] Cf. also Job 27:8.

192 Heaven as a muslin curtain 48:22

This is an alternative to the conception of the firmament as a sheet of metal (see above, §4). Similarly, in the Egyptian *Book of the Dead* (ch. 85), mention is made of "the firmament which constitutes a skin (*šet*),"[1] and in the Greek (Septuagint) and Vulgate's rendering of Psalm 104:2, "who stretchest out the heavens like a curtain," the latter word is translated "skin." The Indic Rig Veda says likewise that the sky is stretched out like a hide;[2] in parts of Africa it is called a cloth;[3] as again in the Finnish Kalevala.[4] The Assyrians called it "the piece of embroidery";[5] and in German riddles it is a curtain.[6]

193 Battle vaunts 42:13

> The LORD sallies forth like a champion
> like a warrior vents (his) passion,
> shouts and raises his war cry,
> vaunts himself over his foes.

193a The combat against the Dragon 51:9–10
See above, §186.

194 The Suffering Servant 53

> The prophet comforts his oppressed compatriots by reminding them of a certain character who, though traduced, smitten, tortured, and

vilified, bears all this in equanimity, as a kind of human scapegoat serving to make expiation for public sin and wrongdoing. A feature of this martyr is that he is of unsightly appearance, like "one from whom men turn their face."

(a) We need not enter here into the vexed question of who the Suffering Servant was intended to be—a problem as chronic and as seemingly insoluble as the identity of the Dark Lady of the Sonnets.[1] Our concern is solely with the folkloristic background of this image.

The picture is drawn, we suggest, from the widespread institution of the *human scapegoat,* usually a misshapen person or one already under sentence of death, upon whom is saddled the taint of all sins and offenses which might otherwise be visited on the community, but precise responsibility for which cannot be placed, for one reason or another, on any particular individual.[2]

In Babylon, a condemned felon (*bêl ḫiṭṭi*) was paraded through the streets, scourged and expelled at the New Year (*Akîtu*) festival.[3] At Athens in times of drought or calamity, a misshapen man and woman were driven out of town as a public expiation; they were called *pharmakoi*.[4] At Chaeronea, during a famine, a slave was ceremoniously beaten with twigs of *agnus castus* (a kind of willow);[5] and at Marseilles, this was done in time of plague.[6] At Ephesus, Apollonius of Tyana, the shamanistic "prophet" and charlatan, had a beggar stoned to relieve pestilence;[7] and a similar use of human scapegoats is recorded from Abdera.[8] In Athens, the misshapen man and woman were scourged with squills;[9] while similarly in Rome, an old man known as Mamurius Veturus was clad in skins and beaten with white rods annually on the Ides of March, evidently an ancient method of forefending evil at the beginning of the year.[10] At Oritsha, on the Niger, two sickly persons act as human scapegoats in moments of public crisis;[11] while in Thailand, purification is effected by parading on a litter a woman broken down by debauchery, pelting her with offal, and subsequently throwing her on a dunghill.[12] Among the aboriginal tribes of China, a man of great muscular strength is expelled in times of crisis, his face having first been disfigured by paints.[13] In Switzerland, a lad disguised as a witch, goat or ass is driven out of town on the second Thursday before Christmas;[14] and at Munich, Germany, the same custom used to prevail on Ascension Eve.[15]

Now observe how perfectly all this chimes with the prophet's description of the Suffering Servant. He is disfigured and sickly (Isa. 52:14; 53:2–3). He bears physical sickness and pain on behalf of the community (53:4, 10). He is expelled, "cut off" (53:8).[16] He is treated as a felon (53:9). He is subjected to stripes, i.e., trounced (53:5).

53:3

(b) The Suffering Servant is described also as *one from whom men hide their face*. On this expression too Comparative Folklore sheds interesting light.

The Servant is a sick man, and, in ancient and primitive thought, sickness implies possession by a demon; indeed, he is said expressly (53:4) to be "smitten of God (i.e., demon-struck) and afflicted (i.e., plagued)."[17] Now, such demonic influences can be relayed to others by a mere glance. Hence, those who wish to avoid being so "infected"—especially persons possessed of some special or divine power—customarily veil their faces.[18] Moses, we are told (Exod. 34:33), veiled his face when addressing the people after his descent from Mt. Sinai. However, it may later have been re-interpreted, the real purpose of this action was to protect from untoward and demonic glances that divine glory with which he had become suffused. In the same way, the kings and sultans of several African peoples often keep their faces veiled;[19] and in ancient Persia only the seven highest courtiers were normally permitted to look upon the countenance of their sovereign at all times.[20]

Alternatively, the person who is demonically possessed had to keep *his* face covered, lest he pass the evil to others. In ancient Greece, for example, a man guilty of unwitting homicide had to keep his head covered;[21] and among West African primitives, human sacrifices are often veiled.[22] Not improbably, this is also the true basis of the law which anciently required lepers to wear hoods. Sometimes too, as in the case of the human scapegoats described above, the necessary disguise is effected by *whitewash*.[23]

195 The faery city   54:11–12

> *O thou forlorn, storm-racked, disconsolate,*
>   *Lo, I—even I myself—*
> *will yet lay thy stones with carbuncles,*[1]
>   *and thy foundations with sapphires;*
> *and I will make thy pinnacles of agate,*
>   *gleaming like little suns,*[2]
> *and thy gates of crystal,*
>   *and thine every boundary-mark of precious stones.*

This picture of the future Jerusalem is modeled after the *faery or heavenly city of folktales*.

Alike in the Old Testament itself (Exod. 24:10) and in Mesopotamian sources the floor or lowest register of heaven is said to be made of sapphires or lapis lazuli.[3] In Canaanite myth, the palace of Baal, built on the holy mountain of the gods, is made of silver and gold and ornamented with gems and lapis,[4] and in Ezekiel's description of the paradisal abode (Eden) on the sacred hill, those who inhabit it "walk about amid flashing gems" (Ezek. 28:14, 16; see below §**213**).

The theme enjoyed great popularity in later Jewish and Christian literature. The Greek version of Enoch speaks of the crystal palace and bdellium walls of heaven,[5] and the pseudepigraphic Testament of Abraham of God's crystal throne and table.⁶ Tobit's "prayer of rejoicing" celebrates the future Jerusalem as a city built of sapphires, emeralds, and precious stones, with towers and battlements of pure gold, and streets paved with beryl, ruby, and "stones of Ophir."⁷ The Book of Revelation elaborates the description by speaking of twelve foundations made of twelve different precious stones like those in the breastplate of Aaron, and adds the touch of the pearly gates and of the street "of pure gold, as it were transparent glass."⁸

The hymnographers virtually run riot with the picture. To quote but a few examples, one recalls first the famous lines of Hildebert of Lavardin, in the eleventh century:

> What joy the blessèd find in thee!
> Oh, how deep their revelry!
> Oh, what thrill unites them all!
> Oh, what gems adorn thy wall!
> What agates there and jacinths glow,
> None but they who dwell there know.⁹

Similar are the words of his great contemporary, Peter Damiani:

> Pearly mansions rise and, lo.
> Golden rooftops gleam and glow;
> Banquet-halls all crystal bright
> Twinkle in the morning light.
> Fashioned not of common stone,
> But of precious gems alone.
> The streets whereon the blessèd pass
> Are purest gold, transparent glass.¹⁰

To the same century belongs also the description of Paradise in a celebrated Jewish hymn entitled *Aqdamûth*. Composed in Aramaic by a certain Meir ben Isaac Nehorai (probably of Orleans), this is customarily recited in the synagogue on Pentecost:

> Lo, when the exiles He hath led
> To Jerusalem, there shall be shed
> Upon that city, day and night,
> The splendor of his radiant light;
> And silver-linèd clouds shall be
> Spread o'er it for a canopy.
> When He doth like a bridegroom ride
> At last, at last, to claim His bride.
> Then round about, on golden chairs
> (Each one approach'd by seven stairs)
> The righteous as His guests shall dine,
> And perfect bliss shall be their wine;
> And o'er their heads, for chandeliers,
> Shall hang the radiance of the spheres;

> A beauty which no lips can tell,
> Whereon no earthly eye can dwell,
> A starry glory which of old
> No prophet's vision could unfold.[11]

The picture appears, indeed, almost everywhere in world folklore. Thus, for example, in the Celtic legend of Sir Owayne, Paradise is enclosed by shining walls of glass; and in the fairy land of Ogygia, whither Meriddin Emorys sails, there is a glass palace of souls.[12] A Bosnian tale tells similarly of a faery castle made of diamonds,[13] in modern Greek tales it is wrought of gold and silver,[14] and in a Russian tale it is fashioned with columns of silver and steps of mother-of-pearl, and is ornamented with precious stones.[15] The Caribs and Arawaks of America spoke in the same vein of the fabulous realm of El Dorado with its imperial capital Manoa, "abounding in precious metals and all manner of gems."[16]

On the theme in general, see also above, §15.

196 Gad and Meni   65:11

> *In castigating his countrymen for forsaking Yahweh and forgetting his holy mountain, Isaiah describes them as men who* spread a table for Gad [RSV: Fortune] and fill cups of mixed wine for Meni [RSV: Destiny].

Gad was the Canaanite god of luck.[1] When her handmaid Zilpah bore a son to Jacob, Leah exclaimed, (*This comes*) *through Gad*, and the child was named after that god.[2] The deity figures in several Biblical personal names, e.g., Gadi-el, a Zebulunite (Num. 13:10), Gaddi (Num. 13:11), and Gadi (II Kings 15:14, 17), as well as in the toponyms, Baal-Gad (Josh. 11:17) and Migdal-Gad, "tower of Gad" (Josh. 15:37).[3] A man named Gad-yô is mentioned several times in the celebrated Samarian ostraca (778–770 B.C.),[4] and such names as Gad-melek, "Gad is king,"[5] Gad-ram, "Gad is exalted,"[6] and Gad-naʻim, "Gad is kindly,"[7] are found on Palestinian seals. The latter, however, are of uncertain date.

In Hellenistic and Roman times, when national religons broke down and men turned increasingly to the more personal mystery cults, the adoration of the Emperor, and the worship of such cosmic forces as the heavenly bodies or of such universal abstractions as Fate, special prominence was given to Tyche, or Chance.[8] In the Semitic area the ancient deity Gad came to serve as her masculine equivalent. He is accordingly mentioned with some frequency in Nabatean[9] and Palmyrene[10] inscriptions of this later period, and in the Greek (Septuagint) Version of our Biblical passage the name Gad is indeed rendered Tyche.

Eventually, the name of the god developed, by metonymy, into a common noun meaning "fortune, luck."[11]

Among the Jews a particularly interesting development took place. The expression, *couch of Gad,* came to be applied to a table decked with delicacies, or to an ornamented sofa, especially set aside, on the occasion of a circumcision. This was simply an imitation of the *lectus* which the Romans used to spread for Hercules or Juno at the birth of a boy or girl.[12] A parallel to this exists in modern Greece, where, on the third or fifth night after a child's birth, a table laden with honey, almonds, bread, and water, as well as with jewelry and coins, is set out for the three Fates, who are believed then to visit the house.[13]

The Talmud mentions also a popular custom of consigning the leavings of a meal to Gad, or Fortune[14]—a usage which survived among superstitious persons in Jerusalem as late as the nineteenth century.[15]

Moreover, as in ancient times, Gad continued to be invoked for prosperity, the popular expression, *Gad, spread luck and be not laggard about it,* being quoted in rabbinic sources.[16] In the same way, too, the Arabs sometimes called upon him when swearing oaths.[17]

Meni was a god who allotted fates.[18] His name derives from the Semitic word, *m-n-y,* "apportion," on the exact analogy of the Greek Moira, "Fate," which is connected with *meros,* "portion," and this inspires the prophet's declaration that Yahweh will *apportion* the worshipers of that deity to the sword.

Apart from our present passage, Meni is not mentioned in earlier Semitic sources. Like Gad, however, the deity became popular (evidently as an equivalent of Moira) in the Graeco-Roman age, appearing, in the form M-n-w-t-w, in Nabatean inscriptions.[19] It is mentioned also, in the feminine form Manat, in a passage of the Koran.[20] Tradition asserts that Mohammed at first countenanced the recognition of this goddess, describing her (along with the pre-Islamic Allat and Al-'Uzza),[21] as one of the three "exalted ladies" who might be expected to make intercession for the faithful. Later, however, his attitude toward such relics of heathendon stiffened, and he excised the conciliatory reference.

Jeremiah

197 Man from stones *Jeremiah 2:27*

Saying to a stock, Thou art my father:
and to a stone, Thou hast brought me forth.

That mankind sprang from stones or rocks is a commonplace of popular belief in many parts of the world.[1] The Khasis of Assam, for instance, assert (with obvious sexual symbolism) that the Great Mother of the race is represented by cromlechs (called "female stone"), and the Great Father by menhirs (called "male stone").[2] In New Caledonia, Malekula, Achin, and other parts of Polynesia, stones were regarded as ancestral deities;[3] and among both the Zulus of Africa[4] and the Indians of Colombia[5] it is held that the first men either were or emerged from stones. The Paressi Indians of Matto Grosso say that the first man, a certain Darakavaitere, was made of stone, being born of a stone mother named Maiso.[6] Stories of particular men born from stone are common in the folklore of North Caucasian peoples;[7] while the Arab tribe of the Beni Sahr, in Moab, fancifully derive their name from the belief that their prime ancestor was a *ṣahr*,[8] or rock. Readers of the classics will at once recall the myth of Deucalion and Pyrrha, which relates how the world was repeopled after the Flood from stones which those two survivors cast behind their backs;[9] and that this story did not originate simply from the similarity of the Greek words, *laas* "stone," and *laos*, "people" (as the ancient mythographers supposed) is evidenced by the primitive parallels which we have cited.[10] In Tahiti, the wife of the first man is called *Papa*, or "Rock."[11]

There is an interesting survival of the belief in a famous passage of the Odyssey, where, before he has revealed his identity, Penelope says to the re-returning Odysseus:

> Say whence thou art, for not of fabulous birth
> Art thou, not from the oak nor from the rock.[12]

198 Land made barren through unchastity *3:2–3*

See above, §144.

199 Passing children through fire *7:31; 19:5*

Usually explained as a form of human sacrifice and sometimes so described by the Biblical writers themselves,[1] the heathen practice of passing children through fire is really something quite different. Fire purifies as well as consumes, and what is here involved is the widespread custom of passing children (and adults) through fire in order to "sain" them—that is, to purge them of human imperfections and (in myth and story) render them immortal.²

In ancient Greece, newborn males were carried around the hearth for this purpose,³ and a similar rite was performed in the cult of Artemis Perasia at Kastabala, in Asia Minor.⁴ Plutarch tells us that a certain Malkandros, king of Byblus (in Syria), was passed through fire to make him immortal;⁵ and the Roman custom of leaping through fire at the festival of Palilia—a rite paralleled in many European harvest celebrations—is similarly interpreted by several modern scholars.⁶ In reference to such usages, the neo-Platonic philosophers speak figuratively of "the ascent through fire" as a means by which devotees of theurgy sought to escape fate and ensure the immortality of the soul.⁷

The custom is well attested in many parts of the world.⁸ Jakun tribes of the Malay Peninsula, for example, pass newborn children over fire.⁹ Moreover, although the custom is proscribed in the classic lawbook of India,¹⁰ it still persists in various parts of that country;¹¹ while a nocturnal ceremony of the same order has been witnessed among the Ali-Ilahis of Persia.¹² So too the practice is (or was) by no means uncommon in the Scottish Highlands,¹³ and Jamieson, in his famous Scottish Dictionary, thence derives the English popular expression, "to haul over the coals."¹⁴ In Siberian shamanism, boiling or roasting in a pot signifies rejuvenation or regeneration. "A Teleut woman," we are told, "became a shamaness after a vision in which unknown men cut her body to pieces and boiled it."¹⁵ Similarly, an Avam-Samoyed shaman, while stricken with smallpox, dreamed that a naked man on a mountain chopped up his body and boiled it in a kettle for three years.¹⁶ In various Australian tribes, initiation includes being roasted in or at a fire in order to achieve new birth.¹⁷ This is also a frequent motif in folktales.¹⁸ Indeed, Christ himself is said in one such tale to have rejuvenated an old woman by putting her on the fire.¹⁹

In ancient mythology, the idea underlies the story of how Demeter tried to make the infant Demophoon immortal by passing him through fire at night;²⁰ while of the same tenor is the tale of Thetis burning six of her and Peleus' sons in order to ensure their deathlessness.²¹

More often, the process is represented as that of being boiled in a Cauldron of Immortality.²² Classical instances of this are the stories of Medea and Aison,²³ and of Thetis and Achilles;²⁴ while in the Welsh *Mabinogion Branwen*, Bendigeldfraen offers Matholoch a magic cauldron of this type.²⁵ The motif recurs also in more modern folktales from Sicily and Wallachia.²⁶

An inscription of the Roman emperor Elagabalus (reigned A.D. 218–22) found at the foot of Mt. Hermon describes him as having been "deified in the cauldron," and this has been interpreted in reference to the same notion.²⁷ In early Christian thought, regeneration was likewise believed to be accomplished by baptism in fire.²⁸

The children are said to have been passed through fire to Molech—a statement repeated elsewhere in the Old Testament. The usual view is that Molech is a tendentious misvocalization of the word *Melech,* "King," the original vowels being replaced by those of the word *bosheth,* "shame," just as Baal himself was called Bosheth by Israelite writers, and just as Ashtareth was vocalized Ashtoreth in the same way.[29] An Ammonite god named M-l-ch (or Milcom) is indeed mentioned in the Old Testament,[30] and a deity of the same name appears in an Amorite text of the eighteenth century B.C. from Mari,[31] in texts from Ras Shamra-Ugarit,[32] in documents from the Third Dynasty of Ur[33] and from Drehem.[34]

O. Eissfeldt has contended, however, that the Biblical *molech* is not the name of a god at all, but a common noun to be connected with a Phoenician (Punic) word, *molk* meaning "votive offering."[35] This view is today accepted by a large number of scholars, though dissident voices have indeed been raised.[36] As I see it, the difficulty with Eissfeldt's view lies not so much in the evidence elsewhere of a god M-l-ch as in the fact that the rite mentioned in the Old Testament need not have been sacrificial at all.

200 Creation of heaven and earth 10:12

> *It was He who formed the earth by His might,*
> *Who by His wisdom formed the firm ground,*
> *Who by His discernment stretched out heaven.*

These lines, together with those which immediately follow, recur at Jeremiah 15:15, and this particular sentence is quoted also in Psalm 135:7. It may therefore be assumed that it derives from a familiar hymn or other form of popular literature.

Now, it is significant that earth and sky (i.e., the firmament) are here said to have been created by a combination of Yahweh's physical prowess and mental shrewdness—of his brawn and brain—for exactly the same combination recurs in Job 26:12, where his primordial victory over the monster Sea (alias *Rahab,* the Blusterer) is described in the words:

> *By His strength He stilled Sea,*
> *by His perspicacity smote Rahab.*

We are therefore able to recognize in the prophet's words (i.e., in those of the popular poem he is quoting) an allusion to a cosmogonic myth parallel to that related in the Mesopotamian Epic of Creation (iv. 136–38), where, after subduing the analogous Tiamat, the victorious Marduk is said to have created heaven and earth by slitting her body lengthwise, suspending the upper half to form the firmament and submerging the lower half to constitute the bedrock of the earth. This is described expressly not only as an act of heroic prowess but also as the product of a "cunning plan," i.e., as a manifestation of his perspicacity!

201 "The wind and the rain"   10:13; 51:16
(a) Fissures for the rain

> When He gives forth His voice,
>   there is surging of water in heaven;
> out on the far horizon
>   He causes vapors to rise;
> Lightnings He makes for the rain,
>   and brings forth the wind from His stores.

The phrase, *Lightnings he makes for the rain,* is readily explicable from the fact that in Palestine and Syria the advent of the "early rains" in October is heralded by electric storms.[1] Indeed, the native Arabs have a saying, "The lightning is a presage of rain."[2] Similarly, in the Canaanite *Poem of Baal* the imminent return of that god of rainfall, after he has been lured beneath the earth, is indicated by a display of lightning from his holy hill; and it is said of him also that "he will send his rain in due season . . . and give forth his voice from the clouds (and) his gleam earthwards as lightning-flashes."[3]

On the other hand, it has been ingeniously suggested[4] that in place of the word, *lightnings,* we should read, by a very slight change in the Hebrew text, (viz., $b^eD\bar{a}q\hat{i}m$ for $b^eR\bar{a}q\hat{i}m$), *chinks, fissures.* The reference will then be to a popular belief that the rain was precipitated through chinks in the firmament, conceived as a solid dam holding back the upper waters of the cosmic ocean.[5] In the aforementioned Canaanite *Poem of Baal,* that god is indeed said to send rain through "chinks" in the sky, a form of the same word (viz., *bdqt*) being employed.[6] The concept of the celestial "chinks," it may be added, is an alternative to that of the celestial "grilles" or sluices (EV: "the windows of heaven"), often mentioned in the Old Testament (Gen. 7:113; 8:2; II Kings 7:2, 19; Isa. 24:18; Mal. 3:10). These are the supernal counterparts of the clefts in the surface of the earth through which springs gush forth. The former release the upper; the latter, the nether waters. The Deluge was caused by the opening of both simultaneously (Gen. 7:11; 8:2).

Similarly, according to Herodotus, it was believed in Libya that rain was precipitated by piercing the sky;[7] while some of the aborigines of New Zealand entertain the fancy that heaven is a solid septum provided with cracks through which the rain descends.[8]

(b) Promptuaries for the wind

The notion that meteorological phenomena are stored in promptuaries recurs elsewhere in the Old Testament: in Job 38:22, hail is so stored, and in Isaiah 45:3, reference is made to "storehouses of darkness." An elaborate description of the treasuries of the winds is given in the pseudepigraphic Book of Enoch.[9]

There is an interesting twist to this idea in the Dead Sea *Hymns of Thanksgiving.* Because the Hebrew word for winds also means spirits, it is there stated that sensate spirits (subsequently transformed into angels) were appointed by God to regulate natural phenomena and were stored in promptuaries. In the same way, man is guided by such a spirit, placed in his flesh![10]

The celestial promptuaries of the winds are a Hebrew counterpart to the widespread belief that the winds are imprisoned in *caves* or special houses. This idea is most familiar, of course, from the Greek story of Aeolus, who so guards them on an island,[11] but it occurs also among primitive peoples of the present day. The New Zealanders assert, for instance, that the god Maiu keeps the winds in check by rolling boulders over the mouths of caves in which they are confined.[12] Similarly, the Iroquois say that the god Gaoh imprisons them in a "home of the winds";[13] and the Eskimos identify the abode of the dead with a "house of the winds" and offer prayers to a spirit known as "Owner of the Winds (*Sillam Innua*)."[14]

202 Rites of mourning 16:6; 48:37
▲ (a) Cuttings for the dead

The customs of cropping or shaving the hair and cutting or mutilating the body in mourning have been very widespread among mankind.

Among Semitic peoples the ancient Arabs, like the ancient Jews, practised both customs. Arab women in mourning rent their upper garments, scratched their faces and breasts with their nails, beat and bruised themselves with their shoes, and cut off their hair. When the great warrior Chalid ibn al Valid died, there was not a single woman of his tribe, the Banu Mugira, who did not shear her locks and lay them on his grave.[1] To this day similar practices are in vogue among the Arabs of Moab. As soon as a death has taken place, the women of the family scratch their faces to the effusion of blood and rend their robes to the waist.[2] And if the deceased was a husband, a father, or other near relation, they cut off their long tresses and spread them out on the grave or wind them about the headstone. Or they insert two stakes in the earth, one at the head and the other at the foot of the grave, and join them by a string, to which they attach their shorn locks.[3]

Similarly in ancient Greece women in mourning for near and dear relatives cut off their hair and scratched their cheeks, and sometimes their necks, with their nails till they bled.[4] Greek men also shore their hair as a token of sorrow and respect for the dead. Homer tells how the Greek warriors before Troy covered the corpse of Patroclus with their shorn tresses, and how Achilles laid in the hand of his dead friend the lock of hair which his father Peleus had vowed that his son should dedicate to the river Sperchius whenever he returned home from the war.[5] So Orestes is said to have laid a lock of his hair on the tomb of his murdered father Agamemnon.[6] But the humane legislation of Solon at Athens, like the humane legislation of Deuteronomy at Jerusalem, forbade the barbarous custom of scratching and scarifying the person in mourning,[7] and though the practice of shearing the hair in honour of the dead appears not to have been expressly prohibited by law, it perhaps also fell into abeyance in Greece under the influence of advancing civilization; at last it is significant that both these forms of mourning are known to us chiefly from the writings of poets who depicted the life and manners of the heroic age, which lay far behind them in the past.

Assyrian and Armenian women in antiquity were also wont to scratch their cheeks in token of sorrow, as we learn from Xenophon,[8] who may have witnessed these demonstrations of grief on that retreat of the Ten Thousand which he shared as a soldier and immortalized as a writer.

Nor was the custom unknown in ancient Rome; for one of the laws of the Ten Tables, based on the legislation of Solon, forbade women to lacerate their cheeks with their nails in mourning.[9] (The learned Roman antiquary Varro held that the essence of the custom consisted in an offering of blood to the dead, the blood drawn from the cheeks of the women being an imperfect substitute for the blood of captives or gladiators sacrificed at the grave.[10] The usages of modern savages, as we shall see presently, confirm to some extent this interpretation of the rite.) Vergil represents Anna disfiguring her face with her nails and beating her breasts with her fist at the tidings of the death of her sister Dido on the pyre,[11] but whether in this description the poet had in mind the Carthaginian or the old Roman practice of mourners is open to question.

When they mourned the death of a king, the ancient Scythians cropped their hair all round their heads, made incisions in their arms, lacerated their foreheads and noses, cut off pieces of their ears, and thrust arrows through their left hands.[12]

Among the Huns it was customary for mourners to gash their faces and crop their hair; it was thus that Attila was mourned, "not with womanish lamentations and tears, but with the blood of men."[13]

"In all Slavonic countries great stress has from time immemorial been laid on loud expressions of grief for the dead. These were formerly attended by laceration of the faces of the mourners, a custom still preserved among some of the inhabitants of Dalmatia and Montenegro."[14] Among the Mingrelians of the Caucasus, when a death has taken place in a house, the mourners scratch their faces and tear out their hair,[15] according to one account they shave their faces entirely, including their eyebrows.[16] However, from another report it would seem that only the women indulge in these demonstrations of grief. Assembled in the chamber of death, the widow and the nearest female relations of the deceased abandon themselves to the vehemence, or at all events to the display, of their sorrow, wrenching out their hair, rending their faces and breasts, and remonstrating with the dead man on his undutiful conduct in dying. The hair which the widow tears from her head on this occasion is afterwards deposited by her in the coffin.[17] Among the Ossetes of the Caucasus on similar occasions the relatives assemble: the men bare their heads and hips, and lash themselves with whips till the blood streams forth; the women scratch their faces, bite their arms, wrench out their hair, and beat their breasts with lamentable howls.[18]

The Turks of old used to cut their faces with knives in mourning for the dead, so that their blood and tears ran down their cheeks together.[19]

In Africa the custom of cutting the body in mourning, apart from the reported practice of lopping off finger-joints, appears to be comparatively rare. Among the Abyssinians, in deep mourning for a blood relation, it is customary to shear the hair, strew ashes on the head, and scratch the skin of the temples till the blood flows.[20] When a death has taken place among the Wanika of East Africa, the relations and friends assemble, lament loudly, poll their heads, and scratch their faces.[21] Among the Kissi, a tribe on the border of Liberia, women in mourning cover their bodies, and especially their hair, with a thick coating of mud, and scratch their faces and their breasts with their nails.[22] In some Kafir tribes of South Africa a widow used to be secluded in a solitary place for a month after her husband's death, and before she returned home at the expiration of that period she had to throw her clothes away, wash her whole body, and lacerate her breast, arms, and legs with sharp stones.[23]

On the other hand, the laceration of the body in mourning, if rarely practised in Africa, was common among the Indian tribes of North America. Thus on the death of a relative, the Tinneh or Déné Indians of North-Western America used to make incisions in their flesh, cut off their hair, rend their garments, and roll in the dust.[24] Again, on the occasion of a death among the Crees, who ranged over a vast extent of territory in Western Canada, "great lamentations are made, and if the departed person is very much regretted the near relations cut off their hair, pierce the fleshy part of their thighs and arms with arrows, knives, etc., and blacken their faces with charcoal."[25] Among the Kyganis, a branch of the Tlingit Indians of Alaska, while a body was burning on the funeral pyre, the assembled kinsfolk used to torture themselves mercilessly, slashing and lacerating their arms, thumping their faces with stones, and so forth.[26] With the Chinooks and other Indian tribes of the Oregon or Columbia River it was customary for the relations of a deceased person to destroy his property, to cut their hair, and to disfigure and wound their bodies.[27]

Among the Indians of the Californian peninsula, "when a death has taken place, those who want to show the relations of the deceased their respect for the latter lie in wait for these people, and if they pass they come out from their hiding-place, almost creeping, and intonate a mournful, plaintive *hu, hu, hu!* wounding their heads with pointed, sharp stones, until the blood flows down to their shoulders.[28] In some tribes of Californian Indians the nearest relations cut off their hair and throw it on the burning pyre, while they beat their bodies with stones till they bleed.[29]

To testify their grief for the death of a relative or friend the Snake Indians of the Rocky Mountains used to make incisions in all the fleshy parts of their bodies, and the greater their affection for the deceased, the deeper they cut into their own persons. They assured a French missionary that the pain which they felt in their minds escaped by these wounds.[30] The same missionary tells us how he met groups of Crow women in mourning, their bodies so covered and disfigured by clotted blood that they presented a spectacle as pitiable as it was horrible. For several years after a death the poor creatures were bound to renew the rites of mourning every time they passed near the graves of their relations; and so long as a single clot of blood remained on their persons, they were forbidden to wash themselves.[31]

Among the Arapaho Indians women in mourning gash themselves lightly across the lower and upper arms and below the knees. Mourners in that tribe unbraid their hair and sometimes cut it off; the greater their love for their departed friend, the more hair they cut off. The severed locks are buried with the corpse.[32] After a bereavement the Sauks and Foxes, another tribe of Indians, "make incisions in their arms, legs, and other parts of the body; these are not made for the purposes of mortification, or to create a pain, which shall, by diverting their attention, efface the recollection of their loss, but entirely from a belief that their grief is internal, and that the only way of dispelling it is to give it a vent through which to escape."[33] The Dakotas or Sioux in like manner lacerated their arms, thighs, legs, breast, and so on, after the death of a friend; and the writer who reports the custom thinks it probable that they did so for the purpose of relieving their mental pain, for these same Indians, in order to cure a physical pain, used frequently to make incisions in their skin and suck up the blood, accompanying the operation with songs,[34] or rather incantations, which were no doubt supposed to assist the cure.

Among the Kansas, a branch of the Siouan stock who have given their name to a State of the American Union, a widow after the death of her husband used to scarify herself and rub her body with clay; she also became negligent of her dress, and in this melancholy state she continued for a year, after which the eldest surviving brother of her deceased husband took her to wife without ceremony.[35] The custom was similar among the Omahas of Nebraska, another branch of the Siouan family. "On the death of the husband, the squaws exhibit the sincerity of their grief by giving away to their neighbours every thing they possess, excepting only a bare sufficiency of clothing to cover their persons with decency. They go out from the village, and build for themselves a small shelter of grass or bark; they mortify themselves by cutting off their hair, scarifying their skin, and, in their insulated hut, they lament incessantly. If the deceased has left a brother, he takes the widow to his lodge after a proper interval, and considers her as his wife, without any preparatory formality."[36] But among the Omahas it was not widows only who subjected themselves to these austerities in mourning. "The relatives bedaub their persons with white clay, scarify themselves with a flint, cut out pieces of their skin and flesh, pass arrows through their skin; and, if on a march, they walk barefoot at a distance from their people, in testimony of the sincerity of their mourning."[37] Among these Indians, "when a man or woman greatly respected died, the following ceremony sometimes took place. The young men in the prime of life met at a lodge near that of the deceased, and divested themselves of all clothing except the breechcloth; each person made two incisions in the upper left arm, and under the loop of flesh thus made thrust a small willow twig having on its end a spray of leaves. With the blood dripping on the leaves of the sprays that hung from their arms, the men moved in single file to the lodge where the dead lay. There, ranging themselves in a line shoulder to shoulder facing the tent, and marking the rhythm of the music with the willow sprigs they sang in unison the funeral song—the only one of its kind in the tribe. . . . At the close of the song a near relative of the dead advanced toward the singers and, raising a hand in the attitude of thanks, withdrew the willow twigs from their arms and threw them on the ground."[38] Further, as a token of grief at the death of a relative or friend, the Omahas used to cut off locks of their hair and throw them on the corpse.[39] Similarly among the Indians of Virginia the women in mourning would sometimes sever their tresses and throw them on the grave.[40]

Among the Indians of Patagonia, when a death took place, mourners used to pay visits of condolence to the widow or other relations of the deceased, crying, howling, and singing in the most dismal manner, squeezing out tears, and pricking their arms and thighs with sharps thorns to make them bleed. For these demonstrations of woe they were paid with glass beads and other baubles.[41] As soon as the Fuegians learn of the death of a relative or friend, they break into vehement demonstrations of sorrow, weeping and groaning; they lacerate their faces with the sharp edges of shells and cut the hair short on the crowns of their heads.[42] Among the Onas, a Fuegian tribe, the custom of lacerating the face in mourning is confined to the widows or other female relations of the deceased.[43]

Among the Orang Sakai, a primitive pagan tribe, who subsist by agriculture and hunting in the almost impenetrable forests of Eastern Sumatra, it is customary before a burial for the relations to cut their heads with knives and let the flowing blood drip on the face of the corpse.[44] Again, among the Roro-speaking tribes, who occupy a territory at the mouth of St. Joseph River in New Guinea, when a death has taken place, the female relations of the deceased cut their skulls, faces, breast, bellies, arms, and legs with sharp shells, till they stream with blood and fall down exhausted.[45] In the Koiari and Toaripi tribes of New Guinea mourners cut themselves with shells or flints till the blood flows freely.[46] So in Vate (or Efate), an island of the New Hebrides, a death was the occasion of great wailing, and the mourners scratched their faces till they streamed with blood.[47] Similarly in Malekula, another island of the New Hebrides, gashes are or were cut in the bodies of mourners.[48]

The Galelarese of Halmahera, an island to the west of New Guinea, make an offering of their hair to the soul of a deceased relative on the third day after his or her death, which is the day after burial. Should the survivors fail to offer their hair to the deceased and to cleanse themselves afterwards, it is believed that they do not get rid of the soul of their departed brother or sister. For instance, if some one has died away from home, and his family has had no news of his death, so that they have not shorn their hair nor bathed on the third day, the ghost (*soso*) of the dead man will haunt them and hinder them in all their work. When they crush coco-nuts, they will get no oil: when they pound sago, they will obtain no meal: when they are hunting, they will see no game. Not until they have learned of the death, and shorn their hair, and bathed, will the ghost cease thus to thwart and baffle them in their undertakings.[49] Customs of the same sort appear to have been observed by all the widely spread branches of the Polynesian race in the Pacific. Thus in Otaheite, when a death occurred, the corpse used to be conveyed to a house or hut, called *tupapow,* built specially for the purpose, where it was left to putrefy till the flesh had wholly wasted from the bones. "As soon as the body is deposited in the *tupapow,* the mourning is renewed. The women assemble, and are led to the door by the nearest relation, who strikes a shark's tooth several times into the crown of her head: the blood copiously follows, and is carefully received upon pieces of linen, which are thrown into the bier. The rest of the women follow this example, and the ceremony is repeated at the interval of two or three days, as long as the zeal and sorrow of the parties hold out. The tears also which are shed upon these occasions, are received upon pieces of cloth, and offered as oblations to the dead; some of the younger people cut off their hair, and that is thrown under the bier with the other offerings. This custom is founded upon a notion that the soul of the deceased, which they believe to exist in a separate state, is hovering about the place where the body is deposited: that it observes the actions of the survivors, and is gratified by such testimonies of their affection and grief."[50]

Among the women of Otaheite the use of shark's teeth as a lancet to draw blood from their heads was not limited to occasions of death. If any accident befell a woman's husband, his relations or friends, or her own child, she went to work on herself with the shark's teeth; even if the child had only fallen down and hurt itself, the mother mingled her blood with its tears. But when a child died, the whole house was filled with kinsfolk, cutting their heads and making loud lamentations. "On this occasion, in addition to other tokens of grief, the parents cut their hair short on one part of their heads, leaving the rest long. Sometimes this is confined to a square patch on the forehead; at others they leave that, and cut off all the rest: sometimes a bunch is left over both ears, sometimes over one only; and sometimes one half is clipped quite close, and the other left to grow long: and these tokens of mourning are sometimes prolonged for two or three years."[51] This description may illustrate the Israelitish practice of making bald places on the head in sign of mourning.

Similarly the Tongans in mourning beat their teeth with stones, burned circles and scars on their flesh, struck shark's teeth into their heads until the blood flowed in streams, and thrust spears into the inner parts of their thighs, into their sides below the arm-pits, and through their cheeks into their mouths.[52]

In the Samoan Islands it was in like manner customary for mourners to manifest their grief by frantic lamentation and wailing, by rending the garments, tearing out the hair, burning their flesh with firebrands, bruising their bodies with stones, and gashing themselves with sharp stones, shells, and shark's teeth, till they were covered with blood. This was called an "offering of blood" (*taulanga toto*).[53] Similarly in Mangaia, one of the Hervey Islands, no sooner did a sick person expire than the near relatives blackened their faces, cut off their hair, and slashed their bodies with shark's teeth so that the blood streamed down.[54] So, too, in the Marquesas Islands, "on the death of a great chief, his widow and the women of the tribe uttered piercing shrieks, whilst they slashed their foreheads, cheeks, and breasts with splinters of bamboo."[55]

Among the Maoris of New Zealand the mourning customs were similar. "All the immediate relatives and friends of the deceased, with the slaves, or other servants or dependants, if he possessd any, cut themselves most grievously, and present a frightful picture to a European eye. A piece of flint (made sacred on account of the blood which it has shed, and the purpose for which it has been used) is held between the third finger and the thumb; the depth to which it is to enter the skin appearing beyond the nails. The operation commences in the middle of the forehead; and the cut extends, in a curve, all down the face, on either side: the legs, arms, and chest are then most miserably scratched; and the breasts of the women, who cut themselves more extensively and deeper than the men, are sometimes woefully gashed."[56]

Nowhere, perhaps, has this custom of cutting the bodies of the living in honour of the dead been practised more systematically or with greater severity than among the rude aborigines of Australia, who stand at the foot of the social ladder. Thus among the tribes of Western Victoria a widower mourned his wife for three moons. Every second night he wailed and recounted her good qualities, and lacerated his forehead with his nails till the blood flowed down his cheeks; also he covered his head and face with white clay. If he loved her very dearly and wished to express his grief at her loss, he would burn himself across the waist in three lines with a red-hot piece of bark. A widow mourned for her husband for twelve moons. She cut her hair quite close, and burned her thighs with hot ashes pressed down on them with a piece of bark till she screamed with agony. Every second night she wailed and recounted his good qualities, and lacerated her forehead till the blood flowed down her cheeks. At the same time she covered her head and face with white clay. This she must do for three moons on pain of death. Children in mourning for their parents lacerated their brows.[57] Among the natives of Central Victoria the parents of the deceased were wont to lacerate themselves fearfully, the father beating and cutting his head with a tomahawk, and the mother burning her breasts and belly with a firestick. This they did daily for hours until the period of mourning was over.[58] Widows in these tribes not only burned their breasts, arms, legs, and thighs with firesticks, but rubbed ashes into their wounds and scratched their faces till the blood mingled with the ashes.[59] Among the Kurnai of South-Eastern Victoria mourners cut and gashed themselves with sharp stones and tomahawks until their heads and bodies streamed with blood.[60] In the Mukjarawaint tribe of Western Victoria, when a man died, his relatives cried over him and cut themselves with tomahawks and other sharp instruments for a week.[61]

Among the tribes of the Lower Murray and Lower Darling rivers mourners scored their backs and arms, sometimes even their faces, with red-hot brands, which raised hideous ulcers; afterwards they flung themselves prone on the grave, tore out their hair by handfuls, rubbed earth over their heads and bodies in great profusion, and ripped up their green ulcers till the mingled blood and grime presented a ghastly spectacle.[62] Among the Kamilaroi, a large tribe of Eastern New South Wales, the mourners, especially the women, used to plaster their heads and faces with white clay, and then cut gashes in their heads with axes, so that the blood flowed down over the clay to their shoulders, where it was allowed to dry.[63]

In the Kabi and Wakka tribes of South-Eastern Queensland, about the Mary River, mourning lasted approximately six weeks. "Every night a general, loud wailing was sustained for hours, and was accompanied by personal laceration with sharp flints or other cutting instruments. The men would be content with a few incisions on the back of the head, but the women would gash themselves from head to foot and allow the blood to dry upon the skin."[64] In the Boulia district of Central Queensland women in mourning score their thighs, both inside and outside, with sharp stones or bits of glass, so as to make a series of parallel cuts; in neighbouring districts of Queensland the men make a single large and much deeper cruciform cut in the corresponding part of the thigh.[65] Members of the Kakadu tribe, in the Northern Territory of Australia, cut their heads in mourning till the blood flows down their faces on to their bodies This is done by men and women alike. Some of the blood is afterwards collected in a piece of bark and apparently deposited in a tree close to the spot where the person died.[66]

In the Kariera tribe of Western Australia, when a death has occurred, the relations, both male and female, wail and cut their scalps until the blood trickles from their heads.[67]

In the Arunta tribe of Central Australia a man is bound to cut himself on the shoulder in mourning for his father-in-law; if he does not do so, his wife may be given away to another man in order to appease the wrath of the ghost at his undutiful son-in-law. Arunta men regularly bear on their shoulders the raised scars which show that they have done their duty by their dead fathers-in-law.[68] The female relations of a dead man in the Arunta tribe also cut and hack themselves in token of sorrow, working themselves up into a sort of frenzy as they do so, yet in all their apparent excitement they take care never to wound a vital part, but vent their fury on their scalps, their shoulders, and their legs.[69] In the Warramunga tribe of Central Australia widows crop their hair short, and, after cutting upen the middle line of the scalp, run firesticks along the wounds, often with serious consequences.[70] Other female relations of the deceased among the Warramunga content themselves with cutting their scalps open by repeated blows of yam-sticks till the blood streams down over their faces; while men gash their thighs more or less deeply with knives. In addition, some Warramunga men in mourning cut off their hair closely, burn it, and smear their scalps with pipeclay, while other men cut off their whiskers.[71]

It deserves to be noticed that in these cuttings for the dead among the Australians the blood drawn from the bodies of the mourners is sometimes applied directly to the corpse, or at least allowed to drop into the grave. Thus among some tribes on the Darling River several men used to stand by the open grave and cut each other's heads with a boomerang; then they held their bleeding heads over the grave, so that the blood dripped on the corpse lying in it. If the deceased was held in high esteem, the bleeding was repeated after some earth had been thrown on the corpse.[72] Similarly in the Milya-uppa tribe, which occupied the country about the Torrowotta Lake in the north-west of New South Wales, when the dead man had been a warrior, the mourners cut each other's heads and let the blood fall on the corpse as it lay in the grave.[73] Again, among the Arunta of Central Australia the female relations of the dead used to throw themselves on the grave and there cut their own and each other's heads with fighting-clubs or digging-sticks till the blood, streaming down over the pipe-clay with which their bodies were whitened, dripped upon the grave.[74] Again, at a burial on the Vasse River, in Western Australia, a writer describes how, when the grave was dug, the natives placed the corpse beside it, then "gashed their thighs, and at the flowing of the blood they all said, 'I have brought blood,' and they stamped the foot forcibly on the ground, sprinkling the blood around them; then wiping the wounds with a wisp of leaves, they threw it, bloody as it was, on the dead man."[75]

Further, it is deserving of notice that the Australian aborigines sometimes apply their severed hair, as well as their spilt blood, to the bodies of their dead friends. Thus, Sir George Grey tells us that "the natives of many parts of Australia, when at a funeral, cut off portions of their beards, and singeing these, throw them upon the dead body; in some instances they cut off the beard of the corpse, and burning it, rub themselves and the body with the singed portions of it."[76] Comparing the modern Australian with the ancient Hebrew usages in mourning, this writer adds, "The native females invariably cut themselves and scratch their faces in mourning for the dead; they also literally make a baldness between their eyes, this being always one of the places where they tear the skin with the finger nails."[77]

Among the rude aborigines of Tasmania the mourning customs appear to have been similar. "Plastering their shaven heads with pipe-clay, and covering their faces with a mixture of charcoal and emu fat, or mutton-bird grease, the women not only wept, but lacerated their bodies with sharp shells and stones, even burning their thighs with a firestick. Flowers would be thrown on the grave, and trees entwined to cover their beloved ones. The hair cut off in grief was thrown upon the mound."[78]

The customs of cutting the body and shearing the hair in token of mourning for the dead have now been traced throughout a considerable portion of mankind, from the most highly civilized nations of antiquity down to the lowest savages of modern times. It remains to ask, What is the meaning of these practices? A clue is perhaps afforded by the Nicobarese custom (to which we have elsewhere referred) of shaving the hair and eyebrows in mourning for the alleged purpose of disguising oneself from the ghost, whose unwelcome attentions they desire to avoid, and whom they apparently imagine to be incapable of recognizing them with their hair cut. Can it be, then, that both customs originated as devices for deceiving or repelling the ghost of the deceased?

How does this hypothesis square with the facts which we have passed in review? The fear of the ghost certainly counts for something in the Australian ceremonies of mourning; for we have seen that among the Arunta, if a man does not cut himself properly in mourning for his father-in-law, the old man's ghost is supposed to be so angry that the only way of appeasing his wrath is to take away his daughter from the arms of his undutiful son-in-law. Further, in the Unmatjera and Kaitish tribes of Central Australia a widow covers her body with ashes and renews this token of grief during the whole period of mourning, because, if she failed to do so, "the *atnirinja,* or spirit of the dead man, who constantly follows her about, will kill her and strip all the flesh off her bones."[79] In these customs the fear of the ghost is manifest, but there is apparently no intention either to deceive or to disgust him by rendering the person of the mourner unrecognizable or repulsive. On the contrary, the Australian practices in mourning seem to aim rather at obtruding the mourners on the attention of the ghost, in order that he may be satisfied with their demonstrations of sorrow at the irreparable loss they have sustained through his death. The Arunta and other tribes of Central Australia fear that if they do not display a sufficient amount of grief, the spirit of the dead man will be offended and do them a mischief. And with regard to their practice of whitening the mourner's body with pipe-clay, we are told that "there is no idea of concealing from the spirit of the dead person the identity of the mourner; on the other hand, the idea is to render him or her more conspicuous, and so to allow the spirit to see that it is being properly mourned for."[80] In short, the Central Australian customs in mourning appear designed to please or propitiate the ghost rather than to elude his observation or excite his disgust. That this is the real intention of the Australian usages in general is strongly suggested by the practices of allowing the mourner's blood to drop on the corpse or into the grave, and depositing his severed locks on the lifeless body; for these acts can hardly be interpreted otherwise than as tribute paid or offerings presented to the spirit of the dead in order either to gratify his wishes or to avert his wrath. Similarly we saw that among the Orang Sakai of Sumatra mourners allow the blood dripping from their wounded heads to fall on the face of the corpse, and that in Otaheite the blood flowing from the self-inflicted wounds of mourners used to be caught in pieces of cloth, which were then laid beside the dead body on the bier. Further, the custom of depositing the shorn hair of mourners on the corpse or in the grave has been observed in ancient or modern times by Arabs, Greeks, Mingrelians, North American Indians, Tahitians, and Tasmanians, as well as by the aborigines of Australia. Hence we seem to be justified in concluding that the desire to benefit or please the ghost has been at least one motive which has led many peoples to practice those mutilations with which we are here concerned.

To say this, however, is not to affirm that the propitiation of the ghost has been the *sole* intention with which these austerities have been practised. Different peoples may well have inflicted these sufferings or disfigurements on themselves from different motives, and amongst these various motives the wish to elude or deceive the dangerous spirit of the dead may sometimes indeed have played a part. We have still to inquire how the offering of blood and hair is supposed to benefit or please the ghost? Is he thought to delight in them merely as expressions of the unfeigned sorrow which his friends feel at his death? That certainly would seem to have been the interpretation which the Tahitians put upon the custom; for along with their blood and hair they offered to the soul of the deceased their tears, and they believed that the ghost "observes the actions of the survivors, and is gratified by such testimonies of their affection and grief." Yet even when we have made every allowance for the selfishness of the savage, we should probably do injustice to the primitive ghost if we supposed that he exacted a tribute of blood and tears and hair from no other motive than a ghoulish delight in the sufferings and privations of his surviving kinsfolk. It seems likely that originally he was believed to reap some more tangible and material benefit from these demonstrations of affection and devotion. Robertson Smith suggested that the intention of offering the blood of the mourners to the spirit of the departed was to create a blood covenant between the living and the dead, and thus to confirm or establish friendly relations with the spiritual powers.[81] In support of this view he referred to the practice of some Australian tribes on the Darling River, who, besides wounding their heads and allowing the blood from the wounds to drop on the corpse, were wont to cut a piece of flesh from the dead body, dry it in the sun, cut it in small pieces, and distribute the pieces among the relatives and friends, some of whom sucked it to get strength and courage, while others threw it into the river to bring a flood and fish, when both were wanted.[82] Here the giving of blood to the dead and the sucking of his flesh appear undoubtedly to imply a relation of mutual benefit between the survivors and the deceased, whether or not that relation be properly described as a covenant. Similarly among the Kariera of Western Australia, who bleed themselves in mourning, the hair of the deceased is cut off and worn by the relatives in the form of string. Here, again, there seems to be an exchange of benefits between the living and the dead, the survivors giving their blood to their departed kinsman and receiving his hair in return. The fact is, however, that these indications of an interchange of good offices between the mourners and the mourned are too few and slight to warrant the conclusion that bodily mutilations and wounds inflicted on themselves by bereaved relatives are always or even generally intended to establish a covenant of mutual help and protection with the dead. The great majority of the practices which we have surveyed in this chapter can reasonably be interpreted as benefits supposed to be conferred by the living on the dead, but few or none of them, apart from the Australian practices just cited, appear to imply any corresponding return of kindness made by the ghost to his surviving kinsfolk.

There is a simpler and more obvious explanation. We have seen that the practice of wounding the heads of mourners and letting the blood drip on the corpse was prevalent among the Australian tribes of the Darling River. Now among these same tribes it is, or rather used to be, the custom that on undergoing the ceremony of initiation into manhoood "during the first two days the youth drinks only blood from the veins in the arms of his friends, who willingly supply the required food. Having bound a ligature round the upper part of the arm they cut a vein on the under side of the forearm, and run the blood into a wooden vessel, or a dish-shaped piece of bark. The youth, kneeling on his bed, made of the small branches of a fuchsia shrub, leans forward, while holding his hands behind him, and licks up the blood from the vessel placed in front of him with his tongue, like a dog. Later he is allowed to eat the flesh of ducks as well as the blood."[83] Again, among these same tribes of the Darling River, we are informed, "a very sick or weak person is fed upon blood which the male friends provide, taken from their bodies in the way already described. It is generally taken in a raw state by the invalid, who lifts it to his mouth like jelly between his fingers and thumb." I have seen it cooked in a wooden vessel by putting a few red-hot ashes among it."[84] Again, speaking of the same tribes, the same informant tells us that "it sometimes happens that a change of camp has to be made, and a long journey over a dry country undertaken, with a helpless invalid, who is carried by the strong men, who willingly bleed themselves until they are weak and faint, to provide the food they consider is the best for a sick person."[85] Now, if these savages gave their own blood to feed the weak and sickly among their living friends, why should they not have given it for the same purpose to their dead kinsfolk? Like almost all savages, the Australian aborigines believed that the human soul survives the death of the body; what more natural, then, than that in its disembodied state the soul should be supplied by its loving relatives with the same sustaining nourishment with which they may have often strengthened it in life? On the same principle, when Ulysses was come to deadland in the far country of Cimmerian darkness, he sacrificed sheep and caused their blood to flow into a trench, and the weak ghosts, gathering eagerly about it, drank the blood and so acquired the strength to speak with him.[86]

But if the blood offered by mourners was designed for the refreshment of the ghost, what are we to say of the parallel offering of their hair? The ghost may have been thought to drink the blood, but we can hardly suppose that he was reduced to such extremities of hunger as to eat the hair. Nevertheless it is to be remembered that in the opinion of some peoples the hair is the special seat of its owner's strength,[87] and that accordingly in cutting their hair and presenting it to the dead they may have imagined that they were supplying him with a source of energy not less ample and certain than when they provided him with their blood to drink. If that were so, the parallelism which runs through the mourning customs of cutting the body and polling the hair would be intelligible. That this is the true explanation of both practices, however, the evidence at our command is hardly sufficient to enable us to pronounce with confidence.

So far as it goes, however, the preceding inquiry tends to confirm the view that the widespread practices of cutting the bodies and shearing the hair of the living after a death were originally designed to gratify or benefit in some way the spirit of the departed; and accordingly, wherever such customs have prevailed, they may be taken as evidence that the people who observed them believed in the survival of the human soul after death and desired to maintain friendly relations with it. ▼

16:7

(b) Funeral meats

> *No one shall break bread for the mourner, to comfort him for the dead; nor shall any one give him the cup of consolation to drink for his father or his mother.*

The custom of serving and partaking of funeral meats is virtually universal. However much they may later have been interpreted as mere "pick-me-ups" in a time of grief and dejection, their original purpose was, on the one hand, to recement by commensality the ruptured ties of kinship, and on the other to forge a link with the dead by sharing a meal with his spirit.[88]

The custom is mentioned elsewhere in the Old Testament. When the wife of the prophet Ezekiel dies, in token of the grief and mourning which God has in store for Israel, he is admonished to dispense with the usual rites of mourning and not to eat "the bread of mourners";[89] while Hosea warns his recalcitrant compatriots that their offerings of food are unwelcome to Yahweh and are "like the bread of mourners, all who eat of which are defiled," i.e., with the contagion of death.[90]

Amorite texts of the eighteenth century B.C. mention the funeral meal (*ukkulum*) beside the wake (*maṣṣartum*) and the lament (*naḫādum*) as standard rites of mourning;[91] and in Mesopotamia, the proffering of food (*kasap kispi*), pouring of water (*niq mê*), and invocation of the name (*zikir šumi*) of the dead—together amounting to an invitation to a commensal meal with the survivors—likewise constituted the prescribed duties of mourners.[92] The same offices are likewise enjoined in a Phoenician inscription from Zenčirli, where we are told also that a son was expected to "eat in the presence" of his departed father.[93] Similarly in the Ugaritic *Poem of Aqhat,* filial duties are said to include that of eating funeral meals in the sanctuary in connection with the cult of ancestors.[94]

Lucian of Samosata, in the second century C.E., cannot eschew his usual touch of satire in describing such meals. "The funeral meal," he writes, "is a universal custom. Neighbors come around and comfort the relatives of the deceased and induce them to take a bite. To be sure, the latter are not pressed unduly, but they are none the less somewhat worn down by three days of continuous hunger (between the demise and the obsequies). 'How long,' they ask, 'are we going to keep up this moping? Let the spirits of the departed have a rest! Even if you want to go weeping your heart out, that's no reason for going without food, and you shouldn't lose weight through grief.' What's more, they start reciting the verses in Homer about Niobe's at last realizing that she was hungry and about the Achaeans' not 'mourning the dead with their bellies.' Thereupon the bereaved indeed touch the food, though at first they are a bit bashful about it, wary lest they may seem to be lacking in human feeling after the demise of their loved ones."[95]

Clement of Alexandria[96] and Chrysostom[97] both attest the custom as current among the early Christians, and it has been suggested that the bench-lined "anterooms" sometimes found in the Christian catacombs at Rome originally served this purpose. So too, at the present day, Arabs conclude funeral ceremonies by slaughtering a lamb of which all the bereaved then partake.[98]

In traditional Jewish usage, a meal (*habra'ah*) of hard-boiled eggs, bread, and lentils (or beans) is served to mourners on their return from the cemetery.[99] This is especially interesting because eggs and beans appear elsewhere as characteristic funeral fare. In Rome, for example, eggs were a common offering to the dead[100]—a usage which still survived in the nineteenth century at Beihingen, in Germany.[101] In the Ukraine, eggs are given to the dead on St. Thomas' day;[102] and the Maori place an egg in the hands of the deceased.[103] Beans, says Pliny,[104] were commonly eaten at Roman funerals, and they were offered to the dead at the Lemuria, the annual Feast of Ghosts.[105] During the Middle Ages, it was customary in the Tyrol to eat bean soup on All Souls' Day.[106] The funeral fare of the Jews is thus identical with that believed to be consumed by the dead themselves; and this once again strengthens the view that the original purpose of the rite was to sustain relationship with them by an act of commensality.

A secondary motive, however, should not be overlooked: in many cultures mourners are indeed required to fast until burial has taken place.[107] To cite but a few representative examples, this custom is attested in the Andaman[108] and Fiji islands,[109] in Samoa,[110] China[111], Korea,[112] and among several African peoples.[113] Orthodox Jews likewise abstain from food on the day of interment, until they come home from the graveyard. Such fasting seems originally to have been a method of expressing the fact that, though death happens to a particular person, it happens in a group, and everyone else is therefore sympathetically affected by it and temporarily in a state of suspended animation. This explanation is supported by the fact that fasting is likewise a common custom at all times when an individual is thought to "put off" his personality and assume a new one, e.g., at initiation and marriage.[114]

Sometimes, to be sure, the custom of "eating with the dead" was regarded in Israel as a heathen rite, evidently smacking of ancestor worship. Thus, in Psalm 106:28, eating the meals of (not, as RSV: sacrifices offered to) the dead is classed with attaching oneself to the Baal of Peor.[115]

203 The ritual lament 22:18

> They shall not lament for him:
> "Ah, my brother!" or "Ah, sister!"[1]
> They shall not lament for him:
> "Ah, Lord [Heb.: adôn]!"..

The prophet is quoting a standard form of lamentation, for it recurs at 34:5. This identical form is found again in a Mesopotamian text describing and explaining the rites of the New Year (Akitu) Festival. At a certain point of the proceedings, we are told, a wailing woman paraded around crying *ma-a aḫu-u-a, ma-a aḫu-u-a,* "Ah, brother! Ah, brother!"[2]

Moreover, a fragment of Sappho[3] preserves the analogous lamentation, *Oh, for Adonis!* where Adonis is, of course, simply the Semitic *adon,* "lord." This form of lament was likewise standard, for it is cited also by Aristophanes[4] and Bion,[5] and later also by Ammianus Marcellinus.[6]

204 Invoking the Earth 22:29

> O Land, land, land,
>   hear the word of the LORD!

The threefold repetition of the word, *Land* (or, *earth*), suggests that this reproduces an incantatory or liturgical formula. We may therefore pertinently compare the words of a Mesopotamian incantation: *Earth, earth, earth, Gilgamesh casts a spell upon you!*[1]

205 Rachel weeping for her children   31:15

> RSV: Thus says the LORD:
> "A voice is heard in Ramah,
> Lamentation and bitter weeping.
> Rachel is weeping for her children;
> she refuses to be comforted for her children,
> because they are not."

Since Rachel in fact died in childbirth (Gen. 35:16–20), it has been suggested that these famous lines reflect the common belief that women who suffer this fate haunt the earth in search of their babes, or return to suckle and tend them.[1]

A Mesopotamian magical text classes among errant spirits that of the woman who has died in childbirth,[2] and among Arabs of the present day the notion prevails that she returns in the form of an owl.[3] In Malaya, the nightjar, called Langsuyar, is thought to embody such a hapless mother;[4] while among the Banks Islanders it is held that the spirit of such a woman cannot go to Panoi, a ghostland, but must roam the earth.[5] Similarly, in the Pelew Islands, she is thought to wander eternally, crying: "Give me my child!"[6]

This is, of course, merely one particular form of the belief, widely attested in ancient Greek sources, that those who have died an untimely or violent death (*aōroi* or *biaiothanatoi*) are not admitted to Hades, but must wander.[7] In German folklore, the ghosts of little children are said to flit around as jack-o'-lanterns.[8]

It is possible, however, to interpret the lines in quite a different manner. Seeing that the prophet has just used the image of the ingathering of scattered sheep (31:10), the word *Rachel* may be no proper name at all, but simply the regular Hebrew word for *ewe-lamb,* while Ramah could be a common noun meaning *height, upland.* The passage would then read:

> Thus says the LORD:
> "Hark! in the upland is heard
> Lamentation and bitter weeping—
> a ewe-lamb weeping for her young,
> refusing to be solaced for her young,
> because they are not."

As a matter of fact, the affection of the ewe for her lamb was proverbial in Ancient Near Eastern literature. A Mesopotamian magical text says expressly: "As a ewe loves its lamb, a gazelle its young, a she-ass its foal . . . so do I love thee, mine own body";[9] while a Hittite text declares likewise: "as the ewe loves the lamb, the cow its calf, parents the child, so, O Sun-god, do thou also . . . etc.[10] The simile recurs also in Egyptian[11] and Sumerian[12] literature.

Even more to the point is the picture drawn in the Canaanite *Poem of Baal* of the goddess 'Anat's distress at his disappearance from the earth: "Like the heart of a cow for her calf, like the heart of a ewe for her lamb, so is the heart of 'Anat on account of Baal."[13] Moreover, precisely the same image is used by Ovid in describing Demeter's search for Persephone. *Ut vitulo mugit sua mater ab ubere rapto Et querit fetus per nemus omne suos, Sie dea nec retinet gemitus et concita cursu Fertur.* (Even as the ewe lamb lows when the calf is snatched from her udder, and goes seeking her offspring through every grove, so the goddess restrains not her sighs and is borne along on her headlong course.)[14]

205a David redivivus 34:23-24

> *And I will set up over them one shepherd, my servant David . . . and my servant David shall be prince among them.*

Here, as again in Ezekiel 37:24 and in Hosea 3:5, the name David is used to denote the future king of a restored Israel.[1] The notion of the heroic king who will reappear in the hour of his people's need is widespread.[2] In Rome it was applied even to Nero.[3] The Welsh held the same belief about Arthur,[4] and the motif appears also in the Finnish Kalevala[5] and in Danish and Norse lore.[6] It is likewise attested among North American Indians and among the Aztecs,[7] while during World War I, the British attached this superstition to Lord Kitchener after he had drowned in the sinking of H.M.S. *Hampshire*.

Ezekiel

206 Cherubim   **1**
See above, §19.

207 Ezekiel's vision of heathen worship   **7–9**

I

In the fifth or sixth[1] month of the Hebrew year, at the season when vines were pruned and summer fruit was reaped,[2] the prophet Ezekiel was transported in a vision to the precincts of the temple of Yahweh in Jerusalem. This is what he saw:

(i) At the northern gate of the inner courtyard, a seat had been set up for an idol whom he calls ironically "the idol of jealousy (or, of passion)."[3]

(ii) In a frescoed cavern,[4] a small congregation of men—described in round figures as seventy in number—was engaged in performing certain rites.

(iii) At the northern gate, women were sitting weeping for "the Tammuz," i.e., the god of vegetation and fertility, who was believed to withdraw from the earth during the summer months, and whom the prophet, living in Babylon, designates by his characteristic Babylonian name.

(iv) In the inner courtyard, between the porch and the altar, a group of men were turning toward the east and prostrating themselves before the rising sun.

The prophet denounced these rites as heathen abominations. Comparative Religion and Folklore now help us to understand what they were.

(a) **The "seat of the idol of jealousy"**

Among the Canaanite documents unearthed at Ras Shamra, in North Syria, is one which sets forth the ritual and accompanying myth of an agricultural and viticultural festival.[5] A rubric in this text[6] prescribes that at a certain stage of the proceedings, "seats" are to be set up for various deities—precisely the same term being used as is employed by the prophet. Moreover, in another document from the same site, the erection of such seats for gods is again mentioned as part of a ritual ceremony,[7] while elsewhere we read of "a throne for Elath" and a "tribune for 'Ashtareth."[8] A much later inscription from Teima likewise makes reference to such a "seat," again using the same word.[8a]

What is here implied is a *lectisternium,* or spreading of couches (seats) for the divine guests at a *theoxenia,* or seasonal banquet. This was a common feature of calendar festivals.[9] Thus, the so-called Egyptian Ramesseum Drama ends with the installation of the revived Horus and the celebration of a banquet attended, on the durative and mythic level, by the gods, and on the punctual and ritual level, by the princes of the several nomes of Upper and Lower Egypt.[10] In the Hittite myth designed for the annual "Festival of the Earth (Puruli)," the weather-god is installed at Nerik, with the gods around him;[11] while in the Telepinu myth, that god's return is celebrated at a banquet.[12] In the Babylonian New Year (Akîtu) myth, Marduk, duly installed as king, presides at a banquet of the gods;[13] and at Asshur, the ancient capital of Assyria, the festival itself is described as a "banquet (kirêtu)."[14] Further, we know from Assyrian sources that once a year the king invited the gods to a banquet and invoked them to bless himself, the city, the land, and the people. This ceremony was termed "the collation (tâkaltu)."[15] Couches which were probably used in such a ceremony have actually been found at Palmyra and in the Hauran;[16] and inscriptional evidence attests the same usage in the Asianic cult of Attis, wherein it was the duty of the priest to "spread the couch" for the gods at annual panegyries.[17] Lastly, as F. M. Cornford has pointed out, Greek comedies, which evolved out of the primitive seasonal drama, often end in a scene of banqueting and in this we may perhaps recognize, albeit through a glass darkly, a lingering trace of the original *lectisternium*.[18]

In the mouth of Ezekiel, the expression "idol of jealousy" probably stigmatizes the divine occupant of the "seat" as a mere image destined to evoke the passionate jealousy of Yahweh. Not impossibly, however, the prophet uses this strange designation with particular satirical intent, for in the aforementioned Canaanite text the rubric prescribing the setting up to the "seats" is followed immediately by the opening words of a hymn then to be recited; and these words are: *I am jealous for the names of the gods*.[19] The implication would be, therefore, that the gods which excite the jealous devotion of their worshipers are but idols which excite the jealous wrath of Yahweh!

(b) The frescoed cavern

The prophet speaks of a "hole in the wall," through which he is told to dig. On doing so, he sees walls frescoed with pictures of "creeping things and loathsome beasts, and all the idols of the house of Israel." Before them stands a crowd of men holding smoking censers, but a discreet veil is drawn over what they were doing. Perhaps Comparative Religion can illuminate what "the elders of the house of Israel were doing in the dark, each in his frescoed chamber."

The first thing to observe is that the Greek (Septuagint) Version omits all reference to a *wall*, and that the Hebrew word (*ḥôr*) translated "hole" can also mean "cave." Not impossibly, therefore, the prophet misunderstood what was really taking place, and interpreted a rite in a subterranean vault as something which he knew in other connections, namely, the adoration of animals depicted, as in prehistoric caves, on the walls of such chambers.[20] But what was really going on? Could it perhaps have been something in connection with the cult of the "dying and resurrected god," symbolically placed in an underground cavern, or a symbolic union of worshipers with the earth?

What lends plausibility to this suggestion is the importance of such subterranean caverns in the later mystery cults. Thus, a scholiast on the *Alexipharmakon* of the Alexandrian poet Nicander explains the curious expression, "marriage-bowers of Rhea Lobrinē," as denoting subterranean chambers used in the rites of that mother-goddess and of her paramour, Attis;[21] while an epitaph on a priest of Cybele, preserved in the Greek Anthology, speaks of his having "descended into the evening darkness, gone down into the cavern."[22] Similarly, the lexicographer Hesychius defines the word *Cybela* as meaning "both caverns and marriage-chambers";[23] and the church father Arnobius, fulminating against the heathen mysteries, scornfully describes how the Mother of the gods "carries off the pine-log [representing Attis] into her cavern."[24]

Descent into a subterranean vault was also regarded, in several mystery cults, as symbolizing an *unio mystica* with the regenerative powers of Mother Earth.[25]

(c) Women weeping for Tammuz

Further researches on Sumerian texts have cast doubt on the old view (espoused especially by Frazer) that Tammuz was a "dying and reviving" god of fertility, of the order of Osiris, Attis, and Adonis. It now seems probable—if not altogether certain—that the Tammuz myth really ran on somewhat different lines.[26] Nevertheless, there is definite evidence that the god was indeed bewailed in annual rites. In the Mesopotamian Epic of Gilgamesh, that hero, rejecting the advances of the goddess Ishtar, brusquely points out to her that her lover Tammuz came to a bad end, and is now the subject of "wailing" year after year.[27] Similarly, in the *Poem of Ishtar's Descent to the Netherworld* there is a reference, albeit obscure, to male and female wailers who annually greet the goddess on the day when Tammuz "jubilates" over her arrival to rescue him.[28] Furthermore, an Old Babylonian text[29] and another of Arsacid date[30] describe the midsummer month of Tammuz as a period of wailing, ritual lamentation, and weeping; while an Old Assyrian almanac prescribes weeping for the second day in it.[31]

These rites have their counterpart, of course, in the well-known ritual laments for the Egyptian Osiris, the Phrygian Attis, and the Syrian Adonis (see above, §203). It survived in the Middle Ages at Harran, where women annually bewailed a log called Ta'uz, i.e., Tammuz.[32]

A modern parallel may also be cited. In Roumania, on the Monday before the Feast of Assumption (in August), groups of girls go out from the villages, carrying under a pall a miniature coffin in which is deposited a clay image called Kalojan. The coffin is subsequently interred, and for two days the girls ceremonially bewail it. Kalojan—i.e., *kalos Ioannēs* (beautiful John)—is here but a Christian substitution for the more ancient *kalos Adonis* (beautiful Adonis).[33]

The women who weep for Tammuz play the role of professional mourners at a funeral ceremony. Such female mourners are, of course, familiar enough, especially from modern Arab usage,[34] but it is noteworthy that they occur already not only in ancient Egypt[35] but also among the Hittites,[36] while in the Canaanite *Poem of Aqhat,* they are said to enter the house of King Daniel in order to perform a keening for his slain son.[36a] Homer likewise mentions them in his account of the obsequies of Hector.[37] They are the later Roman *praeficae,*[38] who lead the dirge; and in modern Armenia they are known as "dirge-mothers."[39]

In illustration of the fact that the lamentation is performed *at the entrance* of the temple, it may be noted that in modern Anatolia rites of mourning take place in the courtyard of the deceased's house and are attended by professional wailing women and relatives; the public exercises, which take place at the actual interment, are quite distinct.[40]

On the significance of the fact that the rite is performed at the *northern* gate, see below, §233.

(d) The adoration of the rising sun

Festivals which evolve around the concept of the dying and reviving god of fertility *are often made to coincide with the solstice or equinox.*[41] The mysteries of Attis, for example, culminated in the triumphant re-emergence of that god on the day of the vernal solstice (March 25); while an Old Assyrian calendar for the month of Tammuz prescribes signficantly that the "weeping" for him, which is to take place on the first day in it, is to be followed immediately, on the second by "the presentation of gifts to the sun-god."[42] A Babylonian hymn belonging to the Tammuz cycle represents the sun-god as assuring his sisters that he himself would restore to her "the verdure which hath been removed" and "the crushed grain which hath been carried away."[43] Similarly, in a Hittite text celebrating the discomfiture of "Jack Frost (*Hahhimas*)," joint honors are paid to Telipinu, the genius of vegetation, and the sun-god;[44] while in the Canaanite *Poem of Baal,* it is the sun-goddess that retrieves Baal from the netherworld and urges his rival Môt, genius of drought and sterility, to give up the fight against him.[45] Similarly, the *Poem of the Gracious Gods,* which was designed for a spring festival, includes a liturgical invocation in which in addition to those deities, the sun-goddess too is adored.[46]

Significant also is the fact that among the Israelites both the vernal festival of Pentecost and the autumnal festival of Ingathering fell in the months of the equinoxes, the latter being explicitly associated with that event in the ritual calendar of Exodus 34:22.[47]

Again, it should be observed that in Syria and in the eastern portions of the Roman Empire the Festival of the "new Age" was likewise combined with an important solar date, viz., the alleged birthday of the sun on November 18.[48] The same date, it may be added, was claimed by Clement of Alexandria as the birthday of the Christian Savior.[49] Indeed, so firmly established was the connection between festivals of the new life and the worship of the sun that the Church was obliged to fix Christmas on what had originally been the birthday of the solarized savior Mithra and to associate the date of Christ's resurrection (Easter) with the vernal equinox.[50] Similarly, the Irish celebration of Lammastide, in August, was associated with the worship of Lug, the sun-god.[51] As the Pervigilium Veneris puts it, *vere natus orbis est*.[52]

II

(e) Ezekiel's satire

If, then, we assume that Ezekiel's sermon was directed against pagan practices at a harvest festival, it becomes possible to recognize throughout his discourse sly allusions to features of that occasion. We may suppose, in fact, that the prophet used the same technique as is today a standard tactic of "hot gospellers" and evangelical revivalists: he drew metaphors from the familiar symbols of the heathen cult, giving to each a peculiar homiletical twist.

Thus he opens his discourse (7:2) with the words, *The end is coming*. The Hebrew word for "end" is *qêṣ,* and he would have been preaching at the very season of the year anciently called *qêṣ,* "the reaping of summer fruit." Is it not possible, therefore, that in these striking words he is giving a forceful meaning to a traditional cry of the season, viz., "Late Summer (*qêṣ*) is icumen in?" If anyone think this suggestion bizarre, let him turn to Amos 8:3, where exactly the same pun is employed: *The LORD God showed me, and behold, there was a basket of summer fruit* (qaiṣ, *i.e.,* qêṣ). *And he said, What seest thou, Amos? And I said, A basket of summer fruit. Then said the LORD unto me: The end* (qêṣ) *is coming for my people Israel. . . .* We may represent the point by rendering "fall," i.e., *The fall is coming!*

The prophet continues (7:7): *Doom is coming.* Here the Hebrew word rendered "doom" is *ṣᵉfîrah,* which does not occur in this sense elsewhere in the Old Testament. In several of the cognate Semitic languages, however, the basic root *ṣ-f-r* means "make a circuit." The sense will thus be, *"The cyclic point has come,"* i.e., things have come round full cycle, and the term will be an exact synonym of *tᵉqūfah,* which means literally "cyclic point" (from root *q-w-f*) and then comes to denote "equinox." We may represent the effect by rendering "turning-point," i.e., *the turning-point is coming* (or, *has come*)!

The fateful day is described (*ibid.*) as one in which *tumult, and not joyful sound, will re-echo on the hills*. It has been recognized by all commentators that the rare Hebrew word *hēd,* rendered "joyful sound," is simply an alternative form of *hēdād,* elsewhere (Isa. 16:10; Jer. 25:30; 48:29) stated to be the cry used by vintners when treading the grape. Thus it is apparent again that the prophet is alluding to features of the season, for an ancient agricultural calendar from Gezer (ninth century B.C.) tell us expressly that the period of *qêṣ* was preceded immediately by that of *zmr,* "trimming vines," when the dominant thought in everyone's mind would have been that of the coming vintage; while in Ezekiel 3:17 there is (apparently) reference to a ceremony in which a vine branch (z^e*mōrah*) was used. We may convey the point by rendering freely, *Horror and not hurrah will re-echo on the hills.*

In verses 10–11, despite the uncertainty of the text, it is at least clear that the prophet is likening the wickedness and violence of his coreligionists to a shoot which grows up apace and, apparently, is destined eventually to wither.[53] Here again it seems not impossible that he is alluding slyly to a feature of the pagan ceremonies—namely, the custom of carrying or erecting garlanded poles or branches at harvest festivals. Such a pole, called *eyan,* is frequently mentioned in Hittite ritual texts;[54] and its most familiar analogues are, of course, the *eiresione* of the Greeks,[55] the palm branch (*lulab*) of the Jewish Feast of Ingathering, and the European maypole. According to both Johannes Lydus[56] and Julian,[57] a prominent feature of the later "mysteries" of Attis was the introduction of a pine log into the sacred precincts. One of the days of the festival was called, in fact, "Day when the Log comes in (*canna intrat*), and the priests who bore it were known as "carriers of the tree" (*dendrofori*).[58] Analogous rites were performed also, according to Firmicus Maternus, in the "mysteries" of Isis, Adonis, and Persephone.[59] In modern times, we may recognize a survival of the rite in the custom reported, at the end of the nineteenth century, from Banga, in Asianic Georgia, where a felled oak was brought into church during the last days of April.[60] Significant also is the fact that on the famous "Minoan" signet-ring discovered by Sir Arthur Evans at Thisbe, in Crete, the Mother and Child are depicted receiving adoration from armed priests (cf. Ezek. 9:1!) who hold flowering reeds in their hands.[61] These Evans rightly identifies with the priestly "reed-bearers" (*cannoforoi*) mentioned in divers sources concerned with the cult of Rhea and Attis.

The prophet's diatribe gains momentum. *They sound the trumpets,* he cries, *and there is general preparation, but no one goes out to battle!* The outward purport of the words is clear enough: we know that the trumpet was sounded at the beginning of a military campaign. What, however, inspired the image? Perhaps, once again, the answer may come from the analogy of the Attis "mysteries," for the priests were there called "spear-bearers" (*aichmoforoi;* Latin, *hastiferi*),[62] and Lucretius, in describing analogous rites, says distinctly that the priests carried weapons (*telaque praeportant*).[63] Moreover, as stated above, on the signet ring from Thisbe, in Crete, the votaries of the Great Mother are shown armed.

As for the sounding of the trumpet, it is sufficient to note that such blasts are a common method of scaring demons, especially at New Year and seasonal festivals.[64] The Hebrews, for example, sounded the ram's horn on such occasions,[65] as also at every new moon[66]—a time when the "princes of darkness" are believed to be particularly rampant. Similarly, it is customary in the Isle of Man to blow trumpets on the mountains at the Feast of Laa Boaldyn, on May 1, first to summon the demons, and then to drive them home;[67] and a similar practice obtains at religious gatherings in Bali.[68] On the same basis too, the Cheremiss use long trumpets of lime-tree bark to scare Satan[69]—a usage recorded in rabbinic literature as current also among the Jews.[70] The Aymara Indians employ the same device to forefend hail.[71]

Trumpets are also blown, in order to arouse dormant or "dead" gods of fertility. Julian tells us that they were so sounded at the annual festival of Attis;[72] while both Pausanias and Plutarch attest that the Argives used year by year to summon Dionysus from the Alyconian lake through which he descended to Hades by blowing trumpets on its shores.[73]

In the light of such comparative material it does not seem far-fetched to assume that Ezekiel may have been satirizing a specific heathen rite.

The prophet now passes on (v. 20) to a pointed jibe at the gaudy raiment and the parade of statuettes (Heb.: $ṣ^e lāmîm$) which characterized the pagan ceremonies.

> *Their silver shall they cast into the streets,*
> *and their gods shall become an unclean thing;*
> *neither their silver nor their gold shall be able to save them,*
> *in the day of the LORD'S wrath.*
> *Their hunger shall they not satisfy,*
> *their bellies not fill,*
> *for this iniquity of theirs shall prove a stumbling block.*
> *The finery which went with it*
> *they assumed for proud show,*
> *and images of their loathsome idols*
> *did they make in connection with it.*
> *Therefore I will make it an unclean thing unto them!*

It is not difficult to recognize in these words an allusion to the *masquerade* typical of a pagan festival,[74] and to the custom of carrying images of the gods in a ceremonial procession. Herodian tells us expressly that at the celebration of the mysteries of Attis, "unlimited permission was given to all for all manner of frivolity, and everyone donned whatever raiment he liked";[75] and a similar practice marked the festival of Anthesteria in Greece.[76] Indeed, even at the present day, "Sunday best" is considered *de rigueur* in religious occasions.

The parading of special statuettes of the gods, called by the same term (viz., ṣalmê) as in our Biblical text, is mentioned in a Babylonian document as a feature of the great New Year (Akîtu) Festival; and we are informed also that on the same occasion images of the god Marduk and of his bride Zarpanitum were made by craftsmen.[77]

Again, verse 22 emerges in a new light, if read as a satire on specific pagan practices. Says the prophet, in the name of Yahweh:

> *I shall turn my face from them,*
> *and men shall profane my hidden place;*
> *intruders shall enter it and profane it.*

In the first part of this statement we may now detect a pointed reference to the so-called *epopteia,* or "beholding of the (divine) face," which was a central element of pagan festivals. In several Babylonian texts, votaries are said then to have proceeded to the temple in order to "see the face" of the god;[78] while in the Israelitic laws concerning the pilgrim feasts (Exod. 23:17; 34:23) the beholding of the face of Yahweh is likewise expressly mentioned. On Greek soil, the *epopteia* is best known to us from the Eleusinian Mysteries,[79] but it is attested also in Samothrace[80] and in other parts. It is with reference to this feature of the pagan ceremonies that Yahweh here pointedly declares, *I shall turn my face from them.*

In the reference to the profanation of "my hidden place" (for so the Hebrew word may fairly be rendered), we may see an allusion to the adyton, where the holiest part of the pagan ceremony took place. Similarly, in Babylonian texts, this adyton goes by the strictly comparable name of "place of the mystery, secret (*ashar puzri*)."[81] The unusual Hebrew word may be, in fact, a translation of this technical term.

The word rendered "intruders" likewise has special point. Usually rendered "robbers," it means literally "men who break through," and it is therefore by no means implausible that in this context it denotes the uninitiated who break in unlawfully upon the sanctity of the innermost shrine.

The prophet's final taunt may be recognized in the words of verse 25:

> *Spasm[82] shall ensue; and they shall seek peace,*
> *but it shall not be.*

Here, it may be suggested, he is alluding slyly to the pagan seasonal ceremony of seeking the lost or ousted god of fertility. The expression, "to seek" the god, was, in fact, a cardinal *terminus technicus* alike in the Egyptian cult of

Isis and Osiris and in the Greek worship of Demeter and Persephone.[83] It occurs also in the Canaanite *Poem of Baal,* when the goddess 'Anat declares her intention of setting forth to "seek" that vanquished deity.[84]

The reference to "spasm" which will overtake the participants in the heathen rites will then fall readily into place in the light of Themstius' description of the scene attending the "resurrection" of the god in the mysteries of Attis; the event was received, he tell us, with "tremor and trembling and perspiration and amazement." The prophet of Yahweh is scornfully satirizing such a scene.[85]

▲ 208   Trapping the soul   13:18

> *Woe to the women who sew fillets upon all wrists and make scarves for the heads of all upstanding people, thereby to entrap souls! The souls which belong to my people you entrap, but your own you keep alive! You also profane Me to My people by (using) handfuls of barley and pieces of bread in order to bring about the death of souls [persons] which ought not to die and to keep alive those which ought not to live. . . .*
>
> *Wherefore thus says the LORD God: Behold, I am against your fillets with which you go trapping souls, and I will tear them from your arms and release the souls which you would entrap, that they may fly away like birds.*[1]

The nefarious practices which the prophet here denounces apparently consisted in attempts to catch stray souls in fillets and cloths, and so to kill some people by keeping their souls in durance vile, and to save the lives of others, probably of sick people, by capturing their vagabond souls and restoring them to their bodies. Similar devices have been and still are adopted for the same purpose by sorcerers and witches in many parts of the world. For example, Fijian chiefs used to whisk away the souls of criminals in scarves, whereupon the poor wretches, deprived of this indispensable part of their persons, used to pine and die.[2] The sorcerers of Danger Island, in the Pacific, caught the souls of sick people in snares, which they set up near the houses of the sufferers, and watched till a soul came fluttering into the trap and was entangled in its meshes, after which the death of the patient was, sooner or later, inevitable. The snares were made of stout cinet with loops of various sizes adapted to catch souls of all sizes, whether large or small, fat or thin.[3] Among the Negroes of West Africa "witches are continually setting traps to catch the soul that wanders from the body when a man is sleeping; and when they have caught this soul, they tie it up over the canoe fire and its owner sickens as the soul shrivels. This is merely a regular line of business, and not an affair of individual hate or revenge. The witch does not care whose dream-soul gets into the trap, and will restore it on payment. Also witch-doctors, men of unblemished professional reputation, will keep asylums for lost souls, *i.e.* souls who have been out wandering and found on their return to their body that their place had been filled up by a Sisa, a low-class soul. . . . These doctors keep souls, and administer them to patients who are short of the article."[4] Among the Baoules of the Ivory Coast it happened once that a chief's soul was extracted by the magic of an enemy, who succeeded in shutting it up in a box. To recover it, two men held a garment of the sufferer, while a witch performed certain enchantments. After a time she declared that the soul was now in the garment, which was accordingly rolled up and hastily wrapped about the invalid for the purpose of restoring his spirit to him.[5] Malay wizards catch the souls of women whom they love in the folds of their turbans, and then go about with the dear souls in their girdles by day and sleep with them under their pillows by night.[6] Among the Toradjas of Central Celebes the priest who accompanied an armed force on an expedition used to wear a string of seashells hanging down over his breast and back for the purpose of catching the souls of the enemy; the shells were branched and hooked, and it was supposed that, once the souls were conjured into the shells, the branches and hooks would prevent them from escaping. When the warriors had entered the hostile territory, the priest went by night to the village which they intended to attack, and there, close by the entrance, he laid down his string of shells on the path so as to form a circle, and inside of the circle he buried an egg and the guts of a fowl, from which omens had been drawn before the troop set out from their own land. Then the priest took up the string of shells and waved it seven times over the spot, calling quietly on the souls of the enemy and saying, "Oh, soul of So-and-So, come, tread on my fowl; thou art guilty, thou hast done wrong, come!" Then he waited, and if the string of shells gave out a tinkling sound, it was a sign that the soul of an enemy had really come and was held fast by the shells. Next day the man, whose soul had thus been ensnared, would be drawn, in spite of himself, to the spot where the foes who had captured his soul were lying in wait, and thus he would fall an easy prey to their weapons.[7]

[In the South Celebes[7a] and among the Minangkabau of Sumatra,[7b] the body of a woman in childbirth is bound tightly lest her soul escape—a practice which has parallels in European folklore[7c]—and when a man falls sick, the latter people fasten fishhooks to his nose, navel, and feet for the same purpose. Similar practices obtain among the Toradjas[7d] and the Olu Dusun Dayaks of southern Borneo.[7e] In the same way, the Minahassa of the Celebes tie the soul of an ailing man to his head;[7f] while the Belong Mongondo of the same area lure it into a doll which is then wrapped in a cloth bound around his temples.[7g] The Papuans of Geelrink Bay, in New Guinea, bind cords around the wrists of sick persons, and retrieve their souls in a bag which is then emptied over their heads.[7h] In Thailand, when a child has intermittent fever, or when its mother is obliged to leave it overnight, she or somebody else binds both its wrists with a piece of unspun thread, tying the knot tightly. Such an operation is termed "binding the soul" (*phuk khwan*). "The sign of life," it is explained, "is visible on either wrist, for the pulse throbs. If a binding is made, the fickle soul (*khwan*) will not play truant.[7i] In Fiji, corpses are trussed up, lest the departed soul walk by night and harm the living.[7j] Siberian shamans and spiritualistic mediums are likewise adept at "binding souls" with cords;[7k] and it is not without significance that in ancient Mesopotamian magical texts a sorceress is sometimes called "a woman who goes catching by night."[7l]

Of special interest also is the prophet's reference to the practice of encompassing the death or preservation of souls by *handfuls of barley and pieces of bread*. On the face of it, this looks like a denunciation of those who try to starve their enemies by scant rations and to preserve their friends by handouts of food, and this is how it is commonly interpreted. Since, however, these words are closely conjoined with an excoriation of magical practices, and since the divine subversion of this device is said to consist in releasing the trapped souls like flying birds, it may be suggested that here too the prophet is alluding to a piece of magic. In that case, it may perhaps be explained in the light of the widespread belief that the soul has the form of a bird (see below, §274), so that it can be entrapped or enticed by the symbolic act of strewing grain or breadcrumbs. Such a magical practice is in fact common in Indonesia and the Malay Peninsula, where it is customary to strew rice on a man's hand in order to prevent his soul from "flying away like a bird."[7m] There, to be sure, the idea is to *hold in* the soul of a sick person, but it is not difficult to see that by the same line of thought the practice could have been employed in "black" as well as "white" magic, and have served, like the fillets and scarves, to bind an enemy's soul in captivity.] ▼

209 Yahweh's scourges   14:12-20

In predicting imminent disaster upon Judah, the prophet warns, in the name of Yahweh, that while the righteous might be delivered, they will not be able to achieve expiation for the people in general. To illustrate this message, he observes that even if such paragons of piety as Noah, Daniel, and Job were to be living in a sinful land doomed to destruction, and if Yahweh were to inflict that punishment in the form of famine, noisome beasts, the sword, or plague, they would not be able to deliver anyone but themselves.

The prophet living in Babylon appears to have in mind a passage in the Babylonian Epic of Gilgamesh. After the Deluge, we read,[1] the god Ea objected to Enlil, the supreme deity, that such wholesale destruction of mankind was unnecesary and involved the innocent as well as the guilty. Enlil, he says, should have taken counsel and adopted a more selective form of punishment, such as the dispatch of a *lion* or a *wolf*, or of *famine* or *plague*.

The specific reference to Noah, the hero of the Hebrew story of the Deluge, suggests that Ezekiel was indeed alluding to this passage.[2] Moreover, in the so-called *Little Genesis* (*Biblical Antiquities*), a paraphrase of early Biblical history composed (probably) in the first century c.e., it is stated expressly[3] that, after the Flood, God assured Noah that in the future He would punish mankind only by *famine, sword, fire,* or *pestilence*.[4]

210 The righteous Daniel   14:14

> *Even if these three men, Noah, Daniel and Job, were in it (i.e., the land), they would deliver but their own lives by their own righteousness, says the Lord GOD.*

We now know that the Daniel who is here classed among the paragons of righteousness is not the prophet of that name nor the "Daniel come to judgment" of the legend of Susanna, but a figure drawn from an ancient Canaanite folktale, the *Poem of Aqhat,* discovered in 1930 at Ras Shamra-Ugarit. King of H-r-n-m, in southern Syria, he is given a male heir (Aqht) as a reward for his piety in serving as a humble scullion in the temple of Baal for seven days. For this reason, the supreme god El issues the order that "the soul of Daniel is indeed to be kept in life" (I Aqhat, i.35–38). He is described also (*ib.,* v. 8) as dispensing justice to the widow and the fatherless.

211 Salting newborn children   16:4

> *On the day you were born your navel string was not cut nor were you washed with water to cleanse you, nor rubbed with salt nor swathed with bands.*

Salt, being incorruptible, averts demons and protects against black magic.[1] As an old writer puts it, witches and warlocks "like their master, the Devil, abhor salt as the emblem of immortality."[2]

Both the Talmud[3] and St. Jerome[4] attest the salting of newborn babies as standard procedure among the Jews in the early centuries of the Common Era; while, according to the physician Galen (130–c. 200 c.e.), this practice obtained also among the ancient Greeks.[5] The Arabs protect their children from the evil eye by placing salt in their hands on the eve of the seventh day after birth; the following morning the midwife or some other woman strews it about the house, crying, "Salt in every envious eye!"[6] "To salt" is a regular expression for "to rear a child";[7] and a Palestinian proverb declares that "the skin which is not salted will suppurate."[8] In standard Catholic ritual, salt is applied to the lips in baptism to exorcize the Devil,[9] and in medieval Sweden it was then put under the infant's tongue.[10] The Germans did the same thing immediately after the child had been delivered,[11] and salt was also placed near the child to forefend demons.[12] In the Balkans[13] and among the Todas of Southern India,[14] newborn children are immediately salted; while Laotian and Thai women "wash" with salt after childbirth to immunize themselves from demonic assault.[15] In the northern counties of England, it is customary to tuck a small bag of salt into a baby's clothing on its first outing.[16] As late as 1946, a couple was arraigned at Trowbridge, Wiltshire, for burning salt over a child in order to stop its hysterical crying. The father attributed the cries to witchcraft and pleaded in defense that "he felt he had to counteract the evil influences that were around."[17] In Italy, salt is often placed under the pillow of a woman in labor;[18] and at Marsala, in Sicily, it is put behind the door, on the day after delivery, to prevent the entry of the evil spirit, 'Nserra. Says a local proverb:

> Water and salt: no matter what they say,
> Thereby can the witches never thee affray
> (Acqua e sali: e zoccu dicinu li magari
> non possa guivari)![19]

The apotropaic quality of salt underlies also the modern Egyptian custom of rubbing a bride with it to protect her against the evil eye;[20] while in Morocco, Jewish women used to dip their hands in it before embarking on a journey.[21] In the Isle of Man, an application of salt in the churning of butter is thought to keep away the "bad people" (*queeltah*).[22]

212 Rites of divination   21:26
(a) Crossroads

The king of Babylon stands at the parting of the two ways, to practice divination.

A man who stands at the crossroads has several alternative courses before him, each beset with its own hazards. In the idiom of ancient thought, therefore, the crossroads are a meeting place of demons and spooks and also of witches and warlocks who would enlist their powers.[1] Thus, among the Greeks, Hecate, divine queen of the witches, appeared where three roads met,[2] as did her Roman counterpart, Trevia;[3] and there too—as in ancient Iran[4] and today in the Abruzzi[5]—superstitious persons propitiated the dead. In India, *bhuts*;[6] among Arabs, jinns;[7] and in Africa,[8] evil spirits in general frequent crossroads; while in German grimoires they are mentioned often as the haunt of demons.[9] It is there that witches dance with the Devil,[10] that he appears at midnight as a black cat,[11] that he concludes his bargain with Faust,[12] and that the Wild Hunt foregathers.[13] Similarly, in Slavonic folklore, it is at the crossroads that sorceresses brew their hell-broth and spin their magic threads;[14] while according to the pseudepigraphic *Testament of Solomon*, it is there that the beldam Envy lurks.[15]

If, however, roads part at the crossways, they also converge there; which means, in primitive idiom, that divers potencies there coalesce. Accordingly, anything associated with crossways is endowed, in popular belief, with especial "virtue" and efficacy. In medico-magical recipes, herbs gathered there are especially potent.[16] In Bombay, a charm against the evil eye is to carry seven pebbles picked up at a spot where three roads meet;[17] and in a Judaeo-German work of the fifteenth century, the burial there of a jet-black hen is recommended as a means of bringing one's true love to one's side.[18]

By the same reasoning, however, devils can themselves be bedeviled at crossroads. A widespread notion in this respect is that ghosts and witches are rendered powerless at places where roads meet, and that furies cannot pass such a spot.[19] A story from Mecklenburg relates, for instance, that a man once eluded a one-legged elf who was pursuing him by reaching the crossroads first; beyond that point he could not be followed.[20] In parts of India, demons are exorcized at crossroads by drawing a circle, protecting it with iron and water, and sitting inside it mumbling spells.[21]

Because they are intrinsically numinous, or haunted by otherworld beings, crossroads are a favorite spot for divination. An excellent illustration of this is the Japanese practice known as *tsujiura*. At dusk, when the spirits convene, a stick is planted in the ground at a crossroads. It represents Funado, the staff which the mythical hero Izanagi similarly emplanted to check the pursuit of infernal demons when he was escaping from the netherworld after his attempt to rescue his sister Izanami. Questions are then asked, and the casual remarks of passers-by counted as the oracular responses. Alternatively, a number of women foregather at the crossroads and draw a line of demarcation. Then, after sprinkling rice against evil spirits, each turns to a different road and summons the otherworld beings by blowing on a boxwood comb held between her teeth. The questions are then posed, and anything said by chance by the first person to pass within the line is taken as the answer.[22] A similar practice is recorded from Iran,[23] while again in India it is not uncommon usage to resort to divination at a crossroads when lost objects are sought. The location is believed to be indicated by the manipulation of some twenty-one pebbles which are there placed on the ground after a benedictory formula from the Atharva Veda has been pronounced over them.[24]

(b) Belomancy

Divination by shaking arrows from a quiver and then drawing omens from the way they fall is well attested in antiquity.[25] Quintus Fabius Maximus, we read, used this method when moving his camp from Tarentum to Metapontum;[26] while Macrobius recalls the same practice among the Etruscans.[27] A Jewish legend says that Nero did likewise before attacking Jerusalem,[28] while Arab tradition relates that the device was adopted by Imr-al-Qais before his expedition against Asad, but was prohibited by Mohammed.[29] "The custom was," says Pockocke, "that when anyone was about to undertake a journey or to marry or to embark on any important project, he would seek an oracle from three arrows which he put in a container. The first of these was inscribed, *God has commanded me;* the second, *God has forbidden me;* the third was blank. If he drew out the first, he would proceed with alacrity, as though ordered by God; if the second, he would desist; if the third, he would replace it and try again."[30]

Arrowheads of the Middle Bronze Age found in Palestine sometimes bear a legend beginning with the Hebrew word, ḥ-ṣ. At first blush, this would appear to be simply the normal term for *arrow*. It has been suggested, however, that it is rather to be connected with a similar Semitic word meaning "fortune," and that the arrows were used in belomancy, or the type of divination described above.[31]

The present writer has himself seen a similar practice, performed with little sticks from a "quiver," at the Wat Po in Bangkok; and it is current also among the Dakotas of North America.[32]

(c) Hepatoscopy

On *hepatoscopy*, or inspection of the liver, as a technique in Mesopotamian divination, see: Von Oefele, in ZAW (1900), 311–14; J. Hunger, Babylonische Tieromina nebst griech.-rom. Parallelen (1909); A. Ungnad, in Babyloniaca 2 (1908), 257–74; G. Furlani, in SMSR 4 (1929), 243–85.—For Greek parallels, see A. G. Bäckström, De hieroscopia Graecorum (1910). The custom was common also among the Etruscans: CIL vi. 32328.78; Servius, on Vergil, Aen. 4.56; Macrobius, Sat. iii.5.1.—It survived among the Arabs until the fourth century: A. Marmorstein, in ARW 15 (1912), 320.

213 The fallen paragon   28:11–19

When Nebuchadnezzar laid siege to the proud emporium of Tyre—a siege which lasted thirteen years (585–73 B.C.)—the prophet Ezekiel, in anticipation of the city's downfall, addressed to its king the following scornful and satirical "dirge":

> *Thou wast the crowning achievement of art,*
> *the sum of wisdom,*
> *the total of beauty.*
> *In Eden, the garden divine, thou wast,*
> *sheathed in all precious stones,*
> *carnelian, topaz and jasper,*
> *chrysolite, beryl and onyx,*
> *sapphire, carbuncle and emerald;*
> *thy bosses and sockets were made of gold,*
> *set upon thee on the day thou wast created.*
> *I placed thee upon the holy mount,*
> *a guardian cherub with wings outspanned;*
> *thou wast a being divine;*
> *amid flashing gems didst thou walk.*
>
> *Blameless, indeed, thou wast in thy ways,*
> *from the day thou wast created*
> *until vice was discovered within thee.*
> *Through thine abundant trading*

> thou hadst filled thyself inwardly with crime,
>   and didst fall afoul.
> So, I cast thee out as a thing profane
>   from the mountain divine;
> guardian cherub though thou wast,
> I banished thee from amid those flashing gems.
> By reason of thy beauty,
>   thy heart had grown proud;
> not only thy radiance didst thou tarnish,
> but also the wisdom that thou hadst!
> So I flung thee upon the earth,
>   exposed thee before kings
>   to feast their eyes upon thee.
> Because of thy manifold wrongdoing,
>   thy vicious trafficking,
> thou hadst profaned the holiness thou hadst.
> So I brought forth fire from within thee
>   —this it is that hath consumed thee!—
> and I turned thee to ashes on the ground
> before the eyes of all who beheld thee.
> All they among the nations
>   who once acknowledged thee
>   became appalled at thee;
> thou hadst become a portent horrendous
>   —gone for evermore!

It has been commonly supposed in recent years that this passage, in which affluent Tyre is likened to some denizen of Paradise eventually cast out for his sins, reflects a variant (probably Phoenician) version of the expulsion of Adam from the Garden of Eden.[1] Anyone who reads it attentively, however, will see at once that the differences are so cardinal as to preclude such a comparison. In the Adam story, Adam is expelled for aspiring to divine prerogatives and in order to prevent his acquiring divine knowledge, whereas the mythological subject of our dirge possesses both from the start and is punished for profaning them. In the Adam story, Adam is condemned to spend the rest of his days on earth, working for his daily bread in the sweat of his brow, and the story is told precisely in order to account for that condition. The subject of our dirge, on the other hand, is doomed to immediate and summary extinction. Furthermore, there is here no mention of such crucial elements of the Adam story as the forbidden fruit and the temptation.

It may be suggested, therefore, that what we have here is a parallel not to the Adam story but to the myth of Prometheus. The culprit is not a man at all, but a divine being, who somehow defiles his divine status and privilege. Just how is not quite clear, for in order to make the parable more applicable, the prophet substitutes for any reference to the mythic offense a direct condemnation of Tyre's commercialism and huckster frame of mind. It is significant, however, that just as the subject of our dirge is characterized as originally "blameless," so Prometheus is specifically described by Hesiod as originally "without evil,"[2] and just as the subject of our dirge is distinguished for his wisdom (which he eventually pollutes), so Prometheus was the teacher of arts and sciences to mankind.[3] (Indeed, his powers of sapience and insight are implicit in his very name, which means properly, Forethought.) Suggestive also of a connection of our hero with some prototype of Prometheus is the prophet's emphasis on his fiery character—the flame which destroys him is extracted, apparently, from his own body—for Prometheus is, of course, associated preeminently with fire and was even worshiped at Athens as a god of that element.[4] Nor need it be objected that Prometheus, after all, did not die in flames or that he was subsequently released. In the first place, there actually existed a tradition that he *was* blasted by lightning and thrust into Tartaros[5]—a tradition elsewhere associated with his brother Menoetius, who is said to have suffered this fate on account of his "savage insolence and overbearing boldness,"[6] comparable with the "proud heart" of our "hero" in Ezekiel's dirge. Second, the tradition that Prometheus was eventually released seems to have been a later innovation—some scholars even credit it to Aeschylus[7]—for Hesiod says clearly that his punishment was to last forever.[8]

Several subsidiary features of Ezekiel's "myth" lend themselves to illustration from Comparative Folklore.

1. The paradisal abode is here located not, as in Genesis, at the source of four rivers, nor in the east, but on the top of a mountain. On this concept, see above, §**13**.

2. The inhabitants of that realm are compact of precious stones and of gold.[9] The latter is strongly reminiscent of the ancient notion that divine beings have golden limbs. Thus, in the famous Egyptian Hymn of Ani, Osiris is said to possess "limbs of gold, head of lapis, and crown of turquoise";[10] while in the inscription of Redseyeh "the god's flesh is of gold" (*nbw ḥ‘w ntrw*),[11] and in the Middle Kingdom *Legend of the Contendings of Horus and Set,* the former is similarly described.[12] A story preserved in the Westcar Papyrus asserts that royal children of the Fifth Dynasty had golden limbs,[13] and in inscriptions at Thebes, Ramses II and III are credited with the same distinction.[14] So too a statue of Baal discovered at Ras Shamra is covered with gold leaf,[15] and it still is the custom of the faithful to attach little patches of golden trefoil to the image of the reclining Buddha at the Wat Po in Bangkok.

3. The statement that the denizen of Paradise walks about "amid flashing gems"[16] reflects the notion that the divine abode or garden is a place of jewels. On this notion, see above, §**15**.

4. The fiery character of our "hero," if not directly derived from some prototype of the Prometheus myth, perhaps reflects the belief that divine beings are enveloped in a perpetual sheen—a belief which obtains alike in Ancient Near Eastern and Classical lore, and which survives in the Christian idea that angels are made of fire.[17]

5. Finally, the idea that the wicked can be punished by being suddenly reduced to ashes finds several parallels in myth and story. The rebellious Titans, for example, are said in Greek legend to have been cast into Tartaros, where their bodies were burned to cinders.[18] Man, adds one version, arose out of those ashes.[19] Similarly, a modern Greek folktale, current alike on the islands of Zacynthos (Zante)[20] and Chios,[21] tells how, after the War against the Giants, one of their number tried to ascend to heaven, but was promptly smitten with a thunderbolt and reduced to ashes, as were several others who subsequently followed his example.

Sometimes, to be sure, it is not an offender that is threatened with this fate. Thus, in the ancient Egyptian Tale of the Shipwrecked Sailor, the serpent whom he encounters on a lonely island at first terrifies him with such a threat;[22] and the same motif occurs in Indian folklore.

214 Pharaoh and the Nile

29:3

(a) *Thus saith the Lord GOD: Behold, I am against thee, Pharaoh king of Egypt, the great dragon that croucheth in the midst of his Nile, which saith, My Nile is my own, and it is I that made it!*

Comparative Folklore enables us to bring out the subtle point of the prophet's words. The Egyptian pharaoh, as the embodiment of the divine norm, or order of nature (*ma'at*), was considered to be responsible for the annual rising of the Nile and consequently for the fertility of his country.[1] Thus, an encomium addressed to Ramses II says explicitly, albeit in fulsome tones: "If thou say to the water, rise to the crest of the mountain, the flood straightway ensues in obedience to thy word";[2] while a similar statement is made also in the same monarch's so-called "Marriage Stele" at Abu Simbel.[3] Moreover, the power extended even to the dead pharaoh.[4] When Thothmes III passed away at a season of year when the Nile was at its lowest, scarabs were put into circulation, bearing the reassuring legend that the river was nonetheless at his command since he had now become one with Osiris.[5]

Basically, of course, this is simply a facet of the widespread idea that the king is the responsible agent of nature—especially of the weather, rainfall, and fertility—in his area.[6]

32:2–9

(b) *Raise a lament over Pharaoh, king of Egypt, and say unto him:
Thou wast like the Dragon in the seas,
puffing amid thy streams,*

> *muddying the waters with thy feet,*
> *turning their streams to mud.*
>
> *Thus saith the Lord GOD:*
> *I will spread My net over thee,*
> *and haul thee up in my drag,*
> *and cast thee upon the land,*
> *fling thee out on the fields,*
> *and make all the fowl of the air settle on thee,*
> *and sate all the beasts of the earth on thee.*
> *I will lay thy flesh on the hills,*
> *and fill the dales with thy rot,*
> *and drench the earth with what oozes from thee,*
> *and fill the watercourses with thy blood.*
> *When thou thyself art extinguished,*
> *I will cover the heavens too,*
> *and clothe their stars in mourning black;*
> *I will cover the sun with a cloud,*
> *and the moon shall not give forth its light.*
> *All the bright lights of heaven*
> *will I shroud in mourning for thee,*
> *and set darkness upon thy land. . . .*
> *Peoples far and wide will I make aghast over thee,*
> *and their kings will bristle with fright*
> *on account of thee,*
> *when I wave My sword in their face.*

Reading these verses, the student of folkore can scarcely resist the suspicion that what the prophet has at the back of his mind is not only the aforementioned concept of Pharaoh as master and controller of the Nile, but also the Egyptian Myth of 'Apep, the dragon who lives in the cosmic ocean and who tries daily to swallow up the sun (Re') as he crosses the sky in his bark, but is daily subdued and pierced with his adversary's sword.[7] Basically, this myth links up with the common belief that eclipses and obscurations of the sun and moon are caused by a dragon or similar monster who temporarily gobbles them up.[8] "Thus, in Indic belief, it is the dragon Rahu (who in this capacity bears the name Svarbhanu) who periodically swallows the sun or moon;[9] and this piece of mythology was adopted in turn by the Buddhists.[10] In China, eclipses were likewise attributed to the devouring of sun or moon by a monstrous beast; and in the Confucian classic, *Tsun Tsiu* ("Springs and Autumns"), the word "eat" is employed to describe the eclipse of April 20, 610 B.C.[11] Similarly, in Scandinavian lore, the sun is believed to be pursued constantly by a wolf called Skoll.[12] The Tartar tribe of Chuwashes use the phrase "a demon has eaten it" to denote an eclipse.[13] The Estonians have a similar expression; while the Lithuanians assert that quasi-serpentine creatures lie in wait for sun and moon; and in the region south of Lake Baikal it is held that the king of hell tries to swallow the moon.[14] In Jewish folklore, the sun was said to be swallowed by a great fish;[15] and the same notion was entertained by spectators of a lunar eclipse at Hastaya, west of Hermon, in 1891.[16] Lastly, the Negritos of Borneo say that eclipses are caused by a python who attempts to swallow the sun or moon;[17] and the idea is attested also in ancient Greek mythology.[18] In the Canaanite *Poem of Baal,* after the sun-goddess (Shapash) has succeeded in retrieving that god from the netherworld, she is promised that ever after she will enjoy the escort of Kôthar-wa-Ḥasis, the god who once "tossed the Dragon into the sea."[19]

In the light of this fairly universal belief, the prophet's words take on an added subtlety: the Lord God will not only subdue the Dragon but also punish the land of Egypt by Himself, obscuring *all* the lights of heaven!

215 The parable of the cedar   31

The most obvious analogue to this parable is the story related both by Herodotus[1] and by Valerius Maximus[2] that when Cyrus was about to be born, his grandfather Astyages had a dream in which he saw his own daughter Mandane in the form of a vine which grew so tall that it overshadowed all the provinces. A similar story is related also concerning Xerxes.[3] Moreover, the comparison of a king to a cypress or palm appears in sundry Babylonian inscriptions.[4]

In a more general setting we are reminded of a passage in the Finnish Kalevala which tells of a gigantic oak which obscured both sun and moon and obstructed the course of the clouds until a dwarf rose from the sea, was transformed into a giant, and felled it.[5] Stories of similar import are told in Syriac,[6] Hungarian,[7] and German[8] sources;[9] and the image is used again, within the Old Testament itself in the Book of Daniel.[10]

Hermann Gunkel (to whom the citation of these parallels is due) has made the interesting suggestion that Ezekiel's parable reflects a folktale concerning a wondrous tree, "child of the deep (*tehôm*)," which shot up to heaven and grew so proud that it had to be felled; whereupon its mother wore mourning, as did also the whole of Lebanon, which had seen it in its glory. Moreover, all the trees that had previously been felled took comfort when they realized that they were not alone in their fate. Gunkel further identifies the tree with the world-tree (e.g., Yggdrasill) of familiar legend.[11]

There is, however, another possibility. Since the prohpet lived in Babylon, this passage may contain a reminiscence of the Mesopotamian story concerning the felling of the sacred cedar(s) by the hero Gilgamesh and his companion(s). This story is known not only from the famous Humbaba-Huwawa episode of the Akkadian Epic of Gilgamesh (III-IV),[12] but also from a far older Sumerian version, the so-called myth of *Gilgamesh and the Land of the Living*.[13] There are some arresting points of similarity:

1. Although this prophecy is addressed to the Pharaoh of Egypt, the scene is set in Lebanon, and it is now generally agreed that the Humbaba episode is to be located in that area.

2. The region is described specifically as a "shady thicket" (v. 3), and this accords perfectly with the description of the grove of Humbaba in the Epic of Gilgamesh (vv. 2–3).

3. The proud cedar is destroyed by the "hero (paladin) of the nations" (Hebrew, *êl goyîm*) and by the "violent men of the nations" (vv. 11–12), and this accords with the description of Gilgamesh in the Sumerian tale (88: ur-sag$^{d d GIŠ}$gibil-ga-meš) and with the fact that *he is accompanied by fifty braves* (99–100).

4. The fellers of the cedar are said to "leave it upon (LXX) the mountains" (v. 12).[14] In the Sumerian tale (139–42), the stalwarts "hew down its crown, bundle it, and lay it at the foot of the mountain."

5. It is said of the felled cedar that it will henceforth lie in the netherworld "among the uncircumcised" (v. 18). The Hebrew word for "uncircumcised" is *'arēlîm*, and it is therefore not impossible that the prophet was playing (as again in 32:19, 24–29, 30, 32) on the Mesopotamian name of the netherworld, viz., *Arallû*.

The background of the story lies in the taboo on felling trees beside a shrine. This still obtains in respect of Moslem holy places in Palestine.[15]

(Not impossibly, this was originally a parable directed against *Assyria*, and then boldly transferred to the Pharaoh of Egypt. This would account for its curious opening phrase, *Behold*, Assyria *is a cedar in Lebanon*—a phrase which has otherwise to be emended, as for instance in RSV.[16] The allusion to the Mesopotamian Gilgamesh legend would then have been more telling.)

216 The dimming of the sun   32:7–8

In predicting the downfall of the Egyptian monarch, Ezekiel declares that the heavens will be covered and the stars obscured; the sun will be veiled with clouds, and the moon will not give light.

The sentiment recurs elsewhere in Biblical prophecy. Joel declares, for example, that on the coming Day of the Lord, sun and moon will be darkened, and the stars withdraw their shining.[1] In the present passage, however, two different ideas are combined. The first is that the heavenly lights will go into mourning for the fallen pharaoh and be clothed, as it were, in funereal raiment.[2] The second is that the sun grows dim in times of disaster. This latter notion has an interesting Classical parallel, for several Roman writers tell us that after the assassination of Julius Caesar, the sun was dim for about a year,³ and Pliny adds that the same thing happened during the subsequent war between Octavian and Mark Antony. Vergil elaborates on this theme in a famous passage of his *Georgics:*

> Is there a man would venture to declare
> The sun plays false? Nay, for oftimes it warns
> When tumult stirs in darkness or when crime
> And wars are surging to the bursting point
> To break into the open. Thus it was,
> When Caesar's light was dimmed, the sun itself
> Grew sad for Rome, and with a veil opaque
> Covered its shining head, so that men feared
> Lest times so lost to ancient loyalties
> Would be enveloped in eternal night.⁴

In the same vein Ovid asserts that

> Sad Phoebus' face showed clouded eyes,⁵

and Tibullus that

> The year beclouded saw the sun
> Shorn of its light.⁶

217 Kôshar, the god of minstrelsy   33:32

The people listen to the words of the prophet, but pay no heed. Yahweh therefore characterizes him as *one that sings* (Heb.: *kᵉshîr*) *with a beautiful voice and plays well on an instrument* (RSV), i.e., as being treated like a performing artist rather than as a messenger of God.

Since the Hebrew word *shîr*, which is here employed, usually means *song* rather than *singer*, the reading and rendering have alike been questioned. The clever suggestion has been made, however,¹ that the word should be vocalized *kôshar* rather than *kᵉshir*, and that we should therefore recognize an allusion to the Canaanite god Kôshar (*K-t-r*) of the Ugaritic texts,² who is said by the Phoenician mythographer Sanchuniathon³ to have been expert in "tricking out words in song."⁴ A common noun *kôsharôth* (*k-t-r-t*) indeed means "professional singing women."⁵

(This ingenious suggestion, however, is not really necessary, for the word *shîr* could indeed mean "singer" as well as "song," the formation being like that of *ṣîr*, "messenger."⁶ Indeed, the feminine plural *shîrôth* seems to occur in this sense in Amos 8:3.)

218 The thread of life   37:11

> *Our bones are dried up, and our hope is lost;*
> *we are clean cut off.*

An interesting folkloristic suggestion has been made about this verse.¹ The Hebrew words (*NiGZaRNW LaNU*) rendered *We are clean cut off* can be so rendered only by torturing the normal rules of syntax. If, however, the letters of which they are compounded be differently divided (viz., *NiGZaR NaWLeNU*), we may obtain the sense *Our thread is cut off*,[2] and this would connect at once with the familar conception of *life or fate as a thread* (see above, §**191**).

The imagery may be detected again in the Old Testament in Isaiah 38:12: *Like a weaver have I rolled up my life; God cuts me off from the loom.* Moreover, in further support of the proposed interpretation, it may be observed that the word here rendered *our hope* actually lends itself to a double-entendre, for it can also mean, *our skein*.[3]

See also, below, §311.

219 The navel of the earth   38:12
See above, §**113**.

The Minor Prophets

220 Introduction

A Hebrew prophet was more than a mere predictor. His role was to interpret passing events in terms of God's ongoing plan and purpose. To do this, he had to look backward as well as forward, to see what had led up to them as well as how they were likely to turn out. Moreover, in order to trace God's hand in the present, he had to recognize comparable operations in the past. That past, however, was not always historical. Traditional myth likewise told many a story of how God (or, in pagan versions, this or that particular god) had acted in primeval or primordial times, and it was sometimes possible to recognize in such mythical exploits precedents for what he was actually doing on the stage of history. These more ancient myths have become known to us only in recent times with the recovery, through archaeological excavations, of so much of Ancient Near Eastern literature; and one of the major contributions which Comparative Folklore has now to make to the interpretation and understanding of the Old Testament is to detect allusions to them in the sacred text. In the following pages, therefore, special attention is paid to these parallels.

The Hebrew prophet was essentially a *speaker,* not a writer. This means that he had always to be on the lookout for an audience, and one of the best ways of ensuring one was to wait for occasions when crowds would gather for the celebration of seasonal festivals or the performance of public rites of religion. Against this background it is possible, I suggest, to discern in many a prophetic utterance (particularly in the twelve Minor Prophets) pointed jibes at standard pagan rites and ceremonies and to recognize *satire* as a cardinal element of the prophetic technique. *Mutatis mutandis,* and on a far more exalted level, this technique was the same as that which is employed in our own day by revivalist preachers and "hot gospelers" who frequent ball games and boxing matches, holding aloft among the spectators or pacing the sidewalks bearing such messages as "Kick off with Jesus" or "the Lord will K.O. the Devil." If, for instance, the people were performing the traditional rite of pouring water as a rain charm, the Hebrew prophet, standing as it were on the sidelines, might hurl at them the taunt that Yahweh would shortly pour upon them the vials of his wrath (Hos. 5:10), or if they paraded around the town in a torchlight procession—a familiar feature of popular festivals—he might warn them that Yahweh too was carrying his torch—to search out sin in every nook and cranny (Zeph. 1:12). Other standard elements of the pagan festivals which lent themselves likewise to satirical castigation are the nocturnal vigil (Joel 1.13), the ululation for the vanished god of fertility (Joel 2:17; Zeph. 1:11; Zech. 12:11–14), the search for him (Hos. 5:6, 15; 6:3; Zeph. 2:3), and the divine banquet (Zeph. 1:7). Sometimes too the assurance of Yahweh's eventual triumph and favor is couched in terms of what was conventionally attributed to the pagan gods in the myths associated with seasonal festivals: he will free his people from the grasp of Death—the Canaanite Môt, genius of sterility (Hos. 13:14), assert his kingship (Zeph. 3:15; Zech. 14:9, 16), and restore rainfall and fertility (Hos. 14:6–8; Joel 2:21–24; 4:18; Zech. 14:8). Thus, by aligning the successive metaphors employed by a Scriptural prophet with the successive elements of a standard seasonal festival, it becomes possible in several instances to recover a sustained satire and in this way to add a new dimension to Hebrew prophecy. Such an approach tends also to offset the tendency of modern Biblical scholars to fragmentize the prophetic discourses by attributing to different authors passages which exhibit a rapid transition and diversity of themes. This too is one of the major contributions which Comparative Folklore has to offer to the interpretation of the Old Testament, and this too receives particular attention in the following pages.

The prophets did not write in a study; they spoke in a passion. Images, metaphors, and tropes came tumbling out of them, and almost every sentence they uttered was charged also with subconscious associations and with suggestions drawn from traditional lore. If, for example, a prophet spoke of the sun's being dimmed in the Last Days (Joel 2:10), he was not simply inventing this picture out of his head; he was drawing, albeit subconsciously, on the storehouse of inherited popular fancies, and he was relying on his listeners' doing the same. The full impact of his words—as, indeed, of those of any creative author—depended therefore at least as much on what was suggested as on what was stated; on what was, so to speak, subliminal as on what was patent. Consequently, it is the business of a modern exegete to try to bring out the implicit as well as the explicit meaning. Accordingly, I have made a special point, in the following pages, of trying to illustrate images and metaphors from folklore. Admittedly, this involves a process of reading into the text (*eisegesis*) as well as out of them (*exegesis*), and the danger of subjectivism is ever-present; but this is, in the last analysis, a danger implicit in attributing meaning to anything, and the notion that there is such a thing as the objective interpretation of literature or art is—at least to me—itself meaningless, the tired cliché of tired scholars. Moreover, even if some of the material here assembled may eventually turn out to be irrelevant to the correct explication of a particular passage, the collection may perhaps prove of service in other contexts.

Hosea

221 Hosea and the pagan festivals

Much of the Book of Hosea may be read as a sustained satire on pagan seasonal festivals.[1] Not only are there significant references to sowing, plowing, and reaping,[2] threats of drought and sterility and promises of dewfall and increase,[3] but there seem also to be a number of sly allusions to standard seasonal rites and myths. The following are the more arresting instances.

Hos. 5:6

(a) *Israel will go seeking Yahweh, but will not find him, since he will have "slipped away" from them.*

The reference here is to the ritual search for the vanished god of fertility. In the Egyptian "mysteries" of Osiris, "seek" was a technical term.[4] In the Canaanite *Poem of Baal,* which is basically a seasonal myth, the goddess 'Anat says expressly that she will "go in search" (*b-q-š*) of the ousted lord of the rains.[5] In the Hittite myth of Telipinu, that god is said to have "taken himself off . . . flown into a rage, and carried away everything good";[6] while the search of Demeter for Persephone is familiar to every reader of Classical literature.[7]

The prophet chooses his words exquisitely. In the original Hebrew, the god is said not merely to depart or withdraw, but to slip away (Heb.: *ḥalaṣ*), suggesting graphically the gradual disappearance of the green summer.[8]

5:8

(b)
> *Blow the horn in Gibeah,*
> *the trumpet in Ramah.*
> *Sound the alarm at Beth-aven;*
> *they are after you,[9] Benjamin!*

The prophet is obviously thinking in terms of warfare, the trumpet being the signal for battle. It should be observed, however, that the trumpet was also sounded at festivals, to scare away the demons, and it is to this pagan rite that he may here be giving an ironic twist (see above, §**207**).

5:10

(c) *The princes of Judah have become like men who remove landmarks;*
I will pour out my wrath upon them like water.

The effect of this image is enhanced if it is read as a satire on the common practice of pouring water as a rain-charm at seasonal festivals (see above, §158). This took place, for instance, in the Jewish ritual for the Feast of Ingathering at Jerusalem,[10] and twice yearly at the Syrian temple of the Great Goddess at Hierapolis-Membij.[11]

6:1-2

(d) *Come, let us return to the Lord;*
though he has torn, he will heal us;
though he has stricken, he will bind us up.
After two days he will revive us;
on the third day he will raise us up,[12]
and we shall be revived in his presence.

A not uncommon feature of seasonal festivals is the staging of a mock funeral and subsequent resurrection of the spirit of fertility.[13] In Egypt, it was Osiris who was thus buried and revived;[14] in Syria, it was Adonis,[15] and in Asia Minor it was Attis.[16] In Russia, the interment and resurrection of Kostrubonko, deity of the spring, was solemnly celebrated in popular custom at Eastertide;[17] and in Roumania, on the Monday before Assumption (in August), a clay image of the analogous Kalojan is deposited in the earth, to be dug up after a few days.[18] The prophet's words may well have been inspired by such a spectacle.

6:3

(e) *Let us know, let us press on to know, the Lord;*
his emergence is as sure as the dawn;
he will come to us as the showers,
as the spring rains that water the earth.

These lines receive added significance when it is borne in mind that seasonal festivals are often made to coincide with the solstice or equinox.[19] The Asianic mysteries of Attis, for example, culminated in the triumphant reemergence of that god of fertility on the day of the vernal equinox (March 25).[20] Similarly, in Mesopotamia, the rites of Tammuz were held in the month of the spring solstice;[21] and the prophet Ezekiel expressly associates the weeping for that god with a ceremony of adoring the rising sun.[22] Moreover, an Old Assyrian calendar for the month of Tammuz prescribes significantly that the weeping for that god, which is to take place on the first day, is to be followed immediately, on the second, by "the presentation of gifts to the sun-god";[23] while a Babylonian hymn belonging to the Tammuz cycle represents the sun-god as assuring the sister of the dead genius of fertility that he himself would restore to her "the verdure which has been removed" and "the crushed grain which has been carried away."[24] In a Hittite ritual myth, the restoration of Telipinu, the god of fertility, is associated with the worship of the sun,[25] and in the Canaanite *Poem of Baal* a particularly important role is assigned to the sun-goddess. It is she that retrieves Baal from the netherworld,[26] and it is she that urges his rival Môt, genius of drought and sterility, to give up the fight against him.[27] Indeed, so cardinal a part does she play in the action that she is formally commended in words which sound uncommonly as though they had been incorporated by the poet from some traditional hymn.[28] Again, it should be observed that in Syria and the eastern portions of the Roman Empire, the Festival of the "New Age" was likewise combined with an important solar date, viz., the alleged birthday of the sun on November 18.[29] The same date was claimed by Clement of Alexandria as the birthday of the Christian Savior.[30] Indeed, so firmly established was the connection between the festivals of the new life and the worship of the sun that the Church was obliged to fix Christmas on what had originally been the birthday of the solarized savior Mithra and to associate the date of Christ's resurrection (Easter) with the vernal equinox.[31] Significant also is the fact that among the Israelites themselves, both the spring festival (Pentecost) and the autumn Festival of Ingathering fell in the months of the equinoxes, the latter being expressly associated with that event in the ritual calendar of Exodus 34:22.[32]

7:14

(f) *For grain and new wine they gash themselves,*[33] *against Me they rebel.*

Gashing the flesh was, as we have seen (above, §158), a standard procedure in rites of mourning, and the vanished god of fertility was everywhere lamented in this manner.[34] Once again, therefore, the prophet is alluding to pagan seasonal practices.

9:1

(g) *You have made love for a harlot's hire on all the threshing floors.*

Ritual promiscuity, designed to promote increase of men, cattle, and crops, is everywhere a standard feature of seasonal festivals.[35] According to Herodotus, it took place both at Babylon[36] and in Cyprus,[37] and it is attested also in the cult of the Great Goddess (Ma) at Comana, in Pontus.[38] In Java, as also among the Fan of West Africa, the Hereros, the Garos, and the natives of Amboyna, men and women are expected to copulate openly in the fields at major agricultural festivals; while the Indians of Peru do so as soon as the alligator pears ripen.[39]

12:9

(h) *I am the Lord your God
from the land of Egypt;
I will again make you dwell in tents
as on the days of the seasonal festival.*

Dwelling in tents is, of course, a natural concomitant of pilgrim festivals. The Samaritans, for instance, still do so when they repair to Mt. Gerizim for the celebration of the Passover. An inscription from the island of Cos, dated in the second century B.C., mentions an annual religious festival at which worshipers were required to erect booths (*skênopagisthôn*),[40] and the rare Greek word which denotes this practice is actually employed by the Septuagint to render the Hebrew "Feast of Booths" (*ḥag ha-sukkôth*), the Feast of Ingathering.[41] The custom is well attested elsewhere in Classical antiquity.[42] Tibullus tells us, for example, that at the Roman festival of Sementivae Feriae (in January) "the crowd makes merry and erects wattled cabins."[43] Somewhat similarly, the celebrated *Pervigilium Veneris,* which really has reference to the festival of Venus Verticordia and Fortuna Virilis, in April, says specifically: *Cras amorum copulatrix inter umbras arborum / Implicat casas virentes de flagello myrteo,* and this, as Clementi has pointed out, bears allusion to the same custom.[44] Yet again, therefore, the prophet's words may have been suggested by the sight of such temporary structures at a pagan festival.

Nor is it only to the *ritual* of these occasions that Hosea appears to allude. Some of his images seem likewise to be drawn from the *myths* associated with such ceremonies. It has been suggested,[45] for instance, that his celebrated picture of Yahweh's marriage to Israel (chs. 1–3) may have been inspired by the fact that a cardinal element of seasonal festivals was often a mimetic "sacred marriage" between god and goddess, customarily impersonated by the king and a hierodule (see above, §**176**). The prophet lifts this primitive rite to a sublime spiritual plane. Similarly, when he declares in the name of Yahweh (5:14)

*I will be like a lion to Ephraim
and like a young lion to the house of Judah;
I, even I, will ravin and depart,
carry off, with no one to rescue,*

he may be drawing his image from a myth which related that the missing god of fertility had been savaged by a boar or some similar wild beast.[46] This, for example, is said to have been the fate of Adonis,[47] Attis,[48] Hyas,[49] Linos,[50] Bormos,[51] and Idmon,[52] all of whom are regarded by Gruppe as variants of the fertility-spirit.[53] To be sure, the evidence here is late and, in some cases, dubious,[54] yet it is significant that, at a far earlier date, the Canaanite Baal himself is said, in a poem from Ras Shamra-Ugarit, to have been attacked by wild beasts called "renders" (*'qqm*) and "devourers" (*aklm*).[55] Thus, what the prophet would be saying is that the horrible doom which attended the hero of the pagan seasonal myth would yet be visited upon recalcitrant Israel, and that he himself ("I, even I") would be the attacker.

That Hosea has in mind specifically the traditional usages and myths *of Canaan* is suggested further by the statement in 13:14 that Yahweh has been provoked beyond compassion, so that he will not redeem his people from Death (Heb.: *Maweth*). For here we may detect a reference to the Canaanite god of that name (Môt), from whom Baal was eventually redeemed, after he had been trapped in the netherworld. The implication thus is that the "happy ending" of the pagan ritual pantomime will not be repeated in the case of rebellious Israel, because "compassion is hidden from my eyes."

A final example of how Hosea may have been alluding to pagan myth is afforded in 14:8. The Hebrew text of this verse is notoriously obscure and has been variously translated and emended. RSV's *It is I who answer and look after you* can scarcely be extracted from it.[56] Some scholars, by different vocalization of the consonants, obtain the sense, *It is I that have bound and will now set loose.* In view, however, of the preceding, *What has Ephraim to do more with idols?* (LXX text), a better sequence results by adopting a clever emendation by Julius Wellhausen, who for the Hebrew *'ªNî 'ANîTHî Wᵉ-'AŠûReNNû* suggests the very similar *'ªNî 'ANāTHô Wᵉ-AŠRāTHô*, "I am his 'Anat and his Asherah." These were the two primary goddesses of the Canaanites.[57] The implication is, therefore, that Yahweh will do for Israel all that these deities were popularly credited with doing in the pagan myth and cult.

That the prophet was indeed indulging in a series of sly allusions is seemingly indicated by his own concluding words (14:9): *Whoever is wise will understand these things; whoever is discerning, will know them.*[58] A similar formula occurs in Psalm 107:43, and it resembles one subjoined to the Mesopotamian Epic of Creation. As Oppenheim has shown,[59] this is representative of standard practice. It is the equivalent of the classic tag, *Verbum sapienti sat,* and harks back to the notion that cultic texts contain a symbolic as well as a literal meaning.

222 Gomer, daughter of Diblaim   1:3

Diblaim is either the lady's father or else her hometown.[1] Since, however, the whole story is told as a parable, it is not improbable that the writer chose this name on account of some latent signficance.[2] Now, Diblaim (a dual form) at once suggests the Hebrew word, *dᵉbelah,* "a cake of pressed figs," and what may have been implied by calling a woman a "two-fig-cake wench" is perhaps suggested by a statement made, several centuries later, by the Arabic writer, Jabir ibn Abdullah, concerning popular usages during the early days of Islam. Until Abu Bekr forbade it, he tells us, it was possible to contract a temporary alliance (*"mota‘*-marriage") with a woman for "a handful of dates or a small quantity of grain"[3]—just as in World War II soldiers overseas could "pick up" accommodating girls for a pack of cigarettes. Nor need we depend only on such late evidence. The Assyrian king Ashurbanipal (699–633 B.C.) informs us, in somewhat similar vein, that after he had suppressed the insubordinate Arabs, there ensued among them such an economic slump that a farmer was able to acquire a camel for the paltry price of "a basket of fresh dates."[4] To call a woman a "two-fig-cake wench" might therefore very well have been the ancient equivalent of calling her a "two-bit whore."

It should be observed, however, that this has nothing whatsoever to do with the common English expression "not worth a fig," for there the word "fig" is connected rather with the Spanish *fico,* and refers to the obscene gesture of contempt made by thrusting the thumb between the first and second fingers in imitation of coitus.[5] Nor has it any relation to the ancient Greek use of the term "fig-like" (*sykinos*) to denote "worthless,"[6] for that derives from the fact that the wood of the fig-tree is too soft to be used in carpentry.[7] Indeed, in Greek popular lore, it was deemed unlucky.[8]

223 Gomer's children   1:6–9

Two of the children of Hosea's union with Gomer are to be called respectively Lo-Ruḥamah and Lo-‘Ammi. Within the context of the parable, these names mean simply, "Unpitied" and "Not-My-people." But they too may also conceal a more subtle point, for *ruḥamah* could also mean "a woman united to one by kinship" (cf. Arabic *raḥîm,* and Heb. *reḥem,* "womb");[1] while *‘ammî* may be compared with the Arabic *ibn ‘amm,* "a man of the same stock-group."[2] Hence, besides their symbolic connotation, Lo Ruḥamah and Lo ‘Ammi could both mean simply, *bastard.*

224 Stripping a divorcee   2:2–3

It was an Ancient Near Eastern custom to strip a woman of her clothing when she was divorced or if she was discovered to be unfaithful.[1] An Old Babylonian letter has a man declare that if, after his death, his wife take another man, his own sons are to strip her and expel her from the house.[2] Legal documents from Nuzi, of the sixteenth century B.C., attest the stripping of a wife who is put away;[3] while in a late Aramaic charm against the demon Lilith, a writ of divorce is symbolically served upon her and she is ordered to go forth stripped.[4] Tacitus tells us that among the ancient Germans faithless wives were similarly treated.[5]

The practice was based on the ancient and primitive notion that *clothes* *symbolize their wearer's person.*⁶ In Mesopotamia, for example, an illiterate could "sign" a legal document by pressing the fringe of his (or her) garment against the wet clay of the tablet on which it was inscribed;⁷ while the Greek poet Theocritus (third cent. B.C.) tells how a lovesick woman tried to bewitch the object of her passion by shedding and burning the fringe (or tassel) of his garment, which had come by chance into her possession.⁸ Analogous, too, is a modern tale from Prussia, which relates how a man who had been caught looting shed his coat while trying to escape, but fell dead the moment he heard that it was being cut to pieces by the man he had robbed.⁹ To strip the clothing from a divorcee was therefore to *cancel her out*. By precisely the same symbolism the Babylonian king was annually stripped of his robes at the Akîtu (New Year) festival, in order to show that he was temporarily deposed;¹⁰ and in the same way too—as in the notorious case of Captain Dreyfus—an army officer is stripped of his epaulets and buttons when he is "drummed out" in disgrace. The idea leaves its trace in popular parlance, for we still speak of *divesting* (or *stripping*) a person of authority or dignity.

Other ideas, however, also come into play, and these are even more clearly articulated in a variant form of the custom, wherein the faithless wife's garment is not stripped from her, but merely *cut*. Thus, a Babylonian who divorced his wife might sometimes content himself with snipping off the fringed hem of her robe;¹¹ while among the Chuwash, Chremiss, Mordvinians, Votyaks, and Voguls of Russia, a husband who desires to part from his wife does so by tearing her veil;¹² and in Wales, a woman who could not clear herself of a charge of adultery had her shift torn.¹³ In such cases, what is thereby symbolized is not merely the diminution or annulment of her person, but also the severance of it from any further association with her husband: he *cuts her off*.

Then, too, it should be borne in mind that in several cultures, husband and wife are portrayed figuratively as each other's *raiment*.¹⁴ Mohammed, for instance, in permitting sexual intercourse on the night of the Fast—a concession directly opposed to Jewish law—tells his followers that, after all, "your wives are your garments, and you are theirs";¹⁵ while, in more cynical vein, a Chinese proverb remarks that "a wife is like one's clothes—replaceable when worn out!"¹⁶ To remove the clothing of a divorcee was thus a symbolic gesture of *shedding* her—a figure of speech still affected by gossip columnists in our own day. This aspect of the custom is brought out arrestingly in a marriage contract from the Ḫabur Valley, dating around 1700 B.C. There it is stipulated that if *either party* unilaterally repudiate the other, *he or she* is to leave the house "naked."¹⁷ Similarly, it is not without significance that an early Arabic term for "divorce" was *ḥol'*, which means properly, *divestiture*.¹⁸

Lastly, it should be observed that the stripping of the divorced wife is, in fact, the converse of the widespread custom whereby the husband casts his mantle over her during the marriage ceremony (see above, §**121**). This is at once a gesture of protection and of covenant. Among the Moslems of Morocco, for example, it symbolizes not only a voluntary but also a compulsory bond; for when a man casts an *'ar,* or "conditional curse," upon another, he sometimes moves toward him a fold of his garment, or throws his cloak over him.[19] The withdrawal of the wife's raiment would thus represent the withdrawal of that protection and the termination of the bond.

225 Marriage formulas   2:19-20

> *I will betroth thee unto me for ever;*
> *I will betroth thee unto me in righteousness, and*
> *in judgment, and in loving-kindness, and in mercies.*
> *I will betroth thee unto me in faithfulness:*
> *and thou shalt know the LORD.*

Note the threefold repetition of *I will betroth thee,* suggestive of a legal (or ritual) formula. The conventional rendering does not bring out the full meaning, for the word translated "in righteousness" really means "by due protocol," that rendered "in judgment" means "by legal process," that rendered "in loving-kindness" means "by mutual bond," and that rendered "in mercies" means "by ties of kinship." Lastly, "in faithfulness" is an inaccurate translation of a word which really means "by pledge." Hence, all are juridical terms.

> *And I said unto her, Thou shalt abide for*
> *me many days; thou shalt not play the harlot,*
> *and thou shalt not consort with another man;*
> *so will I consort with thee.*

This too was probably a standard marriage formula, possibly only for a temporary alliance. The expression "thout shalt abide for me" corresponds to the technical term for marriage in the legal documents from Nuzi.

226 Ephôd and teraphîm   3:5

> *The children of Israel shall dwell many days without king or prince, without sacrifice or pillar, without* ephôd *or* teraphîm.

It has been commonly supposed that *ephôd* and *teraphîm* denote objects used in divination. This, however, is scarcely correct. The *teraphîm,* as we have seen (above, §**68**), are images of the household gods. While they were certainly objects of cult, there is nothing to show that they were used in divination. The *ephôd* is simply a wrap worn in ritual ceremonies. Not only was it part of the official garb of the priests of Israel,[1] but it is said also to have been worn by the young Samuel when he served as an acolyte in the sanctuary at Shiloh,[2] and by David when he performed religious exercises.[3] In the form, *epadâtum* the word has now turned up in the sense of "mantle, wrap" in Old Assyrian texts. It has also been recognized in a poetic text from Ras Shamra-Ugarit.[4]

The combination, *ephôd and teraphîm,* therefore constitutes a merism meaning simply, "regular worship"—the equivalent, so to speak, of "vestments and ikons." Older views about them can now be safely discarded.[5]

227 David redivivus 3:5

> *Afterward the children of Israel shall return and seek the Lord their God and David their king.*

See above, §205, a.

228 El the Bull 8:6

> KJV: *For from Israel was it:*
> *the workman made it;*
> *therefore it is not God:*
> *but the calf of Samaria shall be broken in pieces.*

It is generally recognized that the traditional text of this verse is corrupt and barely translatable. Modern scholars join the opening clause to the last words of the preceding verse and, by slight emendation, obtain the sense, *How long will they be unable to obtain cleanliness (or, acquittal) in Israel?* Comparative Religion, however, comes to the rescue. As H. Tur-Sinai has acutely discerned, by mere redivision of the Hebrew consonants, the verse may be made to read:

> *For who is El the Bull?*
> *Something a workman made.*
> *No god is he!*
> *That Samarian calf will eventually be dashed to splinters.*[1]

"El the Bull" is a stock title of the supreme god in the Canaanite texts from Ras Shamra-Ugarit[2] and finds a counterpart also in the "Bull-Baal" ($\underline{T}r$-$B'l$) of early South Arabian inscriptions.[3] The "calf of Samaria," which was supposed to represent him, was thus an idolatrous image (cf. Hos. 10:5; 13:2; I Kings 12:28; II Kings 10:29),[4] here held up to scorn.

229 The bread of mourners 9:4

> *Theirs shall be bread like that of mourners;*
> *all that eat of it shall be deemed unclean.*

See above, §202.

230 Oil in the making of covenants 12:1

> (Of Ephraim:) *They make a covenant with Assyria,*
> *and oil is carried to Egypt.*

Interesting light is cast on these words by the observation that in neo-Assyrian business contracts the sincerity of the parties is sometimes said to be put to the test by means of a rite performed by a professional diviner (*barû*) "with water and oil."

(If the prophet is indeed alluding to this practice, it is probable that, by deriving the relevant Hebrew word from a different root, the second line should rather be rendered, *And oil* is poured *for Egypt*.)[1]

Joel

231 Joel and the pagan festivals

Comparative Folklore illustrates the Book of Joel in the same way as it does that of Hosea (see above, §**221**), suggesting that it may be read as a sustained satire on a pagan seasonal festival. Each of the characteristic features of that occasion serves, by a homiletic twist, to convey a message from Yahweh to his enemies and to apostates in Israel, while at the same time certain elements are exploited to bring tidings of hope to the oppressed.[1] The following are the more arresting instances.

Joel 1:5

(a) *Drunkards and winebibbers are bidden "wail over the juice which has been cut off from their mouths."*

The reference here is to the ritual wailing for the discomfited god of the vine. The most familiar example of this comes from ancient Greece, where the "passion" of Dionysus was a common theme of vintage ritual. Thus, Diodorus mentions a *"linos*-song," or threnody, in ancient "Pelasgian" script, which recorded it;[2] while Clement of Alexandria speaks of a "rustic song dealing with the dismemberment of Dionysus,"[3] and Plutarch refers to the practice of intoning a dirge (*eleleu*) at the Attic vintage festival of Oschophoria, in June–July.[4] The pruned vine was personified as Dionysus, and the idea was, indeed, taken over into Christianity. Thus Clement speaks of Christ as "that great grape-cluster . . . which was crushed for our benefit"; while a Middle German paternoster by Johann von Krolewitz refers to him as *gemen und gebunden als man ein Garben tut.*[5] In the same way, too, it is recorded in an Arabic source that when plague raged in Iraq in 1204, the warning was issued that all who failed to participate in the time-honored rite of bewailing the lost son of the mythical Um Unkud, "Mother of the Grape," would inevitably fall victim to it.[6] Of the same tenor also is a modern French song chanted at the pruning of vines:

Vignon, vignette,
Vignon, vignette,

> Qui te planta il fut preudon,
> Tu fus taillée à la serpette![7]

The practice was certainly known among the ancient Canaanites, for a vintage song of similar purport is embedded in a mythological text of the fourteenth century B.C. from Ras Shamra-Ugarit:[8]

> Death-and Rot has sat enthroned,
>   firm ensconced in regal sway,
> In his either hand a rood—
>   Loss of Children, Widowhood;
> Yet, when men now prune the vine,
>   *he* it is that they entwine;
> When they grub the soil all round,
>   'tis from *him* they pluck the ground!

1:8

(b) *Israel is bidden wail for "the husband* (Heb.: baal) *of her youth."*

Here the prophet is again satirizing the ritual ululation for the vanished god of fertility, actually named Baal among the Canaanites. "Such howling and wailing is well attested throughout ancient civilizations." The Egyptians, says Diodorus,[9] used to shed tears and cry upon Isis at the first cutting of the corn; and their summer festival was marked, according to Herodotus,[10] by the chanting of a doleful lay called Maneros. This latter, it is believed, is a distortion of the Egyptian words, *maa n per.k,* "come to thy house," which constitute the opening phrase of a seasonal dirge, that has actually come down to us.[11] The custom is attested also, at a much later date, by Firmicus Maternus, who reproaches the pagan Egyptians for "lamenting over the crops and wailing over the growing seed."[12] In Mesopotamia, the harvest was likewise accompanied by the utterance of a ritual cry known as *alalu* or "ululation"—corresponding exactly to the *eleleu* of Plutarch.[13] Similarly, according to a writer quoted by Athenaeus, ritual dirges called *iouloi* (or *houloi*), i.e., howls, characterized the mysteries of Demeter and Kore (Persephone).[14]

1:9–12

(c) *The land is portrayed as suffering from drought and blight. This has denied Yahweh his wonted offerings.*

Seasonal festivals are everywhere introduced by a period of "mortification," in which life and fertility are represented as suffering a temporary standstill.[15] The language in which this is described in the seasonal myth is more or less stereotyped, and it looks uncommonly as though the prophet is playing on the traditional phraseology. Thus, in the Hittite myth of Telipinu, god of vegetation and fertility, it is said that when he withdraws from the earth in a temper, not only do "the hillsides, trees and pasturelands become bare, and the springs dry up, but the gods themselves are threatened with starvation."[16] So too in the Homeric *Hymn to Demeter,* that goddess is said to have kept the seed buried in the ground while she mourned for Persephone, with the result that not only would the entire human race have perished of starvation but also that "they who dwell on Olympus would have been deprived of their offerings," had not Zeus intervened.[17]

For the rest, the terms in which Joel describes the sterility on earth accord closely with the ancient myths. Thus, in the Hittite "Yuzgat Tablet," which describes the ravages of Hahhimas (Torpor, or perhaps Jack Frost), he is said to have "paralyzed plants, oxen, sheep, hounds and pigs" and to be about to do the same to human beings and vegetation;[18] while in the Canaanite *Poem of Baal,* the disappearance of that god into the netherworld evokes the cry, "The furrows of the fields have gone dry. . . . Baal is neglecting the furrows of the plowlands!"[19]

1:13

(d) *In consequence of this disaster, the priests of Yahweh are bidden to don mourning garb and "pass the night in sackcloth."*[20]

Here it is possible to detect a satirical allusion to the seasonal custom of keeping an all-night vigil for the lost god of fertility, somewhat like the Catholic *tenebrae*-service in Holy Week. The mystery cults both of Dionysus[21] and Attis[22] celebrated some of their main rites at night, while at Eleusis a nocturnal vigil on Boedromion (roughly, September) 19 was taken to represent the wandering of Demeter through darkness in search of Persephone.[23] In Roman Egypt the faithful gathered in an underground chamber at the winter solstice and emerged at dawn carrying the image of a man-child (like the Bambino in the Christmas ceremonies at the church of Aracoeli in Rome) and proclaiming, "The Virgin has given birth! Light has increased!"[24] That ceremonies of this kind indeed go back to far earlier times is indicated by the fact the prophet Ezekiel expressly mentions rites in a cavern in connection with the annual bewailing of Tammuz, and there too they are associated with an adoration of the rising sun![25]

2:15

(e) *A sacred fast and period of abstinence* (Heb.: *ʿaṣārāh*) *are ordained.*

This, to be sure, does not come out clearly in the English Version, because the Hebrew word for "period of abstinence" has been confused by the translators with another meaning "solemn assembly."[26] Periods of abstinence are, however, the usual thing before a harvest festival. They indicate that one lease of life has come to an end, before the beginning of another.[27] Thus the Babylonians recognized the first week or even the first sixteen days of the New Year month of Teshrit as a lenten period;[28] while among the Israelites the autumnal Feast of Ingathering was preceded by a solemn Day of Catharsis (*Yôm ha-kippurîm,* "Day of Atonement"), when all activity stopped.[29] In Greece, the festival of Thesmophória, in October, was characterized by fasting; indeed, the third day was called specifically "the Fast,"[30] and in Cyprus, abstention from food obtained throughout the preceding nine days.[31] So too, the Feast of the Yellow Grain-Mother (Demeter Chloē), held in Athens in mid-May, was marked by rites of mortification.[32] In the Attis-cult, the annual resurrection of that spirit of fertility was introduced by a few days of fasting and ceremonial austerity (*hagisteiai, castus*);[33] and at Rome, the Festival of Ceres, in April, was prefaced by a fast.[34]

Modern parallels abound.[35] In Cambodia, for instance, the first three days of the year (which begins in mid-March) are a period of solemn abstinence.[36] Among the Cherokees and Choctaws of America, the New Year festival in August is called *Busk,* "the Fast," and no food is consumed for two nights and one day before the eating of the new crops.[37] The Mao of Manipur observe a *genna,* or period of taboo, for four days at the beginning of the harvest.[38] In South Massam, fasting takes places before the Walaga festival;[39] among the Natchez of Mississippi, for three days before harvest;[40] in New Guinea, before the yam festival;[41] and in Peru before the summer festival of Raymi.[42]

2:20

(f) *The "northerner" will be expelled and driven into parched and desolated land, "his front into the eastern sea, and his rear into the western sea."*

In the immediate context of the prophet's message, this evidently denoted an historical foe. Nevertheless, there is also a subliminal mythological allusion. The prophet is likening that invader to the figure of Death, Blight, or the like ceremonially expelled in seasonal ceremonies.[43] The Incas of Peru, for example, used ceremonially to expel disease at the festival of Situa, celebrated just before the onset of the rainy season in September.[44] Similarly in Thailand,[45] and likewise among the Wotyaks of East Russia,[46] the forces of evil are solemnly banished on the last day of the year, and among the Hos of Togoland (W. Africa)[47] and the Kiriwina of southeastern New Guinea,[48] they are exorcized before the eating of new yams. At Cape Coast Castle the demon Abonsam is driven forth annually after a four-week period of mortification;[49] and in Tonquin, there is a similar expulsion once a year.[50]

The custom survives, as we shall see later (§**238**), in many parts of Europe, and it is significant, in connection with the prophet's words, that the dread spirits are often driven *into the sea.*

3:9–12

(g) *There will be a final warfare of Yahweh against his enemies.*

This is simply a projection into eschatology of the seasonal defeat of Death, Blight, Old Year, Winter, Chaos, and similar beings. The Ritual Combat, as has long been observed, is a standard element of seasonal festivals and is considered a necessary prelude to the restoration of rainfall and fertility. For this reason it is likewise retrojected into cosmogony, for what happens at the beginning of each year had obviously to have happened also at the beginning of time. Marduk defeats the rebel forces of Ti'amat and her allies before being installed as king and as lord of fertility (*bêl ḫegalli*); Baal similarly defeats Yam and Môt (Death) in the corresponding Canaanite myth; and the Hittite storm-god discomfits the dragon Illuyankas. Ritual equivalents of this myth are legion; the reader may find any number of examples in Frazer's *Golden Bough*[51] or in the present writer's *Thespis*,[52] and it is scarcely necessary to cite them. Representative of them all is the custom observed by women in the Brahmi Confederacy of Baluchistan of staging a ritual combat whenever rain is needed.[53] Similarly, in parts of Malaya, such a combat takes place every three or four years in order to expel demons.[54]

3:12

(h) The consequence of victory in the Combat is the holding of an assize at which the triumphant god is installed as king (e.g., Marduk at Esagila) and the order of "nature" reestablished for the ensuing year.[55] This involves the determination of the individual destinies of men. At the Babylonian New Year Festival, for example, the gods so assembled in the Chamber of Destinies (*parak shimātē*),[56] and to this day Jewish belief asserts that the fates of men are reviewed in heaven on New Year's Day. The ritual equivalent of the myth is the installation of a new king or the formal reinduction of the old one.

Out of this myth and ritual Joel develops the warning that the Last Days will be marked by Yahweh's pronouncing judgment[57] upon the enemies of his people. This, he adds, will take place appropriately in the Valley of Jehosaphat, since that name means properly "Yahweh (Jehovah) judges."

3:18

(i) But harvest and fertility *do* follow. Baal, or the vanished god, returns and brings rainfall and increase, and it is this that marks the concluding stage of the seasonal festival. In the Canaanite *Poem of Baal* the imminent return of the deity is harbingered by a dream in which "the skies rain fatness, and the wadies run with honey."[58] So here, harking back to these ancient words, the prophet declares that in the end

> *The mountains shall drip sweet wine,*
> *and the hills be awash with milk,*
> *and all the wadies of Judah shall flow with water.*

232 The dimming of the sun   2:10
See above, §**216**.

233 The foe from the north   2:20
The prophecy that Israel's enemy will be driven into the sea harkens back to a popular custom of so expelling demons and noxious powers (see below, §**238**). The designation of that enemy as "the northerner" likewise combines a mythological with an historical allusion,[1] for it is a widespread belief that the north is the natural habitat of such spirits.[2]

This belief is attested, for instance, among such ancient peoples as the Indians of the Vedic period[3] and the Iranians.[4] It survived later among the Mandeans[5] and the Jews;[6] indeed, a Jewish tradition asserted specifically that certain sacrifices were slaughtered in the north of the temple area at Jerusalem in order to protect Israel from demons who lived there.[7] The Manichaeans too regarded the north as especially sinister.[8]

Nor is the idea confined to Oriental cultures. In late Greek magical literature, demons are conjured from the north,[9] and it is there that Plutarch locates the monster Typhon.[10] Similarly, in Mexican mythology, Mictlan, "the Country of the North," is the home of demonic spirits called *tzitzimitles*.[11]

The concept prevails especially in European folklore. Thus, in Chaucer's *Frere's Tale,* the fiend who comes in disguise declares that he lives "in the north countree": while in the English ballad entitled *Riddles Wisely Explained,* the riddle-mongering wooer—a fiend in disguise—lives in the north, and in some versions of *Lady Isabel and the Elf-Knight* the supernatural suitor hails from "the north lands."[12] Michael Behaim of Sulzbach, a German poet of the fifteenth century, expressly ridicules the superstition that devils live in Norway[13]—a popular notion mentioned also in a contemporary Jewish source.[14]

The north side of a church is often held to be unlucky, and the northern door is left open at baptism to give egress to the Evil One.[15] By the same token, burial on the north side of a cemetery is commonly disdained, this situation being reserved for unbaptized infants, persons excommunicated, executed criminals, and suicides.[16]

Amos

234 Amos and the pagan festivals

Like those of Hosea (§221) and Zephaniah (§243), the prophecies of Amos appear to be studded with jibes at pagan seasonal practices, suggesting that they may have been delivered at festive assemblies.

Amos 4:4, 6–9

(a) Thus, when the prophet ironically summons Israel to present its daily sacrifices and its "three-day tithes" at the pagan shrines of Bethel and Gilgal, he may perhaps be alluding to the fact that the seasonal festivals seem sometimes to have lasted for three days, beginning with a mock funeral, and ending with the "resurrection" of the god of fertility (see above, §**221, d**).[1]

(b) Similarly, when he threatens famine, blight, and drought as the punishment for such apostasy, it is not difficult to recognize a sly reference to the fact that the pagan festivals were designed primarily to ensure regular rainfall and fertility.[2]

4:12

(c) Again, when he urges his brethren to "prepare to meet your God," he may well be playing on the fact that a main reason for repairing to pagan sanctuaries was to "see the face of the god" (see below, §**251**). Moreover, in the later mystery religions, the proceedings often culminated in the "vision" (*epopteia*) of the risen lord of fertility.[3]

4:13

(d) The pointed declaration that the Lord of Hosts is the real creator of the mountains[4] and of the wind, and the real fructifier of the soil, may have been designed more specifically as a counterblow against the pretensions of the Canaanite Baal, whose command of the rains and fertilization of the earth were the particular theme of seasonal myths and ceremonies.[5]

5:6

(e) So too, when the people are bidden "seek" the Lord so that they may "live," we are reminded once again of the ritual "search" for the vanished spirit of vegetation in the pagan seasonal ceremonies (see above, §**221, e**).

5:16–17

(f) The assertion that there will be public wailing in the streets, and that the farmer especially will participate in it, likewise recalls a characteristic feature of the pagan ceremonies—the ululation over the dead or vanished deity (see above, §§**158, 203**).

5:24

(g) The famous statement,

> Let justice roll down like the waters,
> and righteousness like a perpetual stream (êthan),

assumes added force if it is read as a satire on the rite of pouring water as a rain-charm (see above, §**221, c**). This took place at Jerusalem during the month of "perpetual streams" (*Ethanîm*), i.e., September–October.

9:11

(h) Again, when the future restoration of Israel's fortunes is described as the raising of the fallen booth (*sukkah*) of David, the prophet may well be drawing his imagery from the temporary booths or tents which studded the landscape at the pilgrim festivals (see above, §**221, h**). Frail structures, they would often have been blown down by the wind.

A further allusion to the ritual of pagan festivals may perhaps be recognized in the prophet's call to his countrymen (5:15) to "set up justice in the gate." The Hebrew word rendered "set up" is usually employed of erecting statues, and nowhere else does it occur in a metaphorical sense. The phrase is therefore somewhat strained and bizarre. But perhaps it is a deliberate "dig" at the pagan practice of putting up statues of the gods beside the gate of a city or temple in seasonal processions.[6] Such gates were statutory places of judgment,[7] and this would, of course, lend added force to the prophet's words.

That the prophet was indeed alluding to pagan festivals seems also to be indicated by the express declaration which he puts into the mouth of the Lord (5:21):

> *I hate, I reject your festivals,*
> *and take no delight in your days of restraint.*[8]

235 Judgment by fire

7:4

RSV: *Thus the Lord GOD showed me: behold, the Lord GOD was calling for a judgment by fire, and it devoured the great deep and was eating up the land.*[1]

The notion of a final judgment of the world by fire recurs elsewhere in the Old Testament. Thus, the so-called farewell song of Moses (Deut. 32:22)—

which is dated by Eissfeldt to the eleventh century B.C.[2]—includes a prophecy that the fire which has been kindled in Yahweh's wrath and which "burns down to deepest hell" will yet "devour the earth and its produce and set the foundations of the mountains ablaze." Similarly, Isaiah speaks of Yahweh's "day of vengeance, the year of settling accounts in his suit against Zion," when "rivers will be turned into pitch, and dust to brimstone, and when the soil of Zion will become burning pitch."[3] Malachi[4] and Daniel[5] likewise paint a grim picture of a final conflagration, but it is possible that they were influenced more directly by Iranian ideas (see below, §247).

The conflagration became a prominent element of the eschatological nightmare portrayed in intertestamental literature. The Book of Enoch, for instance, threatens the heathen with the prospect of being "cast into the judgment of fire,"[6] and one of the Psalms of Solomon refers in a vivid passage to "the flame of fire and wrath" destined for the unrighteous.[7] In the same vein, too, the Manual of Discipline found among the Dead Sea Scrolls prescribes that at the ceremony of initiation into the brotherhood the levites are to pronounce the curse that all who have cast their lot with Belial "shall be damned in the gloom of the fire eternal,"[8] and in one of the Qumran hymns there is a lurid description (indebted partly to our passage) of the final conflagration.[9]

The New Testament likewise speaks in several places of the final "Gehenna (RSV: hell) of fire."[10]

Nor is the idea confined to the Bible. It features prominently in Zoroastrian doctrine,[11] although there the fire is regarded as purificatory as well as punitive. One of the Yashts, in predicting it, portrays it as the medium whereby the imperfections or dross of the world will be purged away;[12] and the later Bundahishn depicts in horrendous terms this coming disaster.[13]

According to Berosus (as quoted by Seneca),[14] the Neo-Stoics likewise espoused the belief in a final conflagration (*ekpyrōsis*), and it seems to have enjoyed considerable popularity in Imperial Rome.[15] Some scholars believe that this was borrowed, albeit indirectly, from the Iranians, while others see in it a moralizing development of Heraclitus' view that, since all things spring from fire, they will ultimately return to the same element.[16]

According to Eliade, ideas of a similar character are entertained by the Mayas of Yucatan and the Aztecs of Mexico.[17]

It may be suggested that in articulating this age-old belief our present passage also works in an allusion to traditional myth. Eschatology is, after all, simply cosmogony in the future tense: the new world will be born in much the same way as was the present one.[18] *Magnus ab integro saeclorum nascitur ordo.*[19] Hence, the concept of an eschatological world-fire ought to correspond to some cosmogonic event or incident of the same order, and traces of such a mythical event can indeed be detected in Ancient Near Eastern literature. A commentary on the ritual of the Babylonian Akîtu (New Year) festival interprets the ceremonial act of firing an oven as symbolizing the burning of Kingu, husband of the marplot Tiamat and commander of the rebel hosts in the primordial battle of the gods.[20] This lends added point to Amos' specific reference to the burning of "the great deep," seeing that the Hebrew word for "deep" is in fact *tehôm*, the equivalent of Tiamat.[21] Similarly, too, the act of burning the heads of two statues at the same festival is taken to represent the burning of the dragon Mušḫuššu and of the "scorpion man"—two monsters subdued by the god Ninurta in an earlier version of the cosmogonic myth.[22] True, these incidents do not appear in the more or less standardized form of the myth (*Enuma Elish*) which was actually recited at the festival, but we may be reasonably sure that Mesopotamian popular lore knew also of variant tales concerning these primordial events.

In view of the frequent appearance in rabbinic literature of the concept of a final "deluge of fire" (*mabbūl shel 'esh*)[23] it has recently been suggested that it is more specifically to this that Amos here refers, and the suggestion has been bolstered by the further proposal that the traditional text's *QôRē' La-RîB Ba-'ESH*, "calling *for a judgment by* fire," should rather be read (by mere redivision of the consonants) *QôRē' Li-RᵉBîB 'ESH*, "calling for a *rain of* fire."[24] This, however, misses the point of the prophet's phrase. The word, *QôRē'*, "calling," is here used, as in Isaiah 59:4, in the technical sense of *summoning to a court of law;* hence, the traditional *La-RîB*, which properly means "to litigation" (rather than "for a judgment"), is both apposite and necessary. Moreover, the sentiment finds a perfect parallel in Isaiah 34:8–9, where, as mentioned above, the final conflagration is explicitly associated with the year in which Yahweh will settle accounts in his long-standing litigation, or lawsuit (*RîB*) against Zion.[25]

Jonah

236 The story of Jonah

▲ We have all been familiar from childhood with the story of the prophet Jonah, who, fleeing from the presence of the Lord, took passage in a ship for Tarshish, where he evidently expected to be beyond the reach of the deity. However, he miscalculated the power of the Lord; for while he was still at sea, the Lord sent a great wind in pursuit of him, and the storm was such that the ship, in which the renegade prophet had taken his passage, was like to be broken in pieces. But, amid all the tumult of the tempest, Jonah slept soundly in his bunk down below, till the skipper came and, waking him from his slumber, bade him betake himself to prayer as the only way to save the ship. However, when he came on deck, the prophet found that the question with the crew was not so much one of prayer as of pitching somebody overboard as a propitiatory offering to the raging waters, or to the god who had lashed them into fury. So they drew lots to see who should perish to save the rest, and the lot fell upon Jonah. Accordingly with his consent, indeed at his own urgent request, and not until they had very humanely exhausted every effort by hard rowing to make the land, they took up the now conscience-stricken prophet and heaved him over the gunwale into the foaming billows. No sooner did he fall with a splash into the water than the sea went down. But the Lord had mercy on the repentant prophet, and prepared a great fish which swallowed up Jonah; and Jonah was in the belly of the fish three days and three nights. And Jonah prayed to the Lord out of the fish's belly, and the Lord spoke to the fish, and it vomited up Jonah, safe and sound, on the dry land. ▼

The story lends itself to considerable illustration from Comparative Folklore.

(a) Sailing with an "unholy" person

Jonah 1:4–7

It is a common superstition that *it is dangerous to sail with an impious or wicked person,* since his presence aboard will inevitably provoke an outraged god to embroil the sea and possibly wreck the ship. Aeschylus, for example, declares explicitly that

> The pious man who on a ship embarks
> With hothead crew or other villainy
> Goes to his doom with that god-hated brood;[1]

while the orator Antiphon asserts in similar vein that persons suffering from physical or moral contagion can imperil the lives of other passengers on a voyage.[2] So too Theophrastus characterizes the timid and cowardly man as one who, when a great wave breaks against a ship, immediately inquires whether any of his companions is "tainted";[3] while Plautus, in his comedy *Rudens,* has one of the characters twit another with the taunt that any ship in which he sailed would be likely to founder,[4] and Horace asserts that he would not risk letting anyone who had divulged the secret rites of Ceres set foot on his boat.[5]

Nor is the belief confined to ancient times. A well-known anecdote relates that when the late Olive Schreiner was about to be lowered into a lifeboat at the wreck of the *Titanic,* some of its occupants objected, "Don't put her in here; she's an atheist and will wreck us."[6]

1:11–12

(b) *The guilty passenger, once identified, is usually thrown overboard.*[7]

Thus, in a Buddhist story, a certain Mittavindaka, son of a merchant of Benares, who has been disobedient to his mother, is put out on a raft because he might spoil the luck of a ship on which he has embarked.[8] Similarly, in the Scottish ballad of *Bonnie Annie,* a ship will not move because "fey folk" are aboard. Lots are cast to determine who should be sacrificed, and the lot falls, quite unreasonably, on Annie instead of on the captain who has in fact betrayed her. At first he refuses to throw her to the waves, but eventually

> He has tane her in his arms twa, lo, lifted her cannie;
> He has thrown her out owre board, his ain dear Annie.[9]

In the same vein, in the English ballad, *Brown Robyn's Confession,* that "hero" guilty of incest is tied to a plank and cast adrift because his presence prevents the ship from sailing. His "fair confession," however, brings him the aid of the Blessed Virgin and her Son, and he is ultimately translated to heaven.[10] Analogues to such tales are to be found also in Scandinavian folklore (especially in Lappland);[11] while in a French version, it is not one of the passengers but the ship's cat that is thrown as a sop to the angry billows.[12]

1:17; 2–10

(c) *The person cast overboard is sometimes said to be swallowed by a sea monster and subsequently disgorged intact.*[13]

An ancient Indian tale relates, for example, that once upon a time there lived a princess who refused to marry anyone except the man who had set eyes on the Golden City of Legend. The hero Saktidêva accepted the challenge, and proceeded to roam the world in search of that fabulous place. In the course of his travels he set sail for the island of Usthala, to seek directions from the king of the fishermen who dwelt there. On the way, a storm arose, and the ship capsized. Saktidêva, however, was swallowed by a great fish which carried him to the isle. When the king of the fishermen slit it open, the hero emerged unharmed.[14] The same story is told in Ceylon about the hero Bahudama;[15] while an ancient Greek legend relates that Heracles was once swallowed by a whale near the port of Jaffa—Jonah's own point of embarkation!—and remained within the animal's belly for three days.[16] Similar stories are current to this day in the popular lore of Melanesia and Indonesia[17] and among the French Canadians,[18] and there is a parallel even in Basile's famous *Pentamerone*.[19]

A less artistic, but equally veracious, variant of the Biblical story is told by the natives of Windesi, on the northern coast of New Guinea. The inhabitants of the island of Jop, they say, formerly dwelt at Batewaar. One day five of them rowed in a canoe across to Waropen to fetch sago. But out on the high sea a whale swallowed them, canoe and all, and they sank with the fish to the bottom. As they sat in the fish's belly, they cut slices of its liver and guts, hacked the canoe in pieces, and, lighting a fire, roasted the liver and guts and ate them. But the fish, thus mangled in its vitals, died, and its carcass drifted to shore. Thereupon, the men, sitting in the fish's belly, heard the cry of a hornbill. They said, "Is that land?" They opened the fish's snout, they saw that it was land, and they went forth. Then the bird came to them and said, "I did it; it is my doing that you people are still alive. Go now home; fetch your people and dwell on this island." So to sea they went, fetched their people, and took up their abode on the island. That is why the inhabitants of the island of Jop do not eat any hornbills.[20]

What is alleged to be an authentic counterpart to Jonah's adventures is related on the authority of no less redoubtable a man of science than Linné. In 1758, we are informed, a shipwrecked sailor in the Mediterranean had the ill fortune to be swallowed by a shark. When, however, the latter was subsequently harpooned and opened, the sailor emerged intact![21]

Bible scholars often cite as parallels to the story of Jonah the classical legend of Phalanthus, the mythic hero of Brundisium and Tarentum, who was saved from shipwreck by a dolphin,[22] as well as the similar tales of Eikadios,[23] Korianos,[24] and Arion.[25] These stories, however, are really quite irrelevant, since in none of them is the hero swallowed, much less disgorged, by a sea monster. On the other hand, it is indeed permissible to see in our tale a maritime variant of the same motif as is represented, for instance, in the story of Red Riding Hood and the Wolf and of Tom Thumb extricated whole from a crow.[26]

In ages[27] less enlightened than our own, when it was considered blasphemous to see in the stories of the Bible anything but the record of historical fact, commentators and ecclesiastics were often put to considerable pains to "authenticate" our bizarre narrative, and wondrous and ingenious were some of the explanations they propounded. What troubled them especially was that the more common type of whale or shark does not in fact possess a gullet wide enough to swallow a human being whole. The creature in question, it was pointed out, was a special kind of whale—the so-called right whale, described in *Moby Dick* as having a mouth which "would accommodate a couple of whist-tables and comfortably seat all the players." But even if the prophet was swallowed by such a monster, how, it was asked, could he have managed to survive in its belly for three days and three nights, seeing that its gastric juices would surely have poisoned him? Not so, replied the learned Bishop Jebb; the "great fish" which the Lord prepared was a *dead* fish, in which all such noxious elements had already ceased to function. That, too, was why the prophet eventually emerged unchewed and undigested!

Others found even more fantastic explanations. "Great Fish," they said, was the name of a ship which God provided to rescue his servant, and its "belly" was simply the hold or steerage. Maybe, it was added, the vessel was so named because it carried the figure of a fish on its prow! Alternatively, could not *Great Fish* have been the name of an inn at which Jonah put up when he reached land?

2:1–9

(d) *While he is in the belly of the "great fish," the prophet passes the time by intoning a prayer.*

Any attentive reader of the Bible will recognize at once that this consists largely of standard clichés many of which are actually to be found in the Psalter. What we have, then, is simply another example of the *cante-fable*, concerning which see above, §31. Until Jonah is disgorged, the action of the story comes to a standstill. When that story is recited, the intermission is filled by "audience participation" in the form of chanting a well-known hymn, artfully put into the mouth of the prophet.[28]

3:6–8

(e) *Animals dressed in mourning.*

When Jonah proclaims the impending doom of Nineveh, the king decrees a public fast and orders that *beasts as well as men be clad in the sackcloth of mourning*.

Animals are part of the "topocosm"—that is, of the aggregate of living beings and inanimate objects which together constitute the corporate entity and "atmosphere" of a place.[29] Hence, in popular belief, they participate in its fate and fortune. It is in this spirit, for instance, that cattle as well as men are victims of the plagues inflicted upon Egypt at the time of the exodus,[30] and that the prophet Joel can declare, when disaster befalls his country, that "the flocks of sheep too are held guilty."[31] Accordingly, animals can be made to share in any national mourning. The Persians, we are told, shaved the manes of their horses and mules when Masistius fell at Plataea,[32] and Alexander ordered a similar token of mourning after the death of Hephaistion.[33] Plutarch relates that the priests of Egypt shrouded the gilded ox with a linen veil, when they performed rites expressing their participation in the mourning of Isis for Osiris;[34] and somewhat similarly in a modern Greek folktale the king's chargers are said to have been dyed black in a time of national grief.[35]

In our Biblical narrative, the animals not only wear mourning but also *fast;* and this finds a parallel in the medieval Irish romance of Lebar Brec,[36] and even in ancient Mesopotamian sources.[37]

Micah

237 Prophecy by puns — Micah 1

Nomina omina sunt. In ancient and primitive thought, a name is more than an appellation; it is an integral element of being. Accordingly, the very name of a person or object can betoken his or its fate and fortune.[1] One can curse a man by reading a derogatory or sinister meaning into his name, and the same can be done to hostile or impious cities and peoples. The first chapter of Micah is based largely on this practice, though the point is inevitably obcured in translation.

Tell it not in Gath (1:10), for example, is a proverbial expression—it recurs in II Samuel 1:20—depending on the similarity in sound between the name of that city and the Hebrew word, *ta-gidh-ū,* "tell." Similarly, when the city of Beth-le-'aphrah is told (*ib.*) to *"roll" in dust,* the point lies in a pun between its name and the Hebrew word *'aphar,* meaning "dust." Again, when it is said (1:11) of Za'anan (Heb.: Ṣa'anan) that its inhabitants, being beleaguered, *will not be able to come forth,* there is a play of sound between that name and the word *yaṣa,* "come forth"; and when the inhabitants of Lachish are warned (1:13) to *harness the steed to the chariot* and make their escape, the point lies in the similarity of the name Lachish to the word *rechesh,* "pack-horse," as who should say, *Latch on the horses in Lachish.* So too when the houses of Achzib are likened (1:14) to a "deceptive brook (RSV: wrongly, a deceitful thing)," i.e., one that dries up in summer, the English reader must be told that the Hebrew word for such a brook is the likesounding *achzab.* Finally, when the prophet declares (1:15) that *God will bring a dispossessor* (RSV: *conqueror*) *to Mareshah,* his audience saw at once that he was reading into the name of that city a play on the word *yarash,* "(dis)possess."

Puns, however, are often tortured, and the punster is driven to the use of rare and recondite words. In course of time the true meaning of these tends to be forgotten. Therefore, if the prophecy is to retain its message, a contemporary synonym must be substituted, even at the sacrifice of the original play on words. This, it appears, has sometimes happened in the present case.

Thus, when we are told (1:11) that *the wailing of Beth-ezel* (Heb.: *eṣel*) *shall take from you its standing-place*—words which are in any case difficult to interpret—it may well be that in place of the Hebrew word rendered "standing-place" the prophet employed an archaic term *eṣel* (recoverable from the cognate Semitic languages)[2] which meant "grounding, origin." And when he said (*ibd.*), *Pass on your way, inhabitant of Shaphir*—words which in the Hebrew original contain no pun and have, indeed, been variously emended by modern scholars in order to introduce one—it may well be that in place of the more usual and intelligible word *'ibrî*, he used for "pass on your way" an archaic word *sh-p-r,* "travel along," recoverable from Arabic, as who should say, *shift yourselves, inhabitants of Shaphir.*[3]

Sometimes, too, the play on words is implicit rather than overt. Thus in the statement (1:12) that *the inhabitants of Maroth wait anxiously for good* (*bliss*), the point may well lie in the fact that Maroth is the Hebrew word for "sorrow(s)," i.e., *Sorely she waits for bliss, who dwells in Sorrowtown.* Similarly, when the prophet's listeners are bidden (1:14) to *give parting gifts to Moresheth-gath,* the point depends on the resemblance of the name Moresheth to the Hebrew word *me'oreseth* meaning "betrothed" and on the fact that what is conventionally rendered "parting gifts" properly denotes "instruments of divorce." Finally, when he declares (1:12) that *Evil has come down from the Lord* to the gate of Jerusalem, it is not difficult to see that he is ironically interpreting the name of that city to mean "city of peace (Heb.: *shalôm*)."

The same device as is here employed by Micah was used also by other Old Testament prophets. Isaiah, for example, in castigating the Moabite city of Dibon (15:9), deliberately distorts its name to *Dimon,* in order to permit the declaration that it will be filled with *dam,* or blood. Jeremiah (48:2) fulminates against Ḥeshbon by warning that men are *ḥashab*-ing—that is, plotting—evil against it, and against Madmen that *it will be reduced to silence,* for which the Hebrew word is the like-sounding *tid-dom-mî.* Ezekiel (25:16) tells the Cherethim (Cretans?) that *God will curtail them* (Heb.: *k-r-t*); Amos (5:5) warns Gilgal that *it will be driven into exile,* for which the Hebrew word is *galah;* and Zephaniah (2:4–5) has a string of puns on the names of excoriated Philistine cities.

Examples of the same technique may be found also outside of the Bible. Thus, one of the so-called Sibylline Oracles (written during the Hellenistic age) condemns the island of Samos to the state of a sandy beach, the Greek for "sand" being *psammos.* Delos, says the same prophecy, will become *a-dêlos,* that is, "undistinguished," and Rome will be but a *rumê*—an alley.[4]

Illustrative of the same principle and technique is the Arabic story of how Omar, hearing a certain Jamrah ibn Shihâb (Coal, son of Flame) declare that his tribal and local names were both connected with fire, foretold that his house and family would be burned; and this actually happened.[5] One recalls also Catullus' scurrilous puns on the names of his personal enemies.[6]

238 Casting sins into the sea 7:19

> RSV: *He will again have compassion upon us;*
> *he will tread our iniquities under foot.*
> *Thou wilt cast all our[1] sins*
> *into the depths of the sea.*

In the original Hebrew these verses are a jingle, the general effect of which may be reproduced as follows:

> *He will show us his mercy once more,*
> *stamp our misdeeds to the floor,*
> *and all their sins shall be*
> *tossed in the depths of the sea.*

The words may perhaps be those of a traditional chant which accompanied a symbolic ceremony, for the casting of death, blight, noxiousness, contagion, and the like into the waters is a widespread seasonal rite in several parts of the world.[2] At Nuremberg, in Germany, for example, an image of Death used annually to be carried out of the city and plunged into a neighboring stream, the bearers chanting the words, "We are carrying Death to the waters."[3] Similarly at Tabor, in Czechoslovakia, the effigy of Death was transported out of town and then floated downstream;[4] while at Chrudim it was flung into the waters on "Black Sunday."[5] At Bielsk, in Podlachia,[6] and among the Serbs of Upper Lausitz, it was drowned in a nearby pool or marsh.[7] In Silesia, children used to throw a puppet into the river;[8] and a similar practice obtained in various parts of Thüringen.[9] At Leipzig this was done by the local prostitutes and bastards;[10] at Dobschwitz, near Gera, the rite was performed on March 1,[11] and in a number of villages near Erlangen on the fourth Sunday in Lent.[12]

The custom can be traced to far earlier times. On March 15 the Roman vestal virgins flung puppets into the Tiber,[13] just as Indians cast them into the Ganges during the festival in honor of the goddess Kali.[14]

But we can go even further back. In the Canaanite *Poem of Baal,* that god's rival Yam, genius of sea and river, is apparently cast "into the sea with the streams." In terms of the story, he is, of course, merely shoved back where he belongs, but since the entire myth seems to reflect the pattern of seasonal ceremonies, this incident may well have been suggested by a ritual practice.[15]

Alike among the Semites and the Greeks, moral as well as physical impurity was often cast into the sea or into running water.[16] Thus the carcass of the ram used in the purification (*kuppuru*) rite of the Babylonian New Year was subsequently tossed into the river;[17] while in the Iliad, Agamemnon orders his men to perform rites of purgation and to cast their impurities into the sea.[18] So too, in the *Supplices* of Aeschylus, the chorus beseeches Zeus to cast into "the darkling deep" the black fate which hangs over the daughters of Danaus.[19]

In Sophocles' *Oedipus Rex* there is a prayer that the spirit of war (Ares) may be plunged "into the great chamber of Amphitrite (i.e., the sea) . . . and into the Thracian billows."[20] In Euripides' *Iphigenia in Tauris* that hapless maiden expresses a wish to bathe in the sea because "the sea whirls away all mortal ills,"[21] and in the same writer's *Hercules Furens* the chorus voice the prayer that "grievous old age may vanish 'neath the waves."[22] Both Plutarch and the comic dramatist Diphylos expressly describe the sea as purificatory.[23] Indeed, even objects used in rites of purification were often cast subsequently into the sea;[24] so among the Romans, were *prodigia* and monstrous births,[25] while in Car Nicobar it is the custom, when a man is sick, to rub him with pigs' blood and beat him with leaves, and then to throw the leaves into the sea.[26]

The spirit of all these ceremonies is summed up by the Roman poet Tibullus in the well-known lines:

> Whatsoe'er of evil there may be,
> and whatsoe'er of sorrow that we dread,
> May sea and rapid rivers bear away.[27]

Nahum

239 The burden of Nineveh

The historical background of Nahum's prophecy is the capture of Nineveh, the proud capital of Assyria, by a coalition of Medes, Babylonians, and Scythians in the summer of 612 B.C. The details can be pieced together from a Babylonian chronicle now in the British Museum[1] and from later accounts by the Classical writers, Xenophon and Diodorus.

The siege lasted from June (Sivan) until August (Ab).[2] Three assaults were mounted by the Medes; the second of these began under cover of night, and though highly successful, was not conclusive.[3] The eventual sack of the city was facilitated by a vehement storm, which caused the River Tigris to rise in flood and sweep away some twelve hundred feet (twenty stadia) of the embankment.[4] A force of Bactrians sent to lift the siege were won over to the enemy's cause by the Median commander. The Assyrian king, ignorant of this defection, was lulled into a sense of security and passed the time regaling his troops at lavish entertainments. During one of their carousals, Median partisans attacked by night, destroyed the camp, put large numbers of its inmates to the sword, and drove others back into the city.[5] The Assyrian king then set his palace afire, and died in the flames.[6]

In a graphic portrayal of the disaster (2:3-8) the Hebrew prophet describes the final agony of the city—the fruitless defense and the desperate but frustrated hopes of its king, recalling the past glories of his "stalwarts" only to see them routed and the palace flooded:

> *Reddened are the shields of his warriors,*
> *his troops incarnadined,*[7]
> *on the day he makes his preparations.*
> *Aflame are the wheel-spokes of his chariots;*
> *the fir-trees are rustled (as they pass).*
> *Through the streets the chariots dash,*
> *jostle one another in the squares.*
> *Like firebrands—so they seem;*
> *like lightning-flashes they dart.*

He recalls (the past glories of) his braves,
  they come scurrying to the wall,
pitching and lurching as they go;
  and the mantelet is set up.
But the sluice-gates have been opened,
  and the palace now rocks and is awash.[8]

Like a lady she is
  stripped and carried off,
while her maids lead the way before her.
  <moaning>[9] *like doves,*
taboring—but on their own breasts!
  Yea, Nineveh is like a pool
whose waters are ebbing away;
  "Halt, halt!" (men cry),
but none can turn them back!

In these events the prophet saw the hand of Israel's champion, Yahweh, performing in the manner of the familiar storm-god of the Mesopotamians themselves and translating into history the feats traditionally ascribed to him in myth. The prophet brought home his message by prefixing to his denunciation of Nineveh a poem of more general tenor (ch. 1) in which these feats were recited, with sidelong glances, as it were, toward the main features of the city's fall. (The poem appears to have been adapted from an older hymn, composed in the form of an alphabetical acrostic, in which the prowess of the storm-god was related; but this was freely adapted, so that the original alphabetic form and order of the verses has sometimes been disturbed.)[10]

1:2–3

A passionate, vengeful god,
  vengeful and wrathful is he,
taking revenge on opponents,
  nursing rage against foes.
Patient though he be,
  yet he is great in strength,
and lets not the guilty go free.

In gust and gale in his way,
  and clouds are the dust at his feet.

Yahweh plays the role of an Adad, Marduk, or Ninurta; he rides the storm. So Baal-Hadad is described in the Canaanite texts from Ras Shamra as "Rider on the Clouds,"[11] and in Mesopotamian hymns the storm-god is likewise the "rider on the great cloud"[12] or the "lord of the avalanche."[13] In the Babylonian Epic of Creation, Marduk is said specifically to ride the storm against Tiamat.[14]

1:4a

> *'Tis he that rebuked the sea*
> *and dried it up,*
> *and made all the rivers parched.*

The reference is, in the first place, to the general action of the stormwind on ocean and stream. It is to be noted, however, that the succeeding verbs are all in the past tense. The allusion is, therefore, to specific occasions when the prowess of the storm-god was evinced, i.e., to specific exploits attributed to him in the traditional myth.

In the Canaanite *Poem of Baal* (Hadad) that god conquers Yam, "Sea," alias Ṯ-p-ṭ N-h-r, "Prince Stream." Allusion to this is made also in a Hittite version of the Canaanite myth, where the storm-god is described as "he who vanquished the Sea."[15] Old Testament poetry also contains several allusions to this exploit, there attributed to Yahweh: see Isa. 50:2; 51:10; Pss. 74:13; 89:10; 93; Job 7:12; 26:12; 38:10.

There is no clear parallel in Ancient Near Eastern texts to the drying up of sea and streams, but allusions to this as a cosmic event is indeed made in Psalm 74:15. Elsewhere in the Old Testament, this exploit is seen *historically* rather than *mythically,* and is referred to the parting of the Sea of Reeds at the Exodus: Isa. 50:2; 51:10; Ps. 106:9. But the Hebrew poets may well have viewed this as the "actualization" in history of an archetypal mythical event.

1:4b–5

> *Awilt*[16] *were Bashán and Carmél,*
> *and the flowers of Lebanon drooped.*
> *Mountains were shaken before him,*
> *and hills were aquake.*
> *The earth was laid waste*[17] *before him,*
> *the world and all that dwell in it.*

So, in the aforementioned Canaanite poem, it is said of Baal-Hadad:

> When Baal's holy voice rings out,
>   when Baal's thunders peal,
> the earth doth shake   the mountains quake,
>   the highlands rock and reel.[18]

Similarly, one of the celebrated Tell Amarna Letters declares that "when Pharaoh gives forth his voice like Haddu (Hadad), all the mountains quake.[19] This is echoed in turn by a Mesopotamian hymn:

> When Baal rages, heaven is commov'd,
> When Hadad storms, the mighty mounts are rent;[20]

or again:

> Hadad doth his thunder send,
> and [sha]ken are the mounts.[21]

1:6
> *His fury who can withstand?*
> *who abide the blaze of his wrath?*
> *His anger was poured out like fire;*
> *the rocks were riven by him.*

In the Sumerian poem *Lugal-u₂-me-lám-bi-nir-gal*, Ninurta, the warrior-god, is described as assailing the mountains with his special weapon(s).[22] He declares explicitly—in agreement with the opening verse of our poem!—that he wreaks vengeance on them; and he is described as "unrivalled destroyer of mountains."[23]

1:7–8
> *Good is he as a refuge*
> *in the day of distress,*
> *and duly takes note of them*
> *that seek their shelter in him.*
> *Yet, with a flood overflowing*
> *he makes a full end of them*
> *that rise up against him*
> *and chases his foes into darkness.*

The storm-god is, of course, the god of inundations, Adad it was who brought the Deluge,[24] and one of his stock epithets is "lord of the avalanche" (*bêl abûbi*).[25] So too Marduk's word is described as "an advancing flood" (*mīlum tebū*).[26] The prophet, however, cleverly employs these standard clichés in order to show that the unusual rising of the Tigris, which has facilitated the fall of Nineveh (*see above*) is indeed the characteristic work of a deity—but this time, of Yahweh!

The reference to the god's chasing his foes into darkness likewise has special meaning when it is remembered that the final destruction of the Assyrian army took place at night (*see above*). Furthermore, according to Herodotus, the fall of the city coincided with a solar eclipse![27] The prophet sees in these events a translation into history of what was related in myth concerning the Deluge:

> From the horizon rose a darkling cloud . . .
> All that had been bright was turned to dark . . .

No man could see his neighbor, and the view
Of humankind from heaven was black'd out.²⁸

1:9–10

What (more) would ye plot against him?..
  a full end it is that he makes;
  rebellion ne'er rises twice!
See, it is come to the point
  that, tangled like thorns though they were,
  and sodden with drink,
    yet have they been consumed
    as though they were straw!

The prophet is perhaps harking back to the mythical defeat of the sea-god and his confederates.

In the Babylonian Epic of Creation, Tiamat and her allies are said to "plot" (*kapdū*) against the authority of heaven,²⁹ and the victorious Marduk is described expressly as "the crusher of rebellion" (*ḫalaš tuqmati*).³⁰ Moreover, the Hebrew word (viz., *ṣārāh*) here rendered "rebellion" is identical with that which is there employed (iii.15; iv.80, 116–18) to describe the activity of Tiamat's horde, just as in the Canaanite *Poem of Baal* (V AB. D. 36) it describes that of the contumacious Yam ("Sir Sea").

1:11, 14, 12–13

The subsequent words of this verse are so terse and compact that their meaning and point have escaped most commentators, and various emendations of the text have been proposed. But when we recall that the final attack of the Medes was made while the Assyrian generals and troops were in fact carousing and "sodden with drink," and that, according to Diodorus and Abydenus, the Assyrian king finally committed both himself and his palace to the flames, the brilliant irony of the prophet's words becomes apparent: in these events he sees a parallel to the action of lightning upon thick thorn bushes! Even though damp and sodden, and densely knit, they still burn!

*Was it not out of thee,*³¹
  (O Nineveh), that he came
who plotted mischief against him
  —that devilish counsellor?
*So*³² *the LORD has commanded about thee:*
  "No seed of thy name shall be sown.
Out of the house of thy gods
  will I cut off image and idol;

> thy very grave will *I turn*
> *into a desolate place,*[33]
> *for thou art disgraced!"*
>
> (*Yet, to Israel*) *thus saith the LORD:*
> "*What though whole oceans gushed,*
> *yet have they ebbed and passed o'er;*
> *though I afflicted thee,*
> *I shall afflict thee no more.*[34]
> *Now burst I his bonds from thee,*
> *and rend asunder his cords!"*

Here again the prophet is playing on the fact that Nineveh met its doom, to no small extent, through an exceptional flooding of the Tigris.

The siege of Nineveh lasted, as we have seen, from June (Sivan) until August (Ab). It therefore covered the month of July (Tammuz, Dûzu), and this month was regarded by the Mesopotamians as sacred to the storm-god and divine warrior, Ninurta.[35] What happened during this period might therefore be attributed, with peculiar appropriateness, to the action of a god operating as a zealous warrior and as the lord of storm and tempest!

240 "The mills of God grind slowly" 1:3

Assyria had been supreme for a long time, and the retribution had been slow to come. In his opening hymn, therefore, Nahum is careful to assure his listeners that

> *Patient, yet great in strength is the Lord;*
> *he lets not the guilty go free.*

This notion of God's slow but inexorable justice ("The mills of God grind slowly, yet they grind exceeding small")[1] is a commonplace of Greek literature,[2] and it is not impossible that our Scriptural writer was echoing a corresponding Oriental proverb. Says Sophocles, for instance:

> Whene'er a man casts off the things of God
> And turns to mad unreason, then the gods,
> Albeit slowly, yet do see it clear.[3]

And Euripides observes to the same effect:

> The gods may bide their time, but are not weak
> In moving to their ends.[4]

The sentiment was likewise common among Roman writers. Tibullus, for example, declares roundly that

> At first, indeed, a man may hide his crimes,
> Yet with soft steps doth Retribution come,
> Albeit late;[5]

and Horace that

> Though she be lame, yet Vengeance seldom fails
> To follow crime;[6]

while, more directly in consonance with our Biblical poet, Seneca affirms that "the immortal gods may take their time but they can nevertheless be relied upon to exact retributions on the human race,"[7] and Juvenal, more succinctly, that

> Great, though tardy, is the wrath of gods.[8]

Valerius Maximus likewise speaks of the slow-footed anger of the gods,[9] and his statement is echoed in Voltaire's famous dictum that *La peine suite le crime; elle arrive à pas lents.*[10]

Habakkuk

241 "Hush before the Lord"   Hab. 1:20

Before the presence of the Lord in his temple, or when he stirs therefrom (Zech. 2:17), or when he prepares his banquet and invites his guests (Zeph. 1:7), all men are to keep silent. Why? Not merely because silence is the natural concomitant of awe—"the positive expression of the inexpressible, the language of the unutterable"[1]—but also because words have power, and untoward or inappropriate words can therefore impair holy things or defile sacred occasions. To utter unseemly words, or even to make unseemly noises, in the presence of sacred beings is tantamount to sacrilege or blasphemy, or to appearing before them in dirty clothes or in a state of physical impurity.

The Egyptian *Maxims of Ani* declares explicitly that noise in the house of God is an abomination;[2] while both Greeks and Romans (the former already in Homeric times) prefaced the performance of public rites with an order for silence ($εὐφημεῖτε$; *favete linguis*).[3] In the Ion of Euripides, when a slave hurls unseemly invective at the hero while the latter is serving in the temple, that slave is at once replaced, lest the sacred rites be thereby impaired.[4] Somewhat similarly after the slaying of their mother Clytaemnestra, both Orestes and Electra may neither speak to, nor be addressed by, anyone lest in conversation they transmit their own "contagion."[5] For the same reason, too, tombs of ancient worthies had to be passed in silence—a custom attested alike in Classical antiquity,[6] in German popular usage,[7] and among savages in West Africa.[8] Jews who follow orthodox tradition prepare corpses for burial and attend funerals in absolute silence—today interpreted as a mark of respect.[9] Magical rites, and the gathering of magical herbs, must likewise often be performed in silence.[10]

242 The prayer of Habakkuk   3

(a) To the main prophecy of Habakkuk there is appended a "prayer" (ch. 3) in which the prophet envisages the imminent discomfiture of Israel's foes as a repetition in history of the deeds attributed to Yahweh in time-honored myth and legend.[1] Many of these are in turn adaptations of still older legends associated with the pagan gods:

3:2

> *I have heard tell of thee, LORD;*
> *LORD, I am filled with awe*
> *at what thou hast done.*
> *Now, in this present time,[2]*
> *make it a living thing,[3]*
> *show, in this present time,*
> *that even when thou art raging*
> *thou rememberest ties of love!*

3:3–4

(b) *In the dark night of Israel's despair, Yahweh is about to appear as a rising sun:*

> *Here comes he, a very godhead,*
> *out of the Southern Land,*
> *yea, a being divine,*
> *from the hillsides of Parán.[4]*
> *His splendor has mantled the heavens,*
> *and the earth is filled with his sheen.[5]*
> *It is as the glow of the dayspring;*
> *rays shoot forth from his side,*
> *though still in the darkness yonder*
> *lies hid the full force of his strength![6]*

The description of the theophany is based on the conventional portrayal of the sun-god (Shamash) in Mesopotamian art, e.g., on cylinder seals. He rises between twin mountains, with rays issuing from his shoulders or sides.[7] The glow betokens the approach of a god or otherworldly being.[8] In Mesopotamian belief, gods were enveloped in a sheen, called "luster" (*melammu*) or "terror" (*puluḫtu*),[9] or were said to be "clothed in light."[10] In the Epic of Creation, Marduk is described, indeed, as invested with the luster of ten gods.[11] The Hittites too envisaged their gods as wreathed in a nimbus called "terror" (*hatugatar*);[12] and a characteristic of Iranian deities was their *khvareno* (Old Persian, *farnah*), or brilliant radiance.[13] In the Old Testament itself this is evidently what is meant by "the glory of Yahweh";[14] and it is significant that the divine being whom Ezekiel describes as having been cast out of the divine assembly is said to have been distinguished not only by wisdom and beauty but also by "the sheen of a rising sun" (Heb.: *yif'ah*).[15] Greek gods too were signalized by a dazzling brightness,[16] though in sculpture this is portrayed only after the fifth century B.C.[17] Jamblichus (c. A.D. 250–325) preserves the ancient tradition in the statement that "when archangels appear, certain portions of the world are thrown into convulsion, and at their approach a light precedes them, but divided (i.e., forked)."[18] The divine light, it should be added, is not merely a sign of inner radiance; it symbolizes also the bedazzlement of men at the sight of that which is otherworldly. It is therefore also a divine weapon, appropriately known as "the terror."

3:5

(c) *When Yahweh takes to the warpath he is attended by two escorts:*

> *Catastrophe is his vanguard;*
> *Pestilence brings up the rear.*

What is here reflected is an ancient notion that major gods are attended, when they stir abroad, by two servitors. Thus, in the Mesopotamian Epic of Gilgamesh, when Adad brings the deluge, he is accompanied by the two gods Šullat and Ḫaniš.[19] In the Iliad, Phoebus and Ares are accompanied by Deimos, "Dread," and Phobos, "Fear";[20] and in Roman mythology Mars is similarly escorted by Pallor and Pavor. Somewhat analogously, in Czech folklore, the two demons Trâs, "Tremor," and Strakh, "Terror," leap on foes in battle.[21]—A poetic twist is given to this ancient concept in Psalm 89:14, where it is said that Steadfast Love (*Ḥesed*) and Faithfulness (or Truth: *Emeth*) attend upon Yahweh like courtiers.[22]

The concept is based on the ancient practice of dispatching messengers in pairs, lest one alone meet with mishap en route. Thus, in the Canaanite myths from Ras Shamra-Ugarit, Baal has two messengers, Gpn ("Sir Vine") and Ugr ("Sir Field"), just as the goddess 'Anat has at her command the pair Q-d-š and A-m-r-r.[23] In the Egyptian *Poem of Pentaur,* describing the battle of Kadesh in 1286 B.C., *two* bedouins (Šaśu) come from the Shabtuna district to speak with Ramses II, and *two* scouts are dispatched by the Hittite king.[24] In the Iliad, Talthybios and Eurybates are the two regular heralds of Agamemnon.[25] Indeed, the tradition that such envoys went in pairs was so ingrained that even when Homer is in fact speaking of *three* messengers, he automatically employs the dual form of the relevant verbs![26] In the Iranian national epic, Ayatar-i-Zareran, two messengers come from Arzasp to Vishtasp to urge him to give up Mazdaeism.[27]

There is a trace of the same notion elsewhere in the Old Testament itself in Gen. 19:1 ff., where *two* angels (messengers) visit Lot in Sodom (in contrast to the *three* mentioned in the preceding chapter).

In the original Hebrew, the escort here rendered "Pestilence" is named *Resheph.* This is a clear mythological allusion, for Resheph is is now well attested as the Canaanite god of plague.[28] He is portrayed in numerous figurines standing erect and brandishing a lance, but he also assailed his victims with arrows.²⁹ Indeed, in a text from Ugarit he is styled explicitly "Resheph the archer" (*bʻl ḥẓ Ršp*),³⁰ and in a far later Phoenician-Greek bilingual inscription from Cyprus (363 B.C.) he is called "Resheph of the arrow" (*Ršp ḥṣ*) and is equated with "far-darting Apollo."³¹ The arrows are, of course, the faery darts of disease and disaster such as Apollo indeed hurled upon the Achaeans at Troy (Iliad, 1.40) and are familiar to all students of folklore (see below, §275). In the ritual texts from Ugarit, Resheph is associated with the goddess ʻAnat,³² just as is Apollo with her Greek counterpart, Artemis.

In Phoenician texts from Zenčirli (9th cent. B.C.) Resheph is conjoined with El, the supreme deity, Hadad, god of the storm, and a certain Rkb-el, evidently a divine charioteer.³³ In the inscription of King Azitawadda from Karatepe (approximately the same date, or a little earlier), the god is associated with Baal and is styled "Resheph of the *ṣ-p-r-m*."³⁴ Some scholars explain this epithet from the Hebrew *ṣippôr*, "bird," and refer to the fact that at Ischiali, terra-cotta figurines supposedly representing Resheph's Mesopotamian counterpart Nergal, show a heavily armed god encased in feathers and with talons for feet.³⁵ Similarly in Greek lore, Eurynomos, a god of the netherworld, is sometimes portrayed with a vulture's head,³⁶ and at Lipsos in Ephesus, Apollo— Resheph's equivalent—was indeed called "Vulturine Apollo" (Apollōn Gypaieas).³⁷ In further support of this explanation it is pointed out that in Job 5:7 the "sons of Resheph" (KJV: wrongly, "sparks"!) are said to fly, and the Septuagint Version actually renders the expression "fledglings," while in Deuteronomy 32:24 it translates Resheph by "birds." It should be observed, however, that the Hebrew word *ṣippôr* properly refers to a twittering songbird (cf. Akkadian *ṣapāru*, "twitter") and can thus scarcely be applied to a vulture or bird of prey. It would seem preferable, therefore, to connect the epithet with the Hebrew *ṣaphîr*, "buck," seeing that Resheph is indeed sometimes associated with gazelles.³⁸

Resheph was known in Egypt as early as the time of Amenhotep II.³⁹ That monarch is described in one inscription as "striding across the River Orontes with all the fury of Resheph"⁴⁰ and in another, dealing with his association with the Great Sphinx at Gizeh, the god is again mentioned.⁴¹ A hymn to Resheph in Egyptian is also extant.⁴²

The name is sometimes used, by metonymy, in the plural to denote various forms of affliction. In Psalm 76:3 arrows are described as "Rocksheps of the bow" (RSV, wrongly: "flashing arrows"), i.e., satanic shafts; and in Song of Songs 8:6 the pangs of love are "fiery Reshephs" (RSV: "flashes of fire"). In Job 5:7, the "sons of Resheph" is a generic term for demons who hover in the air, in contrast to the "trouble" which seems to sprout out of the very earth. A similar usage appears in Egyptian.⁴³

The derivation of the name is obscure.⁴⁴ Certainly, it has no connection, as was once supposed, with the Semitic *š-r-p*, "burn"—an idea which was evidently inspired by false exegesis of Song of Songs 8:6. Most probably it is connected with an Akkadian word *rašāpu* which seems to mean "assail."[45]

In the original Hebrew, the other escort of Yahweh, here rendered "Catastrophe," is Deber, who is likewise a demonic figure of ancient folklore (see below, §275).

3:6–7

(d)
> He has halted, and shaken[46] the earth,
> looked and convulsed[47] the nations.
> Age-old mountains are riven,
> time-hallow'd hills sink low,
> as again he takes to those highways
> he trod so long ago.[48]
> When Cushan's tents were rustled,
> when Midian's tent-cloths shook.[49]

This description of Yahweh on the warpath echoes standard clichés which would have been familiar to the prophet's audience. In an Egyptian hymn to Amon, dating from the time of the New Kingdom, it is said of him that

> Earth trembles when his word resounds;
> all peoples shudder at his might;[50]

while elsewhere we read of the same god that

> When he rages, mountains tremble;
> when he roars, the earth doth shake.[51]

Similarly, in Mesopotamian hymns:

> When Adad rages, earth doth shake
> and peoples are a-tremble;[52]

and

> When he walks abroad,
> heaven and earth do quiver.[53]

Of the god Ninurta it is related specifically that he attacks mountains.[54]

3:15

Yahweh rides the waves, which are likened to his chargers:

> Thou hast trodden the sea; thy chargers
> the foam of the ocean waves.[55]

Waves are often so described in popular lore. In Old Irish poetry, for instance, "sea horse" is a common expression for "billow,"[56] and in Celtic verse, raging breakers are "the son of Ler's horses."[57] In the French district of Tréguier, an embroiled sea is called "the white mare,"[58] and the Italians speak of the waves as "charging like horses" (*acavallarsi delle onde*).[59] In English idiom, foaming waves are known popularly as "wild horses"; one recalls Matthew Arnold's lines:

> The wild horses play,
> Champ and chafe and toss in the spray.[60]

Connected with this is the representation of sea-gods and of the spirits of lakes and rivers in equine form. Poseidon, for example, is often styled "equine" (*hippios*), and the famous fountain on Mount Helicon was named "Fountain of the Horse" (Hippocrene).[61] In Scotland, the kwelpis, or spirits, who inhabit lochs are thought to be horses.[62] In Ireland, the same is said of the corresponding pookas;[63] and in Iceland, lakes are believed to be infested with sea horses called *vatnahesturs*.[64] A white horse, it is said, appears at dusk at the source of the River Seine.[65]

3:8

(e) Yahweh's onslaught is seen by the prophet as a repetition in history of the storm-god's primordial defeat of the contumacious god of the sea—the theme of the celebrated Canaanite *Poem of Baal* discovered at Ras Shamra-Ugarit.

> *Is it against the rivers,*[66]
> *against the rivers, O LORD,*
> *that thine anger (again) has been kindled,*
> *or thy wrath against the Sea,*
> *that thou comest riding thy chargers,*
> *(riding) thy chariots in triumph?*

The myth appears to have been widespread throughout the Ancient Near East. An Egyptian text, the Hearst Papyrus, alludes to the combat between Seth (i.e., Baal) and the Sea;[67] and a Hittite myth, probably redacted from a Canaanite original, has the personified Mt. Pisaisa, in Syria, exclaim: "See with what [vehemence] the storm-god attacked the sea!"[68]

The picture of Yahweh riding a chariot into battle is taken directly from more ancient pagan mythology. The Canaanite Baal is described as "he that chariots upon the clouds" (*Rkb 'rpt*)[69]—a concept likewise applied to Yahweh in divers passages of the Psalms and by the prophet Zechariah.[70] Similarly, in the Mesopotamian Epic of Creation, Marduk launches his chariot against his adversary Tiamat,[71] and such an attack is indeed portrayed on a cylinder seal of the Akkadian period (c. 2360–2150 B.C.) now in the Morgan Library in New York.[72] Chariots are likewise associated in Hittite myth with the attack of the gods upon the stone monster Ullikummi;[73] and reliefs at Imankulu and Malatya portray the weather-god riding an ox-drawn chariot.[74] In Teutonic mythology, Thor is sometimes styled Rheidhertyr, "god of the chariot";[75] and the Greek lexicographer Hesychius (4th cent. A.D.) says that "lightning is regarded as the chariot of Zeus."[76]

3:9–11

(f)
> No sooner thy bow is filled
> with the shafts at thy command,
> than lo, it is empty again![77]
>
> Thou hast carved out streams in the earth;
> Mountains have seen thee and quailed;
> the torrent has overflowed;
> loudly the deep has roared.
> The sun has forgotten to shine;
> the moon has stood still in the height,
> at the flash of thy darts as they speed,
> at the lightning glint of thy spear.

In the Canaanite (Ugaritic) myth of the fight against the Sea, Baal is armed with *clubs*,[78] but in the Mesopotamian counterpart, Marduk does indeed carry bow and arrows against Tiamat.[79]

The arrows are simply shafts of lightning. Indeed, in several poetic passages of the Old Testament (Pss. 18:15; 77:18; 144:6; Zech. 9:14), "arrows" is a synonym for "flashes of lightning." Parallels to this notion are legion. In Finnish folklore, lightning is called "the shaft of the storm-god Juoma" (*Jumolan nuoli*); in Lithuanian, it is "the arrows of Perkunos" (*Perkuno strelos*); and in Estonian, *pikse nool*. The Russians call it analogously *gromovaya strela*, and the Hungarians say that it is the dart of the god Isten (*istenyala*).[80] The Ewe of Togoland assert that the thunder-god Sogba forges arrows;[81] and a similar belief is held by the Peruvians.[82] Among both the Cheyenne and Arapaho Indians of North America, "the thunder (*bá á*) is a large bird, with a brood of smaller ones, and carries in its talons a number of arrows with which it strikes the victims of lightning."[83]

The reference to cleaving out the rivers continues the reminiscence of the ancient cosmogonic myth: after the defeat of the dragon (Sea), the waters which would otherwise have flooded the earth are confined in rivers. There is a similar allusion to this in Psalm 74:13–15:

> Thou it was shattered Sir Sea by thy strength,
> brake the heads of the dragons on the waters.
> Thou it was crushed Leviathan's heads,
> gave him as public food to hyenas.[84]
> Thou it was cleaved out fountain and river. . . .

Similarly, in a Sumerian myth, after the god (or, in another version, the goddess) has subdued the demon of the subterranean floods, the waters are channeled between the banks of the Tigris and Euphrates.[85]

There is an interesting reference to this myth in the Egyptian Leyden Magical Papyrus.[86] Hadad and his consort Shala are there said to have made ḥʿpy burst forth by striking a mountain. Now, the word ḥʿpy normally means "Nile," but to give it that sense in the passage in question would be plainly absurd because there are in fact no mountains in Egypt! It has therefore been suggested—particularly in view of the mention of the Semitic god Hadad—that this is simply a Syrian myth mechanically translated. In the original version, the word which was rendered ḥʿpy, i.e., Nile, would probably have been the common noun for "river," for in Syria and Canaan rivers are indeed opened up by lightning's striking mountains![87]

By a change of but a single letter in the consonantal Hebrew text, a parallel passage in Psalm 77:18 substitutes for the words, *The torrent has overflowed*, the clause, *(The) clouds poured water in torrents*, and this is adopted by many modern scholars. But it misses the mythological allusion, which is to the upsurging of the nether waters, eventually subdued by the storm-god when he defeats the dragon (see below, §258, on Ps. 29:10). Moreover, this meaning is developed in the parallel clause: *Loudly the deep has roared.*

3:11

(g) *Sun and moon stood still*

Notice the poet's artistry: he has just described the effect of Yahweh's actions upon mountains, rivers, and deep (vv. 6–10ᶜ), and later he portrays his furious march through the earth and his "threshing" of the nations (v. 12). Between these two passages he deftly introduces a picture of what happens meanwhile in heaven (vv. 10ᵈ–11). Unfortunately, the traditional Hebrew text is here corrupt, but a very simple emendation[88] restores yet another cliché drawn from the traditional vocabulary of pagan theophanies. In very similar terms, a Mesopotamian hymn declares that when the storm-god Adad raged,

> The sun sank to the foundation of heaven;
> the moon rose to its height.[89]

The prophet, however, also has in mind the historic realization of this scene in the incident connected with Joshua's defeat of the Amorites, when "the sun stood still in Gibeon, and the moon in the Valley of Ajalon" (Josh. 10:12–14)—an incident which must have been especially familiar through its incorporation into the popular repertoire of ballads known as the Book of Jashar (*loc. cit.*).

3:12–14

(h) *The prophet now passes to Yahweh's triumphant march through the earth:*

> In fury the earth thou bestridest,
> in anger art threshing the nations,
> as forth to the fray thou hast sallied,

> *for the victory of thy people,*
> *the victory of thine anointed,*
> *unroofing the home of the wicked,*
> *as though striking him on the head,*
> *razing it down to bedrock,*
> *as though stripping him top to toe.*[90]
> *Thou hast split the heads of his braves (?),*[91]
> *as down like a whirlwind they sweep,*
> *ready to blow us away,*
> *raising their gleeful cry*
> *like < a lion poised > to*[92] *devour*
> *some hapless wretch in the dark.*

The threshing of enemies is mentioned also in early Arabic poetry. Says 'Adi ibn Riqâ:

> When the battle raged at Rial,
> like chaff our chariots threshed the foe.[93]

Yahweh, says the prophet, has sallied forth into the battle for the victory of his people and his anointed. The latter expression would refer most naturally to the *king*. However, it is not impossible that it here refers to warriors anointed before battle. In the Canaanite *Poem of Baal,* the goddess 'Anat is anointed by that deity before embarking on a warlike mission;[94] and in the Hittite myth of Kumarbi, the chariot and equipment of an attacking god are anointed before he goes into combat.[95] Such anointment would be but a stylized conventionalization of the widespread custom of smearing warriors with animal fat in order to give them added vigor.[96]

3:16

(i) *Through all the turmoil the prophet waits with confidence:*

> *Though, when I heard the sound,*
> *mine inwards were all aquiver,*
> *my lips did twitch,*
> *my bones began to crumble,*
> *my foothold gave way,*[97]
> *yet will I wait with calm*
> *till the day of disaster break*
> *on the horde now sweeping upon us!*

Note again the poet's consummate artistry: the reference to the day which is about to break balances the initial description of Yahweh as a god who appears like sunrise in darkened skies. But there may also be a touch of satire in his words, for it was the practice of bedouin raiders to creep up on their victims under cover of night and then sweep down on them at daybreak;[98]

and that this tactic was employed also in ancient times is shown by the fact that in the Canaanite *Epic of K-r-t*, the attack on the cities of Udum is mounted at daybreak (*špšm*).[99] Hence, the prophet's meaning would be that in the present case daybreak will bring defeat, not victory, to the marauding hosts.[100]

3:17–19

(j)
>Though fig-trees blossom not,
>   nor fruit be on the vines,
>though olive-crop has failed,
>   and fields produce no food;
>though sheep from pen have dwindled,[101]
>   nor cattle remain in the byres,
>I even now will go singing
>   paeans unto the LORD,
>cry in joy to the God
>   who wins my battles for me:
>"LORD, LORD, my riches thou!"[102]
>   For he will yet send me pacing
>light-footed like a hind
>   upon my native heights!

Once again, Comparative Folklore throws unexpected light on the prophet's words: he is drawing on traditional popular poetry associated with the cult and myth of the god of fertility, whose annual disappearance caused the earth to languish, but who eventually returned to usher in a new lease of prosperity and increase. The words read, in fact, like a string of standard clichés from the liturgy of such cults. Here, for instance, are typical laments for the Mesopotamian Tammuz:

>The wailing is for the plants . . . they grow not.
>The wailing is for the barley; the ears grow not.
>The wailing is for homes and flocks; they produce not.
>. . . . .
>The wailing is for the fields of men; the *gunu* grows no more.
>. . . . .
>The wailing is for the garden storehouse: honey and wine fail.[103]

And when Tammuz is restored, it is said (in another poem):

>The figs grew large; in the plains the trees thrived(?).[104]

In the same vein, the Canaanite Baal is thus bewailed:

>The furrows of the field have gone dry. . . .
>the furrows of (all) the vast fields have gone dry!
>Baal is neglecting the furrow of the plowlands.

> Where now is Baal Puissant?
> Where is his Highness, the lord (baal) of the earth?[105]

Of the Hittite Telipinu, it is said analogously:

> Off stalked Telipinu.
> Grain and . . . increase and abundance he took away from field and meadow.
> . . . .
> Forthwith the seed ceased to yield produce;
> forthwith oxen, sheep and men ceased to breed,
> while even those that had conceived did not give birth.
> Hillsides were bare;
> trees were bare and put forth no new boughs;
> pastures were bare; springs ran dry.[106]

And this in turn recalls the description, in the Homeric *Hymn to Demeter,* of the languor which befell the earth through the rape of Persephone:

> No shoots did the earth put forth, for the fair-crowned Demeter kept the seed hidden in the ground. And many a crooked plow did the oxen drag in vain across the fields and many a stalk of barley fell fruitless and unripened to the ground. The goddess would, indeed, have destroyed the entire race of mortal men with grievous famine and have deprived of their offerings them that dwell in the Olympian mansions, had not Zeus taken thought and reflected.[107]

Zephaniah

243 Zephaniah and the pagan festivals

Comparative Folklore does for the Book of Zephaniah what it does for those of Hosea and Joel: it presents a good case for assuming that the prophet spoke against the background of a pagan seasonal festival, the principal features of which served as pegs on which to hang his message.

1:2–3

(a) The prophet opens with the words:

> Yes, I will make an ingathering ('-s-f),
> quoth the LORD,
> of all things off the face of the earth—
> an ingathering of man and beast,
> of fowl of the air and fish of the sea,
> . . . .
> and I will cut off all earthlings
> from the face of the earth!

These opening words would have sounded with special effect if the prophet were addressing the crowds at the Feast of Ingathering ('Asîf)—the autumnal harvest home. They parody the standard descriptions of the languishing earth in myths connected with the "vanished and returning" (or "dying and reviving") deities of fertility, e.g., the Canaanite myth of Baal, the Hittite myth of Telipinu, the Babylonian Tammuz dirges, and the Homeric *Hymn to Demeter* (see above, §242).

Moreover, that they were indeed uttered against the background of ritual practices is shown clearly by the reference, in the very next verse, to the eunuch priests of Baal and to the custom, attested also in a Canaanite text from Ras Shamra-Ugarit,[1] of worshiping the host of heaven on rooftops.

1:7

(b) Yahweh has arranged a banquet[2]
 has invited his guests.

A common feature of seasonal festivals is a banquet of the gods, designed originally to recement by commensality their ties of "kinship" with their worshipers.[3]

The Mesopotamian New Year (Akîtu) Festival is sometimes characterized as a "banquet" (*kirêtu*)[4] or "collation (*tâkaltu*).[5] This is mythologized in the Epic of Creation, then recited, as the banquet of the gods after Marduk has defeated Tiamat and been installed in his newly built palace (temple), Esagila.[6] Similarly, in the Canaanite *Poem of Baal,* that god, after vanquishing his rival Yam, regales the gods in a newly built palace.[7]

In the Hittite myth of Telipinu, the return of that lord of fertility to the earth is celebrated by a banquet attended by the gods, notably by the Ladies of Fate (Gulses), the goddess of increase (Miyantazipas) and the god of grain (Halkis).[8] So too, in the cult-text of the Puruli-festival, after the Weather-god has subdued the Dragon the gods convene, and food (*galaktar*) is served to them.[9]

In Greece, an annual regalement of the gods (*theoxenia*) was held at Delphi in the month of Boedromion (Sept.-Oct.);[10] and such a banquet was likewise a feature of the later mysteries of Attis.[11]

A vivid description of such feasts, as seen through Canaanite eyes in the second millennium B.C., is afforded by three mutually complementary (or parallel) texts discovered at Ras Shamra-Ugarit.[12]

The occasion is the return to the earth and the installation of Baal, lord of rainfall and fructifier of the soil. It takes place at the season when summer fruits are gathered, i.e., in September-October.[13] Various gods are invited to a banquet lasting several days. The affair is designated a "council" or "moot" (*sd*).[14] They come riding to their host's "place" (*atr*) in chariots, or mounted on asses, and foregather appropriately at the threshing floors or plantations, where they are regaled by the mortal king Daniel, known to us also from the *Poem of Aqhat.*[15] They are accompanied by their sons (*bn*) and grandsons (*bn bn*), and each of the youngsters (*sǵr*) is assured that the beautiful goddess 'Anat herself will clasp his hand and kiss his lips.[16] At the scene of assembly they find a mighty host of their divine brethren engaged, "shoulder to shoulder," oldsters and youngsters alike, in various kinds of diversion, and forming a bodyguard for (or: paying honor to) the newly appointed lord and king.[17] 'Anat herself—the Canaanite Diana—fares forth to catch game for the repast, and herself flushes fowl from the bushes.[18] The fare consists of oxen, fatted sheep, lambs, and tender yearling kids. Olive branches shimmer like silver,[19] and dates gleam like gold before the eyes of all who frequent the scene, and the table is fragrant with vine blossoms fit for kings. The wine is of the finest, not just such as comes from spare gleanings.[20] Crescent-shaped loaves of fine Lebanese flour are served,[21] and the drink is so profuse that one might fancy all the wells of Lebanon had poured forth their contents.[22] The guest of honor has been appointed by divine decree to reign over the land of Amurru,²³ i.e., Syria, and, as the divine cultivator of the soil,²⁴ he is regaled with new wine fresh as dew.²⁵ Oil is poured over his head, and on the seventh day of the feast—the Israelite Feast of Ingathering lasted seven days—he apparently addresses his colleagues (the text is here defective) and formally announces to them that "My father [has appointed me your king]."²⁶

Jewish popular lore projected this annual banquet into eschatology: just as at the beginning of each year, so at the beginning of the New Age, Yahweh would tender a banquet to the faithful, the viands being the flesh of the monsters Leviathan and Behemoth.²⁷ Says a liturgical poet of the eleventh century:

> Then round about, on golden chairs
> (Each one approach'd by seven stairs)
> The righteous as His guests shall dine,
> And perfect bliss shall be their wine;
> And overhead, for chandeliers,
> Shall hang the radiance of the spheres,
> A beauty which no lips can tell,
> Whereon no earthly eye can dwell,
> A starry glory which of old
> No prophet's vision e'er foretold.²⁸

1:5

(c) *Punishment will be meted out upon those who have sworn allegiance to Yahweh, yet now take oaths by their king.*

In the seasonal myths, the banquet provides an opportunity for acknowledging the new divine king—evidently a projection of the rite in which the sovereign was annually reinstated or reconfirmed.²⁹ Once this is realized, the standard modern emendation of the Hebrew word, *malkam*, "their king," to *Milkôm*, the god of the Ammonites, is seen to be unnecessary and, indeed, to spoil the point of the prophet's words!³⁰

(d) *Likewise destined for punishment are those "who have not gone seeking the LORD or inquiring after him."*

The words are suggested by the ritual *search* for the departed god of fertility—a common feature of pagan seasonal rituals (see above, §221).

1:8ᵃ

(e) *When Yahweh tenders his banquet, he will* lay charges against (RSV: *punish*) *the attendant officials and the royal entourage.*

Banquets were the regular concomitants, in antiquity, of parliamentary assemblies. This was the case, for instance, in Mesopotamia³¹ and it finds mythological expression in the aforementioned episode of the Epic of Creation.

Similarly, in the Egyptian *Ramesseum Drama*, which celebrates the installation of Horus as king (i.e., on the punctual level, the reconfirmation of the pharaoh), the proceedings end with a regalement of the lords of the realm.[32]

The "parliamentary banquet" was likewise a regular institution among the Persians,[33] the Homeric Greeks,[34] and the Teutons.[35]

At such assemblies the king would give his orders to his ministers (mythologically, the norms of the world would be determined) for the ensuing year.

The prophet plays satirically on this usage, for the Hebrew word for "laying charges *against*" (RSV: "punish") also means "laying charges *upon*."[36] What he is saying, therefore, is that, in accordance with established custom, Yahweh will indeed charge his guests—but with their sins!

The members of the royal entourage are designated "sons of the king,"[37] and this at once recalls the fact that in the Canaanite "banquet" text discussed above, the guests are expressly invited to bring their sons and grandsons. The lesser members of the court are likened satirically to these youngsters at the divine banquet.

1:8ᵇ

(f) *Punishment will be visited also on "all who dress in foreign raiment."*

In the context of the prophet's message this means, of course, all who affect alien modes. The particular image may have been suggested, however, by the spectacle of the pagan worshipers wearing "fancy dress" at the seasonal festival. Designed originally to deceive the demons who were thought to be rampant on such critical occasions, this widespread custom survives in European Carnival masquerades.[38]

The general tone of the prophet's words, it may be added, find their counterpart in the contemptuous jibes leveled by Roman and Christian writers at the foppish and exotic garb affected by the devotees of Attis and Adonis.[39] In a religious medium, it is the superpatriot's cry against "foreign isms."

1:9

(g) *Likewise destined for punishment is "everyone who leaps over the threshold—men who fill their master's house with crime and fraud."*

The expression, "everyone who leaps over the threshold" is simply the Hebrew equivalent of our own colloquial "gatecrasher," and refers to those who are so eager to gain entrée into court circles that they virtually rush into the palace without decency or decorum. Once again, however, there is exquisite satire in the prophet's choice of words, for they are evidently suggested by the widespread practice of stepping over the threshold in order not to tread on the household spirits or the sainted dead, who lie beneath it. Elsewhere it is said expressly that this custom was observed by the Philistine priests when they entered the temple of Dagon at Ashdod (I Samuel, 5:5). It is clearly to some such ritual practice that the prophet alludes. Not impossibly, however, this was also standard etiquette at court. If so, we may aptly compare Marco Polo's account of the same custom at the court of the Great Chan.[40]

1:10–11

(h)   *It shall come to pass in that day*
that a loud cry will resound from the Fish-gate,
and a howl from the Second Quarter
. . . .
Howl, ye that dwell in Maktesh. . . .

A satirical allusion to the ceremonial *howling* for the vanished god of fertility (see above, §**221**).

1:12

(i)   *Yahweh "will search out*
Jerusalem with lamps."

The transition of thought, otherwise somewhat abrupt and inconsequential, becomes immediately intelligible when it is remembered that a very common feature of seasonal festivals was a *torchlight procession*.[41] This was an element, for instance, of the Babylonian New Year (Akîtu) ceremonies,[42] and an ancient Mesopotamian oracle mentions it as standard festal procedure.[43] In Greek usage, when the god Iacchos arrived in procession at Eleusis on Boedromian 20, he was welcomed by a nocturnal torchlight dance at the Callichoron,[44] and such dances were, indeed, a prominent feature of the cult of Dionysus.[45] At the festival of Thesmophoria, women paraded across the fields carrying torches,[46] and it has been suggested that it is this rite that is mythologized in the Homeric *Hymn to Demeter*, where that goddess and Hecate are portrayed as searching by torchlight for the lost Persephone.[47] Torchlight processions were likewise a feature of the mysteries of Attis.[48] The original motivation of this practice was, in the opinion of several modern scholars, to fructify the fields by warmth.[49]

As the procession wends its way through the streets, the prophet, standing as it were on the sidewalk, comments sardonically that Yahweh too has his torches—wherewith to search out sin from every nook and cranny!

1:14

(j)   *Bitter is the sound of the day of the LORD;*
('tis that of) a warrior raising his war-cry!

A further reference to pagan seasonal ceremonies may perhaps be dug out from under the traditional Hebrew text of this verse. To be sure, as it stands it yields eminently intelligible sense, and may well be correct. It has been suggested, however, that by a change of but a single letter and the regrouping of others to form different words, these lines may be made to yield the sense:

> *Swifter than a racer comes the day of the LORD,*
> *and quicker than a champion!*[50]

If this is right, it is not impossible that the words were suggested by the spectacle of a ritual *race*—a not uncommon feature of seasonal festivals. Such a race was run—to cite but a few examples—at the Babylonian New Year,[51] at the Greek Eleusinian mysteries,[52] and at the Roman festival of Robigalia,[53] and the practice is still widespread in European and Oriental calendar customs.[54] Moreover, in the Canaanite "banquet text" from Ras Shamra, which we have discussed above, there is an obscure passage which seems to say that the gods engaged in races.[55] I confess, however, that I drop this suggestion and run for my life.

3:15–19

(k) In spite of all his dire warnings, Zephaniah concludes his prophecy on a note of hope. But this too is conveyed through a skillful use of the traditional pagan pattern. Just as Baal and the other "vanished" gods of the pagan myths and rituals eventually subdue their enemies and return as conquering heroes and kings, to restore the fortunes of the languishing earth and bring "salvation" to their worshipers, so will Yahweh:

> *The LORD hath removed those things*
> *   that were as judgments upon thee;*[56]
> *He hath swept away thy foes.*
> *   The LORD shall yet be in thy midst*
> *   as king of Israel;*
> *thou shalt fear evil no more.*
> *   In that day shall it be said unto Jerusalem:*
> *"The LORD thy God is in thy midst,*
> *   a hero triumphant."*
> *He will rejoice over thee with gladness.*
> *   Though now he keep silent about his love,*
> *he then will exult over thee in a burst of song,*[57]
> *   (saying) "Them that I thrust forth from the assembly*
> *   I now have gathered in;*
> *Albeit they were the cause*
> *   of insults levelled at me,*
> *yet, withal, they came from thee.*[58]
> *   See, I will press hard*[59] *at that time*
> *on all who have oppressed thee;*
> *   The lame will I rescue, the lorn retrieve,*
> *and make them praised and renowned*
> *   who were shamed throughout the earth!*

The reference in these lines to "them that I thrust forth from the assembly" may perhaps echo the Canaanite myth of the divine banquet, for it is significant that when the gods are invited to that repast, their host declares: "Eat, ye gods, and drink: drink wine to satiety, new wine unto drunkenness. . . . He that acknowledges (lit. knows) me—let food be set for him, but he that does not acknowledge me—let them batter him under the table with a stick!"[60]

244 Ravens in ruins   2:14

> *The raven and the hedgehog shall lodge in her capitals;*
> *the owl shall hoot in the window,*
> *the raven croak[1] on the threshold.*

An ancient Arabic name for the *owl* is "mother of ruins" (*imm el-ḥarâb*).[2] The *raven* is everywhere regarded as a prophet of woe (see above, §47). In the Semitic world, the idea appears already in Babylonian literature[3] and it has counterparts in modern Arabic proverbial lore. Says one popular saying: "He is like a raven, bespeaking nothing but ruin." Says another: "Follow the raven, and he will show you nothing but ruin."[4] Such birds, haunting ruins, were thought to be demons. The Syriac writer Thomas of Marga tells us, for instance, that "while a certain man was passing at night along the road by the side of a fire temple of the Magians which had been a ruin for some time, devils sprung out upon him in the form of black ravens."[5]

Zechariah

245 Zechariah and the pagan festivals Zech. 9–12

Zechariah is yet another of the minor prophets who evidently spoke against the background of pagan seasonal festivals—in this case, the Feast of Ingathering which inaugurated the rainy season. Thus, when he describes the final Day of Doom as *a singular kind of day . . . neither day nor night, seeing that at eventide it shall be light* (14:7), the image may well have been suggested by the fact that ancient seasonal festivals were commonly celebrated at solstice or equinox.[1] In Mesopotamia, for example, the rites of Tammuz were held in the month of the vernal solstice,[2] and the prophet Ezekiel—though he seems to have muddled his dates—expressly associates the weeping for that god with a ceremony of adoring the rising sun (Ezek. 8:14–16). Similarly, the Ugaritic *Poem of the Gracious Gods,* which can be shown to have been the "book of words" for a spring festival, includes a liturgical invocation addressed not only to the gods responsible for grain and wine, but also to the Sun-goddess;[3] while in the *Poem of Baal,* which is really the cult-myth of the autumn festival, a particularly important role is assigned to that same deity. She is, in fact, formally commended for the part she plays in retrieving Baal from the netherworld.[4] Significant also is the fact that among the Israelites themselves both the spring festival (Pentecost) and the autumnal Feast of Ingathering fell in the months of the equinoxes.[5]

The Asianic "mysteries" of Attis likewise culminated on the day of the vernal equinox (March 25);[6] while it should be observed also that in Syria and the Eastern portions of the Roman Empire, the Festival of the New Age (Aiōn) was combined with the alleged birthday of the sun on November 18.[7] Indeed, so firmly established was the connection between festivals of the New Life and these crucial solar dates that the Church was eventually obliged to fix Christmas on what originally had been the birthday of the solarized hero Mithra, and to associate the date of Christ's resurrection with the vernal equinox.[8]

Again, when the prophet holds out to his people the hope that eventually *Living waters shall go out from Jerusalem, in summer and winter alike* (14:8), his words are probably motivated by the thought that at the season of the autumn festival the riverbeds have not yet been replenished and the soil still depends for its moisture on those "perpetual streams" (Heb.: *'ethanim*) after which the relevant month was indeed named. Moreover, when he adds to this assurance the dire warning (*ib.*) that the punishment of the impious will consist of a dearth of winter rains (Heb.: *geshem*), what he clearly has in mind is that the autumnal festival marks the official beginning of the rainy season.[9] So too, when he describes how pilgrims will *come annually to pay homage to the King, the Lord of Hosts at the Feast of Booths* (14:16, 18), he is quite obviously thinking of the fact that an essential feature of Ancient Near Eastern seasonal festivals was the ceremonial installation of the god as king, or of the mortal king as his human embodiment or viceroy.[10]

Nor is it only by inference and innuendo that the prophet alludes to these pagan rites, for when he admonishes his listeners that in the last days *the mourning in Jerusalem will be as great as that for Hadad-Rimmon in the plain of Megiddo* (12:11), he is making direct reference to the standard ritual wailing for Baal-Hadad, the god of rainfall and fertility, who is ousted from the earth during the dry summer.[11] In the Canaanite (Ugaritic) *Poem of Baal,* the goddess 'Anat is said to roam the uplands (like Demeter in search of Persephone), gashing her flesh and crying, "Baal is dead!"[12]

246 Teraphîm   10:2

The teraphîm utter nonsense,
and the diviners claim visions falsely.

The teraphîm are the household gods, from whom oracles were sought (see above, §68).

Malachi

247 Malachi's picture of the Last Days

The prophecies which go under the name of "Malachi" were composed in the fifth century B.C., when, after the conquest of Babylon by Cyrus (539), the Jews had come under Persian rule. This brought them into direct contact with Zoroastrian and earlier Mazdean lore and—at least on the popular level, profoundly influenced the traditional patterns of religious thought. From the Persians the Jews adopted and adapted an extensive folklore of angels, archangels, spirits, and demons. Ahriman, captain of the evil ones, became Satan, "the Obstructer," or Belial, "the Good-for-Nothing"; Druj, the spirit of falsehood, who constantly opposed Asha, "the Right," became Mastemah, the female demon of Hostility. The elaborate and lurid eschatology of the Iranians also found its way into popular Jewish thought: there would be a final ordeal by fire, in which wickedness would be purged, to be followed by the appearance of a savior or champion who would bring about the regeneration of the world and usher in a golden age of prodigious increase and prosperity. These apocalyptic ideas, which are extensively developed in the intertestamental literature and in the Dead Sea Scriptures,[1] have long been recognized in the Biblical Book of Daniel, written during the Hellenistic period, but they may also be detected, if one look closely, in the graphic description of the Last Days which forms the concluding portion of the prophecies of "Malachi."[2] The following are the more arresting parallels:

3:1

(a) *Yahweh will send his messenger, to prepare the way before him.*

The Renewal of the World (*frashokereti*) will be inaugurated by the appearance of a "savior" (*saoshyant*).[3]

(b) *The Lord* (Heb.: 'ādôn), *for whom people are looking, will then return suddenly to his palace,*
The 'messenger (angel) of the covenant'[4] *is already on his way.*

Ahura Mazdāh, "the Wise Lord," will reassert his sovereignty over men.

A leading aide of Ahura Mazdāh, often regarded as virtually his equal, is *Mithra*, who is the genius of covenants or contracts.[5] (In Avestan literature *mithra* indeed occurs as a common noun meaning "covenant").[6]

3:2

(c) *The Final Day (era) will be "like a refiner's fire, and like fuller's soap."*

The Iranians held that the Renewal of the World would be preceded by an "ordeal of molten metal" (*aya khshusta*) in which the wicked would be refined, while to the righteous it would be like warm milk.[7] The Book of Daniel (12:10) speaks similarly of a final "refinement" of "many men"; and in the Dead Sea Scrolls, the "era of refinement" is a specific eschatological period.[8]

The doctrine easily gets confused, alike in the intertestamental literature and in the New Testament, with the alternative notion that the present world will end in a conflagration (*ekpyrōsis*)[9] — a notion common also in Neo-Stoic speculation.[10]

3:5

(d) *This will be followed by a Judgment in which Yahweh will appear as a "swift (or, expert?) witness" against sorcerers and other evildoers.*

In Iranian doctrine, the Ordeal of Molten Metal is followed in short order by a Last Judgment.[11]

Moreover, the specification of sorcerers is especially interesting in view of the fact that Zoroastrianism made a particular point of denouncing sorcery as an evil creation of Angra Mainyu (Ahriman). Not only is it condemned in native works of all periods,[12] but testimony to the same effect is also borne unanimously by Greek writers. Dino, for example, states in his *Persica* that the Magi abhorred divination;[13] and Sotion, on the authority of the same writer and Aristotle, says that sorcery was unknown among them.[14]

3:6

(e) *The pious and God-fearing have been registered in God's special record.*

In later Pahlevi works of Zoroastrianism it is said that thrice daily, the spirit Vohuman ("Good Mind") notes down the good and evil deeds of everyone in the Book of Life.[15] True, the idea does not seem to be attested in earlier Iranian sources. Nevertheless, it appears not infrequently in intertestamental literature and is therefore certainly of higher antiquity.[16]

248 The sun of righteousness — 4:2

After the annihilation of the wicked by fire, the "sun of righteousness" will rise for the God-fearing "with healing in its wings."

The "sun of righteousness" is a Hebrew counterpart of Mithra, who is also the lord of light and the champion of righteousness and truth.[1]

The notion is influenced also by the pagan notion that the savior-god or savior-king will appear at the dawn of the New Age in the form of an effulgent sun.[2] The idea originated in the fact that the Festival of the New Age—itself a projection of the seasonal regeneration—often coincided with the winter solstice, when the sun began its ascent from the nether regions.[3] The major festival of Mithra was celebrated on that date,[4] as was also the birthday of Aion (the New Age) in Hellenistic times.[5] In Imperial Rome, this was likewise the birthday of Sol Invictus,[6] and at Durostorum in Silestria, the Roman troops held the festival of Kronos-Helios on that day.[7] The Egyptians said that Osiris had been born at the winter solstice,[8] and the Nabateans said the same of their god Dusares.[9] It was, indeed, on account of such time-honored associations that Pope Julius, in the fourth century, chose December 25 as the birthday of him who was to the Christians *lux mundi*.[10]

The solar disc is often portrayed with wings in Ancient Near Eastern art,[11] and this form of representation is increasingly common in Achaemenian times.—An interesting parallel to the notion occurs among the Ibo-Itsi of Africa, where one of the tribal scarification marks is a winged sun.[12]

Mithra is indeed a god of healing,[13] but the notion of the sun with healing in its wings is probably indebted also to ideas associated with the Semitic Shamash, who is frequently invoked in Mesopotamian texts to provide cures for ailments.[14] Similarly, too, in a Canaanite text from Ras Shamra-Ugarit, the sun-goddess is besought, while on her daily round, to bring a charm against snakebite to various cities whose own gods have remained powerless against it.[15]

A more familiar parallel is afforded by the healing powers of the Greek Phoebus-Apollo.[16]

Not impossibly, the prophet's words are also inspired by a popular belief, attested elsewhere, that the sun is refreshed nightly by a healing draught or by some other substance hidden in the nether waters.[17]

249 The Second Coming of Elijah 4:5

The "savior" and regenerator in the Last Days is identified as the prophet Elijah.

The immediate reason for this identification is that Elijah was translated to heaven in a fiery chariot (see above, §159). He therefore never died, but will eventually return—a notion which is commonplace in later Jewish folklore.[1] It is significant, however, that in this manner of disappearance Elijah duplicates Mithra, who was likewise carried aloft in the chariot of the sun, but who will likewise return in the Last Days to do battle against the forces of evil and help bring about the Renewal of the World.[2]

In Christian art, the ascent of the soul after death is sometimes symbolized on sarcophagi by the portrayal of Elijah ascending in the fiery chariot. Not impossibly, this mode of representation was influenced, or even suggested, by similar portrayals on the tombstones of the followers of Mithra.[3] This would then be an excellent parallel to what Malachi is here doing.

NOTES

ISAIAH

171 Whispering in charms

1. T. H. Gaster, in Orientalia 11 (1942), 64.
2. Andrew Lang, Custom and Myth (1885), 43; A. Dieterich, Mithrasliturgie³ (1910), 42; W. Gesenius, Thesaurus, s.v. ṣ-f-f; P. Lagarde, Ges. Abh. (1866), 45, n.4.
3. Maqlû, ed. Tallquist, ii.17, 68, 91 (šaptu muṣṣapratu); IV R 16, rev. 60 f.; P. Jensen, in ZK 2 (1885), 310.
4. I. Goldziher, in Noeldeke Festschrift (1906), i.306; cf. also: Bar Bahlul 337.
5. Lucian, Dial. meretr. iv.5; cf. Ovid, Met. xiv.57; Apuleius, Met. 23.
6. Grimm-Stallybrass, TM 1224.
7. A. Dieterich, Abraxas (1891), 177.6–7; id., Mithrasliturgie³, 5.23; S. Eitrem, Papyri Osloenses i (1925), i.356; K. Preisendanz, Papyri magici Graeci (1928–31), #12.40, 49; E. Riess, in Latomus 2 (1938), 173.
8. J. Montgomery, Aramaic Incantation Texts from Nippur (1913), 60.
9. S. Euringer, in ZS 6 (1925), 178.25 (and 185n.).
10. Tibullus, i.2, 47.
11. V. Lanternari, The Religions of the Oppressed (1965), 199; Robert Louis Stevenson, In the South Seas, 274 f.

172 Soul-boxes

1. Isa. 3:16–24.
2. Isa. 3:20.
3. "Johnson's learned sock" was on when he wrote these beautiful verses, for the idea was borrowed from Philostratus, Epist. ii: "I have sent thee a wreath of roses, not to honor thee but to grace them, that they wither not." Similarly, the thought of the first stanza derives from Philostratus, Epist. xxxiii.

173 Waistcloths and shoestrings

1. I*AB i.4; T. H. Gaster, Thespis², 201 f.
2. Superstit. 109, Kock.
3. Policrat. ii.8.
4. Cf. A. S. Pease, on Cicero, De Divinatione ii.84 (abruptio corrigiae).
5. HN viii.221.
6. Folk-Lore 13 (1902), 50.

174 Seraphim

1. Herodotus, ii.75; iii.109.
2. Max von Oppenheim, Der Tell Halaf (1943–50), Pl. xxxib.
3. Gesenius-Buhl, HWb 794ᵇ.

176 "A virgin shall conceive": Immanuel

1. *Literature:* Aziz, in Al Mashriq 24 (1900); C. F. Burney, in JTS 10 (1909), 580 f.; K. Fullerton, in JBL 35 (1916), 134 ff.; id., in AJSL 34 (1918), 256–83; F. C. Ackerman, in AJSL 35 (1919), 205–14; E. G. Kraeling, in JBL 50 (1931), 277–97; K. Budde,

in JBL 52 (1933), 22–24; A. von Bulmerincq, in Acta et Commentationes Univ. Tartuensis, B 37/i (1935), 1–17; E. Hamershaib, in Studia Theologica 3 (1949), 124 ff.; J. Coppens, in Analecta Lovanensiana bibl. et or. ii/35 (1952); J. J. Stamm, in VT 4 (1954), 20 ff.; id., in ZAW 68 (1956), 46 ff.; id., in TZ (Basle) 16 (1960), 439–55; L. Koehler, in ZAW 67 (1955), 48 ff.; J. Lindblom, A Study in the Immanuel Section in Isaiah (1957–58); F. L. Moriarty, in CBQ 19 (1957), 226 ff.; H. L. Ginsberg, in J. N. Epstein Denkschrift (1950), 29–32. See also: G. Gutknecht, Das Motiv der Jungfraugeburt in religionsgesch. Beleuchtung (Diss. Greifswald 1953).

2. Nikkal 7 (*hl ǵlmt tld b[n]*).
3. E. Norden, Die Geburt des Kindes (1924).
4. For the evidence, see: T. H. Gaster, Thespis[2], 414 f.
5. Mrs. E. D. von Buren, in Orientalia 13 (1944), 1–72.
6. Statue E, 51–53.
7. Cyliner B, iv.23–v.19.
8. S. Langdon, PBS X.1 (JRAS 1926.36 ff.)
9. VAT 633, obv. 1–10.
10. Ib., 14–21; G. Reisner, Sum.-bab. Hymnen (1896), ii.12–32; R. Pfeiffer, State Letters of Assyria (1935), #217 (reign of Esarhaddon, 681–668 B.C.).
11. Syria 19 (1938), 23.
12. H. Frankfort, OIC 17, p. 48, fig. 42.
13. H. Junker, Die Onurislegende (1917), 116 ff.
14. W. Wolf, Das schöne Fest von Opet (1931), 72 ff.; A. Blackman, Luxor and Its Temples (1923), 70.
15. K. Sethe, Untersuchungen, iv (1905), 219 f.
16. De rep. ath. iii.5.
17. Alexander, 38.
18. Philosophoumena, p. 170, ed. Cruice.
19. Strabo, x.3, 11.
20. R. M. Dawkins, in JHS 26 (1906), 191; M. Beza, Paganism in Roumanian Folklore (1928), 51.
21. E.g., CIS I.86, B 9 (from Citium, Cyprus). Note, however, that L. Koehler (loc. cit.) would interpret the word in Isaiah as a collective, i.e., "Young women, when they bear sons, will give them such significant names as Immanuel (God-is-with-us)."
22. See: O. S. Rankin, The Origin of the Feast of Hanukkah (1930), and cf. Macrobius, Sat. i.18; Claudian De iv. Caes. honor. 570 ff.; Norden, op. cit., 25; Schol. Greg. Naz.: *hê parthenos tetoken, auxei phôs* ("the virgin has given birth; light will increase"); cf. K. Holl, in Sitzb. Berlin. Akad. 1917.427, n.4.
23. L. Duchesne, Christian Worship[2], tr. McClure (1904), 261 f.—In an earlier period, the solstice fell on January 6–7; hence, the birth of the Savior or New Aion was celebrated on that date: Epiphanius, haeres. li.22, 8 f.; cf. H. Engberding, in ALW 2 (1952); L. Fend, in TLZ 78 (1953), i.1–10; R. J. Z. Werblowsky, in RHR 145 (1954), 35 ff.
24. Isa. 9:1.

177 Gibbering ghosts and mediums

1. E. B. Tylor, Primitive Culture, ii.540; Nicolaus Remigius, Daemonolatria (1596), i. ch. 8 (on the authority of Psellus).
2. Iliad 23.100; Odyssey 23.101; 24.5.
3. Vergil, Aeneid vi.492.
4. Sat. i.8, 40.
5. Phars. vi.23.
6. Theb. vii.770.

7. Fasti v.458.
8. Satyricon 122, 137.
9. In Ruf. i.126.
10. H. Callaway, Religious Systems of the Amazulu (1868–70), 265, 348, 370.
11. E. Shortland, Traditions and Superstitions of the New Zealanders[2] (1856), 92.
12. E. Crawley, The Idea of the Soul (1909), 102.
13. W. Ellis, Polynesian Researches[2] (1832–36), i.406.
14. Fr. Lejeune, in Relations des Jesuites 1634.13; 1639.43.
15. R. F. Burton, First Footsteps in East Africa (1910), 42 (*sifr*).

178 Cursing by king and god

1. This is commonly rendered, after Septuagint and Vulgate, *They . . . will curse their king and their god,* though RSV, in a footnote, concedes the alternative translation. The common rendering, however, involves a grammatical anomaly in the Hebrew text, for nowhere else is the word for "curse," viz., *q-l-l*, construed, as here, with the preposition *b-* of the direct object. Indeed, the true meaning comes out very clearly from the next verse, where that preposition is omitted in speaking of the cursing of the territories of Zebulun and Naphtali (direct object). A distinction in sense must therefore be implied by the variant constructions, and this can be elucidated from the fact that the preposition *b-* is similarly employed after the same verb in I Samuel 17:43, to indicate that *by which* one curses.—Interestingly enough, the Greek (Septuagint) Version, according to the best reading, renders "his gods" by the word *patakhra*, "idols"—a loan-word from Iranian which is widely employed in Aramaic and Mandaean magical incantations: see J. A. Montgomery, Aramaic Incantation Texts from Nippur (1913), 72.
2. See: E. Westermarck, The Origin and Development of the Moral Ideas[2] (1912–17), i.564; E. Crawley, Oath, Curse and Blessing [reprint of art. Oath in ERE] (1934), 36 f.
3. R. H. Codrington, The Melanesians (1891), 51.
4. Ib., 217.
5. G. Furlani, La religione babilonese e assira (1929), ii.292 ff.; J. Pedersen, Der Eid bei den Semiten (1914).
6. S. A. B. Mercer, The Oath in Babylonian and Assyrian Literature (1912), 7 ff.
7. Cf. H. Liebesny, in JAOS 61 (1941), 62–63.
8. See: J. A. Wilson, in JNES 7 (1948), 129–56; J. G. Frazer, GB[2], i.419.

179 The dawn of salvation

1. VAT 8896.1.

180 "Lucifer, son of the morning"

Literature: N. König, in ET 1907.479; K. Schmidt, in ThZ 3 (1951); T. H. Gaster, Thespis[2], 412; B. Bamberger, Fallen Angels (1952); R. de Vaux, in RB 46 (1937), 546 f.
1. J. Lewy, in RHR 110 (1934), 43 f.
2. E. R. Hodges, ed., Cory's Ancient Fragments (1876), 12. The comparison was made by O. Eissfeldt at the Twentieth International Congress of Orientalists, Brussels, 1938.
3. H. G. Güterbock, Kumarbi (1946); A. Goetze, ANET 120 ff.; T. H. Gaster, The Oldest Stories in the World (1952), 110.
4. A. Goetze, Verstreute Boghazköi-Texte (1930), #58; T. H. Gaster, Thespis[2], 270 ff.
5. Hesiod, Theogony 154–210, 453 ff.
6. H. G. Güterbock, in AJA 52 (1948), 123–34; N. O. Brown, Hesiod's Theogony (1953), 36 ff.; F. M. Cornford, Principium Sapientiae (1952), 209 ff.; F. Vian, La

guerre des géants (1952); A. Lesky, "Hethitische Texte und griechischen Mythos"; "Osterreichische Anzeiger 51 (1952), 137–59.

7. Cf. J. Morgenstern, in HUCA 14 (1939), 70, n.4; 112, n.153; Gaster, op. cit., 412.

8. Enoch 1:5; 10:9; 12:2; 13:10, etc., and esp. 15:8; II Enoch 18:1–6; 24:4–5; Vita Adae et Evae, chs. 13–16; Qumran Genesis Aprocryphon, tr. T. H. Gaster, The Scriptures of the Dead Sea Sect in English Translation (1957), 330.

181 The fate of Sargon

1. For the traditional text's *mi-qibreka* read simply *mi-qeber* (with prefix in privative sense). The final letter of the traditional reading is simply dittography from the next word.

2. Heb. *ke-neṣer nitcab*. There is no need to emend the text, as is usually done. Heb. *neṣer* means "twig," as in Isa. 60:21; Dan. 11:7 (cf. also Aramaic *niẓrâ*; Arabic *n-ẓ-r*, "be green"). The proud king is likened to foliage once blossoming gloriously but eventually fallen, sodden and mired. Moreover, if, as some scholars think, the prophecy really refers to Nebuchadnezzar, rather than to Sargon, the word *neṣer* would contain a pun on the second element of his name, as written in Hebrew. The Septuagint Version, however, has *nekros* ("corpse"); Aquila has *ichôr*, and the Vulgate *sanies*, while the Syriac and Aramaic versions render "untimely birth." This may point to a variant reading *neṣel* (as in post-Biblical Hebrew) or even to *nephel* (cf. Ps. 58:9; Eccles. 6:3).

3. R. C. Thompson, Semitic Magic (1908), 17; W. A. I. 17; P. Haupt, Akkad. und Sumer. Keilschrifttexte (1881), 11.ii, 6; K. 2175.i, 6–8 = Thompson, in PSBA 1906.219 ff.

4. Josephus, Contra Apionem 1.20.

182 Flying serpents

1. Herodotus, ii.75; iii.109.

2. Lucan, Phars. vi.677.

3. C. Clermont-Ganneau, in Réc. d'archéol. orientale 4 (1880), 319; C. Landberg, Hadramout (1901), 137. Cf. A. Lods, Israël (1930), 275.

4. S. Baring-Gould, Curious Myths of the Middle Ages (New York 1884), 201.

184 The gardens of Adonis

1. Scholiast, on Theocritus, Id., xv.112. See further: Greve, De Adonide (1877), 37–41; Rochette, in Rev. archéol. 8 (1881), 97–123; W. von Baudissin, Adonis und Esmun (1911), 87 ff., 139 ff.; W. H. Engel, Kypros (1841), ii.548 ff.; Ohnefalsch-Richter, Kypros, die Bibel und Homer (1893), i.139 f.

2. Frag. 514 (Melanippe).

3. Phaedrus, 276B.

4. Hist. plant. vi.7, 3.

5. E.g., Zenobius i.29; Philostratus, Vita Apoll. vii.32; Julian, Conviv. 423 Hertlein; Suidas, Lex. s.v.

6. Rashi, on TB Shabbath 81ᵇ. (The boxes are called *p-r-p-s-y-a*, which is the Greek *paropsis*.)

7. A. Neppi Modena, in Bylinchis: fascicolo in ommagio al Congresso internat. di storia delle religioni a Parigi, 1923.

8. G. Pitré, Spettacoli e feste populari siciliani (1881), 211; E. Caetani-Lavatelli, Antichi Monumenti (1889), 61 ff.; Frazer-Gaster, NGB §216.

9. A. Bresciani, Dei costumi dell' isola di Sardegna (1886), 427 f.; W. Baumgartner, in Archives suisses des traditions populaires 43 (1946), 122–48; V. Dorsa, La tradizione greco-latina negli usi populari della Calabria Citeriore (Cosenza 1884), 50.

10. A. Mariette, Denderah (1873–80), iv.35; A. Moret, Rois et dieux d'Égypte

(1922), 102; id., La mise à mort du dieu en Égypte (1927), 39; N. G. Davies and A. H. Gardiner, The Tomb of Amenemhet (1915), 115; H. Carter, The Tomb of Tutankhamen (1923–27), iii.161, pl. 64.

11. E. Thurston, Ethnographic Notes in Southern India (1906), 2.

12. E. T. Dalton, Descriptive Ethnography of Bengal (1872), 259; S. C. Roy, The Oraons (1915), 243.

13. F. C. Movers, Die Phönizier (1841–56), i.217; A. Jirku, in VT 7 (1956), 201 f.

14. J. Wellhausen, Reste d. arab. Heidentums² (1897), 110. Cf. Ovid, Met. x.735; Servius, on Vergil, Aen. v.72. This etymology, however, is disputed by Wellhausen, op. cit., 70, and by I. Löw, Aramäische Pflanzennamen (1881), 201n.; 411, n.90.

185 The rebel constellations

1. Enuma Elish vii.27.

2. S. Langdon, The Epic of Creation (1923), 34 ff. See also the text published by T. G. Pinches in PSBA 1908.53 ff.

3. Rev. 12:7–9.

4. Hesiod, Theog. 617 ff.; Apollodorus, Bib. i.2, 4.

5. Enoch 86:1; 88; 90:20–21; J. Morgenstern, in HUCA 14 (1939), 100; T. H. Gaster, Thespis², 412; B. Bamberger, Fallen Angels (1952).

6. Enoch 21:3 ff.; cf. also ib., 18:13 ff.

7. Jude 13.

8. J. Montgomery, Aramaic Incantation Texts from Nippur (1913), #4.4–5.

9. Qolasta, 75; M. Lidzbarski, Liturgien, 127; E. S. Drower, The Canonical Prayerbook of the Mandaeans (1959), 75.

10. For this sense of the verb *p-q-d,* cf. Isa. 38:10.

11. Enuma Elish, loc. cit.

12. PSBA 1908.53, col. i.

13. Enoch 21:3 ff.

14. Montgomery, loc. cit.: *w'd š'tâ rbty dprqnâ.*

15. For the verb *'a-s-f* in this sense, cf. I Sam. 14:52; 17:1; Zech. 14:2.

186 Leviathan

1. Cf. T. H. Gaster, Thespis², 249 f.

2. S. N. Kramer, Sumerian Mythology (1944), 80 ff.; T. Jacobsen, in JNES 5 (1946), 146–47.

3. Enuma Elish, tab. iv.

4. KBo III.7; KUB XII.66; XVII.5–6; tr. A. Goetze, ANET 125–26; T. H. Gaster, op. cit., 245–67.

5. The so-called Poem of Baal; cf. Gaster, op. cit., 134–244.

6. I*AB, 1–2; Gaster, op. cit., 201 f.

7. J. Montgomery, Aramaic Incantation Texts from Nippur (1903), #2.4, 6. The word here rendered "fate" is the Aramaic *š-m-t-â* = Akkadian *šimtu.*

8. Rig Veda i.32; cf. A. A. Macdonell, Vedic Mythology (1897), 56–60, 158 f.

9. Hesiod, Theogony 820 ff.; Aeschylus, Prometheus Vinctus 351 ff.; Apollodorus, Bib. i.6, 3; Ovid, Met. v.319 ff.; Hyginus, fab. 152. Cf. Porzig, in KlF 1 (1930), 376–86.

10. L. Bechstein, Thüringer Sagenbuch (1885), #190.

11. Ugaritica V (1967), #7. The explanation of the name is my own.

12. Egyptian *djeser tep* (Chicago Oriental Institute, #16881.14); cf. K. C. Steele, in JNES 6 (1947), 47, n.56.

187 The "Name of the LORD" as his agent

1. II AB, B 8; Krt c, vi.55.

2. G. A. Cooke, A Text-book of North Semitic Inscriptions (1903), 37.

3. Cf. Stith Thompson, MI, F. 531.3.8; B 14.1.
4. Gilgamesh iii.109–111.
5. Hesiod, Theogony 820 ff.; cf. Aeschylus, Prometheus Vinctus 351 ff.

188 The haunts of demons

1. R. C. Thompson, Semitic Magic (1908), 92; K 4347, obv. ii.50–51 = S. Langdon, in AJSL 28 (1911), 222. See also: A. Smythe Palmer, Babylonian Influences in the Bible, etc. (1897), 72 ff.; A. Lods, Israël (1930), 276.
2. J. Wellhausen, Reste d. arab. Heidentums[2] (1897), 135–40.
3. Zohar i.188a–b; Sepher ha-Yashar, Wa-tišlaḥ, 70a; L. Ginzberg, Legends of the Jews (1909 sqq.), v.322.
4. ii.599, ed. Budge.
5. E. W. Budge, Lady Meux MSS, Nos. 2–5.216.
6. T. H. Gaster, Thespis[2], 218, n.9.
7. Matt. 12:43; Luke 4:1–2.
8. R. Trench, Studies in the Gospels (1867), 7.
9. John Milton, Comus 207–9.
10. R. Burton, Anatomie of Melancholy, i.2, 2.
11. I, p. xxix, and ch. 57 sub init., ed. Yule.
12. N. Prejevalsky, Mongolia (1876), i.194.
13. F. Lenormant, Chaldaean Magic (1877), 245 f.
14. K. Tallquist, Namen der Totenwelt (1934), 17 ff. See also (but with caution): A. Haldar, The Notion of the Desert in Sumero-accadian and West Semitic Religions (1950).

189 Hairy devils

1. J. Montgomery, Aramaic Incantation Texts from Nippur (1913), #5.4.
2. Maimonides, Guide for the Perplexed, iii.46, says that the Sabaeans regarded certain demons as goats and so called them.
3. Jewish Encyclopaedia, i.605.
4. E. S. Drower, The Mandaeans of Iraq and Iran (1937), 349–50.
5. Grimm-Stallybrass, TM ii.478 ff.; J. Schmidt, "Der Schkrat," in Edda 4 (1892), 218–21, 251–54.
6. Cf. W. Roscher, Ephialtes (1900), 29 f., 62, 285; O. Gruppe, Griech. Mythologie (1906), 1386, n.2.

190 Lilith

1. R. C. Thompson, The Devils and Evil Spirits of Babylonia (1904), i. p. xxxvii; KAT[3] 460; J. Montgomery, Aramaic Incantation Texts from Nippur (1913), 75 ff.; T. H. Gaster, in Orientalia 11 (1941), 40 ff.; C. Frank, Bab. Beschwörungsreliefs (1900); id., Lamashtu, Pazuzu, und andere Dämonen (1940); D. Myhrman, Labartu-Texte (1901); F. Thureau-Dangin, in RA 18 (1921), 161–98; H. Klengel, "Neue Lamaštu-Amulette," in MIOr 7 (1960), 334–55.
2. R. C. Thompson, Semitic Magic (1908), 65 ff.
3. T. H. Gaster, The Holy and the Profane (1955), 18–27.
4. Id., in Orientalia 11 (1942), 41–76.
5. See: M. Gaster, in Folklore 1900.126–62; I. Zolli, in Filologische Schriften 2 (1929), 121–42; G. Kittredge, Witchcraft in Old and New England (1929), 224 ff., 522, nn.104–8; A. H. Krappe, Balor with the Evil Eye (1927), 87 ff.; H. A. Winkler, Salomo und die Karina (1911).
6. T. H. Gaster, in SMSR 25 (1951–52), 154–57.
7. C. Frank, Bab. Beschwörungsreliefs (1900), 78.

8. VAB XI.17, 4 f. (not yet published, but quoted, in another connection, by A. Goetze, in JCS 11 [1957], 81).
9. Frank, Beschwörungsreliefs, 77 f.; Myhrman, op. cit. 11.44–48a.—The Babylonians observed a similar practice in exorcizing demons from a new or renovated house or temple: text and translation in P. Jensen, KB vi/2.
10. Frazer-Gaster, NGB §454.
11. ANET 328.
12. S. G. Oliphant, in TAPA 44 (1913), 127 ff.; L. Oppenheim, in WZKM 30 (1908), 158 ff.; W. Klinger, in Philologus 66 (1907), 344, cites modern parallels.
13. Aristophanes, Frogs 294–95; Suidas, Lex., s.v. Empousa.
14. Aristophanes, Acharn. 574; Theocritus, Id., 15.40.—The name survived in English folklore as a "bogey-word" used to scare unruly children: Notes and Queries, 5/xi (1879), 427; 5/xii (1879), 18.
15. Aristophanes, Thesm. 417; Plato, Phaedo 77E.
16. Diodorus, xx.41; Photius, s.v. LAMIA; Oliphant, loc. cit., Sappho, 94 Wharton. Cf. Gaster, The Holy and the Profane, 229, n.13.
17. On the ominous character of the owl, of Kirby Smith, on Tibullus, i.5, 52.
18. Ib.
19. Gaster, The Holy and the Profane, 21 ff.
20. Hesiod, Theogony 267; cf. Apollodorus, Bib. i.9.21.
21. III.iv.
22. W. W. Skeat, Malay Magic (1900), 325.
23. J. Trachtenberg, Jewish Magic and Superstition (1939), 278, n.34.

191 The loom of life

1. B. Schmidt, Das Volksleben der Neugriechen (1871), 220.

192 Heaven as a muslin curtain

1. BD 85; cf. P. le Page Renouf, in PSBA 16 (1894), 182.
2. Rig Veda, viii, 6.5.
3. R. F. Burton, West and West from Africa, 454.
4. H. Güntert, Von der Sprache der Götter (1921), 142.
5. Cf. KB i. 174–175; P. Jensen, Kosmologie (1890), 6 ff.
6. L. Strackerjan, Sagen aus dem Herzogtum Oldenburg³ (1909), ii. 108.

194 The Suffering Servant

1. The Suffering Servant has been identified by some scholars with the mythological "dying and reviving god": H. Gressmann, Der Ursprung d. israel.-jüdische Eschatologie (1905), 312–33; id., Der Messias (1929), 287–323; H. Gunkel, RGG, col. 1543; W. Staerk, in ZAW, N.F. 3 (1926), 259 f.; A. Jeremias, The Old Testament in the Light of the Ancient East (1911), ii.278; G. H. Dix, in JTS (1925), 241 ff.; S. Mowinckel, in ZAW, N.F. 8 (1931), 259 f. These views are rejected—in my opinion, on inadequate grounds—by H. Orlinsky, The so-called Suffering Servant in Isaiah and alleged Near Eastern Parallels. Gittelson Lecture, 1965.—An interpretation approximating my own is offered by L. Dürr, Ursprung und Ausbau d. israel.-jüd. Heilandserwartung (1925), 125 ff.

(a)

2. See fully: Frazer-Gaster, NGB §§456–67, and Additional Notes thereto.
3. VAT 9555, rev. 10–11; S. Langdon, The Babylonian Epic of Creation (1923), 34 ff.
4. Texts are assembled and discussed in Gilbert Murray, The Rise of the Greek Epic

(1907), Appendix A, pp. 253-58. See also: Jane Harrison, Prolegomena to the Study of Greek Religion³ (1922), 95 ff., 105 f.

    5. Plutarch, Quaest. symp. vi.8.
    6. Servius on Vergil, Aen. iii.57; Lactantius Placidus, Comm. on Statius, Theb. x.793 p. 452, ed. Jahnke; Petronius, fr. 1, Buecheler.
    7. Philostratus, Vita Apoll. vi.10.
    8. Harpocration, s.v. *pharmakos;* cf. J. Töpfer, Beitraege zur griech. Altertumswissenschaft (1897), 130 ff.; M. P. Nilsson, Griechische Feste (1906), 105 ff.
    9. Helladius, cited by Photius, Bib. 534; Lysias, Orat. vii.53; Hesychius, s.v. *pharmakos.*
    10. Joannes Lydus, De mensibus iii.29; iv.36; Varro, De lingua Latina vi.45; Festus 131 Müller; Plutarch, Numa 13. See: L. Preller, Röm. Mythologie³ (1881-82), i.360; W. H. Roscher, Apollon und Mars (1873), 49; H. Usener, Kl. Schriften (1913), iv.125 f.
    11. S. Crowther and J. C. Taylor, The Gospel on the Banks of the Niger (1859), 344-45; Frazer-Gaster, NGB §459.
    12. Turpin, "History of Siam," in J. Pinkerton's Voyages and Travels (1808-14), ix.579.
    13. J. H. Gray, China (1875), ii.306; Frazer-Gaster, NGB §456.
    14. H. Herzog, Schweizerische Voksfeste (1884), 293 f.
    15. L. Curtius, in ARW 14 (1911), 307.—To be sure, the rite was sometimes interpreted as a means of flogging *in* fertility and increase, just as parents today speak alternatively of beating the nonsense *out* of their unruly children or of beating sense *into* them. For this alternative view, see: W. Mannhardt, Mythologische Forschungen (1884), 113-40; S. Reinach, Cultes, Mythes et Religions (1905-12), i.180-83; L. R. Farnell, The Cults of the Greek States (1896-1909), v.163.—Women were struck for fertility in the Arcadian rites of Dionysus and of Demeter: Pausanias, viii.23, 1; Hesychius, s.v. Morotton.—Beating with thongs likewise figured prominently in the Roman rite of the Lupercalia: A. M. Franklin, The Lupercalia (1921), 59 f.—The custom is well attested in European folklore. In Croatia, people beat one another for "freshness and health" after church on Good Friday and the two previous days: F. S. Krauss, Kroatien und Slavonien (1889), 108; while in some parts of Russia people returning from church on Palm Sunday beat with their branches the children and servants who have stayed at home, saying "Sickness into the forest, health into the bones"; W. Mannhardt, Baumkultus (1875), 257. A similar custom, known as "Easter smacks," prevailed around Eastertide in several parts of Germany: Frazer-Gaster, NGB §470. Jews perform a similar rite on the seventh day of the autumnal festival of Ingathering (Booths): H. Graetz, in MGWJ 36 (1887), 509-21.
    16. Heb.: *nigzar.* The expression echoes the wording of the scapegoat ritual in Lev. 16:22, where the beast is ordered to be dispatched to "a land of cutting off" (Heb.: g^ezerah), i.e., a desert.

(b)

    17. For similar conceptions in Classical antiquity, see: T. Wächter, Reinheitsvorschriften (1910), 39 ff. Cf. especially: Iliad 1.413; 5.394 ff.; Herodotus, i.138 (lepers among the Persians). So too among African primitives: J. Spieth, Die Ewe-stämme (1906), 255.
    18. See: J. Heller, "Hiding the Face" (Isa. 53:3), in Communio Viatorum 1 (1958), 263-66.—In Arabia, the face is veiled against the evil eye: J. Wellhausen, Skizzen (1889), iii.146. Alternatively, a disguise is adopted: W. Mannhardt, Antike Wald- und Feldkulte (1904), i.543; E. Nestle, in Philologus, N.F. 4 (1891), 502; M. Grünbaum, in ZDMG 21 (1877), 263.
    19. E.g., the Darfur: Mohammed ibn Omar el-Tunisi, Voyage en Daufar (1845),

203; BORNU: Ibn Batutah, ed. Deffrémery-Sanguinetti (1855–58), iv.441; CHONGA: Mattei, Bas-Niger, etc. (1895), 90 f.; JEBU: A. B. Ellis, The Yoruba-speaking Peoples of the Slave Coast (1894), 190. See Frazer-Gaster, NGB §162.

20. Cf. L. B. Paton, ICC on Esther 1:14.
21. Scholiast on Iliad 24.480; Ap. Rhod., Argon. iv.697 f.; Euripides, Iphigenia in Tauris 1206 f. Cf. Wächter, op. cit., 70.
22. G. Parrinder, La religion en Afrique centrale (1950), 95.
23. O. Gruppe, Griech. Mythologie (1906), 903, n.2, would so explain the Graeco-Roman custom of besmearing with gypsum initiants to the mysteries. See on this: Demosthenes, xiii.239; Plutarch, Superstit. 3; Apuleius, Met. vii.27; Augustine, De civ. Dei viii.26. Cf. also: A. Dieterich, in Rhein. Mus. 48 (1893), 279.

195 The faery city

1. Reading, with LXX, *ba-<no>phek* for the traditional *ba-pūk* ("with stibium"). It occurs to me, however, that this widely accepted emendation may be, in fact, a little too facile and obscure the true sense. The prophet likens Zion to a "forlorn, storm-tossed, disconsolate" woman who will yet be restored to her former glory and beauty. This verse, therefore, may really contain an extension of that metaphor, involving a subtle double-entendre: the very stones of the city will be, in their new brilliance, like a woman whose features are enhanced by cosmetic "eye-shade," for which stibium is regularly employed in the Near East. Similarly, when he describes the gleaming pinnacles as "suns," he may be intending an allusion to the familiar brooches in the form of sun discs. Bizarre as this may sound to Western ears, it is in keeping with the common extravagance of Oriental poetry.
2. Literally, "And I will make thy suns of agate." Cf. Akkadian *šamsātê*, "ornaments in the form of solar discs."
3. KARI #307.30 ff.; B. Meissner, Babylonien und Assyrien (1925), ii.108.
4. II AB, iv-v.77–81.
5. Enoch 14:9 ff.
6. Test. Abraham, ch. xii; tr. Box (1927), 19.
7. Tobit 13:16 f.
8. Rev. 21:18 f., 21 f.
9. Cf. F. Brittain, ed., The Penguin Book of Latin Verse (1962), 191.
10. Ib., 176.
11. Tr. T. H. Gaster, Festivals of the Jewish Year (1953), 72; id., in Commentary, June 1953.
12. Ib., 405 f.; E. Davies, Myths and Rites of the British Druids (1809), 522; R. Southey, Madoc, ix.
13. M. Preindlsberger-Mrazović, Bosnische Volksmärchen (1905), 110 f.; cf. H. Gunkel, Das Märchen im AT (1925), 63 f.
14. J. G. von Hahn, Griechisch und albanesische Märchen (1864), i.147, 194.
15. A. N. Afansjev. Narodnyja russkija skazki[3] (1897), 73.
16. D. G. Brinton, The Myths of the New World[3] (1905), 105.

196 Gad and Meni

1. See: F. Baethgen, Beitraege zur sem. Religionsgeschichte (1888), 76 ff.; W. C. Wood, in JBL 35 (1916), 266 ff.—The name is strangely absent from the Canaanite texts from Ras Shamra-Ugarit.
2. Gen. 30:11. The Masoretes, however, took the Hebrew word *be-Gad* to stand for *bā' Gad*, "Gad (Fortune) has come!"
3. On the other hand, the name 'Azgad (Ezra 2:12; 8:12; Neh. 7:17; 10:16), which

might appear at first blush to be the Semitic 'az-Gad, "Gad is strong," could equally well be the Iranian izgad, "messenger."

4. Nos. 2, 4, 7, 18, etc.
5. M. Lizbarski, Ephemeris fuer Semitische Epigraphik, i (1902), 15.
6. A. Reifenberg, in PEQ 70 (1938), 114.
7. M. Lidzbarski, Handbuch der nordsemitischen Epigraphik (1898), 249.
8. Cf. Pliny, NH ii.5.22; G. A. Cooke, A Text-book of North Semitic Inscriptions (1903), 269; S. A. Cook, The Religion of Ancient Palestine in the Light of Archaeology (1930), 226 ff.—Significantly enough, Jacob of Serug states explicitly (ZDMG 29.138) that the Christians turned many of the sanctuaries of Tyche (in Syriac: *beth gadde!*) into churches.
9. E.g., Cooke, op. cit., 245n. (from El-Qanawat, in the Ḥauran).
10. Ib., 79; 112.4 (A.D. 140).
11. So, for instance, in Nabatean (Cooke, op. cit., 145.4–5: "He shall have neither seed nor *gad* for ever!"); Syriac, Ethiopic, South Arabian, and Mandaean (*gada ṭaba*, "good luck").
12. TB Mo'ed Qatan 27a; N^edarim 56a; Sanhedrin 20a. See: Joseph Karo, Shulḥan 'Aruk, Yoreh De'ah §170.7 (with H. J. D. Azulai, Birkê Joseph [1774–76] in loc.); M. Schul, Superstitions et coutumes populaires du judaïsme contemporaine (1886), 6; T. H. Gaster, Folkways of Jewish Life (1965), 64 f.—On the Roman custom, cf. Varro, cited by Servius, on Vergil, Aeneid 10.76; G. Wissowa, Religion und Kultus der Römer (1932), 357, n.1.
13. G. F. Abbott, Macedonian Folklore (1903), 125 f.; J. C. Lawson, Modern Greek Folklore (1910), 125 f.; Kamporouglou, Historia tôn Athēnôn, iii.67 f.
14. TB Shabbath 92b; cf. also Yalquṭ Shime'oni §509 (on our passage from Isaiah).
15. A. Berliner, Aus dem leben der deutschen Juden im Mittelalter (1900), 105.
16. TB Shabbath 67b; Yalquṭ Shime'oni, §587.
17. Th. Noeldeke, Beitraege zur sem. Sprachwissenschaft (1904), 94.—On Gad among the Arabs in general, see: J. Wellhausen, Reste des arabischen Heidentums[3] (1897), 146; R. Dussaud, Les Arabes en Syrie (1907), 147 ff.; Th. Noeldeke, in ERE i.662a.
18. See: H. Zimmern, in Islamica 2.574–84; S. H. Langdon, in JRAS 1930.21–29.
19. Cooke, op. cit., 79 (from El-Hejra, 1st cent. B.C.); 80.4 (A.D. 1); 86.8 (A.D. 26).
—The form *M-n-w-t-w* appears to be feminine. I. Goldziher (in Archäol. epigr. Mitteilungen aus Oesterreich 6 [1882], 109) reads it as a plural (*maniyat*).
20. Koran 53:20.
21. *M-n-w-t-w* is indeed associated with the ancient goddess Allat in the Nabatean inscription, Cooke, op. cit., 80.4.

JEREMIAH

197 Man from stones

1. Stith Thompson, MI, T 544.1; M. Eliade, Patterns in Comparative Religion (1958), 237; M. Semper, Rassen und Religionen im alten Vorderasien (1930), 179–86; J. Layard, Stone Men of Malekula (1942); G. Dumézil, Légendes sur les Nartes (1930), 75–77; W. J. Perry, Children of the Sun[2] (1926), 255 ff.; W. Jackson Knight, Cumaean Gates (1936), 9 ff.
2. R. Pettazzoni, Dio i (1922), 10.
3. R. W. Williamson, The Social and Political System of Polynesia (1924), ii.242–43; M. Leenhardt, Notes d'éthnologie néocaledonienne (1930), 183.

4. H. Callaway, The Religious System of the Amazulu (1868–70), 34.
5. D. G. Brinton, Religions of Primitive Peoples (1899), 147.
6. T. H. Gaster, The Oldest Stories in the World (1955), 125.
7. A. v. Löwis of Menar, in ARW 13 (1910), 509–24.
8. J. A. Jaussen, Coutumes des arabes au pays de Moab (1908), 107.
9. Ovid, Met. i.125–415; Lucian, De dea Syria, 12 ff.; Apollodorus, Bib. i.7.2.
10. Cf. Stith Thompson, MI, T 544.1.
11. Fornander, The Polynesian Race, as quoted by Brinton, loc. cit.
12. Odyssey 19.163; cf. also: Juvenal, vi.12.

199 Passing children through fire

1. Note that in II Chron. 28:3, which parallels our passage, the Hebrew word for "pass through fire" is replaced by "burned." Cf. also Jer. 7:31 and 19:5, which speak of *burning* children.
2. J. G. Frazer, The Fasti of Ovid (1925), iii.293 ff.; G. Glotz, L'ordalie dans la Grèce primitive (1904), 105 f.; O. Gruppe, Griech. Mythologie (1906), 898, n.4.
3. Preuner, Hestia-Vesta (1864), 60; A. Mommsen, Feste d. Stadt Athen (1898), 274; W. R. Halliday, in CR 25 (1901), 8 f. Cf. also: E. H. Meyer, Indogermanische Mythen, ii (1877), 512 f.
4. Strabo, xii.2, 7.
5. Plutarch, De Iside et Osiride 16.
6. Ovid, Fasti iv.423 ff.; Tibullus, ii.5, 89 f.; Propertius, v (iv).4, 77 f.; Dio Hal., Ant. i.88; Pliny, HN vi.19.
7. Jamblichus, De mysteriis clxxix.8; Proclus, In Rem. i.152, 10. Cf. E. R. Dodds, The Greeks and the Irrational (reprint, 1957), 305, n.66.
8. J. G. Frazer, Apollodorus (1921), ii.311–17; A. Lang, "The Fire Walk," in his Modern Mythology (1897); J. Grimm, DM² i.592; W. Mannhardt, Antike Wald- und Feldkulte (1877), i.497 ff.; ii.302 ff.
9. Journal of the Indian Archipelago 2.264.
10. E.g., Yajnavalk i.137.
11. Meyer, loc. cit.
12. H. Massé, Persian Beliefs and Customs (1954), 499 (citing Layard).
13. T. Pennant, in J. Pinkerton's General Collection of Voyages and Travels (1808–14), iii.383.
14. *s.v.* coals.
15. M. Eliade, Birth and Rebirth (1950), 91.
16. A. Popov, Tavagijcy: Trudy Instituta Antropologii i Etnografi (Moscow-Leningrad), i/5 (1936), 84 ff., as quoted by Eliade, *op. cit.,* 90.
17. B. Spencer and F. Gillen, The Northern Tribes of Australia (1904), 389 ff.; id., The Arunta (1927), i.295 ff.; W. L. Warner, A Black Civilization (1937), 325; F. Speiser, in Verhandlungen der Naturforschenden Gesell. in Basel, 1929, 216–18; A. P. Elkin, Aboriginal Men of High Degree (1946), 91, 193.
18. See below, n22.
19. A. Aarne and S. Thompson, Types of the Folk Tale. FCC #74 (1928), #753.
20. Homeric Hymn to Demeter, 237 ff. (v. Allen-Sikes-Halliday, in loc.).
21. Apollodorus, Bib. iii.13.6.
22. Stith Thompson, MI, D 1885–86; Grimm, ##81, 147; Bolte-Polivka, i.412; iii.198; O. Dähnhardt, Natursagen (1907–12), iii.154; 162 ff., 288; R. Kohler, Kl. Schriften (1894), i.298; J. G. Frazer, Apollodorus (1921), i.121, n.4; A. Ritterhaus, Die neuisländischen Volksmärchen (1902), 338 (Iceland); Hartung, in Zs. f. Volkskunde 8.89; Piger, ib., 10.84 (Germany); P. Sébillot, Incidents, s.v. "four" (Breton); W. Mannhardt, Germanische Mythen (1858), 64–75; A. B. Cook, Zeus ii (1925), 210 ff.;

O. Gruppe, Griech. Mythologie (1906), 546; M. Eliade, Birth and Rebirth (1958), 90 f.; A. H. Krappe, La genèse des mythes (1938), 209; J. G. Frazer, GB iii.872; iv.96; R. B. Onians, The Origins of European Thought about the Body, etc. (1952), 289, n.5.
23. Pausanias ii.3, 2; Ovid, Met. vii.297–349.
24. Apollodorus, loc. cit.; Ap. Rhodius, Argon. iv.869.
25. G. and T. L. Jones, The Mabinogion (Everyman's Library ed.), 29 ff.
26. A. B. Cook, Zeus i (1923), 786.
27. R. Dussaud, in RHR 58 (1909), 309 (*apotheôsis en tô lebêti*).
28. Matt. 3:10; Luke 3:16. See fully: C. Edsman, Le baptême du feu (1949).
29. Concerning Moloch, cf. Daumer, Le culte de Moloch (1842); G. E. Moore, in JBL 16 (1897) 161 ff.; E. Dhorme, in Anatolian Studies 6 (1956), 57–61; H. Cazelles, in Suppl. Dict. de la Bible, cols. 1337–46; cf. also: H. Donkert, Het Mensenoffer in de OTsche Wereld (Baarn 1955).
30. II Kings 23:15; Jer. 49:1; Amos 5:26.—For *mlk* in Phoenician names, cf. G. A. Cooke, A Text-book of North Semitic Inscriptions (1903), 49; S. R. Driver, ICC Deuteronomy, 223.
31. A. Bea, in Biblica 20 (1939), 415; E. Vogt, ib., 38 (1957), 471 f.; H. Cazelles, ib., 485 f.; R. Dussaud, in Syria 35 (1957), 349 f.
32. Ugaritica V (1967), #7.
33. N. Schneider, in Biblica 18 (1937), 337–43.
34. Id., in Biblica 19 (138), 204.
35. O. Eissfeldt, Molk als Opferbegriff im Punischen und Hebräisch, und das Ende des Gottes Moloch (1935), W. Kornfeld, in WZKM 1952.287–313 (against Eissfeldt); cf. also: J. G. Février, in JA 248 (1960), 167–87; C. Virolleaud et al., in CRAIBL 1956.61, 67.—J. Hoftzijzer, in VT 8 (1958), 92 interprets a Punic inscription reading *mlk adm bšrm b(n) btm* to mean "A human sacrifice—his own child in perfect health," but this is very dubious.
36. See: W. Kornfeld, in WZKM 1952.267–313; A. Jirku, in ARW 53 (1938), 178; N. Schlögl, in WZKM 45.203–11.

201 "The wind and the rain"

(a) Fissures for the rain

1. G. Dalman, Arbeit und Sitte in Palästina (1928–37), iii/i.114.
2. Ib.
3. II AB, iv–v.68–71.
4. J. Kissane, in JTS 1952.214 f.
5. See above, §4.
6. II AB, vii. 19; cf. T. H. Gaster, Thespis[2], 195.
7. Herodotus, iv.158, 185.
8. E. B. Tylor, Primitive Culture, ii.157.

(b) Promptuaries for the wind

9. Enoch 17:3; 18:1; 41:4; 60:12–24; 71:4, 9.—Note also the reference in Aeschylus, Eumenides 813 ff., to a mansion of the lightning.
10. Hymn; tr. T. H. Gaster, The Dead Sea Scriptures in English Translation[2] (1964), 135.
11. Iliad 23.192; Odyssey 20.66, 77; Apollodorus, Bib. i.9.21; cf. F. G. Welcker, Griechische Götterlehre (1857–62), i.707; iii.67. Cf. also: Vergil, Aen. i.56.
12. W. Ellis, Polynesian Researches[2] (1832–36), i.329; E. B. Tylor, Primitive Culture, ii.360.
13. H. R. Schoolcraft, Algic Researches (1839), i.139; ii.214.
14. D. G. Brinton, Myths of the New World[3] (1905), 93.

202 Rites of mourning

▲ (a) Cuttings for the dead

1. J. Wellhausen, Reste d. arab. Heidentums[2] (1897), 181 f.; I. Goldziher, Muhammedanische Studien (1888–90), i.248; G. Jacob, Das Leben der vorislamischen Beduinen (1897), 139 ff.
2. A. Jaussen, Coutumes des arabes au pays de Moab (1908), 96; S. Merill, East of the Jordan (1881), 51.
3. Jaussen, op. cit., 94.
4. Euripides, Electra 145 ff.; Hecuba 650 ff.; Hesiod, Shield of Heracles 242 ff.; Lucian, De luctu xii; cf. Ovid, Met. xiii.427 ff.; Heroides ix.91 f., 115 ff.
5. Iliad 23.135–53.
6. Aeschylus, Choephoroe 4 ff.; Sophocles, Electra 51–63, 900 ff.; Euripides, Electra 90 ff., 513 ff.
7. Plutarch, Solon 21.
8. Xenophon, Cyropaedia iii.1, 13, iii.3, 67.
9. Cicero, De legibus ii.23, 59; Festus, De verborum significatione 273 Müller; Pliny, HN ii.157; Fontes Juris Romani Antiqui[7], ed. Bruns-Gradenwitz (1909), 36.
10. Servius, on Vergil, Aen. iii.67; xii.606.
11. Vergil, Aen. iv.672 ff.
12. Herodotus, iv.71.
13. Jornandes, Romana et Getica, ed. Mommsen (1882), 124.
14. W. R. S. Ralston, The Songs of the Russian People[2] (1872), 316.
15. A. Lamberti, in Recueil de Voyages au Nord, vii (1725), 153.
16. G. M. Zampi, ib., 221.
17. G. Mourier, in RHR 16 (1887), 90, 93.
18. J. von Klaproth, Reise in den Kaukasus und nach Georgien (1814), ii.604 ff.
19. Stanislas Julien, Documents historiques sur les Tou-Kioue [Turcs] traduits du Chinoise (1877), 10, 28; L. Cahun, Introduction à l'histoire de l'Asie, Turcs et Mongols (1896), 59.
20. E. Rüppell, Reise in Abyssinien (1838–40), ii.57.
21. J. L. Krapf, Reisen in Ost-Afrika (1858), i.325.
22. H. Néel, in L'anthropologie 24 (1913), 458.
23. L. Alberti, De Kaffers aan de Zuidkust van Afrika (1910), 201; H. Lichtenstein, Reisen im südlichen Africa (1811–12), i.421 ff.; S. Kay, Travels and Researches in Caffraria (1833), 199 ff.
24. E. Petitot, Monographie des Déne-Dindijé (1876), 61.
25. A. Mackenzie, Voyages from Montreal through . . . North America (1801), p. xcviii.
26. H. J. Holmberg, in Acta Societatis Scientiarum Fennicae 4 (1856), 324; cf. also: W. H. Dall, Alaska and Its Resources (1870), 417; H. H. Bancroft, The Native Races of the Pacific States (1875–76), i.173.
27. A. Ross, Adventures of the First Settlers on the Oregon or Columbia River (1849), 97.
28. J. Baegert, in Annual Report of the Board of Regents of the Smithsonian Institution for the year 1864, p. 387.
29. Bancroft, op. cit., i.397, n.142.
30. Father de Smet, Voyages aux Montagnes Rocheuses (1873), 28.
31. Ib. 66.
32. A. L. Kroeber, in Bull. Amer. Museum of Natural History 18/i (1902), 16 ff.
33. W. H. Keating, Narrative of an Expedition to the Source of St. Peter's River (1825), i.232.

34. Ib., i.433.
35. Edwin James, Account of an Expedition from Pittsburgh to the Rocky Mountains (1823), i.116.
36. Ib., i.222 ff.
37. Ib., ii.2.
38. Alice C. Fletcher and F. la Flesche, in XXVIIth Annual Report of the Bureau of American Ethnology (1911), 592–94.
39. Ib., 591.
40. J. F. Lafitau, Moeurs des sauvages amériquains (1724), ii.441.
41. T. Falkner, A Description of Patagonia (1774), 118.
42. P. Hyades and J. Deniker, Mission scientifique du Cap Horn, vii (1891), 379.
43. J. M. Cooper, Analytical and Critical Bibliography of the Tribes of Tierra del Fuego and Adjacent Territory. Bull. Amer. Bureau of Amer. Ethnology, #63 (1917), 160.
44. J. A. van Rijn van Alkemarde, in Tijdschrift van het Nederlandsch Aardrijkskundig Genootschap, II Ser. ii (1884), 238 ff.; H. A. Hijmans van Androoij, in TITLV 30 (1885), 347–49.
45. V. Jouet, La Société des Missionaires du Sacré-Coeur dans les Vicariats Apostoliques de la Mélanésie et de la Micronésie (Issoudin 1887), 292; Father Guis, "Les Canaques. Mort-deuil," in Les Missions Catholiques 34 (1902), 186.
46. J. Chalmers, "New Guinea, Toaripi and Koiari Tribes," in Report of the Second Meeting of the Australasian Association for the Advancement of Science (1890), 316, 322.
47. G. Turner, Samoa, a Hundred Years Ago (1884), 335.
48. T. W. Leggart, "Maleluka, New Hebrides," in Report of the Fourth Meeting of the Australasian Society for the Advancement of Science (1892), 700.
49. M. J. van Baarda, in BTLVNI 69 (1913), 64 ff.
50. The Voyages of Captain Cook Round the World (1809), i.218 ff.
51. J. Wilson, Missionary Voyage to the South Pacific (1799), 352 ff.
52. Voyages of Captain James Cook, v.420.
53. Ch. Wilkes, Narrative of the U.S. Exploring Expedition[2] (1851), ii.139; Turner, op. cit., 144; J. B. Stair, Old Samoa (1897), 182; G. Brown, Melanesians and Polynesians (1910), 401 ff.
54. W. W. Gill, "Mangaria Hervey Islands," in Report of the Second Meeting of the Australasian Society for the Advancement of Science (1890), 344.
55. C. Clavel, Les Marquisiens (1885), 39, 44. Cf. also: M. Radiguet, Les derniers sauvages (1882), 284.
56. W. Yate, An Account of New Zealand (1835), 136 ff.; E. Dieffenbach, Travels in New Zealand (1843), ii.62; W. Brown, New Zealand and Its Aborigines (1845), 19; A. S. Thomson, The Story of New Zealand (1859), i.186; E. Tregear, in JAI 19 (1890), 104 ff.
57. J. Dawson, Australian Aborigines (1881), 66.
58. W. Stanbridge, in Trans. Ethnological Soc. of London, N.S. 1 (1861), 298.
59. R. Brough Smyth, The Aborigines of Victoria (1878), i.105.
60. A. W. Howitt, The Native Tribes of S. E. Australia (1904), 459.
61. Ib. 453.
62. P. Beveridge, in Journal and Proc. of the Royal Society of New South Wales for 1883 (1884), 28 f.
63. W. Ridley, Kamilaroi and Other Australian Languages (1875), 160; Howitt, op. cit., 467.
64. J. Mathew, Two Representative Tribes of Queensland (1910), 115; E. M. Curr, The Australian Race (1886–87), iii.165; A. McDonald, in JAI 1 (1872), 216, 219.

65. W. E. Roth, Studies among the North-West-Central Queensland Aborigines (1897), 164.
66. B. Spencer, Native Tribes of the Northern Territory of Australia (1914) 241 ff. (The writer's account of the use made of the blood is not quite clear.)
67. A. R. Brown, in JRAI 43 (1913), 169; E. Clement, in Internat. Archiv für Ethnographie 16 (1904), 8 ff.
68. B. Spencer and F. Gillen, The Native Tribes of Central Australia (1899), 500.
69. Ib., 510.
70. Ib., 500, n.1.
71. Ib., 516–23; id., Across Australia (1912), ii.426–30.
72. F. Bonney, in JAI 13 (1884), 134 ff.
73. J. A. Reid, in E. M. Curr, op. cit., ii.179.
74. Spencer-Gillen, Native Tribes, 507, 509 ff.
75. G. Grey, Journals of Two Expeditions of Discovery in North-West and Western Australia (1841), ii.332 (quoting a letter from a certain Mr. Bussel).
76. Ib., ii.335.
77. Ib.—For other evidence of cuttings for the dead among the Australian aborigines, see: T. L. Mitchell, Three Expeditions into the Interior of Eastern Australia[2] (1839), ii.346; J. Fraser, in Journal and Proc. of the Royal Soc. of New South Wales 16 (1882), 229, 231; E. Palmer, in JAI 13 (1884), 298; J. F. Mann, in Proc. Geogr. Soc. of Australia 1 (1885), 47; E. M. Curr, op. cit., i.330; ii.249, 346, 443, 465; iii.21, 29.
78. J. Bonwick, Daily Life and Origin of the Tasmanians (1870), 97 ff.
79. Spencer-Gillen, Native Tribes, 507.
80. Ib., 510 f.
81. W. R. Smith, The Religion of the Semites[3] (1927), 322 ff.
82. Bonney, loc. cit.
83. Ib., 128.
84. Ib., 132.
85. Ib., 133.
86. Odyssey 11.13 ff. The drinking of the blood by the ghosts is mentioned explicitly in verses 98, 153, 232, 390.
87. See above, §117.

(b) **Funeral meats**

88. Cf. E. Bendann, Death Customs (1930), ch. ix, pp. 147–61, where examples are quoted from Melanesia, Barthe Bay, Koita, Massim, Santa Cruz, etc. The feasts take place variously two, ten, forty, or a hundred days after death, and are often repeated at spaced intervals.—In the New Hebrides, the dead are believed to join the feast: R. H. Codrington, The Melanesians (1891), 259.—The Greeks held such feasts on the third, ninth, and thirtieth day after a death: Pollux, xiii.146.—The Roman funeral feast took place on the ninth day after a death, and on the birthday of the deceased: E. Aust, Die Religion der Römer[2] (1899), 288 ff.; G. Wissowa, Religion und Kultus der Römer[2] (1912), 235. Cf. also: T. Klaufer, Die Cathedra im Totenkult der heidnischen und christlichen Antike. Liturgesch. Forschungen 9 (1927), 54, 82.—The Patagonians hold funeral feasts every three years: Koch, in Internat. Archiv 13 (1900), suppl. 103.
89. Ezek. 24:17; Heb.: *leḥem* ^{a}*nāšîm*, lit. "bread of men." This is usually "corrected," after Vulgate, Targum, and Hos. 9:4, to *leḥem ônîm*, "bread of mourners." But the emendation is unnecessary, for the received text can stand in the sense of "bread of fellowship, communion" (cf. Arabic *'-n-s* in precisely this sense): T. H. Gaster, Communication to the New York Oriental Club, October 1964 (unpublished).
90. Hos. 9:4.

91. G. Dossin, Archives Royales de Mari, i (1946), 8.14. The terms are absent from Akkadian texts: L. Oppenheim, in JNES 11 (1942), 131.
92. CT XVI, p. 10, v.10–14.
93. G. A. Cooke, A Text-book of North Semitic Inscriptions (1903), #61.14–18.
94. T. H. Gaster, Thespis², 334.
95. Lucian, De luctu 24.
96. Clem. Alex., Const. viii, c.24.
97. Chrysostom, Homil. in Matth. 37.
98. E. W. Lane, Manners and Customs of the Modern Egyptians (Minerva Library ed.), 488.
99. T. H. Gaster, The Holy and the Profane (1955), 176 f.
100. Varro, Nonn. i.235; Servius, on Vergil, Aen. v.92; cf. ARW 11 (1909), 330–46.
101. H. Höhn, Sitte und Gebräuche bei Tod, etc. (1913), 333.
102. Am Urquell 6.26.
103. P. Sartori, Die Speisung der Toten (1913), 11.
104. Pliny, HN xviii.12, 30.
105. Ovid, Fasti vi.438 (v. Frazer, in loc.).
106. P. Sartoti, Sitte und Brauch iii (1914), 262, n.16.
107. T. H. Gaster, Thespis², 29 f.
108. JAI 12 (1882), 142.
109. T. Williams and J. Calvert, Fiji and the Fijians (1858), i.169.
110. G. Turner, Samoa a hundred years ago and long before (1884), 142.
111. Ki Li, in SBE xxvii.87.—Ting Ho-Nien (1335–1424) abstained from salt and lao (a milk product) for five years after the death of his mother: L. C. G(oodrich), in Draft Ming Biographies (MBHD), 1964, a.2.
112. J. Ross, A History of Corea (1897), 222.
113. ERE v.760ᵇ; JAI 19 (1890), 28.
114. Gaster, Thespis², loc. cit.
115. In this passage, the word *zebaḥ* means "meal" not "sacrifice," as in Zeph. 1:7 and as sometimes in Ugaritic.

203 The ritual lament

1. LXX omits, "Ah, sister!" M. Dahood has suggested that *adôn* here means simply "daddy," after Ugaritic *ad,* etc. But the parallel from Sappho shows that he is mistaken.
2. VAT 9555.29.
3. Sappho, fr. 63, 108 Wharton.
4. Aristophanes, Lys. 365–66.
5. Bion, Epitaphion Adônidos 1, 40.
6. Ammianus Marcellinus, xix.1, 11; xxii.9, 15.

204 Invoking the earth

1. K 43, obv. 37 (cited by P. Jensen, KB VI/i.270): *EN irṣitum, irṣitum, irṣitum,* ᵈ*Gilgameš bêl ma-mi-ti-ku-nu.*

205 Rachel weeping for her children

1. R. C. Thompson, Semitic Magic (1908), 19 ff.; J. G. Frazer, GB v (Spirits of the Corn and Wild), ii.97 ff.
2. Utukkê Limnûti IV.v.25; V.i.53 (*bakîtu mušeniqtu*); R. C. Thompson, The Devils and Evil Spirits of Babylonia (1903), i.40, 54.
3. C. M. Doughty, Travels in Arabia Deserta (1888), i.305.
4. W. W. Skeat, Malay Magic (1900), 325; id., and C. O. Blagden, Pagan Races of the Malay Peninsula (1906), i.153 (the Sakai of Perak).

5. R. H. Codrington, The Melanesians (1891), 275.
6. J. Kubary, in A. Bastian's Allerlei aus Volks- und Menschenkunde (1888), i.9.
7. S. Wide, in ARW 12 (1909), 224–33; cf. BCH 12 (1888), 297; Pap. Paris Mag. 322 ff., 342 f., 1410, 2215, etc.; O. Dilthey, in Rhein. Mus. 27 (1872), 387 ff.; O. Gruppe, Griech. Mythologie (1906), 761.
8. A. Wuttke, Deutsche Aberglaube d. Gegenwart (1900), 447 ff.
9. Maqlu vii.25.
10. KUB XXX.70, iii(?).14 ff.
11. W. Spiegelberg, Sonnenauge (1917), 7.31.
12. SRT #5.34–36.
13. T. H. Gaster, Thespis[2], 220.
14. Ovid, Fasti iv.495 ff.; cf.; Lucretius, ii.355–63.

205a David redivivus

1. Cf. H. Schmidt, Der Mythos vom wiederkehrenden König im AT (1925); A. W. Hands, in International Journal of Apocrypha, 1916.39.
2. Cf. Stith Thompson, MI, A 580; T. Norlind, Skattsänger (1916).
3. Suetonius, Nero 57; cf. J. Geffcken, in Gött. Gelehrt. Nachrichten, 1899.441–62.
4. J. A. McCulloch, Celtic Mythology (1918), 194.
5. Kalevala, runo 50.
6. Cf. J. Bolte, in ZfVK 29.74; H. Feilberg, Bidrag til en Ordbog over Jyske Almusmal (1886–94); A. Olrick, Ragnarök, tr. Ranisch (1922), 103 ff., 478 [Balder].
7. Stith Thompson, Tales of the North American Indians (1929), 274, n.11a; N. Alexander, Latin American Mythology (1920), 66.

EZEKIEL

207 Ezekiel's vision of heathen worship

1. LXX says "fifth"; Massoretic text, "sixth."
2. The Gezer Agricultural Calendar (10th cent. B.C.?) assigns these months to *zmr*, "late trimming of the vines," and to *qṣ*, "reaping of summer fruits." A Canaanite gloss in a letter from Tell el Amarna (97.11, Winckler) gives *qêṣ* (*gi-e-zi*) as a statutory season, and the Ugaritic text, I Aqhat i.41 describes it as the time of the early rain (*yr*).
3. The Masoretic text adds the gloss, "which provokes (Yahweh's) jealousy." LXX and Syriac (Peshitta) omit.
4. The Masoretic text, taking the Hebrew word *ḥôr* to mean "hole," explains that this was a hole *in the wall*. LXX omits this gloss.

(a) The "seat of the idol of jealousy"

5. The Gracious Gods (SS); cf. T. H. Gaster, Thespis[2], 406–35; id., in JBL 60 (1941), 290, n.9.
6. The Gracious Gods, 19.
7. RS 1929, #33.
8. RS. 1929. #48, r.2.
8a. CIS ii.114.
9. H. Hepding, Attis (1903), 136–37; E. Rohde, Psyche[7] (1921), i.129, n.3; Gaster, op. cit., 64, 311 f.
10. The Ramesseum Drama = K. Sethe, Dramatische Texte zu altägyptischen Mysterienspiele, ii (1928), lines 132–133ª; Gaster, op. cit. 398.
11. KBo III.7; KUB XII.66; Gaster, op. cit. 265 f.
12. KUB XVII.10, iii.20–34; Gaster, op. cit., 311.

13. Enuma Elish vi.53–54.
14. MDOG 38 (1908), 19; S. A. Pallis, The Babylonian Akitu Festival (1926), 173.
15. Cf. T. Frankema, Tâkultu (1954). Two recensions of the ritual are extant, viz. (*a*) II R 66 (duplicate, KAVI 57), of the reign of Sennacherib; and (*b*) KARI 214 (duplicates, KAVI 83; KARI 325). The ceremony is mentioned in inscriptions of Adad-nirari and of Shalmaneser I; cf. R. Labat, Le caractère réligieux de la royauté assyro-babylonienne (1939), 286–87.
16. H. Seyrig, in Syria 14 (1933), 262 f.; R. Dussaud, Mission dans les regions désertiques de la Syrie moyenne (1903), #19; M. Lidzbarski, Ephemeris für Semitische Epigraphik (1902–15), ii.356.
17. CIA II.i.624, 662; IV.ii.624b; cf. Livy, xxix.14, 13.
18. F. M. Cornford, The Origins of Attic Comedy (1934), 99.
19. Gracious Gods, 21–22.

(b) The frescoed cavern

20. Such pictures have been found in caves at Gezer.
21. Schol. on Nikander, Alexipharmakon 7–8.
22. Dioscorides, in AP vi.220, 3.
23. Hesychius, s.v. KYBELA: *kai antra kai thalamai*.
24. Arnobius, Adv. nationes, v.7.
25. H. Hepding, Attis (1903), 195–96; A. Dieterich, Mithrasliturgie^2 (1910), 157 ff.

(c) Women weeping for Tammuz

26. See: O. Gurney, in JSS 7 (1962), 147–60; S. N. Kramer, in Studia Biblica et Orientalia 3 (1939), 198n.; id., in Trans. XXVth Internat. Congress of Orientalists, i (1962), 169–73; W. W. Hallo, in JBL 82 (1963), 339.
27. Epic of Gilgamesh vi.46–47.
28. CT, XV 48. rev. 56–57.
29. G. Reisner, Sumerisch-babylonische Hymnen aus Tontafeln Griechischer Zeit (1896), 145, iii.12–15.
30. ZA 6 (1891), 243.24.
31. KARI 178.vi, 10.
32. D. Chwolson, Die Ssabier (1856), ii.27.
33. M. Beza, Paganism in Roumanian Folklore (1928), 27 ff. It should be observed, however, that the name of the puppet is given by other authorities as Scalojan, which is the Roumanian word for "drought, dearth": cf. E. Fischer, in Globus 93 (1908), 13–16.
34. E. W. Lane, Manners and Customs of the Modern Egyptians (Minerva Library ed.), 478.
35. M. Werbrouck, Les pleureuses dans l'Égypte ancienne (1939).
36. KUB XXX.15, 27.
36a. III D 170 ff.; Gaster, op. cit., 368 f.
37. Iliad 24.746.
38. Festus, 223 Mommsen; Ovid, Met. ii.340–43; J. E. B. Mayor, on Juvenal, x.261.
39. M. Ananikian, Armenian Mythology (1920), 95.
40. W. M. Ramsay, Asianic Elements in Greek Civilisation^2 (1928), 93 ff.

(d) The adoration of the rising sun

41. Gaster, op. cit. 47 f.
42. R. Labat, in RA 38 (1941), 28.
43. S. Langdon, Tammuz and Ishtar (1914), 32.
44. Yuzgat Tablet (= A. Goetze, Verstreute Boghazköi-Texte [1930], #58), rev.; Gaster, op. cit. 272 f., 291 f.

45. I AB, i.8–16; vi.22–29.
46. Gracious Gods, 23–27.
47. Cf. also: TJ Sanhedrin 18ᵈ.
48. O. S. Rankin, The Origin of the Festival of Hanukkah (1930), 205 f.
49. Cf. O. Weber, in ARW 19 (1916–19), 325 f.
50. O. S. Rankin, op. cit., 201 f.
51. E. Hull, Folklore of the British Isles (1928), 280.
52. Pervigilium Veneris, 3.

(e) **Ezekiel's satire**

53. For suggestions concerning the text, see: T. H. Gaster, in JBL 60 (1941), 299 f. In verse 11, for the traditional text's *qām lᵉmaṭṭeh resha'* I read, with Cornill, *qāmal maṭṭeh resha'*.
54. Cf. KUB XXV.31, 7; cf. also: H. Ehelolf, KUB XXIX, Vorwort, iii; C. G. von Brandenstein, in Orientalia 8 (1939), 75 f.
55. Cf. M. Nilsson, Greek Folk Religion (1940), 36 f.; Frazer-Gaster, NGB §§108–10 (with Additional Notes).
56. Joh. Lydus, De mensibus iv.59.
57. Julian, Orat. V, p. 188C.
58. Hepding, op. cit., 152 ff.
59. Firmicus Maternus, c.27.1–2; Hepding, op. cit. 51.
60. C. F. Lehmann, in Die Zeit 2 (1902), 468.
61. Arthur Evans, The Early Religion of Greece in the Light of Cretan Discoveries (1931), 35.
62. Hepding, op. cit., 169 ff.
63. Lucretius, ii.598.
64. See: I. Scheftelowitz, in ARW 15 (1912), 485 ff.; A. Eberharter, in Zs. für katholische Theologie 52 (1928), 492–518; H. Feilberg, in ARW 4 (1901), 170–77; 274–89; J. G. Frazer, GB ix.116 f., 156.
65. Lev. 22:24; Num. 29:1.
66. Num. 10:10; Ps. 81:4.
67. Hull, op. cit. 251.
68. Standard Dict. of Folklore, etc., 1127ª.
69. P. von Stenin, in Globus 58 (1890), 204.
70. TB Rosh ha-Shanah 28ª; Rashi, in loc.; Yalqut, Zech. §578.
71. Standard Dictionary of Folklore, etc., 1127ᵈ.
72. Julian, *Eis tēn Mētera tôn theôn*, 169C; cf. Catullus, 63.9.
73. Cf. Plutarch, Is. 35; id., Quaest. conviv., 4.6, 2; Pollux 4.86; O. Gruppe, Griech. Mythologie (1906), 180.
74. See below §243.
75. Herodian, i.10, 5–7.
76. C. A. Lobeck, Aglaophamus (1829), i.173 ff. Cf. also: T. Trede, Das Heidentum in der römischen Kirche (1889–91), iii.70.
77. Pallis, op. cit. 123, 201.
78. Cf. F. Nötscher, 'Das Angesicht Gottes schauen' nach babylonischer und alttestamentlicher Auffassung (1924).
79. Plato, Phaedrus 250C; Plutarch, Demeter 26; Dittenberger, Sylloge², 646.40.
80. Dittenberger, op. cit., 657–59.
81. CT IV.5, 18; cf. B. Landsberger, Das kultische Kalender der Babylonier und Assyrer (1915), 124.
82. Heb.: *qᵉfādah*. The root of the word means primarily "constrict."
83. See: A. Moret, La mise à mort du dieu en Égypte (1927), 18. Cf. also: Hos. 5:15.

84. V AB iii.41; cf. T. H. Gaster, in Iraq 6 (1939), 138, n.183.
85. Themistius, quoted by Stobaeus, Anthol. iv.52, 49 (*phrikē kai tromos kai hidrôs kai thambos*).

▲ 208 **Trapping the soul**

Literature: H. Torczyner, in JPES 1934.257-60; W. H. Brownlee, in JBL 69 (1950), 367-73.

1. The traditional text of the passage appears to be corrupt. In v.20, the first *lephorehôth* ("like birds," KJV) is here omitted [with RSV] as a mere doublet of the second, and the obscure words, *eth nephāshîm* ("the souls," KJV) are emended, [again with RSV and many modern scholars,] to the very similar *ôtham ḥôpshîm* ("them free"). [LXX, it may be observed, missed the point entirely by confusing the Hebrew word ṣ-w-d, "hunt, entrap," with the like-sounding ṣ-d-d and ṣ-d-h, "turn aside"—a confusion influenced, perhaps, by the association of the latter word with the *soul* in I Sam. 24:12.]
2. T. Williams, Fiji and the Fijians² (1860), i.250.
3. W. W. Gill, Myths and Songs from the South Pacific (1876), 171; id., Life in the Southern Isles (London, n.d.), 181 ff. (Cimet is cordage made from the dried fibre of coconut husk.)
4. Mary Kingsley, Travels in West Africa (1897), 461 ff.
5. M. Delafosse, in l'Anthropologie 11 (1900), 558.
6. W. W. Skeat, Malay Magic (1900), 576 ff.
7. N. Andriani and A. C. Kruijt, De Bare'e-sprekende Toradja's van Midden-Celebes (1912-14), i.233 f., 236 f.

[7a. B. F. Matthes, Bijdragen tot de Ethnologie vun Zuid-Celebes (1875), 35, 56, 59; id., Ouer de Bissie's of heidensche priesters en priesteressen da Boeginezen (1872), 24; A. E. Crawley, The Idea of the Soul (1909), 118.]

[7b. J. L. van der Toorn, in BTLVNI 39 (1890), 48-49, 56, 58; Crawley, op. cit., 114 f.]

[7c. T. H. Gaster, The Holy and the Profane (1955), 12 f.; Folk-Lore 9 (1898), 79.]

[7d. Crawley, op. cit. 117.]

[7e. A. C. Kruijt, Het Animismus in der Indischen Archipel (1906), 120.]

[7f. N. Graffland, De Minahassa (1867), i.248, 321 f., 331; J. G. F. Riedel, in TITLV 18 (1872), 523.]

[7g. N. P. Wilken and J. A. Schwarz, in Med. van wege het Nederlandsche Zendeling-genootschap 7 (1863), 263 f.]

[7h. A. B. Meyer, in Jahresber. des Vereins für Erdkunde 12 (1875), 26; Crawley, op. cit. 104.]

[7i. Phya Anuman Rajadhon, Chao Thi, or Some Traditions of Thai. Thailand Culture Series, #6 (Bangkok 1952), 15.]

[7j L. Fison, in JAI 10 (1881), 145 f.]

[7k. Fr. Dummeruth, in VT 13 (1963), 228-29.]

[7l. Maqlu iii.46, 59-61 (*ba'artum ša muši*).—A further allusion to this may perhaps be detected in Nah. 3:4 if, with several modern scholars, we emend the traditional text's "mistress of magic arts, who *sells* (Heb.: *ha-môkereth*) whole nations with her harlotries, and families with her charms," to "who *entraps* (Heb.: *ha-kômereth*) whole nations," etc.]

[7m. G. A. Wilken, Verspreide Geschriften (1912), i.20; B. F. Matthes, op. cit., 33; G. K. Nieman, in BTLVNI 38 (1889), 281; W. W. Skeat, Malay Magic (1900), 47.]

209 Yahweh's scourges

1. Epic of Gilgamesh xi.180-94; tr. Speiser, ANET 95.
2. Cf. S. Daiches, in JQR 17 (1905), 441 f.

3. The Biblical Antiquities of Philo 3.19; cf. L. W. King, Legends of Babylon and Egypt in Relation to Hebrew Tradition (1918), 132 ff.
4. Literally, "death," but since the work seems to have been composed in Hebrew or Aramaic, this evidently reflects *môtânâ* or the like in the original text—a word which means both "death" and "plague."

211 Salting newborn children

1. See: I. Scheftelowitz, Altpal. Bauernglaube (1925), 78–79; E. Samter, Geburt, Hochzeit und Tod (1911), 151–61; T. Ploss, Das Kind[3] (1911–12), i.227 ff.; I. Löw, "Das Salz," in G. A. Kohut Memorial Volume (1935), 429–62; Notes and Queries V/xi (1879), 206.
2. Cf. T. H. Gaster, The Holy and the Profane (1955), 14.
3. TB Shabbath 129[b]. So too among modern Arabs: ZDPV 4.63.
4. Wieser, Scholien, ii.248.
5. Galen, De sanitate tenenda, i.7.
6. E. W. Lane, Arabian Society in the Middle Ages (1883), 188.
7. J. Wellhausen, tr., Al-Wākidî al-Madani, Muhammad in Medina (1882), 378.
8. T. Canaan, in JPOS 19 (1944), 239.
9. Cf. W. Kroll, "Alte Taufgebräuche," in Beiheft ARW 8.32 f.—In Britain, salt is sometimes carried around a child at baptism: ERE viii.592[a].
10. Globus 89.587.
11. J. Grimm, DM[2] (1844), ii.999; A. Wuttke, D. deutscher Volksaberglaube der Gegenwart[3] (1900), 91; E. Mogk, in ERE ii.633[b].
12. Grimm-Stallybrass, TM 1049.
13. E. Samter, Geburt, Hochzeit und Tod (1911), 52, A.6.
14. W. H. Rivers, The Todas (1906), 263 ff.
15. C. Bock, Temples and Elephants (1884), 260.
16. Notes and Queries VI/iii (1881), 73 f.
17. Times (London) Weekly Edition, Oct. 16, 1946; Manchester Guardian Weekly, May 22, 1947.
18. G. Finamore, Credenze, usi e costumi Abruzzesi (1890), 69.
19. G. Pitré, Usi e costumi . . . del popolo Siciliano (abridged reprint, 1963), 31.
20. A. Kremer, Aegypten (1863), i.59, 151.
21. J. Richardson, Travels in Morocco (1860), ii.21.
22. Notes and Queries I/viii (1853), 617.

212 Rites of divination

(a) Crossroads

1. See: Stith Thompson, MI, D 1786; ERE iv.330–36; E. Westermarck, The Origin and Development of the Moral Ideas (1912–17), ii.256 ff.; J. G. Frazer, GB ii.340; iii.59; ix.61, 68 ff.; x.229; N. M. Penzer, The Ocean of Story (1923 ff.), iii.37 f.; S. Eitrem, Papyri Osloenses, i (1930), 95; E. Riess, P–W, s.v. Aberglaube; Theophrastus, Characters, 28; Pap. Bib. Nat. 2943; Pap. Mag. London cxxv.3.
2. Orphic Hymns i.1; Athenaeus, vii.126; Cornutus, c.34; Scholiast on Aristophanes, Plut. 594; Lucian, Dial. mort. i.1; Eupolis, Dem. 120, Koch; O. Gruppe, Griech. Mythologie (1906), 760, n.1.
3. A. Wunsch, ERE, s.v. Crossroads; cf. Vergil, Aen. iv.609.
4. SBE xxxi (1887), 291.
5. G. Finamore, Credenze, usi e costumi Abruzzesi (1890), 180–82.
6. W. Crooke, The Popular Religion and Folklore of Northern India (1896), 65, 126–7, 140, 157, 201; cf. H. Oldenberg, Die Religion des Veda (1894), 267 ff.
7. E. W. Lane, Arabian Society in the Middle Ages (1883), 37.
8. J. G. Frazer, The Fasti of Ovid (1925), vol. ii, p. 459 ff.

9. Düntzer, in Scheible's Das Kloster V (1847), 120, n. 42.
10. Grimm-Stallybrass, TM 1074, 1115, 1799, 1803.
11. P. Drechsler, Sitte, Brauch und Kolksglaube in Schlesien (1903–6), 234.
12. Goethe, Faust III.i.40.
13. F. Panzer, Beitrag zur deutschen Mythologie (1845–55), i.16, 93, 98, 198 ff., 260.
14. F. S. Krauss, Volksglaube und religiöser Brauch der Südslaven (1890), 116.
15. F. C. Connybeare, in JQR 11.26.
16. E. Samter, op. cit., 145; S. Seligmann, D. böse Blick (1927), 151 ff.; A. Wuttke, D. deutsche Volksaberglaube der Gegenwart[3] (1900), 89; J. Trachtenberg, Jewish Magic and Superstition (1939), 207.
17. J. Campbell, Spirit Basis of Belief and Custom (1855), 208.
18. F. Perles, in Heinrich Graetz Jubelschrift (1887), 24–25.
19. H. Feilberg, Bijdrag til en Ordbog over Jyske Almuesmal (1886–1914), ii.277a.
20. E. S. Hartland, The Science of Fairy Tales (1891), 142.
21. Folk-Lore 34.281 f.
22. ERE iv.802[a].
23. J. Atkinson, Women of Persia (1832), 11.
24. ERE iv.828[b].

(b) Belomancy

25. See: F. Schwally, in ZAW 11.170 ff.; W. R. Smith, in JOP 13.276–87. For Sumerian evidence, cf. W. W. Struve, in Trans. XXIVth Internat. Congress of Orientalists, i (1962), 178–86. Cf. also: F. Lenormant, La divination et la science des présages chez les Chaldéens (1875), 17–32; A. Ungnad, in AO X/ii (1909), 15.—For the practice in China, cf. J. B. du Halde, The General History of China[2] (1741), iii.§100.
26. Livy, xxvii.16, 15.
27. Macrobius, Sat. iii.5, 1; cf. Servius, on Vergil, Aen. iv.56.
28. TB Gittin 56[a]; M. Gaster, The Exempla of the Rabbis (1924), #70.
29. Koran 5:92; cf. J. Wellhausen, Reste d. arab. Heidentums[2] (1897), 132.
30. E. Pocock, Specimen historiae Arabum (1806), 323 ff.
31. S. Iwry, in JAOS 81 (1961), 27–34.
32. A. Lang, Cultes, Mythes et Religions (French tr., 1896), 94.

213 The fallen paragon

THE TRANSLATION: In the opening verse, I take the Hebrew words *attah ḥôtem taknîth* to mean literally, "Thou wast the one that set the seal on (all) design," i.e., wast the crowning masterpiece of art. No emendation is required. In v. 14, I derive *mimšaḥ* from *m-š-ḥ* II, "extend, spread," rather than from *m-š-ḥ* I, "anoint." I suspect also that we should read *kᵉrūb-ma/i mošeᵃḥ* (with archaic enclitic *-ma/i*) in place of the traditional *kᵉrūb mimšaḥ*. In the same verse, I construe *'elôhîm hayyîthā* as a separate clause, viz., "Thou wast a being divine," for metrical and syntactical reasons. In v. 16 I read, with most modern scholars, *mille'tā* for *māl'ū*, though it has occurred to me that the correct reading may be *mill'ūkā tôk wᵉ-ḥamas*, "trickery and crime had filled thee." In v. 18, I read *ḥillalta-ma(i) qôdšᵉkā*, though *ḥullaltā mi-qôdšᵉkā* would also be possible.—It should be observed that, according to LXX and the Syriac (Peshitta) Version, the expelled denizen of Paradise was not himself a guardian cherub; he was placed on the divine mountain *along with* (or, *beside*) such a creature, and it was that creature that eventually banished him therefrom (v. 16).

1. See in particular: H. Gunkel, Genesis[5] (1922), 34; T. H. Robinson, in Myth and Ritual, ed. S. H. Hooke (1933), 180 ff.; G. W. Widengren, Psalm 110 (1941), 15 ff.; id., Myth, Ritual and Kingship, ed. S. H. Hooke (1958), 164 ff. But see also on this passage: K. Yaron, in ASTI 3 (1964), 28–57; F. L. Moriarty, in Gregorianum 46 (1965), 83–88; H. G. May, in Essays for J. Muilenburg (1962), 166–76.

2. Hesiod, Theogony 614.
3. Hesiod, Theog. 565–616; Aeschylus, Prometheus Vinctus 218, 282, 445 ff., 478 ff.; Theophrastus, apud Ap. Rh. ii.1248 (philosophy); Servius, on Vergil, Ecl. vi.42 (astronomy); I. Bekker, Anecdot. ii.781, 28 (letters); O. Gruppe, Griech. Mythologie (1906), 1025, n.4.
4. An early name for him was Ithas, which may be connected with Greek *aithô*, Sanskrit *idh-*, "burn."
5. The tradition seems to be mentioned in Horace, Odes ii.18, 34 ff.; cf. S. Reinach, in Rev. archéol. 1903.176.
6. Hesiod, Theog. 507 ff.; Apollodorus, Bib. i.11.3. Apollodorus uses the word *katatartaroô*, with which may be compared *tartaroô*, used of the expulsion of the rebel angels, in I Pet. 2:4.
7. Cf. H. Weil, in RÉG 6 (1893), 304; Gruppe, op. cit. 1026, n.1.
8. Hesiod, Theog. 613–16.
9. I take the "bosses" and "sockets" mentioned in v. 13 to denote the protuberances and orifices of the body.—E. Lipinski, in Syria 42 (1965), 49–52, suggests that the "socket" (read as sg.) is the vagina, and the "boss" the *membrum virile*, the king of Tyre being thus portrayed as a hermaphrodite! This interpretation seems to me to emasculate the point.
10. E. A. W. Budge, The Egyptian Book of the Dead (1895), 14.6–7.
11. Bibl. Aegyptiaca, iv.27, 16.
12. The Contendings of Horus and Seth, 14 = G. Lefebvre, Romans égyptiens (1949), 197.
13. Westcar Papyrus, App. iv.10, 11 = Lefebvre, op. cit. 87, n.78.
14. Ch. Maystre, in BIFAO 40 (1941), 53–73; A. Erman, Literatur der Aegypter (1923), 47–49; J. A. Wilson, in ANET 10–11.
15. F. A. Schaeffer, The Cuneiform Texts from Ras Shamra-Ugarit (1939), Pl. xxxv.1, p. 93.
16. The Hebrew is usually rendered "stones of fire," about which wondrous theories have been spun. My translation rests on the fact that in an Akkadian lexical text (CT XIX.5, obv.5) the expression "stone of fire" identifies a particular gem called *ḫipindû*. What this was, however, is as yet unknown. The name has been connected with the Semitic *pindu* = *pêmtu*, "coal," but this leaves the first syllable unexplained. I suspect that *ḫipindû* is an Anatolian word with the same ending as in ja*cinth*, hya*cinth*, etc. (The long final -*û* suggests, in any case, that the word is a loan.)
17. Cf., for example, Pseudo-Epiphanius, Hexaemeron 226, ed. Trumpp (Abh. Bay. Akad. Wiss. 16, 1882): "God took fire and made garments of light for the angels."
18. Nonnus, Dionys. vi.260 ff.; Proclus, on Plato, Timaeus i.188.26 ff.; id., in Rep. i.93, 22 f.; Eusthathius in Iliadem, pp. 231 f., 332.
19. Olympiodorus, on Plato, Phaedo 61E (p. 227 f., ed. Norwin).
20. B. Schmidt, Griechische Märchen, etc. (1887), 131.
21. J. C. Lawson, Modern Greek Folklore and Ancient Greek Religion (reprint, 1966) 73.
22. Tale of the Shipwrecked Sailor, 73–74 Lefebvre, op. cit., 35.

214 Pharaoh and the Nile

1. See: H. Frankfort, Kingship and the Gods (1948), 58 f.
2. Kubban Stele, 17–18 = Breasted, AR iii.§288.
3. Breasted, op. cit. §423.
4. E. Drioton, in Egyptian Religion 1 (1933), 39 ff.
5. Frankfort, op. cit. 94–95.
6. See: Frazer-Gaster, NGB §§65–75; P. Hadfield, Traits of Divine Kingship in

Africa (1949), 17 ff.; C. Seligman, Pagan Tribes of Nilotic Sudan (1932), 329 ff.; S. S. Doran, "Rain-making in South Africa," in Bantu Studies 3 (1927-29), 185-95; W. E. R. Cole, "African Rain-making Chiefs," in Man (1910); O. Petersson, Chiefs and Gods (1953).

7. Book of the Dead, ch. 29; Papyrus of Nesi-Amsu, ed. Budge, in Archaeologia 52 (1890), 502 ff.; id., The Gods of the Egyptians (1904), 324-28; G. Roeder, Urkunden zur Religion des alten Aegyptens (1923), 98-115. Useful also, even though partially antiquated, is P. le Page Renouf's article in TSBA 8 (1883), 217 ff.

8. See: E. Tylor, Primitive Culture³ (1891), 325 f.; H. Gunkel, Schöpfung und Chaos in Urzeit und Endzeit (1895), 41-69.

9. Rig Veda v.40.

10. Buddhagosa i.9; Samyutta i.50, tr. C. A. F. Rhys Davids, Kindred Sayings (1918), i.71.

11. T. Fu, in ERE xii.77.

12. E. Welsford, ib., 102ª.

13. W. Schott, De lingua Tschuwaschorum (1841), 5.

14. Grimm-Stallybrass, TM (1880), 707.

15. Sa^{c}adyah, Introd. to *Emunôth w^e-De^{c}ôth;* L. Ginzberg, Legends of the Jews (1909 sqq.), v. 108, 116. Cf. also: Maximus of Turin, in Migne PL vii.337; Hrabanus Maurus, Op. v. 606, Colyr.; Tacitus, Ann. i.28.

16. G. A. Smith, The Book of the Twelve Prophets² (1904), ii.524.

17. C. O. Blagden, Pagan Races of the Malay Peninsula (1906), ii.203-4.

18. R. Lasch, in ARW 3 (1900), 136.

19. T. H. Gaster, Thespis², 228 f.

215 The parable of the cedar

1. Herodotus, i.108.

2. Valerius Maximus, i.7, extr. v.7.

3. Herodotus, vii.19.

4. E.g., R. F. Harper, Assyrian and Babylonian Letters (1902), #656, rev. 6 ff.; KARI #324.9.

5. Kalevala, runo ii.111-224; tr. Kirby (Everyman's Library ed.), i.13-16.

6. Vita Ephraem, cited in Brockelmann, Syr. Gr. 29** 16 ff.

7. E. Sklarek, Ungarische Volksmärchen, N.F. (1901), 13 ff., 26 ff.

8. P. Zaunert, Deutsche Märchen seit Grimm (1919), 1 ff.; cf. W. Wundt, Völkerpsychologie² (1915), ii/3, 192.

9. Concerning this motif in general, see: Deonna, in RHR 84 (1921), 36 ff.; E. Meyer, Ursprung und Anfänge des Christenthums, iii (1921), 36 ff.; E. L. Ehrlich, Der Traum im AT (1953), 117 f.

10. Dan. 4:10-12.

11. H. Gunkel, Das Märchen im AT (1921), 24 ff.—On the world-tree, see: Stith Thompson, MI, A 652.

12. Trans. Speiser, ANET 78-82.

13. S. N. Kramer, in JCS 1 (1947), 3-56; id., ANET 47-50.

14. The traditional Hebrew text reads: *Unto* (sic!) *the mountains and in all the valleys, after its branches have fallen, will its boughs lie broken.* Reading, with LXX, *upon* (Heb.: ^{c}al) for *unto* (Heb.: '*el*), I construe the first clause with the preceding *will leave it.*

15. Cf. T. Canaan, in JPOS 4 (1929), 35 ff.

16. The Hebrew for "Assyria" is *'aššûr.* By a very slight emendation this can be made to yield *t^e'aššûr,* "pine"—a reading which many modern scholars adopt. Another suggestion is to read *'ašw^{e}kā,* "I will liken thee (to a cedar)" which is followed by RSV.

216 The dimming of the sun

1. Joel 2:10; 4:15.
2. On dark raiment in Semitic mourning, see: A. J. Wensinck, Some Semitic Rites of Mourning and Religion (1917), 60 ff.; E. W. Lane, Arabic Lexicon, i.86. Cf. also: T. H. Gaster, Thespis², 214.
3. Pliny, HN ii.98; Plutarch, Caesar 68; Dio Cassius, xlv.17, 5; Appian, Bellum civile iv.4, 14; Servius, on Vergil, Georgica i.472.
4. Vergil, Georgica i.462 ff.
5. Ovid, Met. xv.785 f.
6. Tibullus, ii.5, 75 f. (F. Kirby Smith, in his commentary ad loc., attributes the darkness to an eruption of Mt. Etna, and compares the effects of the volcanic disturbances in the Pacific in 1883. The Italian sun, he adds, was unusually dim in the summer of 1906, after a great eruption of Vesuvius.)

217 Kôshar, the god of minstrelsy

1. M. Dahood, in Biblica 44 (1963), 531–32.
2. See fully: T. H. Gaster, Thespis², 162 f., 339.
3. Quoted, from the Greek rendering by Philo of Byblus, in Eusebius, Praep. evangelica i.10, 1 f.
4. It should be observed, however, that—strictly speaking—Sanchuniathon speaks of *incantations* (*epōdai*), not of songs in general. This connects with the fact that Kôshar was primarily the god of smithcraft, and the smith is commonly regarded as a master of magic; see above, §22. In exactly the same way, the Greeks regarded the mythical Daktyloi as both the discoverers and first workers in iron and as the founders of the magical arts.—The point, however, need not be pressed, for the analogous *kôsharôth* certainly meant "songstresses" in general, and there are good parallels (e.g., Greek *poiêtês*, Sanskrit *takś-*, German *Reimschmied*) for the transference of meaning from *artisan* to *artist;* see: Gaster, loc. cit.
5. Cf. H. L. Ginsberg, in BASOR 72 (1938), 13–15.
6. Cf. J. Barth, Die Nominalbildung in der semitischen (1889–91), §127c.

218 The thread of life

1. F. Perles, in OLz 12 (1909), 251 f.
2. The word rendered *thread*, vix., *nawel*, does not recur in the Old Testament, and this would readily account for the misreading of it. It is, however, not uncommon in post-Biblical Hebrew, and possesses an Akkadian cognate in *nam/wālu*.
3. Cf. Jos. 2:18,21 (RSV: cord).—Such double-entendre, called *tawriyya* by Arab rhetoricians, is a common device in Biblical and Semitic poetry: see J. Finkel, in Joshua Starr Memorial Volume (1952), 29 ff.

HOSEA

221 Hosea and the pagan festivals

1. Cf. E. Jacob, "L'héritage canaanéen dans le livre du prophète Osée," in RHPR 43 (1963), 250–59; H. G. May, "The Fertility Cult in Hosea," in AJSL 48 (1932), 93–98.
2. Israel sows the wind and reaps the whirlwind (8:7). She is likened to grapes and new figs (9:10); Ephraim, to blighted fruit (9:16). She was originally like a spreading vine (10:1). Judgment will spring up like noxious weeds (10:4). Judah must plow,

and Israel harrow for herself (10:10). Israel has planted iniquity, reaped injustice, and fed on the fruit of lies (10:13).—If the text be read against the background of a harvest festival, added point is given also to the words of 6:11: *Also, O Judah, he (Yahweh) hath set a harvest for thee*"—words usually "emended" by modern scholars.

3. Hos. 13:15. Cf., conversely, the promise of eventual dewfall and fertility in 14:5-8.
4. A. Moret, La mise à mort du dieu en Égypte (1927), 18n.
5. I AB, v.23; cf. V AB, iii.41.
6. T. H. Gaster, Thespis², 303 f.
7. Cf. the Homeric Hymn to Demeter.
8. There is also, of course, the notion of "giving us the slip"; cf. Akkadian *ḫalāṣu*.
9. Heb., simply, "Behind you!" which means properly, "Look to your rear!" There is a good Arabic parallel to this idiom, and the text need not be emended (as in RSV).
10. Mishnah, Sukkah iv.9; cf. D. Feuchtwang, in MGWJ 54 (1910), 535 ff.; I. Scheftelowitz, Altpal. Bauernglaube (1925), 93-95.
11. Lucian, De dea Syria 3, 48.
12. The Hebrew word does not refer to resurrection, but simply to bringing a sick man to his feet.
13. Frazer-Gaster, NGB §§207, 231-32.
14. Plutarch, De Is. et Os. 39; Frazer-Gaster, NGB §259.
15. Plutarch, Alcibiades 18; Lucian, De dea Syria 6.
16. Diodorus, iii.59, 7; cf. H. Hepding, Attis (1903), 131 f.
17. Frazer-Gaster, NGB §207.
18. M. Beza, Paganism in Roumanian Folklore (1928), 30. Analogous is the Pietro Pico of the Abruzzi: E. Canziani, in Folk-Lore 39 (1928), 218.
19. This paragraph is taken substantially from the writer's Thespis², 47 f.
20. Arnobius, Adversus nationes v.42; Macrobius, Sat. i.21, 7-11; cf. H. Hepding, Attis (1903), 44, 63.
21. S. Langdon, Babylonian Menologies and the Semitic Calendars (1935), 119 f.
22. Ezek. 8:14-16.
23. R. Labat, in RA 38 (1941), 28.
24. S. Langdon, Tammuz and Ishtar (1914), 32.
25. The so-called "Yuzgat Tablet" = A. Goetze, Verstreute Texte (1935), #58; cf. T. H. Gaster, Thespis², 273.
26. I AB, i.8-16.
27. I AB, vi.22-29.
28. I AB, vi.40-52.
29. Cf. O. Rankin, The Origin of the Feast of Hanukkah (1930), 205 f. Cf. also: F. Boll, in ARW 19 (1916-19), 240, 342; O. Weber, ib., 315 f.
30. Weber, op. cit., 325 f.
31. Rankin, op. cit., 201 f.
32. Cf. also: TJ Sanhedrin, 18d.
33. Reading *yithgôDᵉDŪ* for the traditional text's *yithgôRāRū*.
34. Cf. Hepding, op. cit., 159.
35. Gaster, Thespis², 41.
36. Herodotus, i.199; cf. Strabo, xvi.1, 20.
37. Herodotus, ib.; cf. Athenaeus, xi.11; Justin, xviii.5, 4.
38. Strabo, xii.3, 32-36.
39. Gaster, Thespis², loc. cit.
40. J. Toepfer, in Athenische Mitteilungen, 1898.415.
41. A. Deissmann, Light from the East² (1911), 116.
42. Toepfer, loc. cit.
43. Tibullus, ii.i., 24.

44. Pervigilium Veneris, 5.
45. Cf. May, op. cit.
46. A similar metaphor occurs in 13:7-8.
47. Apollodorus, Bib. iii.14, 4; Bion, i; Athenaeus, ii.80; Plutarch, Quaest. conviv. iv.5, 3 §8; Ovid, Met. 10.710 ff.; Hyginus, #248. Cf. O. Gruppe, Griechische Mythologie (1906), 1277.
48. Hermesianax, cited by Pausanias, vii.17, 9; Scholiast on Nikander, Alex. 8.
49. Hyginus, #192; Gruppe, op. cit., 950, n.1.
50. Schol. in Iliad 18.570; Propertius, iii (ii.13), 4; Gruppe, op. cit., 968, n.3.
51. Pollux 4.55; Eustathius, on Iliad 4.791.
52. Apoll. Rhod., Argon. 2.815-50; cf. Kraack, in GGA 1896.873.
53. Gruppe, op. cit., 968.
54. W. von Baudissin, Adonis und Esmun (1911), 142, gives reasons for believing that in the myth of Adonis this element is a later intrusion.
55. Gaster, Thespis[1], 217 ff. (omitted in the second ed.).
56. The usual Hebrew word for "look after" is *p-q-d*, not *šûr*.
57. Concerning these goddesses, cf. T. H. Gaster, "The Religion of the Canaanites," in V. Ferm's Ancient (Forgotten) Religions, 125-29; E. Pilz, in ZDPV 47 (1924), 129-68; J. Pritchard, Palestinian Figurines in relation to Certain Goddesses known through Literature (1943).
58. Or, *Whoever is wise,* let him understand, etc.
59. L. Oppenheim, in Orientalia 16 (1947), 237.

222 Gomer, daughter of Diblaim

1. So far, no Semitic personal name is known containing the element *d-b-l*, whereas, as a place-name, Diblaim may be compared with (Beth) Diblathaim, in Moab, and with Dibl, in Galilee.
2. We may compare how Joel (3:12) locates the final judgment on the nations at the Valley of Jehoshapat, i.e., "Yahweh judges," and how Hosea himself declares (2:15) that the Valley of Achor, i.e., "tribulation," will yet become a "gateway of hope."
3. E. Nestle, in ZAW 29 (1909), 233 f.
4. Rassam Cylinder, §ix.; tr. L. Oppenheim, in ANET 299[b]. The American equivalent would be "a row of beans."
5. On this gesture, see HWbDA, s.v. *Feige*.
6. Theocritus, x.45; Antiphon, Cleoph. ii.4; Lucian, Indoct. vi.
7. Scholiast on Theocritus, loc. cit.–T. Gaisford, Poetae Minores Graeci (1830), iv.152 f.; Hemsterhuis, on Aristophanes, Ploutos, p. 328.
8. Comicorum Atticorum Fragmenta, ed. Koch, Anon. 7.

223 Gomer's children

1. W. R. Smith, Kinship and Marriage in Early Arabia[2] (1903), 32, 37, 72, 177. The expressions *'akka 'l-raḥim* and *kata'a 'l-raḥim* mean "to rupture the ties of kinship." The Hebrew equivalent is *š-ḥ-t raḥᵃmîm* (RSV: "cast off all pity"), in Amos 1:11. It seems to me that meter and sense alike demand the restoration of this idiom in Ps. 78:38, where for the traditional text's *wᵉhû' RaḤūM yᵉkapper 'āwôn wᵉlô' yaŠḤîTH* we should read, by transposition, *wᵉhû' yᵉkapper 'awôn wᵉlô' yᵉŠaḤeTH RaḤᵃMāw*, thus obtaining the sense, "But He—He shrives wrongdoing, and breaks not the ties of love," in place of the usual, "But He, being compassionate, forgave their iniquity, and did not destroy them."
2. Smith, loc. cit.; J. Wellhausen, Ehe bei den Arabern (1893), 480, n.4; G. Jacob, Studien in arabischen Dichtern, I: Noten zum Verständniss der Mu'allaqat (1894), 92.

224 Stripping a divorcee

1. Cf. L. Kohler, in ZAW 34 (1914), 146, who sees further allusions to this custom in Isa. 47:4 and Ezek. 16:35. See also: S. Smith, Isaiah xl–xlv (1944), 98, n.90.
2. A 3534.26 (unpublished; cited in CAD, s.v. ḫamāṣu).
3. JEN 444.22. The late Isaac Mendelsohn referred me also to HSS XIX.10.13–15; 19.22–24.
4. J. A. Montgomery, Aramaic Incantation Texts from Nippur (1913), 158.
5. Tacitus, Germania xix; cf. C. H. Gordon, The Living Past (1941), 171, 215 f.
6. Cf. A. E. Crawley, in ERE v.51[b].
7. A. T. Clay, in BEUP XV.55, 10–11; A. Ungnad, in OLz 9.163 f.; 12.479; G. R. Driver, Semitic Writing (1948), 63.
8. Theocritus, ii.53–55. The Greek word is *kraspedôn*, which in LXX Num. 15:36 renders Heb. *ṣiṣîth*, the tassel on the fringe of a robe. It is therefore of interest to observe that in a modern Hebrew charm from Mossul the *ṣiṣith* is likewise used for purposes of *envoûtement*. Theocritus says explicitly (line 162) that the lovelorn woman learned her magic from "an Assyrian (i.e., Semitic) stranger."
9. Tetian-Temme, Volksagen Ostpreussens (1837), 883 f.
10. F. Thureau-Dangin, Rituels accadiens (1921), 127–54, lines 415 ff.; tr. A. Sachs, ANET 334.
11. B. Landsberger, Die Serie *ana ittišu* (1937), 99, ii.50; cf. also: L. Boyer, in Studies and Documents, ii.208–18; Driver, loc. cit., n.5.
12. J. Georgi, Russia (1780–83), i.42.
13. F. Nork, in Das Kloster 12 (1849), 1136; J. Grimm, Deutsche Rechtsalterthümer[3] (1881), 712.
14. W. Gesenius, Thesaurus, 742[b], s.v. *l^ebūš*. Gesenius would recognize this sense in Mal. 2:16, which he would render: *But the Lord God of Israel has declared that he has always hated divorce and always been prepared to hide* (lit. *has always hidden*) *the* (*signs of*) *crime on a man's garment* (i.e., *his wife*). This has been followed by many more recent interpreters, but I think the whole passage (14–16) has been commonly misunderstood or "emended" out of its plain sense. I would suggest the following rendering: *Yahweh himself was the witness* (*to the troth*) *between you and the wife of your youth, whom you have betrayed, even though she was your comrade and the woman to whom you had pledged your faith. There is no one man* (*on earth*), *who has a vestige of spirit within him, who has ever acted like that. What would such a man be seeking? Some sort of divine offspring? . . . Nay, let no man betray the wife of his youth! For Yahweh, God of Israel, has declared that he has* (*always*) *hated divorce and been ready to cover up* (lit. *has always covered up*) *the* (*marks of*) *crime which are* (*all too patently visible*) *on such a man's garment*, i.e., the man is all too often himself culpable, but God prefers to help him conceal his faults rather than be exposed to the scandal and recriminations of divorce. The expression, *signs of crime on his garment*, thus refers to *his*, rather than his wife's, guilt. Consequently, his *garment* cannot here stand for his *wife*, for that would yield just the wrong sense.
15. Koran 2:183.
16. Indo-Chinese Gleaner (Malacca 1818), i.164.
17. C. H. W. Johns, in PSBA 29 (1907), 180.
18. W. R. Smith, Kinship and Marriage in Early Arabia[2] (1903), 112 f.
19. E. Westermarck, Pagan Survivals in Mohammedan Civilization (1933), 68 f.

225 Marriage formulas

1. Exod. 25:7; I Sam. 14:3; 22:18, etc.
2. I Sam. 2:18.

3. II. Sam. 6:14.

4. RŠ 67.i, 4–5; Gordon: *ttrp šmm krs ipdk*, where *ttrp* is a verb and has nothing to do with *teraphîm*. The passage probably means "the heavens will sag like the girdle [read *kr<k>s;* cf. the verb *r-k-s* used of the fastening of the ephôd in Exod. 28:28; 39:21] of thy wrap"; cf. W. F. Albright, in BASOR 83 (1941), 40 f.—In Isa. 30:22, the golden *'ªphūdah* of a molten image is probably a sheath of gold plating, or a covering of gold leaf such as has actually been found on a statue of Baal at Ras Shamra.

5. E.G., W. R. Arnold, The Ephôd and the Ark (1917); E. Sellin, in Nöldeke Festschrift (1906), 699 ff.; J. Morgenstern, in HUCA 18 (1944), 1–17.

228 El the Bull

1. EBB I, col. 31a. What is involved is the change of *Kî M-YŠRaEL* to *Kî My Šôr EL*.

2. E.g., I AB, iii–iv.34; vi.37; II AB, ii.10; iii.31; iv–v.47; V AB, E 18, 43; I Krt, 41, 59, 76, 169. Cf. M. Pope, El in the Ugaritic Texts (1955), 35 f.; F. L. Løkegaard, "A Plea for El the Bull," in Studia Orientalia J. Perdersen (1953), 219–53.

3. Cf. T. H. Gaster, Thespis², 172. E. Burrows, in PEFQS 1935.87 ff., finds the divine name *Šw[r]*, "Bull," on the celebrated Tell ed-Duweir Ewer.

4. Note, significantly, the personal name *'glyw,* composed of *'gl*, "calf," and the shorter form of Yahweh, on a Samarian ostracon of the 8th cent. B.C.

230 Oil in the making of covenants

1. Cf. K. Deller, in Biblica 46 (1965), 349–52. Cf. also: D. J. McCarthy, in VT 14 (1964), 215–21.

JOEL

231 Joel and the pagan festivals

1. Cf. T. H. Gaster, Thespis², 71–76. The same idea underlies A. S. Kapelrud's Joel Studies (1948).

(a)

2. Diodorus Siculus, iii.67 (from Dionysus Skythobracchion).
3. Scholiast on Clem. Alex., Protrept., p. 297.4, Stählin.
4. Plutarch, Theseus 22.
5. Clem. Alex., Paidag. II.1.ii, 2; Johann von Krolewitz, ed. Lisch, in Kirchner's Bib. d. deutsch. Nationalliteratur 19 (1839), 26; cf. R. Eisler, Orphisch-Dionysische Mysteriengedanken (1925), 226 ff.
6. Ibn al-Athir, 10.28, ed. Toraberg.
7. K. Bücher, Arbeit und Rhythmus⁶ (1924), 124.
8. The Poem of the Gracious Gods (52, Gordon), 8–11; cf. Gaster, op. cit., 420 f.; J. Finkel, in Joshua Starr Memorial Volume (1952), 29 ff.

(b)

9. Diodorus Siculus, i.14.
10. Herodotus, ii.79; cf. Julius Pollux, iv.54; Pausanias, ix.29, 7; Athenaeus, xiv.11, p. 620A.
11. See J. de Hoorack, Les lamentations d'Isis et Nephthys (1866); E. A. W. Budge,

Osiris and the Egyptian Resurrection (1911), ii.59–66; A. Moret, Mystères égyptiens (1913), 24–26.
12. Firmicus Maternus, De errore profanarum religionum ii.7; cf. also: A. Moret, La mise à mort du dieu en Égypte (1927), 19 ff.
13. A. L. Oppenheim, in BASOR 103 (1946), 11–14.
14. Semus, quoted by Athenaeus 618E; cf. E. Spanheim, In Callimachi hymnos observationes (1697), 649.

(c)

15. T. H. Gaster, op. cit., 26–28.
16. KUB XVII.10, i.16–18; Gaster, op. cit., 303; A. Goetze, in ANET 126[b].
17. Hymn to Demeter, 302–13.
18. Gaster, op. cit., 286.
19. I AB, iii–iv.25–27, 36–38; Gaster, op. cit., 223; H. L. Ginsberg, in ANET 141[a].

(d)

20. The Hebrew word *ba-śaqqîm*, "in sackcloth," goes with the preceding verb *ḥigrū*, "begird yourselves," as well as with *lînū*, "pass the night."
21. Sophocles, Antigone 1146 f.; Euripides, Bacchae 485–86, 862 ff.; Aristophanes, Frogs 340. Cf. also: Herodotus, iv.76; Pindar, fr. 79.
22. Firmicus Maternus, De errore prof. relig. xxii.1–3.
23. Vassits, Die Fackel in Kult und Kunst der Griechen (1900), 18 ff.; Allen-Sikes-Halliday, The Homeric Hymns[2] (1936), 120 f.
24. Macrobius, Sat. i.18, 10; Epiphanius, Panarion 51; cf. E. Norden, Die Geburt des Kindes (1924), 25; Gaster, op. cit. 276.
25. Ezek. 8:7–16.

(e)

26. Gaster, op. cit. 30 f., 52, n.60.
27. Ib., 27 f.
28. KAV p. 20, ii.22–28; KAR 177, rev. 3; cf. R. Labat, Le caractère religieux de la royauté assyro-babylonienne (1939), 315.
29. Leviticus, ch. 16.
30. Aristophanes, Birds 1519; Plutarch, De Iside et Osiride 69.—In corresponding myth, Demeter was said to have abstained from food while searching for Persephone: Homeric Hymn to Demeter, 49–50; Callimachus, Demeter 17 (cf. Spanheim, op. cit., 671 f.)
31. Diodorus Siculus, v.4; Plato, Epist. 349D; Allen-Sikes-Halliday, op. cit., 135.
32. L. R. Farnell, Cults of the Greek States (1896–1909), iii.34.
33. Julian, Or. v.173D, 177A; Arnobius, Adversus nationes v.16; Tertullian, Adversus physicos, de jejunio, c.16; cf. H. Hepding, Attis (1903), 182 ff.; G. A. Lobeck, Aglaophamus (1829), 247 ff.
34. For the fast in October, cf. Livy, xxxvi.37; cf. also: Ovid, Met. x.432; id., Fasti iv.535; G. Wissowa, in P-W, iii.1780.
35. Gaster, op. cit., 27 f.
36. Cabaton, in ERE iii.161[a].
37. L. Spence, in ERE iii.507[a], 568[b].
38. T. C. Hodson, The Naga Tribes of Manipur (1911), 167; id., in JAI 36 (1906), 94 f.
39. C. Seligman, The Melanesians of British New Guinea (1910), 590.
40. Chateaubriand, Voyage en Amérique (1870), 130 f.

(f)

43. Frazer-Gaster, NGB §§444–52.
44. G. Gay, in Bull. soc. géogr. de Paris, III/19 (1843), 29 f.
45. J. G. Frazer, GB, one-vol. ed., 554.
46. M. Buch, Die Wotjäken (1882), 153 f.
47. J. G. Frazer, GB, one-vol. ed., 555.
48. G. Brown, Melanesians and Polynesians (1910), 413 f.
49. Frazer, op. cit., 555.
50. Ib., 558.

(g)

51. Frazer-Gaster, NGB §206.
52. T. H. Gaster, Thespis^2, 37–40, 63, 77, 89, 268.
53. Census of India 1911, IV/i.65 ff. (as quoted by J. G. Frazer, Aftermath [1936], 75–77).
54. R. O. Winstedt, Shama, Saiwa and Sufi (1925), 92.

(h)

55. H. Frankfort, Kingship and the Gods (1948), 168–69, 183–84, 320.
56. S. A. Pallis, The Babylonian Akîtu Festival (1926), 183–97; mythologized in Enuma Elish vi.69 ff.
57. Note that the Hebrew word here employed is *šaphaṭ*, which refers to the rendering of legal decisions, rather than *dîn* (elsewhere used of God's rule: Gen. 49:16; Deut. 32:36; Pss. 9:9; 72:7, etc.), which refers to general administration and government.

(i)

58. I AB, iii.7; Gaster, op. cit., 222.

233 The foe from the north

1. For the historical implications, see: Stocks, in NKZ 1908.725–50; K. Budde, in OLz 22 (1919), 1–5.
2. Stith Thompson, MI, G 633; T. H. Gaster, Thespis^2, 182.
3. Satapatha Brahmana I.2, 4, 10; XII. 5, i, 11, etc.
4. I. Scheftelowitz, Die altpersische Religion und das Judenthum (1920), 59.
5. W. M. Brandt, Die mandäische Religion (1889), 67 ff.
6. J. L. Lauterbach, in HUCA 2 (1925), 364; n.31; Sepher Raziel (1701), 15^a; Chronicles of Jerahmeel, i.17 (p. 6, ed. M. Gaster).
7. Moses Isserles, *Torath ha-'olah* (1858), ii.25.
8. G. Flügel, Mani, seine Lehre und seine Schriften (1862), 101.
9. Pap. Bibl. Nat. 269; Pap. Leyden W, col. xviii.27.
10. Plutarch, De Iside et Osiride 21; cf. S. Eitrem, Papyri Osloenses, i (1925), 34.
11. L. Spence, The Mythologies of Mexico and Peru (1907), 24.
12. L. C. Wimberly, Folklore in the English and Scottish Ballads (reprint, 1959), 137 ff.; F. B. Gummere, Germanic Origins (1892), 418n.
13. J. Hansen, Quellen und Untersuchungen zur Gesch. des Hexenwahns ... im Mittelalter (1901), 208.
14. Menahem Ziyyuni of Speyer, Sepher Ziyyuni 48^d; cf. J. Trachtenberg, Jewish Magic and Superstition (1939), 34.
15. T. H. Gaster, Customs and Folkways of Jewish Life (1964), 61.
16. Brand-Ellis, Popular Antiquities of Great Britain (1900), ii.292.

AMOS

234 Amos and the pagan festivals

1. Cf. T. H. Gaster, Thespis[2], 68; H. Hepding, Attis (1903), 44, 49, 54.
2. Gaster, op. cit., 66, 124, 195 ff.
3. Cf. Hepding, op. cit., 165 f.
4. LXX reads "thunder" (Heb.: *hara'am*) for "mountains" (*hārîm*). If this is correct, it is worth noting that the Canaanite Baal was recognized as the lord of thunder, his alternative name being Hadad (or Hadd), "the Crasher." The LXX reading, however, involves an odd use of the Hebrew word (*y-ṣ-r*) rendered "creator." This means primarily "moulder, shaper," and although it is sometimes employed in an extended sense (as in Isa. 47:5; Ps. 74:17), one can scarcely *mould* a noise.
5. Gaster, op. cit., 124 f.
6. Cf. G. Furlani, Rel. bab. e assira (1929), ii.216 f.
7. Gaster, op. cit., 342; S. Smith, in PEQ 78 (1946), 5–14.
8. Heb. *'aṣārah*, often rendered "solemn assembly," is here derived from '*-ṣ-r*, "restrain." The reference is to the characteristic austerities (Greek: *hagisteiai*; Latin: *castus*) of seasonal ceremonies; cf. Gaster, op. cit., 26 ff., 62.

235 Judgment by fire

1. The rendering "earth" is approximate, but not exact. The Hebrew word (*ḥeleq*) means properly "field, groundplot" (cf. Akkadian *eqlu*, etc.), but by a clever play it also suggests that the field or territory in question is the peculiar "portion" (Heb. *ḥeleq*), or estate, of Yahweh; cf. Deut. 32.9. For a parallel picture, cf. Isa. 27:4.
2. O. Eissfeldt, The Old Testament: an Introduction (1965), 227. I. Seligmann, in VT 14 (1964), 75–92, dates it to "pre-regnal times."
3. Isa. 34:8–9.
4. Mal. 3:19.
5. Dan. 7:10 f.
6. Enoch 91:9.
7. Psalms of Solomon, 15:14 f.
8. Manual of Discipline, ii.8 = T. H. Gaster, The Dead Sea Scriptures[2] (1964), 48.
9. Hymns, iii.19 f. = Gaster, op. cit., 146.
10. Matt. 18:9; Mark 9:43; Luke 17:28; II Pet. 3:7 ff.
11. It is called "the ordeal of molten metal" (*aya khshusta*); cf. Yasna 31:3; 43:4; 47:6; 51:9; Yasht 22:33. See especially: R. Mayer, Ist die biblische Vorstellung vom Weltenbrand eine Entlehnung aus dem Parsismus? (1947); C. Clemen, Primitive Christianity and Its non-Jewish Sources (1912), 161 f.
12. Yasht 19:14, 89.
13. Bundahisn 30:18.
14. Seneca, Nat. Qu., ii.29.1.
15. Cf. F. Cumont, The Oriental Religions in Roman Paganism (1911), 210.
16. H. Diels, Die Fragmente der Vorsokratiker[1] (1903), 62 f. (quotations from Theophrastus and Aetius).
17. M. Eliade, The Myth of the Eternal Return (1954), 88.
18. Cf. T. H. Gaster, "Cosmogony," in IDB.
19. Vergil, Ecl., 4.5.
20. S. Langdon, Semitic Mythology (1931), 320.
21. This quasi-mythological designation recurs in Ps. 36:7 (also, in the Masoretic text, in Gen. 7:11, but the Greek Version there omits the adjective).

22. Langdon, op. cit., 315.
23. Cf. L. Ginzberg, Legends of the Jews, v.149–50.
24. D. R. Hillers, in CBQ 26 (1964), 221–25.
25. Others have emended *La-RîB* to *Li-ŠeBîB*, i.e., "to a spark," or to *LaHaB*, "a flame." These emendations too miss the point.

JONAH

236 The story of Jonah

(a) Sailing with an "unholy" person

1. Aeschylus, Septem contra Thebas 602 ff.
2. Antiphon, De caed. Herod. 82.
3. Theophrastus, Characters xxv.l.
4. Plautus, Rudens 505.
5. Horace, Odes iii.2, 26.
6. The Times Literary Supplement, Dec. 13, 1957, as quoted in R. G. Ussher, The Characters of Theophrastus (1960), 211.

(b) Man cast overboard to allay storm

7. Stith Thompson, MI, S 264.1.
8. Jataka #439; cf. E. G. Hardy, in ZDMG 50 (1896), 153.
9. F. J. Child, The English and Scottish Popular Ballards (1882–98), #24; F. B. Gummere, The Popular Ballad (reprint, 1959), 214; L. C. Wimberly, Folklore in the English and Scottish Ballards (reprint 1959), 98.
10. Child, op. cit., #57; ib., v.496; Gummere, loc. cit.
11. A. Aarne and S. Thompson, The Types of the Folktale (1928), #973*. Cf. also: V. Chauvin, Bibliographie des oeuvres arabes (1892–1909), vii.30, #212, n.2.
12. Notes and Queries I/x (1854), 26.

(c) Swallowed and disgorged intact

13. Stith Thompson, op. cit., F 911.4; J. MacCulloch, The Childhood of Fiction (1905), 50; W. A. Clouston, Popular Tales and Fictions (1887), i.403 ff.
14. Somadeva, Katha Sarit Sagara, ch. 25, 139 f. ed. Brockhaus (1839); N. M. Penzer, The Ocean of Story (1923–29), ii.193; iv.154, n.3.
15. H. Schmidt, Jona (1907), 127 f.
16. Tzetzes, Scholiast on Lycophron, 34; Scholiast on Iliad 20.146. This is a variant of the story of how Heracles rescued Hesione, daughter of Laomedon (cf. Apollodorus, Bib., II.5.9, and Frazer, in loc.)
17. R. B. Dixon, Oceanic Mythology (1916), 69.
18. E. Petitot, Trad. ind. du Canada Nord-ouest (1886), 319; M. Barbeau, in JAFL 39.11.
19. G. Basile, Pentamerone v.8.—There are also variants from Samoa (G. Turner, Samoa a hundred years ago and long before [1884], 331, 337) and Guiana (F. Im Thurm, Among the Indians of Guiana [1883], 385).
20. J. A. van Balen, in BTLVNI 70 (1915), 465.
21. Quoted by J. G. Einhorn, Einleitung in das AT (1780–86), 249, from Müller's translation of Linné. Cf. also: E. Perowne, Jonah, in the Cambridge Bible for Schools, App. ii.
22. Probus, on Vergil, Georgica ii.197; cf. Pausanias, x.13, 10.
23. Servius, on Vergil, Aen. iii.332.
24. Koiranos was on his way between Naxos and Paros. A brigand crew threw him

overboard, but a dolphin rescued him and carried him to Sikunthos (? Sikenos): Plutarch, De sollert. animalium xxxvi.12; Aelian, De natura animalium viii.3.

25. Herodotus, i.24; Pausanias, iii.25, 5; Hyginus, fab. 194.

26. Aarne-Thompson, op. cit., ##333, 700; Penzer, op. cit. vi.154, n.3; P. Saintyves, Les contes de Perrault (1923), 227 ff.; Bolte-Polivka i.37, 40, 389.

27. The following two paragraphs are adapted from my Festivals of the Jewish Year (1953), 174 f. Cf. also: Notes and Queries 1/iv (1851), 45, 178 f.

(d) Jonah's prayer

28. In 2:7 I read: *ha-areṣ bᵉrîḥêhā baʿadî Nᵉʿūlîm* for the traditional text's *ha-areṣ bᵉrîḥêhā baʿadî Lᵉʿôlam*, i.e., "Earth's bars *were bolted* against me." The roots of the mountains are likewise mentioned in Babylonian literature as the bars of the earth: cf. M. Jastrow, Rel. Bab. und Ass. (1905-12), i.30.4.

(e) Animals dressed in mourning

29. On this concept, see: T. H. Gaster, Thespis[2], 24; W. R. Smith, The Religion of the Semites[3] (1927), 271 ff.

30. Exod. 8:8; 9:3, 6, 9–10, 19, 25; 11:4; 12:12, 29.

31. Joel 1:18. This is the correct rendering. RSV's "are dismayed" depends on an emendation (supported by LXX), which in fact destroys the point.

32. Herodotus, xi.24. For further examples, see: C. G. Rawlinson, History of Herodotus (1880), iv.389, n.7.

33. Plutarch, Aristides 14.

34. Plutarch, De Iside et Osiride 29.

35. P. Kretschmer, Neugriechische Märchen (1917), 2.

36. Lebar Brec, 259, cited by Whitley Stokes in The Academy, Aug. 15, 1896, p. 155.

37. Schaumberger, in Misc. Bib. 2 (1934), 123–34.

MICAH

237 Prophecy by puns

1. See above, §98; cf. also: A. S. Pease, on Cicero, De Divinatione i.102; E. S. McCartney, in Classical Journal 14 (1919), 343–58; id., in Papers of the Michigan Academy 16 (1932), 120 f.

2. Cf. Arabic *'-ṣ-l,* "be firmly rooted"; Nabataean *'aṣlâ,* "foundation, bedrock"; Heb. *'aṣîlîm,* "chief men," in Exod. 24:11 is probably related, in the sense of "the Establishment."

3. There is a further pun in this verse, for the subsequent words, usually rendered, (*in*) *nakedness and shame,* should probably be translated, *Exposed is* (*thy*) *shame,* playing on the fact that the name Shaphir suggests a Hebrew word for "beautiful," as who should say contemptuously, *Shift along, Miss Shapely, your ugly spot is bared.*

4. Oracula Sibyllina iii.363–64; iv.165–66; cf. Tertullian, De Pall. 2; Lactantius, vii.25. Note also Shakespeare's pun in *Julius Caesar,* I.ii: *Is it* Rome *indeed, and* room *enough,* etc.

5. Muwatta (Cairo, A. H. 1280), iv.205, as quoted by D. S. Margoliouth, in ERE ix. 140[a].

6. E.g., 55 (*Camerius: camerium;* see F. O. Copley, in AJP 73 [1952], 295–97); 94; 105 (*mentula*).

238 Casting sins into the sea

1. The traditional (Masoretic) Hebrew text reads, their *sins.* RSV follows the ancient Greek, Syriac and Aramaic versions. The mistake is, to be sure, very simple in archaic

Hebrew script. Nevertheless, *praestat arduor lectio*. If we assume that the prophet was quoting a traditional formula, the anomalous *their* could have been a part of that formula, referring originally to the attendant crowds. It should be observed also that by reading *their*, the jingle in the Hebrew is preserved.

2. Frazer-Gaster, NGB §203.
3. Grimm-Stallybrass, TM, 767.
4. Ib., 771.
5. Th. Vernaleken, Mythen und Bräuche des Volkes in Oesterreich (1859), 29 ff.
6. Grimm-Stallybrass, op. cit., 771.
7. Ib.
8. P. Drechsler, Sitte, Brauch und Volksglaube in Silesien (1903–6), i.70.
9. A. Witzschel, Sagen, Sitten und Gebräuche aus Thüringen (1878), 193.
10. P. Sartori, Sitte und Brauch (1910–14), iii.131, n.2.
11. J. G. Frazer, GB, one-vol. ed. 308.
12. Bavaria: Landes- und Volkskunde des Königsreiches Bayern (1860–67), iii.958.
13. Ovid, Fasti v.62 ff.; Varro, De lingua Latina v.45; Plutarch, Quaest. Rom. 32, 86. For varying modern interpretations, see: L. Preller, Römische Mythologie³ (1881–83), iii.134 ff.; W. W. Fowler, The Roman Festivals of the Period of the Republic (1899), 111 ff.; J. G. Frazer, GB viii.107 f.
14. J. G. Frazer, The Fasti of Ovid (1925), iv.53, 74 ff.
15. T. H. Gaster, Thespis², 175 f. (But H. L. Ginsberg, in ANET 132, translates the passage somewhat differently.)
16. See: I. Goldziher, in ARW 13 (1910), 20 ff.; R. Wuensch, in Festschrift d. Schles. Gesell. für Volkskunde (1911), 25; O. Gruppe, Griechische Mythologie (1906), 895, n.5; L. Radermacher, in Anzeiger d. oesterr. Akad. Wiss., Phil.-hist. Kl. 1949/xvi, 307–15.
17. F. Thureau-Dangin, Rituels accadiens (1921), 127 ff., lines 350–60; trans. A. Sachs, in ANET 333.
18. Iliad 1.312–13.
19. Aeschylus, Supplices 529 f.
20. Sophocles, Oedipus Rex 193.
21. Euripides, Iphigenia in Tauris 1191–93.
22. Id., Hercules Furens 649 ff.
23. Plutarch, Superst. 3; Diphylos, Incert 126, Koch.
24. Pausanias, viii.41, 2; cf. P. Stengel, Die griechische Kultusaltertümer² (1920), 163.
25. Cicero, Rosc. Am. 70; Livy, xxxi.12, 8; Tibullus, ii.5, 80 (with Kirby Smith's note); Valerius Maximus, i.1, 13.
26. V. Solomon, in JAI 32 (1902), 227.
27. Tibullus, iv.4, 7.

NAHUM

239 The burden of Nineveh

1. BM 21, 901, obv. 24–30; C. J. Gadd, The Fall of Nineveh (1923); ANET 304.
2. Gadd, op. cit., 17.
3. Diodorus, ii.25, 6.
4. Diodorus, ii.26, 9–27, 1; Xenophon, Anabasis iii.4, 7–12; Gadd, loc. cit.; P. Haupt, in JAOS 28 (1907), 99–107.
5. Diodorus, ii.26, 1–4.
6. Id., ii.27,2; Abydenus, cited by Eusebius, Chron. i.35, 28–37, 13.

7. What the prophet means, of course, is that the shields and uniforms of the soldiers were bloodstained. But, by a clever choice of words, he likens these braves to princes stoled in scarlet.

8. I follow Gesenius in deriving Heb. *huṣṣab* (RSV, arbitrarily: "its mistress") from a root *ṣ-b-b*, "flow," and joining it to the end of the preceding verse.

9. Inserting *hôgôth*, which has dropped out through haplography.

10. Note especially that in vv. 2, 3, 7, and 11 the divine name YHWH overloads the meter. This suggests that it has been interpolated into an older hymn in which the name of the god was not mentioned or in which he was specified, once for all, in an opening verse which has been suppressed. (In v. 12, *Thus saith YHWH* is, of course, a prose insertion; while in v. 9 the present text's *'el YHWH* may have been originally *'elāw*.)

11. T. H. Gaster, Thespis², 194, n.4.

12. K. Tallquist, Akkadische Götterepitheta (1938), 175.

13. CT XXIV.40, 43; cf. KAT², 448.

14. Enuma Elish iv.50.

15. KUB XXXIII, 18.17; cf. J. Friedrich, in Jahrb. für kleinas. Forschung 2 (1952), 148–49.

16. For the sake of the acrostic, read *dālū* (or some other word beginning with *d*) in place of the traditional text's erroneously repeated *'umlallū*.

17. For the traditional text's *wa-tiśśa'* read *wa-tiššá'*.

18. II AB, vii.29 ff.

19. EA 147.14–15.

20. IV R², 28.2 = S. A. Strong, in PSBA 20 (1891), 61.

21. L. W. King, Babylonian Magic and Sorcery (1896), 21.83.

22. S. N. Kramer, Sumerian Mythology (1944), 117 ff.; S. Langdon, Semitic Mythology (1931), 119 f., 125, 128; M. Jastrow, Rel. Bab. u. Ass. (1905–12), i.461.

23. F. Hrozný, Sumerisch-babylonische Mythen von dem Gott Ninrag, i.e., Ninurta (1903), #4.14–21; K 4829; Jastrow, op. cit., i.458.

24. Epic of Gilgamesh ix.17, 102; cf. E. Dhorme, in RB 39 (1930), 489, 495.

25. See above, n.13.

26. M. Witzel, Tammuz-Liturgien und Verwandtes (1935), 208.31; 269.71; cf. also: A. Haldar, Studies in the Book of Nahum (1946), 106.

27. E. Mahler, in Sitzb. Akad. Wien, Abt. ii, 93 (1886). Mahler's conclusions, however, are disputed.

28. Epic of Gilgamesh xi.96, 106, 111–12.

29. Enuma Elish iii.20, 74.

30. Ib., ii.95.

31. For the traditional text's *mālē'* read, with many modern scholars, *hᵃlô'*, and join to the next verse.

32. Verses 12–13 must be placed after v. 14, since the latter is the logical sequel to v. 11, addressed to Nineveh, whereas the former are clearly words of comfort directed toward Israel.

33. For the traditional text's *'āšîm* read *'aššîm*.

34. For the traditional text's notoriously obscure *'im šᵉlēmîm wᵉ-kēn rabbîm wᵉ-kēn nāgōzū wᵉ-ᶜabār wᵉ-ᶜinnitik* read, by mere re-division of the consonants and omission (with LXX) of the first *wᵉ-kēn: 'im šālū mayyim rabbîm wᵉ-kēn gāzū wᵉ-ᶜabārū ᶜinnitik*, etc. The word *šālū* means "overwhelm with flood"; cf. in Akkadian, Shalmaneser I, Asshur Inscription (KAVI, p. 24), iv.22: *ina šamni tâbi e-ri-ni dišpi ù ḫimêti še-la-ar-šu a-še-el* (cf. M. Kmosko, in ZA 31 [1917–18], 83); Arabic *sayyil*, "flood"; see: T. H. Gaster, in JBL 63 (1944), 51 f.

35. IV R 33, iv.13.

240 "The mills of God grind slowly"

1. Plutarch, ii.549 f.; Paroemiographi Graeci, ed. E. Leutsch and F. G. Schneidewin (1839–51), i.444.
2. Cf. Kirby Flower Smith, The Elegies of Albius Tibullus (1913), 360 f.; J. E. B. Mayor, on Juvenal, xiii.100.
3. Sophocles, Oedipus Coloneus 1536 f.
4. Euripides, Ion 1615.
5. Tibullus, i.9, 4.
6. Horace, Odes iii.2, 31.
7. Seneca, Rhet. controv. x, praef. 6.
8. Juvenal, xiii.100.
9. Valerius Maximus, 1.1, ext. 3.
10. Other Classical references are: Plato, Legg. 899A; Livy, iii.56, 7; Persius, ii.24–30.

HABAKKUK

241 "Hush before the Lord"

1. G. van der Leeuw, Religion in Essence and Manifestation (1963), §63.3; "Silences in worship," says Amiel, "are not the empty moments of devotion, but the full moments." See also: G. Mensching, Das heilige Schweigen (1926).
2. Maxims of Ani, §xi.
3. Iliad 9.171; Aristophanes, Thesm. 39 f.; see: E. Spanheim, In Callimachi hymnos observationes (1697), on Apollo 17–18; F. Stengel, Die griechische Kultusaltertümer² (1920), 111. Cf. also: Cicero, De Div. i.45, 102; Horace, Odes iii.1, 2; Ovid, Fasti ii.654; Tibullus, ii.1, 1; ii.2, 2; Pliny, HN xxviii.11.
4. Cf. W. Kroll, Antiker Aberglaube (1897), 32.
5. Kroll, loc. cit.
6. Scholiast on Aristophanes, Birds 1490; cf. E. Rohde, Psyche⁷ (1921), 244, n.1.
7. J. Grimm, Deutsche Mythologie⁴ (1875–78), iii.463, #830.
8. J. Reville, Les religions des peuples non-civilisées (1883), i.73.
9. T. H. Gaster, Customs and Folkways of Jewish Life (1965), 138.
10. W. Kroll, Antiker Aberglaube (1897), 32.

242 The prayer of Habakkuk

1. See: F. J. Stephens, in JBL 43 (1924), 290–93; U. Cassuto, in Ann. Stud. ebrei 1936–37 (1938), 7–22; W. A. Irwin, in JNES 1 (1942), 10–40; 15 (1956), 47–50; W. F. Albright, in Theodore H. Robinson Volume (1950), 1–18; S. Mowinckel, in ThZ 9 (1953), 1–23; J. H. Eaton, in ZAW 76 (1964), 144–71.
2. Literally, *amid years*, i.e., in actual time.
3. The traditional text's *ḥayyêhū* has point: the mythic exploits are to be actualized in history. The commonly accepted emendation, *ḥawwêhū*, "reveal it," is both unnecessary and banal.
4. Not, as commonly rendered, *God came from Teman, and the Holy One from Mount Paran*. The point is that the sheen indicates that he who is approaching is a god or otherworldly being; *god* and *holy one* are therefore common nouns. For the latter in this sense, cf. the Canaanite inscription from Arslan Tash and the Yeḥimilk inscription from Byblus. So too sometimes in O.T. (e.g., Hos. 16:3; Zech. 14:5; Pss. 16:3; 89:8; Job 5:1; 15:15); see: J. Wellhausen, SBOT Psalms, on Pss. 29 and 58; S. R. Driver, ICC Deut. 4:19; P. Haupt, in Hebraica 20 (1904), 161, 172; T. H. Gaster, in Orientalia 11 (1942), 17; C. Shedl, in VT 14 (1964), 310–18.

5. Heb. *t*ᵉ*hillātô* here derives from *h-l-l* I, "shine" (Isa. 13:10; Job 41:10), not from *h-l-l* II, "praise," as usually rendered.

6. I.e., the first glow of the sun has already appeared over the horizon, but its full strength still lies *yonder* (Heb.: *šām*—deictic) beneath it. No emendation is needed!

7. O. Weber, Altorientalische Siegelbilder (1920), i.101–103; ii. ##373–76; G. Furlani, Rel. bab. e ass. (1925), i.167 f.

8. L. Stephani, "Nimbus und Strahlenkranz," in Mém. de l'Acad. des Sciences de St. Petersbourg, Vi sér., Sc. pol.-hist. et phil. ix (1859); R. B. Onians, The Origins of European Thought about the Body, etc. (1951), 165 ff.; A. Smythe-Palmer, Jacob at Bethel (1899), 47 ff.

9. L. Oppenheim, in JAOS 63 (1943), 31–33; G. Furlani, "L'aureola delle divinità assire," in Rendiconti Acad. Lincei 6–7 (1931), 223–37.

10. JVAI 39.24: *illabiš nûri*.

11. Enuma Elish i.103; iv.57–58. Tiamat so arrays her monsters: ib., ii.22–23, 117–18.

12. KBo III.21, ii.14; J. Friedrich, in AO 25/ii, 190; G. Furlani, Rel. degli Hittiti (1936), 24.

13. Iranian *khvarenah;* Yasht 19; cf. A. Christensen, Die Iranier (1933), 229.

14. Isa. 4:5; 10:16 f.; 24:23; Ezek. 10:19; 11:1; 43:2; Zech. 2:9. Cf. J. Morgenstern, in ZA 25 (1910), 139–93; 28 (1913), 15 ff.; id., in HUCA 6 (1929), 34 ff.; T. Paffrath, Das Gotteslicht im AT (1936); W. F. Albright, From the Stone Age to Christianity[2] (1957), 262.—The O.T. passages in which light is associated with God need, however, to be carefully sifted, for they reflect various conceptions: (*a*) in Micah 7.8; Pss. 27:1; 80:20, all that is meant is that God will dissipate spiritual darkness, as sunrise dissipates the shades of night; (*b*) in Isa. 2:5 the idea is simply that God will be like a torch lighting a path; (*c*) in Num. 6:25; Pss. 4:7; 31:17; 44:4; 67:2; 89:16 the light of God's countenance is simply a Semitic idiom for "favor, benevolent mien" (cf. Prov. 16:15; Eccles. 8:1); (*d*) in Deut. 33:2; Ps. 76:5, the poet is expressly comparing the theophany to sunrise; (*e*) in Ps. 104:2 the light is simply the bright sky, as in Rig Veda I.25, 13 and in the Iranian Avesta, Yasht xiii.3; cf. T. H. Gaster, Thespis[2], 201 f.

15. Ezek. 28:7, 17.

16. Hom. Hymns, Apollo 444; Demeter 189, 278; Aphrodite 173 f.; Euripides, Bacchae 1083 (Dionysus); Aristophanes, Birds 1709–13; Bacchylides xvii.102 (Nereids). Cf. also: Ovid, Fasti i.94; vi.251–52; Vergil, Aeneid ii.615; x.634; Horace, Odes i.2, 31.

17. O. Gruppe, Griechische Mythologie (1906), 382.

18. Jamblichus, De mysteriis ii.4.

19. Epic of Gilgamesh ix.98–100; cf. I. Gelb, in AOr 18/iii (1950), 189–98.

20. Iliad 4.440; 15.119.

21. Grimm-Stallybrass, TM 208.

22. Heb. *y*ᵉ*qad*ᵉ*mū pānāw*, "stand before him," is a technical expression for the office of a courtier; cf. Akkadian *nazāzu ina pani*.

23. Cf. H. L. Ginsberg, in BASOR 72 (1938), 13–15.

24. Breasted, AR iii.144–45, §§319, 321–22.

25. Iliad 1.320–21.

26. Iliad 9.181 ff.; cf. C. H. Whitman, Homer and the Homeric Tradition (1958), 344, n.25.

27. E. Pagliaro, Epica e romanzo nel medievo persano (1927), 4.

28. Concerning RESHEPH, see: W. D. van Wijngaarden, in Internat. Archiv fuer Ethnographie, Oudheidkundige Medeeling 31 (1931), 28–42; A. Caquot, in Semitica 6 (1956), 53–68; W. K. Simpson, in JAOS 72 (1953), 86–89; id., in Bulletin of the Metropolitan Museum of Art 10 (1952), 182–87; P. Matthiae, in Oriens Antiquus 2 (1963), 27–43; A. Eisenlohr, in PSBA 14 (1892), 368 f.; W. Spiegelberg, in OLz 11 (1908), 529–31; S. A. Cook, The Religion of Ancient Palestine in the Light of Archaeology (1925), 112 f.; W. F. Albright, in Paul Haupt Festschrift (1926), 143–58.—

Resheph occurs in proper names from Mari in the forms Rashap and Rushpan: J. Lewy in Mélanges Dussaud i (1939), 275; also at Ḥana: ib., 274; M. Schorr, in Babyloniaca 3 (1910), 266 f. A n. pr. 'Ebed-Resheph occurs in a text from Elephantine: P. 11438 = Sachau, Pl. 70, No. 13.

29. L. Vincent, in RB, 1938.512 ff.

30. RS 15.134; C. Virolleaud, in CRAIBL 1952.30.

31. G. A. Cooke, A Text-book of North Semitic Inscriptions (1905), #30. A Resheph of Amyclae (Mkl) is mentioned in CIL I.89; 91.2. Arsippos, father of Aesculapius, mentioned in Cicero, De natura deorum iii.22, 57, is identified by Clermont-Ganneau (Réc. vii.173) with Resheph. Arsuf, near Jaffa, was the Seleucid Apollonias.

32. RS i.7; iii.16; Krt B ii.6. So in the Hurrian Text, RS.4.42, 44–45, *Iršpn* precedes *'nt Amrn*, "Amorite 'Anat."—Drexler, in Roscher's Lex. Myth. ii.1117, identifies the Cypriotic Keraunios and Keraunia with *Ršp ḥṣ* and *'Anat*.

33. Panamuwa inscription, 2–3, 11.

34. Aztwd Inscription, iii.89–9.

35. H. Frankfort, in OIC, figs. 69–70; id., in Afo 12 (1938), 134.

36. Pausanias, x.28, 7.

37. O. Gruppe, op. cit., 1231.

38. T. H. Gaster, *apud* C. H. Gordon, in JQR, N.S. 39 (1948), 50; see: E. Meyer, Gesch. des Altertums³ (1910), ii.134; W. K. Simpson, in JAOS 72 (1953), 86–89.

39. Concerning Resheph in Egypt, see: B. Grdsellof, Les débuts du culte de Resef en Égypte (1942); W. C. Hayes, in JNES 10 (1951), 234, and fig. 34, No. R. 43; M. Leibovitch, in ASAE 39 (1939), 145 ff.; PSBA 1901.83, #339 (name on 18th Dyn. scarab); J. M. A. Jaussen, in Chronique d'Égypte 50 (1950), 209–12.

40. Stele of Amenhotep II at Mit-Rahineh: A. Badawi, in ASAE 42 (1943), 1 ff; E. Drioton, ib., 45 (1947), 61–64.

41. S. Hassan, in ASAE 37 (1937), 129–34.

42. H. R. Hall, Hieroglyphic Texts from Egyptian Stelae in the British Museum (1925), Pl. vii.

43. W. Edgerton and J. A. Wilson, Historical Records (Medinet Habu), 27. 25*d*; also in n.pr. 'pr-Ršpw in a papyrus dated 1743 B.C., now in the Brooklyn Museum No. 35, 1446. (For these references I am indebted to Professor W. K. Simpson.)

44. W. F. Albright, in Archaeology and the Religion of Israel (1942), 79, derives the name from a root *r-š-p*, "burn," but this meaning of the word is not entirely certain.

45. A. H. Sayce, in PSBA 39 (1917), 207, citing a syllabary (CT XVIII.27, 27): *rašāpu*||*rašu*. But Sayce's interpretation is uncertain.

46. Heb.: *wa-y^{e}môded*. There is no need to emend this word, as do most modern scholars. It connects with Arabic *mâda*, "shake, convulse," rather than with Heb. *m-d-d*, "measure," as usually understood.

47. Heb. *wa-yatter*, to be derived from *n-t-r*, "leap," or vocalized *wa-yater*, from *t-r-r*, Akkadian *tarāru*, Arabic *t-r-t-r*, "quiver."

48. I eschew all emendations of these lines, because they all rest on the assumption that the Hebrew word *h^{a}līkah* means "path," whereas it really denotes *the process of going*. What is implied, therefore, is simply that Yahweh has marched against his foes in his ancient manner; and this makes perfect sense.

49. Cushan is simply Cush, the ending being added for the sake of euphonious harmony with Midian. In the traditional text the verse is corrupt and ungrammatical. I read simply: *rat^{e}tū 'oholê Cushan, t^{e}ḥat'enā y^{e}rî‘ôth Midian*. (The ungrammatical *yirg^{e}zū* is a gloss.)

50. New Leyden Papyrus, ed. A. Gardiner, in ÄZ 42.14 ff.; A. Erman, Die Literatur der Aegypter (1923), 367, Abschnitt 50.

51. Erman, op. cit., 371, Abschnitt 500.

52. IV R², ii.*a*, 11–12.

53. II R 19a, 3–4.
54. F. Hrozný, Sumerisch-babylonische Mythen von dem Gott Ninrag (1903), 8 ff.; P. Jensen, Kosmologie (1890), 455, 460.
55. Heb. *mayyîm rabbîm*, "many waters," is a common expression for "ocean," like Akkadian *mê rabbûti*.
56. K. Meyer, Selections from Ancient Irish Poetry (1911), 3, 7.
57. J. A. MacCulloch, Celtic Mythology (1918), 128.
58. P. Sébillot, Le folklore de France (1904–07), ii.12.
59. R. Battaglia, in Rivista di Antropologia 27 (1925), 25; cf. I. Zolli, in Actes du XXeme Congrès des Orientalistes (1940), 284.
60. Matthew Arnold, The Forsaken Mermaid, 6.
61. O. Gruppe, op. cit., 1147; U. von Wilamowitz-Moellendorf, Griechische Tragödien ii (1907), 230; H. J. Rose, in Folk-Lore 45 (1933), 21.
62. J. F. Campbell, Popular Tales of the West Highlands (1860–62), iv.331, 337, 342; J. MacDougall, Folk Tales and Fairy Lore (1910), 309; J. F. Black, Orkney and Shetland Folklore (1905), 189 ff.; Teutonia 2 (1902), 72.
63. W. B. Yeats, Irish Faery and Folk Tales (n.d.), 100.
64. Powell-Magnusson, Icelandic Legends (1866), i.106 ff.
65. Sébillot, op. cit., ii.207; A. H. Krappe, La genèse des mythes (1938), 203 (whence many of the foregoing examples are taken).
66. Heb.: *ha-bin^{e}hārîm*. Since the plural of the word *nahar*, "river," occurs in the very next verse in the form *n^{e}hārôth*, it has been suggested that we should read here *h^a-ba-Nahar-ma/mi* (with archaic enclitic -*ma/mi*), and see a direct reference to the proper name Nahar, the alternative designation of Yam (Sea) in the Canaanite myth.
67. Hearst Papyrus, ed. G. Reisner (1905 ff.), ii.13.
68. KUB XXXIII.108, 16–17; cf. H. Güterbock, Kumarbi (1946), 112; J. Friedrich, in Jahrb. fuer kleinas. Forschung 2 (1952), 147–50.
69. II AB iii, ii, 18; I*AB ii.7; III AB, A 29, 33; IV AB i.7; iii.22, 37; cf. T. H. Gaster, Thespis², 124, 211.
70. Ps. 18:15; 77:18; 144:6; Zech. 9:14.
71. Enuma Elish iv.40 f.
72. ANEP, #689.
73. H. Otten, Mythen vom Gott Kumarbi (1950), #12, 1 ff. (pp. 23 ff.); KUB XXXIII.106, 1, 3 ff.; Güterbock, op. cit., 24, 76.
74. H. Bossert, Altanatolien (1942), Nos. 563, 778.
75. Grimm-Stallybrass, TM 166 f.
76. Hesychius, Lex., s.v. *elasibronta*.
77. This verse has been variously emended, but it makes perfect sense if only MT's obscure *š^{e}bū'ôth* be vocalized *šibb'athā* or *š^{e}bē'ath*. The word is exquisitely chosen, for it plays by hyperbole on the common expression *malle' qešeth* (also in Akkadian), lit. "*fill a bow*," in the sense of charging it with an arrow. Translate literally, *Utterly empty is thy bow, replete though it was* (or, *which thou hadst constantly filled*) *with the arrows of* (*thy*) *command.*—For '*omer* in the sense of "command," cf. Pss. 68:12; 106:34; I Sam. 24:11; Job 9:7, and the Arabic equivalent in Koran 10:25; 11:42; 16:1.
78. T. H. Gaster, Thespis², 164 f.
79. Enuma Elish iv.35 ff.
80. For these examples, cf. M. Haavio, in Journal of the Folklore Institute 1 (1965), 45 f.
81. E. Dammann, Die Religionen Afrikas (1963), 24.
82. W. Krickberg, Märchen der Azteken und Inkaperuvianer Maya und Muesca (1928), 285.
83. J. Mooney, The Ghost-Dance Religion (reprint, 1965), 218.
84. Heb.: *titt^{e}nennū ma'^{a}kal le'am l^e-ṣiyyîm*. There is no need to emend the text;

ma'ᵃkal lᵉ'am go together, with the meaning of "food for (the) people, for public consumption," while ṣî is the Arabic word for "wild cat, hyena."

85. S. N. Kramer, Sumerian Mythology (1944), 80, 82 f.
86. Leyden Magical Papyrus, ed. Mossart, 84–85.
87. E. Drioton, in BOr. 12 (1955), 165.
88. For *rôm yadêhū nāśā': šemeš* I read *hôdêhū* (cf. v. 2) *našah šemeš*. The initial *rôm* is either a gloss on *zᵉbul*, "height, zenith," at the end of the verse, or else vertical dittography from (*ze*)*rem* in the preceding line. One wonders, however, whether *yadêhū našah*, lit. "forgot its hands," may not be an idiomatic expression for "lost its power."
89. IV R² 28.ii, 22–26.
90. The sense of this verse depends on a double-entendre. The point is that Heb. *rô'š* means both "head" and "top of a building," so that the unroofing of buildings—called "slighting" in medieval England—is likened to beheading. Similarly, the word *yᵉsôd* means both "heel" (Ugaritic *ysd*) and "foundation," so that the act of razing down to bedrock (cf. Ps. 137:7) is compared to stripping a person from head to toe.
91. The meaning of Heb. *pᵉrāzāw* is uncertain.
92. The defective meter shows that a word has dropped out. I restore *'ᵃrî*, "lion," on the basis of the similar expression in Ps. 10:9; Lam. 3:10.
93. G. Jacob, Altarabische Parallelen zum AT (1897), 17.
94. IV AB, ii.22–23.
95. Otten, op. cit., No. 12, iii.3–4.
96. J. Wellhausen, in ARW 7.33; 9.140; Weinel, in ZAW 18.1 ff.; E. Crawley, in ERE i.550.
97. I retain the traditional text, rendering literally, "and where I stand, I tremble, I who . . ." The conventional emendation of *'ašer to ašūr(a)i*, overlooks the fact that *'ašūr* means "foot*step*, foot*print*," not simply "foot."
98. G. Jacob, Studien in arabischen Dichtern, ii (1894), 119; id., Das Leben der vorislamischen Beduinen (1895), 124.
99. Krt A, 108 ff.
100. The point is reinforced by the use of the verb *yᵉgudennū*, which refers properly to marauding raids.
101. Heb. *gazar*, here to be explained from Arabic *j-z-r*, "dwindle."
102. That these are the actual words of the paean is shown by the iterated "LORD, LORD," since this corresponds to the Semitic form of address: cf. Gen. 22:11; Exod. 3:4; 34:6, and cf. in the Canaanite Poem of the Gracious Gods (#52 Gordon), 32–33, *ad ad*, "Daddy, daddy," and *um um*, "Mummy, mummy!"—The context demands that the Heb. word *ḥeylî* here mean "my substance, wealth," rather than "my strength," as usually rendered.
103. S. Langdon, Sumerian and Babylonian Psalms (1909), 332. 1–21; id., Tammuz and Ishtar (1914), 11.
104. S. Langdon, Tammuz and Ishtar (1914), 23.
105. I AB, iii–iv.25–27, 36–38; T. H. Gaster, Thespis², 223.
106. KUB XVII.10, i.16–18; Gaster, op. cit., 303.
107. Homeric Hymn to Demeter, 302–13.

ZEPHANIAH

243 Zephaniah and the pagan festivals

1. RS. 3.50 ff.
2. Heb. *zebaḥ* here means "meal, banquet," (not "sacrifice"). For this meaning, cf. Prov. 7:14 and the Ugaritic Epic of Keret = 128 Gordon vi.5.

3. T. H. Gaster, Thespis[2], 93 f.
4. B. Landsberger, Der kultische Kalendar der Babylonier und Assyrer, i (1915), 14; S. A. Pallis, The Babylonian Akitu Festival (1926), 173; D. Luckenbill, ARAB ii.§456.
5. R. Labat, Le caractère religieux de la royauté assyro-babylonienne (1939), 286 f.; T. Frankema, Tâkultu (1954).
6. Enuma Elish vi.72–81. A similar situation obtains earlier when Kingu claims sovereignty: iii.61–62.
7. II AB, vi–vii; tr. H. L. Ginsberg, in ANET 134 f.; Gaster, op. cit., 190 f.
8. KUB XVII.10, iii.30 ff.; Gaster, op. cit., 311.
9. KBo III.7; Gaster, op. cit., 265 ff.
10. Pindar, Paeans vi; cf. R. Pfister, in P-W V/ii, 2256–58.
11. H. Hepding, Attis (1903), 136 f.
12. Rephaim (Rp), i–iii; C. Virolleaud, in Syria 22 (1946), 1–30; Gordon, UH ##121-24; G. R. Driver, Canaanite Myths and Legends (1946), 66–70.
13. II Rp A.4: *bym qẓ*. Cf. *yrḫw qṣ*, Sept.-Oct. in the Gezer Agricultural Calendar (10th cent. B.C.). In the Amarna letter 131.15 *gi-e-zi* (= *qêẓ*) is the Canaanite equivalent of *eburu*, "harvest," and in the Ugaritic Poem of Aqhat 1.41, *q-ẓ* is the season of the early rain (*yr*).
14. I Rp a.4: *tʿrb sd* (cf. Gen. 49:6). For the basic meaning of *s-d* (Heb.: *sôd*) cf. L. Kohler, Hebrew Man (1956), 87 ff.
15. I Rp B 7–11. The reason why Daniel is introduced may be that the divine guests are characterized as *rpum*, and he himself usually bears the title *mt Rpi*, "rpuman." He would therefore be regarded as an appropriate mortal host.
16. III Rp, B 2–4. For ʿAnat as a paragon of beauty, cf. the Ugaritic of K-r-t, i.145 (ANET 144[b]).
17. The passage is still obscure in details.
18. In the Poem of Aqhat II r. 25–30, ʿAnat offers to teach him the art of archery; see: Gaster, Thespis[2], 351.—The word here rendered "flushes" is *tštr*, which I interpret as a causative form of *t-r-r* = Akkadian *tarāru*, or of *n-t-r* = Heb. id., "startle"; cf. Vergil, Georgica i.56: *sonitu terrebis aves*.
19. III Rp, B 14–17. The lower leaves of the Syrian olive are silvery, and from a distance create the effect of a shimmer: G. E. Poste, in Hastings' Dictionary of the Bible, s.v. Olive.
20. III Rp, B 17–18: *yn bl d-ġll*. The interpretation is due to Gordon.
21. Ib., 19–20: *ᶜnq smd Lbnn*. Cf. Arabic *ʿanāq*, "croissant." This is the *zalabiyeh*, still eaten in the Hejaz: see: W. R. Smith, Lectures and Esays (1912), 511. Crescent-shaped loaves, called *armanni*-bread (cf. *armas*, "crescent moon") are mentioned in Hittite texts. *Smd* is the Arabic and Neo-Hebrew *samîd*, Turkish and Georgian *simidi*, and Greek *semidalis*, whence our *semolina*.
22. III Rp. B 25: *bṣq birt Lbnn*.
23. Ib., A 13–15: *prst . . . [ym]lk . . . ʿl Amr*, "My decree (cf. Akkadian *purussu*) it is that he shall rei[gn] over Amurru."
24. Ib., B 20: Baal is hailed as *y ḥrt Il*; cf. I AB iv.27 f.
25. Ib.: *ṭl mrṭ* cf. Syriac-Aramaic *meritâ*; Heb. *tîrôš*, "new wine." For the idiom, cf. Pindar, Ol. vii.2: *drosos ampelou*. A modern Irish liquor is called "dew-mist."
26. Ib., 26–27.
27. Syr. Apocal. Baruch 29:3–8; IV Ezra 6:32; TB Baba Bathra 74[a]–75[b]; Targum Ps.-Jon. to Num. 9:26 ff.
28. Moses ben Isaac of Orleans(?), *Aqdamuth*, recited in the Ashkenazic liturgy on the first day of Pentecost: trans. T. H. Gaster, in Commentary, June 1953; id., Festivals of the Jewish Year (1953), 72.

29. So the gods acknowledge Marduk at the banquet described in Enuma Elish, loc. cit.

30. This also chimes with the subsequent description of the guests (i.8) as "sons of the king"; see below, n.37.

31. T. Jacobsen, in JNES 2 (1943), 167, n.49.

32. K. Sethe, Dramatische Texte, ii (1928), Ramesseum Drama, lines 89–90, 132–33; Gaster, Thespis², 392 (Scene xxx), 398 (Scene xliii).

33. Herodotus, i.133.

34. G. Glotz, The Greek City and Its Institutions (1930), 37.

35. Tacitus, Germania 22; O. Schrader, in RIA², ii.30.

36. Cf. II Chron. 36:23; Ezra 1:21; Job 36:23, and nouns $p^eqûdîm$ (Num. 31:14, 48; (II Kings 11:15) and $piqqûdîm$ (Pss. 19:9; 103:18; 117:7; 119 passim).

37. Note that the Hebrew says "sons of *the* king," not "sons *of* kings." The expression need not be taken literally; it may be a title, i.e., "members of the royal entourage": cf. Jer. 36:26; 38:6.

38. On festal garb, see: ERE, s.v. Dress (reprinted in E. Crawley, Oath, Curse and Blessing, Thinker's Library, #40, 113–15); C. A. Lobeck, Aglaophamus (1829), 173 ff.; P. Stengel, Die griechischen Kultusalterthümer² (1898), 209; T. H. Gaster, in JBL 60 (1941), 302.—The Hebrew word rendered "foreign" is *nôkrî*. In a text from Mari the same word (*nukru*) is used to denote exotic hand-made articles produced in Anatolia: see W. F. Albright, in BASOR 77 (1940), 31.

39. E.g., Dionysius of Halicarnassus, Antiqu. Rom., ii.19, 5; Ovid, Met. iv.339; Herodian, Post Marcum i.10, 5; Sallustius, De diis et mundo, iv.—In the mysteries of the Syrian Goddess the castrated votaries (*galli*) wore female raiment: Lucian, De de Syria xv. Cf. H. Hepding, Attis (1903), 169.

40. Marco Polo, Travels, tr. R.E. Latham (Penguin 1958), 107 f.

41. Vassits, Fackel (1900), 18 f.; Gaster, Thespis², 465, n.22. Zephaniah's specific mention of *lamps* indicates that he is referring to the torches rather than to seasonal bonfires.

42. K. 3476.5, 29 H. Zimmern, in BSGW 58 (1903), 130, 133. Cf. also F. Thureau-Dangin, Rituels accadiens (1921), 118 ff., obv. 28, rev. 2, 13, 15, 19, 20; K 3050 (VAB vii/2. 252 ff.), iii.5–20 (Ashurbanipal).

43. IV R 61.54a ff. (oracle of the Arbelite priest Ladagilili to Esarhaddon).

44. Euripides, Ion 1074; Aristophanes, Frogs 340.

45. Pindar, fr. 79; AP; vi.173 (Rhianus); Cornutus 6.

46. Aristophanes, Thesm. 101, 1151.

47. Homeric Hymn to Demeter, 48 f. (see: Allen-Sikes-Halliday, in loc.)

48. Julian, Crat. v.179B; Hepding, op. cit., 129, 165.

49. H. Diels, Sibyllinische Blätter (1890), 47 f.; L. R. Farnell, Cults of the Greek States (1896–1909), iii.103; J. G. Frazer, GB x.329.

50. I.e., instead of *QôL YôM YHWH MaR ṢōReaH ŠaM GiBBôR* read *QaL YôM YHWH Me-RāṢ We-ḤaŠ Mi-GiBBôR*. For the speed of the "champion," cf. Ps. 19:6.

51. VAT 9555, rev. 7–9 (*lismu*); H. Zimmern, in BSGW 70 (1918), fasc. 5, p. 6.

52. J. G. Frazer, GB viii.72 f.

53. C. Fries, in MVAG 15 (1910), ii.4.

54. Gaster, Thespis², 40 f.

55. III Rp, B 5–6.

56. Literally, "thy judgments." Some scholars prefer to read, "The Lord hath removed them that wrought judgment upon thee."

57. For this interpretation, cf. T. H. Gaster, in ET 78 (1967), 27.

58. RSV, by emendation of the text, renders: *He will exult over you with gladness;*

he will renew (i.e., *yḥdš*, with LXX, for *yḥrš*) *in his love;* / *he will exult over you with loud singing* / *as on the day of the festival* (i.e., *kym m‘d*, with LXX and Peshitta, for *nūgê mi-mô‘ed*). / *I will remove disaster* (i.e., *hôwah* for *hāyū*) *from you,* / *so that you will not bear* (i.e., *mi-ś‘eth* for *maśś‘eth*) *reproach for it*. In my judgment, this is wrong for several reasons: (*a*) the change of *yḥrš*, "keep silent," to *yḥdš*, "renew," overlooks the pointed contrast between now being silent and eventually breaking into song; (*b*) the emendation of *nūgê mi-mô‘ed*, "them that were thrust forth from the assembly," overlooks a mythological allusion; (*c*) the word *hôwah*, "disaster," which is read in place of *hāyū*, "they were," means properly "a fall," so that the concrete verb "remove" cannot be applied to it; (*d*) the emendation of *maśś‘eth* to *mi-ś‘eth* overlooks the fact that *maśś‘eth ḥerpah* is the nominal equivalent of the verbal *naś‘a ḥerpah*, "to heap insults." All that is really necessary to make sense of the passage is simply to vocalize *nūgai* for *nūgê*, deriving from *y-g-h* I, "thrust away," and to read *maśś‘eth ‘alai ha-ḥerpah* for *maśś‘eth aleihā ḥerpah*, with pointed contrast between *mi-m^{e}kā hāyū*, i.e., from *you* they came forth who brought insult to *me*. (Note that *mi-m^{e}kā* goes with *hāyū*, not with *'asaftî*.)

59. Heb. *‘ōśeh*, here to be derived from *‘-ś-h* II, "press" (cf. Ezek. 23:3, 21).
60. Ugaritica V (1967), #1.5–6.

244 Ravens in ruins

1. The traditional (Masoretic) text reads *ḥôreb*, "ruin, devastation," but this is simply a scribal error for *‘oreb*, "raven"—the reading actually presupposed by the Greek (LXX) and Latin (Vulgate) Versions.
2. Ad-Damiri, i.135.
3. Zs. für Volkskunde 1913.386 ff. So too in Jewish lore: Tosefta, Shabbath vi.6; vii.17; cf. I. Scheftelowitz, Altpalestinensicher Bauernglaube (1925), 140.
4. T. Canaan, Dämonenglaube im Lande der Bibel (1929), 15.
5. Thomas of Marga, The Book of Governors, ed. E. A. W. Budge (1893), ii.599.

ZECHARIAH

245 Zechariah and the pagan festivals

1. Cf. T. H. Gaster, Thespis², 47 f., 66.
2. S. Langdon, Babylonian Menologies and the Semitic Calendars (1935), 119 ff.
3. Gordon #52.23–27; Gaster, op. cit., 426.
4. I AB vi.40–52; Gaster, op. cit., 227 f.
5. Cf. Exod. 34:22; TJ Sanhedrin 18d.
6. Arnobius, Adversus Nationes v.2; Macrobius, Sat. i.21, 7–11; cf. H. Hepding, Attis (1903), 44, 63.
7. Cf. O. S. Rankin, The Origin of the Festival of Hanukkah (1930), 205 f.; O. Weber, in ARW 19 (1916–19), 315 f., F. Boll, ib., 342.
8. Rankin, op. cit., 201 f.
9. Rain-making ceremonies took place in the temple at Jerusalem on the first night of the festival: Mishnah, Sukkah iv.9; D. Feuchtwang, in MGWJ 54 (1910), 535 ff.; cf. also: Tos. Sukkah iii.18, p. 197 f.; P^{e}siqtâ d^e-Rab Kahana 193^b, Buber. Prayers for rain are still offered in the synagogue on the first day.
10. Gaster, op. cit., 49, 63, 78, 300.
11. On ritual ululations at seasonal festivals, cf. Gaster, op. cit., 30 f.
12. I*AB i.6.

MALACHI

247 Malachi's picture of the Last Days

1. Cf. T. H. Gaster, The Dead Sea Scriptures in English Translation[2] (1964), 24–27; id., IDB, s.v. Angels, Demons, Resurrection.
2. On Malachi's eschatology, cf. E. Margolioth, in Studies in the Bible: M. H. Segal Festschrift (1964). Our presentation is independent of this study.
3. Yasna 48.9; 53.2; 49.9; Yasht 13.129, 142; 19.32; Vendidad 19.5. Cf. M. Dhalla, Zoroastrian Theology (1914), 60, 181 f.; J. H. Moulton, The Treasure of the Magi (1917), 43 f., 105.
4. The Iranian parallel disposes of the facile emendation of Heb. *mala'k*, "messenger, angel," to *melek*, "king"—yet another of those tiresome "corrections" which, by missing an allusion, destroy an author's point.
5. Yasht 10.2.
6. Yasht 10.116–17; Vendiad 4.2–16.
7. Yasna 30.7; 31.3, 19; 32.7; 34.4; 43.4; 47.6; 51.9; Dhalla, op. cit. 291 (Pehlevi).
8. Dead Sea Scrolls, Comm. on Ps. 37, *b* 4; Florilegium 2.1.
9. Dead Sea Scriptures, Hymns 3.29; War 14.17; Manual of Discipline 2.8; Dan. 7:10; Enoch 77:6; Psalms of Solomon 15:14; Or. Sib. 2.253 f.; 3.542, 689; 4.176; Luke 17:28; II Pet. 3:6 f.; II Thess. 1:7 f.; Rev. 19:20; 21:10, 14 f.; 21:8. See: R. Mayer, Ist die biblische Vorstellung vom Weltenbrand eine Entlehnung aus dem Parsismus? (1947).
10. Berosus, quoted by Seneca, Nat. Quaest. ii.29, 1; cf. C. Clemen, Primitive Christianity and Its Non-Jewish Sources (1912), 161 f.; M. Eliade, The Myth of the Eternal Return (1954), 87–88.
11. Dhalla, op. cit., 60f.
12. E.g., Videvdat i.14, 5; cf. Dhalla, op. cit., 173.
13. Dino, Persica 5 (FHG ii.90).
14. Diogenes Laertius, Proaem. 8.
15. Dadistan-i-Denak (West, SBH xviii), 14.2; Dhalla, op. cit., 162.
16. Dan. 12:1; DSS Hymns 1.23–24; 16.10; Slavonic Enoch 50.1; Odes of Solomon 9.12. For rabbinic parallels, cf. L. Ginzberg, Legends of the Jews (1909 ff.), v.128, n.141.

248 The sun of righteousness

1. Dhalla, Zoroastrian Theology (1914), 106; M. J. Vermasseren, Mithras (Urban Bücher 1965), 75 ff.
2. O. S. Rankin, The Origin of the Festival of Hanukkah (1930), 200 f.
3. T. H. Gaster, Thespis[2], 47 f.
4. CIL I, p. 410.
5. Joh. Lydus, De mensibus 4.1; Macrobius, Sat. 1.18,9.
6. G. Wissowa, Religion und Kultus d. Römer[2] (1912), 367.
7. F. Boll, in ARW 19 (1916)–19), 342; O. Weber, ib., 315 f. On the identification of Kronos with Helios (the sun), see: Rankin, op. cit., 206 f.
8. Plutarch, De Iside et Osiride 12.
9. K. Holl, in Sitzb. Berl. Akad. 1917.428; O. Weber, in ARW 18 (1919), 300 ff.; E. Norden, Die Geburt des Kindes (1924), 27, n.2.
10. L. Duchesne, Christian Worship, tr. McClure (1920), 261 f. Cf. Philip le Grève's hymn, *In nativitate Christi*, quoted in Gaster, Thespis[2], 280, n.18.

11. See: S. A. Cook, The Religion of Ancient Palestine in the Light of Archaeology (1925), 47–48; F. v. Bissing, in ZÄS 64 (1929), 112; B. Perring, in AfO 8 (1933), 281–96; V. Christian, ib., 9 (1934), 30; O. Eissfeldt, in Forsch. und Fortschritte 18 (1942), 145–47; J. Pritchard, ed., ANEP ##442, 443, 493.
12. M. O. W. Jeffreys, in Africa 31 (1951), 94–111.
13. Yasht 10.5.
14. E. Dhorme, Les religions de Babylonie et d'Assyrie (1945), 61; B. Meissner, Babylonien und Assyrien, ii (1925), 20.
15. Ugaritica V (1967), #7.
16. See fully: O Gruppe, Griechische Mythologie (1906), 1237 ff.

249 The Second Coming of Elijah

1. E.g., TB Menaḥoth 45a; Baba Meṣi'a 3a; Aboth de-Rabbi Nathan 24.4; cf. also: Matt. 11:14; 17:10 ff.; Mark 9:11 f.
2. M. J. Vermasseren, Mithras (Urban Bücher, 1965), 84 f.
3. Ib., 85.

THE HOLY WRITINGS

Psalms

250 The divine adoption of kings   Ps. 2:6–7

This psalm was designed for the installation of a king. In ancient times, the primary function of a king (as it still is among primitive peoples) was to mediate what *we* call "nature" to the community. The king was responsible for the weather, the rhythm of the seasons, and, in general, the life and increase of his people. He was therefore a representation in present time of the god, who exercised the same office on a continuous plane, extending over all generations.[1] To articulate this relationship in intelligible terms, various images and symbols were employed: the king could be envisaged as the god in the flesh, or as an offspring of the god's body, or as the recipient of insignia and tokens of authority handed to him from "on high." These images and symbols condition the forms of installation ceremonies.

In the present case, the pattern used is that of genealogy. The king is formally acknowledged by the god as his son: *Yahweh hath said unto me, Thou art my son; this day have I begotten thee.* Parallels to this are to be found throughout the Ancient Near East. An Egyptian text has the god Re' declare to Sesostris III (c. 1880–40 B.C.): "Thou art the son of my body, whom I have begotten";[2] while elsewhere the Pharaoh is described explicitly as "the son of his (Re"s) body."[3] The Babylonians conveyed the same idea by having the king placed on the knees of a divine image during a solemn ceremony in the temple[4]—an act which in secular life, signified acknowledgment of paternity.[5] In a Canaanite myth from Ras Shamra-Ugarit, the imminent death of the king excites surprise on the grounds that he is "a son of God (El)," and therefore presumably immortal;[6] while among the Iranians all kings were deemed descendants of the god Mithra,[7] and in ancient South Arabia as the sons of gods.[8]

(The idea could be expressed also by saying that the king had been suckled at the breasts of the major goddess. Two Egyptian texts have Hathor make such a statement to the Pharaoh;[9] and a relief at Abydos portrays Seti I (c. 1318–01 B.C.) imbibing from the udders of that cow-deity.[10] Similarly, the early Babylonian king Entemena is "nourished by the life-giving milk of the goddess Ninḫursag";[11] while Ashurbanipal (668–63 B.C.) is informed by the divine messenger Nabu that he is indeed a suckling of divine teats.[12])

Alternatively, a god is said to have contrived the human birth of the sovereign and thus to be, in a sense, his real father. Thus Hatchepsut, Ramses II and Amenhotep III of Egypt are alike represented as "adopted" by Amun.[13]

We have seen above (§**122**) that a standard method of adopting a child was to clasp it to the bosom, in imitation of suckling by the mother. This too appears as part of our present ceremony of installation. Unfortunately, however, the point is obscured in the traditional text because the ancient editors, unaware of it, put the wrong vowel points to the Hebrew consonants and also ventured a slight emendation, thereby obtaining a false meaning. In place of the words (v. 7), *I will publish the decree* (a translation which is, in any case, grammatically untenable), we must read, by a very slight restoration, *I will gather thee unto My bosom*.[14]

King installed on holy mountain

The king is said (v. 6) to be installed on the holy mountain, here identified as Mt. Zion. This, again, reflects a piece of ancient symbolism. As the punctual representation of the god, the king had to imitate him on the present scene. Gods—especially supreme gods—characteristically dwell on the top of a mountain regarded as the axis of the world.[15] We think immediately of the Olympus of the Greeks, but there are also the Uttarakuru of the Hindus,[16] the Haraberezaiti (Elburz) of the Iranians,[17] the Meru of the Aryans, the Himavata of the Tibetans, the Kwan-lun of the Chinese, the Mtemnoh Toung of the Burmese,[18] the Northern Mountain of the Caucasian Khevsurs[19] and of the North American Dakotas,[20] and countless others. In religious cult, these mythical mountains were usually localized at the most prominent peak in the area, e.g., Casius in Syria, Tabor, Zion, Gerizim; and where no such peak existed, fiction supplied it by identifying the local cult center, albeit low-lying, with this eminence. The Egyptian queen Hatchepsut, for example, extols Karnak as representing "the light-mountain, the favorite place of Re‘,"[21] and similar praise is lavished also on the cities of Thebes and Hermonthis.[22] The Mesopotamians appear to have identified their stepped temples (ziggurats) with the mythical cosmic mountain,[23] as the Javanese do their famous temple at Barabudur.[24] Nor, indeed, is the idea unattested in the Old Testament itself; for in Psalm 48:2, Mt. Zion is hailed as something called "the far extremes of the North," and we now know from the Canaanite texts discovered at Ras Shamra that this was a standard designation of the mythical mountain of the gods. So too in Psalm 87:1, the temple on Zion was apostrophized as "the structure founded by God on the holy hills," and here again the point is that it is fancifully identified with the mythical mansion which the god (e.g., Baal in the Ras Shamra texts) upreared on the mythical mountain where the divine hosts convened.[25]

Accordingly, when the king is here said to be installed on "Zion, My holy hill," the meaning is not merely that Zion, by virtue of the Temple's being upon it, happens to be a cultically sacred spot, but rather that it stands for the mythical mountain of the god, the king thus reproducing on the real plane the status of the god on the ideal one.[26]

A further significance may also be involved. Since, as we have seen, the king was but a punctual embodiment of the sempiternal, continuous god, the beginning of his reign could be envisaged as the repetition of the primordial beginning of all things. The ceremony of installation would therefore have had to reproduce the primordial archetype. Now, the belief was entertained by many ancient peoples (as it is also by many modern primitives) that the earth had risen out of the primeval waters in the form of a hill or mound.[27] Accordingly, at his coming into power, the new king would have had symbolically to stand on such a hill or mound—a practice which we have already discussed (above, §148) in connection with the installation of Solomon.

251 Seeing the face of God   17:15

I shall behold Thy face in righteousness
when I awake, have full enjoyment of thy visage.

This psalm is written for the occasion when a man seeks refuge at a sanctuary from men who are bringing charges against him or actually pursuing him in order to wreak vengeance.[1] Such suppliants were regarded as the temporary "guests" (Heb.: *gērim*) of the god, claiming from him the customary rights of hospitality and protection (see above, §149). They slept in the sacred precincts and trusted to wake up safe and sound in the morning. It is to this rather than to the resurrection or judgment after death—as has been commonly supposed—that our concluding verse alludes.[2] The immediate reference is to what came later to be termed the *epopteia*—that is, the vision of the god in a dream or ecstatic experience,[3] though here it is conceived rather as the act of beholding the divine host's friendly countenance on awaking. The *epopteia* later became a prominent element of the Graeco-Roman mystery cults,[4] though it is mentioned already in connection with the Eleusinian mysteries.[5]

A further reference to this usage may be detected in the concluding words of Psalm 11—likewise a "psalm of asylum," viz., *The upright shall see his face.*[6]

252 The breakers of Death   18:4–5

"Death" is here used by metonomy, as elsewhere in the Old Testament,[1] for the netherworld. The river (or rivers) of the netherworld figure ubiquitously in world folklore.[2] Usually, it is regarded as a barrier at the edge of the world of the living.[3] There is evidence of such a concept among the Egyptians, though admittedly of doubtful interpretation.[4] The Mesopotamians, however, spoke clearly of an infernal stream named Ḫubur, which all mortals were destined to cross.[5] In one Mesopotamian text, a man's deliverance from misfortunes is described as being plucked from the waters of Ḫubur.[6] Gilgamesh, in his quest for immortality, is eventually directed to a distant island beyond "the waters of death," where dwells the ancient worthy Utnapishtim, survivor of the Flood.[7] The Greeks spoke likewise of a river (Acheron) which compasses the realm of the dead;[8] and the figure of the ferryman (Charon) who rows souls across it is, of course, a commonplace of Classical mythology and survives in modern Greek folklore.[9] King Arthur of England was transported on a barge to the Land of the Dead, and the hapless Lady of Shallot requested that, after her death, "her body be placed in a skiff and left to drift to the underworld, led only by the winds"[10]—a faded reminiscence of the same concept. The gravedigger in *Hamlet* also alludes to it when he declares that old age "hath *shipped* me into the Land";[11] while the old English Ballad of Johnnie Cock speaks significantly of "the *ford* of Hell."[12]

Attempts were sometimes made to determine the earthly location of this River of Death. German popular belief, for instance, identified it with the Rhine;[13] Procopius, the Byzantine historian, writing in the early sixth century, says that the English Channel was once so regarded;[14] while according to Pliny, the Cimbri—the ancient inhabitants of Jutland—called an arm of the North Sea "the sea of the dead."[15] Similarly, in France, an arm of the River Tréguier was known popularly as *le passage de l'enfer*.[16]

Nor is this fancy confined to ancient peoples. In a funeral dirge current among the Badaga of the Nilgrit Hills, the departing soul is said to encounter the "sea rising in waves" before it reaches the bridge dividing this world from the next.[17] The infernal or otherworld stream figures also in the popular fancy of many North American Indian tribes, such as the Ojibwas, the Araucanians, the Algonqins, and the Sioux of Dakota.[18] The Aztecs speak of "Nine Rivers (Chicuroapa)";[19] the Greenlanders sail after death to an unfathomable abyss;[20] and analogous beliefs obtain among the Tupis of Brazil[21] and the Caribs.[22]

(If the Biblical writer is indeed referring to this Barrier Stream, the plural *rivers* [KJV: floods] must be understood as mere poetic idiom, like ῥοαί so used by Homer [e.g., Il. 19.229; Od. 6.216] or *rivi* by Latin authors [e.g., Horace, Odes 3.13.7; Tibullus 1.1, 28; Juvenal 6.490].)

To be sure, the concept is fluid in more than one sense, and the River (or Rivers) of Death are sometimes envisaged not as barriers but as actually flowing in the netherworld; and it is equally possible that this is what the Psalmist has in mind. Especially familiar in this respect are the four rivers of Hades in Greek myth—possibly an infernal counterpart of the four rivers of the Earthly Paradise (see above, §14).[23] But these are by no means the only examples. In the Hindu Rig Veda we hear similarly of the "hellish" Vaitârâṇi river;[24] and in the Finnish Kalevala, the gruesome realm of Tuonela contains a "murky lake" and a "raging whirlpool."[25] The funeral liturgy of the Mandaeans of Iraq and Iran includes mention of a river which the dead must cross;[26] while Dante, gilding the Classical lily (if one can use such a metaphor of such darkling things), speaks of "infernal rivers fed by human tears."[27]

253 The bonds of Death

If Death can be portrayed mercifully as a shepherd (Ps. 49:14), he can also be pictured more harshly as a huntsman armed with snares and toils. This concept is by no means the peculiar invention of the Hebrew Psalmist. A Mesopotamian magical text likewise speaks of a man's being "bound in death."[1] In Hindu belief, Yama, the god of death, comes equipped with nets,[2] and among the Iranians the demon Astoridhotush stalks abroad in this fashion.[3] A Mandaean text speaks in the same way of "the bonds and toils of Death."[4]

The picture is common also in European lore. It is said, for instance, in the poem *Beowulf* that if any man gazed upon Thryth "he might reckon death-bonds prepared for him,"[5] and in the Anglo-Saxon *Exodus,* when Moses slays the Egyptian (Exod. 2:12), the latter falls "in dede's bond."[6] Shakespeare too speaks of the "bonds of death,"[7] and in medieval German poetry, Death is armed, like the Devil himself, with traps and bonds.[8]

The same is said too of Death's brother, Sleep. Sophocles speaks of "almighty Sleep who binds men,"[9] and Plato of being "fettered by Sleep."[10] In one of the Orphic Hymns, Hypnos (Sleep) is said to "tie men in indissoluble bonds";[11] and the Roman poet Ennius expresses a similar sentiment.[12] A Jewish prayer, still recited on retiring at night, alludes to "the bonds of sleep,"[13] and everyone familiar with English literature will at once recall Thomas Moore's "Oft in the stilly night, Ere slumber's chain hath bound me."

The idea is, of course, simply a variation on the common motif of *demoniacal binding,*[14] concerning which see above, §208.

(Most versions obscure the point by confusing the Hebrew word for "bonds" or "snares" with that which means "sorrows" (KJV) or "pangs." The word is *ḥebel,* and it is here to be associated rather with the Akkadian *naḫbalu,* "snare.")

254 Riding a cherub 18:10

We have already seen (above, §18) that a cherub is not a nightgowned angel, but a griffonlike monster; and since the words, *He mounted a cherub and flew,* here stand parallel to *He darted on the wings of the wind,* it is apparent that the reference is to the mythological storm-bird—the Im. Dugud of the Sumerians,[1] the Anzu (formerly read Zu) of the Akkadians,[2] the Hraesveglr of the Eddas,[3] the Garuda-bird, mount of Vishnu, of the Hindus,[4] and their congenors in other mythologies (*loc. cit.*).[5]

That gods ride the winds is a commonplace of Mesopotamian religious literature.[6] Ninlil, for instance, is described expressly as "rider on the great storms."[7] A variant of the idea is that gods are shod with the winds. They are said in the Hittite myth of Kumarbi to be so accoutred;[8] and a dim echo of the same notion may perhaps be heard in Homer's statement that Hermes and

Athene flew with the aid of winged sandals,[9] for this may represent a conflation of the originally distinct ideas that (a) gods were shod with the winds and (b) the winds were winged. In Sassanian and Byzantine iconography, gods are often portrayed riding in chariots drawn by griffons or similar mythical beasts.[10]

255 The heavenly sieve 18:11

> *His pavilion round about*
> *were dark waters and thick clouds of the skies* (KJV)

Comparison with the parallel passage in II Samuel 22:12 shows that the Hebrew word rendered *dark* (viz., *ḤeŠKaT*) is simply a substitution for a very similar archaic word (viz., *ḤaŠRaT*) which does not occur elsewhere in the Old Testament and which the ancient editors therefore could not understand. Now, this rarer word is identical in outward form with one which occurs in post-Biblical Hebrew and in other Semitic languages with the meaning, *sieve*. It has therefore been suggested[1] that the Psalmist is here alluding to a widespread popular notion that rain is precipitated through a celestial sieve. Among the Kandhs of India, for example, it is believed that rain is sent in this manner by the god Pidzin Pennu;[2] while the Greek comedian Aristophanes has one of his characters declare ribaldly that it is Zeus urinating through a sieve;[3] and even at the present day, in certain districts of Boeotia, "God is plying his sieve" is a common popular expression for "it is hailing."[4]

The belief also underlies a very common practice of weather magic. In times of drought, the Ainus of Japan scatter water through a sieve in order "homeopathically" to influence the precipitation of rain.[5] German witches used to do likewise;[6] and it is recorded that in the middle of the nineteenth century the inhabitants of the Tarashchansk area of Russia poured water through a sieve over an exhumed corpse to the same end.[7]

This interpretation of the Biblical verse has, however, itself to be passed through a sieve, for it turns out to be a parade example of how Comparative Folklore can be *wrongly* invoked in the exegesis of Scripture. The stark and prosaic fact is that the obscure word *ḥašᵉrah*, which has been taken to mean *sieve*, and which stands parallel in the text to *thick clouds of the skies*, is really to be connected with a quite distinct Arabic *ḥathara*, "condense," and therefore means no more than *condensation*, i.e., thick mass, *of waters!*[8]

256 Lightning as an arrow 18:14
See above, §242.

257 Walking round the altar 26:6

> *I will wash my hands in innocency,*
> *and compass Thine altar*

Circumambulation is a common device in folk custom for keeping noxious spirits from a place or person. The object is to make a closed circle which they cannot penetrate.[1]

The custom is well attested in Semitic antiquity.[2] The Akkadian word *saḫāru*, which comes to mean, "to resort to a shrine, perform cultic practices, worship," means literally, "to circuit," and probably referred in the first place to ritual circumambulation.[3] Similarly, in ancient South Arabian inscriptions, a not uncommon term for "altar" or "cultic standing stone" is *q-y-f* or *m-q-f*, the literal meaning of which is "object of circuit";[4] while a prominent feature of pre-Islamic worship was the rite known as *tawwaf*, in which the altar was solemnly circuited, in a peculiar limping gait, amid wild ejaculations of praise (*tahlil*).[5]

As with so much of primitive usage, the idiom may be rude and antiquated, but the content is profound and meaningful: the holy must be protected by a spiritual *cordon sanitaire*, and that cordon must be provided by human beings who are on their feet and moving.

258 A Canaanite psalm?   29

It is now commonly recognized that the Babylonian poem *Enuma Elish*— the so-called "Epic of Creation"—is really the cult-myth of the New Year (Akîtu) Festival, as part of the ceremonies of which it was indeed recited.[1] The sixth tablet of that poem relates how, following his victory over the monster Tiamat, the god Marduk (or, in the earlier Sumerian version, Ninurta)[2] was acclaimed king of the divine hosts and how, after being installed in an especially constructed palace, he received the adoration of his subjects. This episode of the myth evidently corresponded to that stage of the ritual in which the image of the god was conducted ceremoniously to his temple and there enthroned.

Precisely the same thing is represented also in Hittite myth and ritual. A text discovered at Boghazköi[3] which preserves the cultic legend and ritual of the annual Puruli festival held in spring deals with the triumph of the god of storm and weather over a dragon (*illuyankas*) and describes how, as the climax of that festival a parade was organized to the city of Nerik and how, on arrival at that cultic center, the victorious god was enthroned as king.[4]

The same pattern obtained likewise in the Canaanite world. In the *Poem of Baal*, the story is told how that god, after defeating the monster Yam (Sea) was acclaimed king of the gods and how, duly installed in an especially constructed palace, he received the adoration of his divine subjects.[5] The *Poem of Baal*, like its Mesopotamian and Hittite counterparts, was in all probability the cult-myth of a seasonal festival, its main episodes corresponding to the main stages of the ritual.[6]

In both cases the pattern is the same: the god of the weather defeats a rebellious dragon or monster, thereby acquires dominion and is installed in a new palace; and in both cases the occasion is marked by the recitation of a paean rehearsing his glory and prowess.

This mythological situation certainly finds expression in the Old Testament, for, as we shall see later, it provides the true interpretation of Psalm 93.[7] That psalm begins with a reference to Yahweh's having acquired kingship and to his being arrayed in the robes of majesty. It then alludes to the firm establishment of his throne and of the world order, and to his prowess over the raging force of Sea (*Yam*) and Streams (*Nºharōth*), the very antagonists specifically mentioned in the Canaanite *Poem of Baal*.[8] Next it makes reference to the reliability of his decrees—a phrase readily explicable from the fact that, in the analogous Babylonian myth, Marduk inaugurates his new regime by issuing orders and decrees designed to regulate the world.[9] Lastly, there is an allusion to a "house" which Yahweh is destined to occupy for all eternity.

Psalm 29 may be regarded as of the same order and as being really the typical "hymn of laudation" detached from its mythic context, Yahwized and preserved as an independent liturgical composition.[10] There is a complete correspondence in details between the Hebrew psalm and the texts to which we have referred, and several passages of the former which are at present difficult of interpretation are at once clarified and illuminated by comparison with the latter.

The psalm begins (v. 1) with an invocation to the *bºnê elim* or members of the pantheon, to pay homage to Yahweh.[11] Now, in *Enuma Elish* it is the company of the gods who render homage to Marduk after his victory,[12] while in the Canaanite *Poem of Baal* it is the "threescore and ten sons of Asherat,"[13] identical with what are elsewhere called specifically the *bn ilm*,[14] who are summoned to the new-built palace to perform the same function.

These lesser gods are invited (v. 2) to ascribe unto Yahweh "the glory of His name." This last expression recurs elsewhere,[15] and the whole phrase is usually taken to mean that the divine hosts are summoned to acknowledge the innate majesty of Yahweh. But it is significant that in *Enuma Elish* the adoration takes the particular form of reciting the god's honorific name and titles,[16] and that there is repeated reference in that poem to the celebration of Marduk's *name;* cf. vi, 117: "verily, we will acclaim his name in our assembly"; *ib.* 143-44: "in their convocation they acclaim his essence; in the fane they all of them celebrate His name." Hence, it would appear plausible that the expression "glory/honor of His name" possesses a more specific meaning and denotes the recitation, with appropriate laudatory embellishments, of his honorific names.[17] In other words, the ensuing description of Yahweh's prowess as a "god of glory" who convulses nature by his storms would be the actual "glory of his name" which the divine hosts are bidden recite.

The gods are invited (v. 2b) to "prostrate themselves" in "holy awe." Now, for the latter phrase (Heb.: *bºhadrath qōdeš*) the Septuagint and Peshitta Versions read, significantly, "in the court of the/His sanctuary (*beḥad/ṣrath* qōdeš),[18] and this links up at once with the fact that in *Enuma Elish* the gods are said explicitly to render homage to Marduk "in the great court (*paramaḫḫu*) of his temple Esagila in Babylon (vi, 51) and "in the fane" (*ib.* 144). while in the *Poem of Baal* they are invited into the "mansion" (II AB vi, 44: "he invited his brethren into his mansion, his kinsmen into the midst of his palace, he invited the seventy sons of Asherath").

There follows (vv. 3–9b) a vivid description of Yahweh's prowess in storm and tempest. This, as suggested above, must be regarded as the actual honorification which the lesser gods are invited to recite; it is not merely a series of laudatory observations by the poet. Yahweh's thunder (lit. "voice") is said to convulse forest and ocean; it comes with strength and awe-inspiring vehemence. Particularly, it is stated that by means of it Yahweh shatters the cedars of Lebanon. Now, the language of this laudation runs parallel, to a remarkable degree, with that of the paean recited to Baal in the Canaanite poem. The latter is put into the mouth of Kôshar, the divine architect,[19] who, after some argument, has at last received Baal's consent to install windows and skylights in the new palace. The plan is that whenever the latter are opened it will be a sign to Baal correspondingly to open "a rift in the clouds" and send rain. Kôshar is so delighted at Baal's final acquiescence in this plan that he breaks out into a hymn of glory celebrating the powers of the god as genius of the storm. The hymn reads as follows:[20]

> When Baal opens a rift in the clouds,
> When Baal gives forth his holy voice,[21]
> When Baal keeps discharging the utterances of his lips
> His ho[ly] voice [convul]ses the earth,
> . . . . the mountains quake,
> A-tremble are the . . . .
> East and west the high places of the e[arth] reel;
> The enemies of Baal take to the woods,
> The foes of Hadad to the sides of the mountains!

Baal replies:

> The eyes of Baal mark down, then his hand strikes,[a]
> Yea, cedars quiver at the touch of his right hand![22]

That this paean is based upon standard hymns to the storm-god is shown by the fact that parallel phrases are indeed quoted by Abimilki of Tyre in the Tell Amarna letter 149:14–15 Winckler:

> Who giveth forth his voice in heaven like Hadad,
> And all the mountains quake at his voice.

Similarly, a hymn to Hadad printed in King's *Magic and Sorcery,* 21:22 contains the directly comparable expression:

> Hadad giveth forth thunders,
> The mountains are shaken.

In the light of these parallels the conclusion seems inescapable that the "glory of his name" of our Hebrew psalm reproduces the mythic laudation uttered by the lesser gods, itself projected from a standard hymn recited at the festival in the ceremonies of which the myth was recited or enacted.

At the end of the laudation (v. 9c) occur the obscure words "and in His palace all of it saith, Glory." The abruptness of this clause has been duly observed by most modern commentators, and the usual way of surmounting the difficulty is to assume an immediately antecedent lacuna, which must have also contained the subject to which the expression "all *of it*" referred.[23] With this solution we may readily agree, but exactly how the lacuna should be filled is indicated clearly by a comparison with *Enuma Elish* vi, 144. There we are told that the gods, duly assembled in the new-built palace of Esagila, *sat in the fane and recited the "name" of Marduk.* The words are a virtually exact translation of our Hebrew phrase, "all of them" answering precisely to "all of it" (*kullô*) and thus showing that the missing subject is the assembly of the gods. Indeed, the preceding verse in *Enuma Elish* (vi, 143) reads explicitly: "in their convocation they celebrated his essence." Hence it is apparent that we must restore something like:

> The congregation of the holy ones[24] praise him
> And in his palace all of it recites the Glory.

The Glory is, of course, the foregoing laudation.

"Yahweh," continues the Psalmist (v. 10), "sat (enthroned) at the stormflood, and Yahweh will sit (enthroned) for ever." The abruptness of this statement is likewise perplexing, while scholars have also been exercised to determine whether the reference to the stormflood is to the specific Noachic Deluge or to *any* inundation caused by the display of Yahweh's powers. The difficulty is removed, however, when the mythological background of the psalm is kept in mind. In *Enuma Elish* it is stated *specifically* (vi, 47, 51) that Esagila, the newly-built palace of Marduk, *was upreared upon the nether sea*;[25] while the temple of E-ninu at Lagash was said likewise to have been founded on the nether ocean,[26] and that in Eridu was termed "House of the nether sea."[27] In the sanctuary at Hierapolis (Membij), Lucian was shown a chasm into which the waters of the Deluge were supposed to have gathered,[28] and Jewish tradition asserted that the foundation stone of the temple at Jerusalem held down the flood.[29] An analogous myth was current in the sanctuary of Olympian Zeus at Athens.[30] Even more pertinent is the fact that in the Hittite cult-myth of the Puruli festival, the god who vanquishes the dragon (*illuyankas*) is said subsequently to be enthroned in the temple "over the well."[31] As for the phrase "and Yahweh will sit (enthroned) for ever," this must be regarded as something like a "God save the king!" In precisely the same way, the divine ancestors of Marduk are said, in *Enuma Elish* iv 28, to hail him with the cry "Marduk is king", while in the Canaanite *Poem of Baal* (III AB, A 32) the defeated monster Yam explains: "Let Baal be king."[32]

The concluding verse (11) of the Psalm ("Yahweh giveth strength to His people; Yahweh blesseth His people with peace") is usually regarded as an addition made when the poem was incorporated into or adapted for the public liturgy, and analogies to it may certainly be found in Psalm 28:8; 68:36, etc. It should be observed, however, that an exactly comparable expression occurs in *Enuma Elish* vi 113, where the minor gods hail their new king Marduk in the words "Verily, Marduk is the strength of his land and of his people." This suggests that it was part of the original mythological hymn. In itself, of course, it was a liturgical formula, probably used at ceremonies of enthronization and therefore adopted into the liturgy whenever a god was hymned in the role of king; this would account for its substantial recurrence in Psalms 28:8; 68:36, etc. The point is, however, that its presence in our psalm is not due to such adoption at a later date; on the contrary, it was adopted already in the original composition.

Thus it would appear that Psalm 29 is a form of the ritual laudation of the victorious god which formed part of the seasonal pantomime of the New Year Festival. It must be emphasized, however, that this in no way implies that the seasonal pantomime actually obtained in official Israelitic cultus, as has been so frequently supposed. All that we are here suggesting is that certain hymnodic patterns, derived from these earlier usages, survived in literary convention.[33] This is, of course, a very different thing, and the difference is salient. At the same time, we would not deny that the survival often involved more than a mere persistence of forms. Evidence is increasing daily that many of the psalms were conscious and deliberate Yahwizations of current "pagan" compositions; and we believe that this was the case in the present instance.[34] It can scarcely be doubted that beside the official cult of Yahweh in Jerusalem there existed a more primitive folk-religion throughout the length and breadth of Palestine. This may have taken the form of mere folkloristic and unmeaning customs rather than of formal religion, but it must certainly have had its influence upon the cult of Yahweh, and it is not unreasonable to suppose that the zealous propagandists of the latter may frequently have tried to "fetch the public" by adopting and adapting the songs and airs current in the former, on the same principle as induced Rowland Hill to suggest that hymns be set to popular melodies on the grounds that "the Devil shouldn't have the best tunes." Has not Professor Soothill told us[35] that he once heard children in India singing enthusiastically in imitation of a well-known Christian hymn:

> Buddha loves me; this I know
> For the Sutras tell me so?

259 Paradisal bliss   36:7–9

> O LORD, how precious is Thy loving-kindness!
> Gods and men take refuge under the shadow of Thy wings.
> They are sated on the richness of Thy house,
> and Thou givest them to drink of the River of Thy delights.
> For with Thee is the Fountain of Life;
> in Thy light do we see light.

The Psalmist is painting a picture of paradisal bliss, and draws on characteristic mythical traits. The "river of delights" is the celebrated Paradisal Stream, source of the world's rivers (see above, §**14**). The word rendered *delights* is the plural of *'eden*, "luxuriance," and pointedly suggests the Garden of Eden. The "fountain of life" is the paradisal Fountain of Immortality or Eternal Youth, so ubiquitous in world folklore (see above, §**14**). The "light" is the special glow of the paradisal realm, derived in large measure from the fact that it lies near the rising sun (see above, §**13**).

(The traditional rendering misses the mythological allusion by construing the word "gods" in the second line as a vocative, i.e., "O God"; it really provides the complement to "and men," and is simply a poetic vestige of ancient pagan myth.

The words, "with Thee is the Fountain of Life, in Thy light do we see light," are often emended by modern scholars who have simply failed to drink from it. Once the underlying mythology is appreciated, there is no need to "correct" the text.)

260 Magical waters   41:7–9

> RSV: *All who hate me whisper together about me;*
>   *they imagine the worst for me.*
>   (*They say,*) "*A deadly thing has fastened upon him;*
>   *he will not rise again from where he lies.*"

This rendering again misses the underlying folklore. The word "whisper" refers specifically to the murmuring of spells (see above, §**171**), and the phrase translated, (*They say,*) "*A deadly thing has fastened upon him*," is really a direct statement meaning, *A noxious thing is poured upon him.*[1] The allusion is then clarified by a famous passage in the Babylonian Epic of Creation (*Enuma Elish* 1.61 ff.), where the rebellious god Apsu is finally dispatched (perhaps "liquidated" would be the better word) by Ea, genius of all arts, knowledge, and magic, by having a magical concoction poured over him in his sleep, so that he never wakes! The passage runs:

> Ea, the all-wise, divined their plan.
> A master design he contrived and wrought.

> Cunningly wrought he his spell, high and pure.
> He . . . ed it, set it in water.
> Then, while he (Apsu) was lying in a cavern,
> he poured sleep over him.
> He made Apsu lie supine, drenched with sleep.

(In the light of this parallel it is apparent that the Hebrew words usually rendered, *They imagine the worst for me,* really mean more specifically, *They devise an evil plot against me.*)

261 An ancient Hebrew wedding song 45

Psalm 45 is expressly entitled "a song of loves," and if one reads it attentively in the light of Comparative Folklore it becomes immediately apparent that it is in fact an ancient Hebrew hymeneal.[1]

Unfortunately, the true sense of the poem has been but imperfectly perceived and is therefore not brought out clearly in the standard English translations. Because it is said to have been indited for a "king" (v. 1), and because it refers to his anointment (v. 2) and enthronement (v. 6), and makes specific mention of a "princess" (v. 12), it has been commonly assumed that it was composed for the marriage of a particular monarch, and scholars have broken their heads to determine who he may have been.[2] Once we bear in mind, however, that in the Near East, as elsewhere, it is a common convention to treat a bridal couple as royalty,[3] it becomes apparent that "His Majesty" is simply an ordinary bridegroom and the princess an ordinary bride, and that the reference to their regal status and dignity are no more than *jeux d'esprit.*

Oriental weddings invariably involve the presence of a professional poet or minstrel (Arabic: *sha'ir*) who improvises songs in honor of the bridal couple and leads the guests in chanting them. Accordingly, our poem begins with the songster's reaction to the summons for his services. He playfully expresses his excitement at being called to a "command performance":

> *My heart is a-flutter—oh joy!*
> *'Tis for a king himself*
> *I am now to indite my works!*
> *My tongue shall be like the pen of a fluent scribe!*

The scene then turns to the bridegroom's house. He is being robed and perfumed for the ceremony, and each stage of the procedure is accompanied by appropriate verses. As the unguents are poured over him, the poet exclaims:

> *Fairer thou wast than human kind,*
>   *with a magic*[4] *shed o'er thy lips!*
> *Some godhead must have endowed thee*
>   *with an immortal grace!*

In these words the poet plays on the custom of sprinkling date juice, clarified butter, or honey on the lips of a child shortly after birth.[5] No ordinary juice or honey was it that was shed on *your* lips, he says in a graceful compliment to the bridegroom, but rather divine magic or charm. You were born superhumanly handsome; some god must have conferred upon you the quality of immortal grace (Heb.: *berakah,* "blessing").[6]

The idea that privileged beings were fed at birth on heavenly food or that they were especially annealed by gods is commonplace in the folklore of many peoples. It may be illustrated especially from ancient Greek poetry. In the Homeric *Hymn to Demeter* we read how that goddess anointed the newborn Demophoon so that he resembled a god.[7] Apollonius Rhodius relates how Thetis tried by similar means to render Achilles immortal;[8] and Theocritus asserts that Aphrodite likewise "immortalized" Berenice.[9] So too Athene poured ambrosial grace on the infant Telemachus,[10] and so too was Penelope endowed;[11] while Ovid declares of Aeneas that his divine mother (Venus) touched his baby lips with nectar and ambrosia and "thus made a god of him."[12] True, none of these references comes from an Oriental source, but that the basic idea was not foreign to Ancient Near Eastern thought is attested by the frequent insistence in both Mesopotamian and Egyptian documents that the king "imbibed" divinity at birth by being suckled at the breasts of a goddess (see below, §**284**).

Once attired, the bridegroom buckles on his sword. Such a sword is a standard article of equipment at Arab weddings.[13] Thus, when a Palestinian Arab bridegroom goes out to usher his bride into his house, he usually carries a sword, which he presses against her face and with the tip of which he eventually raises her veil.[14] Alternatively, he stands on the flat roof and waves a sword over the bride as she crosses the threshold.[15] The purpose in either case is to forefend demons.[16] Sometimes, to be sure, the sword is carried by a groomsman.[17] Indeed, the Song of Songs expressly alludes to this custom when it speaks of the threescore "mighty men" who escort the bridegroom's palanquin, "each with his sword on his thigh against the Terror at Night" (i.e., demon; cf. Ps. 91:15);[18] and the usage survives in modern times in the crossed swords held over the bridal couple when they leave the church at a military wedding. Sometimes, too, it is the bride rather than the groom who carries a sword. This is not uncommon among the Arabs,[19] and readers of Norse literature will recall that in pagan Norway, Erik's daughter carried a sword at her marriage to Rolf.[20] In medieval Egypt, Jewish brides not only carried a sword but also wore a helmet;[21] and it is reported that in the Usambara territory of East Africa, the chief bridesmaid, dressed as a man, carries a sword before the bride.[22]

Likening the bridegroom to a king, the poet identifies the sword with that carried by a warrior monarch or handed to him—as in the British coronation ceremony—at the time of his investiture. He therefore bids him gird it on by way of insignia and regalia:

> *Champion that thou art,*
> *gird the sword on thy thigh*
> *as thy regal array and adornment!*[23]

The "conquering hero" is now ready to go forth to meet the bridal procession in order to lead it into the house. The bridegroom usually goes mounted on a horse or a camel.[24] As he mounts, the minstrel, playing on that action and continuing the comparison with a valiant monarch, bids him:

> *Ride forth, fare on, in the cause of Truth!*

As he leaves the precincts of his house, the bridegroom customarily distributes largesse to the poor, who crowd around the gate.[25] Now, in Hebrew popular speech such largesse was called "righteousness" ($ṣ^ed\bar{a}q\bar{a}h$).[26] Accordingly, by a neat double-entendre, the minstrel likens this act of charity to the typical duty of a king (cf. Pss. 72:2–4; 82:3), bidding him

> *do the right thing by the poor.*[27]

Finally, as the party is about to move off, minstrel and friends exclaim:

> *May thy right hand guide thee on thy way*
> *by awe-inspiring feats!*
> *May thine arrows (well-sharpened, to boot)*
> *sink into the heart of thy Majesty's foes!*
> *May (whole) peoples fall at thy feet!*

In these words there is, it would seem, yet another artful allusion to a wedding custom, for among the Arabs and among several other peoples it is a common practice for the bridegroom and/or his escorts to shoot arrows in order to ward off malevolent spirits.[28] At ancient Indian weddings, for example, he used to shoot them while he cried out, "I pierce the eyes of the demons who are surrounding the bride!"[29] The modern equivalent is the firing of rifles.[30] Moreover, it is worth noting that, according to some authorities, discharge of arrows was likewise an element of Egyptian coronation ceremonies,[31] and it still obtains at the installation rites of the Bar-Kitara of Africa.[32] If, therefore, such a rite could be attested in ancient Palestine or Syria, we might find in the minstrel's words a further parallelism between the features of wedding ceremonies and those of enthronement.

As the bridegroom rides through the courtyard, looking to all the world like a king, the bystanders—again led by the chief minstrel—chant appropriate verses extolling his regal state:

> *Thy throne hath some god <set firm>*[33]
> *to endure for all time!*
> *A sceptre of equity is the sceptre of thy kingship!*
> *Because thou hast loved the right,*
> *and hated the wrong,*

> *some god with (this) festive oil*[34]
> *hath now anointed thee (king)!*

These verses deliberately imitate the kind of salutation which loyal subjects were wont to address to their sovereign. We need quote only such common expressions in the state letters of Assyria as: *May the royal throne of my lord stand firm for ever,*[35] or *May the gods Nabu and Marduk . . . grant unto my lord, the king of countries, a sceptre of equity and an enduring throne!*[36]

The bride's procession is now in view, or at least within earshot. The bridegroom's party therefore feels called upon to give him a special "build-up" as an enviable "catch." Accordingly, with typical Oriental exuberance, it pays tribute to his former triumphs in the lists of love:

> *Among thy lady loves,*
>   *who have brought delight unto thee*
> *have been very princesses themselves*
> *hailing from ivory halls!*
> *At thy right hand hath stood*
>   *(full many) a harem-queen*
> *Decked in the gold of Ophir!*[37]

Meanwhile, corresponding ceremonies have been taking place in the home of the bride, and the next verses of our poem represent the snatches of song sung by *her* relatives and friends as she is being prepared for the ceremony. As they dress and undress her, they seek to allay her apprehensions and to overcome that bashfulness which convention demands of her:[38]

> *Hearken, maiden, and see,*
>   *and incline thine ear;*
> *forget thy kith and kin;*
>   *His Majesty craves thy beauty;*
> *He is thy lord—make obeissance to him!*

Then, as a counterpart to what the bridegroom's friends have been chanting about *him* while they have been preparing him for the ceremony, they make a point of complimenting the girl on her powers of captivation:

> *Thyself a Tyrian heiress,*[39]
>   *the richest men of the people*
> *have come courting thee with gifts!*[40]

This is followed, in turn, by what the Arabs call the *jelwe*—that is, the formal display of the bride in all her finery.[41] As they turn her this way and that and take in the various details of her costume, they break out into enthusiastic cries:

> *Very princess that she is,*
> *her finery is of pearls*[42]
> *set amid braids of gold!*
> *She is clothed in broidered robes!*[43]

The general sentiment of these verses is well illustrated by the modern Arab practice of referring to the bride's trousseau as "royal garments,"[44] while the mention of the pearls and the braids of gold alludes to the fact that the bridal crown often consists of strings of pearls set amid golden braids or chains of golden coins.[45]

When all is in readiness, the procession moves off to conduct the bride into the presence of the groom. The procession is accompanied by gay music, and the guests shout in chorus:

> *Let her be led to the king!*
> *Let virgins, walking behind her,*
> *escort her with gladness and glee,*
> *bring her into his Majesty's halls!*

After the ceremony, the company turns once more to shower congratulations upon the bridegroom:

> *In place of thy fathers be thy sons!*
> *Mayest thou make them to be lords throughout the earth!*
> *May they keep thy name in remembrance*[46]
> *for age upon age!*
> *May peoples heap upon thee*
> *everlasting praise!*

Such outspoken wishes for offspring—reminiscent of the Italian greeting, *figli maschi*—were and still are quite common at Syrian weddings. In the Canaanite (Ugaritic) *Poem of K-r-t*, The supreme god El himself, on behalf of the divine guests, proposes such a toast to the hero at his marriage to the princess Ḥurraya.[47] The point to be observed, however, is that the formula here employed reproduces at the same time the type of salutation customarily addressed by courtiers to their sovereign. In one of the state letters of Assyria, for example, we find the expression, *May the gods grant kingship to thine offspring, to thy seed, for all time!*[48] Comparable also is the Homeric formula addressed by Odysseus to the queen of the Phaeacians: *May the gods grant these thy friends that they may be prosperous while they live and that each may rear up children to inherit the wealth which lies in his halls and the honorable place which the people have given him!*[49]

262 Mountains in midsea 46:2

> *We shall not fear though God rock*[1] *the earth,*
> *though mountains totter into midsea.*

This hyperbole finds an excellent parallel in an Icelandic poem by the skald Kormak (10th cent.): *Flagstones will float like corn on water, and great mountains move out into the deep sea ere there be born again a lady so illustrious and fair as Steingard.*[2]

263 The far reaches of the North   48:2

> *His holy hill, towering superb,*
> *joy of the whole earth,*
> *Mt. Zion, thou "far reaches of the North,"*
> *an emperor's citadel!*

Mt. Zion is here likened to the mythical northern mountain of ancient lore, on which the gods held session and where their overlord sat ensconced in his palace.[1] Thus, in the Canaanite texts from Ras Shamra-Ugarit, the abode of El and the seat of the divine parliament lies in the "far reaches of the North," popularly identified with neighboring Jebel el Akra (ancient Mt. Ḥazzi, Casius), the tallest peak in Syria;[2] and this belief is echoed in Isaiah 14:13, where the rebellious "Lucifer" declares, "I will sit throned on the Mount of Assembly, in the far reaches of the North." The Babylonian supreme god Anu dwelt atop a great mountain—the "axle of the world"—near the North Star.[3] The celestial Uttarakuru of the Hindus,[4] the Himavata of the Tibetans, the Meru of the Aryans, the Kwan-lun of the Chinese, the Myemnoh Toung of the Burmese, and the Asaheim of the Norsemen likewise lay in the north.[5] In the north too, on the summit of a mountain, sat Heyoka, the weather-god of the North American Dakotas,[6] and there also the Khevsurs of the Caucasus locate the lord of storms.[7] The Masai believe in a northern paradise,[8] as do also the Finns.[9] In the Syriac Alexander-legend, that hero sees Paradise from a place in the north;[10] and in the Scandinavian Flatey-book (14th cent.), the hero Holge Thoresen goes to the north in order to join the blessed.[11]

The numinous quality of the north also inspires the belief that it is the seat of demons. This idea obtained among the Iranians,[12] the Mandaeans of Iraq and Iran,[13] the Hindus of the Vedic age,[14] the Greeks,[15] Jews,[16] and Mexicans,[17] and was a tenet also of Manichaean belief.[18] In late Greek magical spells, demons are conjured from the north,[19] and Plutarch there locates the monster Typhon.[20] Milton, in his *Paradise Lost,* makes the rebel angels muster in the north; and in Shakespeare's *I Henry the Sixth* (v. 3), La Pucelle invokes the aid of spirits "under the lordly monarch of the north." In English popular superstition, the north door of a church is sometimes regarded as that through which the Devil enters.[21]

264 Death as a shepherd   49:14

The conception of Death as a shepherd is not so common in folklore as one might suspect.[1] Nevertheless, this Biblical image has interesting parallels. In Greek mythology, Menoetēs, the son of Keuthonymos, is said to herd sheep at the far western entrance to Hades;[2] and a statement by Plato that the soul is shepherded has been so interpreted.[3]

265 Bottled tears 56:8

Put Thou my tears in Thy bottle!

This curious image may well have been suggested by the widespread practice of conserving tears in a bottle at funerals and other occasions of lamentation. Thus, when the Shi'ite Moslems of Iran celebrate the annual Commemoration of Hosein, their tears are often wiped with a cloth or a piece of cotton-wool and then squeezed into a bottle. They are held to possess amuletic virtue, and popular superstition asserts that an angel keeps them until the Day of Judgment.[1] Originally, such tear-bottles were buried with the dead, the idea being that the moisture would preserve their desiccated bodies and compensate for the vital fluids that had ebbed out of them. This custom obtained, for instance, in many parts of Germany until recent times;[2] while in Russia tear-stained handkerchiefs were often thrown into graves.[3] In ancient Egypt, the tears shed by Isis and Nephthys were believed to revive Osiris,[4] and similar notions appear in several Indonesian folktales.[5] A frequent theme of Greek and Latin poetry is the craving of the dead for tears;[6] what was really besought was not a token of grief but a means of "survival." Analogous is the common idea that "Blessed are the dead whom the rain rains on."[7]

On the other hand, such tears are sometimes regarded as an encumbrance to the deceased. There are, for example, many European folktales which tell how the ghosts of children return and complain of being troubled by the presence of tear-bottles in their graves;[8] while the Iranians say that the tears of mourners form a river which impedes the passage of the dead to the other world.

266 Yahweh's processional 68

(a) It was the custom both among the Mesopotamians and the Hittites solemnly to induct the major national or local god as king during the New Year ceremonies. He was led to his palace in a festal parade, accompanied by the lesser gods who had come to pay him homage. The procession assumed the form of a triumph, for the god was thought to have secured his dominion by vanquishing the contumacious dragon of the waters, who might otherwise have flooded the earth.[1] Whether such a ceremony actually occurred also among the Canaanites is at present unknown, but it was certainly represented by them in myth, for the conquest of the draconic Sir Sea (Yam), and the consequent induction as king of his victor, Baal, form the central theme of a mythological poem discovered at Ras Shamra-Ugarit.[2]

It is not necessary to suppose that the actual ceremony persisted in Israel. The type of liturgical composition which originally accompanied it may well have survived simply as a conventional genre of hymns, and it is on this assumption that the long and otherwise disjointed Psalm 68 becomes at once coherent and intelligible. The psalm moves, as it were, through the successive moments of the celebration and may be read as a kind of "processional." Indeed, this is explicitly indicated by the words of v. 25: *How awe-inspiring*[3] *are thy processions, O God, the processions of my God, my King, into the sanctuary.*

> 1. *When God but takes the field,*[4]
> *his enemies are scattered,*
> *and his foemen flee from his face.*

These proud opening words echo the traditional cry uttered when the ark (palladium) of Yahweh moved forward: cf. Numbers 10:35. The ark, we know, represented the presence of Yahweh on the field of battle: cf. I Samuel 4:5–7. Accordingly, this verse places us in imagination at the scene of the combat wherein the god vanquished his adversary and thereby acquired kingship.

> 4. *Cast up a way*[5] *for him*
> *who chariots through the deserts*

The Hebrew for "chariots through the deserts" is *Rokeb 'ărābōth*. This is simply a popular distortion of *Rokeb 'araphôth* "He that chariots upon the clouds"—the constant epithet of Baal in the mythological texts from Ras Shamra-Ugarit.[6] It is clear, therefore, that the Hebrew poet has this ancient myth in mind.

> 6. *God . . . leads out prisoners to prosperity.*

It was the custom among the Babylonians to release a prisoner at the New Year festival;[7] and this usage prevailed also at several Greek festivals.[8] Moreover, Livy tells us that at the celebration of a *lectisternium*, or "banquet offered to the gods," the bonds of prisoners were untied.[9]

A more familiar example of this custom is afforded by the incident of Barabbas in the New Testament.[10] The Psalmist plays on this standard element of the ceremonies, using it to point up the clemency and mercy of God in general.

> 9. *A liberal rain dost thou shed, O God,*
> *over thine estate;*
> *and when it waxes faint,*
> *thou dost hold it firm.*

The victory of the newly inducted god is everywhere associated with the securing of adequate rainfall for the ensuing year. Thus, in the Canaanite myth, Baal's triumph over Yam and over Mot (Death, Sterility) culminates in his "furnishing his rains in their due seasons";[11] and when, in the corresponding Babylonian version, Marduk has subdued Tiamat, he is hailed as "Lord of luxuriance" (*bêl ḫêgalli*).[12] Similarly, too, the victory of the Hittite storm-god over the dragon Illuyankas—the theme of the annual Puruli festival—is associated with the supply of rain.[13]

> 16. *Why look ye askance, ye many-peaked hills,*
> *at the mount which (this) God has favored*
> *as his dwelling?*
> *Surely, Yahweh too can take up an eternal*
> *dwelling!*

In the Canaanite *Poem of Baal,* that victorious god is installed on his holy mountain;[14] just as is Marduk in the lofty ziggurat of Esagila, especially built for him.

> 17. *The chariotry of God is twice ten thousand;*
> *bowmen there are by the thousands;*
> *Yahweh comes from Sinai into the sanctuary!*[15]

The allusion is to the triumphal march (Babylonian *tebû*)[16] of the divine victor into his palace, or temple. This is conceived of in terms of a military parade.

The word rendered "bowmen" (viz., Heb.: *šin'an*) has long proved a puzzle to commentators and, by false etymology, is usually rendered "thousands *twice-told*." But the word has now turned up as a military term in documents from Alalaḫ[17] and it has been recognized as the equivalent of the Egyptian *snni,* which means bowmen who fought from chariots.[18]

> 18. *Thou hast ascended the height.*

The expression occurs in reference to a conquering hero, in Psalm 7:8.[19] It echoes the technical language of the ancient myth, for Baal too is said after his victory to ascend the "height" (*mrym*) of Zaphon, i.e., Mt. Casius.[20]

> 20. *To God, the Lord, belongs escape*
> *from death* (RSV).

The Hebrew word rendered "escape" also means "ruin, discomfiture."[21] The poet is giving a universal meaning to the fact that in the ancient myth Baal secured his sovereignty by discomfiting Môt, the god of death.

> 21. *God smites the head of his foes.*

Again the poet is giving a general meaning to a specific feature of the celebrations. A commentary on the Babylonian New Year ceremonies mentions that at one stage of the proceedings a felon (*bêl ḫiṭṭi*) was marched through the streets and beaten about the head.²² He probably served as a human scapegoat (see above, §**194**).

> 22.   Said Yahweh; I will muzzle Bashan,
> capture Yam in the depths!
> (RSV: *I will bring them back from Bashan,
> I will bring them back from the depth of the sea.*)

At first blush one would assume that Bashan meant the volcanic plateau east of the Jordan (as in v. 15), and that what the poet intended to convey was that Yahweh delivers from loftiest height to lowest depth. We now know, however, from the Canaanite texts discovered at Ras Shamra that another word B-sh-n (vocalization uncertain) was one of the names of the mythological dragon muzzled and subdued by Baal.²³ We know also that another of his names was simply "Sea" (Yammu) and that the archaic Canaanite word for "muzzle" was very similar in form to that usually rendered "I will bring (them) back."²⁴ Accordingly, what the first line of our verse really meant was: *Said Yahweh, I will muzzle the Dragon!* To this the second line now provides an appropriate parallel, for here the Hebrew word usually rendered, *I will bring back,* is identical in form (in the original spelling) with one meaning, *I will capture*,²⁵ and this is in fact the very term used in the Canaanite myth to describe the discomfiture of Sea (Yammu) at the hands of Baal!²⁶ Hence, the second part of the verse really means, *Yea, I will capture Sir Sea in the depth!*

In the Canaanite poem, Baal shatters the multiple heads of his adversary with a bludgeon;²⁷ while in the corresponding Babylonian myth, the victorious Marduk does likewise to the monster Tiamat.²⁸ That the myth was familiar to the Hebrews is clear from the explicit allusion to it in Psalm 74:14: *Thou it was that didst crush the heads of Leviathan.*

By a natural association, therefore, the poet connects the belaboring of the condemned felon (see above §**194**) with the similar punishment inflicted, in the traditional myth, upon the god's adversary.

> 35.   *Awe-inspiring is God amid the holy beings.*²⁹

The poet is here alluding to the fact that when the victorious god is finally enthroned, he is surrounded by the lesser gods, who come to pay him homage and to participate in the divine "parliament" at which the fates of the ensuing year are determined.

This is the culminating scene of the Babylonian myth;³⁰ while in the corresponding Hittite version there is even a description of the protocol which is to govern the order of seating!³¹ Baal too, when he is finally enthroned in his new-built palace, tenders a banquet to the gods.³²

(In the traditional Hebrew text the point of this verse is obscured by the false reading: *Awe-inspiring art thou, O God, from thy sanctuary.* The correct reading can, however, be elicited from a variant in the Greek Septuagint Version.)

(b) Yellow garments 68:13

> Shall ye still go lying 'mid the slagheaps,
> ye wings of a dove silver-spangled,
> whose pinnions are yellow gold?[33]

The poet is addressing the womenfolk of Israel who are thus exhorted to emerge from their gloom and dejection and preen themselves in celebration of Yahweh's triumph over His and their enemies.

The imagery becomes even more effective when it is observed that yellow was highly favored in the costume of women alike in Oriental and Classical antiquity. "Like all Oriental women," we are told of the Arabian 'Aisha, "they love yellow. Often they dress entirely in that color. . . . Their garments are dipped in saffron whenever they are laundered."[34] In Malaya, yellow is the regal hue;[35] and in the famous Syriac *Hymn of the Soul*, it wears a yellow robe.[36] Cassandra, says Aeschylus, was clothed in yellow at the sack of Troy;[37] and in the same poet's *Persians*, the ghost of Darius is bidden rise from the netherworld clothed in yellow.[38] Greek courtesans and temple women affected yellow garb[39] as did also the eunuch priests of the Syrian Goddess whom Lucian saw at Hierapolis (Membij)[40] and as do Buddhist monks (*bhikkus*) and Indian ascetics at the present day.[41] The wife of the priest of Jupiter (*flamen Dialis*) at Rome likewise wore yellow,[42] and, on a less exalted plane, such Roman poets as Catullus, Tibullus, and Ovid frequently make mention of the yellow raiment of brides, ladyloves, and mythological heroines.[43]

Yellow is considered also to have special virtue in forefending demons,[44] and this too is a reason for its popularity. Modern brides in India, for example, wear tattered yellow raiment for six days before marriage, to avert evil spirits;[45] and a wife who greets her husband after his return from a long absence wears yellow.[46] Similarly, the Mundas and Santals of Bengal smear yellow dye on bridal couples;[47] and the Hindus of western India rub their bodies with yellow turmeric against assault by the "princes of darkness."[48] In Sicily, yellow threads (*nastro gallo intrecciato*) are worn against the evil eye.[49]

Since, in popular usage, anything that excites observation usually does so ambivalently—that is, for evil as well as for good—yellow comes to be regarded also as an ominous and evil color. In medieval Germany, a yellow badge was placed around the neck of a condemned heretic; and this, of course, is the origin of the infamous "Yellow Badge" imposed on Jews.[50] Furthermore, in medieval art, Cain and Judas were often portrayed with yellow beards.[51] Says Simple in Shakespeare's *Merry Wives of Windsor: He hath but a little wee face, with a little yellow beard—a Cain-colour'd beard.*[52]

267 The Book of Fate   69:29

The concept of a Book of Fate was not uncommon in the Ancient Near East.

The Babylonians believed that Nabu, the divine scribe, kept such a record. Ashurbanipal, for instance, addresses to him the words, "My life is inscribed before thee,"[1] and similar expressions occur in other texts.[2]

Among the Hittites, the goddesses who presided over individual destinies were called Gulses, a name which is probably to be derived from the verb GUL-, "write, inscribe."[3] Similarly, both the Roman Parcae and the Teutonic Norns are said to have kept a written record of men's fates,[4] the latter being sometimes designated Die Schreiberinnen.[5] In the same vein, too, Tertullian tells us that at the conclusion of a child's first week of life, prayers were offered to Fata *Scribunda*.[6]

In the Old Testament itself, the notion reappears in Psalm 139:15:

> *My frame was not hidden from thee,*
>   *when I was being fashioned in secret,*
>   *knit together (as though) in the depths of the earth.*
> *Thine eyes beheld mine unformed substance,*
>   *and in Thy book were all of them written*
>   *—the days when men were to be created,*
>   *and among them was one (assigned) thereto.*[7]

A further allusion to it has been recognized in a Punic inscription of the second or third century B.C., which has been interpreted to read: "Moreover, the gods have . . . my name; my mark . . . along with their names have they inscribed, and the glory and splendor of my name have they recorded for all time right from the beginning."[8]

268 The combat against the Dragon   74:13–14
See §§**186**, **299**, **310**.

269 Demon shafts   76:3

RSV: *There He broke the flashing arrows*

The Hebrew says nothing about *flashing arrows;* it speaks of *Reshephs of the bow*. Resheph was the Canaanite god of pestilence. He was popularly regarded as being armed (like Cupid) with arrows—a concept which survived in the medieval notion of *elf-shot* (see below, §**275**). In a cuneiform text from Ras Shamra-Ugarit he is designated "Resheph the archer,"[1] and in a far later Phoenician-Greek bilingual inscription from Cyprus, where he is equated with the arrow-shooting Apollo, as "Resheph of the arrow."[2] In the plural, the word came to be used as a general term for "demons."[3] Accordingly, there is here an allusion to popular lore, the reference being to "the slings and arrows of outrageous fortune," particularized as the hazards of war.

(A similar mistake has converted the fiery *reshephs* of love mentioned in Song of Songs 8:6 into *flashes* [or *coals*] of love [see below, §**338**].)

270 Food of angels 78:25

Man did eat angels' food

The word traditionally rendered *angels* means simply, *divine beings*. The reference is, of course, to the manna supplied in the wilderness; and on manna as the Hebrew equivalent of the Classical nectar and ambrosia and of the Indic soma and amrita, see above, §§**16, 88**.

▲ 271 The bird sanctuary 84:1-3

How dear is thy dwelling place,
O LORD of hosts!
My soul longeth, yea, even fainteth
for the courts of the LORD;
my heart and flesh sing for joy
unto the living God.
Even the sparrow hath found a house,
and the swallow a nest for herself,
where she may lay her young
—thine altars, O LORD of hosts,
my King and my God.

These words seem to imply that birds might build their nests and roost unmolested within the precincts and even upon the very altars of the temple at Jerusalem. There is no improbability in the supposition, for the Greeks in like manner respected the birds which had built their nests on holy ground. Herodotus tells us that when the rebel Pactyas, the Lydian, fled from the wrath of Cyrus and took refuge with the Greeks of Cyme, the oracle of Apollo commanded his hosts to surrender the fugitive to the vengeance of the angry king. Thinking it impossible that the god could be so merciless, we may almost say so inhuman, as to bid them betray to his ruthless enemies the man who had put his trust in them, one of the citizens of Cyme, by name Aristodicus, repaired to the sanctuary of Apollo, and there going round the temple he tore down the nests of the sparrows and all the other birds which had built their little houses within the sacred place. Thereupon, we are told, a voice was heard from the Holy of Holies saying, "Most impious of men, how dare you do so? how dare you wrench my suppliants from my temple?" To which Aristodicus promptly retorted, "So you defend your own suppliants, O Lord, but you order the people of Cyme to betray theirs?"[1]

Again, we read in Aelian that the Athenians put a man to death for killing a sacred sparrow of Aesculapius.[2] In the great sanctuary of the Syrian goddess at Hierapolis on the Euphrates, the doves were held to be most sacred, and no man might touch, far less molest or kill them. If any person accidentally harmed a dove he was deemed to be in a state of ceremonial pollution or taboo for the rest of that day. Hence the birds became perfectly tame, entering into people's houses and picking up their food on the ground.[3] We must remember that in antiquity the windows of temples as well as of houses were unglazed, so that birds could fly freely out and in, and build their nests, not only in the eaves, but in the interior of the sacred edifices. In his mockery of the heathen, the Christian Father, Clement of Alexandria, twits them with the disrespect shown to the greatest of their gods by swallows and other birds, which flew into the temples and defiled the images by their droppings.[4]

The reason for not molesting wild birds and their nests within the precincts of a temple was no doubt a belief that everything there was too sacred to be meddled with or removed. It is the same feeling which prompts the aborigines of Central Australia to spare any bird or beast that has taken refuge in one of the spots which these savages deem holy, because the most precious relics of their forefathers are there deposited in the holes and crannies of the rocks.[5]

The divine protection thus extended to birds in the ancient world and particularly, as it would seem, in the temple at Jerusalem lends fresh tenderness to the beautiful saying of Jesus, "Are not two sparrows sold for a penny, yet not one of them will fall to the ground without your Father's will?" (Matt. 10:29). We may perhaps indulge the fancy that these words were spoken within the sacred precinct at Jerusalem, while the temple sparrows fluttered and twittered in the sunshine about the speaker.

[Every living being that lodges in a sanctuary is automatically a guest of the god and therefore sacrosanct under his protection (see above, §**149**). In many parts of the world, this status extends to animals and birds. Thus, among the protestations of innocence (the so-called "negative confession") which the Egyptian dead were required to make before the judges in the afterworld was the statement, "I have never driven cattle from the gods' pastures . . . never netted birds in the gods' manors."[5a] Artemidorus, author of a famous Greek dream book, says similarly that fowl nesting beside an altar are inviolable;[5b] while in German,[5c] Russian,[5d] and English[5e] folklore, birds found in a church enjoy the same immunity.] ▼

272 The heavenly and earthly Zion

Zion, says the Psalmist, is a structure reared by God (Yahweh) "on holy hills." These hills, however, are not (as usually supposed) merely the hills of Jerusalem. The phrase contains a subtle mythological allusion and is charged with far deeper import. What the Psalmist is really saying is that the habitation of Yahweh on Zion is the earthly counterpart of the glorious mansion which, in traditional popular lore (e.g., the Canaanite *Poem of Baal*), the divine overlord is said to have built for himself on the supernal hill of the gods.[1] The statement is, in fact, exactly parallel to the identification of Zion, in Psalm 48:2, with the mythical "far reaches of the north"—a standard synonym for that mountain (see above, §**263**).

The comparison reflects a basic tenet of all ancient and of much primitive thought: things on earth correspond to things in heaven or in the otherworld; the real has its counterpart in the ideal; the immediate and punctual is but an aspect of the continuous and durative.[2]

In accordance with this idea, for instance, the Babylonians worked out a comprehensive celestial geography, in which the counterparts of such prominent earthly cities as Babylon, Ashur, and Susa were recognized in the constellations;[3] while Judeo-Christian literature is full of the "Jerusalem on high," counterpart of the "Jerusalem below," which will eventually come down to earth, "prepared like a bride adorned for her husband" (Rev. 21:2).[4] So too, during the Han period in China (206 B.C.–221 C.E.), popular fancy traced an equivalent of the capital city in the stars.[5]

What held good for cities held good also for *temples*. Gudea of Lagash claimed that the blueprint of the major sanctuary in that city had been conveyed to him by the goddess Nisaba and followed a celestial archetype.[6] Hammurapi says that the temple at Sippar corresponded to one in heaven;[7] and the same is affirmed concerning Esagila, the great fane of Marduk in Babylon.[8] Moses, we are told, saw the model of the Tabernacle while he was standing before God on Mt. Sinai.[9]

Just as the relation between durative god and punctual king was often articulated by the fiction that the former had handed down the insignia to the latter (see below, §**284**), so that between the celestial and terrestrial temple was often conveyed by the notion that the latter had actually been built by the god who inhabited it. Egyptian temples, for example, were commonly held to have been designed by the gods;[10] while a Babylonian hymn to Enlil of Nippur hails him as the builder of his local shrine,[11] and Ishtar herself is said to have upreared one of her major shrines at Nineveh.[12] Similarly too, the ancient song preserved in Exodus 15 speaks (v. 17) of "the place, O Yahweh, which Thou hast made for Thine abode, the sanctuary which Thine own hands have established"; while Moslem tradition asserts that the Haram (sacred enclosure) at Mecca was planned by the angels.[13]

Against this background, other phrases in our psalm acquire new point and significance. Thus it now becomes apparent that in v. 3, which is usually rendered, *Glorious things are spoken of thee, O city of God,* the last phrase is really not a vocative at all, but means rather, *City of the gods,* and itself constitutes the "glorious things" spoken of, i.e., the glorious epithet applied to, Zion. Thereby it is likened to the celestial city.

Similarly, in v. 6, the words usually rendered, *For the Most High himself will establish her,* really carry an even richer meaning. For while it is true that *'elyôn,* the Hebrew original of *Most High,* is indeed attested as the name of a specific deity,[14] the word itself means simply "supernal being" and was applied also to any celestial god, in contrast to those who were believed to dwell on or under the earth.[15] Hence, what the Psalmist is really saying is that an added distinction of Zion is that *He* (virtually pointing upward)—a celestial being, and no mere mortal—is its founder! Note, in confirmation of this, that in Isaiah 14:14 the typical inhabitant of the celestial "Mount of Assembly" is similarly designated an *'elyôn* (*I will mount the back of a cloud, be like an* '*elyôn*).

Excursus. Because the psalm has, in my opinion, been persistently misunderstood, I append a new translation (bald and literal, to be sure) showing what I believe to be its true meaning:

1   *It is, it is the structure*
       which He Himself upreared
       upon the holy mountains!

2   *Yahweh loves the gates of Zion*
       more than Jacob's dwellings all!

3   *Glorious words applied to thee:*
       "City of the gods!"

                                Selah

4   *Unto my friends I tell the fame*
       of Egypt proud and Babylon;
       say, "Here is Philistia, Tyre and Cush:[a]
       Such-and-such was born there!"

5   *But when it comes to Zion,*
       each man born therein is mentioned,
       for He, yes He, a heavenly being,
       it is that founded it!

6   *'Tis Yahweh who Himself records,*
       in writing up peoples and princes:[b]
       "Such-and-such was born there."

                                Selah

7   *Within thee all of them together*
       like minstrels raise their song.[c]

[a] I.e., Ethiopia.

[b] With the Greek (LXX) Version, I transfer the obscure *wešārîm* of v.7 to this place, reading *weśārîm*. For the contrast of "peoples" with "princes," cf. Jer. 25:19; 26:11, 12, 16; II Chron. 24:10.

[c] For *kôl ma'yanai bak* I read, by redivision of the consonants, *kullam 'ānū bak*.

273 The throne founded on righteousness   89:14

> *Right and Justice are the foundation of Thy throne*

This metaphor is admirably illustrated by the fact that the Egyptian hieroglyphic sign for "right, normalcy" (*mu'at*), viz., ▭, originally meant *the base of a throne*.[1]

274 The winged soul   90:10

> *The days of our years are threescore years and ten,*
> *or even by reason of strength fourscore years;*
> *yet is their pride but toil and trouble,*
> *for swiftly it passes, and we fly away.*

Among peoples which believe that the soul of the departed goes to heaven, it is often depicted as winged.[1] Thus, among the Egyptians, both the *ba* and the *akh*, two aspects of the essential self, were alike portrayed as birds,[2] and in the *Tale of the Two Brothers*, preserved in the famous D'Orbiney Papyrus, the dead pharaoh is said to have "flown aloft."[3] Similarly, in India, the *pitaras*, or spirits of the ancestral dead, were believed to hover around the offerings presented to them in the form of birds.[4] Homer too pictures the souls of the deceased as birds;[5] and the psyche is often so represented in paintings on Greek vases.[6] The pre-Islamic Arabs entertained the same fancy,[7] and it survives in the folklore of the Moslems of Abyssinia[8] and likewise among the Mandaeans of Iraq and Iran.[9] The idea is further attested in China[10] and in several parts of Indonesia (notably, on the island of Bali);[11] while the Semangs of Malacca assert that the soul of the dying often soars aloft in the form of a small bird.[12] German popular lore is full of stories about birds (usually doves) which ascend into the air beside a deathbed;[13] and in the Czech traditional poem of *Czestmir and Wslaslaw*, they are turned after death into nesting doves.[14] In England, white pigeons are sometimes regarded, on the same basis, as omens of death,[15] as are also white moths;[16] and in the Breton ballad of *Le Seigneur Nann et la Fée*, souls appear as white doves perched in the branches of a tree.[17] Readers of Thornton Wilder's *The Bridge of San Luis Rey* will recall the discussion between two Peruvians whether "the soul can be seen like a dove fluttering away at the moment of death."

The notion finds place also in Christian hagiology. To quote but a few instances: the friends of Polycarp maintained that as the martyr died, a white dove flew from his mouth;[18] and the same phenomenon was said to have characterized the deaths of St. Eulalia,[19] of the abbot of Nuria,[20] and of St. Benedict's sister, Scholastica.[21] In Catholic ritual, white doves are released from cages at the canonization of a saint.

275 A coven of demons[1]   91:5–6

> *Thou shalt not be afraid of the terror by night,*
> *of the arrow that flieth by day,*

> *of the pestilence that stalketh in darkness,*
> *of the destruction that ravageth at noon.*

Although the Psalmist is speaking only in a vague and general way, like the famous Cornish prayer with its comprehensive reference to "ghoulies and ghosties and long-leggity beasties and things that go bump in the night," the disasters which he lists are in fact specific demons believed to operate at specific hours. He commences with the "terror by night" because the Hebrew day began at the preceding nightfall.

The TERROR BY NIGHT, who is mentioned again in Song of Songs 3:8 (see below, §335), is simply the *nightmare*. This is a universal figure in folklore.[2] A Mesopotamian magical text speaks expressly of "the terror of the nights,"[3] and in many primitive cultures bad dreams are personified as demons. Among the aborigines of Australia, for example, a demon named Koin is said to throttle people when they are asleep;[4] while the Caribs say the same of a spirit called Mboya,[5] and the Karens of Burma tell of the noxious *na* who crouches on the stomach.[6]

The ARROW THAT FLIETH BY DAY is the "faery arrow" of pestilence and disaster. This concept too is ubiquitous.[7] The anguished Job cries out that "the arrows of Shaddai (EV: the Almighty) are with me";[8] while in the Iliad, Apollo shoots arrows of plague at the Achaeans.[9] The Canaanite god Resheph, genius of plague and adversity, was known popularly as a demonic archer;[10] and in Hindu myth the hero Krishna is finally killed by the arrows of the demon Jara, who personifies old age.[11] In medieval European folklore, diseases were attributed to the shafts of elves,[12] and sudden pain in the side is still called "stitch," i.e., prick of an arrow (cf. German *stechen*). The Scandinavian Eddas speak analogously of an elf-*ray*.[13]

Wielders of these demonic shafts can be thwarted by receiving what they give. Arrows were discharged against them, for instance, as part of the Babylonian New Year (Akitu) ceremonies;[14] and in certain parts of Germany they are still so discharged on January 1,[15] as well as at such crucial seasonal festivals as those of Easter and May Day.[16] An Aramaic magical spell from Nippur inveighs against demons with the threat that "a bow has been drawn against you, and its string pulled taut";[17] while in a Manichaean text from Chinese Turkestan, a conjuror (shaman) is said to fell demons by aiming darts at them.[18]

The DESTRUCTION THAT RAVAGETH AT NOON is *sunstroke,* the demon of the torrid noonday heat in which only "mad dogs and Englishmen" venture abroad.[19] Theocritus, the Alexandrian poet, has one goatherd counsel another not to sit piping at noon for fear of this demon, whom he identifies with Pan.[20] Pliny the Elder likewise discourses about the noonday demon;[21] and belief in him is still very much alive among the peasantry of Greece[22] and Italy.[23] German popular lore also knows of formidable *Mittagsgespenster,*[24] and Slavonic peoples tell of an ominous being (variously named Ozwita, Poludnitza, Preypoludnitza, and Szépassony) who wanders in the woods at noon to strike terror in men.[25]

The noonday demon also figures in legend. The faery mistress of Gilbert, later Pope Sylvester II, is called Meridiana, and he first makes her acquaintance at noon;[26] while Joan of Arc hears her "voices" at midday.[27]

The PESTILENCE THAT STALKETH IN DARKNESS is the demon *Debher,* whose name means simply, "Reverse, Catastrophe"[28] (see above, §242).

276 From Canaanite hymn to Israelite psalm   93

The Chinese scholar Soothill has recorded that he sometimes heard children in India paraphrase a well-known Christian hymn in the words, "Buddha loves me, this I know / For the Sutras tell me so";[1] while of Rowland Hill it is related that he used to set his hymns to catchy music-hall airs on the grounds that "the Devil shouldn't have the best tunes." The ancient Israelites did likewise, and this psalm provides an excellent illustration of their methods.

Yahweh is acclaimed as king of the earth. Why? Because he has subdued the raging and contumacious floods. Where is he enthroned? In his special house which "holiness beseemeth for evermore." What does he do there? He issues decrees which are "very sure." At first blush, this sequence is somewhat bewildering, but to anyone who has read the Canaanite poems from Ras Shamra the implication is obvious: the psalm is an adaptation to the cult of Yahweh of the Canaanite myth of Baal.[2] Baal succeeds to kingship by vanquishing the contumacious Yammu-Nahru, the genius of sea and rivers. Once he has subdued his adversary, he is enthroned "for evermore."[3] He builds himself a special palace on the heights of Ṣaphon, the mountain of the gods.[4] From that eminence he regulates the order of nature, causing the rains thenceforth to fall in due season, rather than by caprice.[5]

The story has several parallels in Ancient Near Eastern literature.[6] In the Mesopotamian Epic of Creation (*Enuma Elish*), for example, the god Marduk (or, in the earlier version, Enlil) attains sovereignty by conquering the marine monster Tiamat and her cohorts, and then builds himself a sumptuous palace whence he issues ordinances for the regulation of the world.[7] Similarly, in the cult-myth of the Hittite Puruli-festival, the god subjugates the marine Dragon (*Illuyankas*) and is therefore installed as king.[8]

Basically, this is a seasonal myth designed to explain how, at the beginning of the agricultural year, increase and the "benefits of nature" can be assured only if the surging streams and upwelling springs can be kept in check (see above, §258). There is no reason to suppose, however, that the battle of Yahweh against Sea and River was necessarily enacted in Israelitic ritual; the theme survives only as a literary relic or fossil.

277 Renewing youth like the eagle   103:5

Thy youth is renewed like the eagle's.

Says the medieval *Bestiary:*

It is a true fact that when the eagle grows old, and his wings become weary, and his eyes become darkened with a mist, then he goes in search of a fountain. . . . At length, taking a header down into the fountain, he dips himself three times in it, and instantly he is renewed with a great vigor of plumage and splendor of vision.[1]

There is an amusing allusion to this traditional belief in the *Heauton Timoroumenos* of the Roman comedian, Terence: in reply to his protest that he has not been drinking too much, the old codger Chremes is told that, in any case, he seems so spry early in the morning that "the old saying seems to hold true; you've got yourself the old age of an eagle!"[2] The Greeks too used the expression "eagle's eld" to denote longevity.

278 Heaven as a garment   104:2

To Thee, to Thee, all royal pomps belong,
  Clothed art Thou in state and glory bright:
For what is else this eye-delighting light
  But unto Thee a garment wide and long?
The vaulted heaven but a curtain right,
  A canopy Thou over Thee hast hung?
            (trans. Mary, Countess of Pembroke)

The portrayal of heaven as a garment or curtain is one of the most widespread images of the world's folklore.[1] It recurs again in the Old Testament itself in the familiar words of Isaiah (40:22) who describes Yahweh as "stretching out the heavens like a muslin curtain, spreading them like a tent wherein to dwell." In Mesopotamia, the cloud-hung sky was called poetically "the heavenly garment,"[2] and the star-spangled firmament "the embroidered robe";[3] while in a Greek magical text, the moon is hailed as "wearing a jerkin of stars."[4] The Sumerians spoke similarly of the goddess Innini's "donning the garment of heaven,"[5] just as in a hymn of the Indic Rig Veda, Indra is said to "wear heaven as a crown";[6] and the Iranians said likewise of the supreme god Mazda that "he takes heaven to himself as a garment star-embroidered, god-woven."[7] In Teutonic mythology, Odin wears a blue or azure mantle representing the sky;[8] while among the Ewe-speaking peoples of Africa the azure sky is the veil with which Maiu, the supreme god, covers his face, and the clouds are his garments and ornaments.[9] Herakles (i.e., Baal) of Tyre is depicted by the Byzantine poet Nonnus as "wearing a jacket of stars" and as being wrapped in a garment which lights up the sky at night;[10] while Daniel Defoe, in his *History of the Devil,* calls the sky "the blue blanket."[11]

The idea is implicit also in the Greek (Septuagint) Version of Job 14:12, where, by vocalizing the Hebrew consonants differently from the received text, an allusion is introduced to "heaven's becoming unstitched."[12] Similarly, in Isaiah 64:1 (Heb. 63:19), where Yahweh is besought to "rend the heavens and come down," and word "rend" is that employed of rending garments.[13] Not impossibly, a further reference to this concept is to be recognized in an obscure passage of the Canaanite *Poem of Baal* which seems to speak of heaven as the *ephod,* or wrap, of Baal.[14]

Because kings were considered to be the punctual incarnations of gods (see above, §250), they were sometimes invested, especially in Sassanian and Byzantine usage, with star-spangled robes;[15] and it has been suggested that even in a more ancient Mesopotamian text, the expression "robe of heaven" really denotes such a royal garment.[16]

279 The wings of the wind — 104:3
See above, §254.

280 The clouds as chariots — 104:3
See above, **ibidem.**

281 The kindly stork — 104:17
The stork has its home in the fir trees.

The Hebrew word for "stork" (viz., $h^a s\hat{\imath} dah$) means literally, "one imbued with loyalty or affection (*ḥesed*)." This reflects a popular belief that the bird in question is especially solicitous towards its parents.[1] "I am a most pious creature," says the stork in one of Aesop's fables, "in that I honor and serve my father";[2] and similar testimony is given by other ancient writers.[3]

282 The bread of angels — 105:40
See above, §270.

283 The right hand — 109:31
He stands at the right hand of the needy,
to save him from those who condemn him to death.

See below, §284.

284 The ritual of enthronement — 110
The LORD said unto my lord,
Sit thou at my right hand,
until I make thine enemies thy footstool.

> *The LORD shall send the rod of thy strength out of Zion:*
> *rule thou in the midst of thine enemies.*
> *Thy people shall be willing in the day of thy power,*
> *in the beauties of holiness from the womb of the morning:*
> *thou hast the dew of thy youth.*
> *The LORD hath sworn, and will not repent,*
> *Thou art a priest for ever after the order of Melchizedek.*
> *The LORD at thy right hand*
> *shall strike through kings in the day of his wrath.*
> *He shall judge among the heathen,*
> *he shall fill the places with the dead bodies;*
> *he shall wound the heads over many countries.*
> *He shall drink of the brook in the way:*
> *therefore shall he lift up the head.*

So, in the stately cadences of the King James Version, runs the famous 110th Psalm. But to whom it is addressed, and what is its wider background has been, throughout the centuries, anybody's guess. Older generations of scholars thought that the man who was to be at once king and priest "for ever" and to sit at the right hand of God, could be only the future Messiah, or Davidic prince (in a Christian interpretation, Jesus); while in recent times it has been suggested that the psalm was composed at a relatively late date and refers to Simon the Maccabee who, in reward for his military prowess and religious zeal, was in fact appointed ethnarch and "perpetual" high priest of the Jews in 141 B.C.[1] Indeed, some scholars have sought ingeniously to detect an acrostic on his name in the first four verses of the Hebrew text![2]

Comparative Religion and Folklore, however, put things in a very different perspective. For if we align the several statements made in the psalm with ancient beliefs and practices relating to the installation of kings, it becomes immediately apparent that what we have before us is really *the "book of words" for a coronation ceremony, each verse being uttered by the officiant as he performed an act of the traditional ritual*.[3] Especially illuminating in this respect is a long inscription describing in detail the coronation of Queen Hatshepsut of Egypt (c. 1500 B.C), for this runs parallel to a remarkable degree with the ideas which inform our Hebrew composition.[4]

The king is the punctual counterpart of the durative god,[5] and the main function of all coronation ceremonies everywhere is to demonstrate in a series of symbolic acts his absorption of divine power and authority.[6]

(a) The proceedings here begin with the actual *installation*. In token of his divine appointment, the new king is conducted to a throne placed to the right of the god's statue. Thereupon the officiant says:

> *The pronouncement of Yahweh to my lord:*
> *"Sit thou at my right hand. . . ."*

This divine summons is couched in terms of a formal *edict*, being introduced in the original Hebrew by the term *n^e'ūm* (attenuated in the King James Version to the colorless "said"), which is the standard technical word for an oracular utterance. In precisely the same way, in the account of Queen Hatshepsut's enthronement, it is Thoth, the spokesman of the supreme god—counterpart of the Greek Hermes—who pronounces the appropriate formula when the royal tiaras are placed on her head.[7] Similarly too, the Assyrian king Ashurbanipal says that his divine appointment was ordained by Ninlil.[8]

Ancient Oriental monarchs frequently articulated their divine character by declaring that thy had been especially selected or commissioned by the gods.[9] Both Hammurapi[10] and Mardukbaladan II,[11] for instance, assert explicitly that they had been nominated by Marduk, god of Babylon; and Esarhaddon that he had been appointed by Ashur, Bel, Nabu, and Shamash jointly.[12] Elsewhere in the Old Testament itself, the new king is formally "adopted" by Yahweh (Ps. 2:6), receives "authorization"[13] from him (Ps. 72:1-2), or "grasps his hand" (Isa. 45:1; cf. 42:6).[14]

(b) To sit at the *right hand* was to sit in the seat of honor. In the Canaanite *Poem of Baal,* the divine architect Koshar sits at the right hand of that god when plans for the latter's temple are drawn up.[15] In Psalm 45:9 the king's favorite odalisque (*not* "queen" as in EV) stands at his right hand; and in I Esdras 4:29 the concubine Apamē sits at the right hand of Darius. According to Josephus,[16] this was likewise the position occupied by Jonathan at the court of Saul; and Jesus, of course, is said to sit at the right hand of God the Father in heaven.

The underlying idea is that the right side is auspicious; the left, ominous.[17] In Psalm 16:11, favors are bestowed by God's right hand, and in Psalm 80:17, one who enjoys them is styled "a man of Thy right hand." Conversely, in Psalm 77:10, misfortune is described as "a change (in position) of the celestial right hand." Rachel, dying in childbirth, calls her last son Ben-oni, "son of my sorrow," but Jacob changes the name to the more auspicious Benjamin, "son of the right hand."[18] In Arabic, "at the right hand (*yamin*)" means "fortunate";[19] and it has been suggested that the Babylonian word for "evil," viz., *limnu,* really stands for *la imnu,* "not (at) the right hand," i.e., sinister.[20] In Chinese script, the notion of "protection, providence" is expressed by a sign composed of the right hand plus the mark of divinity.[21] The right hand was likewise deemed auspicious by the Egyptians,[22] and the notion is also abundantly attested in Greek and Roman literature.[23] The helping hand of a god was the right hand, and it was the ham of the right leg that became the god's share of a sacrifice and was therefore allotted to the priest.[24] In Plato's famous myth of Er, the souls of the righteous pass by a right-hand path to heaven, while the wicked go left to hell.[25] The right foot, said the Romans, was the lucky one, and one should step forth with it foremost or enter a house on it[26]—a superstition which even the rugged Sam Johnson punctiliously observed[27] and which survives also in the widespread notion that "a bride must step over the church sill with her right foot."[28] Finally, among the Yoruba of West Africa, the highest court functionary is called "the right-hand minister."[29]

(c) Next, the *footstool* is placed in position. A symbolic meaning is read into this act, and the officiant, continuing the divine pronouncement, utters the words:

> *. . . while that I set thy foemen*
> *a footstool at thy feet!*

From the ritual standpoint, there is a special significance in these words. As the mediator of what *we* would call "the order of nature" to his people, the king is responsible not only for the positive benefits of weather, fertility, and increase but also for the expulsion or aversion of all noxious influences, whether demonic or human.[30] Accordingly, an essential element of the installation ceremony is that he receive the power to do so, and the purpose of this statement is to serve formal notice that he indeed possesses it. Exactly comparable is the assurance given at the coronation of the Egyptian Pharaoh Thothmes III that "all lands are under thy sandals."[31]

(d) Once enthroned, the king is handed the royal scepter, while the officiant declares:

> *Yahweh extends the rod of thy might;*
> *from Zion exact subjection 'mid thy foes!*[32]

This again is a way of articulating the subtle relationship of punctual king to durative god: the latter bestows the insignia upon him. So, in the Egyptian account, Amon-Re' confers the "magical powers" of the diadem on Hatshepsut, while Thoth recites the accompanying formula.[33] So too, the Sumerian King List asserts that the regalia came down primevally from on high,[34] and the Sumerian Story of the Deluge corroborates the statement;[35] while in the Akkadian Legend of Etana, those marks of kingship are said to be reserved in heaven during a period of divine displeasure.[36] Hammurapi states that he was invested by the mother-goddess;[37] Esarhaddon, by Shamash, Bel, and Nabu;[38] and Nabuna'id (Nabonidus) by Sin and Nabu together;[39] while elsewhere we are told that the insignia are held by the supreme god Anu, who delegates them to mortal kings.[40]

Nor is this idea confined to the Ancient Near East. Homer says in the same vein that the scepter of Agamemnon came ultimately from Zeus;[41] while in Japanese tradition, the Imperial Sword (Kusangi no Tsurugi) is believed to have come, in the first instance, from heaven and to have been acquired, through a feat of gallantry and daring, by the ancestor of the Mikados.[42] Analogously too, in Tahiti, the native king is invested in the presence of the god Oro, and the royal cincture is solemnly addressed as the "parent" or "progenitor" of the king's power.[43]

(e) In contrast to the subdued enemies of the king are his loyal subjects. Speaking, as it were, in their name, the officiant declares that they are willing at all times to take up arms in their royal master's cause:

> Thy people freely volunteer
> whensoever thou musterest thy forces!

(This is the correct translation.[44]) Not impossibly, these words constitute a formal expression of fealty, as in the British coronation ceremony, where the investiture is followed by pledges of allegiance from the peers.[45]

(f) What follows is, as all scholars admit, somewhat obscure. The King James Version's *In the beauties of holiness from the womb of the morning: thou hast the dew of thy youth,* is, perhaps, the best that can be made out of the traditional Hebrew text. This is usually taken to mean that whenever the king sallies forth to war, his youthful warriors, attired in stately and sacred garments, will press forward in his service, countless as dewdrops at dawn.[46] Such an interpretation, however, is open to at least three objections. First, the word rendered *thy youth,* and taken to mean the collective youth of the country, could mean at best *thy childhood,* or the collective children of the country; and children do not go to war.[47] More probably, however, it means simply *thy birth* and connects somehow with the expression, *womb of the morning.*[48] Second, warriors do not normally go into battle dressed in sacred or ecclesiastical vestments. Third, in the Old Testament, as in other literatures, dew is usually a symbol of freshness, or even of fragrance, rather than of innumerability.[49]

Perhaps here again Comparative Religion and Folklore can throw a ray of light. Whatever the verse may mean in detail, it seems to be saying something about the new king's birth or childhood. May it not be, then, that it is really alluding to that cardinal doctrine of ancient and primitive peoples that the king is of divine, "supernatural" birth and predestined for his role? In the ceremony of Queen Hatchepsut's coronation, for example, the supreme god Amon-Re' declares explicitly that he is her true supernal begetter, and the fact is formally acknowledged by the other gods.[50] In line with such ideas, coronation elsewhere involves a symbolic demonstration that the new king, though indeed born of mortal parents, is, from the moment of his investiture, really the incarnation of a divine being. Thus, in ancient India, he was thought, when crowned, to discard his natural parentage and to be born anew, his royal robe being sometimes described as "the caul (or womb) of sovereignty."[51]

Similarly, among several West African peoples, he has on that occasion to renounce his human parents, and is given an official divine pedigree;[52] while in Fiji, the symbolism is carried to such lengths that the new king is nursed as a baby for four days after his installation![53] If this is, indeed, the general purport of our verse, what it seems specifically to be saying is that the new king comes "trailing clouds of glory," like the sun emerging from the womb of dawn, and with all the freshness and fragrance of the morning dew still clinging to him.

This picture too is suffused with ancient and primitive imagery. In Egypt, the king was indeed portrayed as a sun, offspring of the solar deity Re',[54] and in the Tell Amarna Letters, "sun" is one of his regular titles. Similarly, in Hittite hieroglyphic script, the sign for "sun" enters into the names of several kings of the Neo-Hittites.[55] Mesopotamian kings also often affect the same style;[56] while in the New World, the Natchez of Mississippi say that their original culture-hero was a "sun-child," and call his progeny, "suns."[57] Pertinent also is the fact that in a number of modern Greek folktales, maidens who consort with kings or princes are said to give birth to Sun, Moon, or Morning Star, or to offspring with starlight in their faces.[58] Directly comparable with this last is the statement in our psalm that the new king comes bathed with the morning dew of his birth or childhood, especially when it is borne in mind that dew was often regarded in antiquity as an effluvium from the stars.[59] In sundry Egyptian texts, the pharaoh is likewise described as bathed in fragrant and invigorating dew.[60]

Not impossibly, the recital of this verse accompanied the act of anointment, the dew being symbolized by the oil. What makes this suggestion the more plausible is that otherwise there would be a strange omission of any reference to this essential element of the installation ceremony.[61]

(g) As the mediator of the divine order, the king functioned, both in Egypt and in Mesopotamia, as a *priest;*[62] and this, it will be recalled, was likewise the role of Melchizedek, king of Salem, in Genesis 14:18. His formal authorization in this office therefore forms the next element of the coronation ritual:

> *Yahweh has sworn, and will not relent:*
> *"Thou art a priest for ever,*
> *on the pattern of Melchizedek!"*

The royal priesthood is perpetual because the king is the punctual embodiment of a continuous, indesinent being: *Le roi est mort, vive le roi!*[63] In the same way, at the coronation of Queen Hatchepsut, her royal names and titles are bestowed on her by Amon-Re' "for ever."[64]

To be sure, the institution of royal priesthood did not obtain in Israel; the reference to it here is therefore an example of what may be termed "literary atavism"—a mere survival of an element common in the traditional form of composition on which this one is based.

(h) We have already observed that, as steward of the divine order, the king is responsible for "security" in the wider sense of the word—that is, for eliminating all noxious influences from his people, and this includes the subjugation of his enemies. The assumption is, however, that he does the latter not merely through the fortunes of war but necessarily and automatically by virtue of his divine character. If ever he is defeated (or if prosperity fail), it is simply because the vessel is not functioning properly; the king's human shortcomings ("sins") have impaired it. In the long run, therefore, victory comes from the durative god whom the king embodies. It is that god who has stood

> (*ever*) *at thy right hand,*
> *has smitten kings whenso he was angry.*

Moreover, with the defeat of their sovereigns, it is that same god who now himself

> *wields government*[65] *among the nations,*
> *having filled the valleys with corpses,*[66]
> *smashed heads far and wide.*[67]

Again there is an exact parallel in the Egyptian texts describing the coronations of Thothmes III and of Hatshepsut: the gods, we read, "give victory" to the king and fight on behalf of the queen.[68]

(i) In its final verse, the psalm swells to a dramatic crescendo. In contrast to the heads of his enemies which will be smashed, the king, it is said, will always lift his own proudly and triumphantly; and, while *their* corpses fill the valleys and are strewn "far and wide" over the fields, *he* will go drinking nonchalantly from the wayside brook!

The sense (despite the insensitive skepticism of some modern scholars) seems plain enough;[69] but what, we may ask, prompted the introduction of this somewhat bizarre image? The answer, it may be suggested, is that *the recital of this verse accompanied the act of proffering to the new king a ceremonial chalice.*

Such royal chalices are well attested in the Ancient Near East. In the Canaanite *Poem of Baal,* that god is described as "our king, our governor . . . to whom we bring goblet of tribute, to whom we bring cup of tribute";[70] while in the Hittite *Yuzgat Tablet,* Jack Frost (*Hahhimas*) challenges the sovereignty of the supreme god by telling him that his hands no longer "retain firm hold on the chalice," only to receive the retort that they are in fact virtually glued to it![71] Moreover, the literary evidence is supported in turn by artistic representations. Thus, on the sarcophagus of King Ahiram of Byblus,[72] and again on the Megiddo ivories[73] and on two Phoenician bowls, the king is depicted holding a cup in his right hand and a lotus in his left;[74] while on cylinder seals gods are often portrayed holding goblets, while their votaries stand before them.[75] The Holy Grail (in its original form) probably also comes into the picture.[76] The goblet or chalice evidently represents that primordial water which, as we have seen (above, §**148**), the new king had to absorb in order to acquire divine wisdom and power.

* * *

For the reader's convenience, I append a new translation of the psalm embodying the above interpretation:

The king is enthroned

> *1. The pronouncement of Yahweh to my lord:*
> *"Sit thou at my right hand,*

The footstool is placed in position

> *while that I make thy foemen*
> *a footstool at thy feet!"*

The scepter is handed to the king

> *2. Yahweh extends the rod of thy might;*
> *from Zion subdue thy foes!*

The attendant crowd signify their allegiance

> *3. Thy people shall offer ready service*
> *whensoever thou musterest thy host!*

The king is invested and anointed

> *(Clad) in (all) the tokens*
> *of awesome, sacred state,*
> *thou comest besprent from birth*
> *with dew from the womb of dawn!*

The king is consecrated as priest

> *4. Yahweh has sworn, and will not relent:*
> *thou art perpetual priest,*
> *on the pattern of Melchizedek!*

The king is assured of military success

> *5. Yahweh, at thy right hand,*
> *crushing kings whenso he grows angry,*
> *6. will himself bear rule 'mid the nations,*

> *filling <the valleys> with corpses,*
> *crushing heads far and wide;*

A chalice is proffered

> 7. *(yet) he^a will go (calmly) drinking*
> *(meanwhile) from the wayside brook,*
> *(and) by reason of this,*
> *(proudly) lift his head!*

285 Jordan turned back 114:3

> *The sea looked and fled,*
> *Jordan turned back*

The picture is drawn from popular lore: the reversal of rivers betokens world upheaval and a change in the prevailing order of things. In a famous chorus of Euripides' *Medea*, the universal breakdown of things as they were is conveyed by the words:

> Back flow the streams on the ever-running river;
> Life, life is changed, and the laws of it o'ertrod.[1]
> —trans. Gilbert Murray

while the diversion or entire arrest of the rivers was regarded in Classical antiquity as a typical accomplishment of witches.[2]

286 Snares of death 116:3
See above, §253.

287 Tears fertilize 126:5–6

> *They that sow in tears*
> *shall reap with shouts of joy.*
> *Though one go forth weeping,*
> *bearing the trail of seed,*
> *he shall come home with shouts of joy,*
> *bearing his bounden sheaves!*

Though employed in a wide and general sense, this image may well have been suggested by the common practice of bewailing the dead or vanished god of fertility at agricultural ceremonies. The Egyptians, says Diodorus, used to shed tears and cry upon Isis when they began cutting their corn,[1] and their summer festival was marked, according to Herodotus, by the chanting of a doleful lay called Maneros.[2] The latter, it is now known, is simply a distortion of the Egyptian words, *maa n per.k,* "come to thy house," which constitute

---
[a] I.e., the king.

the initial phrase in seasonal lamentations for Osiris which have actually come down to us.[3] The custom is attested also, at a much later date, by Firmicus Maternus, who reproaches the pagan Egyptians for "lamenting over the crops and wailing over the growing seed."[4] The lamentations, say Herodotus and various other Classical writers, were accompanied on the flute,[5] and one of the scenes sculptured on the walls of the Fifth Dynasty tomb of Ti indeed portrays a man piping beside reapers![6]

In Mesopotamia, the harvest was accompanied by the chanting of an ululation (*alalu*),[7] and this is paralleled in other parts of the ancient world. Thus, in the Biblical Book of Judges (9:27) it is stated expressly that the inhabitants of Shechem performed the analogous rite of *hillulim* (RSV: lamely, "held festival") on the occasion of the vintage,[8] and the custom still obtains in parts of the Holy Land;[9] while Plutarch informs us that the traditional cry at the Attic vintage festival of Oschophoria was *eleleu*.[10] Similarly, according to a writer quoted by Athenaeus, the ritual dirges uttered in the mysteries of Demeter and Kore—basically an agricultural rite—went under the name of *iouloi* (or *houloi*), i.e., "howls";[11] and it is possibly to such a cry that the prophet Micah consciously alludes when he exclaims (7:1): "*Al^elai li* (Woe is me!), for I am become as when the summer fruit has been gathered, the vintage gleaned!"

These traditional howlings and wailings were popularly interpreted as dirges over gods or spirits of fertility who were believed to have died or temporarily withdrawn themselves from the earth. The lamentations for Osiris in Egypt, Adonis in Syria, and Attis in Asia Minor are well known. Similarly, in the Babylonian Epic of Gilgamesh,[12] and again in the *Poem of the Descent of Ishtar to the Netherworld*,[13] mention is made explicitly of the annual weeping for Tammuz, and other texts prescribe wailing in midsummer.[14] This seasonal ululation survived, indeed, into the Christian era, for a medieval Arab antiquary records the performance of it at Harran.[15]

Yet, despite these later mythological interpretations, there is reason to suspect that the howlings and wailings in question were not originally signs of mourning at all. First, it is significant that in several cases the gods or spirits who are supposedly lamented bear names which are really nothing but artificial personifications of the wailings themselves! The Greeks, for example, promptly invented a corn-goddess Ioulo whom the *iouloi* or "howls" of the Demeter-cult were supposed to invoke.[16] Similarly, the Phoenician refrain, *ai lanu*, "woe unto us," was transformed into the Greek *ai Linou*, "woe for Linos," and gave birth to the Adonis-like figure of that name;[17] just as among the Basques the traditional *lelo*, or lamentation, has begotten a legendary hero Lelo, for whom they are held to be chanted.[18]

Second, it should be observed that weeping is, in any case, not necessarily evidence of mourning, for it can be produced also by any violent excitement.[19] Accordingly, seasonal weeping may have been but the natural accompaniment of frenzy and hysteria, and the loud cries mere shrieks and yells of agitation. Moreover, it is to be borne in mind that in several cultures—as, for instance, among the Toradjas, Galelarese, and Javanese of Indonesia[20]—tears are regarded (like blood, sweat, semen, and urine elsewhere)[21] as effusions of the "soul-substance," so that the shedding of them serves as a means of reinvigorating the earth and even of reviving the dead. Thus, at Great Bassam, in Guinea, oxen are slaughtered annually as part of a procedure designed to ensure a good harvest, and it is an essential part of the ceremony that they must weep. To this end, manioc meal and palm wine are thrown into their eyes.[22] Again, among the Khonds of Bengal,[23] and likewise in Mexico,[24] the shedding of tears is believed to be a homoeopathic method of producing rain. It is therefore something of this kind that may have underlain the practice reflected in the Psalmist's language.

288 The winds of fortune 143:10

RSV: *Let Thy good spirit lead me on a level path!*

Once again, the conventional rendering obscures an interesting piece of folklore. The Hebrew words translated *good spirit* really mean *goodly wind*, and hark back to the ancient conception of good and bad fortune as favorable and unfavorable winds.[1] Such an image would readily have suggested itself to Phoenicians sailing the Mediterranean or to Mesopotamians plying their crafts along the Tigris and Euphrates.

To cite but a few examples. Ashurbanipal "waits upon a goodly wind."[2] A Mesopotamian magical text includes the invocation that the god "may cause his goodly wind to blow," and prolong a man's life;[3] while in a prayer a suppliant entreats, "May I live through thy wind!"[4] The wind is, of course, the divine breath, so that when Isaiah says of Israel (63:14) that it is guided by the same gentle "breath of Yahweh" as guides cattle which roam the valley for pasture,[5] or when the "Babylonian Ecclesiastes" advises men to "seek ever the good breath of the gods,"[6] the same image is involved. Aeschylus too describes good fortune as the wind, or breeze, of the gods.[7]

Conversely, evil spirits are frequently portrayed as fierce stormwinds,[8] and in an incantation from the time of Hammurapi, winds are bringers of illness[9]—a notion which survives sporadically in European folklore.[10] Euripides speaks analogously of "the blast of Fate."[11]

Job

289 Introductory

The Biblical Book of Job is a poetic and quasi-philosophic treatment of an ancient pagan legend, the outlines of which are sketched in the prose prologue and epilogue. From the fact that all of the principle characters are said to come from Arabian lands,[1] that Job's estate is raided by Arabian Sabaeans,[2] and that many words are used in a sense common in Arabic but unparalleled in classical Hebrew,[3] it has been conjectured that the book emanates from Edom,[4] whose "sages" are indeed mentioned as proverbial in sundry passages of Scripture.[5]

The description of Job's physical sufferings, and his protest of seeming innocence, find a striking parallel in a Mesopotamian poem often styled *The Babylonian Job*.[6] It should be observed, however, that while the Biblical writer has indeed been influenced by that composition, his work is far from a mere slavish imitation of it, for the plight of Job is merely the background, but not the essence, of the book. The latter lies rather in the argument that by virtue of man's finite nature and intellect, there can be no rational discourse between him and God, so that all attempted justifications of God's dealings with him are necessarily futile. In other words, the book is not a philosophical theodicy but rather a protest against any such thing. Viewed in this light, it is quite mistaken to object, as many critics have done, that God answers Job with thunder rather than with reason; the whole point is that this is the only plane on which He can communicate with man, for "justification" implies a satisfaction of purely human standards by that which *ex hypothesi* transcends them. We have in this book the direct antithesis of Greek moral philosophy.[7]

Scholars have assumed that the speeches of Elihu were added later, the reason being that he speaks in a style different linguistically from the rest of the book and says nothing which God himself does not say.[8] I believe this argument to be false and unperceptive. The introduction of Elihu is essential to the real point and irony of the book. He is, so to speak, the brash young theological student who "knows all the answers" and fancies himself superior to the homespun philosophies of Job's middle-class friends.[9] He speaks in a somewhat different dialect precisely in order to point up the difference between his background and theirs; he knows the "seminary jargon." But he gets his eloquent come-uppance from God himself, who exposes the limitations and impudence of "theology," and he is hoisted with his own petard by having his ratiocinations condemned as mere plebeian mortal arguments! Inured as we are to Greek patterns of thought and criteria of discourse, this primitive Oriental line of approach may indeed fail to satisfy our more sophisticated minds, but that is no reason for distorting the author's own attitude, which is precisely that our minds are inadequate vehicles for the comprehension of the problem which Job's experience raises.

290 The Devil's wager

The folktale around which the Book of Job revolves finds an interesting parallel in the Indian legend of King Harischandra. Once upon a time, we are told, at a combined assembly of the gods, saints, and patriarchs, the question was propounded whether any entirely faultless prince could be found on earth. The majority, headed by the god Rudra, said, No, but the sage Vasesta nominated his disciple Harischandra. Rudra accepted this challenge and obtained permission to put the matter to the test. He therefore subjected Harischandra to the most abject poverty, compassed the execution of his only son, and took away his wife. Harischandra, however, withstood all these afflictions without relinquishing his piety. In reward for such virtue, the gods restored his property, revived his son, and brought back his wife, while Rudra retired discomfited. It should be observed, however, that this story—which is told in connection with a passage in the Markandcya Puraṇa—appears to be no older than the third century A.D., and may itself reflect the story of Job, picked up from Christian missionaries.[1]

291 The Sons of God   1:6–12

The opening scene of the book is set in the court of God, which is portrayed in terms of ancient pagan belief, since the story itself is of pagan origin. The "sons of God," therefore, are not angels—which belong to a much later theology; they are simply the junior members of the pantheon, this being their common designation in the Canaanite texts from Ras Shamra-Ugarit,[1] and again in a magical inscription of the eighth century B.C., from Arslan Tash in the Upper Euphrates Valley.[2] The same style recurs, as a mythological relic, in such ancient passages of the Old Testament as Genesis 6:2,4 (see above, §**32**), Deuteronomy 32:8, and Psalms 29:1 and 89:7.

292 Satan

The *satan* in this narrative is not the archfiend, perpetually opposed to God. Such a conception, again, belongs to later thought, when Iranian dualism had made inroads into traditional Hebrew thinking.[1] Here the name denotes simply a member of the pantheon who happens on this particular occasion to "throw a monkey wrench" into the proceedings, but who is subject to God. The word means simply "obstructor."

293 Signs of mourning   1:20
See above, §§135, 202.

294 Mother Earth   1:21

Naked I came from my mother's womb,
and naked I return thither.

(a) No one returns to his mother's womb. Hence, *thither* must be understood deictically: the speaker points to the earth with the added implication that it is the mother of all men.

(On the concept of *Mother Earth* among the Semites, cf. E. Dhorme, in ARW 7 (1905), 550 ff.; Noeldeke, *ib.*, 8 (1906), 161 ff.; Briem, *ib.*, 24 (1926), 179–85; Stein, in *Tarbiz* 9 (1938), 257–77; Volmer, in ZNTW 10 (1910), 324 f.; W. von Baudissin, *Adonis und Esmun* (1911), 20, n. 1, 443 f., 505 f.
On the concept in general, cf.: A. Dieterich, *Mutter Erde*[2] (1913); Dittmar, in ZNTW 9 (1908), 341–44; E. H. Jones, *The Earth Goddess* (1936).)

In token of return to Mother Earth, it is customary in many parts of the world to lay the deceased on the ground shortly after death.[1] The custom can be traced back to ancient India,[2] and Servius, the famous fourth-century commentator on Vergil, tells us that it was likewise the practice of the Romans, when men lay dangerously ill, to place them on the ground outside their houses, "so that they might return their last breath to the earth" whence they sprang.[3] Similarly, Aelfric, the celebrated medieval English churchman, says that in his day it was the custom to spread a sheet of sackcloth on the floor and on this to sprinkle ashes in the shape of a cross. Just as the dying person was in the last agony, he was taken out of bed and stretched on the sackcloth and ashes; it being deemed more becoming "that sinful man should yield up his soul thus than on a soft bed, when his divine Redeemer died on the hard wood of the cross."[4] Moreover, it is related both of Bishop Benno of Osnabruck, in the eleventh century,[5] and of St. Francis of Assisi, in the thirteenth,[6] that they ordered their disciples to deposit them on the ground during their last moments. Nor, indeed, was the custom altogether extinct in more recent times; it was common as late as the nineteenth century in several parts of England and Ireland,[7] and it still obtains sporadically in such regions of Germany as Vogtland, Silesia, and East Prussia.[8] It is also standard usage among Orthodox Jews to lay a corpse on the ground for one hour.

Earth appears as a deity in sundry passages of Ancient Near Eastern literature. She is included, beside various celestial phenomena, in a list of gods from Asshur, the older capital of Assyria;[9] while in the Canaanite myths from Ras Shamra-Ugarit, "Miss Earth" (*Arṣaya*) is one of the brides of Baal.[10] The female Omorka mentioned in Sanchuniathon's account of ancient Phoenician cosmogony is identified by many scholars as *em arqâ,* "Mother Earth," though his Greek translator, Philo of Byblus, says that she is the same as Tiamat, the primordial ocean.[11] In the Book of Enoch mention is made of an angel Arqiel, who is probably a transmogrification of an older god of the earth (cf. Aramaic, *arqâ,* "earth").[12]

(b) Job's pious exclamation finds an arresting parallel, albeit in a somewhat different vein, in an epigram by Palladas of Alexandria (4th cent. C.E.) in the Greek Anthology:

> Naked I came unto earth;
> naked to earth I descend.
> Why should I labor for naught,
> seeing how naked the end?[13]

Similarly too, an old Norse expression for "die" was "fall back into mother's womb" (*i mooturaett falla*).[14]

> The LORD gave, and the LORD has taken;
> blessed be the name of the LORD!

We now know that Job was adapting a traditional proverb, for another version of it has turned up in a Mesopotamian cuneiform text: *The king gave, and the king has taken; long live the king!*[15]

295 Rousing Leviathan 3:8

> May they curse it who pronounce days accursed,
> who will in the future rouse up Leviathan!

Since Job has just expressed the wish that the day of his birth may be shrouded in darkness, it is usually supposed that Leviathan here denotes the celestial dragon who, in many mythologies, causes eclipses by swallowing up the sun or moon.[1]

Thus, in Indic belief, it is the dragon Rahu (Svarbhanu) who periodically swallows the sun or moon,[2] and this notion was adopted also by the Buddhists.[3] In China, eclipses were likewise attributed to the devouring of sun or moon by a monster, and in the Confucian classic, *Tsun Tsiu* ("Springs and Autumns") the word "eaten" is employed to describe the eclipse of April 20, 610 B.C.[4] Among the Burmese, it is a white dog (*shittakwā*) that swallows the moon;[5] and in Scandinavian lore the sun is continually pursued by a wolf named Skoll.[6] The Tartar tribe of the Chuwashes use the phrase, "a demon has eaten it" (*vabur siat*) to denote a lunar eclipse;[7] while the Lithuanians assert that the demon Tiknis (Tiklis) attacks the chariot of the sun.[8] A Mongolian myth says that dragons lie in wait for sun and moon[9]—a belief which possesses a well-known analogue in ancient Egypt.[10] In Iraq, the popular cry at an eclipse is, "O serpent who art swallowing it up, disgorge the moon!"[11] In Jewish folklore, the sun was said to be swallowed by a great fish,[12] and the same notion is mentioned, but refuted, by Maximus of Turin[13] and Hrabanus Maurus.[14] Spectators of a lunar eclipse near Mt. Hermon, in 1891, held that a large fish had devoured the moon,[15] and Tacitus attests a similar belief among the Romans.[16] The Greeks maintained that eclipses were caused in like fashion by a python;[17] and this fancy obtains also among the Negritos of Borneo.[18] In the Canaanite *Poem of Baal,* the sun-goddess is assured of the protection of the god Kothar "who hurls both Monster and Dragon into the sea."[19]

It may be suggested, however, that Job is really alluding to quite a different myth. Leviathan, as we have seen (above, §**186**), is the monster whom the regnant god (Baal, Yahweh) subdues at the beginning of the present era. But, though imprisoned, it is destined to break lose when that era reaches its close, and then the combat will be repeated. A famous passage in Isaiah (27:1) alludes to this coming event; while in the Book of Revelation (20:1-3) we read similarly of "the ancient serpent" (*not* the snake in Eden!) who will break his bonds after a thousand years and "be loosed for a little while." The same picture is painted also in later pseudepigraphic[20] and rabbinic literature.[21] In Iranian myth, the rebellious serpent Azhi Dahak, imprisoned beneath Mt. Demawend, will eventually burst forth, only to be subdued by the hero Keresaspa,[22] while in Classical lore, the volcanic fires of Etna are attributed to the snortings of the dragon Typhon incarcerated beneath it.[23] The curse which Job invokes, therefore, would be that the day of his birth may be deemed so ill-starred that it will be the one on the anniversary of which the Dragon will emerge and "all hell break loose."

296 Father's knees 3:12

Why did knees receive me?
or breasts, that I should suck?

The knees were those of Job's father, for a father acknowledged paternity by setting his child on his knees. In the Hittite myth of Ullikummi, for example, after the god Kumarbi has created the stone monster, he dandles it on his knee and gives it a name;[1] while in reliefs at Der-el-Bahri, Queen Hatshepsut of Egypt is shown perched on the knee of the god Amon in token of her divine parentage.[2] The custom was standard also in pagan Germany[3] and, indeed, throughout Europe:[4] Harald the Dane adopted the son of Erik by placing him on his knees,[5] and Harald Haarfagre wrested the succession from the true offspring of the English king Aethelstan by setting the son of a handmaid on the latter's knee.[6] Even grandfathers sometimes authenticated their descendants in this way; those of Joseph, for example, are said to have been born "on his knees."[7]

The basis of this custom was a widespread belief that the knee was a seat of the seminal fluid—an idea attested by the very etymology of the word (knee-*genu*-generate).[8] Indeed, the word *genuine* meant originally "one whose paternity had been authenticated by his having been placed on his father's knee (*genu*)";[9] and in ancient Mesopotamian speech the word for "knee" (*birku*) was sometimes used in the sense of the male organ.[10]

297 The weary dead 3:17

There the wicked cease from raging,
and there the weary are at rest.

A common euphemism for "the dead" in Egyptian is "the weary" (*nn.y*) or "the languid at heart" (*wrd 'ib*);[1] while the Greeks likewise called them "the weary" or "toilworn" (*hoi kamontes*).[2] The name Rephaim by which they are designated both in the Old Testament and in Canaanite and Phoenician texts has been derived by some scholars from a verbal root (*r-ph-h/y*) of the same meaning, but this is uncertain.[3]

298 The sons of Resheph 5:7

For affliction does not come from the dust,
nor does trouble sprout from the ground;
but man is born to trouble,
as the sparks fly upward.

This familiar rendering must now be given up, for the Hebrew words translated *sparks* really mean *sons of Resheph,* and we now know that Resheph was the Canaanite god of plague and pestilence.[1] The reference is, therefore, to the band of demons who are ever on the wing, hovering over men. Moreover, the words rendered *for not . . . nor* really mean (by an idiom found in the Amarna Letters and sporadically also in the Old Testament itself)[2] *how not?, surely.* Hence, the correct translation is:

Verily, affliction springs from the very dust,
and trouble sprouts from the very ground;
yea, man is born to trouble,
and Resheph's band wings ever on high.

In other words, this is again a mythological allusion, the sense of which is that man is beset on all sides, above and below; he "gets it coming and going."

(On Resheph as winged, see F. Matthiae in *Oriens Antiquus*[2] [1963], 39. Note also that the Greek (Septuagint) Version renders here, "vulture's fledglings," and that the Egyptian *r-sh-f*—perhaps a loanword from Canaanite—denotes a winged being.[3])

299 Guard over Sea and Dragon   7:12

> *Am I, then, sea or dragon,*
> *that Thou shouldst set guard over me?*

Again a mythological allusion. Sea is here personified, the reference being to the contumacious Sir Sea (Yammu) of the Canaanite *Poem of Baal,* where the Dragon (Tannin) is also mentioned (see above, §**186**). The monster represented the raging floods, and had therefore to be clamped down and guarded (see above, §**258**). In the Babylonian Epic of Creation (*Enuma Elish* 4.139) it is said explicitly that after the defeat of Tiamat, Marduk posted guards over her confederates "and ordered them not to let the waters escape."

300 Orion   9:9

> *Who made the Bear and Orion.*

The Hebrew word for Orion (viz., *K^esil*) means properly "a lumbering gawk, clod" (not simply, fool, as commonly rendered).[1] In Classical tradition, Orion was a giant. Homer speaks of him as "prodigious in size,"[2] and he is so portrayed in Greek art.[3] Latin writers call him *Gigas,*[4] and in Arabic literature he is termed analogously, "the Giant" (*al jabar*).[5] The Hebrew name therefore reflects a common ancient belief that giants are gawkish dunderheads. Thus in German folklore they are frequently styled *dumme Lutten,* or "lubbers,"[6] and in Old Norse, *dumbr,* or "numskulls."[7] Some two hundred stories about stupid giants and ogres are listed in Aarne-Thompson's standard *Types of the Folk-Tale.*[8]

301 The whip of God   9:23

> *When a scourge brings sudden death,*
> *He (God) but mocks at the anguish(?) of the innocent.*

It was a common belief in antiquity that disaster and disease were caused by the stroke of a divine or demonic whip. In the Iliad, the Achaeans and Argives are defeated by "the whip of Zeus";[1] while Aeschylus ascribes military reverse to lashes of the whip of Ares, god of war.[2] The Furies too are said to brandish whips;[3] and the hapless Io complains that she is being driven from pillar to post by the "scourge of Zeus."[4] Similarly, the Egyptian demon Seth is often figured wielding a whip, and so too is the cock-headed demon Iao on Gnostic gems.[5] A late Greek magical spell offers protection in the divine name against "any whip's coming near you,"[6] and in a prayer for a sick person composed by Bishop Serapion of Thmuis, in the fourth century, immunity is besought against "every whip (scourge), every pain, every trouble."[7] In medieval folklore, the Devil often carries a whip.[8]

Lightning too was regarded as a lash.[9] Capaneus, who, in Greek legend, was struck by lightning for attempting to scale the walls of Thebes, is said by the Alexandrian poetaster Lycophron—surely the greatest bore in all Greek literature—to have been flailed by the whip of Zeus;[10] and Oppian (c. A.D. 180)—who runs him a close second—describes Zeus as lashing the waves in a sea storm[11]—an idiom which survives, of course, in modern speech. Lightning is similarly conceived in India, China, and Wallachia;[12] while in medieval German folklore it is portrayed as a blue flail.[13]

302 The disappearing shadow — 15:29

> *He shall not grow rich, neither shall the substance which*
> *he has continue,*
> *nor will he strike root in the earth.*

The Hebrew of the second line is obscure, and the text is probably corrupt, but RSV's rendering, given above, is pure conjecture. The Greek (Septuagint) and Old Latin versions have the interesting variant: *Nor will his shadow extend upon the ground.* If this is correct, we are once more in the realm of folklore, for the verse will then reflect a widespread popular belief that the disappearance of one's shadow—regarded as one's alter ego—betokens death. Pausanias, Polybius, and Plutarch all attest the ancient Greek superstition that anyone who trespassed on the sacred precinct of Lycaean Zeus would lose his shadow and die within the year.[1] Similarly, it is believed in various parts of Germany that if one's shadow be invisible on Christmas Eve, one will not live through the ensuing twelve months;[2] and in Jewish popular lore, the same consequence is said to be entailed if one's shadow cannot be seen on the wall of the synagogue during the public devotions on Hoshanna Rabbah, the seventh day of the Feast of Booths.[3] A Japanese proverb says that "When death approaches, a man's shadow fades, although he seems healthy,"[4] and people are warned not to tread on a man's shadow, "for shadow is life."[5]

On the general notion of the shadow as a life index, see above, §94.

303 The hawsers of the heart — 17:11

> RSV: *My days are past; my plans are broken off,*
> *the desires of my heart.*

This conventional rendering obscures an effective metaphor drawn from popular lore and fancy. The Hebrew word rendered *broken off* is usually employed of snapping a rope or thread,[1] and in Isaiah 33:20, specifically of a ship's cable. That rendered *plans,* if derived from a different verbal root, can mean *things that tie, restrain, curb;*[2] while that rendered *desires* can be connected with a Syriac term for *hawser.*[3] The verse would then read:

> *Spent are my days; snapped are my hawsers,*
> *the moorings of my heart.*

The picture now finds a perfect parallel in Shakespeare's *King John,* where that monarch exclaims:

> The tackle of my heart is crackt and burned,
> And all the shrouds wherewith my life should sail
> Are turned to a thread, one little hair:
> My heart hath one poor string to stay it by.[4]

This is a natural counterpart to the familiar figure of "the desired haven."[5] If the fulfillment of life's dreams and ambitions can be described as reaching port, the frustration of them can obviously be represented as a sudden snapping of the hawsers, so that the ship drifts from its moorings.

304 The King of Terrors   18:14

Bildad warns Job that the affluence and security of the impious are short-lived:

> *His strength is hunger-bitten,*
> *and disaster stands poised at his side.*
> *Death's firstborn feeds on his limbs,*
> *feeds on the thews of his flesh.*[a]
> *He is torn from the tent where he felt secure,*[b]
> *to be led in triumphal progress*[c]
> *unto the King of Terrors!*

The last line has greatly perplexed commentators, and various emendations have been proposed.[1] Once again, however, Comparative Folklore clarifies what is otherwise obscure, for the fact is that the expression "King of Terrors" finds its exact counterpart in Sumerian texts where Nergal, lord of the netherworld, is characterized as "king of the land of terror" (*lugal ḫuš-ki-a*),[2] and that realm itself as "the terrible house" (*eš ḫuluḫ*).[3] Similarly too, Vergil describes Pluto as *rex tremendus*.[4] The words are thus a perfect parallel to the personification of wasting disease as "the firstborn of Death."

The picture is completed by the word here rendered "led in triumphal progress," for this refers primarily to *marching in a procession* (cf. II Sam. 6:13). The irony should not be missed: the affluent, but impious, "tycoon," whose greatest ambition is to be "presented at court," finds himself eventually escorted to the court of Hades!

Thus interpreted, the sentiment finds a striking echo in a passage of Aeschylus' *Seven against Thebes,* where the seer Amphiaraus, who has encouraged Polyneikes to attack his paternal city, is castigated by Eteocles as

---

[a] There is no need to emend the text, as is usually done; the subject of *both* clauses is "the firstborn of death."

[b] Or, His security is plucked out of his tent.

[c] For this nuance of the verb *ṣ-ᶜ-d,* cf. Ps. 68:8.

one who is bound in the end to be conducted, along with the impious invaders, to the "far city," i.e., Hades.[5]

305 God's net 19:6
See above, §253.

306 Razed foundations and faery gold 22:15–30

Are you taking note
of the fate that once attended
certain impious men?[1]

Though God himself had filled
their houses with all good things,
they said to him, "Begone!
What can Shaddai[2] *do for us?"*
    (Oh, wicked, wicked counsel!
    Be it ever far from me!)
So they became (like plants)
shrivelled betimes,[3]
their foundation turned to a quagmire.
The righteous looked on and made merry;
the guiltless laughed them to scorn:
"Though our mainstay proves not delusive,[4]
their tent-ropes[5] *are set ablaze!"*

Pay heed, then, to God, and submit;
thereby shall you get rich yield.
Take guidance from his mouth,
and store his words in your heart.
If you return to Shaddai[6]
(and) keep frowardness far from your tent,
you will (again) be built up.
You will find a treasure-trove
lying there in the dust,
and amid the stones of the brook
there will be gold of Ophir!
Shaddai himself will be
that treasure-trove of yours,
and he will be to you
like silver massed in heaps![7]
You will find in Shaddai
a mooring taut and secure,[8]
and be able to face him with calm.

> *When you pray, he will hear you;*
> *you will (live to) fulfill your vows.*
> *When you decide on a matter,*
> *you will find that it comes to fruition,*
> *and sunlight shall shine on your ways.*
> *Though others lower their eyes,*
> *you will say to yours, "Be raised!"*[9]
> *For God is wont to save*
> *a man downcast in meekness.*
> *Even to him whose hands*
> *are soiled with the taint of guilt*
> *God grants a means of escape.*
> *How much more, then, will you escape,*
> *if yours, in fact, are clean!*[10]

It is evident that in these lines (somewhat obscured in the standard translations) the author is alluding to familiar popular lore. The reference in the first part, it may be suggested, is to the widespread tale of the city that was suddenly flooded or burned on account of the impiety of its inhabitants[11]—a tale represented in the Old Testament by the legend of Sodom and Gomorrah (see above, §55). Of the same tenor too is an early Arabic story which tells of a certain Ḥimar who had been practising exemplary piety for forty years when, one day, all of his ten sons were killed by a thunderbolt while they were out hunting. Thereupon their father vowed that he would no longer serve a god who acted so cruelly. In punishment, however, for this impious resolve, his property was destroyed and his valley turned into a desert.[12]

In the second part, the poet seems to be alluding to the popular belief—well attested in European folktales—that "faery gold" can be found in rivers and mountains ("There's gold in them thar hills"),[13] or that the dust of the earth can be turned miraculously into gold as a reward for piety or good deeds.[14]

307 The shades beneath the waters   26:5

> *The Shades (Rephaim) tremble beneath the waters;*
> *so too do they who dwell therein.*

It is a not uncommon belief among primitive peoples that the abode of the dead lies beneath the sea. The Polynesians there locate the underworld, Puloto;[1] while the Eskimos contrast a submarine hell named Adlivum with a celestial paradise, Quidlivum.[2] The Massims of New Guinea know of a realm of bliss under the waters, called Hyoyoa;[3] and similar ideas are entertained also by the Papuans;[4] while in New Caledonia, the domain of the blessed (Tsiabiloum) is likewise thought to lie beneath the ocean.[5]

A curious variation on this theme appears among certain Bantu tribes of West Africa: the submarine paradise, it is held, is White Man's Land, and Negroes who go there become white and happy![6]

Nor are such notions confined to primitive peoples. In the Irish tale of Laegaire mac Crimthainn, related in the fifteenth-century Book of Lisinore, the abode of the blessed is Tir fa Tonn, "the Land under the Waters";[7] and Radermacher has tried to make out a case for such a belief among the Greeks.[8]

To be sure, this was not the usual view of the netherworld among the ancient Semites, but it should be observed that in some of the Mesopotamian hymns relating the fate of Tammuz, he is said to have been dragged down *beneath the waters.*[9]

308 Binding waters in the clouds 26:8

See below, §319.

309 The pillars of heaven 26:11

The notion that heaven rests on pillars is virtually universal.[1] The Egyptians spoke of four columns of iron or alabaster which held up the sky and which were controlled by the four sons of Horus—Mesthi, Hapi, Tuatmutef, and Qebhsenuf—who sat on them. They were regarded as the four cardinal points. This concept was so ancient that even by the time the Pyramid Texts came to be written, the true nature of the pillars was no longer clearly discerned.[2]

The pillars of heaven were likewise a common feature of Indo-European mythology. Not only are they mentioned in a hymn of the Rig Veda[3] and in sundry passages of ancient Iranian literature,[4] but they were also, from very early times, so standard an element of Greek popular lore that they were variously associated with different gods and heroes, being connected now with Atlas, now with Heracles, and now with Briareus.[5] Among modern primitives, the concept is attested in such divers parts of the world as Africa,[6] Indonesia,[7] North and South America,[8] Australasia,[9] and Finland.[10]

If it is true, as has often been asserted, that the temples of the Ancient Near East were built to represent the world in miniature,[11] then the twin pillars which are frequently associated with them (e.g., Jachin and Boaz at Jerusalem) may be taken as further evidence that the sky was believed to rest on such supports.[12]

Two curious survivals of the concept perhaps deserve special mention. Among the Skidi in the southwest region of North America, a "Pole Ceremony" is held periodically in which the posts are supposed to support the sky, represented by a domed roof;[13] while in the medieval right of High Mass, three ministers stood under a domelike canopy, or ciborium, painted blue and ornamented with stars in imitation of the sky, and this rested on four posts.[14]

310 The Dragon in the net 26:12–13

> By his strength he stilled the sea,
>   and by his intelligence smote the Proud Dragon.[a]
> By his breath the heavens were made fair,
>   his hand pierced the Evasive Serpent.

These lines clearly refer to the well-known myth of God's defeat of the primeval Dragon (see above, §186). The third line, however, seems out of place in such a context; yet Comparative Folklore enables us at once to recognize a lost allusion and thus to restore the true sense. For the traditional text's *ShāMaYiM*, "heavens," we must read, by mere redivision of the consonants, *ŚāM YāM*,[1] and we must interpret the Hebrew word *shifrah*, commonly rendered "made fair," from the Akkadian *saparu*, "net."[2] Thus the line will mean *By his wind he put Sir Sea in a net*. The allusion will then be to the incident related in the Mesopotamian Epic of Creation,[3] where the god Marduk subdues the monster Tiamat by driving the "evil wind" into her mouth and the stormwinds into her belly, and by spreading a net to catch her in it.[4]

311 The thread of life 27:8
See above, §191.

312 The legend of the phoenix 29:18

> RSV: Then I thought, "I shall die in my nest,
>   and I shall multiply my days as the sand."

The Hebrew says literally, "I shall die *with* my nest," and this has inspired some ancient translators and commentators with the notion that the word *ḥôl*, rendered "sand," is here to be taken as a homonym allegedly meaning "phoenix."[1] The reference would then be to the legend, recorded by Pliny, that at the close of its long life, the miraculous bird called phoenix (of which there is only one at a time) builds itself a nest out of cassia and frankincense, and dies in it. From its corpse is generated a worm which grows into the young phoenix.[2] (Variations on this legend, in which the long-lived bird is said finally to burn itself alive but subsequently to rise from its own ashes, are related by other Classical authors.[3])

Analogous stories are told in Arabic literature. Kazwini relates, for instance, that a mysterious bird called the *'anka* lives for seventeen hundred years, and that, when it is hatched, the parent of the opposite sex burns itself alive;[4] while Damiri speaks of a long-lived and periodically rejuvenated creature named *samand* or *samandal*, i.e., salamander, variously represented as a quadruped and as a bird.[5] The story also finds place in medieval bestiaries.[6]

---

[a] Heb.: *Rahab*, i.e., Braggart.

It has been suggested that the phoenix is really a transmogrification of the Egyptian mythical *bennu*-bird, regarded as symbolizing the rising sun and often described as "self-generating."[7]

(On the history of the legend, see fully: J. Hubaux and M. Leroy, *La mythe du phénix dans les litteratures grecque et latine* (Liège, Faculté des Lettres, 1939); R. T. Rundle Clark, "The Origin of the Phoenix," in *University of Birmingham Historical Journal*, 2 (1949), 1–29, 105–40.)

Against the proposed interpretation of our verse stand the following facts: (1) There is no evidence of a word *ḥôl* meaning "phoenix" in any Semitic or Ancient Near Eastern language;[8] (2) sand as a symbol of multiplicity is a commonplace of Biblical literature (see above, §59).

On the other hand, the reference in the first line of the verse to "dying with my nest" ought indeed, by normal laws of parallelism, to comport with what is said in the second line and to repeat the same sentiment. Moreover, there are indeed traces in Ancient Near Eastern literature of a belief in the rejuvenation of certain birds. Thus in Psalm 103:5, the Psalmist bids his soul bless the Lord who causes his youth to "renew itself like the eagle," and it is significant that Herodotus (ii.73) actually likens the phoenix to an eagle. Similarly, an inscription in an Egyptian tomb says of the deceased: "Mayest thou have the life of a *ḳḳ*-bird, and mayest thou wax old like the *nʿy*-serpent!"[9]

313 The negative confession 31

Job protests his innocence by reciting a list of offenses for which condign punishment would indeed be merited but each of which he claims never to have committed. These include: practice of fraud and deceit, rape of virgins, liaisons with other men's wives, denial of legal rights to servants, oppression of widows, refusal of hospitality to wanderers, and adoration of the sun or moon.

This catalogue is patterned after a type of composition known in the Ancient Near East as the *Negative Confession*.[1] Egyptian texts dating as far back as the sixteenth century B.C. contain a form of protestation believed to have been uttered by the deceased before the tribunal of the netherworld, and among the offenses of which he claims to be innocent specific mention is made of: blasphemy, sacrilege, assault, theft, perversion of justice, falsehood, trespass, usury, slander, and lust.[2] Such protestations are likewise incorporated into the autobiographical inscriptions found in tombs. Thus, in a Twelfth Dynasty tomb at Beni Hasan the occupant declares that he has never violated the daughter of a fellow-Egyptian, nor forced anyone to labor, nor denied food to the hungry;[3] while in the far older Pyramid Texts, the defunct proclaim in similar fashion that they have never done physical violence to anyone, nor refused succor to the starving or raiment to the naked.[4]

From Babylon too come examples of similar "negative confessions" recited by the deceased before the court of the netherworld;[5] and the analogous "oath of purgation," whereby a person might clear himself of a proffered charge by swearing innocence at an altar or sanctuary, is mentioned expressly in the Book of Kings (I Kings 8:31 f.) and seems to have been a standard judicial procedure among the Semites.[6]

Negative confessions (especially on the part of women in respect of sexual delinquency) are also part of the sun-dance ritual of the Crow Indians, the Cheyennes, the Sarsi, and the Dakota Oglala of America,[7] and obtain likewise among the Negroes of Calabar.[8]

In the Old Testament itself a similar literary imitation of the Negative Confession may be recognized in Isaiah 59:12 ff.:

> Our transgressions have abounded[9] before thee,
>   and our sins have borne witness against us.
> Verily, our transgressions are ever with us,
>   and as for our iniquities—they are our familiars:
> transgression and denial of the Lord,
> backsliding from our God,
> giving utterance to oppression[10] and revolt,
> conceiving and emitting from our hearts
>   words of falsehood.

That the author of Job is indeed imitating the "negative confessions" of the deceased is shown clearly by his telltale reference to the *scales of justice* (vv. 5–6):

> *Have I consorted with fraud,*
>   *or has my foot sped to deceit?*
> *Let God weigh me in the scales of justice,*
>   *and he will know how blameless I am!*

For, although the concept of the scales of justice indeed appears also in Indic,[11] Zoroastrian,[12] and Greek[13] lore, as well as in Japanese Buddhism,[14] the fact is that in ancient Egypt and similarly in Babylon the negative confession was thought to be accompanied in the court of the netherworld by a weighing of the heart or soul;[15] and a similar fancy is entertained to this day among the Negroes of Calabar.[16]

314 Blowing kisses to the sun and moon 31:27

> *If I have looked at the sun when it shone,*
>   *or at the moon passing in beauty,*
> *and my heart has been secretly enticed,*
>   *so that my mouth has kissed my hand,*
>   *this too would be an iniquity. . . .*

This passage is admirably illustrated by the fact that the word *adore* means primarily "to put the hand to the mouth" (Latin: *ad* + *os, oris*) in a gesture of blowing kisses. This form of worship was known already to the ancient Sumerians, for it is portrayed on a statuette of Awil-Nannar of Larsa.[1] In later times, Pliny attests it as a common usage among the Romans.[2]

The origin of the gesture, as of kissing in general, probably lay in the notion that a portion of one's own *élan vitale* could thereby be conveyed to another—even to a god as an act of submission.[3]

315 Man pinched out of clay   33:6

> Behold, I am toward God as you are;
> I too was pinched out of clay.

On this concept, see above, §**8**.

316 Cattle presage storms   36:33

> The peal of his thunder announces him,
> (*as do*) cattle a storm when it is but rising.

This is perhaps the only possible translation of the Hebrew original.[1] The Ancient Versions could make little of it, and modern commentators have resorted to various emendations.[2] Folklore, however, may perhaps clarify the meaning, or (if the text be indeed corrupt) at least what the ancient editors intended, for it is a widespread popular belief that sheep and cattle sense a rising storm and indicate its approach by their behavior. In England, for example, it is said among farmers that when sheep put their feet into the hedges for shelter, this is a sign of impending rain;[3] while the Kashmir goats that were formerly kept in Windsor Park were reputed to remain instinctively in the barn when a downpour was imminent.[4]

317 Gold from the north   37:22

> Out of the north cometh gold;
> round about God is a wondrous sheen.

It was thought by some older commentators that the reference here was to the provenience of gold from northerly countries—a fact attested by Herodotus (iii.116)! The parallelism shows clearly, however, that the "gold" is the luster of divinity. Accordingly, this is a further instance of the popular belief that God (or the gods) dwelt in the far reaches of the north, on the summit of a mountain (cf. Ps. 48:2, and see above, §**263**).

318 Stars divine   38:7

> When the morning stars sang together,
> and all the sons of God shouted for joy.

The parallelism demands that "stars" be regarded as equivalent to "sons of God," i.e., members of the heavenly court (see above, §**32**). Precisely the same parallelism occurs in a Canaanite mythological text from Ras Shamra-Ugarit;[1] while in Mesopotamian belief, each of the main deities had his or her distinctive star.[2]

The picture recurs in Lucian of Samosata's burlesque hymn celebrating the birth of Gout (*Podagra*):

> All the bright heaven into laughter broke,
> And o'er the radiant sky loud thunder pealed.[3]

319 Rain from bottles   38:37

RSV: *Who can number the clouds by wisdom?*
     or who can tilt the waterskins of heaven?

On an enamel of the time of the Assyrian king Tukulti-Ninurta II (c. 890 B.C.) raindrops are depicted stored in skins.[1] In the Indic Rig Veda, the rain-god Parjanya is invoked: "Thine opened waterskin draw with thee downward. . . . Lift up the mighty vessel, pour down water."[2] A Turkish popular expression for rainfall is "the bottles are emptied."[3] The Peruvians believed in a rain-goddess who sat in the clouds and sent rain by emptying a pitcher;[4] while in Teutonic mythology,[5] rain was said to be poured by the gods out of celestial bowls. The same idea occurs also in Edna St. Vincent Millay's poem, "Renascence":

> O God. . . .
> Upset each cloud's gigantic gourd
> And let the heavy rain, downpoured
> In one big torrent, set me free,
> Washing my grave away from me![a]

[a] *Collected Poems* (New York: Harper & Row). Copyright 1917, 1944, by Edna St. Vincent Millay. By permission of Norma Millay Ellis.

Proverbs

320 Introductory

Surprisingly enough, the Book of Proverbs contains but few overt allusions to popular lore, though D. S. Margoliouth (in *The Temple Bible* [1902]) has made the attractive suggestion that some of its maxims which are now obscure to us might have been clarified for their original readers by accompanying tales to which they served as introductory or concluding "morals." That such moral apophthegms were indeed attached to folktales in the Ancient Near East we now know from the case of the Hittite story of Master Good and Master Bad (retold in the present writer's *Oldest Stories in the World*), where the narrative is introduced by a version of the familiar proverb, *One rotten apple in the basket spoils all the others* (*Pomum compunctum corrupuit sibi junctum*).

In several cases, allusions to popular lore may be pretty confidently suspected, even though they cannot yet be precisely identified. Thus, there seem's little doubt that Wisdom's seven-pillared mansion (9:1 ff.) reflects the faery castle of some familiar folktale; while the leech and her two (LXX: three) greedy daughters (30:15) may be safely recognized as a prototype of the child-stealing hag and her nine (or seven) beldams of later folklore. Similarly, the comparison, in 23:34, of the intemperate drunkard to "one who lies on the top of a mast"—a comparison which already nonplused the ancient Greek (Septuagint) translators—looks uncommonly like an allusion to some traditional numskull. An attentive reader will doubtless find many more such possible reflections of popular lore. Here we must perforce confine ourselves to those cases which permit of more adequate illustration.

321 The house that leads down to Death   Prov. 2:18–19
7:27

The house of the wanton woman, who lurks in the street to seduce wayward young men, is said to sink down to Death, i.e., the netherworld.[1]

The late D. S. Margoliouth has made the attractive suggestion[2] that there is here an allusion to the widespread folktale of the castle or mansion which sinks miraculously into the earth.³ More probably, however, the writer is referring to a somewhat different tale, best exemplified by the legend of Tannhaüser and by the ballad of *Thomas the Rhymer*, which tells of a Fairy Mistress who lures her mortal lovers into a subterranean (or submarine) palace or realm, whence they cannot escape.⁴ This story is familiar also from the Celtic *imramas* of Malduin, Bran, Connla, Cuchulainn, Teigue, Guingamor, Lanval, and Desiré, as well as from the legend of Morgan le Fay in the Arthurian cycle. An Indian counterpart is the story of the princess Mrangakavati and Yasahketu in Somadeva's *Ocean of Story*.⁵

322 Ants store food in summer 6:6,8

> Go to the ant, thou sluggard;
> consider her ways, and be wise
> . . . .
> She prepares her food in summer,
> gathers her sustenance in harvest.
> The ants are a people not strong,   **30:25**
> yet they prepare their food in summer.

That ants store food in summer against the lack of it in winter is stated also by Ovid:

> Be sparing of the grain on which ye prey,
> Ye ants; thereby, when harvest-time is o'er,
> Ye will enjoy a larger wealth of loot;¹

while Vergil likewise alludes to the prudence with which the ant provides for its needy old age.²

The truth of this popular notion, it may be added, was denied, in the nineteenth century, by the entomologist Grimes,³ but it is said to have been amply confirmed by observations made in Southern Europe, India, and America.⁴

323 Pointing the finger 6:13

> A vicious person, a mischievous man,
> goes about with a twisted mouth,
> winking with his eyes, scraping with his feet,
> pointing with his finger.
> Perversion is in his heart;
> he fabricates evil;
> sows discord every moment.

The prophet Isaiah (58:9) likewise denounces pointing with the finger as a wicked act, associated with "uttering mischief." In many cultures, this gesture is one not merely of insult but also of black magic, the idea being that a potential victim is thus indicated to the demons.[1] In Mesopotamian magical texts "stretching out the finger" is listed among noxious acts,[2] and in modern Algeria the gesture strikes positive terror in the person at whom it is directed.[3]

Nor is it only persons who can be thus affected. Among the Ilocoans of Luzon, in the Philippines, it is forbidden to point at the seeds of cucumbers, on the grounds that this will prevent their growth;[4] and in several parts of Europe, fishermen grow angry when anyone points at them or at their catch, since this is deemed the equivalent of casting the evil eye.[5]

(That the Biblical writer indeed had a magical practice in mind is suggested also by the fact that the Hebrew words here rendered "mischievous man" are, literally, "man of *'awen*," and it has been pointed out that the analogous expression, "workers of *'awen*," when it occurs in the Psalms [e.g., Ps. 5:6], often means "magicians": see N. M. Nicolsky, Spuren magischen Formeln in den Psalmen [1927]; S. Mowinckel, Segen und Fluch in Israels Kult und Psalmendichtung [1924.])

324 Wisdom as God's master craftsman   8:30–31

> *Then was I* [Wisdom] *beside him like a master craftsman;*
> *I was his daily playmate,*
> *making merry before him every moment.*

In the conventional rendering, Wisdom is described as God's *nursling,* but it is now commonly agreed among Biblical scholars that the Hebrew word (*'amôn*) so translated really means, *expert, master craftsman,*[1] like the corresponding Babylonian *ummanu;*[2] and this interpretation is supported by a passage in the apocryphal Wisdom of Solomon, where it is styled "the *artificer* of all things."[3]

There is, however, more to the picture than this. The Babylonian *ummanu* was also a court official, and one of the functions of such officials was to cheer up their royal masters when the latter were depressed or overburdened by the cares of state.[4] Thus the vizier of Sennacherib (704–681 B.C.) is described as "the one who puts him in good humor,"[5] and elsewhere we read of a court secretary who served as the "cheerer" of his lord—a kind of court jester.[6] In the so-called Epic of Creation (*Enuma Elish*), Mummu plays this role before the god Apsu.[7] Accordingly, the words, *I was his daily gossip,*[8] *making merry in his presence at all times,* may refer to Wisdom's duty as God's *ummanu.*[9]

325 The seven pillars of Wisdom   9:1

> *Wisdom is said to have embellished her house with a portico of seven pillars.*[1]

It has been suggested that this picture reflects a traditional type of Ancient Near Eastern temple, for on the site of the very ancient "holy place" at

Bab ed-Dra', in Moab (third millennium B.C.), seven such menhirs have indeed been found lying on the ground.[2] Moreover, a later Greek inscription from Amathus, in Cyprus, records the dedication of a seven-pillared shrine to the local Aphrodite (i.e., Astarte?).[3]

An alternative view[4] is that the Biblical writer is portraying Dame Wisdom's mansion in terms of the "stately homes" of ancient Palestine, for a later rabbinic source states expressly that these were sometimes adorned with seven pillars,[5] as were indeed their counterparts in India.[6]

Perhaps, however, the whole picture is simply a folkloristic cliché—what the Greeks called a *topos*—for the number seven often figures in descriptions of ancient buildings and furnishings merely as a symbol of grandiose multiplicity.[7] Thus, according to Herodotus, the famous stepped temple (*ziggurat*) at Babylon had seven tiers.[8] In the Old Testament itself, Solomon's throne is said to be mounted upon seven steps,[9] and in medieval Jewish lore the seats of the righteous at the celestial banquet tendered them by God are each reached by seven stairs.[10] The Mandaeans of Iraq and Iran say that Jerusalem rests on seven pillars;[11] and the pseudepigraphic Book of Enoch goes so far as to assert that the Sovereign of the universe is enthroned upon seven jewelled hills.[12] Similarly, the *śakra* of the ancient Indic Ruler of the World rises to the height of seven palmtrees,[13] and the goddess Śri inhabits a palace adorned with seven kinds of jewels.[14]

The folkloristic seven likewise enters into architectural convention. The walls of ancient Persian palaces were colored in seven hues,[15] and the first Armenian church was raised on seven pillars.[16] At Rostock, in Germany, the Church of the Lady Mary has seven doors; there are seven bridges across the river; and the Rathaus has seven towers. A similar predilection for seven can be observed in the architectural layout of Jena, Lübeck, Altmark, and several other cities.[17]

326 The Fountain of Life 10:11

The mouth of the righteous is a fountain of life

13:14

The teaching of the wise is a fountain of life

Concerning the mythological Fountain of Life, see above, §**14**.

327 The lamp of the soul 20:27

RSV: *The spirit of man is the lamp of the Lord, searching all his inner parts.*[a]

[a] Several modern commentators, who have found difficulty in this expression, have suggested that the Hebrew word *nēr*, "lamp," is a scribal error for *n<ôṣ>er*, "preserves," i.e., *The Lord preserves the spirit of man, searching all his inner parts.* But the juxtaposition of the words "lamp" and "search" in Zephaniah 1:12 seemingly confirms the traditional text.

The author of this proverb is probably giving a special twist to the widespread notion that the soul, or *élan vitale,* is a light or candle. This notion is virtually ubiquitous in European folklore,[1] and there are many stories which revolve around the idea that life ends when a light goes out.[2] Related too is the motif, exemplified especially by the well-known stories of Meleager[3] and of Olger the Dane,[4] that the life of a hero is bound up with a blazing torch.

Because of its symbolic significance, says Plutarch, the Romans had an aversion to snuffing a lamp; they preferred to let it go out by itself.[5]

In Greek mysticism of the sixth century B.C. it was commonly held that the soul itself was made of the fire stolen from heaven by Prometheus.[6]

328 Coals of fire on the head   25:21–22

> *If thine enemy be hungry, give him bread to eat,*
> *and if he be thirsty, water to drink,*
> *for (so) wilt thou be heaping coals of fire on his head,*
> *and the Lord will reward thee.*

A late Egyptian text speaks of a custom of pouring coals of fire on the head of an offender as part of the ritual ceremony of penitence.[1] This was evidently a kind of ordeal, comparable with that which underlies our own popular expression, "to rake over the coals,"[2] and which may be paralleled also from the practice of throwing fire over the heads of novices in certain Australian initiatory rites.[3] Since Egyptian influence can be traced elsewhere in the Book of Proverbs,[4] it has been suggested that the proverb alludes to this usage, the general meaning then being that charity shown to an enemy in need will be just as effective in moving him to expressions of regret and contrition.

To this ingenious interpretation it may be objected, however, that the Hebrew word rendered "heaping" means properly "shoveling," and is usually used of shoveling coals *off* a fire rather than *on* to it.[5] This suggests quite a different picture. In the Oriental,[6] as in the Classical,[7] languages and in English, anger, jealousy, love, and similar passions are commonly portrayed as fires burning in the heart or soul. In Egyptian, an intemperate man is a "hot man," or, as we would say, "incensed";[8] and in Arabic, "coals of the heart" is a popular expression for strong emotion.[9] Sometimes, however, the fire is said to rage *in the head*—a concept which survives, indeed, in our own colloquial "hothead"—because the head was regarded as the seat of personality or of the *élan vitale.*[10] Thus, in one of the comedies of Plautus, when a pander complains to the slaves who have tricked him that his heart is incensed, they at once suggest that he should be given a drink lest "his head too catch fire!"[11] Similarly, a man in love declares that if the tears in his eyes did not prevent it, his head would already be blazing.[12] In the Iliad and Odyssey, flames of valor are seen over the heads of heroes,[13] and in Vergil's *Aeneid,* when Turnus rages for combat, it is said that sparks leaped from his face.[14]

Nor is the idea confined to Classical authors. Of the Irish Cuchulain it is said that when he was enraged "you might have thought that a spark burned on his every hair."[15]

Thus, all that our proverb might really mean is that an act of charity toward an enemy in need will not only douse the flames of his passion or enmity but also earn reward from God.[16]

329 Mythological riddles   30:4

> Who went up to heaven and came down?
> Who gathered the wind in his fists?
> Who tied up the waters in a garment?
> Who upheld all the ends of the earth?
> What is his name, and what is his son's name?
> Surely you know!

It is commonly supposed that these are merely rhetorical questions and that the answer to each of them is, God. In that case, however, the words, *What is his name, and what is his son's name?* sound strangely odd from Hebrew lips. It may therefore be suggested that, however the Scriptural compiler may later have understood them, they were originally riddles employed, on a well-known pedagogical principle, to teach that special knowledge of which the writer professes himself ignorant (vv. 2–3). Each would then refer to a standard myth.

(a) *Who went up to heaven and came down?* would refer to Etana, the central figure of a famous Mesopotamian story which related how he was persuaded to attempt ascent to heaven on the back of an eagle, but eventually slipped off and plunged into the sea[1]—an Ancient Near Eastern variant of the Classical tale of Icarus and his waxen wings and, indeed, of the widespread motif of "Borrowed Plumes."[2]

(b) The second question should probably be read, after the Greek (Septuagint) Version and with a change of but a single letter in the consonantal Hebrew text,[3] *Who gathered the wind in his bosom* (or rather, *in the sinus of his robe*)?[4] The allusion will then be to a mythological figure like the Classical Aeolus, who kept the winds tied in a bag.[5] This in turn is simply a translation into myth of a practice attributed to witches and warlocks in several parts of the world.[6] In the Isle of Man, for instance, witches are said to tie up the winds with three knots of thread; when these are loosened, fresh breezes ensue.[7] In Lapland and Finland they sell bags of wind to sailors.[8] Similarly, a priest of the Bagaba in Togoland was credited with the power of shutting up the wind in a pot.[9] A Norwegian tale relates that a witch once sunk a ship by opening a bag in which she had imprisoned the wind;[10] and in Mecklenburg, whenever a storm blew up, local sailors were wont to exclaim, *Nu hebben de Jungens den Sack wedder open makt* (The youngsters have gone and opened the sack again)![11]

(c) *Who tied up the waters in a garment?* This might refer to a folktale which accounted for a drought on the supposition that someone had maliciously kept the rainwaters tied up. That rain was indeed believed to be bound in skins is stated expressly in Job 38:37 (see above, §**319**), and God himself is said to tie it up in the cloudbanks (*ib.*, 26:8). Australian folklore likewise knows of waters tied in a bag.[12] The story would be a variant of the well-known motif of Impounded Waters (see above, §**258**). I must confess, however, that I have thus far been unable to identify a particular story of this nature.

(d) *Who upheld all the ends of the earth?* The word "upheld" (Heb.: *heqim*) is nowhere else applied to the "ends of the earth," and the seeming strangeness of the expression has led several modern scholars to suspect that the traditional text is corrupt and should be emended (after the Greek Version) to read, *Who has laid hold of all the ends of the earth?* It was, however, common Hebrew belief that the earth rested on pillars (see above, §**309**), so that the allusion may be to some mythological figure like Atlas, who was sometimes believed to support not only the heavens but also the earth.[13] Such a figure appears indeed in Ancient Near Eastern mythology in the Hittite *Myth of Ullikummi*, where the giant Upelluri carries the world on his shoulder.[14] Similarly, too, the Chibchas (Muyscas) of Colombia say that the earth is upheld by a giant named Chibchachum,[15] and the Tlingits and Athapascans of North America by Hayicanako, "the Old Lady beneath us."[16]

330 'Aluqah the vampire 30:15

RSV: *The leech has two daughters; "Give, give," they cry.*[1]

This conventional rendering misses an interesting piece of folklore. The Hebrew word rendered "leech" is 'Aluqah, and in Arabic the corresponding word, 'Alauq, is the name of a vampyric demon.[2] Accordingly, this may be a reference to a Lilith-like creature with her attendant gang. Note that in Jewish charms Lilith is usually accompanied by a band of nine beldams,[3] just as in Shakespeare's *King Lear,*

> Saint Withold footed thrice the [w]old,
> He met the night-mare and her nine-fold.[4]

The Song of Songs

331 Introductory

The Song of Songs has been interpreted traditionally as an allegory of the union between God and Israel, Christ and the Church, or even of the intellect and the soul.[1] Such homiletic exegesis, however, is now, by and large, a thing of the past. Among modern scholars three principal views prevail.

(1) The song is a pastoral drama. A girl from the village of Shunem (i.e., the Shulamite; cf. 7:1) has been abducted by the king to his harem in Jerusalem (1:4). Her lover, a peasant lad, visits her, "peers through the lattice" (2:9), and sings his love for her. She reciprocates, and they are eventually reunited.[2]

This view, however, rests on a flimsy foundation. For one thing, such secular drama does not appear elsewhere in the whole range of ancient Semitic literature, and was therefore probably unknown to the Hebrews. For another, to interpret the Song in this manner entails making some of the scenes consist only of a single verse or even less! And in the third place, the crucial verse *The king hath brought me into his chambers; we will exult and rejoice in thee* (1:4) can equally well be rendered, *Were even the king to have brought me to his chambers, 'tis in thee we would exult and rejoice.*

(2) It has been suggested that the Song represents, *au fond,* a repertoire of love-poems originally chanted in the pagan worship of such divine lovers as Ishtar and Tammuz or Astarte and Adonis.[3] The fact is, however, that the parallels which have been adduced between the wording of the Song and the ritual chants of such cults are scarcely convincing,[4] and it must be borne in mind in any case that the language used in such cultic songs would be bound to imitate that current among ordinary human lovers.

(3) Comparative Folklore has furnished a third interpretation. This derives from observations made nearly a century ago by the German consul, Johann Gottfried Wetzstein, among the Syrian peasantry. Wetzstein noticed that Syrian wedding festivities lasted for seven days, and that during this period bride and groom were enthroned as king and queen. Each danced before the other, while

the assembled company joined them in outspoken eulogies of their bodily charms. The Song of Songs, it is held, is a collection of such chants, known as *waṣfs*.[5] The long descriptions of bodily charms (e.g., 4:1–7; 5:10–16; 6:4–7; 7:2–10) would then fall into place, while the references to the king and to Solomon would be complimentary allusions to the bridegroom. Similarly, "Shulamite," the name given to the bride (7:1), would be a dialectical pronunciation of Shunemite, and the point of the compliment would be to liken her to Abishag, the Shunemite beauty who comforted David in his old age (cf. I Kings 1:1–4; see above, §147). Again, the obscure lines, *What see ye in the Shulamite? As it were, the dance of Mahanaim* (6:13) would be an allusion to the customary sword dance performed by the bride, seeing that Mahanaim could mean "the two camps."

It must be admitted that this theory is, at first blush, not unattractive. However, a closer comparison of the Syrian usages with the Hebrew text of the Song does not fully bear it out. We need cite but two glaring discrepancies. The sword dance is performed *barefoot*, whereas the Song declares expressly, *How fair are thy feet in sandals* (7:1). The Syrian bridegroom is not crowned, whereas the Song speaks specifically of *the crown with which his mother crowned him on the day of his espousals* (3:11).[6]

Nor is it necessary to assume that the descriptions of bodily beauties necessarily indicate an origin of the Song in some earlier analogy of the Syrian *waṣfs*. Such descriptions are the stock-in-trade of love lyrics all over the world and in all ages. Many of the phrases and images used in the Song find parallels, for instance, in ancient Egyptian love songs. The following are representative examples drawn from S. Schott's *Altägyptische Liebeslieder* (1950):

1:2:	Thy caresses are better than wine	Schott, 66.5
2:6:	Oh that his right hand would embrace me!	ib., 52.5
2:9:17:	the lover is likened to a gazelle	ib., 44.3
4:9:	Thou hast ravished my heart with one glance of thine eyes	ib., 44[b]
4:11:	Thy lips drop honey	ib., 57.2
4:12–16:	A garden locked is my sister, my bride	
	Let my lover come to his garden,	ib., 56.2
	and eat his choice fruits!	Pap. Harris, 500
7:5:	The king is held captive in thy tresses	Schott, 63.3
8:6:	Set me as a seal upon thy heart	ib., 67.6

Other arresting parallels can be culled from both ancient and modern Arabic poems.[7] The Arabs too, for example, take the gazelle as the paragon of grace and beauty,[8] liken the tresses of the beloved to waving palms (Song 5:11),[9] and compare the legs of the beloved to marble pillars (5:15).[10]

Equally striking, though less familiar, are the parallels afforded by the love songs of modern primitive peoples.[11] Thus, the comparison of the beloved to "a mare of Pharaoh's chariots" (1:9) is echoed both in a song of the Kirghiz of Siberia, where she is likened to "the steed of nobles,"[12] and in a chant of the Fulbé of the Sudan, where she is addressed as "the steed of the king of all kings."[13] Somewhat analogously too, a popular chant of the Hausa speaks of her as "a camel with slender neck."[14] Again, in a popular ditty from Malaysia, the maiden's locks are likened to palms;[15] and the Jaggas of East Africa speak of the lips of cherished friends as having "the savor of honey, the sweet savor of honey from the Sahara."[16]

The aforementioned Malayan chant may serve as a representative example of these primitive parallels:

> Mabrûka is a camel with slender neck.
> Her teeth are like gold,
> her hands are of gold,
> her ring is of gold.
> Her arm is pliant like a rush;
> her nose is like a rose,
> her face like a mirror.
> Her shoulders are of gold,
> her shawl is of gold,
> her locks are like gold.
> Her apron is broidered with silver,
> her blouse is broidered all over with silver,
> her drawers are of silk.
> Her locks are tightly bound;
> her breasts are like silver cups;
> look on those breasts, and it dazzles your eyes!
> look too on her body, how it sways
> like a reed!

Is this derived from a Syrian *waṣf?*[17]

It would be safer, then, to say only that certain portions of the Song may have been taken from wedding chants, but to regard the book as a whole as simply a collection of Palestinian love songs. These need not have been written in any one single place nor at any one single time. Moreover, the fact that certain verses recur does not prove unity of authorship, for the incorporation of popular lines from one song to another is a commonplace of all folk poetry.[18]

Naturally, in the course of transmission through the ages the original wording would often have been "modernized"—as happens in all popular songs—so that we cannot cite the relatively late language of the present Hebrew text as evidence for the original date of composition.[19]

332   The banner of Love

> *He brought me to the banqueting house*
> *and his banner over me was love.*

It has been suggested that these words contain an allusion to the custom of marking taverns with distinctive banners. Inns were certainly so marked by the pre-Islamic Arabs,[1] but there appears to be no evidence of the usage in the Ancient Near East. If the interpretation is correct, the banner would be comparable to the old English ale-stake, a pole set up before an alehouse by way of sign, often surmounted by a bush or garland (cf. the proverbial saying, "Good wine needs no bush"). In the Prologue to *The Canterbury Tales*, Chaucer refers to this custom in the words:

> A garland hath he set upon his head
> As great as it were for an ale-stake. . . .[2]

An alternative suggestion is that this is a military metaphor: when the girl is "taken places" by her escort, she sallies forth under the banner of his love, like an army under that of its commander. The difficulty with this interpretation is, however, that the Hebrew word (*degel*) traditionally rendered "banner," probably means simply "regiment," or division of the army.[3]

This brings us to the third view, which is that the word in question is rather to be connected with an Akkadian word meaning "look at." The sense will then be that the escort casts loving looks on his inamorata.[4]

333   Apples and love   2:5

> *Comfort* (RSV: *refresh*) *me with apples,*
> *for I am sick with love.*

In the folklore of many peoples the apple has erotic associations. In Classical antiquity, to throw apples at a person was an invitation to dalliance.[1] Thus, in the *Clouds* of Aristophanes, young men are warned not to frequent the houses of dancing girls, where "while they are gaping at some cute strumpet, she might get them involved by tossing an apple at them." Similarly, in Vergil's *Third Eclogue,* the goatherd Damoetas boasts that Galatea, "that wanton minx," keeps egging him on by throwing apples at him;[3] and in one of Lucian's *Conversations of Harlots,* a jealous courtesan complains that her fickle lover keeps pelting her rival with apples.[4] In the story of Acontius and Cydippe, the former sends a love note to the latter by inscribing it on an apple which he arranges to have cast at her feet.[5] A similar erotic quality is attached to the apple even at the present day in the popular lore of Kentucky, in the United States;[6] and it has been suggested that it was this association that inspired the medieval identification of the forbidden fruit of Paradise with an apple.

Among the Mesopotamians, apples and pomegranates were thought to give sexual potency;[7] and a Jewish superstition asserts that the sap of an apple tree can induce conception in a barren woman.[8]

Our passage is commonly interpreted in the light of these ideas. But it is difficult to see why a girl who is already lovesick should demand an aphrodisiac. Besides, the text says distinctly that she asks for apples in order to *restore*, not *lose*, her equilibrium; for the Hebrew word rendered *comfort* (or *refresh*) means properly *stabilize, support*. Hence it would seem more apposite to regard the apples as a kind of restorative "smelling salt," and this is supported by the fact that the Hebrew word so rendered (viz., *tappuᵃḥ*) actually derives from a verbal root (*n-p-ḥ*) meaning "blow," i.e., diffuses aroma. Moreover, we may aptly compare what the ancient botanist Simeo Sethus says of apples: "They are a useful aid against failure of spirit and irregular heartbeat."[9]

(This interpretation also surmounts the difficulty that Heb. *tappûsh* may in fact be a more generic term than our *apple,* including quince and apricot, since it is still an open question whether apples grew in the Holy Land in ancient times. [Note, incidentally, that in English itself, *apple* originally possessed a wider meaning.])

Further support for this interpretation comes from the parallel phrase, *Sustain me with raisins,* for this would reflect a popular belief that raisins and other dried fruits are effective against fatigue and nervous debility. In 1881, Sir William Gull, M.D. testified before the Committee of the House of Lords on Intemperance that he had always found raisins useful to this end![10]

334 Solomon's groomsmen 3:7–8

> *Behold, here is Solomon's litter;*
> *threescore warriors stand around it,*
> *of the warriors of Israel,*
> *all of them girt with swords,*
> *trained for battle;*
> *each with his sword at his thigh,*
> *against terror by night.*

This little song was probably designed to accompany the procession of a bridegroom to his wedding, much of the Song of Songs being a repertoire for such occasions. In Oriental weddings, as elsewhere, the bridal couple is likened to a king and queen;[1] in Malaya, for example, they are called "sovereigns for a day" (*raja sari*).[2] Hence the bridegroom is here fancifully identified with King Solomon—the Harun al Rashid of ancient Israelitic folklore.

The bridegroom, as also the bride's procession, is customarily escorted by an armed bodyguard, designed originally to ward off those hovering demons who, in the fancy of ancient and primitive peoples, personify the hazards of marriage.³ Often the bride herself carries a sword;⁴ and in medieval Jewish usage, she sometimes wore a helmet.⁵ In the Usambara region of West Africa, an armed bridesmaid procedes her with drawn sword.⁶

Analogously, because demons also hover at death, Baltic funeral corteges used anciently to be escorted by an armed bodyguard.⁷

335 The "Terror by Night"   3:8

In the Hebrew, this is an extended use of a term which, in a stricter sense, denoted the nightmare; cf. Ps. 91:5 (see above, §275). It finds an exact parallel in the description of Zaqar, god of dreams, as "the terror of the nights" (*puluḫtu ša lilâti*) in an ancient Mesopotamian magical incantation.¹

Two ideas are here combined. On the one hand, the "terror by night" denotes simply the dangers which may beset the wedding procession, since weddings are usually celebrated in the East at nightfall. On the other, however, it alludes slyly to untoward happenings during the bridal night,² and to nightmare in general.³

336 The separable soul   5:6

My soul failed when he spoke

The Hebrew word rendered *failed* means literally *went out*. The idiom thus reflects the widespread notion that the "soul," or inner self, leaves the body in sleep, trance, ecstasy, or unusual excitement.¹

337 The dance of Mahanaim   6:13 [Heb. 7:1]

What see ye in the Shulamite?
As it were, the dance of Mahanaim.

W. F. Albright has suggested that "Shulamite" is here the Hebrew equivalent of the Mesopotamian Shulmanitu, a title of the goddess Ishtar at Ashur.¹ Now, since Ishtar was also a goddess of battle, and since the word Mahanaim could conceivably mean "camps," the meaning would be that the gyrations of the girl in her dance resemble those of the goddess in her war dance.

An alternative interpretation might start from the legend that Mahanaim was the place where Jacob saw "the camp of otherworldly beings" (Gen. 32:1–2). As we have seen (above, §71), this was simply a Hebrew variant of the Wild Hunt, or Furious Host. Now, alike in Greek and European folklore, the latter is often associated with such goddesses as Artemis or Berchta and her troupe of ghostly dancers.² Thus the meaning would be that the wild gyrations of the girl in her dance are such as to suggest to the onlookers that they are witnessing the "furious rout." (It might then be significant that the word rendered "see" often denotes *prophetic or imaginative vision*.)

338 The Reshephs of love 8:6

> *The flashes* (KJV: *coals*) *thereof are flashes of fire,
> a most vehement flame.*

It seems a pity to eliminate this familar and graphic description of love. The stark fact is, however, that the Hebrew word does not mean flash (or coal). It is the name *Resheph,* which designates the Canaanite god of plague and pestilence (see above, §242) and which came to be used in the plural to denote demons in general.[1]

The point of the picture is brought out more clearly when it is borne in mind that in Arab folklore, *demons are often believed to be made of fire.*[2]

Lamentations

339 Dirges over cities; the weeping "daughter of Zion"

A common feature of Oriental funerals was (and is) the employment of professional wailing women.[1] Not only is this usage well attested among the Egyptians,[2] but likewise in a description of Hittite funeral rites the leading role is said to be played by women.[3] In the Canaanite *Poem of Aqhat* "weeping women" (*bkyt*) and "female mourners" (*mšspdt*) repair to the palace and perform a keening for the slain prince;[4] and the custom is mentioned also in several passages of the Old Testament itself.[5] So too, in Homer's account of the burial of Hector, the laments are uttered by women, led by the hero's mother, wife, and daughter;[6] and such wailing women appear later in the Roman *praeficae*, who lead dirges.[7] E. W. Lane describes graphically the "crying and shrieking" of women at Moslem funerals, despite the Prophet's express prohibition of such excesses.[8] In Armenia, professional wailing women are known popularly as "dirge-mothers."[9]

Out of this custom there developed a literary convention of composing lamentations over fallen cities in the form of dirges sung by some imaginary female citizen. A song of this type, written partly in the so-called Eme-sal dialect, usually reserved for speeches by females, is preserved on Sumerian cuneiform tablets of the early second millennium B.C., discovered at Nippur. It bewails the destruction of the city of Ur.[10] Later specimens of the same genre, written in the Akkadian language, are also known, one of them being put into the mouth of "the daughter of Sin (the moon-god.)"[11] The Biblical Book of Lamentations, which may indeed have been composed in the exile in Babylon, belongs to the same class of composition, and employs the analogous figure of the weeping "daughter of Zion" (cf. 1:16, 21; 2:19, etc.).

Our Biblical poems follow the older Mesopotamian models, working in more or less standard clichés of this genre. The following parallels will best illustrate this point.

A. Sumerian Lamentation over the Destruction of the city of Ur by the Elamites and Subarians: trans. S. N. Kramer, in *ANET* 455–63.

B. Rm. iv. 97 (3334): trans. T. G. Pinches, in *PSBA* 23 (1901), 197 ff.

C. "The Lament of the Daughter of Sin": T. G. Pinches, in *PSBA* 17 (1895), 64–74.

1.

1. (The city) is become like a widow

   B 5: The woman of Hursag-kalama moans for the husband of her youth

2. Bitterly weeps she at night

   A 100: Because of its [affliction], in my sleeping-place ... verily there is no peace for me

3. She finds no resting place

   B 2, 3: The maiden of Arka weeps ... the daughter of Uruk weeps

6. From the daughter of Zion has departed all her beauty

   B 2: The maiden of Arka weeps, whose youthful grace is departed

9. Her uncleanness is in her skirts

   B 7: The maiden of Masha weeps, whose garment is sullied

10. The foeman has put forth his hand against all her precious things

    A 279: My treasure verily has been dissipated

    They have entered her holy place

    C i.6: He has entered my shrine

13. From on high has God sent fire

    A 180: Enlil brings Gibil, the fire-god, to his aid in destroying Ur

15. He has summoned a battle-line against me to crush my young men

    B 14–15: The maiden of Durilu weeps for all of Qutu, for the son of her city crushed, for her family brought to ruin

16. I weep

    B 1, 18: I lament, I wail

17. Zion stretches out her hands

    A 371: The house stretches out the hands to thee

19. My priests and my elders are dying in the city

    B 8: The maiden of Agade weeps, whose elders are killed

2.

1. The Lord in his anger beclouds the daughter of Zion

   A 190: The day was deprived of the rising of the bright sun, the goodly light

   He has taken no thought of his footstool

   B 22: His platformed throne is overturned

2. The Lord has destroyed ... all the pastures of Jacob

   A 1: He has abandoned his stable, his sheepfold (has been delivered) to the wind

6. He has broken down his booth like that of a garden

   A 128: My house ... like a garden hut, verily on its side has caved in

17. The Lord has done what he purposed, has consummated his word which he ordained of old

    A 168–69: Anu changes not his command; Enlil alters not the command which he had issued

19. Pour out thy heart like water

    A 331: O queen, make thy heart like water!

4.

1. The holy stones (gems?) lie scattered at the top of every street

   A 278: My (precious) metal, stone and lapis lazuli have been scattered about

5. those who feasted on dainties perish in the streets

   A 271 f.: In its boulevards, where the feasts were celebrated, scattered they lay, etc.

8. Blacker than soot is their visage; they are not recognized in the streets

   A 358: Dirt has been decreed for them; verily, their appearance has changed

11. He has kindled a fire in Zion and it has consumed her foundations

    A 180: Enlil calls Gibil, the fire-god, to his aid

5. 15. *Our dance is turned to a dirge* A 359–60: *Thy song has been turned into weeping; thy . . . -music has been turned into lamentation*

18. *. . . Mount Zion which lies desolate; foxes walk upon it.* A 269: *In the rivers of my city dust has gathered; into fox-dens verily have they been made*

340 The limping meter

The first three chapters of the Book of Lamentations are composed in the "limping meter" characteristic of Hebrew dirges. Whereas normal Hebrew verse—there are, of course, variations—consists of two stichs each containing three accentual beats, in the dirge the final beat of the second stich is cut off, e.g.,

> *Outdoórs they líe on the groúnd,
> yoúng men and óld;
> My yóuths and máidens áll
> fáll by the swórd.*
>
> (2:21)

This produces a distinctly limping (scazonic) effect, and it may therefore be suggested that the dirges were originally designed to accompany a limping dance of mourning. An excellent description of such a dance is given by Lane in his famous *Manners and Customs of the Modern Egyptians:*

> It is customary among the peasants of Egypt for the female relatives and friends of a person deceased to meet together at his house on the first three days after the funeral, and there to perform a lamentation and a strange kind of dance. They daub their faces and bosoms and part of their dress with mud and tie a rope girdle . . . round the waist. Each flourishes in her hand a palm-stick or a *nebroot* (a long staff) or a drawn sword [i.e., to forefend demons], and dances with a slow movement and in an irregular manner, generally pacing about and raising and depressing the body.[1]

The custom was current also, we are informed, among the Syrian peasantry, who gave it the name of *ma'îd*, or "limping."[2] (This last, as we have seen above, §**129**, is the real explanation of Agag's "walking delicately" in the famous incident related in I Samuel 15:32.)

Furthermore, it is significant that both in Syriac and Arabic, a word which normally means "skipping" (*r-q-d, r-q-z*) is a technical term for "funeral exercises"; while an Akkadian lexical text lists a cognate word (*ru-qu-ud-du*) among names of professional mourners.[3]

See further, above, §**158**.

341 Sitting apart 1:1

> RSV: *How lonely sits the city that was full of people!*

This rendering misses a subtle point: the reference is not to the contrast between a crowded and a deserted city, for the Hebrew word translated *lonely* really means *apart,* and the allusion is to the ritual seclusion of menstruous women and diseased persons.[1] Exactly the same expression occurs in Leviticus 13:46 in reference to the segregation of lepers; while in verse 8 of this very lamentation Jerusalem is described explicitly as having "become like a menstruous woman" (RSV, wrongly: *therefore she became filthy*).

▲ 342 The silent widow 1:1

[The vanquished city of Jerusalem is likened not only to a leper segregated from the community[1] but also to a *widow*. Comparative Folklore throws interesting light on this comparison.]

Among many, if not all, peoples of the world the occurrence of a death in a family has entailed on the survivors the obligation of observing certain rules, the general effect of which is to limit in various directions the liberty enjoyed in ordinary life; and the nearer the relationship of the survivor to the deceased, the more stringent and burdensome these restrictions become. Though the reasons for imposing them are often unknown to the people who submit to them, a large body of evidence points to the conclusion that many, perhaps most, of them originated in a fear of the ghost and a desire to escape his unwelcome attentions by eluding his observation, repelling his advances, or otherwise inducing or compelling him to acquiesce in his fate, so far at least as to abstain from molesting his kinsfolk and friends.[1a]

The ancient Hebrews observed many restrictions on the occurrence of a death, which are either expressly enjoined or incidentally referred to in the Old Testament.[2] To the list of rules for the conduct of mourners, which can thus be collected from Scripture, may perhaps be added one which, though it is neither inculcated nor alluded to by the sacred writers, is suggested by etymology and confirmed by the analogous usages of other peoples.

The Hebrew word for a widow (*'almanah*) is perhaps etymologically connected with an adjective meaning "dumb" (*'illem*). If this etymology is correct, it would seem that the Hebrew name for a widow is "a silent woman." Why should a widow be called a silent woman? I conjecture, with all due diffidence, that the epithet may be explained by a widespread custom which imposes the duty of absolute silence on a widow for some time after the death of her husband.

Thus among the Kutus, a tribe on the Congo, widows observe mourning for three lunar months. They shave their heads, strip themselves almost naked, daub their bodies all over with white clay, and pass the whole of the three months in the house without speaking.[3] Among the Sihanaka in Madagascar the observances are similar, but the period of silence is still longer, lasting for at least eight months, and sometimes for a year. During the whole of that time the widow is stripped of all her ornaments and covered up with a coarse mat, and she is given only a broken spoon and a broken dish to eat out of. She may not wash her face or her hands, but only the tips of her fingers. In this state she remains all day long in the house and may not speak to any one who enters it.[4] Among the Nandi, of British East Africa, as long as a widow is in mourning she is considered unclean and may not speak above a whisper, though she is not absolutely forbidden to speak at all.[5] In describing the Nishinam tribe of Californian Indians, a writer who knew these Indians well, as they were in the third quarter of the nineteenth century, mentions that "around Auburn, a devoted widow never speaks, on any occasion or upon any pretext, for several months, sometimes a year or more, after the death of her husband. Of this singular fact I had ocular demonstration. Elsewhere, as on the American River, she speaks only in a whisper for several months. As you go down towards the Cosumnes this custom disappears."[6] Among the Kwakiutl Indians of British Columbia, for four days after the death of her husband a widow must sit motionless, with her knees drawn up to her chin. For sixteen days after that she is bound to remain on the same spot, but she enjoys the privilege of stretching her legs, though not of moving her hands. During all that time nobody may speak to her. It is thought that if any one dared to break the rule of silence and speak to the widow, he would be punished by the death of one of his relatives. A widower has to observe precisely the same restrictions on the death of his wife.[7] Similarly among the Bella Coola Indians of the same region a widow must fast for four days, and during that time she may not speak a word; otherwise they think that her husband's ghost would come and lay a hand on her mouth, and she would die. The same rule of silence has to be observed by a widower on the death of his wife, and for a similar reason.[8]

But by no people is this curious custom of silence more strictly observed than by some of the savage tribes of Central and Northern Australia. Thus, among the Waduma and Mudburra, two tribes on the Victoria River in the Northern Territory, not only a man's widows but also the wives of his brothers are under a ban of silence until the final disposal of his bones three or four weeks after death. After that ceremony, animals of the deceased's totem are placed on a fire. While they are cooking, the women who have been under a ban of silence go up to the fire and, after calling out *"Yakai! Yakai!"* put their heads in the smoke. An old man then hits them lightly on the head and afterwards holds out his hand for them to bite a finger. This ceremony removes the ban of silence under which the women had hitherto laboured.[9]

Again, in the Arunta tribe of Central Australia a man's widows smear their hair, faces, and breasts with white pipeclay and remain silent for a certain time, until a ceremony has been performed which restores to them the use of their tongues. The ceremony is as follows. When a widow wishes the ban of silence to be removed, she gathers a large wooden vessel full of some edible seed or small tuber, and smears herself with white pipeclay at the women's camp, where she has been living ever since her husband's death. Carrying the vessel, and accompanied by the women whom she has collected for the purpose, she walks to the centre of the general camp, midway between the two sections occupied by the two halves of the tribe. There they all sit down and cry loudly, whereupon the men, who stand to them either in the actual or in the classificatory relationship of sons and younger brothers of the dead man, come up and join the party. Next, these men take the vessel of seeds or tubers from the hands of the widow, and as many as possible laying hold of it, they shout loudly, *"Wah! wah! wah!"* All the women, except the widow, stop crying and join in the shout. After a short time the men hold the vessel of seeds or tubers close to, but not touching, the widow's face, and make passes to right and left of her cheeks, while all again shout *"Wah! wah! wah!"* The widow now stops her crying and utters the same shout, only in subdued tones. After a few minutes the vessel of seeds or tubers is passed to the rear of the men, who now, squatting on the ground and holding their shields in both hands, strike them heavily on the ground in front of the women, who are standing. When that has been done the men disperse to their camps and eat the food brought in the vessel by the widow, who is now free to speak to them, though she still continues to smear herself with pipeclay.[10]

The significance of this curious rite, by which an Arunta widow recovers her freedom of speech, is explained as follows by Messrs. Spencer and Gillen: "The meaning of this ceremony, as symbolised by the gathering of the tubers or grass seed, is that the widow is about to resume the ordinary occupations of a woman's life, which have been to a large extent suspended while she remained in camp in what we may call deep mourning. It is in fact closely akin in feeling to the transition from deep to narrow black-edged paper amongst certain more highly civilised peoples. The offering to the sons and younger brothers is intended both to show them that she has properly carried out the first period of mourning, and to gain their goodwill, as they, especially the younger brothers, are supposed to be for some time displeased with a woman when her husband is dead and she is alive. In fact a younger brother meeting the wife of a dead elder brother, out in the bush performing the ordinary duties of a woman, such as hunting for 'yams,' within a short time of her husband's death, would be quite justified in spearing her. The only reason that the natives give for this hostile feeling is that it grieves them too much when they see the widow, because it reminds them of the dead man. This, however, can scarcely be the whole reason, as the same rule does not apply to the elder brothers, and very probably the real explanation of the feeling is associated, in some way, with the custom according to which the widow will, when the final stage of mourning is over, become the wife of one of these younger brothers whom at first she has carefully to avoid."[11]

Again, among the Unmatjera and Kaitish, two other tribes of Central Australia, a widow observes the ban of silence until, usually many months after her husband's death, she is released from it by her husband's younger brother. When this takes place she makes an offering to him of a very considerable quantity of food, and with a fragment of it he touches her mouth, thus indicating to her that she is once more free to talk and to take part in the ordinary duties of a woman.[12]

Among the Warramunga, another tribe of Central Australia, the command of silence imposed on women after a death is much more comprehensive and extraordinary. With them it is not only the dead man's widow who must be silent during the whole time of mourning, which may last for one or even two years; his mother, his sisters, his daughters, his mother-in-law or mothers-in-law, must all equally be dumb and for the same protracted period. More than that, not only his real wife, real mother, real sisters, and real mothers-in-law are subjected to this rule of silence, but a great many more women whom the natives, on the classificatory principle, reckon in these relationships, though we should not do so, are similarly bound over to hold their tongues, it may be for a year, or it may be for two years. As a consequence it is no uncommon thing in a Warramunga camp to find the majority of women prohibited from speaking. Even when the period of mourning is over, some women prefer to remain silent and to use only the gesture language, in the practice of which they become remarkably proficient. Not seldom, when a party of women are in camp, there will be almost perfect silence, and yet a brisk conversation is all the while being conducted among them on their fingers, or rather with their hands and arms, for many of the signs are made by putting the hands or elbows in varying positions. At Tennant's Creek some years ago there was an old woman who had not opened her mouth, except to eat or drink, for more than twenty-five years, and who has probably since then gone down to her grave without uttering another syllable. When, however, after a longer or a shorter interval of absolute silence, a Warramunga widow desires to recover her liberty to speak, she applies to the men who stand to her in the classificatory or tribal relationship of sons, to whom, as is customary in such cases, she has to make a present of food. The ceremony itself is a very simple one; the woman brings the food, usually a large cake of grass seed, and in turn bites the finger of each of the men who are releasing her from the ban of silence. After that she is free to talk as much as she likes.[13]

Again, in the Dieri tribe of Central Australia a widow was not allowed to speak until the whole of the white clay, which she had smeared on her body in token of mourning, had crumbled and fallen away of itself. During this intermediate period, which might last for months, she might communicate with others only by means of the gesture language.[14]

But why should a widow be bound over to silence for a longer or a shorter time after the death of her spouse? The motive for observing the custom is probably a dread of attracting the dangerous attentions of her late husband's ghost. This fear is indeed plainly alleged as the reason by the Bella Coola Indians, and it is assigned by the Unmatjera and Kaitish as the motive for covering the widow's body with ashes. The whole intention of these customs is apparently either to elude or to disgust and repel the ghost. The widow eludes him by remaining silent; she disgusts and repels him by discarding her finery, shaving or burning her hair, and daubing herself with clay or ashes. This interpretation is confirmed by certain particularities of the Australian usages.

In the first place, among the Waduma and Mudburra the custom of silence is observed by the widow only so long as the flesh adheres to her late husband's bones; as soon as it has quite decayed and the bones are bare, she is made free of the use of her tongue once more. But it appears to be a common notion that the ghost lingers about his mouldering remains while any of the flesh is left, and that only after the flesh has wholly vanished does he take his departure for the more or less distant spirit-land.[15] Where such a belief prevails it is perfectly natural that the widow should hold her tongue so long as the decomposition of her husband's body is still incomplete, for so long may his spirit be supposed to haunt the neighbourhood and to be liable at any moment to be attracted by the sound of her familiar voice.

In the second place, the relation in which among the Arunta, the Unmatjera, and the Kaitish the widow stands to her late husband's younger brother favours the supposition that the motive of the restrictions laid on her is the fear of the ghost. In these tribes the younger brother of her late husband appears to exercise a special superintendence over the widow during the period of mourning; he sees to it that she strictly observes the rules enjoined by custom at such times, and he has the right severely to punish or even to kill her for breaches of them. Further, among the Unmatjera and Kaitish it is the younger brother of the deceased who finally releases the widow from the ban of silence, and thereby restores her to the freedom of ordinary life. Now this special relationship in which the widow stands to her late husband's younger brother is quite intelligible on the supposition that at the end of mourning she is to become his wife, as regularly happens under the common form of the levirate which assigns a man's widow to one of his younger brothers. This custom actually obtains in all the three tribes—the Arunta, the Unmatjera, and the Kaitish—in which the widow observes the rule of silence and stands in this special relation to the younger brothers of her late husband. In the Arunta it is the custom that on the conclusion of mourning the widow becomes the wife of one of her deceased husband's younger brothers;[16] and with regard to the Unmatjera and Kaitish we are told that "this passing on of the widow to a younger, but never to an elder, brother is a very characteristic feature of these tribes."[17] Similarly in the Dieri tribe, which enforced the rule of silence on widows during the period of mourning, a man's widow passed at his death to his brother, who became her husband, and her children called him father.[18] But among rude races, who believe that a man's ghost haunts his widow and pesters her with his unwelcome attentions, marriage with a widow is naturally thought to involve the bridegroom in certain risks arising from the jealousy of his deceased rival, who is loth to resign his spouse to the arms of another. This may help us to understand why, among the Australian tribes in question, a man keeps such a vigilant watch over the conduct of his deceased elder brother's widow. The motive is probably not so much a disinterested respect for the honour of his dead brother as a selfish regard for his own personal safety, which would be put in jeopardy if he were to marry the widow before she had completely got rid of her late husband's ghost by strictly observing all the precautions usually taken for that purpose, including the rule of silence.

Thus the analogy of customs observed among widely separated peoples supports the conjecture that among the ancient Hebrews also, at some early time of their history, a widow may have been expected to keep silence for a certain time after the death of her husband for the sake of giving the slip to his ghost; and further, perhaps, that the observance of this precaution may have been particularly enforced by her late husband's younger brother, who, in accordance with the custom of the levirate, proposed to marry her when the days of her mourning were over. But it should be observed that, apart from analogy, the direct evidence for such an enforced silence of widows among the Hebrews is no more than a doubtful etymology; and as all inferences from etymology to custom are exceedingly precarious, I cannot claim any high degree of probability for the present conjecture.

*   *   *

[Proceed with caution. It is true that among many primitive peoples a woman is condemned to a period of silence and to other austerities on the death of her husband;[18a] but Frazer's theory that such a practice obtained also in ancient Israel rests solely on a supposed connection of the Hebrew word *'almanah,* "widow," with a like-sounding *'illem,* "dumb," and this, though superficially alluring, is not accepted by the best Semitic philologists, who relate it rather to the Arabic *'a-l-m,* "be in pain, forlorn."[18b] Besides, the word *'illem,* wherever it occurs in the Hebrew Bible, means "to be voiceless by nature or by physical defect," not simply "to be muted, hushed, silenced";[18c] for the doleful silence observed by persons in distress the quite distinct verb *d-m-m* is employed.[18d] It is to be observed also that the cognate of Hebrew *'almanah* has now turned up in Akkadian and in Ugaritic, yet no Akkadian or Ugaritic text speaks of a ritual silence of widows, even though they indeed describe procedures of mourning. Moreover, among primitive peoples such silences are by no means confined to widows, but are usually imposed on *all* mourners and kinsfolk.[18e] Accordingly, philological objections apart, it would be difficult to explain why "the female silent one" should have to mean the widow exclusively.] ▼

343   Cannibalism in a time of famine   2:20; 4:10

Should women eat their offsprings
the babes whom they have dandled?

The hands of compassionate women have boiled their own children:
they (the children) have become as food for them.

Allegations of cannibalism are something of a cliché in ancient literary accounts of famines and sieges. Thus, Ashurbanipal relates that during his campaign against the Arabs "famine broke out among them, and they ate the flesh of their children against their hunger."[1] Similarly, the inhabitants of Tauromenium, in Sicily, are said to have eaten their slaves when they were beleaguered by the Romans during the Servile War of 104 B.C.;[2] and it is reported of the Vascones (Basques) of the city of Calahorra that they ate their children to stave off hunger when they were resisting the Romans after the death of Sertorius in 72 B.C.[3] Procopius, in his Gotica, tells of two women who slew and devoured their offspring during a famine;[4] and Strabo relates that the practice was not unknown, in similar circumstances, among the ancient Irish.[5]

What happened in the time of the Biblical writer seems to have been repeated later when Jerusalem fell to the Romans in 70 C.E., for Josephus reports the unnatural behavior of a woman who then ate her own suckling.[6]

The word rendered above *as food* is *lebārôt*. This has inspired the suggestion that it really conceals the name of Labartu, the cannibalistic child-stealing hag of Mesopotamian folklore, the correct translation being, *They became unto them like child-eating hags.*[7] Since this suggestion has found its way into several modern commentaries, it may be well to point out that the reading of the demon's name as Labartu is in fact erroneous. The cuneiform sign for the syllable *bar* can also be read as *mash,* and that the correct reading in the present case is LaMAShtu is now proved by the discovery of a text in which it is actually spelled out: La-ma-ash-tu.[8]

344 Drinking gall   3:15

> *He hath filled me with gall,*
> *sated me with wormwood.*

This expression recurs twice in the Book of Jeremiah.[1] Drinking gall is frequently invoked as a curse in Classical literature.[2] It was not only a symbol of bitterness, but was believed also to cause madness.

We may aptly compare the famous lines in Shakespeare's *Macbeth*:[3]

> Come to my woman's breasts
> And take my milk for gall, you murdering monsters,
> Whenever in your sightless substances
> You wait on nature's mischief.[4]

345 Gravel and dust in the mouth   3:16

> *He has ground my teeth on gravel,*
> *and made me cower in ashes.*

The Greek (Septuagint) and Latin (Vulgate) Versions render the second clause, *And has fed me on ashes.* There does not appear to be any philological authority for this rendering, but it rests on an interesting piece of folklore. The ancient translators were evidently nonplused by the Hebrew word which, though it can be satisfactorily explained from the cognate Semitic languages, does not in fact recur in the Old Testament.[1] They therefore saw in the phrase an allusion to the custom of stuffing a man's mouth with dust or with a pebble against adverse spells or utterances.[2] This custom is attested by the popular expression, "Dust (or, stone) in thy mouth!" which is found alike in the Talmud[3] and in Arabic[4] and Mandaean[5] sources. The same custom likewise underlies the words of Proverbs 20:17:

> Though the bread of deceit may be pleasant to a man,
> his mouth will thereafter be filled with gravel.

According to Herodotus,[6] Ctesias,[7] and other ancient writers,[8] it was the custom of the Iranians to throw condemned felons into a room filled with ashes, with meat and drink in sight, but out of reach. Similarly, in the *History of Tamurlane*, it is recorded that men sentenced to death were given a cake of dust and ashes.[9]

346 The king as the life-breath of his people   4:20

> *The breath of our nostrils, the Lord's anointed*
> *is taken in their net.*[1]

The portrayal of the king as the *élan vitale* of his people occurs also in Egyptian literature.[2] Sesostris III, for instance, is described as "he that gives breath to his subjects' throats,"[3] and as "the herdsman that gives breath."[4] Elsewhere, the pharaoh is styled analogously, "the breath of our nostrils,"[5] "our life-breath,"[6] and "the *élan vitale* of mankind";[7] while in the Tell el Amarna Letters he is sometimes addressed as the breath of his servant's life.[8]

Similar expressions are also found in Mesopotamian literature.[9]

The idea is applied also to divine beings. In Genesis 2:7 and in Job 27:3; 32:8; and 33:4, it is the breath of God that not only animates man but also gives him intelligence and moral sense. The concept is familiar especially from the great verses of Psalm 104:29–30: *When Thou withdrawest Thy breath,*[10] *they die, and return to their dust. When Thou sendest forth Thy breath, they are created;* (*thereby*) *also Thou renewest* (i.e., by Thy wind) *the face of the earth.*

Two ideas are in fact combined. The first is that the king, as the embodiment of the god,[11] furnishes the breath of life to his people. The second is that, as the embodiment of the community, he is at the same time the epitome, rather than the endower, of its corporate vitality.[12] He is that in which "they live and move and have their being."

347 The king's shadow   4:20

. . . in his shadow we live.

Two ideas are here combined.

(i) The king, as the embodiment of the god, is a *protective shade* to his people. In Mesopotamian belief "to stay (or serve) in the sweet and fine shadow of the king" meant to belong to his immediate entourage. "Persons so described enjoyed special privileges. . . . Officials on missions were considered to be 'travelling in the shadow of the king.'" The notion seems to have originated in Egypt and to have been introduced into Mesopotamia toward the beginning of the first millennium B.C.[1] In a hymn from Kahun, the Northerners are said to exclaim, "Set us in thy shadow, O king!"[2] Elsewhere Pharaoh is described as being "like a shadow in spring, a cooling shade in summer."[3]

In the celebrated Travels of Wen-Amun, when that official is brought before the king of Byblus, he accidentally steps into the latter's shadow. A courtier at once interposes himself, and it has been suggested that the motive for his action was to prevent the stranger's thus coming within the ambit of the royal favor and privilege.[4]

The notion is applied also to the protection afforded by gods. Many Akkadian names begin with the element Şilli, "in the shadow of," followed by mention of a specific deity.[5] A Hebrew name of this type is Bezalel, meaning properly, "In the shadow of God."[6] Similarly, in an Aramaic papyrus from Elephantine, the expression, "in the shadow of Ahuramazda," means "under the protection of that god.[7]

(ii) Associated with this notion is the more basic concept that, since the shadow is a part of the self, to be in the king's (or in anyone's) shadow is to absorb his royal (divine) essence.[8]

Esther

348 Introductory[1]

The Book of Esther relates a story designed to account for a festival named Purim. Scholars are virtually agreed, however, that the story is fiction rather than history, and that the festival must consequently have had quite a different origin.[2] In the first place, none of the Persian kings who bore the name Xerxes (Ahasuerus) had a wife called Esther. Second, there is no mention anywhere but in the Book of Esther of a queen named Vashti, a vizier named Haman, or of a courtier named Mordecai who eventually replaced Haman.[3] Third, there is no Hebrew, Aramaic, or Persian word *pur* denoting "lot"; this explanation of the name Purim could be, at best, a piece of folk etymology by which the exiled Jews attempted to account for the name of an already existent festival through fanciful association of it with a *Babylonian* word of that meaning![4]

Thus the book presents two problems: (*a*) What is the real origin of the story, independent of its connection with Purim? (*b*) What is the real origin of Purim?

(*a*) It is to be noted, first, that the Book of Esther really consists of *two* stories now artificially linked together. The one is the story of Vashti; the other, that of Esther. Now, in each of them the central figure is a woman, and both revolve around the same central theme of how a beautiful woman outwits the designs of kings and princes. Vashti frustrates her lord's plan to make a vulgar display of her; Esther foils the plot of Haman against Mordecai and the Jews. Both stories belong, therefore, to that well-known class of folktales which deal with the wiles of women. Such tales, of course, would have been especially popular with the fair sex, and doubtless have been told and retold with relish in the harems of Persia or wherever else women came together in purely feminine converse. They are, essentially, "Kaffee-klatsch" talk at the expense of the menfolk. It is, accordingly, from a repertoire of such novellae that the Book of Esther may be supposed to have stemmed. Originally, the two stories would have been purely Persian compositions, dealing with intrigues at the Persian court. In course of time, however, it would have been picked up and adapted by the Jews living under Persian rule, and eventually used to explain a popular festival called something like Purim.

The stories have been linked together in the manner of most Oriental romances. They are enclosed in a general cadre of adventures at the court of the Great King. This is the kind of thing which one finds again in such well-known collections as the Pančatantra, the Twenty-five Vampire Tales (Vetalapanchavimsati) of Somadeva, and the Thousand and One Nights.

That the story of Esther was originally independent of that of Vashti is plain on the surface. In the story of Vashti, the succession falls to the next harem favorite (1:19). Esther, however, is chosen only after a nation-wide beauty contest. Moreover, whereas the deposition of Vashti is said to have taken place in the *third* year of the king's reign (1:3), the appointment of Esther occurs in the *seventh* (2:16)—surely, too long an interval, if the events were really connected.[5]

Furthermore, although the story of Esther purports to be of essentially *Jewish* interest, dealing with a situation affecting Jews and explaining the origin of a Jewish festival, the fact is that every detail of its Jewish coloration is either anomalous or incredible. Mordecai and Esther bear non-Jewish names. This is like calling a French heroine, Gretchen. The king authorizes the massacre of the Jews on the grounds that they are a refractory people (3:11); yet, he heaps honors on Mordecai, who openly admits to being a Jew (6:10)!

Lastly, as it now stands, the story bears clear evidence of having been manipulated from some earlier original. The king, for instance, himself approves the plan of Haman (3:10-11); yet, when Esther discloses it to him, he expresses surprise and demands to know the villain's name (7:2-5). So too, although Esther makes a great fuss about the danger of interceding with the king (4:10-11), when she finally musters the courage to do so and is assured explicitly that any request she might make will be granted, she fails to use the opportunity and resorts, instead, to the elaborate and quite unnecessary procedure of inviting the king and Haman to a couple of dinners! Not only is the point of this procedure obscured, but it also remains unexplained why Haman could not just as well have been denounced *in absentia*.

Now, once the Jewish veneer is removed, the earlier pattern begins to emerge, even though some of its features remain but faintly limned. The original story was simply a Persian tale of court life, with a Persian setting and Persian characters; and it was later adapted to account, in terms acceptable to the Jews, for the origin of a Persian festival which they had come to adopt. Moreover, the dénouement is now seen to have involved a motif which is in fact extremely common in folktales throughout the world, namely, that of maneuvering a culprit into an unwitting confession. The most familiar example of this occurs in the play scene of Shakespeare's *Hamlet*.[6]

It is, of course, impossible to be certain about all the details, but the main outlines of the earlier story may be reconstructed somewhat as follows:

Once upon a time, at the court of the Persian king Ahasuerus (Xerxes), a feud broke out between two courtiers, one named Haman, and the other Mardaka (a good Persian name).[7] In consequence of this feud and the intense hatred which he entertained against Mardaka, Haman represented to the king that his rival and his rival's kinsfolk were disobedient and disloyal citizens, and thereby obtained the royal assent to have them put to death.

What Haman did not know, however, was that one of those kinsfolk was the current royal favorite, the beautiful Esther (Persian, Sitireh, "star"; cf. our *Stella*). He did not realize either that she was a girl of great courage, shrewdness, and resource. Esther found a way of foiling his evil designs. She invited him to dine privately with the king and herself and, when the two men were in their cups, she entertained them by telling a seemingly fictitious tale of how a wicked courtier had once plotted the destruction of the reigning favorite and her entire kinsfolk merely to pay off a score against one of his rivals. The king, intrigued by the tale and thoroughly befuddled with drink, thereupon broke in with the rhetorical question, "What kind of man could he have been to fill his heart with such designs?" Haman, however, equally befuddled, interpreted this as a direct and specific inquiry and, his lips loosed by wine, clumsily blurted out, "Why, that's me, of course," thereby betraying himself. Esther's purpose was thus achieved, and the villain was exposed and put to death with all his family—an admirably satisfying illustration of the principle, "measure for measure."

In the Jewish retelling of this tale, the Persian Mardaka was transmogrified into Mordecai, a name (derived from that of the Babylonian god Marduk) actually affected by Jews in the Babylonian Exile,[8] and he was said to descend from one of his coreligionists who had actually been deported to Babylon after the capture of Jerusalem by Nebuchadnezzar.[9] Conversely, Haman was made to trace his pedigree to Agag, king of the Amalekites (cf. I Sam. 15:32) and hence to be a member of that accursed race against whom the God of the Jews had sworn warfare "from generation to generation" (Exod. 17:16).[10]

(b) As for the origin of Purim, here we are confronted with a wide variety of theories. There is no need to waste space mentioning them all.[11] Two, however, invite special comment.

The first[12] asserts that the festival originated not in Persia, but in Babylon, and that it was adopted by the Jews in the Babylonian Exile. Its prototype was the Babylonian New Year festival, held at the beginning of spring. At that festival, it is supposed, a ritual pantomime was enacted portraying the victory of Babylon's leading deities, the male Marduk and the female Ishtar, over those of the neighboring state of Elam, the male Humman and the female

Kiririsha. This pantomime was later transmogrified by the Jews, when Babylon fell under Persian rule, into the story of Mordecai and Esther's triumph over Haman and his wife Zeresh, the setting being changed appropriately to the Persian court. On this hypothesis, the name of the festival would be connected with the Babylonian word *puru*, "lot," but it would originally have referred to the fact that on New Year's the gods were believed to meet in conclave and determine the fates of men by the casting of lots.

Attractive as all this sounds, it is nevertheless riddled with fatal objections. The Babylonian New Year took place in the month of Nisan; hence it could not have been the origin of a festival which is said explicitly to have fallen on the fourteenth and fifteenth days of the preceding month of Adar! Second, there is no evidence that the Babylonian New Year was ever known as "the day of lots," nor that the destinies of men were thought to be determined by this method. Third, although an Elamite Khumban is indeed attested, there is no Humman or Haman, and there is nothing to show that Khumban's consort was Kiririsha (i.e., Zeresh).

The second theory[13] contends that the Book of Esther is really a political squib, and that what it actually celebrates is the victory of Judah the Maccabee over the Syrian general Nicanor on the thirteenth day of Adar, 161 B.C. On this assumption, Xerxes stands for Antiochus IV; Haman for Nicanor; and Mordecai for Judah the Maccabee. But here again there are fatal objections. The Second Book of Maccabees, in the Apocrypha of the Bible, states clearly (15:36) that the victory of Nicanor was celebrated "on the day preceding the day of Mordecai." Furthermore, the name of the festival (viz., Purim) remains unexplained, and there is no historical character to correspond to Esther.

Comparative Religion and Folklore may perhaps lead us out of the labyrinth. A story designed to explain a festival has obviously to account for its leading features. Working backward, therefore, we may attempt to recognize in various features of the story of Esther allusions to characteristic seasonal customs, and thence to reconstruct the nature and pattern of the underlying festival. The factors of the story which then come into consideration are the following:

(1) The selection of a queen and the celebration of her accession by a public holiday (2:17–18).

(2) The parading of an ordinary citizen in the garb of the king (6:1–11).

(3) The observance of a fast (4:15–16).

(4) The execution of a malefactor (7:10; 9:14, 25).

(5) An armed combat between two parties (9:1–17).

(6) The distribution of gifts (9:22).

(7) The celebration of the festival around the time of the vernal equinox (9:18–21).

Now, it so happens that all of these features are characteristic of seasonal festivals in many parts of the world.

(1) The selection of the queen connects at once with the common practice

of appointing kings and queens at the beginning of the year, and of celebrating their nuptials at the seasonal festival.[14] The most familiar example is the election of European kings and queens of the May, but Aristotle informs us that the marriage of a king and queen formed part of the Dionysia at Athens.[15] In Egypt, the wedding of god and goddess was likewise celebrated both at the summer festival in Edfu[16] and at the winter festival in Luxor,[17] and Mesopotamian parallels can also be adduced.[18]

(2) The parade of Mordecai in the royal robes would reflect the equally common custom of appointing temporary kings to reign during the few days which often intervene, in ancient and primitive calendars, between the end of one year and the beginning of the next.[19] Such temporary kings, usually ordinary citizens, are attested, for instance, at Lhasa in Tibet,[20] among the Kwottos of Northern Nigeria,[21] among the Bakitara of Uganda,[22] among the Bastars of the Central Provinces of India,[23] and in Cambodia.[24] We are told also that at the Persian festival of Sacaea, held in July, one of the royal domestics was installed as temporary king and paraded in the royal attire.[25] Even more significantly, the Arab writer al-Biruni (973–1048) relates that it was customary in Persia to lead a thin-bearded man around on horseback, attended by the king's servants, just before the spring festival.[26]

(3) The observance of a fast accords with the fact that New Year is usually preceded by a period of abstinence.[27] The Babylonians, for example, recognized the first six or even sixteen days of the year as a lenten period.[28] The Hebrews prefaced the autumnal feast of Ingathering by the solemn Day of Atonement, observed as a fast. In Rome, the festival of Ceres, goddess of crops, in April, was introduced by a fast.[29] Similarly, in modern Cambodia, the first three days of the year (in March) are a period of abstinence;[30] while among the Cherokees and Choctaws of North America, the New Year feast (in August) is called the Fast.[31] The purpose of such fasts and lents is to express the state of suspended animation in which a community finds itself at the end of its annual or seasonal lease of life.

(4) The execution of Haman would go back to the annual dispatch of a human scapegoat at the beginning of the year, in order to drive out all blight and noxiousness.[32] At the Athenian festival of Thargelia, in May, a male and a female were thus expelled and scourged; and the same thing took place at Abdera.[33] In European usage, the unfortunate wretch is often identified with Death, Disease, Old Year, or the like.[34] Sometimes too the rite is performed in symbolic form, the part of the victim being taken by an effigy which is drowned or burned.[35] In Cambodia for example, such a rite is performed in March;[36] and among the Eskimos of Point Barrow, Alaska, the evil spirit Tuña is driven out with contumely as soon as the sun reappears.[37] (On such usages, see above, §**194**.)

(5) The combat between the Jews and their antagonists is similarly explicable as reflecting the characteristic seasonal combat between Summer and Winter, Old and New Year, Life and Death, Fertility and Drought, or the like, which is a feature of seasonal festivals in many parts of the world,[38] and which is attested even among the ancient Egyptians[39] and Hittites.[40]

(6) The distribution of gifts as a New Year custom still obtains at the present day, so that little need be said about it. It is worth noting, however, that the Romans used likewise to distribute presents, called *strenae,* on the first of January, and that the French term, *jour d'étrennes,* meaning New Year's Day, is thence derived. Indeed, it has been suggested that Purim itself may have a similar meaning, being connected with an assumed Old Persian word, *purti,* and with our own *portion.*

(7) Purim usually falls within the week of the vernal equinox; it has done so, for example, no less than twenty times during the past fifty years. Now, in ancient and primitive calendars, equinox and solstice, or (in lunar systems) the new moons nearest to them, are often regarded as the beginning of the year. Thus, the Babylonians and the Jews reckoned their year from the month of Nisan (roughly, mid-March until mid-April) or Tishri (roughly, mid-September until mid-October). The Roman year, before the Julian reform, likewise began on March 1, and it is significant that the vernal equinox was the beginning of the year in European countries until comparatively modern times. Under Charlemagne, it began on March 25, and it was only in the eighteenth century that January 1 became the official date in Holland, Protestant Germany, Russia, and Sweden.[41] Moreover—and this is especially important—the Old Persian year began at the vernal equinox.

Purim, then, would have been the ancient New Year festival, and in explanation of the name it is noteworthy that in modern Arabic, New Year is indeed sometimes called *phur.* The word has, apparently, no satisfactory etymology in the Arabic language. It must therefore have been borrowed, and a not unreasonable conjecture would associate it with the Persian word for "first," when it would bear the same general connotation as the French *printemps* or as the Spanish and Italian *primavera.*

349 The Iranian background

The Book of Esther is full of little touches which can be illustrated from Persian lore and custom.

(a) The court at Susa 1:2

The incident concerning Vashti is said to have taken place "when King Ahasuerus was occupying his royal throne in Susa the capital." This has a special meaning, for Xenophon tells us that the Persian king used to make the rounds of his three capitals, spending the spring in Susa, the summer in Ecbatana, and the winter in Babylon.¹ What is indicated, therefore, is that the incident took place in the spring, while the court was in residence at the first-named city.

(b) The royal banquet   1:3

The banquet tendered by the king lasted one hundred and eighty days. Scholars have long wondered how officers of state could have absented themselves from their duties so long. The answer is simple: the author modeled his account on the practice which obtained at the annual feasts of Nauroz (New Year) and Mihrajan, when the sovereign entertained his ministers and friends *in relays,* according to order of rank.²

(c) The one hundred and eighty days   1:4

The mention of 180 days is a clever touch. To be sure, in the mouth of one who had lived in the Babylonian Exile, this could be nothing more than a round number, consisting of the basic Babylonian sixty multiplied thrice for exaggeration. There may, however, be more to the matter than this, for the fact is that the ancient Persian year was divided into six parts, called *gahanbars,* and it so happens that 180 days comprise exactly the first three of them, beginning in spring. The scheme is as follows:

maidyoizaremaya (mid-spring) — *maidyoišema* (mid-summer)	45 days
maidyoišema — *paitshaya* (grain-bringing)	60 days
paitshaya — *ayathrima* (home-coming)	75 days
	180 days

The total period lasted from May 1 until October 16.³ The Jewish author, however, was not quite *au fait* with the details, for, as we have seen, Xenophon says that the court moved to Ecbatana over the summer months, whereas it is here represented as spending both spring and summer at Susa.

(d) "Men who knew the law"   1:13

After Vashti has refused to appear at the banquet, the king consults men "who know law and protocol." Cambyses, says Herodotus, married his own sister after consulting the judges, described as "certain picked men, appointed for life or until found guilty of misconduct. It is by them that justice is administered in Persia, and they are the interpreters of the old laws."⁴

The Hebrew word (*dath*) here rendered "law," it should be added, is a *Persian* term.

(e) The seven who saw the king's face   1:14

The king's special counselors are seven men privileged to see his face. Heracleides Commanus, quoted by the antiquarian Athenaeus, informs us that the Persian king used to dine alone behind a curtain, and only seven men had the right to see him.⁵

Similar taboos obtain among the Loango[6] and Coango[7] of West Africa and in Susa, a region to the south of Abyssinia.[8] They are explained by Frazer from the belief that a man's "spirit," or *élan vitale,* can be elicited by ill-wishers when he opens his mouth.[9] Possibly, however, this is simply a particularization of the rule that the king, as the embodiment of deity, must be kept inviolate.[10] The king of Jebu, in West Africa, for example, has always to remain veiled or screened,[11] and among the Ewe-speaking peoples of the same area only three chosen men may have direct converse with him.[12]

(f) The crazy edict 1:22

After Vashti has rebuffed him, the king, fearful lest the other ladies of the realm might be encouraged by her example to defy their husbands, issues a decree that every man is to be "ruler in his own house and (entitled to) speak the language of his people." Scholars have long wondered why Ahasuerus should have had to give special permission to husbands to use their native tongues in their own homes.[13] The answer is really very simple. This is a deliberately humorous touch. The only way in which the proud and ostentatious monarch can guarantee his male subjects authority in their own households is formally to appoint them "governors" therein, and this appointment is made, under full protocol, in the same terms as were used in letters patent accrediting governors to their several provinces! Such letters evidently contained a clause sanctioning the use of native tongues. The diplomatic phraseology is here reproduced with delightful humor, and one can readily imagine that when our story was told and retold in the harems of Persia, this little detail must have roused a particularly uproarious laugh.[14]

(g) The royal crown 2:17

As a mark of favor to Esther, the king places a crown on her head. The crown is called *kether.* Although common in later Hebrew, this word does not occur in the Old Testament except here. The reason is that it is a Persian technical term, for Greek writers mention the *kidaris* (or *kitaris*) as the royal headgear of Persian monarchs.[15]

(h) Haman's boast 5:11

Elated at the impending ruin of Mordecai and the Jews, Haman summons his wife and friends and recounts to them "the splendor of his riches, the number of his sons, and all the promotions with which the king had honored him" (RSV). At first blush, the reference to *the number of his sons* sounds somewhat odd and, as a matter of fact, the historian Josephus was so nonplused by it that he simply left it out in his retelling of the tale! But it is, once again, a genuine Persian touch. "Next to prominence in arms," says Herodotus, the Persians "regarded it as the greatest proof of manly prowess to be the father of many sons. Every year the king sends rich gifts to the man who can show the largest number, since they hold that number is strength."[16]

(i) "Whom the king delights to honor"   6:8–11

As a reward for having saved the king's life from conspirators, Mordecai is paraded around the city wearing a royal robe and mounted on a royal steed. It has been suggested above that this incident was intended to account for the parade of the "temporary king" at the festival which underlies Purim. Within the framework of the story itself, however, it can be illustrated from the assertion of Plutarch[17] that when the Persian king wished to show special favor to a subject, he gave him one of his own robes.

(j) Covering the head   6:12

Thoroughly put out by the honor which he has had to pay to Mordecai, Haman rushes home "in mourning and with head covered." Again a Persian touch. Quintus Curtius informs us that when a Persian wept in mourning, he kept his head covered.[18] The Hebrews, on the other hand, strewed ashes over it.

Ecclesiastes

350 The telltale bird   Eccles. 10:20

A bird of the air shall carry the voice,
and that which hath wings shall tell the matter.

The allusion in this proverbial phrase is to the widespread tale of *The Bird of Truth,* who discloses treachery, murder, marital infidelity, and the like.[1] Tales of this type are to be found in Grimm,[2] in *The Arabian Nights,*[3] in the famous *Legend of the Seven Sages,*[4] and in the English and Scottish ballads.[5] A classic Greek example is the familiar story of the cranes of Ibycus.[6]

The motif is very ancient. In the recently discovered Hittite *Tale of Elkunirša* (which evidently goes back to a Canaanite original), "Ishtar," disguised as a bird, overhears the love-making of Baal and Asherath and reports it to the latter's husband, Elkunirša (i.e., *El qôneh 'eres,* "the god who owns the earth"; cf. Gen. 14:19).[7]

Related to this theme is the popular expression, "A little bird told me,"[8] the prototype of which occurs already in Aristophanes.[9] A popular belief in Norway is that if a bird flies to a window, this signifies news.[10]

NOTES

PSALMS

250 The divine adoption of kings

1. On this concept, see: A. M. Hocart, Kingship (1927); Frazer-Gaster, NGB §§125-27; T. H. Gaster, in Numen 1 (1954), 193-94.—On sacred kingship in the Ancient Near East, see: M. Canney, in JMEOS 10 (1923), 53-58; A. Moret, Du caractère religieux de la royauté pharaonique (1902); R. Labat, Le caractère religieux de la royauté assyro-babylonienne (1939); C. Jeremias, Die Vergöttlichung der bab.-ass. Könige, AO 19/iii-iv (1919); I. Engnell, Studies in Divine Kingship in the Ancient Near East (1943); T. H. Gaster, in Review of Religion 9 (1945), 267-81; C. J. Gadd, Ideas of Divine Rule in the Ancient Near East (1948); H. Frankfort, Kingship and the Gods (1948); A. Bentzen, Det sakrale Kongedomme (1945); S. Smith, "The Practice of Kingship in Early Semitic Kingdoms," in S. H. Hooke, ed., Myth, Ritual and Kingship (1958).—On kingship in Canaan and Israel, see: M. Noth, in Zeitschr. für Theol. und Kirche 47 (1950), 157-91; G. Widengren, Sakrales Königtum im AT und in Judentum (1955); J. de Fraine, L'aspect religieux de la royauté israélite (1954); A. Johnson, Sacral Kingship in Ancient Israel (1959); J. Gray, in VT 2 (1952), 199-220; A. Bentzen, Det sakrale Kongedomme (1945).—For modern African parallels, see: C. G. Seligman, Egypt and Negro Africa (1934); P. Hadfield, Traits of Divine Kingship in Africa (1949); C. Petersson, Chiefs and Gods: Social and Religious Elements in the S. E. Bantu Kingship (1953).

2. Cf. S. A. B. Mercer, The Religion of Ancient Egypt (1949), 248 ff.; H. Nelson, in JNES 1 (1942), 127-55.

3. Inscription of Khenzer, in Breasted, AR i.§786. In the Stela of Kubban (ib., iii.285), 18, he is regarded as "Re 'incarnate," and in Pyramid Texts, Ut. 362, 1146, 1156, as "a vast cosmic figure."

4. T. Paffrath, in Hommel Festschrift (1917), i.157-59; G. Furlani, La religione babilonese e assira (1928), i.353.

5. See below, §296.

6. Krt C = 125 Gordon, 20-22.

7. E. Casartelli, in ERE vii.722-23.

8. M. Lidzbarski, Ephemeris ii (1908), 383 f.

9. E. Naville, Deir-el-Bahri iv (1913), pl. 96.4; id., Osorkon (1892), ii.25.

10. H. Gressmann, ATOB, #88; cf. G. Maspero, in PSBA 14 (1892), 308 ff.; A. Jacoby, in ARW 13 (1906), 547 ff.; K. Sethe, Altaeg. Pyramidentexte ii (1910), §§910-13.

11. ISA 58, g.7-8.

12. P. Jensen, KB vi/2. 140-41; M. Streck, Assurbanipal (1916), ii.348-49, 8; Labat, op. cit., 64-66; A. Boissier, in OLz 1908.234 f.; H. Zimmern, in ZA 36 (1925), 85, n.1; T. H. Gaster, Thespis[2], 179, 254.

13. See below, §284.

14. For the traditional text's 'aSaPP^{e}RaH 'el ḤôQ read 'ôSîPh^{e}KaH 'el ḤêQî.

King installed on holy mountain

15. See: M. Canney, in JMEOS 20 (1936), 25-40; M. Eliade, The Myth of the Eternal Return (1954), 12 ff.; W. Gaerte, in Anthropos 9 (1914), 956-79; T. H. Gaster, Thespis[2], 183 f.

16. Lassen, in ZKM 2 (1839), 62 ff.
17. C. Meinhold, in Baudissin Festschrift (1918), 382.
18. A. Smythe-Palmer, Jacob at Bethel (1899), 17 ff.
19. ERE xii.485b, n.3.
20. D. G. Brinton, Myths of the New World[3] (1905), 95.
21. K. Sethe, Urkunden (1927–30), iv.364.
22. K. Sethe, Amun (1929), §250 f.
23. Sethe, ib., 117–18; A. de Buck, Oersheuvel (1937), 72–84; H. Frankfort, Kingship and the Gods (1948), 151–54. Cf. also: S. Morenz, Aeg. Religion (1960), 45.
24. T. Dombart, Der Sakralturm, I: Zikkurat (1920), 34.
25. P. Mus, Barabudur (1935), i.68 ff., 94 ff.
26. See below, §272; Gaster, op. cit., 156 f.
27. W. Dunbar, in Antiquity 3 (1929), 408–13.—The Egyptians held that earth had been formed from the gathering of primordial sand at Thebes: NK Leyden Papyrus, ed. A. H. Gardiner, in ÄZ 42.14 f. A. Erman, Literatur d. Aegypter (1923), 365, #10.— On Jerusalem as the cosmic hill, see: E. Burrows, in The Labyrinth, ed. S. H. Hooke (1935), 53 ff.—In Ezekiel's blueprint of the future temple (43:15), part of the altar is termed *hril,* which W. F. Albright (Archaeology and the Religion of Israel [1942], 151) identifies as a symbol of the divine mountain (*har el*), in accordance with the notion that the temple was a microcosm.

251 Seeing the face of God

1. The psalm bears all the hallmarks of such compositions. The god is besought to hear the suppliant's defense (Heb.: *ṣedeq:* v. 1); to let the verdict issue in his favor (v. 2); to investigate his state of heart (v. 3). He is addressed as "savior of those that *seek refuge*" (v. 7), and specific reference is made to guilty men (RSV: "the wicked," v. 9), who "despoil" him (ib.) or "track him down" (v.10). Many of these expressions possess a juridical nuance.
2. Cf. T. H. Gaster, IDB, s.v. Resurrection.
3. Cf. F. Nötscher, "Die Angesicht Gottes schauen" nach biblischer und babylonischer Auffassung (1924).
4. Cf. Apuleius, Met. ii.24: *inexplicabili voluptate divini simulacri perfruebar;* cf. F. Cumont, After Life in Roman Paganism (1922), 121 f.; A. D. Nock, Early Gentile Christianity and Its Hellenic Background (1964), 6, 111–13, 139.
5. L. R. Farnell, Cults of the Greek States (1896–1909), iii.126 ff.
6. For the traditional text's *yašar yeḥ^{e}zū panêmô* we should probably read *y^{e}šārîm yeḥ^{e}zū pānāw.*

252 The breakers of Death

1. Isa. 28:15; 38:18; Hos. 13:14; Ps. 6:6; Job 28:22; 30:23, etc.
2. Stith Thompson, MI, A 672; F 93.1.
3. M. Cox, Introduction to Folklore (1897), 184 ff.; T. Waitz, Anthropologie der Naturvölker (1860–77), iii.197; W. Mannhardt, Germ. Mythen (1858), 364 ff. Cf. also the familiar Negro spiritual: "One more river, / And that's the River of Jordan, / One more river, / There's one more river to cross."
4. G. Maspero, in JA, IVème sér. 15 (1880), 161; W. Müller, Egyptian Mythology (1918), 176.
5. *Ludlul bêl nimêqi* iii.16 = ANET 438 f.
6. Ib., iv.6 = ANET, 437.
7. Epic of Gilgamesh x.21–27, 50.
8. Hesiod, Theog. 774 ff; cf. also: Ps.-Plato, Axioch 12, p. 371B; Plutarch, De orac. defec. ii.

9. E.g., Euripides, Herakles 431 ff.; id., Alcestis 253 ff., 440; Aristophanes, Lys. 606 ff.; id., Frogs 185 ff.; Vergil, Aen. vi.290 ff.; Juvenal, iii.260 f.; B. Schmidt, Das Volksleben der Neugriechen (1871), 222, 237; D. Hesseling, Charos (1897).—Neither in Homer nor in Aeschylus, Septem 857 is the ferryman named Charon.

10. Lancelot du lac, ed. 1591, p. 147; cf. F. Nork, Das Kloster xii (1849), 249 ff., 260 ff.

11. Shakespeare, Hamlet, V.i (song).

12. F. J. Child, English and Scottish Ballads (1882–98), #114; L. C. Wimberly, Folklore in the English and Scottish Ballads[2] (1959), 108 ff. Cf. also the ballads of Edward, Lizzie Wan, and The Two Brothers (ib.). For a Slavonic parallel, cf. K. Schwenk, Die Mythologie der Slawen (1853), 334; and for a Finnish parallel, ib., 389.

13. A. Kuhn, Westfalische Märchen, i (1859), 129.

14. Procopius, Goth. iv.20.

15. Pliny, HN iv.27.

16. Cox, op. cit., 188 f.; cf. Villemarqué, Barz. breiz. i.169: "En passant le lac de l'angoisse, elle vit une bande des morts, vetus de blanc, dans les petites barques."

17. E. Martinengo Cesaresco, Essays in the Study of Folk Songs (Everyman's Library ed.), 295.

18. A. B. Alexander, Latin American Mythology (1920), 198; D. G. Brinton, Myths of the New World[3] (1905), 288 f.

19. D. G. Brinton, Essays of an Americanist (1890), 135–47.

20. Id., Myths, loc. cit.

21. Ib.

22. Ib., 290.

23. Odyssey 10.514; Plato, Phaedo 112–13C; O. Gruppe, Griechische Mythologie (1906), 402 f.; C. G. Heyne, Excursus ix. to Comm. on Vergil, Aen. vi.

24. Rig Veda x.63.

25. Kalevala, runo xvi.

26. E. S. Drower, The Canonical Prayerbook of the Mandaeans (1959), 63.4, 5, 9.

27. M. Pope, Job (Anchor Bible, 1965), 218, would recognize a reference to the river of the underworld in the expression "pass over the šelaḥ in Job 33:18; 36:12— both times in allusion to death. The word is commonly rendered "weapon" (i.e., pass away by means of a weapon), but Pope here combines it with the Akkadian šilḫu, šiliḫtu, Heb. šelaḥ (Neh. 3:15), "channel." Cf. also the Coptic loanword šoleḥ, "canal."

253 The bonds of Death

1. Ticᵢ Series, IX.i, 25 = R. C. Thompson, Devils (1904), ii.66 (*itti mûti rakis*).

2. Atharva Veda vi.92, 2; viii.7, 28 (*Yamasya padbiĆa*); id., vii.112, 2; viii.7, 28 (*mtryupâçah*). Cf. I. Scheftelowitz, Schlingen- und Netzmotiv (1912), 6; M. Eliade Images et Symboles (1952), 132 ff.

3. Yasna 53.8; Vendidad 5.8 (*mərəithyaosh*).

4. Alma Rišaia Zuṭa (Drower Coll. 48), 317 (*giṭria usqupata d-muta*).

5. Beowulf, 1936 ff.

6. Genesis-Exodus, 2716.

7. Shakespeare, Cymbeline, I.ii.

8. Grimm-Stallybrass, TM 845 ff., 1557.

9. Sophocles, Ajax 675 f.

10. Plato, Timaeus 71E.

11. Orphic Hymns, 35.85; cf. R. B. Onians, Origin of European Ideas about the Body, etc. (1951), 422, n.5.

12. Ennius, Ann. 5, Vaal. (*somno levi placidoque revinctus*).

13. TB, Ber. 60b (*heblê šênah*).
14. Cf. S. Eitrem, Papyri Osloenses, i (1925), 71; A. Deissmann, Light from the Ancient East (1911), 306 f.; M. Lidzbarski, Ephemeris, i (1902), 31.

254 Riding a cherub

1. F. Thureau Dangin, in RA 24 (1927), 199–202.
2. T. Fish, in BJRL 31 (1948), 162–71; S. Langdon, Semitic Mythology (1931), 115 f.
3. Grimm-Stallybrass, TM 633.
4. Somadeva 2.102.
5. T. H. Gaster, Thespis[2], 168 f.; Stith Thompson, MI, A 284.2.
6. Examples are collected in MAOG xi/1–2.69.
7. R. C. Thompson, in AAA 20.8, 8 (Ninlil).
8. H. Güterbock, in JCS 6 (1952), 34.
9. Iliad 24.341–45; Odyssey 1.97; 5.45–49.
10. H. P. L'Orage, Symbols of Cosmic Kingship in the Ancient World (1953), 49–51.

255 The heavenly sieve

1. S. Feigin, in JNES 9 (1953), 40 ff.—This interpretation is anticipated in TB Ta‹canith 9b (cf. Rashi in loc.).
2. S. C. Macpherson, Memorials of Service in India (1865), 89, 355.
3. Aristophanes, Clouds 367. Cf. also: Plautus, Pseudol. 1.1.100; Pliny, HN xxviii.2 (*imbrem in cribro*).
4. W. W. Hyde, Greek Religion and Its Survivals (1923), 225, n.16.
5. J. Batchelor, The Ainu and Their Folklore (1901), 333.
6. A. Kuhn, Westfalische Sagen, Gebräuche und Märchen (1859), i.18, 203; J. Grimm, DM[4], 231.—In Grimms' Märchen, #178, Master Pfriem sees people in heaven pouring water in a tub full of holes; cf. Stith Thompson, MI, F 171.6.2; H 1023.2; Q 512.1.—O. Gruppe, Griech. Mythologie (1906), 831, suggests that a rain-making rite underlies the myth relating that the daughters of Danaos were compelled to pour water into a perforated jar in the underworld as a punishment for killing their husbands, the sons of Aegyptos. On this myth, see further: Campbell Bonner, in Harvard Studies xxiii.1291 ff.
7. J. G. Frazer, GB i.285.
8. E. Kutscher, in Leshonenu 21 (1956), 252 [Hebrew].

257 Walking round the altar

1. On the subject in general, see: M. Haberlandt, in Correspondenzblatt der. Gesell. für Anthropologie, Ethnologie und Urgeschichte, 21.9; A. Hillebrand, in Festschrift d. schles. Gesell. für Volkskunde (1911), 1 ff.; S. Eitrem, Opferritus und Voropfer der Griechen und Römer (1915), 6–75; F. Nötscher, "Die Angesicht Gottes schauen" nach biblischer und babylonischer Auffassung (1924), 66–67, n.l.; W. Upright, in ET 22 (1911), 563 ff.; F. Heiler, Das Gebet (1918), 176.
2. Cf. Jubilees 16:31; cf. A. J. Wensinck, in Theol. Tidjsk. 1919.103 f.
3. G. Furlani, Rel. bab. e ass. (1928), ii.286. So too in Sabaean: G. Ryckmans, in Le Muséon 71 (1958), 127 f.
4. CIS iv.19, 392, 395; Glaser 425, 1402; Jaussen, Himyar. 120; Mittwoch-Mordtmann, 24.1. Cf. M. Höffner and N. Rhodokanakis, in WZKM 1936.216 ff.
5. J. Wellhausen, Reste d. arab. Heidentums[2] (1897), 110 ff.; W. Robertson Smith, The Religion of the Semites[3] (1927), 340. Full description in H. St. John Philby, A Pilgrim in Arabia (1946).—For a Classical parallel, cf. Ovid, Met. vii.257 f.: Sparsis Medea capillis / Bacchantum ritu flagrantes circuit aras.

258 A Canaanite psalm?

1. Cf. S. A. Pallis, The Babylonian Akitu Festival (1926), 221 f., 249–306.
2. Cf. S. Langdon, The Epic of Creation (1923), 16 ff. For the earlier Sumerian myths, cf, T. Jacobsen, in JNES 5 (1946), 146–47; S. N. Kramer, Sumerian Mythology (1944), 82 ff.
3. See: T. H. Gaster, Thespis[2] (1961), 245–67; A. Goetze, in ANET 125 f. The original texts are: KBo III.7, i.9–27; KUB VII.v.6–24; KBo III.7, iii.4–33. The god is aided by the mortal hero, Hupasiyas.
4. KBo III.7, col. iv.
5. III AB, A; III AB; cf. especially II AB vi.44 ff.
6. Gaster, op. cit. 114–244.
7. Ib. 443.
8. III AB, A. The antagonist is there called Prince Sea (*Zbl Ym*) and Lord Stream (*Tpṭ Nhr*); cf. Hab. 3:8.
9. Enuma Elish vi.32, 56.
10. T. H. Gaster, in Folk-Lore 1933, 382, n.13; id., Thespis[2], 443–46; H. L. Ginsberg, The Ugaritic Texts (1936), 129–31 [Hebrew].
11. Note the *threefold* invocation—a common liturgical device.
12. Cf. vi.47, 51, etc.
13. II AB vi.44. "Threescore and ten" is, of course, merely a round number, signifying multitude.
14. See above, §32.
15. Pss. 66:2; 79:9; I Chron. 16:29.
16. Cf. vi.98–99, 142, 144; vii.118, 120, 124–25.
17. Note that in the Ugaritic texts the verb *k-b-d*, "pay homage," is a regular complement of *q-l*, "fall," and (*h*)*šthwy*, "prostrate oneself"; cf. I AB i.37–38; II AB iv.25–26, etc. The rendering to Yahweh of "the glory (*kabôd*) of his name," accomplished as it is by prostration, might therefore be a formal act of homage consisting in a ceremonial recitation of his honorific names and titles; cf. Enuma Elish vii.120: "he (Marduk) whose name his fathers glorified."
18. So also in Ps. 96:9, where the expression recurs. (Note that the traditional text's *hadrath qôdeš* means "holy *awe*," after Akkadian *adāru*, not "beauty of holiness," as commonly rendered.)
19. Concerning this god, see: T. H. Gaster, Thespis[2], 162 f.
20. II AB vii.27a–41.
21. The "voice of Baal" is mentioned again in II AB iv-v.70 and in III Aqhat 45–46.
22. The translation is, however, uncertain. Ginsberg, in ANET 135, suggests that the meaning of the clause is rather, "A yew-club swings in his right hand." This might be supported by a passage in an Egyptian magical text (Leyden Papyrus 235, recto iv.12 —v.2 = ANET 249), where it is said of Baal that he smites his enemies "with the cedar which is in his right hand."
23. See Kittel, BH[3] in loc.
24. For this expression, cf. Ps. 89:6. It corresponds to the "Assembly of the Holy Ones (*mpḫrt qdšm*)" in the inscription of Yeḥimilk of Byblos (tr. Rosenthal, ANET[2], 499). The term "holy ones" denotes the pantheon in the 8th cent. B.C. Canaanite magical plaque from Arslan Tash, and the same usage may be recognized in Ps. 16:3; Job 5:1; 15:15; Hos. 12:1 and Zech. 14:5; cf. T. H. Gaster, in Orientalia 11 (1942), 59.
25. Similarly, in CT VIII.35, i.17 Marduk is said to have established his dwelling on the waters; cf. also: Ps. 104.3.
26. Gudea Cylinder A, xii.11–13; cf. JNES 2 (1943), 118.
27. Cf. T. Jacobsen, in JNES 5 (1946), 145, n.28.

28. Lucian, De Dea Syria, 13.
29. Targum Ps.-Jonathan, Exod. 28:30; Midrash Tanḥuma, Qedošim, §10.
30. Pausanias, i.18, 7.
31. KBo III.7 (duplicates, KUB XII.66; XVII.5–6); cf. Gaster, Thespis², 251 f., 256.
32. Cf. also: Enuma Elish vi.114–15.
33. Cf. T. H. Gaster, in Folk-Lore 1933. 382, n.13.
34. Cf. particularly Ginsberg's brilliant recognition of a Canaanite grammatical form in v.6, where for the traditional text's *wa-yarqidem* we should read *wa-yarqed-ma* (or, *wa-yirqod-ma?*), with the archaic coordinative enclitic *-ma*. Other instances of this may be detected in Num. 24:17; Deut. 33:3; Isa. 35:1; Joel 1:17; Pss. 42:5; 110:3.
35. The Modern Churchman 12 (1922), 390.

260 Magic waters

1. G. R. Driver has suggested that the Heb. word *dabar*, "thing," should be vocalized *deber*, "plague," the verb being derived, not from *y-ṣ-q* "pour," but from *ṣ-w-q*, "be attached closely." The sense will then be: "A noxious plague has fastened upon him." This, however, is thinking in English, not in Hebrew, for the word *deber* really means "reverse, catastrophe" (cf. Akkadian *dab/pāru*, "thrust back"), so that a very mixed metaphor results!

261 An ancient Hebrew wedding song

1. See: T. H. Gaster, in JBL 74 (1955), 239–51; J. H. Darly, in Ir. E. Rec. 91 (1959), 249–55.—The best accounts of modern Arab wedding customs are: H. Granquist, Marriage Customs in a Palestinian Village (1931–33); W. Rothstein, "Moslemische Hochzeitsgebräuche bei Jerusalem," in Palästinajahrbuch 6 (1910); E. W. Lane, Manners and Customs of the Modern Egyptians, ch. vi.
2. The bridal couple has been identified, for instance, with David and Maacah (Abraham ibn Ezra); Solomon and Pharaoh's daughter (Kirkpatrick); Ahab and Jezebel (Hitzig); Joram and Athaliah (Delitzsch); Alexander Balas and Cleopatra, daughter of Ptolemy Philometer (Olshausen, Haupt); Aristobulus I and Salome (Duhm). These are just wild stabs.
3. See: E. Westermarck, History of Human Marriage (1925), ii.261, n.5; id., Marriage Customs in Morocco (1914), 118, 274; J. G. Wetzstein, in Zeitschr. für Ethnologie 5 (1873), 288. At Malayan weddings, bride and groom are called "sovereigns for a day" (*raja sari*): W. W. Skeat, Malay Magic (1900), 388. In Java too they are treated as royalty: G. Geertz, The Religion of Java (1960), 57. In a wedding song of the Mandaeans of Iraq and Iran the groom is hailed as "king": M. Lidzbarski, Mandäische Liturgien (1920), p. x, n.3.
4. Literally, "grace" (Heb.: *ḥēn*).
5. W. Robertson Smith, in JP 14.125; J. Wellhausen, Reste des arabischen Heidentums² (1897), 173; J. Morgenstern, Rites of Birth, Marriage, etc. among the Semites (1966), 34–35. Photographs of the ceremony appeared in Life magazine, July 12, 1954, p. 52.
6. Literally, "some god hath endowed thee with *berākah*" (RSV: "God has blessed you"). *Berākah* is a kind of magical aura: E. Westermarck, Pagan Survivals in Mohammedan Civilisation (1933), 87 ff.; J. Chalhod, in RHR 148 (1955), 68–88. For this sense of the word in O.T., see: M. Canney, in ET 39 (1928), 381–85. A good example is Isa. 65:8: "When wine is found in a cluster of grapes, men say, 'Destroy it not, for there is *berākah* in it.'" See also: J. Pedersen, Israel i–ii (1926), 198 ff.
7. Homeric Hymn to Demeter, 236 ff.
8. Apollonius Rhodius, Argonautica iv.571 f.
9. Theocritus, Id., xv.106 f.

10. Odyssey 2.12.
11. Ib., 18.193 f.
12. Ovid, Met. xv.606 f.
13. Granquist, op. cit., ii.113, 117.
14. Ib.
15. C. R. Conder, Heth and Moab (1885), 295.
16. E. Crawley, The Mystic Rose[2] (1927), ii.33 ff.; P. Sartori, Sitte und Brauch (1910–14), i.114; E. Westermarck, History, ii.449 ff.
17. Granquist, op. cit., ii.60.
18. Song of Songs 3:7–8.
19. Granquist, op. cit., ii.85 ff.; Rothstein, op. cit., 121, 135; J. A. Jaussen, Coutumes des arabes au pays de Moab (1908), 55.
20. R. Chambers, The Book of Days (1886), i.721.
21. I Abrahams, Jewish Life in the Middle Ages[2] (1927), 267.
22. Notes and Queries VI/ii (1880), 245.
23. The expression recurs in Ps. 21:6 in the specific sense of *insignia and regalia*.
24. Granquist, op. cit., ii.95 ff.
25. Ib., i.124; ii.78; Lane, op. cit. (Minerva Library ed., 1891), 156; H. N. Hutchinson, Marriage Customs of Many Lands (1897), 66.
26. Cf. F. Rosenthal, in HUCA 33 (1950–51), 411 ff. The adjective *ṣadîq* bears this sense in Arabic, and it may be recognized in O.T. in such passages as Pss. 112:4; 116:5.
27. For the traditional text's $w^{e\text{-}c}anwah\ ṣedeq$, which is barely translatable, read, by mere redivision of the consonants, $w^{e\text{-}c}anî\ haṣdeq$ (Melville Scott). The expression recurs in Ps. 82:3; cf. also: Ps. 72:2–4.
28. Crawley, op. cit., ii.37 f.
29. H. Oldenberg, Die Religion des Veda (1894), 271.
30. Granquist, op. cit., ii.90, n.1; Sartori, op. cit., i.92.
31. C. Seligman, Egypt and Negro Africa (1934), 15–18, 59.
32. J. Roscoe, The Bakitara (1912), 134.
33. The traditional text reads literally, *Thy throne God for ever.* This is a famous puzzle. The usual solution is to render, *Thy throne is as God is—everlasting,* or to assume that the word *God* has been substituted for an original YHWH (Yahweh), which was itself a corruption of the similar *yhyh*, "shall be." This, however, overlooks the parallelism of such phrases as "some god (*elohim*) has endowed thee with $b^{e}rākah$" in v. 3, and "some god (*elohim*) has anointed thee," in v. 8, whence it is apparent that *God* (*elohim*) is here likewise the subject of the clause and that a verb describing his action has dropped out. Such passages as I Sam. 13:13; II Sam. 7:12, Isa. 9:6, and I Chron. 17:11, as well as a parallel Akkadian formula of salutation (cited above in the text) show that the missing word was *hêkîn*, "has set firm," as suggested long ago by Street (1790) and Olshausen (1853).
34. The *festive oil* is mentioned also in Isa. 61:3.
35. R. H. Pfeiffer, State Letters of Assyria (1935), #267.3–6.
36. R. F. Harper, Assyrian and Babylonian Letters belonging to the Kouyunjik Collections of the British Museum (1902), #330.3–6.
37. RSV: *From ivory palaces stringed instruments make thee glad; daughters of kings are among your ladies of honor; at your right hand stands the queen in gold of Ophir.* In my opinion, this rendering is impossible. First, the word translated "stringed instruments" (in any case an unusual form) could mean only "strings," and the assumed synechdoche is, at least to my ears, too harsh to be probable. Second, the word rendered "queen" means properly "concubine," and so to describe the bride herself would be, to put it mildly, indelicate! I would therefore make sense by simply deleting the word

rendered "stringed instruments" (viz., *mînî*), as vertical dittography from *li-y^eMINekā* in the line below.—The reference to the ivory halls is admirably illustrated by Euripides, Iphigenia in Aulis 581 f., where Helen is said to have been abducted by Paris "from ivory halls."

38. Granquist has pointed out that such last-minute exhortations and admonitions are a standard element of Arab wedding ceremonies at the present day.

39. Literally, "daughter of Tyre." Tyre was the proverbial "affluent society" of the Ancient Near East; cf. Ezek. 26–27. The implication—allowing for the anachronism—is, so to speak, "Yourself a daughter of Croesus, you have been courted by millionaires!"

40. For the tradtional text's *panāyik yeḥallū*, "now come courting thee," I read, in the past tense, *panāyki ḥillū*.

41. Granquist, op. cit., ii.118, n.11; Rothstein, op. cit., 122, n.2; G. Dalman, Palästinischer Diwan (1908), 254. This is believed to be the background of Song of Songs 7:1 f., *How fair are thy feet in sandals, O prince's daughter*, etc.

42. For the traditional text's *kôl k^ebūdah bath-melek p^enîmah* (KJV: The king's daughter is all glorious within) read *k^elê k^ebôdah bath-melek p^enînîm*. The expression *k^elê kabôd* is matched by *k^elê tiphēreth* (glorious ornaments)—likewise associated with broidery—in Ezek. 16:17; cf. also Isa. 61:10. The emendation *p^enînîm* is due to Krochmal.

43. The word *li-r^eqāmôth* at the beginning of v. 14 really belongs at the end of v. 13.

44. Granquist, op. cit., ii.42.

45. P. Haupt, The Book of Canticles (1912), 31 (on Song of Songs 1:9).

46. So with the Greek Version; the traditional text reads, I *will keep your name in remembrance*.

47. II Krt ii.16 ff. Birth of daughters is also invoked: ib., iii.5 ff.

48. Pfeiffer, op. cit., #125.14–18.

49. Odyssey 7.148–50.

262   Mountains in midsea

1. The Heb. word *b^e-hāmîr* requires no emendation. It is here to be connected with Arabic *m-r-m-r*, "be agitated," used especially of an embroiled sea.

2. Finmor Jónsson, Der norsk-islandike Skaldedighting, BI 79.—On such stylized exaggerations in general, see: S. Eitrem, Papyri Osloenses i (1925), 69.

263   The far reaches of the North

1. T. H. Gaster, Thespis[2], 181 f., 452. Cf. also: B. Alfrink, in Biblica 14 (1933), 60 f.; C. Virolleaud, in CRAIBL 1937.67–68; J. Morgenstern, in HUCA 16 (1941), 65; H. Dunbar, in Antiquity 3 (1924), 408–13.

2. I AB i.57, vi.12, vii.5; IV AB iii.31; V AB i.21, etc. (*ṣrrt Ṣpn*).

3. P. Jensen, Die Kosmologie der Babylonier (1890), 23; A. Jeremias, The Old Testament in the Light of the Ancient East (1911), i.20; F. Delitzsch, Wo lag das Paradies? (1881), 117; Krappe, in JA 1897.86 ff.

4. Lassen, in ZKM 2 (1839), 62 ff.

5. A. Smythe Palmer, Jacob at Bethel (1899), 17 ff.

6. D. G. Brinton, Myths of the New World[3] (1905), 95.

7. ERE xii.485[b], n.3.

8. R. Merker, Die Masai (1904), 197, 199.

9. K. Schwenk, Die Mythologie der Slawen (1853), 386.

10. Pseudo-Callisthenes, ii.32.

11. Gaster, loc. cit.

12. I. Scheftelowitz, Die altpersische Religion und das Judentum (1920), 59.

13. W. M. Brandt, Die mandäische Religion (1889), 67 ff.

14. Satapatha Brahmana i.2, 4, 10; xii.5, 1, 11, etc.
15. O. Gruppe, Griechische Mythologie (1906), 815 ff.
16. Ziyyuni 48d; Jerahmeel i.17 (p. 6, ed. M. Gaster).
17. L. Spence, The Mythologies of Mexico and Peru (1907), 24.
18. G. Flügel, Mani (1862), 101.
19. Pap. Bib. Nat. 269; Pap. Leyden, Wesselski, col. xviii.27.
20. Plutarch, De Iside et Osiride 21.
21. T. H. Gaster, Customs and Folkways of Jewish Life (1965), 61.

264 Death as a shepherd

1. On the theme in general, see: S. J. Lessing, De Mortis apud veteres figura (Diss., Bonn 1866); S. G. F. Brandon, in BJRL 43 (1961), 317–35.—On specifically *Greek* conceptions of Death, see: C. Robert, "Thanatos," in XXXIX Berl Winckelmanns Progr. Arch. März., 170, 175 ff.; E. Gaetani-Lovatelli, Thanatos (1888); Preller-Robert, Griech. Mythologie[4] (1894), i.842 f.

2. Apollodorus, Bib. ii.5, 10; vi.12, 7; see: J. H. Croon, The Herdsman of the Dead (Diss., Utrecht 1952).

3. Plato, Phaedo 62B (*en phrourâ*); cf. Espinas, in Archiv für Ges. der Philosophie 8.452. However, Cicero (Cat. Maj. 73) interpreted Plato's expression to mean simply that souls are "in the keeping of God," and this interpretation is followed by E. Rohde, Psyche[7] (1921), iii.161, n.2.—See also: Euxitheos (a Pythagorean), in Athenaeus, iv.137.

265 Bottled tears

1. S. G. Wilson, Persian Life and Customs[2] (1896), 190 ff.; J. Perkins, A Residence of Eight Years in Persia among the Nestorian Christians (1843), 209; J. Morier, quoted by E. W. Rice, Orientalisms in Bible Lands (1910), 124.

2. J. A. E. Köhler, Volksbrauch . . . im Voigtlande (1867), 492; W. von Schulenburg, Wendisches Volksthum (1882), 280.—The custom was known also in Switzerland: F. Stählin, Die Schweiz in römisch. Zeit (1927), 361.

3. Niederdeutsch. Zs. für Volkskunde 7 (1932), 47.

4. W. Ebers, in Abh. Bay. Akad. Wiss. 1 Kl. 20/i.140 ff.; cf. R. B. Onians, Origins of European Thought about the Body, etc. (1951), 201 f., 283.

5. A. C. Kruijt, in ERE vii.234[a].

6. On tears as generative, cf. Onians, op. cit., 205; Proclus, fr. 354, in Orphicorum Fragmenta, ed. Kern; Pap. Leyden iv.1.395.

7. E. Rohde, Psyche[7] (1921), i.223, n.2; Levi, in Philologus 63.55; A. Wright, English Folklore (1928), 21.

8. Grimm, Märchen #109; Bolte-Polivka, iii.483 ff.; W. Wackernagel, Kl. Schriften (1872–74), ii.400 ff.; A. Wirth, Beiträge zur Volkskunde von Anhalt (Dessau, s.a.), ii/3.67.

266 Yahweh's processional

Literature: T. H. Gaster, Thespis[1] (1950), 87–97; W. F. Albright, in HUCA 23 (1951), 1–39; S. Mowinckel, Der 68te Psalm (1953); P. Haupt, in AJSL 23 (1901), 220–40; R. Podechard, in RB 54 (1947), 502–20; R. Tournay, ib., 51 (1942), 227–45; F. C. Fensham, in JNES 19 (1960), 292–93.

(a)

1. Cf. S. A. Pallis, The Babylonian Akitu Festival (1926). Good popular accounts are: H. Zimmern, AO 25/iii; C. J. Gadd in S. H. Hooke's Myth and Ritual (1933),

47-58.—The procession of the gods is described in the text published by T. G. Pinches in PSBA 30 (1908), 62.—The Hittite material will be found in KBo III.7; cf. T. H. Gaster, Thespis[2], 245–67.

2. Gaster, op. cit., 114–244.
3. Reading with Torczyner (Tur-Sinai), *mah norā'ū* for the obscure *minnēhū rā'ū* of the traditional text.
4. Literally, "arises," but this is also a military term; cf. Num. 10:35; Amos 7:9; Ob 1, etc.
5. Others render, "Raise a song," but this meaning of the word is not well attested, and the context surely supports the normal translation.
6. III AB iii.11, 18; I*AB ii.7; III AB, A 8, 29, 33; IV AB i.7; iii.22.
7. IV R 33*, 21*d*, 22*b*; cf. B. Landsberger, Kultische Kalendar (1915), 116 f.; L. Dürr, Ursprung und Ausbau der israelit.-jüdischen Heilandserwartung (1925), 141.
8. Athenaeus, 639–640A (Crete, Troezen, Thessaly); Schol. on Demosthenes 22.68; 614.23 (Athens); Ephorus, cited by Athenaeus, 263F (Cydonia). See fully: Headlam-Knox, Herodas (1922), 266 f.
9. Livy, v. 13; cf. also: Heliodorus, Aeth. viii.7.
10. Matt. 27:15.
11. II AB vi.68 (*Bᵉl yᶜdn ᶜdn mṭrh*).
12. Enuma Elish vii. 21 (*mukin hêgalli*).
13. Gaster, op. cit., 261–62.
14. II AB iv.19, v.85; I*AB i.11; ᶜnt iv.82, etc.
15. Reading, with most modern scholars, *bā' mi-Sinai* for the *bam Sinai* of the traditional text.
16. Cf. E. Behrens, Assyrisch-bab. Briefe kultischen Inhalts aus der Sargonidenzeit (1906), 31–32; Pallis, op. cit., 202 ff.
17. Nos. 145, 183, 352, ed. Wiseman; cf. also *šnnm* as a military term in the Ugaritic text, Krt A ii.91.
18. Cf. A. R. Schulman, Military Rank, Title and Organization of the Egyptian New Kingdom (1962), 96 ff.
19. For the traditional text's *ᶜalêhā la-mārôm šūbah*, which is barely translatable, I read *ᶜaleh la-mārôm šᵃbeh*, in accordance with the passage in our psalm.
20. See above, n.14.
21. Heb.: *tôṣā'ôth;* cf. Akkadian *ušêṣi* and Aramaic cognate, meaning "bring to ruin."
22. VAT 9555.10–11.
23. I*AB i.1. This is the Akkadian *bašmu*, "serpent." The identification is due to S. Feigin, *Mi-sitrê he-ᶜavar* (1943), 407.
24. Viz. *'ašbm*, confused with *'ašîb;* cf. S. E. Lowenstamm, in IEJ 9 (1959), 260 f.; J. L. McKenzie, in Theological Studies 2 (1950), 275–82; M. Dahood, in RB 43 (1962), 365.
25. I.e., *'ašb* for *'ašîb*.
26. III AB, B 29–30.
27. III AB, A 11 ff.; Gaster, op. cit., 163 ff.
28. Enuma Elish iv.130.
29. "Holy beings" (*qdšm*) is a common name for the gods in general both in Canaanite-Phoenician texts and vestigially also in O.T.: see T. H. Gaster, in Orientalia 11 (1942), 59 f.
30. Enuma Elish vi.70 ff.
31. Gaster, op. cit., 266.
32. II AB vi.39 ff.; Gaster, op. cit., 109 f.

(b) Yellow garments

33. Heb. *yᵉraqraq ḥārūṣ*, sometimes rendered "*greenish* gold"; but the word *w-r-q* is used of gold in S. Arabian, and Ugaritic has the comparable expression *yrq ḥrṣ* (Krt A 138). Strictly speaking, *yrq*, like Greek *chlôros*, oscillates between yellow and green.
34. A. Sprenger, Muhammad (1851), iii.63; cf. Muᶜallaqat, Tarafa 49; G. Jacob, Studien in arabischen Dichtern ii (1894), 90.
35. W. W. Skeat, Malay Magic (1900), 51.
36. Acts of Thomas 5.11; cf. M. R. James, The Apocryphal NT (1924), 411.
37. Aeschylus, Agamemnon 224 f.
38. Id., Persae 662.
39. Kirby Smith, on Tibullus i.7.46.
40. Cf. Apuleius, Met. viii.27.
41. W. Crooke, The Popular Religion and Folklore of Northern India (1896), ii.20, 26; E. Crawley, in ERE v.47.
42. Lucan, Phars. iii.361.
43. Catullus, lxi.9–10; Tibullus, i.7.46; Ovid, Met x.1. Cf. also: Vergil, Aen. ix.614 (Trojan); Seneca, Oed. 421; Pliny, HN xxi.46; Clem. Alex., Paidag. ii.10.
44. Zs. für Volkskunde 23 (1913), 262 f.
45. Crawley, loc. cit.
46. Ib.
47. Zs. für Volkskunde 23 (1913), 262 f.
48. Crawley, loc. cit.
49. G. Pitré, quoted by T. Ellworthy, in ERE v.614ᵃ.
50. J. Grimm, Wörterbuch (1854), iv/i.2883; Goethe, Farbenlehre, §771.—In France, the doors of traitors used to be daubed with yellow paint: St. Swithin, in Notes and Queries VI/8 (1883), 172.
51. T. F. Thiselton Dyer, Domestic Folklore² (s.a.), 75.
52. Shakespeare, The Merry Wives of Windsor, I.iv.

267 The Book of Fate

1. P. Jensen, KB VI/i (1900), 136 f.; J. A. Craig, Assyrian and Babylonian Religious Texts (1895–97), i.5 ff.; ii.ix.
2. H. Zimmern and H. Winckler, KAT³ (1903), 401; A. Jeremias, Babylonisches im Neuen Testament (1905), 69–73.
3. J. Friedrich, in JCS 1 (1947), 283 f.; cf. also: T. H. Gaster, Thespis², 288.
4. A. Klausen, in Zs. für deutsch. Alt. 1840.226.
5. Grimm-Stallybrass, TM 406.
6. Tertullian, De anima c.39.
7. Some details of this passage are still not quite clear, and various emendations of the text have been proposed. The general sense, however, is sufficiently apparent, and that is all that here concerns us.
8. M. Lidzbarski, Ephemeris für semitische Epigraphik (1902–15), i.164 ff.

268 The combat against the Dragon

1. Cf. J. L. McKenzie, in Theological Studies 2 (1950), 275–82.

269 Demon shafts

1. RS 15.134; C. Virolleaud, in CRAIBL 1952.30 (*bᶜl ḥẓ Ršp*).
2. G. A. Cooke, A Text-book of North Semitic Inscriptions (1903), 56 f.
3. Song of Songs 8:6. So too in Ugaritic: Virolleaud, in CRAIBL 1952.62 (*ktᶜrbn ršpm bt mlk*). Also in Egyptian: Edgerton-Wilson, Historical Records of Ramses III,

Medinet Habu i–ii.24 (*snnw shmty.w mi' Ršp*). A "land of Reshephs" (*'rṣ ršpm*) is mentioned in an inscription of the 4th cent. B.C. found near Sidon: Cooke, op. cit., 401.

271 The bird sanctuary

1. Herodotus, i.157–59.
2. Aelian, Var. Hist. v.17.
3. Lucian, De dea Syria, 54.
4. Clement of Alexandria, Protrept. iv.52.
5. B. Spencer and F. J. Gillen, The Native Tribes of Central Australia (1899), 134 ff.
[5a. Book of the Dead 125; tr. J. A. Wilson, in ANET 34. Cf. C. Maystre, Les declarations d'innocence (1937), A.29.]
[5b. Artemidorus, Oneirocrit. 16.]
[5c. P. Sartori, Sitte und Brauch (1910–14), ii.13, n.4.]
[5d. Archiv für Russland 1 (1848), 628.]
[5e. J. Harland and T. Wilkinson, Lancashire Legends, etc. (1873), 143.]

272 The earthly and heavenly Zion

1. II AB iv–v.
2. M. Eliade, Traité d'histoire des religions (1949), 324 f.; T. H. Gaster, Thespis[2], ch. 1; id., in Numen 1 (1954), 195.—Egypt was called "the replica of heaven": Ps.-Apuleius, in Höpfner, Fontes rel. aegypt. 620. The Egyptians spoke of "two heavens" corresponding to the two lands of Egypt: Pyr. Texts 406*b*, 541*c*; S. Morenz, Aeg. Religion (1960), 47. The shrine of a god was called "heaven": J. Cerný, in JEA 34 (1948), 120.
3. Cf. B. Meissner, Babylonien and Assyrien ii (1925), 107, 110, 409 f.; H. Winckler, Babyl. Geisteskultur (1919), 93 f.
4. Test. XII Patr., Dan 5; II Baruch 59:4; Syr. Apoc. Baruch 4:3 ff.; IV Ezra 40:49; cf. G. H. Box, Liber Esdrae (1912), 198 f.; TB Ta^canith 5a, Hagigah 121; L. Ginzberg, Legends of the Jews, v.292. Cf. also: Matt. 5:35; Heb. 8:5; 11:10, 16; 12:22; 13.14.
5. J. Duyvendak, in Proc. Congress Hist. of Religions 7 (1951), 137.
6. F. Thureau Dangin, Die sumerischen und akkadischen Königsinschriften (1907), #140. 19 f.
7. Ḥammurapi, Code iii.29 ff.
8. KARI #164.38 ff.
9. Exod. 25:9, 40.
10. A. Moret, Du caractère religieux de la royauté pharaonique (1902), 13.
11. M. Jastrow, Religion Babyloniens und Assyriens (1905–12), i.542; V. Scheil, in ZA 10.291, 3–4.
12. J. A. Craig, Assyrian and Babylonian Religious Texts (1895–97), i. Pl. 7–8.4.
13. I. A. Matthews, in JPOS 15 (1935), 351; J. Pedersen, Israel, iii–iv (1940), 263, 639.
14. Gen. 14:18; Sujin Inscription (c. 750 B.C.) = ANET[2], 504; Sanchuniathon, apud Eusebius, PE i.6.
15. See above, §180.

273 The throne founded on righteousness

1. Brunner, in VT 8 (1958), 426 ff.; S. Morenz, Aegyptische Religion (1960), 120.

274 The winged soul

1. Cf. G. Weicker, Der Seelenvogel in der alten Literatur und Kunst (1902); O. Waser, in ARW 16 (1913), 337 ff.; V. Aptowitzer, Die Seele als Vogel (1925); O. Dähnhardt, Natursagen (1907–12), iii.476 f.; A. B. Cook, Zeus, ii (1925), 524,

697n., 1132; O. Gruppe, Griechische Mythologie (1906), 1502, n.1; 1618, n.1; A. de Gubernatis, Die Thiere in indogerm. Mythen (1874), 469 ff.; I. Scheftelowitz, Altpal. Bauernglaube (1925), 12 ff.; E. S. McCartney, in Papers of the Michigan Acad. of Science, Arts and Letters 16 (1932), 162 ff.; A. H. Krappe, Balor with the Evil Eye (1927), 95 ff.; Frazer-Gaster, NGB §151 (and Additional Note).

2. H. Kees, Totenglauben und Jenseitsvorstellungen der alten Aegypter (1926), 57–66; L. Klebs, in ZÄS 61 (1926), 104–8; W. Spiegelberg, in OLz 29 (1926), 393–95.

3. Tale of the Two Brothers, xix.3; cf. H. Grapow, Die bildlichen Ausdrücke des Aegyptischen (1924), 93 f.

4. Atharva Veda iv.34, 4; cf. H. Oldenberg, Religion des Veda (1894), 563.

5. Cf. O. Falsirol, in SMSR 1951–52.102–16; McCartney, op. cit., 162 ff.

6. E. Rohde, Psyche[7] (1921), i.244; O. Jahn, Archaeologische Beitraege (1847), 128 ff.—When Alexander died, an eagle suddenly appeared, representing his soul ascending to heaven: Ps.-Callisthenes, iii.33. Similarly, when Peregrinus was cast on the pyre, an eagle rose from it, crying, "I have left the earth, and am going to Olympus": Lucian, Peregr. 39.

7. G. Jacob, Das Leben der vorislamischen Beduinen (1895), 122, n.2, 143, citing Mas^cudi, *Muruj edh-dhahab* iii.311 ff.; Diwan der Hudhaliten, #141.5; ^cOrwa b. al-Ward iii.3–4; cf. also: ZDMG 12 (1858), 63.

8. I. Goldziher, in Globus 83.301.

9. E. S. Drower, The Canonical Prayerbook of the Mandaeans (1959), #73 (p. 62), lines 12, 27; (p. 63), lines 3, 10.

10. Inst. Arch. f. Ethnologie, 11.86 f.

11. H. Tonkes, Volkskunde von Bali (1888), 29; H. Ling Roth, Natives of Sarawak (1896), i.224.

12. W. Wundt, Elements of Folk Psychology, tr. Schaub[2] (1916), 82.

13. Grimm-Stallybrass, TM 828 f.; F. Nork, in Das Kloster xii (1845), 271; R. Kühnau, in Mitt. d. sachs. Ges. f. Volkskunde, Heft 16 (1906), 96 f.

14. K. Schwenk, Die Mythologie der Slawen (1853), 274 f.

15. The Gentleman's Magazine 92 (1822), pt. i.311; Byron, Don Juan, stanza 94; Notes and Queries VI/vi (1882), 269, 452 f.; Thos. Hardy, "The Superstitious Man's Story," in Life's Little Ironies.—In Cornwall, cloughs are protected because the soul of King Arthur is said to have migrated into one. Similarly, stormy petrels ("Mother Carey's chickens") are protected by sailors because they are believed to be the souls of dead mariners: E. Brewer, Dictionary of Phrase and Fable, s.v. Bird.—Other examples—not all of them convincing—are assembled by L. C. Wimberly, Folklore of the English and Scottish Ballads[2] (1959), 44 ff.

16. T. G. Thiselton Dyer, English Folklore (1880), 134 (Yorkshire).

17. T. Keightley, Fairy Mythology (1854), 436.—So too in Armenia, souls are thought to fly near graves in the form of doves: M. Abeghian, Der armen. Volksaberglaube (1899), 10.

18. Letter to the Smyrneans, 16.

19. Prudentius, Perist., #3.

20. Gregory of Tours, Dial. iv.10 (Migne, PL 77, col. 386).

21. Migne, PL 66, col. 196.

275 A coven of demons

1. See on this psalm: W. O. E. Oesterley, in The Expositor, 1907.132–51; Charbel, in REB 17 (1957), 281–300; A. Caquot, in Semitica 6 (1956), 281–300.—In Jewish tradition this psalm is recited at the expiration of the sabbath, when the demons who have been confined during the day of rest are again let loose. It is likewise recited at a funeral—originally to exorcize the princes of darkness both from the deceased and

from the mourners: T. H. Gaster, Festivals of the Jewish Year (1953), 279 f.—Conversely, in a sixteenth century German grimoire, it forms part of a magical ritual for *invoking* spirits: Wahrafter Jesuiten Höllenzwang, reprinted in J. Scheible's Das Kloster v (1847), 110.

2. E. B. Tylor, Primitive Culture, i.275 f.; J. Grimm, DM[4], 1193; A. Wuttke, Der deutsche Volksaberglaube (1869), 122; J. Brand, Popular Antiquities of Great Britain (1882–83), iii.279.

3. KARL ii.58, r.2 (*mušitu puluḫtu ša li-la-a-ti*).

4. J. Backhouse, A Narrative of a Visit to the Australian Colonies (1843), 555.

5. De Rochefort, Histoire naturelle et morale des Iles Antilles[2] (1665), 419.

6. F. Mason, The Karens (1842), 211.

7. M. Höfler, in ARW 2 (1899), 127 f.; S. Eitrem, Papyri Osloenses (1925), 53 f.; Grimm-Stallybrass, TM 23, 443, 846, 1182, 1244 f.

8. Job 6:4.

9. Iliad 1.44. Sudden death was represented by the Greeks as a visitation by painless arrows, shot at men by Apollo, and at women by Artemis: Odyssey 3.280; 5.124; 11.173, 199; 15.140.

10. See above, §**269**.

11. A. B. Keith, Indian Mythology (1917), 125, 225.

12. Notes and Queries I/iv (1851), 500.—The idea appears in the famous Song in Time of Plague by Thomas Nashe (1567–1601): *Fond are life's lustful joys./Death proves them all but toys./None from his darts can fly.*

13. J. A. MacCulloch, Eddic Mythology (1930), 192, 222.

14. K. 3476, obv. 14; S. A. Pallis, The Babylonian Akitu Festival (1926), 215.

15. P. Sartori, Sitte und Brauch (1910–14), iii.67, 68, n.2.

16. Ib., iii.157, 171.

17. J. A. Montgomery, Aramaic Incantation Texts from Nippur (1913), #2.4–5.

18. Sitzb. Berl. Akad. 1908.401 (cited by Montgomery).

19. See: K. Haberlandt, in Zs. für Völkerpsychologie 13 (1882), 310–24; L. Laistner, Das Rätsel der Sphinx (1882), i.1 ff., 310 ff.; W. Mannhardt, Antike Wald- und Feldkulte (1875–77), ii.8, 37, 114, 135; A. H. Krappe, La genèse des mythes (1938), 163 f.; M. Grünbaum, Gesammelte Aufsätze (1901), 96 ff.; O. Crusius, in Philologus 50.70 ff.; B. Caillois, in RHR 115 (1937), 142–73, 116 (1938), 54–63; S. Landersdorfer, in BZ 18 (1929), 294 ff.; J. de Fraine, in Biblica 40 (1959), 372–83; W. H. Worrel, in JAOS 38 (1918), 160–66; W. H. Roscher, in ARW 1 (1898), 76 ff.; O. Gruppe, Griechische Mythologie (1906), 759; K. Schwenck, Die Mythologie der Slawen (1853), 319; T. H. Gaster, in Folk-Lore 1938. 361–63.

20. Theocritus, Id., i.15 ff. Cf. also Lucian, Philos. 22, where the midday spirit is identified with Artemis or Hecate, just as Christian authors sometimes call it Diana: C. A. Lobeck, Aglaophamus (1829), 1092. In Schol. ad Aristoph., Frogs 239 it is equated with Empusa, the child-stealing witch.

21. Pliny, HN xviii.330.

22. J. C. Lawson, Modern Greek Folklore (1910), 79, 139, 143, 148, 150, 160, 164, 168, 170, 172; B. Schmidt, Das Volksleben der Neugriechen (1871), 94 ff.

23. T. Trede, Das Heidentum in der römischen Kirche (1889–91), iv.362.

24. L. Korth, Mittagsgespenster (Cologne 1915); Grimm, DM[4], 342.

25. J. V. Grohmann, Aberglauben und Gebräuche aus Böhmen und Mähren (1864), 108, 111, 125; Grimm, op. cit., ii.778, n.2; B. Caillois, in Revue des études slaves 16 (1936), 18–37; A. Strausz, Die Bulgaren (1898), 152; W. R. S. Ralston, Songs of the Russian People[2] (1872), 147; A.H. Wratislaw, Sixty Folk-tales from exclusively Slavonic Sources (1889), 45; Mitt. d. schles, Ges. für Volkskunde 1 (1894), 6; Am Urquell 3 (1892), 202.

26. K. Liebrecht, Zur Volkskunde (1879), 46 f.
27. Anatole France, Vie de Jeanne d'Arc, in Oeuvres complètes xvi.250 (as cited by Krappe, loc. cit.).
28. Cf. Akkadian *dab/pāru*, "thrust back"; cf. also: Caquot, loc. cit.

276 From Canaanite hymn to Israelite psalm

1. The Modern Churchman 12 (1922), 390.
2. Cf. T. H. Gaster, Thespis², 443.
3. III AB, B 10 (*tqh mlk ᶜlmk*); Thespis², 162.
4. II AB iv–v; Thespis², 185 ff.
5. II AB iv.68 (Thespis², 185); ib., v–vi (Thespis², 195 f.).
6. Thespis², 137–49.
7. Enuma Elish vii.78–79.
8. KBo III.7; KUB xii.66; xvii.5–6; Thespis², 256 ff.

277 Renewing youth like the eagle

1. T. H. White, The Bestiary (1960), s.v. Aquila; cf. S. Bochart, Hierozoicon (1692), II.ii, 1.
2. Terence, Heauton Timoroumenos iii.2, 10 f.

278 Heaven as a garment

1. R. Eisler, Weltmantel und Himmelszelt (1910).
2. B. Meissner, in AJSL 47 (1931), 202 (*nalbaš šamê/urpiti*); but see: E. Weidner, in AfO 7 (1931), 115 f.
3. Akkadian *burrumu* (cf. Heb. *bᵉrômîm*, Ezek. 27:24): P. Jensen, Kosmologie der Babylonier (1890), 6 ff.; cf. II R 48 c–d 54: *šupuk bu-ru-me;* K 3528.38 *šiṭir bu-ru-um-mi;* KB i.174–75.
4. Pap. Paris, Suppl. Gr. 574. 2259 = R. Wuensch, Aus einem griech. Zauberpapyrus (Kleine Texte 84), 15.
5. E. Chiera, Sumerian Religious Texts (1924), iii.17, 37; cf. S. Langdon, in JRAS 1925.717 f.
6. Rig Veda i.173, 6.
7. Yasht 13.3; Yasna 30.5.
8. P. Hermann, Nordische Mythologie (1903), 259; E. H. Meyer, Mythologie der Germanen (1903), 370.
9. A. Blanc, Il sacro presso i primitivi (1945), 71.
10. Nonnus, Dionys. xi.367–577.
11. Daniel Defoe, History of the Devil (1939), 50.
12. I.e., for the traditional text's *ᶜad BiLTî šamāyim* they read *ᶜad BᵉLôT šamāyim*, lit. "until the heavens wear out."—Not impossibly, this image also underlies Isa. 51:6, which RSV renders, "The heavens will vanish like smoke, and the earth will wear out like a garment." The Heb. word rendered "vanish" is *nimlāḥū*, but this meaning is conjectural. If, however, we combine it with Arabic *malāḥa* and with the noun *mᵉlāḥîm*, "tatters," in Jer. 38:11–12, and if we emend the inapposite *kᵉ-ᶜašan*, "like smoke," to *kᵉ-ᶜaš* (error through dittography), we may obtain the sense, "The heavens will become tattered (fretted) as by a moth, and the earth wear out like a garment."
13. Heb.: *q-r-ᶜ*.
14. I*AB i.1–5; cf. T. H. Gaster, Thespis², 201 f.
15. H. P. L'Orage, Studies in the Iconography of Cosmic Kingship in the Ancient World (1953).
16. Weidner, loc. cit.

281 The kindly stork
1. Cf. S. Bochart, Hierozoicon[3] (1692), ii.327 ff.
2. Aesop, Fables, #110.
3. E.g., St. Basil, Hexaëm., hom. viii; St. Ambrose, Hexaëm., c. xvi.

284 The ritual of enthronement
1. Cf. I Maccabees 14:41.
2. R. Pfeiffer, Introduction to the O.T. (1944), 630.
3. T. H. Gaster, in JMEOS 21 (1937), 47–44. Cf. also: J. Coppens, "Les rapports du psaulme cx à l'idéologie royale israélite," in Proc. VIIIth Internat. Congress of the History of Religions (1959); G. R. Driver, "Psalm cx: its meaning and purpose," in Studies in the Bible presented to Prof. M. H. Segal (1964).
4. J. Breasted, AR iii.§§216 ff.
5. On the subject in general, cf. T. H. Gaster, in Numen 1 (1954), 188 f.; id., in RR 9 (1945), 267 ff.; Lord Raglan, The Origins of Religion (1949), 81; Frazer-Gaster, NGB §§70, 73–75.—On divine kingship *in Israel*, see: M. Noth, in Zeitschr. für Theologie und Kirche 47 (1950), 157–91; A. R. Johnson, in ET 62 (1950), 36–42; J. Kroeker, Das Koenigtum und die Theokratie in Israel (1931); C. R. North, in ZAW 50 (1932), 8–38; G. Widengren, in Horae Soederblomianae (1947); F. Gypkens, Koenig und Kult im At (Diss., Emsdetten 1940).
6. Cf. Lord Raglan, "Patterns in the Ritual of Coronation and Royal Funerals," in Folk-Lore 64 (1953), 257 ff.; H. Thurston, The Coronation Ceremony[2] (1911).
7. Breasted, op. cit. §220.
8. S. A. Strong, in BA 2 (1884), 645; tr. Pfeiffer, in ANET 451[a].
9. Cf. K. Tallquist, Der Assyrische Gott (1932), 86 ff.
10. Ḫammurapi, Code v. 11–12; rev. xxiv. *a* 14.
11. F. Delitzsch, in BA 2 (1894), 267.
12. Prism B = ANET 288[a].
13. Heb. *ṣedāqah* means here the quality of preserving the norm (*ṣedeq*).
14. In the celebrated Cylinder Inscription of Cyrus, it is said similarly that Marduk, god of Babylon, selected him as "the upright man whose hand he would grasp": ANET 315.
15. II AB iv–v.109; T. H. Gaster, Thespis[2], 187. Cf. Callimachus, Apollo 29.
16. Josephus, Ant. vi.11, 9.
17. See: C. Meloni, "Sedet ad dexteram patris," in Saggi di Filologia semitica, iii (1913); E. Pottier, in Mélanges Boissier (1903), 405–13; S. Eitrem, Papyri Osloenses i (1925), 96 f.; O. Weinreich, in Göttingen Gelehr. Anzeiger 1912, No. 7–9. 135 ff.; F. Boll, Sphaera (1903), 563 f.; F. Dölger, Die Sonne der Gerechtigkeit (1918), 9 ff., 37 ff.
18. Gen. 35:18.
19. J. Wellhausen, Reste d. arab. Heidentums[2] (1897), 202.
20. P. Haupt, in BA 1 (1889), 170.
21. Tchang, L'écriture chinoise et le geste humaine (1939), 145.
22. G. Roeder, Urkunden z. Rel. d. alten Aegypter (1915), 107, 109, 112.
23. Cf. Iliad 2.353; Odyssey 24.312; A. S. Pease, on Cicero, De Divinatione ii.82; A. P. Wagener, Popular Associations of Right and Left in Roman Literature (Baltimore 1912); E. S. McCartney, in Papers of the Michigan Academy 16 (1932), 140 ff.; S. Eitrem, Opferritus und Voropfer der Griechen und Römer (1915), 29 ff.
24. Exod. 29:22; Lev. 8:25, 26; 9:21; Lev. 7:32–34; Num. 6:20; I Sam. 9:24.
25. This tradition is preserved also in the Koran, Sura 56.
26. See: J. E. B. Mayor, on Juvenal, x.5; M. B. Ogle, in AJP 32 (1911), 254, n.2;

so too in Madagascar: M. Cox, Introduction to Folklore (1897), 9; likewise in parts of the United States: D. L. and L. B. Thomas, Kentucky Superstitions (1920), #1001; C. J. Johnson, What They Say in New England (1897), 93.

27. Jas. Boswell, Life of Dr. Samuel Johnson, end of entries for 1764.
28. F. D. Bergen, Current Superstitions (1896), #355; A. Wuttke, Der deutsche Volksaberglaube der Gegenwart³ (1900), 371.
29. G. Parrinder, La religion en Afrique occidentale (1950), 216.
30. Frazer-Gaster, NGB §§69–76, 86.
31. Breasted, op. cit. §148. Enemies are portrayed as the footstool of Amenhotep III on a wall of tomb #226 at Thebes: N. M. Davies and A. H. Gardiner, Ancient Egyptian Paintings (1936), ii.Pl. 38; ANEP #4.
32. The usual translation is, *Yahweh sends the rod of thy strength out of Zion;* but the scepter is sent from heaven, not from Zion. Hence the words "out of Zion" must go with the verb "exact subjection," making a neat balance of four words in each half of the verse.
33. Breasted, op. cit. §§227, 235, 237.
34. T. Jacobsen, Sumerian King-List, #11.1–2; tr. Oppenheim, in ANET 365ᵇ.
35. Deluge Tablet 88–89; ANET 43ᵇ.
36. Etana Myth, Old Bab. Version A.I. i.11 ff.; tr. Speiser, in ANET 114. Cf. also: KARI i.19, obv. 14 f. = E. Ebeling, in Orientalia 23 (1954), 210 f. So also in the Neo-Assyrian Version, C.I. 13–16.
37. L. W. King, Letters and Inscriptions of Ḥammurabi (1898–1900), #61 f. In Code xxiv, a14, the sovereignty is conferred by Marduk.
38. Prism B; ANET 288ᵃ.
39. ANET 310.
40. AO 6461 = F. Thureau Dangin, Rituels accadiens (1921), 70.108.—In Egypt, the scepter (*sḫm*) was thought to possess divinity: W. Spiegelberg, in Rec. des Trav. 25 (1903), 184; 28 (1906), 136 f.—On the divinity of scepters in general, cf. G. van der Leeuw, Religion in Essence and Manifestation (1963), i.41.
41. Iliad 2.100–108; 204–6; 9.99. Agamemnon's scepter was worshiped at Chaeronea: Pausanias ix.40, 1.
42. N. Muccioli, Lo Shintoismo (1948), 21n. The myth relating to this sword is narrated in the *Kojiki;* cf. R. Petazzoni, La Mitologia Giapponese (1929), 73.
43. W. Ellis, Polynesian Researches (1832–36), iii.103.
44. The correctness of the traditional text's ᶜammᵉkā nᵉdābôth (against LXX's ᶜimmᵉkā nᵉdābôth, "with thee is nobility") is avouched by similar phrasing in Judg. 5:2, and by the effective contrast it provides between the king and his people.
45. On *acclamatio* in ritual, cf. van de Leeuw, op. cit. 431; cf. also: E. Spanheim, In Callimachi hymnos observationes (1697), 647.
46. See Briggs, ICC, in loc.
47. According to Num. 1:3, the minimum age for military service was twenty.
48. For *me-reḥem mišḥar* I read *me-reḥem-ma šaḥar,* with the archaic enclitic *-ma;* a similar error in Joel 1:17 and possibly also in Ezek. 28:14.
49. Deut. 32:1; Hos. 14:6; Prov. 19:12; Isa. 26:19; Mic. 5:6.
50. Breasted, op. cit., §§216–17.
51. Lord Raglan, The Hero (Thinker's Library ed.), 169.
52. G. Parrinder, Les religions de l'Afrique occidentale (1950), 227.
53. Raglan, loc. cit.
54. See above, §251.
55. E. F. Weidner, AOF 1 (1927), 135–37; P. Jensen, in ZA, N.F.i (1924), 267–74; A. Goetze, Kleinasien¹ (1933), 82 f.
56. E.g., Ashurnasirpal (ARAB i, §437); Shalmaneser (ib., §§556, 596).

57. Le Page du Praz, Histoire de la Lousiane (1758), tr. K. T. Preuss, in Bertholet's Religionsgesch. Lesebuch (1926), pt. ii.35 ff.

58. A. B. Cook, Zeus ii (1925), 1003 ff.; cf. T. H. Gaster, Thespis², 431.

59. Cf. Pervigilium Veneris 20; O. Gruppe, Griechische Mythologie (1906), 823–24; J. Wellhausen, op. cit., 210. So also in Ugaritic: Gaster, op. cit., 237.

60. Cf. H. Grapow, Die bildlichen Ausdrücke des Aegyptischen (1924), 39 f.

61. The anointing of kings is mentioned in the Tel el Amarna Letter 34.50 ff. For the custom in Assyria, cf. K. Müller, in MVAG xii/3.9, line 33. See also: F. Steinmetzer, in BZ 1909.17–29.

62. Cf. S. Morenz, Aegyptische Religion (1960), 42 f.; A. Moret, Le rituel du culte journalier en Égypte (1902), 56 ff.; C. Aldred, The Egyptians (1963), 158 f.; G. Furlani, Rel. bab. e ass. (1928), i.355.

63. Cf. J. Jelito, "Tu es sacerdos," in Ruch Biblijny i Liturgiczny (Cracow), 3/i, 1–6 (1951), 251–64; B. Holwerda, De Priesterkoning in het OT (1946).

64. Breasted, op. cit., §§187–212.

65. Heb. *yādîn*, which implies more than merely "judging" (*yišpôṭ*).

66. Reading, *millē' gē'āyôth gewîyôth*—error through haplography. Exactly the same expression occurs in the Victory Hymn of Thothmes III at Thebes: Breasted, op. cit. §660. ad fin.

67. Literally, "Over a great land (area)."

68. Breasted, op. cit. §237.

69. Heb. *minaḥal ba-derek yišteh*. As an example of insensitive *cacoethes emendandi* I record simply (with disgust) the conventional modern "correction," *neḥalîm bedāmām yašqeh*, "valleys will he make to drink of their blood," which is, to boot, bad Hebrew, since *š-q-h* takes the direct accusative (without *b-*) of the substance which is proffered. —Cf. also: P. Nober, in Verbum Domini 26 (1948), 351–53; C. Schedl, in ZAW 73 (1961), 290–97.

70. II AB iv.45.

71. Yuzgat Tablet, obv. 38–41; Gaster, op. cit. 291.—In the Kumarpi myth (KUB XXXIII 120, 1, 11, 17) the divine chamberlain proffers goblets to the divine king. Cf. also: Gen. 40:11 ff. (Egypt).

72. P. Montet, Byblus et l'Égypte (1929), pl. 130; cf. G. Widengren, King and Savior IV (1951), 28 f.; R. Giveon, "King or God in the Sarcophagus of Ahiram?" in IEJ 9/i (1959).

73. G. Loud, The Megiddo Ivories (1939), Pl. 4, 2 *a–b;* Widengren, op. cit. fig. 8.

74. Widengren, op. cit., figs. 10–11.

75. E.g., W. H. Ward, Seal Cylinders of Western Asia (1910), #917; E. Porada, Mesopotamian Art in Cylinder Seals (1947), #44 (III Ur); O. Weber, Altorientalische Siegelbilder (1920), 111.

76. Cf. (but with caution) Jessie Weston, From Ritual to Romance (Anchor reprint, 1957), ch. vi.

285 Jordan turned back

1. Euripides, Medea 410 f.

2. Apollonius Rhodius, Argonautica iii.532; Vergil, Aeneid iv.489; Horace, Odes i.29, 10; Tibullus i.2, 44 (see: Kirby Smith, in loc.); Propertius, i.1, 23; ii.15, 30 f.; cf. also: A. S. Pease, Comm. on Cicero, De Divinatione, pt. ii, p. 288.

287 Tears fertilize

1. Diodorus Siculus, i.14.

2. Herodotus, ii.79. Cf. also: Pausanias, ix.29, 7; Athenaeus, 620A; Julius Pollux, iv.54.

3. Cf. J. de Horrack, Les lamentations d'Isis et Nephthys (1866); E. A. W. Budge, Osiris and the Egyptian Resurrection (1911), ii.59–66; A. Moret, Mystères égyptiens (1913), 24–26.

4. Firmicus Maternus, De errore profanarum religionum, ii.7.

5. Herodotus, ii.48. So too at the festival of Adonis: G. Glotz, in RGG 33 (1920), 206.

6. A. Moret, La mise à mort du dieu en Égypte (1927), 21; P. Montet, Les scènes de la vie privée de l'ancien empire (1925), 201–2, Pl. cvi.

7. A. L. Oppenheim, in BASOR 103 (1946), 11–14.

8. RSV renders neutrally, "held festival."

9. G. Dalman, Arbeit und Sitte in Palästina (1928–37), i.566.

10. Plutarch, Theseus 22.

11. Semus, quoted by Athenaeus, 618E; cf. E. Spanheim, In Callimachi hymnos observationes (1697), 649.

12. Epic of Gilgamesh vi.46–47.

13. Descent of Ishtar, rev. 56–57.

14. G. Reisner, Sumerisch-babylonische Hymnen (1896), #145.iii.12–15; ZA 6 (1891), 243.34; KARI #178.vi.10.

15. D. Chwolson, Die Ssabier (1856), ii.27.

16. See above, n.11.

17. H. Brugsch, Die Adonisklage und das Linoslied (1852); F. C. Movers, Die Phönizier (1841–56), i.246; W. Mannhardt, Antike Wald- und Feldkulte (1904–5), ii.281; O. Eissfeldt, "Linos and Aliyan," in Mélanges Dussaud i (1939), 161 ff.

18. F. G. Welcker, Schriften (1844–47), i.27 ff.; cf. also K. Schwenck, Die Mythologie der Slawen (1853), 227–29.

19. M. Canney, "The Magic of Tears," in JMEOS 12 (1926), 47–54.

20. A. Kruijt, in ERE vii.234a.

21. ERE vii.234; xii.127a.

22. H. Hecquard, Reise an die Küste und in das Innere von West-Afrika (1854), 41–43.

23. S. C. Macpherson, Memorials of Service in India (1865), 113–31.

24. B. de Sahagun, Histoire générale des choses de la Nouvelle-Espagne, tr. D. Jourdanet et R. Siméon (1880), ii.86.

288 The winds of fortune

1. Cf. S. Langdon, The Babylonian Epic of Creation (1923), ad vii.15; T. H. Gaster, in JRAS 1932.892.—In the Sumerian Deluge Tablet (ANET 446) the breath of Enlil brings fertility.—It is worth observing also in this connection that the colloquial term *bonanza* is really a Spanish and Portuguese word for *fair weather at sea*.

2. E. Klauber, Politisch-religiöse Texte aus der Sargonidenzeit (1913), #112, rev.4.

3. L. W. King, Babylonian Magic and Sorcery (1896), #18, rev.3.—A similar petition is made in an Egyptian penitential hymn dating toward the end of the empire: Turin Museum #102; B. Gunn, in JEA 3 (1916), 86–87; tr. Wilson, in ANET 381.

4. BA 5.312.21.

5. For the traditional text's *tered*, "goes down," I read *tarîd*, from the root $*r\text{-}w\text{-}d =$ Arabic *râda*, "roam for pasture." Also, for *TeNiḤeNū*, "gives it rest," I read *TaNḤeNū*, "guides it."

6. "Babylonian Ecclesiastes," 241 = ANET 440.

7. Aeschylus, Septem contra Thebas 688; Persae 604 f.

8. R. C. Thompson, Semitic Magic (1908), 7, 54.

9. T. Fish, in Iraq 6 (1939), 184.

10. R. Corso, in Rivista di Anthropologia 22 (1918), 80; I. Zolli, ib., 27 (1926), 9–10.
11. Euripides, Iphigenia in Tauris 1317.

JOB

289 Introductory

1. Job himself hails from Uz, described in Gen. 10:23 as an Aramean tribe, but said in Lam. 4:21 to have been occupied by Edomites at the time of the fall of Jerusalem in 586 B.C. Two of Job's "comforters," viz., Eliphaz and Bildad, come respectively from Teman, specifically located in Jer. 49:20 and Amos 1:12 in Edom, and from Shuaḫ, which is probably the Šuḫu of Akkadian records, lying on the west of the Euphrates, near the mouths of the rivers Baliḫ and Ḫabur.
2. Job. 1:13. Note that the Sabaean raid is succeeded (v. 17) by one on the part of the Chaldeans of Mesopotamia!
3. See: F. H. Foster, in AJSL 49 (1933), 21–45; A. Guillaume, in S. H. Hooke Volume (1963), 106–27; E. Dhorme, Job (1926), pp. cxl–cxliii.
4. See: R. H. Pfeiffer, Introduction to the O.T. (1941), 669 f. Pfeiffer holds, however, that the prologue was added later by an Israelite writer, since no Edomite would have regarded Yahweh as the supreme god. But Yahweh seems indeed to have had early connections with Edom; cf. Judg. 5:4, and note that the name Yahweh-in-Edom occurs in an inscription of Ramses II at Amarah West: H. W. Fairman, in ILN, April 17, 1948. In Deut. 33:2 Yahweh comes from Seir, which is Edom, and in Hab. 3:3 from Teman.—See, however, J. Pedersen, in RPHR 10 (1930), 317–70, for arguments against the Edomite provenience of the book.
5. Jer. 49:7; Obad. 8.
6. *Ludlul bêl nimêqi*, tr. Pfeiffer, in ANET 434–37; cf. also: R. J. Williams, in Canadian Journal of Theology 2 (1956), 14–26. Analogous Mesopotamian texts are: (a) "The Babylonian Ecclesiastes," tr. Pfeiffer, op. cit. 438 ff.; cf. also: B. Landsberger, in ZA 43 (1936), 32–76; (b) "The Righteous Sufferer," ed. O. Lambert and O. Gurney, in Anatolian Studies 4 (1954), 65–99; (c) the Sumerian poem, "Man and his God," ed. S. N. Kramer, in VT Suppl. 3 (1955), 170–82.
7. The same argument informs T. E. Brown's famous poem, Sunset at Chingford; cf. The Week-End Book (1928), 102 ff.
8. E.g., G. B. Gray and S. R. Driver, Job (ICC), i, pp. xli–xlvii; W. A. Irwin, in JR 17 (1937), 37–47; E. Fohrer, in AFO 19 (1960), 83–94; R. H. Pfeiffer, Introduction, 673 f.; O. Eissfeldt, The O.T.: an Introduction (1965), 458.—On the other hand, the authenticity of the Elihu speeches is upheld, among others, by: C. H. Cornill, Einletung in das AT[4] (1913), 249; N. H. Ridderbos, in GThT 38 (1937), 353–82; L. Dennefeld, in RB 48 (1939), 163–80; R. Gordis, in Biblical Studies, ed. A. Altmann (1963), 60–78.
9. So too Pfeiffer, Introduction, 673 f.

290 The Devil's wager

1. J. Muir, Original Sanskrit Texts i (1872), 179 ff.; cf. K. Schlottmann, in Deutsche Zeitschrift für christl. Wiss. und christl. Leben, 1850, No. 23; A. Jeremias, The Old Testament in the Light of the Ancient East (1911), ii.252 f.; O. Eissfeldt, op. cit., 468, n.44.—Cf. also: M. B. Cook and S. A. Eliot, "Tracing Job's Story," in The Hibbert Journal 60 (1962), 323–29.

291 The Sons of God

1. RS 1929.ii.16 f.; II AB iii.15; III AB, B 20-21; III AB, C 19-20; Krt C i-ii.9-11, etc.
2. T. H. Gaster, in Orientalia 11 (1942), 44.

292 Satan

1. Cf. T. H. Gaster, IDB, s.v. Satan; Faivre, Personalité de Satan d'après la bible (Diss. Montauban-Granié, 1900); S. Kluger, Satan in the OT (1967).

294 Mother Earth

1. This paragraph is excerpted from T. H. Gaster, The Holy and the Profane (1955), 161 f.
2. W. Caland, Altindische Toten- und Bestattungsgebräuche (1896), 8.
3. Servius, on Vergil, Aeneid xii.395.
4. Aelfric, Anglo-Saxon Homilies, ed. B. Thorpe (1841), i.623.
5. A. Dieterich, Mutter Erde (1913), 25 ff.
6. Ib.
7. Notes and Queries VI/ii (1860), 87, 214.
8. Dieterich, loc. cit.; P. Sartori, Sitte und Brauch (1910-14), i.134; Rider, in Zs. für Kulturgeschichte 1.59 ff., 97 ff.; Stolz, in Zs. für oesterreiche Volkskunde 12, fasc. iv-v; E. Rohde, Psyche[7] (1921), 204.
9. VAT 10173, ii.14; O. Schröder, in ZA 33 (1921), 130.
10. II AB i.18; I*AB v.11; V AB, A 24, C 4, E 4, 50; cf. T. H. Gaster, Thespis[2], 128.
11. E. H. Hodge, ed., Cory's Ancient Fragments (1876), 59.
12. J. Lewy, in HUCA 19 (1945-46), 429, n.134, sees a relic of such an earth-god in the name Arqiel (i.e., Earth-god) given to one of the fallen angels in Enoch 6.
13. AP x.58.
14. Grimm-Stallybrass, TM 642.
15. Orientalia 19 (1950), 382.

295 Rousing Leviathan

1. Stith Thompson, MI, A 737.1; E. B. Tylor, Primitive Culture[2], i.325 ff.; H. Gunkel, Schöpfung und Chaos (1895), 41-69.
2. Rig Veda v.40.
3. Buddhagosa i.9; Samyutta i.50; tr. C.A.F. Rhys Davids, Kindred Sayings (1918), i.71.
4. Ti Fu, in ERE xii.77.
5. R. C. Temple, in ERE iii.36ª.
6. E. Welsford, in ERE xii.102ª.
7. W. Scott, De lingua Tschuwaschorum (1841), 5.
8. Grimm-Stallybrass, TM 707.
9. Ib.
10. P. le Page Renouf, in PSBA 7 (1885), 163-70.
11. A. M. Layard, Discoveries in the Ruins of Nineveh and Babylon (1853), 442; B. Meissner, in ARW 5 (1902), 225.
12. Saᶜadya, Introd. to *Emunoth* wᵉ-*Deᶜoth;* L. Zunz, Gesammelte Schriften (1875), ix.245, n.2; L. Ginzberg, Legends of the Jews, v.108, 116.
13. Migne, PL vii.337.
14. Hrabanus Maurus, Opera v.606, Colyr.
15. G. A. Smith, The Book of the Twelve Prophets (New York 1944), ii.524.
16. Tacitus, Ann. i.28.
17. R. Lasch, in ARW 3 (1900), 136.

18. C. O. Blagden, Pagan Races of the Malay Peninsula (1906), ii.203 f.
19. I AB vi.35–52; cf. T. H. Gaster, Thespis², 228 f.
20. E.g., II Esdras 6:49–52; Apoc. Baruch 29: 3–8.
21. TB Baba Bathra 74ᵃ–75ᵃ; Shabbath 30ᵇ; Kethub. 11ᵇ; Pal. Targum, Num. 9:26 ff.
22. Yasht xiii.62; cf. also: W. Bousset, Rel. des Judentums in NTlicher Zeitalter (1903), 271, where Behemoth is compared with the ox Hadhayos.
23. Hesiod, Theog. 820 ff.; Aeschylus, Prometheus Vinctus 351 ff.; Ovid, Met. v.319 ff.; Apollodorus, Bib. i.6, 3.

296 Father's knees

1. KUB XXIV 7 iv.38; XXIV 8 iii.4 ff.; cf. H. Ehelolf, in OLz 1926.767; A. Goetze, in JAOS 69 (1949), 180.
2. Breasted, AR ii, §§187–212.
3. J. Grimm, Deutsche Rechtsaltertümer⁴ (1899), 598; M. Cahen, in Bull. de la Société de Linguistique, Paris 27.56–57; K. Beth, in HWbDA i.195.
4. For its prevalence among the Celts, cf. J. Loth, in Revue celtique 40.143–52.—The custom was known also to the Greeks: B. Haussolier, ib., 43.168–73; P. Suys, ib., 45.322–24.—So too among the Iranians: E. Beneviste, in Bull. de la Soc. de Linguistique 27.51–53.
5. HWbDA, loc. cit.
6. Ib.
7. Gen. 50:23.
8. See: M. W. Déonna, in Rev. arch. 1 (1939), 224–35; R. Meringer, in Wörter und Sachen 11 (1928), 114 ff.; K. Simyoni, "Knie und Geburt," in Kuhns Zeitschrift für vergl. Sprachwiss. i (1923), 152 ff.; R. B. Onians, The Origins of European Thought about the Body, etc. (1951), 174–86. Cf. also: E. Schwyzer, in Antidoron, Wackernagel Festschrift (1923), 283 ff.
9. A. Meillet, in Bull. de la Soc. de Linguistique 27 (1926), 54 f.; id., in CRAIBL 1926.45 ff.
10. Cf. H. Holma, Namen der Körperteile im Assyrisch-Babylonischen (1911), 96.

297 The weary dead

1. A. Erman and H. Grapow, Handwörterbuch d. aeg. Sprache, 38.
2. Odyssey 11.474 f.—In later Roman times, the dead were sometimes termed *securi* (free from care) and were said to enjoy *securitas aeterna:* Dessau, Inscr. sel. #8025, 8149; F. Cumont, After Life in Roman Paganism (1922), 191. Cf. also: Cicero, In Catil. iv.7: *mors laborum et miseriarum quies.*
3. Not impossibly, in view of the antithetical *rogez*, the Heb. word $r^e ša^c îm$, commonly rendered "the wicked" (its usual sense), should here be emended to $ro^{ca} šîm$, "stormtossed, restless."

298 The sons of Resheph

1. See above, §242.
2. E.g., I Sam. 23:5. The words were anciently written *k l*, and in Hos. 14:3 this has been misvocalized as *kôl*, "all," the correct rendering being, *Say unto him, Surely thou wilt remit the penalty of wrongdoing.* Cf. also Neo-Hebrew h^a-*kî lô'*.—For the Amarna usage, cf. H. Holma, in ZA 28.102.
3. W. Müller, apud Gesenius-Buhl, s.v. *r-š-f*.

300 Orion

1. T. H. Gaster, Thespis², 323. It derives from a root meaning properly "to have collops of fat on the loins." Cf. also: G. R. Driver, in JTS 7 (1956), 2.
2. Odyssey 11.572.

3. Cf. E. Babelon, in Rev. belge de numismatique 1898.20 ff.; A. B. Cook, Zeus ii (1925), 430.
4. Cf. R. Allen, Star-names and Their Meanings (1899), 306.
5. The word is rendered similarly (*gabrâ*) in the Syriac (Peshitta) Version of our passage.
6. Grimm-Stallybrass, TM 66.
7. Ib., 525–29.
8. A. Aarne and S. Thompson, Types of the Folktale (1928), #1000–1099.

301 The whip of God

1. Iliad 12.37; 13.812; cf. Hesychius, s.v. *Dios mastigi*. Cf. also: J. E. B. Mayor, on Juvenal, xiii.195; H. J. Munro, on Lucretius, iii.1203; v.1154.
2. Aeschylus, Choephoroe 290.
3. Aeschylus, Eumenides 155–60; Heliodorus, Aethiopica ii.11.
4. Aeschylus, Prometheus Vinctus 681–82.
5. S. Eitrem, Papyri Osloenses: (1930), 53.
6. T. Pradel, Griech, Gebete (1907), 259.
7. Eitrem, op. cit., 52.
8. Grimm-Stallybrass, TM, 1003.
9. R. Harris, Picus who is also Zeus (1916), 57 ff.; A. B. Cook, Zeus ii (1925), 824 f.; T. H. Gaster, Thespis², 165 f.
10. Aeschylus, Septem contra Thebas, 423 ff.; Euripides, Phoenissae 1172 f.; id., Supplices 496 ff.; Lycophron, Alex. 433 ff.
11. Oppian, De pisc. 5.282 ff.
12. Harris, loc. cit.
13. Grimm-Stallybrass, TM 178.

302 The disappearing shadow

1. Pausanias, viii.38, 6; Polybius, xvi.12, 7; Plutarch, Quaest. Graec. 39; cf. J. Negelein, in ARW 5 (1902), 1–37.
2. P. Drechsler, Sitte, Brauch und Volksglauben in Schlesien (1905–6), i.31.
3. Cf. A. Löwinger, in Grunwald's Mitteilungen zur jüd. Volkskunde (Vienna 1910).
4. G. H. Simon, in JAFL 65 (1952), 1920.
5. Ib.

303 The hawsers of the heart

1. Cf. Judg. 16:9; Isa. 5:27.
2. Root *z-m-m*, akin to **ṣ-m-m*.
3. Syriac *maršô*.
4. Shakespeare, King John, V.vii.52 ff.
5. On the universal prevalence of this concept, see H. Campbell Bonner in HTR 34 (1941), 49–68.

304 The King of Terrors

1. The Heb. runs: w^e-$taṣ^cîdēhū$ l^e-$melek$ $balāhôt$. LXX's σχοίη δὲ αὐτὸν ἀνάγκη αἰτίᾳ βασιλικῇ is scarcely translatable, but perhaps presupposes the reading w^e-$taṣ^cîRēhū$ K^e-$melek$ bal-$heyôt$. Vulgate renders: *Et calcet super eum, quasi rex, interitus* = w^e-$taṣ^cîdēhū$ K^e-$melek$ $b^elôt$. The verb $w^etaṣ^cîdēhū$ means literally "thou wilt cause him to march," and may be understood, without facile emendation, in the sense, "you will eventually see him escorted, conducted."
2. CT XXIV 36.52; 47.10.
3. E. Ebeling, Tod und Leben (1931), 166.14.
4. Vergil, Georgica iv.464.
5. Aeschylus, Septem contra Thebas 608 ff.

306 Razed foundations and faery gold

1. Literally, *Of the ancient way, which impious men (once) trod.* If the allusion is indeed to a time-honored story, the word "ancient" is pertinent and need not be emended, as some modern scholars have suggested.
2. EV: the Almighty.
3. RSV: *They were snatched away before their time,* but the precise meaning of the Hebrew verb is *shrink, contract.* The picture is drawn from plant life, and I have therefore inserted the words, *like plants,* to bring out explicitly what is implicit in the original.
4. Another reading is, *Why, their mainstay* (or, *substance*) *has proved delusive.*
5. The context requires that the Hebrew word *yeter* be taken in the sense of *tent-rope* (cf. Job 4:21), rather than *remainder, surplus,* as usually rendered.
6. EV: *the Almighty.*
7. KLV: *You shall have plenty of silver;* RSV: *Your precious silver.* For the true sense of the Hebrew word *to^caphôth,* see Ps. 95:4; cf., by metathesis, Arabic *y-f-^c,* "be high, tower."
8. For this expression, cf. Job 27:10. The Hebrew word (*tith^cannag*) is usually rendered, "thou shalt delight thyself," but it is here better explained from an homophonous root akin to Arabic *^c-n-j,* "moor, tie, attach," and (by metathesis) Neo-Hebrew *^c-g-n,* since the point is that the tents of the pious stand firm, in contrast to what has just been said about the foundation of the wicked.
9. There is no need to emend this verse, as is usually done by modern commentators. The subject of the Hebrew verb *hišpîlū* is *^ceynaim* ("eyes") at the end of the sentence, and the point lies in a contrast between men who cannot "look God in the face" and those who lower their eyes through genuine humility.
10. Here again, no radical emendation is required. The renderings in the Ancient Versions merely indicate perplexity over a difficult phrase. The expression *î-nāqî* means simply "not guiltless," but it also includes the notion of not having clean hands; cf. Ps. 24:4. The traditional text's *nimlaṭ* must be vocalized *nimlaṭâ = nimlaṭ^ethā.*
11. Stith Thompson, MI, F 944.
12. Commentary on First Mu^callaqah, v.49, ed. Arnold, quoted by D. S. Margoliouth, The Relations between Arabs and Israelites Prior to the Rise of Islam (1924), 32.
13. Stith Thompson, op. cit., F 475.
14. Ib., D 1201; HWbDA, s.v. Gold.

307 The shades beneath the waters

1. J. A. MacCulloch, in ERE xii.518.
2. S. Reinach, Cultes, mythes et religions, i (1922), 184–94; A. H. Krappe, La genèse des mythes (1938), 216 f.
3. C. Seligmann, The Melanesians of British New Guinea (1910), 610, 655; cf. also: C. Clemen, Religionsgesch. Europas (1926–31), i.47; MacCulloch, loc. cit.
4. O. Finsch, Neu-Guinea und seine Bewohner (1865), 104 f.
5. R. Lambert, Moeurs et superstitions des néo-Calédoniens (1900), 13 f.; J. G. Frazer, The Belief in Immortality (1913), i.326.
6. R. Nassau, Fetichism in West Africa (1904), 56 ff., 237.
7. O'Grady, Sylva Gadelica (1842), 290; A. McBain, Celtic Mythology (1917), 91; J. A. MacCulloch, in ERE ii.689.
8. L. Radermacher, in Anz. d.Oesterreich. Akad. d. Wiss., phil.-hist. Kl. 1949, #16.307–15.
9. Cf. CT XVI.10*b*; IV R, 30.2.

309 The pillars of heaven

1. Stith Thompson, MI, A 665.2.1; A 841.
2. R. Anthes, in Mythologies of the Ancient World, ed. S. N. Kramer (1961), 31 f.; G. Maspero, in Rev. archéol., N.S. 34 (1877), 322; Guide to the Egyptian Collections in the British Museum (1908), 145.
3. Rig Veda vi.67, 6.
4. J. Scheftelowitz, Das altpers. Religion und das Judentum (1920), 106.
5. Odyssey 1.53–54; cf. O. Gruppe, Griechische Mythologie (1906), 382; A. B. Cook, Zeus ii (1925), 140 ff.
6. L. Frobenius, Erlebte Erdteile (1925), 163.
7. R. B. Dixon, Oceanic Mythology (1916), 163.
8. Stith Thompson, Tales of the North American Indians (1929), 286, n.56; A. B. Alexander, Latin American Mythology (1920), 154 (Mayan).
9. A. Bastian, Inselgruppen (1883), 218 (Maori); C. Strehlow, Die Aranda und Loutja-Stämme in Zentral-Australien (1907–20), i.2.
10. Kalevala, runo xvii.551, tr. W. F. Kirby (Everyman's Library ed.), i.191.
11. Cf. G. B. Gray, Sacrifice in the O.T. (1925), 152 (on Ps. 78:69); H. P. L'Orage, Iconography of Cosmic Kingship in the Ancient World (1953), 9–17; G. Martiny, in OLz 41 (1938), 665–72; F. Jeremias, in Bertholet-Lehmann, Handbuch i.523 ff.; I. Benzinger, Hebräische Archäologie² (1927), 329; R. Patai, Man and Temple (1947), 105 ff.; A. Piankoff, Les chapelles de Toutankhamen (1901), pl. ix; T. H. Gaster, in Numen 1 (1954), 195 f.—Among ancient writers, cf. Josephus, Ant. iii.7, 7; Clem. Alex., Strom. 562 ff.; Justin, Cohortatio ad gentes 29; Heb. 9:8 ff.—Against this view, however, cf. A. Parrot, Ziggurat et Tour de Babel (1949); J. Nougayrol, in Symbolisme cosmique et monuments réligieux, Musée Guimet, July 1953, pp. 13 f.; H. Nelson, in BA 7 (1944), 77.
12. Cf. A. Audin, in AOr 21 (1953), 430–39.
13. J. R. Murie, Anthropological Papers of the American Museum of Natural History 11 (1916), 551.
14. E. O. James, in The Labyrinth, ed. S. H. Hooke (1935), 245.

310 The Dragon in the net

1. This brilliant emendation is due to Tur Sinai.
2. The corresponding verb may be recognized, I suggest, in the Heb. text of Ps. 59:12, where in place of the usual *Let them be trapped in their pride, for the cursing and lies which they utter* ($y^e sapper\bar{u}$), we should render, *Let them be trapped in their pride, and enmeshed in their intrigue and deceit.*
3. Enuma Elish iv. 97 ff.
4. The Greek (Septuagint) Version, by a change of but one letter, obtains the sense, *The bolts of heaven were terrified at him; his hand pierced the Evasive Serpent.* But this destroys the pointed contrast between the actions of God's *hand* and of his *breath*, balancing that between his *strength* and his *understanding* (as if to say, his *brawn* and *brain*) in the immediately preceding line.

312 The legend of the phoenix

1. The tradition that our verse refers to the phoenix is due also to a misunderstanding of the Septuagint's Greek rendering, "I will live a long while like a branch of the *phoinix*," where *phoinix* really means "palm-tree" (cf. Vulgate's *et sicut palma multiplicabo dies*). However, there is no solid basis for this rendering of the Heb. word, *ḥôl;* cf. E. Dhorme, Job (1926), in loc.
2. Pliny, HN x.2.

3. Cf. Herodotus, ii.73; Ovid. Met. xv.391; Tacitus, Ann. vi.34; Aelian, NA vi.58; Statius, Silv. ii.4, 37; Martial v.7, 1. Cf. also: II Enoch 12, 15; III Baruch 6:4 ff.
4. Kazwini, i.420.
5. Damiri, ii.36 f.
6. T. H. White, The Bestiary (1960), s.v.
7. A. Wiedemann, in ZÄS 16.89 f.
8. The word was recognized by Virolleaud in a passage of the Ugaritic Epic of K-r-t (C,109), but this is now otherwise explained; cf. H. L. Ginsberg, The Epic of Keret (1946), 44.
9. A. H. Gardiner and N. G. Davies, Tombs of Menkheperrasonb (1933), 26.

313 The negative confession

1. Cf. R. Pettazzoni, La confessione dei peccati, iii (1935), 1–24.
2. Book of the Dead, ch. 125; tr. J. A. Wilson, in ANET 34. Cf. C. Maystre, Les déclarations d'innocence (1937); E. A. W. Budge, Osiris and the Egyptian Resurrection (1911), i.315 ff.
3. Breasted, AR i (1906), 523.
4. Ib., 252, 281.
5. E. Ebeling, Tod und Leben nach den Vorstellungen der Babylonier, i (1931), 20–21.
6. Cf. S. A. Cook, The Laws of Moses and the Code of Hammurabi (1903), 62 f.
7. Pettazzoni, op. cit., 21.
8. Budge, op. cit., i. 339; Mary Kingsley, Travels in West Africa (1897), 465.
9. Heb.: *rabbū*. But I suspect that we should read *rābū*," have entered suit."
10. Heb.: *cošeq*. It has been suggested that we should read *^{c}oqeš*, "distortion." An alternative might be *cathaq*, "arrogance," as in I Sam. 2:3; Pss. 31:19; 75:6; 94:4.
11. Satapatha Brahmana xi.2, 7.33.
12. Cf. A. W. Jackson, in Actes du Xe Congrès des Orientalistes (1897), II.i.67 ff.— The concept passed thence into Islam (cf. Tor Andrae, Der Ursprung des Islams und des Christentums [1926], 69) and into the lore of the Mandaeans of Iraq and Iran (Left Ginza iii.19, Lidzbarski).
13. Cf. M. Nilsson, in Bull. de la Soc. Royale des Lettres de Lund, 1921–23. 29 ff.
14. Pettazzoni, op. cit., i.186.
15. In the Egyptian conception, the forty-two judges were ranged in equal number on the left and the right, with the scale in the middle: H. Kees, Totenglauben und Jenseitsvorstellungen des alten Aegypten (1926), 450; G. Roeder, Urkunden zur Religion des alten Aegypten (1923), 244.—For the Babylonian view, cf. Ebeling, loc. cit.
16. Budge, op. cit., i.339.

314 Blowing kisses to the moon

1. S. Langdon, in JRAS 1919.531 f.; A. Malraux and G. Salles, Arts of Mankind: Sumer, tr. Giebert-Emmons (1960), fig. 350. Cf. also: A. Goetze, in JNES 4 (1945), 248, n.2.
2. Pliny, HN xviii.2, 5: *inter adorandum dexteram ad osculum referimus.*
3. Cf. E. Crawley, The Mystic Rose^2 (1927), i.343–49.

316 Cattle presage storms

1. Heb.: *yaggîd ^{c}alāw rē^{c}ô miqneh 'af ^{c}al ^{c}ôleh.*
2. By one such emendation (viz., *m^{e}qanne' 'af ^{c}al ^{c}awlah*) RSV obtains the sense, *Its crashing declares concerning Him, Who is jealous with anger against iniquity.* Other suggestions are: (a) *yaggîd ^{c}alāw rē^{c}ô wi-y^{e}hawweh' apô ^{c}aloleh*, i.e., *God's thunder bespeaks him, and the stormwind discloses his anger.* This is simply an arbitrary

rewriting of the text; (b) *yaggîd ᶜalāw rôᶜô miqneh <šō>'ef ᶜaloleh* (Dhorme), *Its shepherd tells of him, (and) the cattle itself snuffs the stormwind(!)*; (c) *yaggîd ᶜAliy rēᶜô maqnî' 'af ᶜal ᶜawlah* (Pope), *ᶜAliy* (i.e., *the High One) speaks with his thunder, venting his anger against evil.* This is barely Hebrew.

The preceding verse, to which this is the logical complement, has also given headaches to commentators. The traditional text reads: *ᶜal kappaim kissah 'ôr wa-yᵉṣaw ᶜalêhā bᵉ-mafgîᶜᵃ*. KJV renders arbitrarily, *With clouds he covereth the light, and commandeth it (not to shine) by (the cloud) that cometh betwixt.* Heb. *kappaim*, however, can only mean "palms, hands," not "clouds." RSV, reading *ba-mifgaᶜ*, improves this to, *He covers his hands with lightning, and commands it to strike the mark.* It seems to me that perfect sense can be obtained simply by revocalizing the word *kappaim* to read *kēfîm*, "rocks," and by assuming a haplography in the second hemistich, to read, *wa-yᵉṣaw ᶜalê lahab mifgaᶜ*, i.e., *O'er rocks he casts the lightning as a mantle, and commands the flash to strike the mark.*

3. W. C. Hazlitt, Dictionary of Faiths and Folklore (1905), ii.624[b].

4. Ib.

318 Stars divine

1. IV AB i.4 (*bn il* || [*p*]*ḫr kkbm*); cf. T. H. Gaster, in Iraq 6 (1939), 125, n.5.

2. G. Furlani, Rel. Bab. e assir., i (1928), 95 f.; A. Deimel, Pantheon babylonicum[1] (1914), passim.

3. Lucian, Tragopodagra 108 f.

319 Rain from bottles

1. H. Gressmann, Texte und Bilder[2] (1926–27), #303; S. A. Cook, The Religion of Ancient Palestine in the Light of Archaeology (1925), 49.

2. Rig Veda v.83, 7–8, tr. R. H. Griffith.

3. G. Jacob, Altarabische Parallelen zum AT (1897), 20.

4. Garcilasso de la Vega, Royal Commentaries of the Yncas, tr. C. R. Markham (1869–71), ii.27.

5. Grimm-Stallybrass, TM 593.

PROVERBS

321 The house that leads down to death

1. For this sense of the word "death" in the Old Testament, see: Isa. 38:18; Pss. 6:6; 9:14; 22:16; Job 28:22; 30:23.

2. Temple Bible: Proverbs, in loc.

3. Stith Thompson, MI, F 941.1; A. Wesselski, Märchen des Mittelalters (1925), 200.

4. Stith Thompson, op. cit., F 302; W. A. Clouston, Tales and Popular Fictions (1887), i.212 ff.; S. Baring-Gould, Curious Myths of the Middle Ages[2] (1869), ch. 10, "The Mountain of Venus"; E. Hoffmann-Krayer, in Zeitschrift für Volkskunde 25.120, n.4; C. A. Williams, Oriental Affinities of the Legend of the Hairy Anchorite (1925), i.13–25; Myra Olstead, "Lancelot at the Grail Gate," in Folk-Lore 76 (1963), 48–55.

5. See above, §11.

322 Ants store food in summer

1. Ovid, Fasti i.685 ff.—A similar observation is made by the Hellenistic poet, Pseudo-Phocylides, 164 ff. (= T. Gaisford, Poeti Minores Graeci [1814], ii.458), but this writer appears to have been a Jew, and his statement seems to be derived directly from

Prov. 30:25, for his description of the ants as *phylon oligon* reproduces to a nicety the Heb. expression, ᶜ*am lôʼ* ᶜ*az* (EV: a people not strong); cf. J. Bernays, in Jahresber. des jüdisch-theologischen Seminars Fraenckelscher Stiftung (Breslau 1856), xxx, n.2.
2. Vergil, Georgica i.186: *inopi metuens formica senectae.*
3. Notes and Queries II/xi (1861), 475 f.
4. J. Lubbock, Ants, Bees and Wasps³ (1882), 59–61, cited by Frazer, Comm. on Ovid, Fasti, loc. cit.; Chambers' Encyclopaedia (1925), i.302, s.v. Ant. Cf. also: S. Bochart, Hierozoicon (1663), ii.591.

323 Pointing the finger

1. See in general: S. Seligmann, D. böse Blick (1910), ii.183; F. G. Groschuff, Abhandlung von der Finger, deren Verichtungen und symbolische Bedeutung (1756), 312 f.; Echtermeyer, Ueber Namen und symbolische Bedeutung der Finger bei den Griechen und Römer (1835); I. Löw, "Die Finger in Literatur und Folklore der Juden," in Gedenkbuch D. Kaufmann (1900), 61–85; Am Urquell 6. 49 ff.—Diogenes affronted Demosthenes by pointing his finger at him: C. Sittl, Die Gebärden der Griecher und Römer (1890), 51, 110 f.
2. Šurpu ii.88; cf. also: Maqlu iii.8, 11, with Tallquist's note, in loc.; KARI #118.4 f.; MDOG 1918/i.78 ff.; A. Jirku, Altor. Kommentar zum AT (1923), 234 f.
3. Seligmann, op. cit., ii.262; cf. I. Goldziher, Abhandlungen zur arab. Philologie (1896–99), i.57.
4. Globus 46.202.
5. Am Urquell 6.10 ff.; F. G. Heins, Seespuk (1888), 142.

324 Wisdom as God's master craftsman

1. Cf. Heb. *'ammān,* Song of Songs 7:2.
2. See fully: F. L. Moriarty, in Verbum Domini 27 (1947), 291–93.
3. Wisdom of Solomon 7:22 (*technitis*).
4. Cf. L. Oppenheim, in Orientalia 16 (1947), 212, n.4.
5. S. Smith, First Campaign of Sennacherib, line 33.
6. D. Luckenbill, ARAB i.§63.
7. Enuma Elish i.30–31.
8. The Heb. word (*šaᶜᵃšūᶜîm*), usually rendered "delight," is connected with a verbal root (*š-ᶜ-ᶜ* II) meaning "converse, chat." Cf. Prov. 19:24.
9. Cf. T. H. Gaster, in Vetus Testamentum 4 (1954), 77 f.

325 The seven pillars of Wisdom

1. For the traditional text's *ḥaṣbah,* "has hewn out," we must read, with LXX, *hiṣṣîbah,* "has set up." (RSV adopts this reading.)
2. W. F. Albright, in Wisdom in Israel and the East: Rowley Volume (1958), 9; cf. id., in BASOR 14 (1924), 10; 53 (1933), 13 ff.; Nelson Glueck, in AASOR 14 (1934), 45 ff.
3. The inscription was discovered by T. B. Mitford in 1948; cf. JHS 66.40; Albright, in Wisdom in Israel, etc., loc. cit.
4. S. Krauss, Talmudische Archäologie (1910–12), i.53.
5. Bᵉrešîth Rabbah 78.
6. I. Scheftelowitz, Die Entstehung der manichäischen Religion (1922), 5.
7. The examples here cited are drawn mainly from I. Scheftelowitz, Altpalest. Bauernglaube (1925), 29 f.
8. Herodotus, i.181.

9. I Kings 10:19.
10. E.g., in Meir of Orleans' poem Aqdamûth; tr. T. H. Gaster, in Commentary, June 1953.
11. Right Ginza xiv.11, Lidzbarski.
12. Enoch, chs. 24–25.
13. Lal. Vist. xiv.11, ed. Lefmann.
14. Scheftelowitz, Altpal. Bauernglaube, loc. cit., n.1.
15. Id., Entstehung, loc. cit.
16. O. Wardrop and F. C. Connybeare, eds., Studia Biblica v (1908), 38 f., 83 f.
17. F. Nork, in Scheible's Das Kloster xii (1849), 765 f.

327 The lamp of the soul

1. J. Grimm, DM[4], 1559; Bötticher, in Philologus 25 (1867), 27 ff.; R. S. Boggs, Index of Spanish Folktales: FCC #90 (1930), No. 708A; J. Jegerlehner, Sagen und Märchen aus dem Oberwallis (1909), 313; C. Plummer, Vitae Sanctorum Hiberniae (1910), #138; Bolte-Polivka i.377 ff., 388.
2. Stith Thompson, MI, E 761.7.4; 765.1.1; J. Bolte, in Zeitschrift für Volkskunde 20.70, n.11; A. H. Krappe, apud N. S. Penzer, The Ocean of Story (1913 ff.), viii.107.
3. Aeschylus, Choephoroe 604 ff.; Bacchylides, v.136 ff.; Apollodorus, Bib. I.7, 2 (see: Frazer, in loc.); Ovid, Met viii.445–525; Hyginus, fab. 171, 174.
4. Cf. E. S. Hartland, The Science of Fairy Tales (1891), 205.
5. Plutarch, Quaest. Rom.
6. Cf. O. Gruppe, Griechische Mythologie (1906), 848, n.10.—For the general notion that the soul was made of fire, cf. Cornutus ii.8; Orphica lxvi.2, 13.

328 Coals of fire on the head

1. S. Morenz, in Theologische Literaturzeitung 78 (1953), 187–92.
2. J. Jamieson, Etymological Dictionary of the Scottish Language[2] (1879–82), s.v. *coal*.
3. M. Gusinde, Die Yamana (Mödling 1937), 942 ff.
4. Thus, it is now recognized that Prov. 22:17—24:22 stand in very close relation to the Egyptian Maxims of Amenemope (ANET 421 ff.); while in Prov. 17:10 the *hundred* blows may be explained from an *Egyptian* form of punishment, seeing that the Deuteronomic law (Deut. 28:3) restricted the maximum to *forty:* cf. B. Couroyer, in RB.1950.331–35.
5. On this point, see fully: F. Vattioni, in Studiorum Paulinorum Congressus Internationalis Catholicus (1963), 341–45.
6. Cf. such verbs as $ḥ$-r-$ḥ$ (blaze, kindle) and c-$š$-n (fume) applied to the passions.
7. Cf. Latin *ignesco*, etc.
8. Cf. H. Grapow, Die bildlichen Ausdrücke des Aegyptischen (1924), 48.
9. W. Gesenius, Thesaurus, s.v. g-$ḥ$-l.
10. R. B. Onians, Origins of European Thought about the Body, etc. (1951), 147 f. (where, however, sound observations are mixed with untenable conjectures).
11. Plautus, Poen. 770.
12. Id., Merc. 590.
13. Iliad 18.207 f.; Odyssey 18.353 ff.
14. Vergil, Aeneid xii.101 f.
15. Táin Bó Cúalnge, quoted by Onians, op. cit., 157.
16. Admittedly, the preposition c*al*, "upon," creates a difficulty, for we should normally expect *min*, "from." However, it might be justified as brachylogical, the meaning being, "You will be shoveling away coals of fire *which are on* his head."

329 Mythological riddles

1. ANET 114 ff.
2. Stith Thompson, MI, K 1041. Variants are to be found in Spain, Indonesia, among the North American Indians, and even in one of the Uncle Remus stories.
3. I.e., b^e-ḥiSnô for b^e-ḥôFnô.
4. For this sense of the word, cf. Neh. 5:13.
5. Cf. Odyssey 10.1–76; Ovid, Met. xiv.223–32; Apollodorus, Epitome vii.10; Hyginus, fab. 125.—On this myth, see: Schwartz, in Zeitschrift d. Vereins f. Volkskunde 1 (1893), 448–51; id., Nachklänge. prähist. Volksglaube (1894), 20; R. Stroemberg, "The Aeolus Episode and Greek Wind Magic," in Symbolae Phil. Goteb. 1950.71–84.
6. Cf. Grimm-Stallybrass, TM 640, 1087; G. Kittredge, Witchcraft in Old and New England (1929), 159, 477, nn.65–66; Gaster-Frazer, NGB §60; Miss Macdonald, in PSBA 13 (1891), 162; L. Gomme, Ethnology in Folklore (1892), 48–49.
7. Higden (14th cent.), Polychronicon, ed. Babington, ii.43.
8. J. Scheffer, Lapponia (1674), 144 f.; Kalevala x.159–84; K. Krohn, Finnisch-Ungrische Forschungen, vi (1906), 173–75.—Elizabethan playwrights allude to this custom. Says Webster: *Henceforward I will rather trust / The winds which Lapland witches sell to men;* and Nashe: *For, as in Ireland and in Denmark both, / Witches for gold will sell a man a wind, / Which, in the corner of a napkin wrapped, / Shall blow him safe unto what coast he will.*
9. H. Klose, Togo unter deutscher Flagge (1899), 189.
10. C. Leemius, De Lapponibus Finnmarchiae, etc. (1767), 454.
11. K. Wehran, Die Sage (1908), 63.—I have a lurking suspicion that the practice here discussed really underlies the difficult Hebrew text of Hos. 4:19.
12. R. B. Dixon, Oceanic Mythology (1916), 296 f.
13. Stith Thompson, op. cit., A 842.
14. A. Goetze, in ANET 125; H. G. Güterbock, The Song of Ullikummi (1952); T. H. Gaster, The Oldest Stories in the World (1952), 122 f., 129.
15. H. B. Alexander, Latin American Mythology (1920), 203.
16. S. Thompson, Tales of the North American Indians (1929), 286, n.56b.

330 'Aluqah the vampire

1. The insertion of the words "they cry," which are not in the Hebrew, spoils the point. The expression "two give-give daughters" is a colloquialism, like the American "a gimme girl," i.e., a "gold-digger."
2. W. Gesenius, Comm. on Isa. 34:14; J. Wellhausen, Reste d. arabischen Heidentums (1897), 149; H. Schneider, in Junker Festschrift (1961), 257–64.
3. Cf. T. H. Gaster, The Holy and the Profane (1955), 25 ff.
4. Shakespeare, King Lear, III.iv (Withold is a popular form of St. Vitalis.)

THE SONG OF SONGS

331 Introductory

1. For a convenient summary of the various interpretations, cf. H. Rowley, in JRAS 1938.251–76. For a popular treatment, cf. T. H. Gaster, in Commentary 13 (1952), 316–22.
2. Cf. W. W. Cannon, The Song of Songs edited as a Dramatic Poem (1913). For recent renderings along these lines, cf. L. Waterman, The Song of Songs translated and

interpreted as a Dramatic Poem (1948); D. de Sola Pool, in The Menorah Journal, Spring 1945.

3. For this view, cf. especially, T. J. Meek, in AJSL 39 (1923), 1–14; id., in The Song of Songs: a Symposium (1924), 48–79; W. Wittekindt, Das Hohe Lied und seine Beziehungen zum Istarkult (1927); H. Schmökel, Heilige Hochzeit und Hohelied (1956). But cf. also: F. Horst's critique, in ThLz 83 (1958), 184–86.

4. Thus, there is no proof that *Dôd*, the Hebrew word for "lover," used throughout the Song, was ever a title of Tammuz or Adonis. Nor does the catalogue of Mesopotamian love-songs (?) cited and translated by Meek (Song of Songs: a Symposium, 70–79) necessarily emanate, as supposed, from the Ishtar-Tammuz cult, so that its phraseological similarities with the Song of Songs prove nothing more than that all lovers speak the same language everywhere.

5. J. G. Wetzstein, "Die Syrische Dreschtafel," in ZE 5 (1875), 270–302. These observations were first applied to the interpretation of the Song of Songs by Karl Budde, in his commentary (1898). For an excellent critique of the theory, cf. Cannon, op. cit., 28–40.

6. Cannon, op. cit., 32, 35.

7. Cf. G. Jacob, Das Hohelied auf arabische und andere Parallelen untersucht (1902); H. Stephan, "Modern Palestinian Parallels to the Song of Songs," in JPOS 2 (1922), 199–278.

8. Cf. G. Jacob, Altarabische Parallelen zum AT (1897), 20 f.

9. Id., Das Leben der vorislamischen Beduinen (1895), 46 f.

10. Cf. Amr's Mu^callaqa, 18 (= Jacob, Altarab. Parallelen, 22).

11. A representative selection of these may be found in E. von Sydow's Dichtungen der Naturvölker. (I have used the Italian translation, Poesia dei Popoli Primitivi [1951]).

12. W. Radloff, Proben der Volkliteratur der türkischen Stämme Süd-Siberiens (1870), iii.155 = von Sydow, op. cit.,

13. Von Sydow, op. cit., #83.

14. R. Prietze, Haussa Sprichwörter und Lieder (1904), 26 = von Sydow, op. cit., #85.

15. H. Overbeck, Malaische Erzählungen (1925), 91 = von Sydow, op. cit., #68.

16. B. Gutmann, "Lider der Dschagga," in Zeitschrift . . . Eingeborenen Sprachen, 17 (1928), 179 ff. = von Sydow, op. cit., #96.

17. Comparisons have also been made with Greek poetry, especially with the Idylls of Theocritus; cf. H. Graetz, Schir ha-Schirim (1871); W. W. Hyde, in The Song of Songs: a Symposium (1924), 31–42. Once again, however, these scarcely show direct indebtedness. Thus, the statement that there is honey under the beloved's tongue (4:11) certainly finds its analogue in Theocritus' description of her voice as sweeter than honey (Id., xx.27), but "mellifluous" is a term applied everywhere to speech or voice and, as we have seen, this expression occurs already in an ancient Egyptian lyric!—Much has been made also of the similarity between the words, *I have likened thee, my beloved, to my mare in Pharaoh's chariot* (1:9) and Theocritus' statement (Id., xviii.30–31) that Helen was to Sparta what a Thessalian mare was to a chariot. But the two statements are not really parallel. In Theocritus, the comparison is between the glory which a cypress lends to a garden or a Thessalian horse to a chariot and that which Helen's beauty lent to Sparta. In the Song of Songs, on the other hand, the lover is likening his peasant inamorata (cf. 1:5–6) to the richly caparisoned mare in some pharaoh's equipage! (The words, *my mare* are therefore pointed, and should not be emended.)

18. Anyone can check this readily by leafing through Child's English and Scottish Popular Ballads or Percy's Reliques.

19. Failure to recognize this essential feature of popular literature bedevils much of modern Biblical criticism. All that the language of the extant Hebrew text can ever indicate is the date of that particular redaction, not of the original composition. It is strange that so blatant an error of method should still persist.

332 The banner of Love

1. Cf. ᶜAntara, Moᶜall, 52 (v. Noeldeke, in loc.); Landberg, Dat., 1432; BGA 8,xxii.
2. Chaucer, Canterbury Tales, Prologue, 666 f.
3. Cf. G. B. Gray, in JQR 11 (1899), 92–101; R. de Vaux, Ancient Israel (1965), 226 f.
4. Some scholars would vocalize the Hebrew word as an imperative of the corresponding verb (Akkadian *dagālu*), thus obtaining the sense, "Look lovingly upon me." The words would then be addressed to "the daughters of Jerusalem."

333 Apples and love

1. See: H. Gaidoz, "La réquisition d'amour et la symbolisme de la pomme," in Annuaire de l'École Pratique des Hautes Études 1902.5–23; B. O. Foster, "Notes on the Symbolism of the Apple in Classical Antiquity," in Harvard Studies in Classical Philology 10 (1899), 39–55; E. S. McCartney, "How the Apple became the Token of Love," in Trans. and Proc. Amer. Philos. Assoc. 56 (1925), 76–81; R. Aigremont, Volkserotik und Pflanzenwelt (n.d.), 59 ff.; A. de Gubernatis, Mythologie des Plantes (1878–82), iii.301 ff.; L. Bianchi, in Hessische Blätter für Volkskunde 13 (1914), 107; Bolte-Polivka iii.11; Zs. für Volkskunde 13.318; M. J. Gurion, Der Born Judas² (1916–22), i.192; T. Menzel, Türkische Märchen ii (1924), 69.
2. Clouds 996–97.
3. Ecl. iii.64; cf. Theocritus, Id. v.88; Propertius, ii.34, 69.
4. Dial. meretr. 12.
5. R. Flacalière, Love in Ancient Greece (paperback ed. 1964), 106, 136.
6. D. B. Thomas, Kentucky Superstitions (1920), 25–26, 41.
7. KARI ii.61, vs. 2–3 = E. Ebeling, Liebeszauber (1925), 12–13 (ᴳᴵŠMA = *ḫašḫuru*-ᴳᴵŠ*nu-ur-mu*, which is also taken to mean *fig;* see: KARI ii.69).
8. R. Patai, in Talpioth 5 (1953), 248.—On apples in magic, see also: K. Helbig, in ZNTW 44 (1953), 111–17.
9. 64, ed. Langkavel.
10. Report, ii.243 (cited by W. Platt, in Notes and Queries, VI/5 (1882), 174).

334 Solomon's groomsmen

1. E. Westermarck, A History of Human Marriage (1925), ii.261, n.5; id., Marriage Customs in Morocco (1914), 118, 274; J. G. Wetzstein, in Zs. für Ethnologie 5 (1873), 288 (Syria); T. H. Gaster, in JBL 74 (1955), 239 ff.
2. W. W. Skeat, Malay Magic (1900), 388.
3. A. E. Crawley, The Mystic Rose² (1927), ii.33 ff.; P. Sartori, Sitte und Brauch, i (1910), 114.
4. H. Granquist, Marriage Conditions in a Palestinian Village, ii (1933), 85 ff.; W. Rothstein, in Palästinajahrbuch 6 (1910), 121, 135; J. A. Jaussen, Coutumes des Arabes au pays de Moab (1908), 295; T. H. Gaster, in JBL 74 (1955), 241 f.
5. I. Abrahams, Jewish Life in the Middle Ages² (1927), 267.
6. Notes and Queries, IX/ii (1880), 245.
7. Jan Malecki, De religione et sacrificiis veterum Borussorum (1551), quoted by V. Pisani, La religione dei Celti e dei Balto-Slavi nell'Europa precristiana (1950), 88.

335 The "Terror by Night"

1. KARI ii.58 (= E. Ebeling, in MVAG 28 [1918], i/3), rev. 10–12.
2. See: S. Krauss, in Orient and Occident: Moses Gaster Anniversary Volume (1936), 323–30.
3. The verse is included in the Jewish prayer recited on retiring at night: S. Singer, Authorised Daily Prayer Book (1890), 296.

336 The separable soul

1. Frazer-Gaster, NGB §§149, 152; Stith Thompson, MI, E 721; A. E. Crawley, The Idea of the Soul (1909), 278, 280; J. J. de Groot, The Religious System of China (1892) sqq.), iv.105.—A. B. Cook (Zeus ii [1925], 1039 f.) would thence derive the Orphic notion of creation from *erôs* (i.e., inner ergative passion) emanating from Zeus.

337 The dance of Maḥanaim

1. Cf. W. F. Albright, in Hebrew and Semitic Studies . . . G. R. Driver (1963), 5–6; cf. also: L. Rost, Tiglathpileser (1893), iii.73.10; K. Tallquist, Akkadische Göttere-pitheta (1938), 34 (where for Di-ni-tu read Šulmanitu).
2. Cf. O. Gruppe, Griechische Mythologie (1906), 840, n.5; Grimm-Stallybrass, Teutonic Mythology (1880–88), 935, 1589.

338 The Reshephs of love

1. The name is likewise used in the plural in Ugaritic (C. Virolleaud, in CRAIBL 1956.60–67, #19.5 J. Nougayrol, ib., 126–35) and, as a loanword, in Egyptian (e.g., Edgerton-Wilson, Historical Records: Medinet Habu 27.25d).
2. Koran, Sura 55.; T. Canaan, Dämonenglaube im Lande der Bibel (1929), 5.

LAMENTATIONS

339 Dirges over cities; the weeping "daughter of Zion"

1. Cf. I. Scheftelowitz, in ARW 19 (1916–19), 221, n.1.
2. Cf. M. Werbrouck, Les pleureuses dans l'Egypte ancienne (1939).
3. KUB XXX.15, 27; cf. H. Otten, in ZA 46 (1942), 206–24; O. Gurney, The Hittites (1952), 164 f.
4. III Aqhat 170 ff.; cf. T. H. Gaster, Thespis², 369 f. Note that the women are called *mšspdt*, which is a causative form of the verb, indicating that they *lead* the dirge, which is then, apparently, taken up by others.
5. Cf. Jer. 9:16, 19; Ezek. 8:14 ("women weeping for Tammuz"); 32:16. Cf. also: H. Jahnow, Das hebräische Leichenlied (1923); P. Heinisch, Die Trauergebräuche bei den Israeliten (1931), 91 f.; id., Die Totenklage in AT (1931).
6. Iliad 24.746.
7. Cf. J. E. B. Mayor, on Juvenal, x.261; cf. also Ovid, Met. ii.340–43. Festus, 223.
8. E. W. Lane, Manners and Customs of the Modern Egyptians (Minerva Library ed., 1890), 478; G. Jacob, Das Leben der vorislâmischen Beduinen (1895), 140 f.; P. Kahle, "Die Totenklage in heutigen Aegypten," in Forschungen zu Religion und Lit. d. AT und NT, 19 (1923), 346 ff.
9. M. Ananikian, Armenian Mythology (1920), 95.
10. Tr. S. N. Kramer, in ANET, 455–63.
11. Rm. iv.97 (3334), translated by T. G. Pinches, in PSBA 23 (1901), 197 ff.; id., "The Lament of the Daughter of Sin," in PSBA 17 (1895), 64–74.

340 The limping meter

1. E. W. Lane, Manners and Customs of the Modern Egyptians (Minerva Library ed., 1890), 488.
2. C. Wetzstein, in Zeitschrift für Ethnologie 5 (1873), 296 ff. For other descriptions of the rite, see: E. Roger, La terre saincte (1664), 265; H. Jahnow, Das hebräische Leichenlied im Rahmen der Völkerdichtung (1923), 75, n.6; A. J. Wensinck, Some Semitic Rites of Mourning and Religion (1917), 43; E. C. Quiggin, ed., Essays and Studies presented to William Ridgeway (1913), 379 ff.; T. H. Gaster, Thespis², 370 f.
3. T. G. Pinches, in PSBA 18 (1896), 253.

341 Sitting apart

1. Concerning menstrual segregation and taboos, see: Frazer-Gaster, NGB §166; W. Robertson Smith, Religion of the Semites³ (1927), 446 ff.; R. C. Thompson, Semitic Magic (1908), 116 ff.; J. Wellhausen, Reste d. arab. Heidentums² (1897), 170 ff.; T. Canaan, Dämonenglaube im Lande der Bibel (1929), 43 f. Cf. also: Koran 2:222; Fihrist 319, line 18 (Syria).

▲ 342 The silent widow

[1. For this nuance of the expression, "sit apart," cf. Lev. 13:46.]
[1a. Frazer-Gaster, NGB §172; J. G. Frazer, Psyche's Task² (1913), 111 ff.]
2. Cf. especially Numbers, ch. 19, with G. B. Gray's Commentary (ICC, 1903), 241 ff.
3. Notes analytiques sur les collections ethnographiques du Musée du Congo I/ii, Religion (Brussels 1906), 186.
4. Rabesihanaka [a native Malagese], "The Sihanaka and their Country," in The Antananarivo Annual and Madagascar Magazine, Reprint of the First Four Numbers (1885), 326.
5. A. C. Hollis, The Nandi (1909), 72.
6. S. Powers, Tribes of California (1877), 327.
7. F. Boas, "Fifth Report of the Committee on the North-Western Tribes of Canada," in Report of the British Association . . . Meeting, 1889, p. 43.
8. Id., Seventh Report . . ." in Report of the British Association . . . Meeting, 1891, p. 13.
9. B. Spencer, Native Tribes of the Northern Territory of Australia (1914), 249 ff.
10. B. Spencer and F. Gillen, The Native Tribes of Central Australia (1899), 500–502.
11. Id., The Northern Tribes of Central Australia (1904), 507 ff.
12. Ib., 502.
13. Ib., 525 ff.; id., Native Tribes, 500 ff.
14. A. W. Howitt, Native Tribes of S. E. Australia (1904), 724 ff.; S. Gason, in JAI 24 (1895), 171.
15. Cf. Frazer-Gaster, NGB, loc. cit.
16. Spencer-Gillen, Native Tribes, 502.
17. Spencer-Gillen, Northern Tribes, 510.
18. Gason, op. cit., 170.
[18a. See fully: E. Bendann, Death Customs (1930), 125, 138, 229 f.]
[18b. T. Noeldeke, Mandäische Grammatik (1875), 128; F. Růžička, in BA 6.44, 104. —For another view, see: H. Bauer, in ZDMG 67.342 f.]
[18c. Cf. Exod. 4:11; Isa. 35:6; 53:7; 56:10; Ezek. 3:26; 24:27; 33:22; Hab. 2:18; Pss. 38:13; 32:2, 9 (I became "like a mute, reduced to silence"); Prov. 3:1, 8.]

[18d. Cf. Lam. 2:10; 3:28.]
[18e. Bendann, op. cit.]

343 Cannibalism in time of famine

1. Ashurbanipal, Rassam Cylinder ix; tr. L. Oppenheim, in ANET 300.
2. Diodorus Siculus, xxxiv.2, 20.
3. Juvenal, xv.92 ff.; Valerius Maximus vii. E §3; Orosius v.23; Prudentius, Perist. i.94.
4. Procopius, Got. ii.20.
5. Strabo, 201.
6. Josephus, Bell. Jud. vi.3, 3–4.
7. F. Peries, in O1z 6.244 f.
8. Cf. A. Ungnad, in ZA 36.108; S. Langdon, Semitic Mythology (1931), 416, n.34.

344 Drinking gall

1. Jer. 9:14; 23:15.
2. Cf. Kirby Smith, on Tibullus I.v, 50 (*Tristia cum multo pocula felle bibit*).
3. Cf. E. Oppenheim, in Wiener Studien, 30 (1908), 146.
4. Shakespeare, Macbeth, I.v.48–51.

345 Gravel and dust in the mouth

1. The word is *k-p-sh*, readily explicable as a bye-form of *k-b-sh*, "tread," on the analogy of Neo-Heb. *c-p-sh*, "shrivel," = *c-b-sh* (Joel 1:17); Heb. *n-p-sh* = Zenčirli *n-b-sh;* Ugaritic *l-p-sh* = Heb. *l-b-sh*.
2. Cf. I. Goldziher, in ZDMG 47.588 f.; id., in Vienna Oriental Journal 16 (1902), 144, n.4.
3. TB Baba Bathra 16 (Resh Lakish to Abbayê).
4. Goldziher, loc. cit.
5. The Canonical Prayerbook of the Mandaeans, ed. E. S. Drower (1949), 137.13; Johannisbuch, 131.8, Lidzbarski (*giṭma ᶜl pumaihun d-kalhun kahnia*).
6. Herodotus, ii.100, 7.
7. Ctesias, Pers. xviii.48.
8. Cf. Ovid, Ibis 317: *Utque necatorum Darei fraude secundi / Sic tua subsidens devoret ora cinis;* Valerius Maximus, ix.27.—In II Maccabees 13:5 ff. this is said to have been the fate of the priest Menelaus.
9. Hist. Timuri ii.124, 142, 926 (cited by Schleussner, Novus Thesaurus [1821], v.569).

346 The king as the life-breath of his people

1. Heb.: *bi-šᵉḥîthôthām;* cf. Akkadian *šêtu*, "net."
2. Cf. H. Grapow, Die bildliche Ausdrücke des Aegyptischen (1924), 122.
3. F. L. Griffith, Hieratic Papyri from Kahun and Gurob (1898), Hymn #4 = Erman-Blackman, The Ancient Egyptians (Harper Torchbook ed., 1966), 186.
4. Ib., Hymn #5 = Erman-Blackman, op. cit., 187.
5. Inscrip. inédit., cited by Grapow, loc. cit.
6. N. de G. Davies, The Rock Tombs of El Amarna (1903), ii.21.
7. Grapow, loc. cit. (Medinet Habu).
8. EA 128.7, 10; 130.7, 9, Winckler.
9. Cf. KAT³, 526.
10. Reading *rûḥᵃkā* for the *rûḥām* ("their wind") of the traditional text.
11. Cf. Frazer-Gaster, NGB §§77–93.

12. On this concept, cf. T. H. Gaster, in Review of Religion, 9 (1945), 270 f.; id., NGB, Add. Note to §1.

347 The king's shadow

1. Cf. A. L. Oppenheim, in BASOR 107 (1947), 7–11, citing R. F. Harper, Assyrian and Babylonian Letters belonging to the Kouyunjik Collection of the British Museum (1892–1914), #264.6–11; #595.4-r.1; #652.12-r.1–3; #886.r.1–4. Cf. also ib., #152.8-r.2; #456.4-r.16; #852.r.2–18; #925.5–7.
2. Kahun Hymn, ii.17 = A. Erman, Literatur, 181.
3. H. Grapow, Die bildliche Ausdrücke des Aegyptischens (1924), 45 f.
4. Text in A. Erman, The Ancient Egyptians, tr. A. M. Blackman (Torchbook ed., 1966), 182. For the interpretation, cf. Oppenheim, loc. cit.
5. Cf. J. Stamm, Die akkadische Namengebung (1939), 276.
6. Cf. G. B. Gray, Hebrew Proper Names (1896), 207.
7. A. Ungnad, Aramäische Papyrus aus Elephantine (1911), #65.5.
8. Cf. Frazer-Gaster, NGB §157, and Additional Note.

ESTHER

348 Introductory

1. Much of this section is condensed from the present writer's Purim and Hanukkah in Custom and Tradition (1950), 6–38.
2. For a resumé of modern critical views, cf. L. B. Paton, Esther (ICC, 1908), 77–94. On the other hand, some scholars have affirmed the historicity of the book: cf. S. Jampel, Das Buch Esther auf seine Geschichtlichkeit kritisch untersucht (1907); J. Hoschander, The Book of Esther in the Light of History (1923).
3. A minor official named Mardukâ, serving at the court of Darius I or of Xerxes at Susa, is mentioned in a cuneiform text cited by A. Ungnad in ZAW 58 (1941), 243; 59 (1943), 219.
4. The Babylonian word *pûru* means properly, "urn," i.e. into which lots are cast. Then, by metonymy, it comes to mean "lot"; cf. A. Bea, in Biblica 21 (1940), 198.
5. The Syriac (Peshitta) Version indeed saw the difficulty and substituted *fourth* for *seventh*.
6. Cf. Stith Thompson, MI, N.275; Bolte-Polivka, ii. 412.
7. Cf. Mardonius, etc. The final *-ka* is a regular Persian ending.
8. Cf. Ezra 2:2; Neh. 7:7.
9. It is not, as modern scholars commonly assert, Mordecai himself, but his ancestor, who is thus described.
10. To enhance the contrast with Agag, Mordecai himself is said to trace his descent from Kish, the father of Saul!
11. Cf. V. Christian, "Zur Herkunft des Purim-Festes," in F. Nötscher Festschrift (1950), 33–37; W. Erbt, Die Purimsage in der Bibel (1900); K. Ringgren, "Esther und Purim," in Svensk Exegetisk Arsbok, 20 (1956), 5–24; N. S. Doniach, Purim or the Feast of Esther (1933); J. Lewy, in HUCA 14 (1939), 127–51.—J. von Hammer (in Wiener Jahrbuch für Literatur, 38 [1872], 49) and P. de Lagarde (Purim [1887]) would derive the feast from the Persian festival of Farvadigan, celebrated in honor of the dead. This theory has been supported by the fact that the Greek (Septuagint) Version calls the feast Furdia, rather than Purim; but this may be merely a scribal error of ΦΟΥΡΔΙΑ for ΦΟΥΡΙΜ.
12. Cf. P. Jensen, in WZKM 6 (1892), 47–70, 209–26; H. Zimmern, KAT³, 514–20.

13. On such theories, cf. R. H. Pfeiffer, Introduction to the Old Testament (1941), 737 ff.; O. Eissfeldt, The Old Testament (1965), 509.
14. Frazer-Gaster, NGB §118; T. H. Gaster, Thespis², 49.
15. Aristotle, Const. Athen. iii.5; cf. Gaster, Thespis², 60, n.260, for further references.
16. Cf. H. Junker, Die Onurislegende (1917), 116 ff.
17. Cf. W. Wolf, Das schöne Fest von Opet (1931), 72 ff.; K. Sethe, Untersuchungen zur Geschichte und Altertumskunde Aegyptens (1902 ff.), iv.219 f.
18. E.g., Gudea Statue E, 51–53; Gudea Cylinder B, iv.23–v.19; S. Langdon, in JRAS 1926.36 ff. (Iddin-Dagan); VAT 633, obv. 1–40; R. H. Pfeiffer, State Letters of Assyria (1935), #217 (Esarhaddon).
19. Cf. Frazer-Gaster, NGB §196.
20. L. A. Waddell, The Buddhism of Tibet (1895), 504 ff.; Frazer-Gaster, op. cit., 462.
21. J. R. Wilson-Hoffenden, in Journal of the African Society 27 (1928), 385 f.
22. J. G. Frazer, The Golden Bough, one-vol. ed., 382 ff.
23. Ib.
24. J. Moura, Le royaume de Cambodge (1883), i.327 f.
25. Ctesias, quoted by Athenaeus, xi.44; cf. Ctesias, ed. F. Baehr (1824), 449 f.; S. Langdon, in JRAS 1924.65–72 (to be read with caution).
26. Cf. P. de Lagarde, "Purim," Abh. d. Kön. Ges. d. Wiss. zu Göttingen, 1887.
27. T. H. Gaster, Thespis², 26 ff.
28. KAV 120, ii.22–28; KAR #177, rev.iii; cf. R. Labat, Le caractère religieux de la royauté assyro-babylonienne (1939), 315.
29. Livy, xxxvi.37; Ovid, Met. x.432; Fasti, iv.353; cf. G. Wissowa, Rel. und Kultur der Römer² (1912), 246.
30. E. Cabaton, in ERE iii.161a.
31. L. Spence, in ERE iii.507a, 568b.
32. Frazer-Gaster, NGB §§456–67; T. H. Gaster, Thespis², 34 ff.
33. Cf. Gilbert Murray, The Rise of the Greek Epic (1907), Appendix A; Jane Harrison, Prolegomena to the Study of Greek Religion (1922), 95 ff.
34. Grimm-Stallybrass, TM 767 ff.
35. Cf. Gaster, Thespis², 175 f.
36. J. G. Frazer, The Golden Bough, one-vol. ed., 559.
37. Ib., 551.
38. Cf. Gaster, Thespis², 37 ff.
39. Cf. Herodotus, ii.63; K. Sethe, op. cit., iii.134; A. Erman, Handbook of Egyptian Religion, tr. F. Griffith (1907), 215.
40. KUB XVII.35, iii.9–17; cf. A. Lesky, in ARW 24 (1927), 73–82; Gaster, Thespis, 267 ff.
41. Cf. T. H. Gaster, Purim and Hanukkah (1950), 17.

349 The Iranian background

(a) The court at Susa

1. Xenophon, Cyrop. viii. 6, 22; Anabasis iii.5, 15.

(b) The royal banquet

2. Al-Biruni, 203 f.; cf. L. H. Gray, in ERE v.872b.

(c) The one hundred and eighty days

3. L. H. Gray, in ERE iii.129a.

(d) "Men who knew the law"

4. Herodotus, iii.31.

(e) The seven who saw the king's face

5. Athenaeus, xii.514*b*. Concerning the *seven* counsellors, cf. Xenophon, Anabasis i.6, 4; A. Christensen, Die Iranier (1933), 256.
6. A. Bastian, Die deutsche Expedition an der Loango-Küste (1874–75), i.262 ff.
7. Proyart's "History of Loango, etc." in Pinkerton's Voyages and Travels, xvi.584.
8. W. C. Harris, The Highlands of Aethiopia (1844), iii.78.
9. Frazer-Gaster, NGB §162.
10. Ib., §146.
11. A. B. Ellis, The Yoruba-speaking Peoples of the Slave Coast (1894), 170.
12. G. Zündel, in Zeitschr. der Ges. für Erdkunde zu Berlin, 12 (1877), 402.

(f) The crazy edict

13. It has been proposed to read *U-M^eDaBbeR KôL SHôVeH ^ciMmÔ*, "and to speak all that beseems him," in place of *U-M^eDaBbeR Ki-L^eSHôN ^caMmÔ*, but this is not Hebrew, for the verb *sh-v-h* is construed with the preposition *l-*, not with ^c*im;* cf. Esther 3:8; 5:13.
14. Cf. T. H. Gaster, in JBL 69 (1950), 381.

(g) The royal crown

15. Cf. P. de Lagarde, Gesammelte Abhandlungen (1866), 207; F. Baehr, Ctesiae Cnidii Operum Reliquiae (1824), 191 f.

(h) Haman's boast

16. Herodotus, i.134.
17. Plutarch, Artaxerxes 5.

(i) Covering the head

18. Quintus Curtius, iv, x.

ECCLESIASTES

350 The telltale bird

1. Cf. Stith Thompson, MI, B 131; Bolte-Polivka, ii.380 ff.; A. Aarne and S. Thompson, Types of the Folktale (1928), #781; V. Chauvin, Bibliographie des ouvrages arabes (1892–1922), ii.107.
2. Grimm's Märchen, #76; cf. Bolte-Polivka, i.275.
3. Ed. Burton, SV 245.
4. Cf. K. Campbell, The Seven Sages of Rome (1907), xcvii.
5. F. J. Child, The English and Scottish Popular Ballads (1882–98), ii.146–55, 260.
6. Cf. Stith Thompson, MI, N 271.3.
7. H. Otten, in MDOG, No. 85 (1953), 33. In the original Canaanite version, the telltale goddess would probably have been Ashtareth (Astarte).
8. Concerning this expression, cf. Notes and Queries, 1/iv (1851), 232, 284, 394; 4/iv (1869), 292; 6/iv (1891), 366; A. de Cock, in Volkskunde 22 (1911), 96–100; W. Wackernagel, Ἔπεα πτερόεντα (1864), 14.
9. Aristophanes, Birds, 600.
10. F. Liebrecht, Zur Volkskunde (1879), 329, No. 140.

ADDENDA

11b Eve

The Hebrew word for Eve is *ḥ a w w a h*. Since this can be connected with a Semitic word meaning "serpent," it has been suggested that the mother of mankind was originally regarded as a serpent—an idea which recurs in many cultures; cf. Th. Noeldeke, in ZDMG 42. 487; J. Wellhausen, Reste[2] (1897), 154; H. Gressmann, in Harnack Festschrift, 24 ff.; W. F. Albright, in AJSL 36 (1928), 284, n.l.—Concerning the ophidian life-goddess of the Mesopotamians, cf. S. Langdon, Tammuz and Ishtar (1914), 114 ff., and note that in a cuneiform text published in BA iii.348, the deity KADI is described as "divine serpent, lady of life." Cf. also: ERE xi.410.—On this hypothesis, the Serpent in Eden would arise from a later differentiation.

13 Localization of Paradise

There are several interesting parallels to the Bible's attempt to localize the mythical Garden. In Classical tradition, the mythical Eridanus (which A. B. Cook [Zeus, ii.1025] would interpret to mean "river of life") was variously identified with the Rhodanne, a stream near Danzig (Rawlinson, Herodotus, iii, pp. 416–17), the Transalpine Rhone, the Italian R. Po (cf. Strabo, 215) and even with the Rhine! Similarly, the Greek Aigle, the mythical "bright land," was located at various places (Preller-Robert, Gr. Mythol.[4] [1894], i.569), as was also Mt. Olympus. Corbenic, the mythical castle of the Grail romances, was likewise localized, in the later *Morte Artu,* at Winchester, Edinburgh, on the R. Humber, on Salisbury Plain, and even at the Tower of London (cf. R. S. Loomis, The Development of Arthurian Romance [1964], 107 f.).

17a The Tree of Life

The tree has also been identified as a fig-tree; cf. L. Ozer, in Acta Antiqua 10 (1962), 1–16.

22 Iron as apotropaic

For this belief in Egypt and Africa, cf. J. Leclant, in Annales de l'Est, Mém. 16. (Nancy 1956), 83–91.

24 Signing of votaries

At Mecca, every male child receives three slashes on the cheek to signify that he is a servant of Allah's house: R. F. Burton, Pilgrimage to Mecca and Medinah[3] (1898), 456.—In India, menials used to be branded on the shoulder: J. A. Dubois, Moeurs, institutions, et cérémonies des peuples de l'Inde (1825), Pt. iii, ch. 3.—Cf. also: Gal. 6:17, "Henceforth let no man trouble me, for I bear branded in my body the marks of Jesus," which does not mean "I share figuratively in the Crucifixion," but "I am God's bondsman."—Witches were often signed at initiation into the coven by being pricked painfully on the shoulder or other part of the body: Margaret A. Murray, The God of the Witches (1952), 99 f.—On the branding of slaves in Babylon, cf. Marx, in BA 4.11.—Cf. also Pseudo-Phocylides 212 (= Gaisford, Poetae Minores Graeci [1824], ii.460): "Do not make brand-marks, thus putting a servant to shame."

25 Corpses of murdered men bleed posthumously

Cf. also Chrétien de Troyes, 'Yvain v. 1195 ff.; K. Lehmann, in Abh. für K. von Maurer (1893), 21–45; W. W. Comfort, Arthurian Romances (1968), 369 f.—The motif recurs in Cervantes' Don Quixote, in Walter Scott's Ballads, and in Schiller's Braut von Messina.—For analogous Jewish legends, cf. TB Giṭṭin 54a; Pesiqta Rabbathi 25; Deut. Rabbah §1; M. Gruenwald, Yalquṭ Sippurîm u-Midrashîm (1923), i. 44.

31 The Song of Lamech

The initial words represent a cliché which recurs in Isa. 32:9.

70 Swearing on stones

Both the Danes and the islanders of Iona swore on stones: J. G. Frazer, GB[3], i.160.— The Samoans swear by the sacred stone of the village: G. Turner, Samoa (1884), 30, 184.

81 The Rod of Moses

Cf. M. Grünbaum, Neue Beiträge (1893), 161–64; P. Saintyves, Essais de folklore biblique (1923), 90 f.; B. Heller, in MGWJ 80 (1936), 47.—For Jewish traditions on the subject, cf. Aaron Rosmarin, Moses im Licht der Agada (1932), 75 f.; I. Löw, Flora der Juden (reprint, 1966), iv.408–10; L. Ginzberg, Legends of the Jews, ii.291; v.411–12.

86 The passage through the Sea of Reeds

Cf. V. Lauha, in VT Suppl. 9 (1963), 32–46.

93 Leprosy as punishment

In Jewish belief, leprosy is the punishment meted out by God for murder, adultery, false suspicion, perjury, impiety, and eight other offenses: cf. Midrash Tanḥuma, Meṣora §4; Tosefta, Nega'im, vii.7; Pirqê de-R. Kahana, 37a. David and Reuben were so chastised for adultery: Ginzberg, Legends, ii.190; iii.266, n.96; vi.305; cf. also: Josephus, Ant. vii.9, 4.

128 Eyes brightened by eating honey

For an Indic parallel, cf. A. B. Keith, Indian Mythology (1917), 158. Also in a modern recipe from Mississippi: W. N. Puckett, Folk Beliefs of the Southern Negro (1926), 276.

129a Youngest son becomes king

David is here said to be the youngest of *eight* brothers; so also in 17:12, 14. But in I Chron. 2:13–15, only *seven* sons of Jesse (Ishai) are mentioned, and David is the seventh. This variant may go back to the familiar folktale motif of the blessed seventh son: cf. Stith Thompson, MI, L 10.—Similarly, in the Welsh Mabinogion, Peredur is the last and sole survivor of the seven sons of the Count of York, and Peredur has much in common with David.

133 The Witch of Endor

On the basis of Sumerian, Akkadian and Hittite evidence, H. Hoffner has suggested (JBL 86 [1967], 385–401) that the Hebrew 'ôb really denotes the pit from which the dead were evoked.

145a Giant with extra fingers and/or toes   II Sam. 21:20

Folklore often equips giants with extra limbs. Thus, "Italian writers of the sixteenth century often call giants *quatromani* ["four-handers"]; giants with thirteen elbows [are mentioned] in Fischart's *Gargantua;* Bilfinger in Swabia are families with twelve fingers and twelve toes": Grimm-Stallybrass, TM 1440.—On the motif in general, cf. Stith Thompson, MI, F 551.2.—For a Celtic parallel, cf. J. A. McCulloch, Celtic Mythology (1918), 143.

150 The Judgment of Solomon

For Indic parallels, cf. W. Kirfel, in Saeculum 7 (1956), 369–84.

157 "Measuring" the sick

The practice seems to be mentioned also in an ancient Mesopotamian text: R. C. Thompson, Devils, ii.56 (*qa-nu-u el-lu lu-qi-e-ma a-me-lu šu(!)-a-tim šum-di-id-ma*, "take a clean rod and measure that man"); cf. K. Frank, Bab. Beschwörungsreliefs (1908), 69.—Cf. also: R. Killan, in BZ, N.F. 10 (1966), 44–56.

158 Elijah on Carmel

The "calling with a loud voice" is a common device in magic, in order to gain the deity's attention: cf. A. Dieterich, Mithrasliturgie^2 (1910), 41.—In orgiastic rites, noise (pandemonium) often imitates the actions of demons: O. Gruppe, Griech. Mythologie (1906), 906. The Pueblo Indians use noise to induce thunder. Certain Bantu tribes clash spears: M. Hunter, Reaction to Conquest (1936), 81. The Navahos use a "groaning stick": W. Matthews, in Fifth Annual Report of the American Bureau of Ethnology (1887), 435 f.

171 Whistling in charms

For an example of this practice from Mahuran, Iran, cf. Percy Sykes, Ten Thousand Miles in Persia (1902), 115.

193a The combat against the Dragon

The description of the dragon as "riddled" (Heb.: *ḥ-l-l*) accords with the fact that the determinative use in writing the name of his Egyptian counterpart Apepi (who, however, is celestial) indicates that he was "sword-smitten," and the epithet "transpierced" (*mdś*) is sometimes applied to him: P. le Page Renouf, in PSBA 1894.295.—In Mandaean lore, Leviathan personifies the submarine monster who will swallow all sinners and demons at the end of the present era: Ginza r., 293.20. (For the netherworld as a fish in Jewish lore, cf. I. Scheftelowitz, Altpers. Rel. und d. Judentum [1920], 198 ff.).— The *seven* heads of Leviathan are mentioned already in the Ugaritic text, I*AB, i. 1 ff. Cf. also the pseudepigraphic Odes of Solomon, 22:5.—G. R. Driver, in Studi Levi della Vida (1956), 238 ff., says that Leviathan is simply "any large serpent."

194 The Suffering Servant

Cf. also: L. Waterman, in JBL 56 (1937), 27–34.

203 The ritual lament

It has been asserted that the figure of Adonis is a Hellenistic creation. To be sure, the so-called "mysteries of Adonis" are known to us only from texts of that age and of the subsequent Roman period, but it should be noted that the wailing for Adonis is attested already by Sappho. What this means is, in a nutshell, that the familiar myth is late, but some earlier story, by means of which the Semitic Adon in the ritual cry was thus transmogrified, must indeed have existed.

209 The righteous Daniel

Cf. also: B. Mariani, Daniel il patriarche sapiente (Rome, Pontificium Athenaeum Antonianum 1945).

211 Salting newborn children

The text mentions not only salting, but also anointing. The latter is a worldwide practice; cf. F. Ratzel, The History of Mankind, English translation (1896), iii.286; A. E. Crawley, in ERE i.522a. It is common among primitive as well as civilized peoples: cf. W. E. Roth, Ethnological Studies among the North-West-Central Queensland Aborigines (1897), 183; T. Williams and J. Calvert, Fiji and the Fijians (1858), i.125; F. Caron, "Account of Japan," in Pinkerton's Voyages and Travels, vii (1811), 635; A. B. Ellis, The Yoruba-speaking People of the Slave Coast of West Africa (1894), 141.

212 Crossroads

For crossroads in ancient Mesopotamian magic, cf. R. C. Thompson, Devils, ii.1, 5; 4.16 (*suq irbitti*).

213 The fallen paragon

Cf. H. G. May in Muilenburg Festschrift (1962), 166–76; G. Widengren, in Myth, Ritual and Kingship, ed. S. H. Hooke (1958), 165 ff. (I find Widengren's interpretation strained and far-fetched.)

224 Stripping a divorcee

A curious parallel to the Babylonian custom whereby a husband who divorces his wife tears the fringe of her garment is afforded by modern Gypsy usage. A Gypsy is outlawed for marrying a non-Gypsy woman. The latter is required to tear a piece of cloth from her dress and throw it at the head of the Rom, after he has been formally condemned by his kinsmen. He is then expelled. Cf. Jean-Paul Clébert, The Gypsies, tr. C. Duff (1967), 160 (on the authority of the Gypsy novelist, Mateo Maximoff).

241 The prayer of Habakkuk

Concerning Resheph, cf. also: F. Vattioni, in Annali dell'Istituto Univ. Orientale di Napoli, N.S. 15 (1965), 39–74.—**n.77.** The Hebrew expression *'eryah te'ôr qaštēka* (lit.: "Thy bow is utterly naked"), which has given trouble to commentators, is admirably illustrated by the Greek γυμνὸν τόξον in Odyssey 11.607 and γυμνὸς οἶστος, ib., 21.417.—A text from Nuzi indicates that a quiver might contain some thirty arrows: Y. Yadin, The Art of Warfare in Biblical Lands (1963), i.82.

259 Paradisal bliss

The phrase, "In thy light do we see light," is usually explained as an imitation of one used conventionally in addressing kings, e.g., in the Tell Amarna Letters, 190.9; 214.11 ff.; 239, 8 ff., Winckler. The Egyptian pharaoh was commonly regarded as an embodiment of Horus, son of the sun-god Re': cf. H. Ranke, Aegypten (1923), 60. Similarly, in Hittite hieroglyphic script, the sign for "sun" appears in the name of kings: cf. E. F. Weidner, in AfO 1 (1927), 135–37; A. Goetze, Kleinasien[1] (1933), 82 f.—Similarly, among the Natchez of Mississippi, the culture-hero is a sun-child, and his offspring are called "suns": Le Page du Praz, Histoire de la Lusiane (1758), ii.331–36. It may be suggested, however, that the expression really continues the description of paradise, or the Faery Garden. In Hebrew folklore this was located in the region of the rising sun (Gen. 2:7; see above §13), and in the Mesopotamian Epic of Gilgamesh (IX.v.45 ff.), the divine garden seems to lie at the point of sunrise.

262a "A river whose streams rejoice the city of God"   Psalm 46:4

A mythological allusion. The "city of the gods" (so we should render) is the celestial city, where they dwell; the term is so used again in Ps. 87:3 (see below, §272). The river is the stream which runs through Paradise and which is sometimes identified astrally with the Milky Way (see above, §14). This pleasant, tranquil river is here contrasted with the raging seas which symbolize the turbulence of the heathen (v.7). It is the river mentioned in Rev. 22:2.—Cf. also: H. Kruse, in Verbum Domini (1949), 23–27; H. Junker, in Biblica 43 (1962), 197–201.

Some scholars have amended the word P^eLaGaW, "its streams," to $G\bar{a}L\bar{a}W$, "its waves." This is silly. First, a river has no waves. Second, this destroys the imagery, the picture of the heavenly city—here in turn equated with the earthly zion (see §272)—being drawn from the analogy of early Mesopotamian cities built on lagoons.

The immediately succeeding clause (RSV: "the holy habitation of the Most High") is somewhat difficult. (Cf. the Countess of Pembroke's quaint and spirited rendering: "For lo, a river streaming joy,/With purling murmur softly slides,/That city washing from annoy,/The holy shrine where God abides.") The traditional text's $Q^eD\hat{o}\check{S}$ $Mi\check{S}K^eN\hat{e}\ {}^cELY\hat{o}N$ involves positing an unusual masculine plural of the word $mi\check{s}kan$ paralleled only in Ezek. 25:4. Elsewhere the plural always has the feminine form, $mi\check{s}k^en\hat{o}th$. The Greek (Septuagint) and Latin (Vulgate) Versions therefore vocalize the words $QidDe\check{S}\ Mi\check{S}K\bar{a}N\hat{o}\ {}^cELY\hat{o}N$ which they understand to mean, "The Most High (i.e., Yahweh) has sanctified his habitation," and this reading is adopted by several modern scholars. It may be suggested, however, that the words, thus read, really contain a more subtle mythological reference: ${}^cELY\hat{o}N$ in this passage is not a proper name, but simply the ancient term for a celestial being (as again in Isa. 14:14 and Ps. 82:6). The meaning will then be that Jerusalem is like the supernal city of ancient myth, a holy habitation which some celestial being has established for himself on earth. The sentiment finds a parallel in Ps. 87:3–4.

265 Bottled tears

On this custom at the annual Hosein-ceremonies in Iran, cf. S. G. Wilson, Life and Customs[3] (1896), 190 ff.

272 The heavenly and earthly Zion

Cf. also: H. Jefferson in VT 13 (1963), 87–91. I cannot accept the treatment of this psalm by E. Beauchamp, in Studii Biblici Franciscani Liber Annuualis 13 (1962–63), 53–75, which seems to me to involve too many arbitrary transpositions of verses.

274 The soul as bird

Cf. also Greek Apoc. Baruch, ch. 10—TB Sanhedrin 91[a] has the soul declare, "After I leave the body, I flutter in the air like a bird."—Abôth d[e]-R. Nathan, Add. 2, p. 160, ed. Schechter, applies Eccles. 12:4 ("one shall rise up at the voice of a bird") to the soul.

276a Eating Ashes   Psalm 102:9

See §245.

283 The accuser at the right hand   Psalm 109–6

Note the subtle point: the guilty will find an accuser standing where *defenders* normally stand; contrast v. 31; Psalm 110:5.

294 Mother Earth

On the concept that earth both bears and ultimately receives all men, cf. Aeschylus, Choephoroe 120–21; Euripides, Supplices 536; Lucretius, v. 319; Pacuvius, fr. 86.—For the concept in Sanskrit literature, cf. S. L. Sütterlin, in ARW 8 (1906), 533 f.—This notion begets the custom of lifting a child from the earth immediately after birth, and of depositing the dead there immediately after death; cf. T. H. Gaster, The Holy and the Profane (1955), 163.

298a Spirits of the field   Job 5:23

The traditional Hebrew text reads:

> *For thou shalt be in league with the stones of the field,*
> *and the beasts of the field shall be in compact with thee.*

It has been objected that there would be no point in a league with the stones of the field, since they could offer nothing as their part of the bargain: L. Köhler, in ARW 7 (1910), 75–79. Accordingly, the words, *'aBNê Ha-SaDeH* ("stones of the field"), have been emended to *'aDôNê Ha-SaDeH*, "lords" of the field" (Rashi, Köhler) or to *BeNê Ha-SaDeH*, "sons of the field," i.e., field-spirits. These would be the spirits of the soil, called in Arabic *ahl el-arḍ*, "earth-folk"; cf. M. Pope, Job (1965), 46.

This seductive interpretation is, however, quite unnecessary. What the poet is saying is that God's chastisements are directed toward the correction, not the destruction, of men. If they are accepted, men can still hope for eventual good fortune. God will ransom them from death in time of famine, and from the sword in time of war. They will be kept in hiding from the scourge of slander and need have no fears when seeming disaster approaches. They can safely "laugh off" any appearance of imminent hunger or ruin, and can feel secure before savage beasts (vv. 17–22). The stony soil—known to the modern fellahin as "devil's land" (*arḍ Iblis;* cf. T. Canaan, in ZDMG 70 [1916], 168)—will not prove an obstacle to their getting earth's produce; they will be, so to speak, on friendly terms with it. Similarly, wild beasts will not assail them; they will, as it were, have come to terms with them. (Heb. *hašlamah* is to be understood in the sense of Akkadian *šulmu*, "agreement"; cf. Obad. 7).

311 The thread of life

It may be suggested that the simile is continued in the second half of the verse, "When God takes away his life," for the Hebrew word (*nafšô*) rendered "his life" may in fact contain a play on a word (**nefš;* cf. Akkadian *napšu;* Aram. and Arabic *n-f-s*) meaning "carded wool," while that rendered "takes away" means properly "pulls off." (This interpretation has the advantage of giving special point to the rare verb, and thus of avoiding capricious emendation.)

314 Blowing kisses to the sun

Lucian says that the Greeks worshiped the sun by kissing their hands to it; cf. Grimm-Stallybrass, TM 1294.

319 Rain from bottles

Cf. Trinculo in Shakespeare's The Tempest, II.ii.20 ff.: *Yond same black cloud, yond huge one, like a foul bombard that would shed his liquor.* (A bombard is a leather jug or a bottle.)

319a Numbering the clouds with wisdom   Job 38:37-38

> *Who can number the clouds with wisdom,*
> *or tilt the waterskins of heaven,*
> *when the dust congeals into a mass,*
> *and the clods stick fast together?*

The parallelism suggests that this refers specifically to measuring the due amount of rainfall, for the Mesopotamians spoke likewise of "measuring" or "weighing out" rain: Atraḫasis Epic, A 11. In omen texts, "weighed rainfall" (*zunnu šaqlu*) means scarce, or measured rainfall, in contrast to a violent downpour: cf. F. R. Kraus, in ZA 43 (1946), 109; T. Bauer, ib., 311; B. Landsberger, MSL II (1937), 228; Lassøe, in Bibliotheca Orientalis 13 (1956), 91.

An alternative suggestion might be, however, that the Hebrew word *YiṢPôR*, "numbers," should be emended to *YᵉSaPpeᵃḤ*, "pours out."

ABBREVIATIONS

AAA	Annals of Archaeology and Anthropology
AASOR	Annual of the American Schools of Oriental Research
AB	The Ugaritic *Poem of Baal* (Virolleaud's numeration)
Abh.BAW	Abhandlungen der Bayerischen Akademie der Wissenschaften
Afo	Archiv für Orientforschung
AJP	American Journal of Philology
AJSL	American Journal of Semitic Languages and Literatures
ALW	Archiv für Liturgiewissenschaft
ANEP	*The Ancient Near East in Pictures*, ed. J. B. Pritchard. Princeton 1955
ANET	*Ancient Near Eastern Texts relating to the Old Testament*, ed. J. B. Pritchard. Princeton 1955
AO	Der Alte Orient
AOF	H. Winckler, *Altorientalische Forschungen*
AOr	Archiv Orientální
APAW	Abhandlungen der Preussischen Akademie der Wissenschaften
AR	*Ancient Records of Egypt*, tr. J. H. Breasted. Chicago 1906
ARAB	*Ancient Records of Assyria and Babylonia*, tr. D.D. Luckenbill. Chicago 1926–27
ARM	*Archives Royales de Mari*, ed. A. Parrot and G. Dossin. Paris 1940–
ARW	Archiv für Religionswissenschaft
ASAE	Annales du Service des Antiquités de l'Égypte
ASAW	Abhandlungen der Sächsischen Gesellschaft der Wissenschaften
ASKT	P. Haupt, *Akkadische und sumerische Keilschrifttexte*. Leipzig 1881
ASTI	Annual of the Swedish Theological Institute in Jerusalem
AT	Alte Testament
ATOB	H. Gressmann, ed., *Altorientalische Texte und Bilder zum Alten Testament*^{2}. Berlin-Leipzig 1926–27
ÄZ	Äegyptische Zeitschrift
BA	The Biblical Archaeologist
BASOR	Bulletin of the American Schools of Oriental Research
BBAE	Bulletin of the Bureau of American Ethnology
BD	The Egyptian Book of the Dead
BEUP	The Babylonian Expedition of the University of Pennsylvania
BIFAO	Bulletin de l'Institut Français d'archéologie orientale
BJRL	Bulletin of the John Rylands Library, Manchester, England
BM	British Museum
BOr	Bibliotheca Orientalis
BoTU	E. Forrer, *Die Boghazköi-Texte in Umschrift*. Leipzig 1922, 1926
BSGW	Berichte der Sächsischen Gesellschaft der Wissenschaften
BTLVNI	Bijdragen Taal, Land– en Volkenkunde van Nederlandsch Indië

ABBREVIATIONS

CAH	Cambridge Ancient History
CBQ	Catholic Biblical Quarterly
CIA	Corpus Inscriptionum Atticarum
CIH	Corpus Inscriptionum Himjariticarum (CIS iv)
CIS	Corpus Inscriptionum Semiticarum
CQ	Classical Quarterly
CR	Classical Review
CRAIBL	Comptes Rendus, Académie des Inscriptions et Belles Lettres, Paris
CT	Cuneiform Texts from Babylonian Tablets in the British Museum
Cult. Bib.	Cultura Bíblica, Segovia
DB	Dictionary of the Bible, ed. J. Hastings
DM	J. Grimm, *Deutsche Mythologie*[4], ed. E. H. Meyer. Berlin 1875
EBib.	Encyclopaedia Biblica, ed. T. K. Cheyne and J. Black
EBrit.	Encyclopaedia Britannica
EEF	Egyptian Exploration Fund
EG	*Epigrammata graeca ex lapidibus collecta,* ed. G. Kaibel. Berlin 1876
ERE	Encyclopaedia of Religion and Ethics, ed. J. Hastings
ET	The Expository Times
ETL	Ephemerides Theologicae Lovanienses
EV	English Version (KJV, RV) of the Bible
FFC	Folklore Fellowship Communications, Helsinki
FHG	*Fragmenta Historicorum Graecorum,* ed. K. Müller. Paris 1868–83
GB	James G. Frazer, *The Golden Bough*
GThT	Gereformeerd Theologisch Tijdschrift
Heb.	Hebrew
HN	Pliny, *Historia Naturalis*
HUCA	Hebrew Union College Annual, Cincinnati
HWb	Handwörterbuch
HWbDA	Handwörterbuch des deutschen Aberglaubens, ed. H. Bächtold-Staubl et al. Berlin 1927–
ICC	International Critical Commentary
IDB	Interpreters' Dictionary of the Bible
IEJ	Israel Exploration Journal
ILN	Illustrated London News
JA	Journal asiatique
JAF	Journal of American Folklore
JAI	Journal of the Anthropological Institute, London
JAOS	Journal of the American Oriental Society
JAS	Journal of the Asiatic Society
JBL	Journal of Biblical Literature and Exegesis
JCS	Journal of Cuneiform Studies
JEA	Journal of Egyptian Archaeology
JHS	Journal of Hellenic Studies
JHUC	Journal of the Hebrew Union College, Cincinnati

ABBREVIATIONS

JJS	Journal of Jewish Studies
JMEOS	Journal of the Manchester Egyptian and Oriental Society
JQR	The Jewish Quarterly Review
JRAI	Journal of the Royal Anthropological Institute, London
JRAS	Journal of the Royal Asiatic Society
JRS	Journal of Roman Studies
JTS	Journal of Theological Studies
KARI	*Keilschrifttexte aus Assur religiösen Inhalts*, ed. E. Ebeling. Leipzig 1919–
KAT	*Die Keilinschriften und das Alte Testament*³, ed. H. Zimmern and H. Winckler. Berlin 1903
KAVI	*Keilschrifttexte aus Assur verschiedenen Inhalts*, ed. O. Schroeder. Leipzig 1920
KB	*Keilinschriftliche Bibliothek*, ed. E. Schrader. Berlin 1889–1915
KBo	Keilschrifttexte aus Boghazköi
KJV	King James (Authorised) Version of the Bible
Kl.Forsch.	Kleinasiatische Forschungen
KUB	Keilschrifturkunden aus Boghazköi
LSS	Leipziger semitische Studien, ed. A. Fischer and H. Zimmern
LXX	Septuagint (Greek) Version of the Old Testament, ed. Rahlfs
MDOG	Mitteilungen der Deutschen Orientalistichen Gesellschaft
MeL	R. Pettazzoni, *Miti e Leggende*
MGWJ	Monatsschrift für Geschichte und Wissenschaft des Judentums
MI	Stith Thompson, *Motif-Index to Folk Literature*¹ (FFC, 106–09, 116–17; Indiana University Studies, 106–12). 6 vols. Helsinki-Bloomington 1932–36
MScRel	Melanges de Sciences Religieuses
MVAG	Mitteilungen der Vorderasiatisch-Aegyptischen Gesellschaft
N.F.	Neue Folge
NGB	J. G. Frazer—T. H. Gaster, *The New Golden Bough*. New York, Mentor Books, 1964
NTT	Norsk Teologisk Tidsskrift
OECT	Oxford Editions of Cuneiform Texts, ed. S. Langdon
OLz	Orientalistische Literaturzeitung
OT	Old Testament
PBS	Publications of the Babylonian Section of the University Museum, Pennsylvania
PE	Eusebius, *Praeparatio evangelica*
PEFQS	Quarterly Statement of the Palestine Exploration Fund
PEQ	Palestine Exploration Quarterly
PG	Patrologia Graeca, ed. Migne
PMLA	Proceedings of the Modern Language Association
PQ	Philological Quarterly
PRE	Realencyclopädie für protestantische Theologie und Kirche³. Leipzig 1896–1913
PSBA	Proceedings of the Society of Biblical Archaeology

ABBREVIATIONS

P–W	Pauly-Wissowa-Kroll, Realencyclopädie der klassischen Altertumswissenschaft
R	H. C. Rawlinson, *The Cuneiform Inscriptions of Western Asia*. London 1861–64
RA	Revue d'assyriologie et d'archéologie orientale
RB	Revue biblique
RBCalz	Rivista Biblica, Villa Calbada (Argentine)
Rev. Celt.	Revue celtique
RGG	Die Religion in Geschichte und Gegenwart. First ed., Tübingen, 1909–13; second ed., Tübingen, 1927 ff.
Rhein. Mus.	Rheinisches Museum für Philologie
RHPR	Revue d'Histoire et de Philosophie Religieuses
RHR	Revue de l'histoire des religions
RIA	Reallexicon der indogermanischen Altertumskunde^2. Leipzig 1929
Riv. Stud. Or.	Rivista degli Studi Orientali
RR	Review of Religion
RS	Ras Shamra text
RSV	Revised Standard Version of the Bible
RV	Revised Version of the Bible
RVV	Religionsgeschichtliche Versuche und Vorarbeiten
SBE	Sacred Books of the East
SBOT	Sacred Books of the Old Testament (the "Rainbow Bible"), ed. P. Haupt
SEG	*Sylloge Inscriptionum Graecarum*^{2}, ed. W. Dittenberger. Leipzig 1898–1901
SMSR	Studi e materiali di storia delle religioni
SOTS	Society for Old Testament Study (Great Britain)
TANAG	Tijdschrift v. h. Kon. Nederl. Aardr. Genootschap
TAPA	Transactions of the American Philological Association
TAPS	Transactions of the American Philosophical Society
TB	Babylonian Talmud
ThLZ (also TLZ)	Theologische Literaturzeitung
TITLV	Tijdschrift voor Indische Taal-, Land en Volkenkunde
TJ	Jerusalemitan (Palestinian) Talmud
TM	J. Grimm, *Teutonic Mythology*, tr. F. Stallybrass (reprint, New York 1966)
TSBA	Transactions of the Society of Biblical Archaeology
TT	Theologisch Tijdschrift
TZ	Theologische Zeitschrift
UCP	University of California Publications in American Archeology and Ethnology
UH	C. H. Gordon, *Ugaritic Handbook*. Rome 1947
UILL	University of Illinois Studies in Language and Literature
VAB	Vorderasiatische Bibliothek, ed. H. Winckler and A. Jeremias
VAT	Cuneiform tablet in the Vorderasiatische Abtheilung of the Staatliche Museen, Berlin

VD	Verbum Domini
VT	Vetus Testamentum
W.A.I.	See R
WO	Die Welt des Orients
WZKM	Wiener Zeitschrift für die Kunde des Morgenlandes
ZA	Zeitschrift für Assyriologie
ZÄS	Zeitschrift für ägyptische Sprache
ZAW	Zeitschrift für die alttestamentliche Wissenschaft
ZDMG	Zeitschrift der Deutschen Morgenländischen Gesellschaft
ZE	Zeitschrift für Ethnologie
ZK	Zeitschrift für Keilschriftforschung
ZKM	Zeitschrift für die Kunde des Morgenlandes
ZNTW	Zeitschrift für die neutestamentliche Wissenschaft
ZS	Zeitschrift für Semitistik
Zs.f.V(1)k.	Zeitschrift für Völkerkunde
ZTK	Zeitschrift für Theologie und Kirche

INDEX OF MOTIFS

Numbers in the left-hand column refer to Stith Thompson's standard *Motif-Index of Folk-Literature;* those in the right-hand column refer to the sections of the present work.

Abandonments and exposures	S 140	78
Ambrosia	A 153	16
Angel helps in battle	V 232	85
Angels entertained unawares	Q 45.1	55
Animals, king of	B 236	112
Atlas	A 692	329
Babel, Tower of	* C 771.1; F 772.1	49
Bell confounds devil/demons	G 303 16.12	91
Bloodbath curative	T 82	161
Branding	P 171	24
Cain, mark of	Q 556.2	24
Chariot of the sun	A 724	170
Circumambulation	* D 1791	257
Clay, man created out of	A 1241	8
Confusion of tongues	* A 1333	50
Crops fail during reign of wicked king	Q 552.3	144
Culture hero asleep in hill	* A 571	83
expected to return	A 530 ff.	205a
Cup, in sack	H 151.4	77
Daughters of men and sons of God	F 531.6.1.1	32
Day magically lengthened	D 2146.1.1	106
Deluge	A 1010 ff.	33–45
caused by gods in conflict	A 1015.1	48
Demons' food taboo	C 242	16
Door, monster guards	* D 1146	19
Eagle renews youth	B 788	277
Ever-blooming garden	F 162.1.1	12
Exposed child	R 131 ff.	78
Fairyland food of, taboo	C 211.1	16
Food of gods taboo	S 261	105
Foundation sacrifice	cf. A 2234.2	16
Fruit, forbidden	* C 621	16

INDEX OF MOTIFS

Garden of gods	A 151.2; * F 111	12
Griffin guards treasure	N 575	19
Honey, rivers of	* F 162.2.3	14
Horns blow down wall	D 1562.3	104
Hunt, Wild	E 50b	71; 337
Inexhaustible cruse	* D 1652 ff.	165
Jonah, swallowed by great fish	F 911.4	236(c)
Joseph and Potiphar's wife	K 2111	76
places cup in sack	H 151.4	77
Ladder to upper world	F 52	64
Lengthening day by magic	D 2146.1.1	106
Leviathan	B 61	186
Lot's wife turned to salt	C 961.1	58
Maimed king must retire	P 16.2	
Mandrake	* D 965.1; B 754.2	67
Manna	D 1030.1.1	88
Milk and honey	F 701.1	14
Moses rescued by princess	R 131.11.1	78
Mutilations	S 161.1	107; 134
Navel of the earth	A 875.1	113
North, abode of demons	G 633	180; 233
Paradise		
on mountain	F 132.1	213
four rivers of	* F 162.2.1	14
serpent in	B 176.1	18
waters of	A 878.1	14
Password, recognition by	H18(ad.)	116
Pillar(s) of heaven	A 665.2	309
Precious stones, city of	F 761	195
Raven	A 2234.1	47, 156
Serpent, immortality of	A 1355(ad.)	18
Seven, formulistic	Z 71.5	
Seventy-seven	Z 71.15	31
Sheba, Queen of, riddles of	H 540.2.1	153
Shibboleth	H 18(ad.)	116
Solomon, judgment of	J 1171.1–2	150
Staff		
blossoming	* F 971.2; H 331.3	95
draws water from stone	D 1549.5	81
Subterranean castle	* F 721.5	321

Tower of Babel	F 772.1	49, 51
to upper world	F 58	49
not to build too high	* C 771.1	49
Tree of immortality/life	D 1346.4; * E 90 ff.	17
knowledge	J 165	17
Twelve	Z 71.8; D 1723.1.4	118
Water		
child cast into	F 321.1.4.1	78
drawn from rock	D 1549.5; * D 1567.6	81
Waters, magically divided	* D 1551 ff.	81
Wind, tied in bag	C 322.1	329

INDEX

Aaron 232, 234, 300
Ababua 288–289
Abarambos 288
Abel 51–75
Abigail 458–459, 461
Abimelech 428–429
Abishag of Shunem 489
Abner 476
Aborigines, Australian 26, 36, 68, 69, 113–114, 234, 596–602, 770
Aborigines as giants 311–312
Abraham 139–156, 161–162
Absalom 479, 480
Abydenus 665
Adah 76, 78
Adam 8–23, 622
Admonitions of Ipuwer 9
Adonijah 489, 490
Adonis, gardens of 573–574
Adoption
  gestures of 448–449
  of kings, by gods 741–742
Aelian 224, 320, 500, 766
Aeneid (Vergil) 19, 140, 805
Aeschylus 71, 72, 129, 159, 300, 464–465, 623, 652–653, 659, 763, 790, 792–793
Aesop's fables 424, 425
Aethiopica (Heliodorus) 506
Agag 455–456
Ahab 513
Ahaziah 514, 515
Ahitophel 480
Ainus 216, 241, 746
Akamba 44–45, 166, 170, 193, 203, 258, 484

Akikuyu 57, 71, 146–147, 166–168, 170, 173, 175, 176, 182, 256–257, 258, 259, 484
Akkadians 145, 236, 306, 307, 456, 745, 747, 776
Albanians 149
Albright, W. F. 475, 813
Alcibiades 320
Alexander the Great 238–239
Alexis 200
Alfoors 103
A-Louyi 42
Altar
  asylum at 490–491
  fire upon 505–506
  settlement of disputes beside 495
  walking round 746–747
'Aluqah the vampire 807
Ami 104
Ammianus Marcellinus 452, 481, 604
Ammonites 430, 433, 476–477
Amorites 414, 415
Amos
  judgment by fire 549–651
  pagan festivals and 648–649
Amoy 473–475
Anals 97, 133–134
Andaman Islands 104–105, 195
Angels
  bread of 242–243, 765, 773
  entertaining unawares 156–157
  escorting 236–237
  guardian 212–214

Angoni 209
Animals
  dressed in mourning 655–656
  punishment of 243–250
Annals of Ashurnaṣirpal 129
Annam 47–48
Ants store food in summer 802
Apollodorus 84–85
Apollonius of Tyana 465
Apollonius Rhodius 754
Apples 811–812
Apuleius 159
Aqdamûth 583
Arabs 36, 53, 64, 66, 70, 77, 129, 130, 139, 149, 150–151, 153, 162, 164, 182, 187, 200, 204, 212, 214, 231, 241, 244–245, 256, 302, 305, 320, 414, 418, 428, 431, 435, 438, 444, 456, 457, 477, 478, 480, 482, 488, 491, 498, 506, 516, 521, 565, 570, 577, 590, 603, 605, 618, 619, 658, 754–757, 769, 794, 796, 809, 826
Arawaks 126
Aristophanes 73, 231, 246, 604, 746, 811, 838
Aristotle 29, 86, 214, 242, 455, 517, 569, 689, 833
Ark of the Lord 453–454, 476
Armenians 131, 213, 425–426, 487, 521, 591, 610
Arnobius 192, 609
Arnold, Matthew 673

896 INDEX

Arrows
 demonic 764-765, 769-770
 divination by 620-621
 lightning as 674, 746
Arunta 62, 422, 460, 597-599, 821-824
Aryans 94, 96, 742, 758
Asahel 476
Ascension of Elijah 511-512
Ascension of Isaiah 214
Ashantis 43-44, 133
Ass, Balaam's 309-310
Assam 97
Assumption of Moses 214
Assyrians 20, 34, 145, 428, 429, 432, 457, 591, 756, 757
Asylum 490-491, 743, 766
Atás 103-104
Athenaeus 432, 454, 509, 510, 643, 782, 835
Augur 303-304
Avesta 245, 525
Awome 144
Azandes 288
Aztecs 18, 25, 26, 27, 437, 650, 744

Baal 504, 505, 507, 567
Baal Zebub 514-515
Babel, Tower of 132-138
Babrius 320, 435
Babylonian Job, The 784
Babylonians 3, 4, 7, 22, 29, 49, 55, 56, 129-130, 138, 145, 158, 159, 201, 211, 225-226, 230, 303, 422, 432, 438, 482, 568-569, 575, 579, 608, 634, 638, 645, 650-651, 741, 760-762, 768, 798, 803, 831-835
Bacon, Francis 269
Badagas 209, 259, 274, 744
Bagandas 208, 252, 254-255, 259, 262, 274, 294, 466
Bagesu 57-58, 141, 502
Bagnouns 281

Bagobo 13
Bahima 176-177, 221, 252, 253, 254, 259, 260, 261
Bahnars 98, 99
Baholoho 52, 212
Baigas 523-524
Bairo 261
Bakongo 59, 483
Balaam 303-310
Balantes 280-281
Baldness 517-518
Baluba 197-198
Balunda 290
Ba-Luyi 132
Bambala 132-133, 289, 421
Bangala 288, 483
Bangongo 289-290
Banks Islands 31, 38, 187-188, 570, 605
Bannavs 99
Banyoro 254, 255-256, 261, 262, 274, 294, 466-467
Baoules 616
Bari 51
Barolong 143, 149
Baronga 46, 47
Barotsé 468
Barrenness of land 71-72, 481, 586
Bashilange 290
Basoga 52, 293-294, 467
Basques 229, 782, 825
Basutos 46, 60, 149, 241
Bataks 100, 131, 185, 471-472
Bateso 269
Bathing
 in blood 513-514, 519-520
 as cure for leprosy, 519-520
Bathsheba 478, 479
Battas 146
Battle taunts 76-78, 457, 580
Bavaria 199, 487
Bawenda 291
Ba-Yaka 60, 244
Bayas 240, 286
Beard, shaven in mourning 573
Bechuanaland 513, 520
Bechuanas 46, 143, 255, 259, 508

Bedars 192
Bedawib 254
Beheading fallen foes 457
Belep 521-522
Bells 263-278
Belomancy 620-621
Ben Sira 182
Benfey, Theodor 494
Beni-Amer 199
Berossus 9, 84, 129, 650
Besisi 187
Bethel 182, 191
Bettaks 213
Bhils 95-96, 437
Bihors 6
Bila-an 12-13
Bion 604
Bird, telltale 838
Birds
 dispatch of 129-130
 sanctuary for 765-766
Birth, new 176-182
Bkerewe 278
Blessings, Jacob steals 165-182
Blinding, for impiety 158-159
Blood
 of Abel 65-69
 bathing in 513-514, 519-520
 contagion of 69-72
 makes soil barren 475
Bloodstained coat 215-217
Blossoming Rod 301
Boaz 448
Bobos 68
Boeotia 148
Bogos 203, 244, 274-275
Boloki 58, 483
Bondei 235
Bonds of Death 745
Book of the Covenant 243, 247, 312
Book of the Dead 3, 84, 580
Book of Enoch 29, 589, 650, 804
Book of Fate 764
Book of Jashar 415, 675
Book of Jubilees 19
Boring of ears 312-316
Bottled tears 759
Bottles, rain from 800

INDEX

Bouras 283
Bowditch Island 189–190
Branding 55–63
Brazil 124–126
Bread
  of angels 242–243, 765, 773
  of mourners 602–604, 640
Breakers of Death 743–744
Breath of God 19–20
Bride, false 199–200
Buddhists 24, 28, 34, 157, 231, 248, 428, 493, 513, 625, 653
Bugis 317
Bulgaria 310
Bulloms 251
Bulrushes, Moses in 224–230
Bundle of the living 457–462
Bunyoro 454
Burmese 272, 742, 758, 787
Burning bush 230

Caffres 68
Cain 51–75
Cairn, covenant at the 201–204
Calabar 45–46
Caleb 301
Callimachus 424–425, 451
Cambodia 457, 833
Canaanite poems 5, 25, 26, 29, 30, 70, 211, 218, 236, 241, 309, 411, 416, 417, 422, 454, 456, 475, 479, 480, 481, 491, 494, 505, 519, 567, 568, 578, 582, 607, 636, 643, 662, 670, 679, 680, 684, 690, 741, 742, 758, 759, 762, 771, 785, 787, 799
Cannibalism during famine 825–826
Cante-fable 241, 655
Captives
  fed on scraps 417–418
  hewn asunder 456–457

Captives (cont.)
  mutilation of 416–417, 475
Caribs 66, 163, 513, 744, 770
Carmel, confrontation on 504–511
Cattle presage storms 799
Catullus 485, 763
Cedar, parable of 626–627
Celsus 455
Celtic folklore 22–23, 25, 28, 29, 34, 49, 77, 210, 243, 311, 439, 442–443, 802
Celts 230, 428
Census, sin of taking 483–488
Chariots
  clouds as 773
  of the sun 524–525
Charms, whispering in 565–566
Cheremiss 14, 186–187
Cherub, riding on 745–746
Cherubim 48, 607
Children
  drawn out of the waters 225–230
  exposed 224–225, 319–320
  passing through fire 586–588
  Rachel weeping for 605
  salting of newborn 618–619
Chinese 6, 27, 34, 190, 218, 229, 235, 269–270, 271, 274, 299, 472–473, 493, 581, 625, 742, 758, 767, 787
Chingpaws 97–98
Chins 147, 149–150, 151
Chiriguanos 127–128
Chronicles (Eusebius of Caesarea) 84
Chubras 197
Cicero 19–20, 567
Circumambulation 411–412, 746–747
City
  dirges over 815–818

City (cont.)
  faery 582–584
  sown with salt 428–429
  submerged 157–158
Clavigero, Francisco 121
Clay, man formed from 8–19, 799
Clouds
  binding waters in 795, 800
  as chariots 773
Coals
  on head 805–806
  on hearth 479–480
Coango 836
Coat
  bloodstained 215–217
  of many colors 216
Code of Eshnunna 250
Code of Hammurapi 250
Codex Chimalpopoca 121
Columella, Lucius 243
Confession, negative 491, 766, 797–798
Constellations, rebel 574–575
Cornford, F. M. 608
Coronation 489–490, 773–781
Corpses, use of in magic 521–522
Covenant
  at the cairn 201–204
  "cutting" a 140–156
  oil in making of 640–641
  of salt 301–302
Covenant, Book of the 243, 247, 312
Crantz, D. 120
Creation
  of heaven and earth 588
  as shaping 3
Crossroads 619–620
"Croucher" 55
Cruse, inexhaustible 518–519
Ctesias 826
Cultic transvestitism 316–318
Cup, Joseph's 218–222
Curse
  by king and god 570

Curse (*cont.*)
  professional 303
  of wandering 72–73
Curtain, heaven as 580
Curtiss, S. I. 477
"Cutting" a covenant 140–156
Cuttings for the dead 590–602
Cyprus 192, 634
Cyrus, King of Persia 225

Dagaris 283
Dahomey 163
Damiani, Peter 583
Dance, limping 455–456, 506–507, 818
Daniel 650
Daniel, righteous 618
Danish folklore 155, 431, 487, 514
Dante 744
Daredevils of Sassoun, The 218
Daughters of man 79–80
David 232, 457, 458–459, 475–483, 489
David redivivus 606, 640
Dawn of salvation 571
Dayaks. *See* Dyaks
Dead
  beneath the waters 794–795
  cuttings for 590–602
  revival of the 503–504, 519
  weary 789
Dead, Book of the 3, 84, 580
Dead Sea Scrolls 213, 306, 307, 589, 650, 688, 689
Death
  bonds of 745
  breakers of 743–744
  house that leads down to 801–802
  of Jacob 214
  of Moses 234–235
  as shepherd 758–759
  snares of 745, 781
Débat 54
Deber 672

Deborah 240
  song of 418–419
Decapitation 457
Dedication of the Temple 494–495
Deissmann, A. 236
Delilah 436–443
Delrio, Martin 268–269
Deluge 7, 82–131
Demons 55, 321, 516–517
  coven of 769–771
  haunts of 577–578
  shafts 764
Demosthenes 70
Devils, hairy 578
Devil's wager 785
Dialogues of the Demi-Monde (Lucian) 565
Diblaim 636
Dictys Cretensis 452
Didriks Saga 165
Dieri 823, 824
Dino 689
Diodorus 176, 432, 643, 661, 665, 781
Dionysius of Halicarnassus 204, 511
Dioscorides 200, 455
Diphylos 660
Dirges over cities 815–818
Divination 218–222
  by arrows 620–621
  rites of 619–621
Divorcee, stripping 637–639
Djaga 32
Dobu 70
Dogon 15
D'Orbiney Papyrus 769
Dragon 575–577, 580, 764, 787–788
  guard over 790
  in net 796
Dreams of gods 182–184
Drinking, modes of 420–422
Druzes 477
Durandus 263–264
Dust in the mouth 826
Dusuns 37, 273
Dyaks 11, 36, 101–102, 186, 235, 272–273, 317, 471, 616

Eagle, renewing youth like 772
Ears, boring of 312–316
Earth
  creation of 588
  invoking 604–605
  Mother 786–787
  navel of 428, 629
  separated from heaven 6
Earthly Paradise 24–25
Eddas 28, 92, 242, 309, 478
Eden, Garden of 24–50
Efe 31–32
Egyptians 5, 6, 9, 20, 21, 25, 26, 33–34, 37, 55–56, 72, 84, 162, 186, 211, 217, 219, 222, 229, 236, 299, 300, 311, 320, 411, 427, 432, 449, 455, 479, 490, 493, 507, 508, 513, 519, 569, 570, 573, 579, 606, 608, 610, 619, 624–625, 632, 633, 640, 671, 672, 675, 682, 690, 741–743, 754, 755, 759, 769, 774–779, 781–782, 788, 795, 797, 798, 805, 815, 818, 827, 833
Ehrenzweig, P. 74
Eissfeldt, O. 461, 588, 650
Ekoi 42–43
El the Bull 640
Eliade, Mircea 650
Elijah 305, 444, 498–513
  ascension of 511–512
  Carmel, confrontation on 504–511
  as man of God 498
  mantle of 512–513
  "measuring" the sick 503–504
  ravens and 498–503
  second coming of 690–691
Eliphaz 77
Elisha 158, 503–504, 511, 512, 516–521
  called "baldpate" 517–518
  inexhaustible cruse and 518–519

INDEX

Elisha (*cont.*)
  purifies water 516–517
  revives dead boy 519
Ellis, William 110
Endor, Witch of 462–475
Engano 100–101
English folklore 23, 25, 31, 80, 157, 160, 165, 222, 249, 411, 422, 446, 480, 486, 487, 488, 618–619, 647, 653, 673, 744, 769, 786, 788, 799, 838
Enoch, Book of 29, 589, 650, 804
Enthronement, ritual of 489–490, 773–781
Enuma Elish. See Epic of Creation (*Enuma Elish*)
Ephôd 639–640
Ephraim Syrus 7
Ephraimites 433
Epic of Creation (*Enuma Elish*) 3, 6, 20, 49, 76, 131, 319, 415, 449, 454, 494, 574, 575, 588, 636, 651, 663, 665, 669, 673, 680, 681, 747–751, 771, 790, 803
Epic of Gilgamesh 9, 22, 24, 28, 36, 48, 55, 73, 76, 82–84, 164, 417, 418, 432, 462, 577, 609, 617, 626, 627, 670, 782
Epic of Keret 73, 233, 454, 481, 677, 757
Esau 162–165, 212
Escorting angel 236–237
Eskimos 4, 15–16, 19, 62, 77, 120–121, 220, 460, 472, 590, 794, 833
Esther 829–837
Esthonians 199, 253, 413, 508
Euripides 25, 573, 660, 666, 668, 781, 783
Eusebius of Caesarea 52, 84
Evans, Sir Arthur 612
Eve 8–23
Ewe-speaking peoples 56, 312, 313, 468–469, 674, 836

Exodus, the 236–278
Exposed children 319–320
Eyes, brightened by eating honey 454–455
Ezekiel 56, 64, 158, 232, 607–629, 644, 669, 686
  dimming of the sun 627–628
  "dirge" over Nebuchadnezzar 621–624
  parable of the cedar 626–627
  Pharaoh and the Nile 624–626
  trapping the soul 615–617
  vision of heathen worship 607–615
  Yahweh's scourges 617–618

Faery city 582–584
Fairy Mistress 22–23
Fallen paragon 621–624
Falling to the ground 451
False bride 199–200
Fans 15, 286, 634
Fate, Book of 764
Fazoql 454
Fijians 62–63, 106–107, 306, 512, 615, 617, 778
Finger, pointing 802–803
Finger of God 236
Finn, Mrs. E. A. 77
Finnish folklore 3–4, 6, 31, 66, 243, 455, 518, 578, 580, 626, 674, 744, 758
Fire
  on altar 505–506
  children passed through 586–588
  judgment by 649–651
  on offender's head 805–806
Firmament 5–6
Firmicus Maternus, Julius 432, 433, 782
Fleece, Gideon's 419–420
Flies, Lord of the 514–515
Flood. *See* Deluge
Flying serpents 573

Food of Paradise 29–32
Fortune, winds of 783
Foundations, razed 793–794
Foundation-sacrifice 413–414
Fountain of Life 804
Fourth generation 156
Foxes, Samson and 434–435, 568
French folklore 31, 49, 164–165, 199, 204, 265, 437, 486–487, 653, 769
Fuegians 594
Funeral meats 602–604, 640
Furious Host 204–205, 511–512, 813

Gabon 4
Gad 584–585
Gadd, C. J. 34
Galen 455, 618
Gall, drinking 826
Gallas 47, 61, 146, 165–166, 169, 253, 303, 484
Garden of Eden 24–50
Gardens of Adonis 573–574
Garment
  covering with 448
  heaven as 772–773
Garos 203, 221, 446, 634
Georgics (Vergil) 628
German folklore 65, 66, 69, 157, 165, 200, 266–267, 320, 411, 430, 451, 480, 487, 514, 516, 520, 521, 581, 605, 618, 637, 659, 744, 746, 763, 769, 786, 790
Ghosts 57–65, 69, 462–475, 570
Giants, aborigines as 311–312
Gibeon 414, 415
Gibeonites 480, 482
Gideon, 233
  fleece of 419–420
  men of 420–422
Gilgamesh and the Land of the Living 627
Giraldus Cambrensis 417

INDEX

God
finger of 236
justice of 666–667
man made in image of 21
net of 793
seeing face of 743
whip of 790–791
"God saw it was good" 6
Gods
cursing by 570
dreams of 182–184
itinerant strangers as 158
Gold
faery 793–794
land of 28
from north 799
Golden Legend (Worde) 229, 264
Golden Meadows (Masʿudi) 7
Goldsmith, Oliver 502
Goliath 457
Gomer 636–637
Gomorrah 156–161, 794
Gonds 273, 275, 523
Gravel in the mouth 826
Grebo 284
Greeks 5, 9, 19, 20, 25, 26, 29, 30, 36, 56, 69–72, 80, 84–92, 129, 135, 136, 145, 148, 159, 162, 164, 177, 183, 191, 205, 207, 211, 213, 219, 224, 227–228, 230–233, 238, 245–246, 275, 311, 320, 413, 414, 416, 418, 422, 423, 428, 430, 432, 438, 439, 445, 451, 453, 455, 462, 478, 480, 487, 498, 510, 514, 515, 516, 522, 525, 569, 572, 579, 581, 582, 585, 587, 590, 618, 619, 624, 642, 645, 654, 659, 666–669, 671, 680, 690, 742, 744, 758–759, 765–766, 772, 775, 778, 782, 787, 788, 795, 805, 838
Greenlanders 120, 303, 744

Grey, Sir George 598–599
Grose, Francis 264
Ground, falling to 451
Guamachucos 163
Guarayos 26
Guardian angels 212–214
Gruppe, Otto 503
Gunkel, Hermann 494, 626

Habakkuk 305
prayer of 668–678
Hair 436–439, 517
Hairy devils 578
Hairy man 164
Haitians 26
Hall, C. F. 120
Hand, withering of 497
Hanun 476, 477
Harlots bathe in Ahab's blood 513–514
Hausas 47, 454
Hawaiians 27, 110, 219–220
Heart
hawsers of 791–792
stealing 201
Hearthfire 479–480
Heathen worship, Ezekiel's vision of 607–615
Heaven
creation of 588
as garment 772–773
as muslim curtain 580
pillars of 795
scaling 132–135
separated from earth 6
Heavenly ladder 184–187
Heavenly sieve 746
Hebrides 202
Heimskringla (Snorri Sturluson) 435
Heliodorus 506
Hellanicus 85
Hepatoscopy 621
Heraclitus 650
Hereros 63, 68, 290, 445, 634
Herodian 506, 613
Herodotus 139, 417, 432, 451, 454, 507, 525, 567, 589, 626, 634, 643, 664, 765–766, 781, 782, 797, 799, 804, 826, 835, 836

Herrick, Robert 266
Hervey Islands 596
Hesiod 207, 243, 525, 572, 580, 623
Hesychius 451, 674
Hewing asunder of captives 456–457
Hildebert of Lavardin 583
Hill, Rowland 751, 771
Hindus 4, 6, 19, 27, 28, 29, 53, 130, 134, 159, 232, 233, 322, 419, 423, 428, 455, 489–490, 520, 742, 744, 745, 758, 763, 770
Historia Danica (Saxo) 478
History of Human Marriage (Westermarck) 199
Hittites 6, 7, 79–80, 129, 135, 145, 158, 159, 237, 302–303, 304, 307, 429, 444, 476, 481, 494, 520, 571, 575, 579, 605–606, 608, 610, 632, 634, 643–644, 663, 673, 676, 679, 745, 747, 759, 761, 762, 778, 779, 788, 815, 833, 837
Hobley, C. W. 146, 167, 168, 258
Homer 3, 4, 6, 27, 29, 65, 72, 73, 92, 144–145, 158, 182, 214, 414, 465, 525, 570, 590, 603, 610, 670, 745–746, 769, 776, 790, 815
Homicides
banishment of 69–71
mark of Cain 56–60
Honey, eyes brightened by 454–455
Hooke, S. H. 74
Horace 30, 213, 300, 465, 500, 570, 653, 667
Horses
of the sun 524–525
waves as 672–673
Hós, 96
Hosea, 233
and pagan festivals, 632–636
House that leads to Death 801–802
Hungarians 65, 210, 265, 478, 514, 518, 674

Huns 591
Hyginus, Gaius Julius 157
Hymn to Demeter 678, 679, 683, 754

Ibn Hishām 67–68
Ibos 209
Icelandic folklore 199, 216, 310, 322, 507, 525
Igalwa 68
Iliad (Homer) 3, 214, 237, 304, 418, 453, 659, 670, 790, 805
Immanuel 568–570
Impiety
 blinding for 158–159
 hand withers for 497
Incas 127, 645
India 13, 24, 94–97, 130, 177–181, 190, 195, 201–202, 226, 228, 232, 241, 273, 277, 295–297, 302, 317, 411, 455, 478, 492–494, 507, 513, 518, 573–574, 587, 619, 620, 659, 763, 769, 777, 785, 786, 833
Indonesia 36, 100–105, 199, 229
Instruction of Amen-em-opet 9
Iranians 25, 29, 130, 228, 245, 320, 525, 578, 620, 647, 650, 670, 673, 688, 689, 741, 742, 758, 772, 788, 795, 826
Irish folklore 49, 210, 222, 233, 422, 439, 521, 786, 795, 806, 825
Iron 52–53
 floating 520–521
Isaac 139
 proposed sacrifice of 161–162
Isaiah 77, 309, 566, 567, 568, 571, 574, 650, 658
Islamic folklore 25–26
Italian folklore 160–161, 183–184, 310, 514, 619

Jabbok, ford of, 205–210
Jacob 162–215
 at Bethel 182–193
 covenant at cairn 201–204

Jacob (*cont.*)
 at ford of Jabbock, 205–212
 last words 214
 at Mahanaim 204–205
 marriage 199–200
 steals blessing 165–182
 at well 193–199
Jacobsen, Thorkild 54
Jains 492
Jakun 187
Ja-Luo 61
Jamblichus 159, 505, 670
Japan 26, 36, 299–300, 422, 498, 620, 776–777
Jashar, Book of 415, 675
Java 235, 422, 438, 445, 448, 455, 508, 517, 521, 585, 603, 604, 634, 647, 668, 742, 783
Jehovistic Document 8
Jephthah, vow of 430–432, 433
Jeremiah 141
Jericho, Joshua at 411–413
Jeroboam 497
Jibaros 126
Joab 475–476, 478, 479, 490
Job 156, 248, 784, 785, 787, 788, 792, 797, 798
Joel, and pagan festivals 642–646
Jonah 240, 652–656
Jonathan 455, 482
Jordan turned back 781
Joseph 215–222
Josephus 200, 238, 303, 413, 775, 825, 836
Joshua 204, 228–229, 231, 301, 411–415
 at Jericho 411–413
Jotham, parable of 423–427
Jubilees, Book of 19
Judas Iscariot 229
Judgement of Solomon 491–494
Judgement by fire 649–651
Juvenal 517, 667

Kaboos 213
Kachins 276
Kaffirs 36, 208, 233, 255, 257, 258, 413

Kagoro 285–286
Kai 38
Kaitish 822–824
Kalevala 3–4, 6, 66, 243, 455, 580, 626, 744
Kalmuk 276
Kamars 96
Kamchadales 100
Kandhs 746
Kaniyans 255
Karaites 251
Karens 69, 135–136, 147–148, 770
Katanga 52
Kavirondo 58, 61, 141, 174, 272
Kayans 148, 471, 481
Kei Islands 155–156, 192, 460
Khasis 13, 586
Khonds 310, 783
Kibanga 454
Kid, seething in mother's milk 250–262
King
 cursing by 570
 divine adoption of 741–742
 enthronement ritual 489–490, 773–781
 installed on holy mountain, 742–743
 as life-breath of people 826–827
 purple of 422–423
 qualifications 454
 shadow of 827–828
 soil affected by misconduct of 481–482
King of Terrors 792–793
Kirantis 272
Kisses to sun and moon 798–799
Kissi 469, 592
Knee 788–789
Knives, gashing with 507–508
Koita 163
Konde 454
Koran 20, 27, 496, 497, 585
Korkus 178–179
Koryaks 150, 151
Kôshar, god of minstrelsy 628
Kratês 518
Kroeber, A. L. 22

INDEX

Kru 284
Kukis 137, 243
Kulwe 133
Kumi 13, 139
Kurkus 13-14
Kurnai 113-114
Kutus 820

Laban 201, 204
Laceration, ritual 507-508
Ladder, heavenly 184-187
Lamech, Song of 76-78
Lament, ritual 604
Lamentations 815-828
Lamp of the soul 804-805
Land of Nod 73-74
Landamas 282
Lane, E. W. 444, 455
Lang, Andrew 452
Language 132, 135-138
Laotians 516, 618
Lapps 486, 653
Law of Moses 71
Laws, The (Plato) 246
Leah 199
Legend of Adapa 5, 29, 30
Legend of Nergal and Ereshkigal 55
Lepchas 96, 134
Leprosy
 bathing as cure for 519-520
 as punishment 300-301
Leviathan 575-577
 rousing 787-788
Levirate marriage 447
Life
 Fountain of 804
 loom of 580
 thread of 580, 628-629, 796
Life of Adam and Eve 30
Life span 79, 80-81, 222
Lifu Island 107-108, 134
Lightning 589, 674-675
 as arrow 674, 746
Lilith 23, 578-580, 807
Limping dance 455-456, 506-507, 818
Lions, Yahweh's 522-524

Lithuanians 93, 131, 141, 222, 431, 674
Liver, in divination 621
Livy 72, 144, 435, 760
Loango 484, 836
Lolos 99-100
London Magical Papyrus 305
Looking back, taboo on 159-160
Loom of life 580
Lord of the Flies 514-515
Lot 156, 157, 159
Lot's wife 160
Love
 apples and 811-812
 banner of 811
 Reshephs of 814
Lucan 465, 570, 573
Lucian 85, 86, 159, 191, 263, 316, 507, 510, 565, 569, 603, 750, 763, 800, 811
"Lucifer, son of the morning" 571-572
Lucretius 612

Macrobius 620
Macusi 320
Madagascar 139, 175, 193, 202, 209, 235, 294-295, 299, 317, 820
Magic
 use of corpses in 521-522
 waving in 520
 whispering in charms 565-566, 570
Magical water 752-753
Mahabharata 28, 226, 497
Mahanaim
 dance of 813
 Jacob at 204-205
Malachi 248, 650
 picture of the Last Days 688-689
Malagasy 146, 192-193
Malays 99, 129, 411, 426, 605, 810, 812
Man
 animated by divine breath 19-20
 formed from earth or clay 8-19, 799

Man (*cont.*)
 formed from stones 586
 hairy 164
 made in the image of God 21
 role of 49-50
 woman formed from rib of 21-22
"Man of God" 498
Mandaeans 30, 56, 139, 232, 461, 519, 575, 578, 647, 744, 758, 769, 804, 826
Mandrake 200
Mangars 186
Manichaeans 647
Manna 242-243
Manners and Customs of the Modern Egyptians (Lane) 444, 455-456
Mantle of Elijah 512-513
Maoris 6, 10, 20, 110-112, 194-195, 303, 469-470, 512, 596
Marcellus of Bordeaux 455
Margoliouth, D. S. 801
Marie de France 427
Marindineeze (Marindanim) 470
Mark of Cain 55-65
Marquesas Islands 457, 470, 596
Marriage
 formulas 639
 of Jacob 199-200
 Levirate 447
Martial 480
Masai 52, 61, 141, 167, 198, 208, 252, 260, 310, 483-484, 758
Masarwas 41-42
Mason, J. A. 22
Maxims of Khety 21
Mayas 650
Measuring the sick 503-504
Meats, funeral 602-604
Mediums 570
Melanesians 10, 31, 38, 39, 47, 107, 187-188, 570
Melchizedek 139-140
Menander 213, 238, 567

INDEX

Meni 584–585
Menkieras 190–191
Mesopotamians 4, 5, 6, 9, 34, 49, 55, 69, 82–84, 129, 131, 160, 162, 212, 229, 235, 250, 305, 307, 308, 321, 479, 481, 500, 524, 565, 570, 577, 578, 579, 582, 603, 605, 633, 637, 643, 662–664, 669, 672, 675, 680, 681, 689, 742, 743, 745, 754, 759, 770, 772, 778, 782, 783, 789, 795, 799, 803, 812, 813, 825, 827, 832
Message, falsified 39–48
Metamorphoses (Apuleius) 159
Mexico 121–124, 135, 232
Miao-Kia 190
Micah 309
 prophecy by puns 657–658
Mice 452–453
Michemis 272
Michoacans 17–18
Middle Assyrian Code of Laws 316
Mikirs 136
Milk, seething of kid in mother's 250–262
Milton, John 266, 308, 578, 758
Miriam 232, 300, 301
Mohammed 6, 36, 53, 68, 448, 585, 620, 638
Mongols 212
Moon
 blowing kisses to, 798–799
 halted 414–415, 675
Morocco 71, 512, 619
Moses 182, 223–235, 582, 767
 in bulrushes 224–230
 death of 234–235
 farewell song 318–321, 649–650
 at Horeb 230–232
 incident at inn 234
 proofs of commission 232
 rod of 233–234
Moslems 251, 455, 520, 638–639, 769
Mossi 220, 282–283, 522–523

Mother Earth 786–787
Mountain
 of deliverance 128–129
 king installed on holy 742–743
 in midsea 757–758
Mourners, bread of 602–604, 640
Mourning 475, 781–783, 786
 animals dressed in 655–656
 beard shaven in 573
 rites of 590–604, 609–610
Mpongwe 182
Mrus 36
Mudburra 820–821, 823
Mummers' Play 73–74, 78
Mundas 14
Muretus 486
Mutilation of captives 475
Mythological riddles 806–807

Naaman 519, 520
Nagas 136–137, 143, 144, 190
Nages 103
Nahum 661–666
Naloos 282
Namaquas 39–40, 41, 421
"Name of the Lord" 577
Names, regnal 479
Nandi 36, 40–41, 61, 141, 144, 170, 175, 182, 198, 253, 255, 256, 261, 313, 502, 820
Naomi 448
Nasamonaeans (Nasamones) 139, 464
Nathan 479
Navel of the earth 428, 629
Nebuchadnezza 621–622
Necromancy 462–475
Negative confession 491, 766, 797–798
Net
 Dragon in 796
 God's 793
New birth 176–182
New Caledonians 31, 80, 421, 586, 794

New Hebrideans 11, 38, 107, 164, 187–188, 469, 594
New Zealanders 590
Neyaux 284
Ngoni 46, 47, 61
Nias 12, 37–38, 100, 145, 438–439
Nicander 609
Nikunau Island 190
Night, terror by 769–770, 813
Nile, Pharaoh and 624–626
Nilus 302, 456
Nineveh 661–666
Nippur 53
Njamwezi 133
Nod, Land of 73–74
Nogais 276
Norse folklore 5, 29, 30, 66, 92, 130, 201, 234, 439, 754, 758, 787, 790
North
 far reaches of 758
 foe from 645, 647
 gold from 799
North American Indians 4, 5, 15, 16–17, 19, 20, 21, 22, 26, 27, 31, 32, 36, 58, 61–62, 63, 69, 114–120, 137–138, 163, 164, 191, 196–197, 210–211, 218, 234–235, 270–271, 317, 322, 413, 417, 423, 438, 446, 485, 501, 508, 514, 570, 590, 592–594, 621, 645, 674, 742, 744, 758, 798, 820, 833
Nounoumas 68

Obadiah 139
Ocean of Story (Somadeva) 24, 478, 513, 520, 802
Odes of Solomon 448
Odyssey (Homer) 4, 158, 159, 309, 453, 480, 481, 586, 744, 805
Ogieg 421
Oil in covenant-making 640–641
Oppenheim, L. 461
Oracles, Balaam's 306–307
Orang Sakai 594, 600
Ordeal, poison 280–300
Orinoco Indians 126–127

Orion 790
Osphresiology 489
Ossetes 148
Ot-Danoms 102
Ovambo 258–259
Ovid 36, 53, 73, 157, 199, 300, 435, 480, 499, 570, 606, 628, 754, 763
Ox that gores 243–250

Pagan festivals
 Amos and 648–649
 Hosea and 632–636
 Joel and 642–646
 Zechariah and 686–687
 Zephaniah and 679–685
Panope 163
Papuans 31, 139, 414, 794
Paradise 582–584, 622–623
 bliss 752
 Earthly 24–25
 cherubim 48
 food of 29–32
 as land of gold and gems 28
 location of 25–26
 revolving sword 48–49
 serpent 35–48
 trees of 32–35
 waters of 26–28
 woman in 22–23
Paragon, fallen 621–624
Paul, St. 158
Pausanias 157, 183, 205, 309, 320, 463, 505–506, 613, 616
Peguans 163
Pelew Islands 10, 112–113, 317, 518, 605
Perrot, Nicolas 196–197
Persians 218, 688, 829–837
Persians, The (Aeschylus) 464–465
Petronius 565, 570
Pettazzoni, R. 508
Phaedrus 427
Phantom Host 204–205, 511–512, 813
Pharaoh and the Nile 624–626
Philostratus 465
Phoenicians 231, 782, 783

Phoenix, legend of 796–797
Pillar of salt 160–161
Pillars
 of heaven 795
 of wisdom 84–804
Pinches, T. G. 575
Pindar 6, 28
Pipiles 445
Plato 57, 70, 182, 214, 246, 573, 759, 775–776
Plautus 653, 805
Pliny 55, 130, 204, 306, 309, 320, 451, 455, 465, 501–502, 509, 513, 517, 519, 521, 567, 603, 628, 744, 799
Plutarch 36, 37, 80, 130, 316, 422, 432, 463–464, 483, 587, 613, 642, 643, 647, 660, 758, 782, 805
Pockocke, E. 620
Poem of Aqhat 29, 70, 71, 140, 158, 422, 456, 460, 505, 603, 610, 618, 680, 815
Poem of Baal 30, 74, 76, 411, 454, 494, 505, 576, 589, 606, 610, 615, 626, 632, 634, 644, 646, 659, 663, 665, 673, 676, 679, 680, 686, 687, 747–749, 751–752, 767, 775, 779, 788, 790
Poem to the Descent of Ishtar to the Netherworld 432, 782
Poem of the Gracious Gods 610, 686
Poem of Pentaur 670
Pointing the finger 802–803
Poison ordeal 280–300
Polo, Marco 578, 683
Polynesians 5, 570, 595, 794
Pope, Alexander 20
Pope, Marvin 461
Popul Vuh 18
Portugal 445
Poseidonius 214
Potiphar's wife 217–218
Priestly Code 243, 280
Priestly Document 8, 64
Primal upsurge 6–7
Primordial water 3–4, 229

Primordial wind 3, 4–5
Procopius 744, 825
Professions, rivalry of 53–54
Prometheus, myth of 622–624
Propertius 507
Puns, prophecy by 657–658
Purple of kings 422–423
Pyramid Texts 25, 186, 201, 320, 795, 797

Qashgai 52
Qazwini 302
Queen of Sheba 495–497
Quiché 4, 25, 138, 498

Rachel 193, 199, 200, 605
Racine, Jean Baptiste 246
Raiatea Island 109–110
Rain
 bottles and 800
 fissures for 589
Rainbow 130–131
Raincloud 511
Rain-stones 509–510
Rape 444–445
Ras Shamra-Ugarit. *See* Canaanite poems
Ravens 129–130
 Elijah and 498–503
 in ruins 685
Reade, Charles 214
Red Sea 237–240
Redheads 164–165
Regnal names 479
Republic, The (Plato) 246
Resheph 670–672, 764–765
 sons of 789
Reshephs of love 814
Reuben 200
Revolving sword 48–49
Riddle, Samson's 435–436
Riddles, mythological 806–807
Riding high 418–419
Rig Veda 5, 48, 243, 525, 580, 744, 772, 800
Righteousness, throne founded on 769

Rivalry of professions 53–54
Rivers, of the netherworld 743–744
Rizpah 482
Rod
 blossoming 301
 of Moses 233–234
Roger, E. 455
Romance of Aḥikar 425
Romans 144, 159, 162, 163, 204, 213, 228, 230, 231, 232, 239–240, 246, 263, 277, 304, 307, 411–412, 413, 416–417, 422, 445, 449, 451, 452, 457, 516, 521, 525, 585, 587, 591, 603, 610, 619, 626–627, 635, 659, 660, 666, 667, 668, 670, 690, 775, 776, 786, 805, 833
Roscher, W. H. 243
Rotti 103
Roumania 164, 609–610, 633
Russian folklore 186, 229, 439–440, 488, 633, 638, 645, 674, 746
Ruth 448

Sacred stone 187–193
Sacrifice, foundation 413–414
St. Cristoval Island 21, 22
Salt
 city sown with 428–430
 covenant of 301–302
 newborn children and 618–619
 pillar of 160–161
 waters purified by 516–517
Salvation, dawn of 571
Samaritans 423, 428, 635
Samoans 189, 203, 421, 596
Samson 433–443, 568
 Delilah and 436–443
 and foxes 434–435, 568
 riddle of 435–436
 as solar hero 434
Samuel 451, 455, 456, 462

Sanchuniathon 37, 52, 571, 628
Sandwich Islands 306
Sappho 604
Saracens 456
Sargon of Agade 225–226
Sargon of Assyria 571, 572
Satan 785–786
Satapatha Brahmana 13, 94–95
Saul 454, 455, 458, 462, 475, 480, 482
Saxo Grammaticus 201
Sayce, A. H. 306
Scapegoats, human 581–582
Scipio the Elder 239
Scottish folklore 25, 31, 80, 204, 221–222, 235, 448, 486, 515, 587, 653, 673, 838
Scourges, Yahweh's 617–618
Scythians 451–452, 514, 591
Sea
 casting sins into 659–660
 foe driven into 645, 647
 guard over 790
 mountains in 757–758
Sea of Reeds, passage through 237–240
Second Leyden Papyrus 565
"Seeing the face of God" 743
Segregation 819
Seneca 667
Seraphim 567
Sereres 281–282
Serpent
 flying 573
 in Paradise 35–48
Servant, Suffering 580–582
Servius 786
Seven circuits of Jericho 412
Seven Evil Spirits, concept of 321
Sexual intercourse, properties conveyed through 79–80

Shadow
 disappearing 791
 of king 827–828
 soul as 301
Shakespeare, William 66, 67, 73, 214, 307, 321, 478, 500, 580, 758, 764, 792, 807, 826
Shans 59
Shaving and shearing 476–478
Sheba, Queen of 495–497
Shepherd, Death as 758–759
Shibboleth 433
Shilluks 14–15, 454
Shiloh, rape of the women of 444–446
Shoes, removal of 231–232, 449–450
Shoestrings 567
Shorthand Islands 38, 235, 485
Siberia 52, 322, 587, 617
Sibylline Oracles 307
Sick, measuring 503–504
Sieve, heavenly 746
Silence
 ritual 668
 of widows 819–825
Sinew, shrinking 206, 210–212
Singhalese 32, 277
Sins, casting into sea 659–660
Sitting low 418–419
Smith, W. Robertson 74–75, 148, 151, 152, 480, 600
Smiths 51–52
Snares of Death 745, 781
Snorri Sturluson 435
Socrates 214, 320
Sodom 156–161, 794
Soil
 affected by king's misconduct 481–482
 made barren through unchastity 586
Solar hero, Samson as 434
Solomon 479, 489, 490, 743
 judgement of 491–494
 Queen of Sheba and 495–496

INDEX

Solomon (*cont.*)
  Temple, dedication of 494–495
Solomon Islands 570
"Solomon's" groomsmen 812–813
Somadeva 24, 28, 478, 513, 520, 802
Somali 66, 514
Song
  of Deborah 418–419
  of Lamech 76–78
  Moses' farewell 318–321, 549–650
  at the Sea 240–241
  wedding 753–757
  at the well 302–303
Songos 290
Sons of God 79–80, 785
Soothill, William Edward 751, 771
Sophocles 72, 159, 214, 660, 666
Sothe 480
Sotion 689
Soul
  lamp of 804–805
  separable 813
  as shadow 301
  trapping 615–617
  winged 769
Soul-boxes 566
Sowing a city with salt 428–430
Spain 204, 265, 320, 446
Span, mortal 79, 80–81, 222
Spindle, holder of the 475–476
Stars, divine 799–800
Statius 507, 570
Steel 53
Stigand, C. H. 421
Stones
  enthronement ritual and 490
  man formed from 586
  oaths sworn upon 201–204
  rain 509–510
  sacred 187–193
Stork, kindly 773
Storms, cattle presage 799
Strabo 130, 452, 513, 569, 825
Strangers, disguised as gods 158

Stripping divorcees 637–639
Submerged city 157–158
Suetonius 505
Suffering Servant 580–582
Suk 198, 256, 261
Sumerians 3, 5, 21, 22, 24, 25, 49, 53–54, 84, 231, 236, 428, 490, 575, 606, 626–627, 664, 674, 745, 772, 776, 792, 815
Sun
  blowing kisses to 798–799
  dimming of 627–628, 647
  halted 414–415, 675
  horses and chariots of 524–525
  of righteousness 689–690
Swabia 266, 267
Swedish folklore 31, 222, 431, 486, 525, 618
Switzerland 581
Sword, revolving 48–49
Sword of Moses, The 517, 519
Syrians 153–154, 232, 321, 428, 429, 456, 514, 520, 633, 634, 808–809, 818

Taboos
  Ark of the Lord and 453–454, 476
  on counting 483–488
  on looking back 159–160
Tacitus 316, 505, 637, 788
Tagalogs 275–276
Tahitians 6, 10, 108–109, 219, 235, 600, 777
Tale of the Armament of Igor 5
Tale of Elkunirša 838
Tale of the Shipwrecked Sailor 26, 624
Tales of the Seven Masters 218
Talmud 305, 308, 319, 419, 420, 446, 491, 521, 577, 585, 826
Tami 36
Tammuz 609–610, 633

Taunts
  battle 76–78, 457, 580
  Elijah's 508–509
Teaching of Ani, The 21
Tears
  bottled 759
  fertilize 781–783
Tell el Amarna Letters 20, 663, 778, 827
Telltale bird 838
Temple, dedication of 494–495
Teraphîm 200, 639–640, 687
Terence 772
Terre Saincte, La (Roger) 455
Terror by night 769–770, 813
Terrors, King of 792–793
Tertullian 319
Testament of Solomon 53, 619
Testaments of the Twelve Patriarchs 30
Thailand 69, 457, 516, 581, 616–617, 618, 645
Tha-thun 163
Theocritus 159, 300, 512, 638, 754, 770
Theogony (Hesiod) 572
Theophrastus 65, 200, 573, 653
Theraka 169
Thonga 60, 253, 255
Thread of life 580, 628–629, 796
Throne founded on righteousness 769
Tiāhā 477
Tibetans 27, 52, 96–97, 514, 520, 742, 758, 833
Tibbu 52
Tibullus 465, 480, 507, 517, 565, 628, 635, 660, 666–667, 763
Tierra del Fuego 128
Timor Island 145–146
Timorlaut Islands 139
Tischlein deck' dich 518–519
To Koelawi 38–39
Todas 192, 257, 258, 259, 516, 618
Toltecs 136

Tongans 26, 32, 480, 596
Tongues, confusion of 132, 135–138
Toradjas 11, 37, 53, 102, 184–185, 209, 210, 233–234, 244, 252, 314–315, 470, 522, 616, 783
Torres Straits Islands 189
Tower of Babel 132–138
Transvestism, cultic 316–318
Travels of St. John of Zebedee, The 414
Travels of Wen-Amun 827
Tree
 of Knowledge of Good and Evil 32–35
 of Life 32–34
Trumpets 413, 612–613, 632
Tuamotu Island 136
Tuaregs 464
Tupis 59, 163, 195–196, 422, 744
Turner, George 188
Tur-Sinai, H. 640
Twelve 443–444
Twins 163–165
Tzetzes, John 263

Unchastity renders soil barren 586
Unmatjera 822–824
Upotos 288
Upsurge, primal 6–7
Uriah letter 478
Uzza 476

Vaca, Cabeça de 196
Valerius Maximus 506, 667
Valmans 105
Vampire 807
Vampire Tales (Somadeva) 22, 28
Varozwe 454
Vergil 19, 140, 214, 500, 506, 568, 570, 591, 628, 805
Virgin birth 568–570
Vishatantra 297
Voguls 93–94
Vuatom 37

Wabende 37
Waboungou 65
Wachaga 141–143, 144, 152–153, 169, 170–172
Waduman 820–821, 823
Wafipa 37, 240
Wa-giriama 169–170
Wagogo 253, 293
Wahumba 253
Waistcloths 567
Wajagga 52
Walls, circuit of 411–412
Wamegi 253
Wandering, curse of 72–73
Wanika 68, 293, 592
Wa-Nobbos 52
Wanyamwesi 293, 502–503
Waralis 192
Warramunga 822–823
Warriors, long-haired 418
Wa-Sania 46, 136, 484
Washamba 168–169, 260–261
Wat Po 621
Water
 children drawn from 225–230
 enthronement ritual and 489–490
 primordial 3–4, 229
 from rock 233–234
Waters
 binding in clouds 795, 800
 dividing of 233, 237–240
 magical 752–753
 of Paradise 26–28
 purified by salt 516–517
 shades beneath 794–795
 sweetening bitter 241–242
Waves 672–673
Waving, in magic 520
Wawanga 60–61, 169, 171, 173–174, 293
Wawira 294
Weary dead 789
Wedding song 753–757
Well
 Jacob at 193–199

Well (*cont.*)
 Song at the 302–303
Wellhausen, Julius 636
Welsh legends 92–93
Westermarck, Edward Alexander 182, 199
Wetzstein, Johann Gottfried 808
Whip of God 790–791
Whispering, in charms 565–566
Widow, silent 819–825
Wild Hunt 204, 511–512, 813
Wind
 primordial 3, 4–5
 promptuaries for 589–590
 wings of 745–746, 773
Wind-bird 5
Winds of fortune 783
Winged soul 769
Wings of the wind 745–746, 773
Wisdom
 as God's master craftsman 803
 seven pillars of 803–804
Wisdom of Solomon 243
Witch of Endor 462–475
Wolofs 313, 314
Woman
 divided into twelve parts 443–444
 formed from man's rib 21–22
 in Paradise 22–23
Worde, W. de 264

Xenophon 214, 591, 661, 834

Yabim 59–60
Yakuts 52
Yellow garments 763–764
Yezidis 274
Yoruba 4, 15, 19, 274, 457, 776
Youth, renewing 772
Yunkas 163
Yurakaré 163

Zambesi 292
Zangas 283

Zechariah 673
   pagan festivals and 686–687
Zephaniah, pagan festivals and 679–685

Zillah 76, 78
Zimmern Chronicle 67
Zion, heavenly and earthly 766–768
Zohar 422

Zoroastrianism 688–689
Zulus 31, 36, 46, 199, 207–208, 255, 257, 291, 317, 454, 480, 570, 586
Zuñi 413, 508

BS 625.G3 1975
GASTER, THEODOR HERZ
MYTH, LEGEND, AND
CUSTOM IN THE OLD TE

WITHDRAWN